AF531691

आ नो भद्राः क्रतवो यन्तु विश्वतः

Let noble thoughts come to us from every side

—Rigveda, I-89-i

BHAVAN'S BOOK UNIVERSITY

THE HISTORY AND CULTURE OF THE INDIAN PEOPLE

VOLUME I

THE VEDIC AGE

BHAVAN'S BOOK UNIVERSITY

THE HISTORY AND CULTURE OF THE INDIAN PEOPLE

THE VEDIC AGE

FOREWORD BY

K. M. MUNSHI

B.A., LL.B., D.LITT. LL.D.

President, Bharatiya Vidya Bhavan

GENERAL EDITOR

R. C. MAJUMDAR

M.A.,PHD., F.A.S., F.B.B.R.A.S.

Ex. Vice-Chancellor and Professor of History
Dacca University

Hon, Head of the Department of History
Bharatiya Vidya Bhavan

ASSISTANT EDITORS

A. D. PUSALKER

M.A., LL.,B., PH.D.

Assistant Director and Head of the
Department of Ancient Indian Culture

Bharatiya Vidya Bhavan

AND

A. K. MAJUMDAR, M.A., D. PHILL

Director
Bharatiya Vidya Bhavan
Delhi Kendra

2025

BHARATIYA VIDYA BHAVAN

Kulapati K. M. Munshi Marg
Mumbai - 400007

First Edition	:	1951
Second Edition	:	1952
Third Edition	:	1957
Fourth Edition	:	1965
Fifth Edition	:	1988
Sixth Edition	:	1996
Seventh Edition	:	2010
Eight Edition	:	2015
Ninth Edition	:	2017
Tenth Edition	:	2021
Eleventh Edition	:	2023
Twelfth Edition	:	2025

Price ₹ 1,275/-

PRINTED IN INDIA

by Siddhi Printers, 13/14, Bhabha Building, 13th Khetwadi Lane,
Mumbai - 400004 and Published by P.V.Sankarankutty, Director,
for Bharatiya Vidya Bhavan, Kulapati K. M. Munshi Marg, Mumbai - 400007.
E-mail: publications@bhavans.info • Website: www.bhavans.info

CONTRIBUTORS

R. C. MAJUMDAR

M.A., PH.D., F.R.A.S.B.

Formerly Vice-Chancellor and Professor of History in the University of Dacca

RAO BAHADUR K. N. DIKSHIT

M.A., F.R.A.S.B.

Formerly Director-General of Archaeology, Government of India

D. N. WADIA

M.A., B.SC., F.G.S., F.R.G.S., F.R.A.S.B., F.N.I.

Special Adviser to the Government of India

G. P. MAJUMDAR

M.SC., PH.D. (Leeds)

Professor of Botany in the Presidency College, Calcutta

B. K. CHATTERJI

M.SC.

Lecturer in Zoology in the Presidency College, Calcutta

H. D. SANKALIA

M.A., LL.B., PH.D. (London)

Professor of History in the Deccan College Post-Graduate and Research Institute, Poona

S. K. CHATTERJI

M.A., D.LITT. (London) F.R.A.S.B.

Khaira Professor of Indian Linguistics and Phonetics in the University of Calcutta

A. D. PUSALKER

M.A., LLB., PH.D.

Assistant Director and Head of the Department of Sanskrit Bharatiya Vidya Bhavan

B. K. GHOSH

D.PHIL. (Munich), D.LITT. (Paris)

Lecturer in Philology in the University of Calcutta

V. M. APTE

M.A., PH.D. (Cantab.)

Professor of Sanskrit in the Karnatak College, Dharwar

M. A. MEHENDALE

M.A., PH.D.

Professor of Sanskrit in S. B. Garda College, Navasari, Bombay

FOREWORD

By Dr. K. M. MUNSHI

In the course of my studies I had long felt the inadequacy of our so-called Indian histories. For many years, therefore, I was planning an elaborate history of India in order not only that India's past might be described by her sons, but also that the world might catch a glimpse of her soul as Indians see it. The Bhāratīya Vidyā Bhavan, an educational society which I founded in 1938, took over the scheme. It was, however, realized only in 1944, when my generous friend Mr. G. D. Birla, one of India's foremost industrialists, lent me his co-operation and the support of the Shrī Krishnarpan Charity Trust of which he is the Chairman. As a result, the Bhāratīya Itihāsa Samiti, the Academy of Indian History, was formed with the specific object of preparing this series, now styled *The History and Culture of the Indian People*.

The Samiti was lucky in securing the services of Dr. R. C. Majumdar, formerly Vice-Chancellor of Dacca University and one of India's leading historians, as full-time editor, and of Dr. A. D. Pusalker, a young and promising scholar, Assistant Director of the Bhāratīya Vidyā Bhavan, as assistant editor. A large number of Indian scholars of repute have lent their co-operation to the scheme. Professor H. G. Rawlinson has been good enough to undertake the task of revising the MS. Messrs. George Allen and Unwin Ltd. rendered my work easy by undertaking its first publication in 1951, despite difficult publishing conditions in England, and have now been good enough to remit the publication rights to the Bhavan. To all of them I owe a deep debt of gratitude which I hasten to acknowledge.

The General Editor in his introduction has given the point of view of the scientific historian, to which category the contributors belong. My own work for the past thirty-five years has lain in the humbler sphere of weaving historical romances and literary and cultural studies out of materials so heroically salvaged by Indian and European scholars. As a result I have seen and felt the form, continuity and meaning of India's past. History, as I see it, is being consciously lived by Indians. Attempts to complete what has happened in the past form no small part of our modern struggle; there is a conscious as well as an unconscious attempt to carry life to perfection, to join the fragments of existence, and to discover the meaning of the visions which they reveal. It is not enough, therefore, to conserve, record and understand what has happened: it is necessary also to assess the nature and direction of the momentous forces working through the life of India in order to appreciate the fulfilment which they seek.

Some years ago, therefore, I defined the scope of history as follows: "To be a history in the true sense of the word, the work must be the story of the people inhabiting a country. It must be a record of their life from age to age presented through the life and achievements of men whose exploits become the beacon lights of tradition; through the characteristic reaction of the people to physical and economic conditions; through political changes and vicissitudes which create the forces and conditions which operate upon life; through characteristic social institutions, beliefs and forms; through literary and artistic achievements; through the movements of thought which from time to time helped or hindered the growth of collective harmony; through those values which the people have accepted or reacted to and which created or shaped their collective will; through efforts of the people to will themselves into an organic unity. The central purpose of a history must, therefore, be to investigate and unfold the values which age after age have inspired the inhabitants of a country to develop their collective will and to express it through the manifold activities of their life. Such a history of India is still to be written."

I know the difficulties which beset the path of any enterprise which seeks to write such a history. In the past Indians laid little store by history. Our available sources of information are inadequate, and in so far as they are foreign, are almost invariably tainted with a bias towards India's conquerors. Research is meagre and disconnected.

Itihāsa, or legends of the gods, and *Purāṇa,* legends of origin, had different spheres in the ancient literary tradition of India. But later, both came to mean the same thing, traditional history. The *Kali Yuga,* the current Iron Age, was considered too degenerate a period to deserve recording. The past was only cherished as the pattern for the present and the future. Works by ancient Indian authors which throw light on history are few. Religious and literary sources like the *Purāṇas* and the *Kāvyas* have not yet fully yielded up their chronological or historical wealth. Epigraphic records, though valuable, leave many periods unrelated.

Foreign travellers from other countries of Asia and from Europe, like Megasthenes of Greece, Hiuen Tsang of China, Al-Masudi of Arabia, Manucci of Venice, and Bernier from France, have left valuable glimpses of India, but they are the results of superficial observation, though their value in reconstructing the past is immense. Chroniclers in the courts of the Turk, Afghan or the Mughal rulers wrote "histories" which, in spite of the wealth of historical material, are partially legendary and partially laudatory. The attempts of British scholars, with the exception of Tod, wherever they have taken these "histories" as reliable source-books, have hindered rather than helped the study of Indian history. Sir H. M. Elliot, the foremost of such scholars, for instance, has translated extracts from Persian and Arabic "histories" with a political objective, viz. to make, to use his own words, "the native subjects of British India more sensible of the immense advantages accruing to them under the mildness and equity of the present rule....." So high an authority as Dr. Maulānā Nadvi, in his Presidential Address at the "Early Medieval India" Section of the Seventh Session of the Indian History Congress, expressed the verdict of modern scholars, that both the selection and translation of these extracts have not been honest. But unfortunately, Elliot's volumes became the source-book for most of our modern histories of Medieval India. As a result, they do not present a true picture of India's past, nor do they explain how Indians resisted the Turk, Afghan and Mughal incursions, how they reacted to the vicissitudes through which in consequence they passed, and how a Renaissance sprang up out of the impact of Indian with Persian and Turkish cultures.

The treatment of the British period in most of our histories is equally defective. It generally reads like an unofficial report of the British conquest and of the benefits derived by India from it. It does not give us the real India; nor does it present a picture of what we saw, felt and suffered, of how we reacted to foreign influences, or of the values and organizations we created out of the impact with the West.

The history of India, as dealt with in most of the works of this kind, naturally, therefore, lacks historical perspective. Unfortunately for us, during the last two hundred years we had not only to study such histories but unconsciously to mould our whole outlook on life upon them. Few people realize that the teaching of such histories in our schools and universities has substantially added to the difficulties which India has had to face during the last hundred years, and never more than during recent years.

Generation after generation, during their school or college career, were told about the successive foreign invasions of the country, but little about how we resisted them and less about our victories. They were taught to decry the Hindu social system; but they were not told how this system came into existence as a synthesis of political, social, economic and cultural forces; how it developed in the people the tenacity to survive catastrophic changes for millennia; how it protected life and culture in times of difficulty by its conservative strength and in favourable times developed an elasticity which made ordered progress possible; and how its vitality enabled the national culture to adjust its central ideas to new conditions.

Readers were regaled with Alexander's short-lived and unfructuous invasion of India; they were left in ignorance of the magnificent empire and still more enduring culture which the Gangetic Valley had built up at the time. Lurid details of intrigues in the palaces of the Sultans of Delhi—often a camp of bloodthirsty invaders—are given, but little light is thrown on the exploits of the race of heroes and heroines who for centuries resisted the Central Asiatic barbarians when they flung themselves on this land in successive waves. Gruesome stories of Muslim atrocities are narrated, but the harmony which was evolved in social and economic life between the two communities remains unnoticed. The Mutiny of 1857—the British name for the Great National Revolt—gave the readers a glimpse of how the brave foreigner crushed India; it is only outside the so-called historical studies that the reader found how at the time patriotic men of all communities in most parts of India rallied round the last Mughal Emperor of Delhi, the national symbol, to drive out the hated foreigner.

The multiplicity of our languages and communities is widely advertised, but little emphasis is laid on certain facts which make India what she is. Throughout the last two millennia, there was linguistic unity Some sort of a *lingua franca* was used by a very large part of the country; and Sanskrit, for a thousand years the language of royal courts and at all times the language of culture, was predominant, influencing life, language, and literature in most provinces. For over three thousand years, social and family life had been moulded or influenced by the *Dharma-Śāstra* texts, containing a comprehensive code of personal law, which, though adapted from time to time to suit every age and province, provided a continuous unifying social force. Aryan, or rather Hindu culture (for there was considerable Dravidian influence) drew its inspiration in every successive generation from Sanskrit works on religion, philosophy, ritual, law and science, and particularly the two epics, the *Mahābhārata* and *Rāmāyaṇa,* and the *Bhāgavata,* underwent recensions from time to time, and became the one irresistible creative force which has shaped the collective spirit of the people. Age after age the best of Indians, from the mythical Vasishṭha to the modern Gāndhījī, found self-fulfilment in living up to an ideal of conduct in accordance with a code of life which may be traced back as far as the *Upanishads.*

The British conquest and the benefits of British rule are generally described in histories in "Rudyard Kipling" style. The impact of western culture, however, came in the wake of the British connection. In our histories we completely lose sight of how this impact awoke the sleeping giant to a consciousness of its ancient strength and modern possibilities; how under the influence of European ideas and British democratic traditions, the Collective Spirit, without losing its grip over the essentials of its culture, adjusted itself to modern conditions, creating new intellectual and artistic movements and making the democratic traditions of Great Britain its own; how, under the European concept of nationalism *Ārya-Dharma* (Indian Culture) slowly broadened out into a powerful neo-nationalism seeking a secular democratic state, Indian in conception and technique.

The older school of historians believed that imperialism of the militaristic political type was unfamiliar to this "mystic land." But the Aryan conquest of India, which forms the subject matter of Vol. I of this series, was as much militaristic-political as religious and cultural. If instead of treating by dynasties, stress is laid on the rise and fall of Imperial power, Magadhan sovereignty and Sātavāhana imperialism from 600 B.C. to A.D. 320 (Vol. II) were, for the age, outstanding phenomena. If the territory involved, the population affected, and the heroism and power of organization displayed and the cultural activities pursued are taken into account, the Classical Age, A.D. 320-750 (Vol. III), which saw the empire of the Guptas and of Śrī Harsha, was one of the culminating points in history. The age between A.D. 750-1000 (Vol. IV) saw the empire of the Pratīhāras, the Rāshṭrakūṭas and the Pālas. Between A.D. 1000 and 1300 (Vol. V), the Paramāras and the Cholas founded empires; different states struggled for imperial power; the barbarian inroads from Central Asia rendered all indigenous efforts at consolidation unfruitful.

The rise of the Turkish Power under Alā-ud-dīn Khiljī founded a new and powerful imperialism, the Sultanate of Delhi, which lasted from 1300 to 1526 (Vol. VI). From A.D. 1526-1707 the Mughals held sway at Delhi (Vol. VII) when the world witnessed one of the most magnificent empires of all time. The Marāṭhā supremacy, which lasted from 1707-1818 (Vol. VIII), brought about the downfall of the Mughal Empire, but before it could consolidate its power, the British stepped in. British domination from 1818-1947 (Vols. IX and X) was a period of complete subjection; but it saw the national resurgence which, on August 15, 1947, under Mahātmā Gāndhī, secured freedom by non-violent means. It also saw the birth of a Renaissance which gave fresh vitality to all that India stood for in history. These militaristic-political movements in India were in no wise less vigorous or worldly than similar movements in other parts of the world in the corresponding age. To say that the country was lost in contemplation all the time would be to ignore the salient facts of history.

The rôle of alien invasions in the history of India, hitherto exaggerated, deserves to be reduced to its appropriate proportions. India, like most other countries, has had its foreign incursions, which, like Mahmūd of Ghaznī's raids between A.D. 999 and 1024, glittering episodes from the raiders' point of view, were at best only shaping influences. Of foreign conquests, which changed the course of history and the texture of life and culture, there were only three. First, the Aryan conquests in pre-historic times, which wove the essential pattern of national life and culture. Second, the Turko-Afghan conquests, which introduced Islamic influence into India and added new colours to the pattern of life. These conquests, however, soon lost their character of foreign military occupation, for the conquerors threw in their lot with the country and produced some of its best rulers and its most powerful political organizations. This so-called Muslim period, scientifically the Turko-Mughal period, dominated the country for about four centuries roughly from A.D. 1300 to 1700. Third, the British occupation from 1818-1947, perhaps the only period of foreign rule in the sense that the country was governed essentially by foreigners from a foreign country and in foreign interests. It brought in its wake contact with Europe, a new awakening and a new cultural synthesis.

But during all this period the vitality of the race and culture, altered from time to time in direction and objective, expressed itself with unabated vigour in resistance movements, military, political, and cultural. The History of India is not the story of how she underwent foreign invasions, but how she resisted them and eventually triumphed over them. Traditions of modern historical research founded by British scholars of repute were unfortunately coloured by their attitude towards ancient Egypt, Greece and Rome, which have a dead past and are, in a sense, museum exhibits. A post-mortem examination of India's past would be scientifically inaccurate; for every period of Indian History is no more than an expression in a limited period of all the life forces and dominant ideas created and preserved by the national culture, which are rushing forward at every moment through time. The modern historian of India must approach her as a living entity with a central continuous urge, of which the apparent life is a mere expression. Without such an outlook it is impossible to understand India, which, though a part of it has seceded in search of an independent existence, stands today three hundred and fifty million strong, with a new apparatus of state, determined not to be untrue to its ancient self, and yet to be equal to the highest demands of modern life.

CONTENTS

LIST OF ILLUSTRATIONS

between pages 176 and 177

MAPS AND PLANS

PREFACE

by R. C. Majumdar, M.A., PH.D., F.R.A.S.B.

The genesis of this work and its scope and nature have been explained in the Foreword. But it is necessary to add a few words about its general planning. After having decided that the work would consist of ten volumes of approximately five hundred pages each, it was not an easy task to distribute the subject-matter among them on a basis which would be both equitable and rational. It has been hitherto customary to divide Indian history into the Hindu, Muslim and British periods, and assign equal space to each. The *Cambridge History of India* has set its seal of approval upon this plan, which has also been adopted by the Indian History Congress for its projected history of India. But it can hardly be regarded as equitable. Looking at the matter from a broad standpoint, it would be difficult to maintain that the 4,000 years of pre-Muslim India, of the history and culture of which we posses a definite knowledge, though in brief outline, should rank in importance as equal with that of the Muslim period of about 400 or 500 years, or the British period of less than 200 years. It is true that we possess more historical material for the later ages, but if we are to judge by that standard alone, the British period should have twice or thrice the number of volumes assigned to the Muslim period. After all, the contribution of different ages to the evolution of national history and culture should be the main criterion of their relative importance, though the space devoted to each should also be largely determined by the amount of historical material available. There is, no doubt, a dearth of material for the political history of ancient India, but this is to a large extent made up for by the corresponding abundance for the cultural side. Taking everything into consideration we have modified the hitherto-accepted plan, and have allotted nearly half of the entire work to the Hindu period.

Some difference will also be noticed in our conception of the beginning and end of the Muslim period. It is usual to regard the accession of Qutb-ud-din to the throne of Delhi in A.D. 1206 as the commencement of this period, and some historians even include within it the period of Ghaznivite supremacy in the Punjab two centuries earlier. It should be remembered, however, that the major part of India remained under Hindu rule almost throughout the thirteenth century A.D. and the same was also largely true of the century following the death of Aurangzeb. To include these two centuries under the Muslim period can therefore be hardly regarded as historically accurate.

These difficulties can best be overcome by avoiding altogether the terms Hindu and Muslim. As a matter of fact, one may rightly question the reasonableness of designating historical periods by the religious denomination of the ruling dynasties. In that case, in order to be consistent, we should style the third period of Indian history Christian rather than British. This is sufficient to demonstrate the absurdity of the present system of nomenclature, deep-rooted though it has become. We have accordingly divided Indian history into three chronological periods—Ancient, Mediaeval, and Modern—which are generally adopted for the history of Europe.

In the case of Europe, the overthrow of the Western Roman Empire by the irruption of barbarian hordes, which brought about the disappearance of classical learning, is taken to be the dividing line between Ancient and Mediaeval periods. In the case of India, there is no general agreement on this subject, but the onslaught of Islam, accompanied by a marked decadence of culture and the disappearance of the creative spirit in art and literature, seems to mark A.D. 1000 as the beginning of the Mediaeval Age.

The decline of the Mughal Empire and the growing power of the European nations in Indian politics may be reasonably regarded as marking the end of one and the beginning of another epoch in Indian history, and hence the eighteenth century has been taken as the commencement of the Modern Period. In Europe the Modern Period dates from the overthrow of the Eastern Roman Empire and the subversion of the age of faith and tradition by the awakening of humanism through the agency of the revival of classical learning. On this analogy one might be inclined to include the eighteenth century within the Mediaeval rather than the Modern period. But the political considerations referred to above, especially the establishment of the British power on a solid basis, are strong arguments in favour of dating the beginning of the Modern Period from the eighteenth century rather than the nineteenth.

For reasons given above, neither the thirteenth nor the eighteenth century A.D. has been included within what is usually described as the Muslim Period. The first is taken as a part of a long period of protracted struggle for political supremacy, both between the Indians and foreign invaders and among the Indians themselves, which ultimately ended in the next century in favour of the Khiljīs. So far as the eighteenth century is concerned there is no doubt that the Marāṭhās were the leading political power in India. These two volumes have been styled accordingly.

So far by way of explanation of the general division into three broad periods—Ancient, Mediaeval, and Modern—and the titles given to Volumes V and VIII, which mark a great departure from current practice. It must be remembered, however, that while specific dates had to be assigned to each volume for the sake of precision and accuracy, they should not be strictly equated with the title given to it. The period of Marāṭhā supremacy, for example, cannot be said to cover exactly the years A.D. 1707 to 1818, but nevertheless these have been taken to be the limiting dates of Volume VIII, which bears that title, because they mark definite events of great importance connected with the central theme, viz. the death of Aurangzeb which facilitated the growth of Marāṭhā power, and the Third Marāṭhā War which put an end to the Marāthā supremacy.

The same is more or less true of the other volumes and the justification for the titles and dates will be discussed in the preface of each. For the present we may confine our attention to the present volume. Although it is entitled the Vedic Age it begins from the dawn of human activity in India, so far as it is known to us. Being the first volume of the series, it contains an introductory section dealing with certain general topics bearing upon the history of India as a whole. As there are some special characteristics which distinguish Indian history from that of other countries, it has been thought desirable to explain at the very outset its meaning and methods of approach as well as the nature of the material from which it has been reconstructed. The first three chapters have been devoted to this subject. The next three deal with the background of Indian history, geological, geographical and biological. These chapters, particularly the first and third, may appear too technical for the historical student, and some may even regard them as too elaborate for a treatise on history at all. But a knowledge of these topics is essential for a proper understanding of the evolution of Indian culture, and being written by acknowledged experts, these two chapters, it may be hoped, will place at the disposal of the reader adequate information on difficult but relevant subjects, which it would not be possible for them to acquire except by the patient study of bulky volumes of a highly technical nature, which few would be disposed to undertake.

The next section, which may be regarded as the beginning of history proper, deals with the period before the Vedic Aryans settled in this country. This, however, involves certain assumptions which are not unanimously accepted. Some scholars hold the view that India was the original home of these Aryans, and that there cannot be any question of their immigration into this country. Some have referred the Aryans to such hoary antiquity—tens of thousands of years ago according to more than one theory—that there can be no question of any historical period prior to them.

Similarly there is a divergence of opinion regarding the question whether the Indus valley civilization was pre-Aryan or post-Vedic. In the present state of our knowledge no dogmatic answer can be given to these questions, and there is no theory that is likely to meet with general acceptance. Even our own contributors do not agree on these points. Dr. Pusalker, who has written on the Indus Valley Civilization, is inclined to regard it as not fundamentally different from the Aryan, and possibly posterior to Rigvedic culture, while Dr. B. K. Ghosh and Dr. S. K. Chatterji, who have written on the Aryan and pre-Aryan peoples, take the opposite view. Such differences are inevitable in a co-operative undertaking of this kind. It has not been thought advisable to suppress these individual view-points, but cross-references have been given in order to impress upon the readers that such questions do admit of different answers and to enable them to judge for themselves the cogency of the arguments on which different theories are based.

It has been the constant attempt of the Editor, by free and frank discussions, to reconcile the different points of view as far as practicable, and where complete agreement was unattainable, to have them presented in a manner which would convey the impression that they are not dogmatic assertions of contradictory views, but alternative solutions, each equally valid, of the problem concerned. Beyond that the Editor did not choose to go, by way of forcing a definite solution of an admittedly controversial problem. It has been thought better to risk even a seeming inconsistency among the different parts of the book rather than convey a false idea of a general agreement of views where no such unanimity really exists, or is possible under the present circumstances.

The third section is devoted to a general consideration of the Indo-Aryans. It begins with a detailed discussion of the chief problems concerning them, viz. their original home, the date and route of their immigration into India, the antiquity of their chief literary production, the *Ṛigveda,* and their relations with the Iranians with whom they must have lived in close and intimate contact long after their separation from the other branches of the Indo-European family. These are some of the most intriguing problems on which opinions differ widely, and an attempt has been made to present the different viewpoints, with emphasis on the one which appears to be most reasonable in the light of the evidence available to us. Although few scholars today believe India to be the original home of the Aryans, this theory has naturally a sentimental appeal to Indians, and has therefore been discussed in some detail in an Appendix to Chapter X.

The fourth section deals with the political history of the period. It has been customary hitherto to rely for such knowledge only on the few scattered historical notices contained in the *Ṛigveda.* Pargiter's attempt to reconstruct a continuous historical narrative from the data, particularly the royal genealogies, contained in the Purāṇas and the Epics, has been systematically ignored in historical works, even in the comprehensive *Cambridge History of India*. But, in spite of obvious shortcomings, Pargiter's theories cannot be altogether discarded even on their merits, and the fact remains that they offer the only fair basis on which the ancient political history of India can be built up. So instead of being content to glean a few isolated facts from the *Ṛigveda,* as has hitherto been done, we have tried to trace a brief outline of the traditional history of early India on the lines laid down by Pargiter. This must not, of course, be confused with history proper, but it possesses none the less great value of its own, both as a tangible framework for connecting a number of well-authenticated facts, and as a basis for further investigation of our historical knowledge of this obscure period. Pargiter has at least successfully demonstrated that it is a mistake to regard such great historical figures of antiquity as Pūru, Māndhātā, Nahusha, Yayāti, Kārtavīrya Arjuna, etc., as mere fanciful and mythological names, and any theory which gives them some sort of historical setting cannot but be regarded as of great value to students of Indian history.

In spite of the limitations of our knowledge of the political history of the period, there can be no doubt that its chief interest and importance lie in the picture of culture and civilization offered by the vast field of Vedic literature. Whereas everything else is but vaguely known, we possess nearly full information about the growth and gradual evolution of the Indian civilization from the well-marked stratification of the mass of literature, collectively known as the Vedas. It is also a matter of general knowledge that this civilization is the common basis on which succeeding generations of diverse races and localities have built up the imposing structure known as the Hindu civilization. This would explain why this volume has been entitled *The Vedic Age,* and detailed study has been made of it in three different sections, corresponding to the three well-marked stages of the evolution of Vedic literature.

There is a general agreement among scholars about the chronological sequence of Vedic literature: the *Ṛik-Saṁhitā* representing the earliest stage, the other Saṁhitās and Brāhmaṇas the next, and the Upanishads and Sūtras the concluding one. But while these chronological divisions are, broadly speaking, accurate, it is to be noted that they are to some extent overlapping, and it is difficult to draw an absolutely rigid line of demarcation between them. It is likely, for example, that some portions of the *Atharva-Saṁhitā* are as old as, if not older than, portions of the *Ṛik-Saṁhitā,* and some of the oldest Upanishads certainly reach back to the Brāhmaṇa period. Nevertheless the general outlook of the three different categories of literature is sufficiently distinct to label them as belonging to three successive chronological periods, and they have been dealt with accordingly in three separate sections.

It is, however, a difficult problem to assign definite dates to the three literary stages of the Vedic period. In spite of extravagant theories about the antiquity of the *Ṛik-Saṁhitā*, the view that it received its present form about 1000 B.C. has much to commend itself. Though mainly based on philological grounds, as enunciated in Chapter XII, this theory finds unexpected support even from Indian traditions. For some of the kings referred to in the *Ṛik-Saṁhitā* seem to be identical with those mentioned in the royal genealogies and occupying a low place in the dynastic list. Further, as Pargiter has pointed out, "the Epic and Puranic tradition unanimously and repeatedly declares that the Veda was arranged by Vyāsa," who flourished about the time of the Bhārata War, which has been dated between 1500 and 1000 B.C. by many scholars. Whatever we might think of this date, it is important to remember that along with the doctrine that "the Veda is eternal and everlasting," there are also ancient traditions to the effect that it was compiled by Vyāsa not long before the great Bhārata War. The view that dates the *Ṛik-Saṁhitā, in its present form*, to about 1000 B.C., cannot therefore be regarded as absolutely wide of the mark and altogether without any basis of support in Indian tradition. But it must be remembered that although the *Ṛik-Saṁhitā* might have received its final shape in about 1000 B.C., some of its contents are much older, and go back certainly to 1500 B.C., and not improbably even to a much earlier date.

There is no doubt whatsoever that the oldest Upanishads are pre-Buddhist, and some of them at any rate belonged to the seventh century B.C., if not earlier still. The later Saṁhitās and Brāhmaṇas accordingly may be placed, generally speaking, in the ninth and eighth centuries B.C. These dates are of course only provisional and are set down here as merely working hypotheses.

No precise date can be assigned to the end of the Vedic Age, for the Sūtras and Upanishads, representing the last stage of Vedic literature, contain texts of varying antiquity. While, as mentioned above, some of them are probably as old as the seventh century B.C., if not older still, others are probably as late as the third or fourth century B.C. Although, therefore, the Vedic Age cannot be regarded, strictly speaking, as having come to an end in 600 B.C. with which this volume closes, this date has been selected mainly for two reasons. In the first place, the sixth century B.C. saw the rise of Buddhism, Jainism, and other religious sects heralding that Protestant movement which was destined to bring to an end the unquestioned supremacy of Vedic religion and culture. Secondly, our knowledge of political history becomes more precise and definite from the sixth century B.C., and we can clearly perceive how the stage was gradually set for the rise of the great Magadha empire which constitutes the most distinguishing feature of the succeeding period.

Although the age of the Sūtras and Upanishads extends beyond 600 B.C., culturally it is a direct offshoot and a continuation of the earlier Vedic civilization, and reflects no special characteristic of the later era, such as we find in the Epics, Purāṇas, or Buddhist and Jaina literature. It has, therefore, been included in the volume dealing with the Vedic Age even in disregard of the strict limitations of chronology.

This volume attempts a picture of what may be regarded as the dawn of Hindu civilization. To continue this metaphor, we may say that the next two volumes reflect its full morning glory and noonday splendour; in the fourth volume we come across the shadows of the declining day, while dusk sets in with the fifth. Then follows the darkness of the long night, so far as Hindu civilization is concerned, a darkness which envelops it even now. This gives a broad idea of the distribution of the first five volumes of this series.

The Editor takes this opportunity of offering his sincere thanks to the contributors of this volume for their hearty co-operation, and to Professor H.G. Rawlinson for having kindly revised the MS.

He notes with great regret that one of the contributors, Rao Bahadur K. N. Dikshit, late Director-General of Archaeology, Government of India, passed away while the book was in the press, and takes this opportunity to convey his condolence to the bereaved family. His death has been a serious loss to Indian Archaeology.

The Department of Archaeology, Government of India, has kindly supplied us with photographs for which we express our hearty thanks to the authorities.

Some amount of repetition or overlapping is inevitable in a book of this kind where different authors deal with literature and the philosophical, religious, and social ideas mainly derived from it, and where the different chapters are closely related to one another.

The system of transliteration adopted in this volume is that followed in the *Epigraphia Indica*. The geographical names have been spelt as in the Imperial Gazetteer, with a few exceptions such as "Krishnā" for "Kistnā," "Narmadā" for "Narbadā." Diacritical marks have not been used, as a rule, in geographical names and oriental words with an English suffix (Puranic, Rigvedic, Brahmanical, etc.) except to indicate the long *a* sound (ā). In the word Aryan, however, the *a* has not been lengthened as it may now be regarded as almost a naturalized English word.

In addition to footnotes, general references have been added at the beginning of some chapters in order to indicate books or articles in periodicals which have been extensively used or frequently referred to in the body of the text. No footnotes have been given in Chapter II as all the works cited therein will be dealt with in detail in subsequent chapters.

A Bibliography has been added for the convenience of those readers who wish to make special studies of any particular topic. As most of our knowledge regarding the history and culture of the Vedic Age is derived from Vedic literature, and a large number of secondary texts also deal with the period as a whole, a General Bibliography has been given at the end which covers the topics dealt with in Books IV, V, VI, and VII. Generally speaking the Bibliography is selective in character and does not aim at giving an exhaustive list of works on the subject. The only exception to this is the Bibliography to Chapter IX where an attempt has been made to give a list of all important contributions on the Indus Valley civilization, as the subject is comparatively new and controversial in character, and it is difficult to assess the proper value of the different theories. As copious footnotes have been given in many chapters, important references indicated therein have not been included.

ABBREVIATIONS

ABIA.	*Annual Bibliography of Indian Archaeology, Leyden.*
ABORI.	*Annals of the Bhandarkar Oriental Research Institute, Poona.*
AE.	*Ancient Egypt, London.*
AIHT.	*Ancient Indian Historical Tradition, by F. E. Pargiter.*
Ait. Br.	*Aitareya Brāhmaṇa.*
AJA.	*American Journal of Archaeology, Philadelphia.*
AL.	*Altindisches Leben, by H. Zimmer.*
Anthrop. Soc. Bom. Jub. Vol.	*Anthropological Society of Bombay, Jubilee Volume.*
AP.	*Aryan Path, Bombay.*
Āp. Dh.S.	*Apastamba Dharma-sūtra.*
Āp. Ś.S.	*Apastamba Śrauta-sūtra.*
ASI.	*Annual Report of the Archaeological Survey of India.*
ĀSS.	*Ānandāśrama Sanskrit Series, Poona.*
AV.	*Atharvaveda.*
Bau. Dh.S.	*Baudhāyana Dharma-sūtra.*
Bau. Ś.S.	*Baudhāyana Śrauta-sūtra.*
BDCRI.	*Bulletin of the Deccan College Research Institute, Poona.*
BEFEO.	*Bulletin de-l'École Française d'Extrême-Orient, Hanöi.*
BIR.	*Bhāratīya Itihāsakī Rūparekhā (in Hindi), Vol. I, by Jaya Chandra Vidyalankar.*
BMFA.	*Bulletin of the Museum of Fine Arts, Boston.*
Br.	*Brāhmaṇa.*
Bṛih.	*Bṛihadāraṇyaka Upanishad.*
BSOS.	*Bulletin of the School of Oriental (and African) Studies, London.*
BV.	*Bharatīya Vidyā, Bombay.*
CAG.	*Cunningham's Ancient Geography of India, Ed. by S. N. Majumdar.*
CAH.	*Cambridge Ancient History.*
CAI.	*Chronology of Ancient India, by S. N. Pradhan.*
Chan-d.	*Chanhu-daro Excavations, 1933-36, by E. J. H. Mackay.*
Chhānd.	*Chhāndogya Upanishad.*
CHI.	*Cambridge History of India.*
Comm. Vol.	*Commemoration Volume.*
CR.	*Calcutta Review, Calcutta.*
CS.	*Current Science, Bangalore.*
Cult. Her.	*Cultural Heritage of India. Published by Śrī Rāmakṛishṇa Centenary Committee, Calcutta.*
Dh. S.	*Dharma-sūtra.*
DKA.	*Dynasties of the Kali Age, by F. E. Pargiter.*
EI.	*Epigraphia Indica, Delhi.*
ERE.	*Encyclopaedia of Religion and Ethics, Ed. by J. Hastings.*

Gau. Dh.S.	*Gautama Dharma-sūtra.*
GD.	*Geographical Dictionary of Ancient and Medieval India, 2nd Edn., by N. L. Dey.*
Geol. Mag.	*Geological Magazine.*
Gṛ. S.	*Gṛihya-sūtra.*
Harappa.	*Excavations at Harappa, by M. S. Vats.*
Hari.	*Harivaṁśa (Bombay Edition).*
HASL.	*History of Ancient Sanskrit Literature, by F. Max Müller.*
HIL.	*History of Indian Literature.*
HIP.	*History of Indian Philosophy, Vol II, Creative Period, by S. K. Belvalkar and R. D. Ranade.*
HOS.	*Harvard Oriental Series, Cambridge, Mass.*
HSL.	*History of Sanskrit Literature, by A. B. Keith.*
IA.	*Indian Antiquary, Bombay.*
IAL.	*Indian Art and Letters, London.*
IC.	*Indian Culture, Calcutta.*
IHQ.	*Indian Historical Quarterly, Calcutta.*
ILN.	*Illustrated London News, London.*
Ind. Antiquities.	*Studies in Indian Antiquities, by H. C. Raychaudhuri.*
Ind. Sc. Congress.	*Indian Science Congress.*
Ind. Stud.	*Indische Studien, by A. Weber.*
IP.	*Indian Philosophy, by S. Radhakrishnan.*
JA.	*Journal Asiatique, Paris.*
JAHRS.	*Journal of the Andhra Historical Research Society, Rajahmundry.*
Jai. G.S.	*Jaiminīya Gṛihya-sūtra.*
JAOS.	*Journal of the American Oriental Society.*
JASB.	*Journal of the Asiatic Society of Bengal, Calcutta.*
JBHS.	*Journal of the Bombay Historical Society, Bombay.*
JBHU.	*Journal of the Benares Hindu University, Benares.*
JBORS.	*Journal of the Behar and Orissa Research Society, Patna.*
JGIS.	*Journal of the Greater India Society, Calcutta.*
JGRS.	*Journal of the Gujarat Research Society, Bombay.*
JIH.	*Journal of Indian History, Madras.*
JISOA.	*Journal of the Indian Society of Oriental Art, Calcutta.*
JMU.	*Journal of the Madras University, Madras.*
JOR.	*Journal of Oriental Research, Madras.*
JRAI.	*Journal of the Royal Anthropological Institute of Great Britain and Ireland, London.*
JRAS.	*Journal of the Royal Asiatic Society of Great Britain and Ireland, London.*
JRASB(L).	*Journal of the Royal Asiatic Society of Bengal, Letters, Calcutta.*
JRASB(S).	*Journal of the Royal Asiatic Society of Bengal, Science, Calcutta.*
JRSA.	*Journal of the Royal Society of Arts, London.*
JSHS.	*Journal of the Sind Historical Society, Karachi.*

ABBREVIATIONS

JUB.	*Journal of the University of Bombay, Bombay.*
JUPHS.	*Journal of the U.P. Historical Society, Lucknow.*
Kaṭha.	*Kaṭha (or Kāṭhaka) Upanishad.*
Kau. S.	*Kauśika Sūtra.*
Kaushi.	*Kaushītaki Upanishad.*
Kena.	*Kena Upanishad.*
KHDS.	*History of Dharmaśāstra, by P. V. Kane.*
KHR.	*Karnatak Historical Review, Dharwar.*
KZ.	*Kuhn's Zeitschrift.*
MAGW.	*Mitteilungun der Anthropologischen Gesellschaft in Wien.*
Mānava G.S.	*Mānava Gṛihya-sūtra.*
Manu.	*Manusmṛiti.*
MASI.	*Memoirs of the Archaeological Survey of India.*
Mbh.	*Mahābhārata (= Bombay Edition, unless specifically stated otherwise).*
Mbh. (Cr. Ed.).	*Critical Edition of the Mahābhārata, published by the Bhandarkar Oriental Research Institute, Poona (used for the first five Parvans hitherto published).*
Mem. Geol. Surv Ind.	*Memoirs of the Geological Survey of India.*
Moh. Exc.	*Further Excavations at Mohenjo-daro, by E. J. H. Mackay.*
Moh. Ind.	*Mohenjo-daro and the Indus Civilisation, by J. Marshall.*
MR.	*Modern Review, Calcutta.*
Muṇḍ.	*Muṇḍaka Upanishad.*
New Light.	*New Light on the Most Ancient East, by V. Gordon Childe.*
NIA.	*New Indian Antiquary, Bombay.*
NR.	*New Review, Calcutta.*
OLZ.	*Orientalische Literaturzeitung, Leipzig.*
P.	*Purāna.*
Pañch. Br.	*Pañchaviṁśa Brāhmaṇa.*
PBA.	*Proceedings of the British Academy.*
PHAI.	*Political History of Ancient India, 4th Edn., by H. C. Raychaudhuri.*
PIHC.	*Proceedings of the Indian History Congress.*
POC.	*Proceedings of the All-India Oriental Conference.*
PPL.	*Das Purāṇa Pañchalakshaṇa, by W. Kirfel.*
Preh. Civ.	*Prehistoric Civilisation of the Indus Valley, by K. N. Dikshit.*
Prolegomena.	*Die Hymnen des Ṛigveda, Vol. I.: Metrische und text-geschichtliche Prolegomena, by H. Oldenberg.*
QJMS.	*Quarterly Journal of the Mythic Society, Bangalore.*
Rec. Geol. Surv. Ind.	*Records of the Geological Survey of India.*
Rivers.	*Rivers of India, by B. C. Law.*
RPVU.	*Religion and Philosophy of the Veda and Upanishads, by A. B. Keith.*

RV.	*Ṛigveda.*
Śāṅkh Śr.S.	*Śāṅkhāyana Śrauta-sūtra.*
Śat. Br.	*Śatapatha Brāhmaṇa.*
SAWM.	*Sitzungsberichte der Bayerischen Akademie der Wissenschaften, München.*
SBA.	*Sitzungsberichte der Berliner Akademie der Wissenschaften.*
SBE.	*Sacred Books of the East, Oxford.*
SC.	*Science and Culture, Calcutta.*
Sript.	*The Script of Harappa and Mohenjo-daro, by G. R. Hunter.*
SD.	*Sanskrit Drama, by A. B. Keith.*
SPAW.	*Sitzungsberichte der Preussischen Akademie der Wissenschaften.*
ŚS.	*Śrauta-sūtra.*
SV.	*Sāmaveda.*
Śve.	*Śvetāśvatara Upanishad.*
Taitt.	*Taittirīya Upanishad.*
Taitt. Br.	*Taittirīya Brāhmaṇa.*
Taitt. Saṁ.	*Taittirīya Saṁhitā.*
Tribes.	*Tribes in Ancient India, by B. C. Law.*
Vas. Dh.S.	*Vasishṭha Dharma-sūtra.*
Ved. Ind.	*Vedic Index, by A. A. Macdonell and A. B. Keith.*
Ved. Myth.	*Vedische Mythologie, by A. Hillebrandt.*
Ved. Stud.	*Vedische Studien, by R. Pischel and K. F. Geldner.*
VM.	*Vedic Mythology, by A. A. Macdonell.*
WZKM.	*Wiener Zeitschrift für die Kunde des Morgenlandes.*
YV.	*Yajurveda.*
ZDMG.	*Zeitschrift der Deutschen Morgenländische Gesellschaft, Leipzig.*
ZII.	*Zeitschrift für Indologie und Iranistik, Leipzig.*

THE VEDIC AGE

BOOK ONE

INTRODUCTION

CHAPTER I

INDIAN HISTORY—ITS NATURE, SCOPE AND METHOD

History has been defined as "the study of man's dealings with other men, and the adjustment of working relations between human groups." The beginnings of the history of India, therefore, go back to that remote period when man first settled in this country. We need not discuss whether he migrated from outside or emerged here by a process of evolution from his animal ancestors. But in any case the earliest man has left little evidence to enable us to investigate his thoughts, desires, activities or achievements. We can only dimly discern his gradual growth as a sentient being amid the geological changes and physical and biological environment in which he found himself. To begin with, he was essentially a part of the plant and animal life that surrounded him, reacting passively to the climate and geographical configuration of the land. But he slowly gained consciousness of those powers and potentialities which distinguished him from other animals and enabled him to dominate over nature rather than remain its slave.

The greater part of this process of evolution, which must have covered a long period of time, is only a matter of inference based on very slender evidence. The study of this fascinating subject has made some progress in Europe, while so far as India is concerned, it is still in its infancy. But the little that is known shows that the prehistoric period in India presents features very similar to what we meet with in Western Asia and Europe. Here, as elsewhere, "man's prehistory merges in the pageant of the animal world," and is largely determined by his natural surroundings.

This volume, therefore, begins with a short account of the geological, geographical, and biological background of primitive man. This setting of the stage is followed by a study of the peoples who played their part therein. In the absence of any written record, the little that we know of their history and culture is based on archaeological finds, such as tools and implements made of stone, bone or metal, potsherds, rude paintings and skeletal remains—exactly the same type of evidence on which the prehistoric study of other countries is based.

As we proceed with our narrative we gradually realize that the different phases of Indian history present a striking parallel to those of other countries which can boast of a culture and civilization going back to remote antiquity. The stone implements and other remains of the palaeolithic and neolithic periods prove that human civilization began here in the same way, if not at the same time, as in other parts of the world. The development of this civilization through the copper and iron ages, presents features which, though not identical, yet offer sufficient similarity in detail with what we know of many other countries. The discoveries in the Indus Valley and adjacent regions have further emphasized the close association between the cultures of India and those of Western Asia, and thereby link up Indian history with that of the most ancient period of the world known to us.

India now takes her place, side by side with Egypt and Mesopotamia, as a country where we can trace the dawn of human civilization and the beginnings of those thoughts, ideas, activities and movements which have shaped the destinies of mankind all over the civilized world. The history of India thus possesses an aspect of universality which so strikingly distinguishes the history of Egypt, Babylonia, and Assyria in the early, and Persia, Greece, and Rome in a somewhat later age. In the case of each of these the universal aspect far transcends in importance the individual or regional aspect. This is not, however, the case with India. This difference has modified the outlook and treatment of the history of India and made it a problem almost *sui generis.*

The chief difference between India and the other ancient countries mentioned above lies in the continuity of her history and civilization. The culture and civilization of Egypt, Sumer, Akkad, Babylon, Assyria, and Persia have long ceased to exist. They are now mere past memories and their history possesses only an academic interest. Indian history and institutions, however, form an unbroken chain by which the past is indissolubly linked up with the present. The modern peoples of Egypt and Mesopotamia have no bond whatsoever with the civilization that flourished there millennia ago and its memorials have no more (usually very very much less) meaning to them than to any enlightened man in any part of the world.

But not so in India. The icons discovered at Mohenjo-daro are those of gods and goddesses who are still worshipped in India, and Hindus from the Himalaya to Cape Comorin repeat even today the Vedic hymns which were uttered on the banks of the Indus nearly four thousand years ago. This continuity in language and literature, and in religious and social usages, is more prominent in India than even in Greece and Italy, where we can trace the same continuity in history. The social and religious ideas of ancient Greece and Rome and their philosophy and outlook on life, in short, some of the most essential factors which give individuality to a nation and preserve its continuity, are almost foreign to the peoples now inhabiting those lands. An artificial continuity is no doubt maintained in these two countries, and the link with the past is not altogether snapped, as in the cases of Egypt and Mesopotamia. Nevertheless, the difference can only be regarded as one of degree and not of kind: and neither

Greece nor Italy offers a parallel to India, in respect of either antiquity or continuity of civilization.

To this difference may be added the present position of India. Her political subjection and lack of material power have relegated her to a position of marked inferiority in the eyes of the world. Both these causes have affected the study of the history of India in more ways than one. It has not been easy, for instance, to bring a detached scientific spirit to bear on the study of the history of India. This spirit, which so conspicuously distinguishes European writers of the history of Egypt and ancient countries in Western Asia, is not seldom lamentably absent while they deal with the history of India. The reason is not far to seek, and may be traced to a psychological instinct or political prejudice. The India of today has cast its shadow on the past, and few writers have been able to disentangle the two and view each of them in its true perspective. The political history of India, even of ancient times, has been almost invariably viewed through the spectacles of the eighteenth and nineteenth centuries. V. A. Smith, the well-known historian of ancient India, and a distinguished member of the Indian Civil Service, never concealed his anxiety to prove the beneficence of the British Raj by holding before his readers the picture of anarchy and confusion which, in his view, has been the normal condition in India with rare intervals. To him, as to many others before and after him, ancient Indian history after the death of Harsha-vardhana was merely a pathetic tale of political chaos and internecine struggles, pointing to the inevitable moral: "such was India and such it always has been till the British established a stable order."

Sometimes the pendulum swings to the opposite extreme, and Indian writers seek to find in ancient India a replica of the most advanced political institutions of the West. From isolated phrases of doubtful import they conjure up a picture of a full-fledged modern democracy and even of an up-to-date parliamentary form of government. This is a counterblast, from the Indian side, to the inveterate belief of European writers in undiluted autocracy as the only form of government that ever prevailed in India. To them "Oriental despotism" is an article of faith that colours their whole outlook. Some have also inherited the classical idea that wisdom and enlightenment were always a sort of monopoly of the West, and the East, comparatively as backward as she is today, must have acquired all the elements of higher culture from the West.

The squalid poverty of modern India colours the outlook on economic conditions in ancient and mediaeval times. Even enlightened historians find it difficult to accept the view that Indians built ships and navigated the seas, for no better reason than that modern Indians show such an aversion from, and ineptitude for, maritime activities. Such instances may be multiplied to almost any extent.

There are no doubt exceptions, but one cannot deny, or overlook, the broad fact that Indian history has suffered much from an instinct to read the present into the past.

The opposite danger of reading the past into the present has been no less a potential factor in distorting the history of India. To many the most glaring imperfections and even the most degrading features of modern Indian social life are sanctified by antiquity. They have a tendency to judge everything they see before them, not by its present form and effect, but by a reference to what they conceive to be its original character, and the part it is supposed to have played in building up an ideal society in the past. This almost necessarily leads to the artificial creation of a golden age which rests mainly on imagination and intuition, independent of historical evidence. This intellectual support of false doctrines and bad institutions in the name of India's past often proceeds from a perverted form of patriotic sentiments or an inborn sense of national pride. In either case it is a wrong interpretation of Indian history, and what is worse, such interpretation is often devised as an instrument for consecrating all deep-seated prejudices.

The student of Indian history must avoid these pitfalls and follow the modern method of scientific research. Our aim should be the discovery of the truth, and nothing but the truth, and in order to attain this goal we must apply our minds fearlessly and without prejudice and preconceptions to the study of all available evidence. We should properly sift these data by all rational methods, handle them in the spirit of a judge rather than an advocate, and formulate our conclusions only as far as they permit us to do so. We may not achieve definite results in many cases, and final and decisive conclusions would probably be few and far between. But it is better to plead ignorance, express doubts and put forward alternative possibilities rather than definitely uphold a view on meagre and insufficient grounds. We must be particularly on our guard where any such view is likely to evoke strong sentiments and passions or affect the interest of any class or community. The history of India's past touches the present life of India on many points, and we may legitimately expect the one to guide and control the other. This makes it all the more difficult, especially for an Indian writer, to take a detached view of the history of India and approach it in a purely scientific attitude. Nevertheless the difficulty, great as it is, must be overcome, and a proper critical spirit should be cultivated, if we are to read aright the story of India's past and correctly understand its implications for the future.

We have so far dealt with the peculiar difficulties that confront us in the study of Indian history in view of its continuity. Another obstacle, also of a somewhat special character, arises from the nature of the evidence on which the study must necessarily be based. The different classes of evidence and their nature, scope and value will be discussed in detail in the next chapter. But some general points must be noted here in order to indicate both the limitations and the specific directions of our study.

The first thing to remember is that for the longest period of Indian history, viz., from the earliest time down to the Muslim conquest in the thirteenth century A.D., a period of about four thousand years, we possess no historical text of any kind, much less such a detailed narrative as we possess in the case of Greece, Rome, and China. The history of ancient India resembles, therefore, that of ancient Egypt and Mesopotamia. In all these cases it has only been possible to reconstruct the skeleton with the help of archaeological evidence discovered in comparatively recent times. This history differs radically from what we normally understand by the word. It is mostly a string of names and incidents, often with wide gaps, and almost always without that fullness of detail which enables us to trace the causes and consequences of specific events, examine the various forces at work in their true perspective, mark the general tendencies of the epoch, explain the inner causes of the rise and fall of kingdoms and empires, or the progress and decay of races and nations, and determine the exact relation between the different elements of the body politic or the different aspects of life and society. These and many other features which make history a social science in the real sense of the term are lacking in the history of ancient India, more or less to the same extent as in that of other ancient civilizations that flourished in Egypt or Western Asia.

But there is one very important difference. Ancient India has bequeathed to us a vast treasury of texts which represent the intellectual and literary activities of more than two thousand years and cover a wide field. The earliest literary work, the Saṁhitā of the *Ṛigveda*, is at least three thousand years old and may be even considerably older. A continuous stream of literature flowing since that remote age, widening in course of centuries, and embracing almost all fields of human endeavour excepting political activity, throws a light on the civilization of India such as we do not meet with in cases of other ancient cultures. This mass of literature deals with philosophy and religion, including ethics, ritual, and ceremonial; cosmogony, cosmology, geography, astronomy, and the allied sciences; political and economic doctrines and practices; and, in a minor way, with almost all branches of secular life. It includes, besides a mass of religious texts, purely literary works such as epics, lyrics, *Kāvyas* (poems), dramas and prose romances, as well as biographies and folk tales. This literature is as bulky in volume as it is varied in its contents. Although it does not help us very much in reconstructing the political history of ancient India, it throws a flood of light on, and enables us to trace the various stages in the development of, culture and civilization in ancient India, such as is not possible in the case of ancient Egypt, Western Asia and China, and even Greece and Rome.

This fact must be borne in mind in any approach to the study of ancient Indian history. We should not expect any critical and detailed narrative of the political events, or a proper estimate of the life and character of great historical personages of whom we catch but fleeting glimpses in the moving panorama of the history of two thousand years that passes before our eyes in a haze of mist or gloom. The galaxy of kings, generals, and statesmen which crowd, for instance, the canvas of the history of Greece and Rome, the moving stories of their lives and activities, the surging mass of internal and external forces that shape the destiny of the state and set it going, sometimes in slow evolution and sometimes in revolutionary ardour, and the ebb and tide of national glory from age to age with its intense human appeal and great lessons for posterity—all these and many other factors which form the spell of the history of Greece and Rome do not constitute the main force or the chief interest of ancient Indian history. That these elements were not lacking in the evolution of Indian history is proved by the occasional glimpses of great men and great events, of the same genre. But these are mostly shadows, without that glow and colour which endow them with life and spirit. Hence the picture is dull and lifeless and, being devoid of general interest, makes no passionate appeal to human mind.

But though admittedly deficient in this respect, Indian history is abundantly rich in its delineation of the progress of the human mind and society from its earliest infancy to a comparatively mature state. Other civilizations must have passed through the same or similar stages, but we lack the means to trace them in such fullness of details. In no other case, for example, can we go back to the dim beginnings of those intellectual and moral ideas which appear to us in full maturity in the shape of a set form of religion, theology, and philosophy. Thanks to the vast mass of Indian literature, we can not only do this but follow, in a general way, the long and tortuous ways which human civilization, at least in a large part of the world, has had to pursue in its weary and tedious onward march for thousands of years. This constitutes a claim for universal interest which should not be less keen than that inspired by the political history of Greece and Rome.

The genius of each considerable group of humanity is perhaps adapted more to one kind of end than to another. It has been argued that the Indians had a bent of mind which looked more to the inner self than the outer body, to matters spiritual rather than the material world. In the absence of a fuller knowledge of the political history or secular life of ancient India, it is difficult to set the final seal of approval to this view, although it is very generally held. But so far as available evidence goes, there cannot be the slightest doubt that Indian civilization manifests itself in a way and a form very different from that with which we are familiar in the rest of the world. We have consequently to approach the history of India in a different spirit, and adopt a different scale of values in order to appraise her culture and civilization. The wars and conquests, the rise and fall of empires and nations, and the development of political ideas and institutions should not be regarded as the principal object of our study, and must be relegated to a position of secondary importance. On the other hand, more stress should be laid upon philosophy, religion, art, and letters, the development of social and moral ideas, and the general progress of those humanitarian ideals and institutions which form the distinctive feature of the spiritual life of India and her greatest contribution to the civilization of the world.

Nevertheless, the political history of each period, as far as it is known to us, must be the starting point of our study, as it forms the backbone of history. Its function may be compared to that of the skeleton in a human body which gives shape and distinctness to the mass of flesh and skin and marks it with the stamp of individuality.

The greatest handicap in the treatment of the history of ancient India, both political and cultural, is the absence of a definite chronology. The dates of political events and of the vast mass of literature which forms the basis of cultural study are but imperfectly known, and the farther back we recede, even a close approximation of these dates becomes more and more difficult and uncertain. This gives scope for endless discussions and wide differences of opinion. We experience a similar difficulty in the interpretation of data, as they are often vague and meagre. It is not always possible, and in many cases neither desirable nor profitable, in a general comprehensive history of India, to review the different standpoints, and the historian is often obliged to adopt one particular view, as against others, with or sometimes even without brief reference to them. For minute discussions of the merits of conflicting views the reader must be referred to special treatises or articles in journals. Great care should, however, always be taken to distinguish clearly the known from the unknown, and the doubtful from the certain, and to indicate, as far as possible, the range of our ignorance and uncertainty. Ignorance may not be bliss in historical studies, but it is certainly folly to be wise where wisdom is based on imperfect knowledge and serves merely as a cloak for dogmatism. As the following pages will show, the path of the historian is beset with difficulties, doubts, and uncertainties; he has often to advance laboriously through dubious tracks and not seldom loses them altogether. His task frequently resolves itself into weighing one set of doubtful evidence against another in order to arrive at what appears to him to be the most reasonable conclusion. More often than not, such theories are all that he can offer. The historian, no less than his readers, must clearly recognize the provisional nature of these hypotheses and be ready to see them modified or upset and replaced by others with the discovery of fresh data. They are slender but necessary foundations on which the history of India has been built up in the past and has to be built in future.

The observations hitherto made apply more particularly to the ancient period of Indian history. With the beginning of the next period the situation is considerably improved by the existence of a series of chronicles, dealing with the history of India from the foundation of the political power by foreign Muslim invaders up to the eighteenth century A.D. These chronicles include detailed narratives of contemporary events as well as compilations of past history from older sources now lost to us. They cannot be regarded as an absolutely authentic account or impartial review of historical events, but supply ample data for the reconstruction of the history of the period. Both in scope and value they are comparable to the chronicles and historical treatises in Europe of the same period. Unfortunately these historical texts concern themselves primarily with the events and fortunes of the principal Muslim ruling dynasties, and dwell only very incidentally on the history of the smaller states, specially the Hindu kingdoms. Nor, with a few exceptions, do they throw much light on the life of the people at large outside the royal courts. Although, therefore, there is a great advance in our historical knowledge over the earlier period, and in some cases we have got a pretty good historical account, it is, generally speaking, neither as definite nor as full as our modern historical sense would demand, in spite of the valuable additional help that the historian gets from other sources such as the archaeological evidence, official documents, contemporary literature, accounts of foreign travellers, etc. Nevertheless it would be unjust to deny that from about 1200 A.D. India possesses a written history which would not suffer very much in comparison with the history of contemporary Europe, and might differ from it in degree, but not in kind. It is a fairly good and detailed history, but of kings and states, not of the country and the people.

The thirteenth century A.D. may be regarded as a broad dividing line in Indian history in more than one sense. The sovereign power passed into the hands of foreigners who belonged to alien races and professed a new religion of somewhat militant type. The establishment, for the first time, of two diverse systems of culture and civilization led to a definite cleavage between the rulers and the ruled such as India had never known before. Indian history gains in content and becomes richer in detail, but loses unity of treatment. The stories of the ruling powers grow in volume, but we know little of the lot of the ruled who formed the vast mass of the people.

The first three or four centuries of Muslim rule in India form a very important period of transition. The foreign rulers and the new religion with its exotic culture took a long time to take root in the soil. But we have little reliable knowledge of the struggle for independence and the steps by which the resistance of the people was broken down. Of the early reaction of Hinduism towards Islam, and the process by which the latter gradually made headway in this land of conservatism and orthodoxy, we know even less. The Muslim chroniclers, our sole source of information, generally speaking, record only a series of cheap military victories over the rebellious or recalcitrant infidels, and these are looked down upon as merely hewers of wood and drawers of water whose life and fortunes are hardly of any consequence to them. They would have us believe that the triumphant banner of Islam merrily floated from one end of the land to the other, and nothing else counted in the country.

But this is merely one side of the picture, and that of the lion painted by himself. We know that there was always a Hindu India, side by side with Muslim India, and it again asserted itself, both in politics and culture, in the fullness of time. It was not dead, but lay dormant in the early centuries of the foreign rule. The history of the Hindus, except in South India and Rājputāna, during this period is, however, almost a blank page. The scanty remains of their literature throw some faint light on the social and religious changes that came over them, but the little that we know merely casts into greater relief the depth of our ignorance.

Light dawns again in the sixteenth century. The establishment of the Mughal power ushers in a new period of Indian history in which our knowledge of India as a whole is much fuller, and we begin to see things in their true perspective. The vision of a new India, built upon the only stable foundation of the love and confidence of the ruled and the fusion of the two great cultures, now emerges in clear light. History, though it still continues mainly to be the court history of the Muslim rulers, begins to visualize India as a whole, and takes note of Hindu India. The rosy dream of a politically united India, on a common cultural basis, is soon shattered, but Hindu India comes to stay and the historian no longer loses sight of it. The balance is restored and the unity of Indian history is securely established. In spite of many vicissitudes, we can trace the fortunes of India as a whole through the pages of history. This unity of treatment is never lost in later times.

It is not necessary to dwell at length upon the modern history of India. Strictly speaking, it offers no peculiarities, in respect of sources of information or method of treatment, save and except the restrictions imposed by political considerations. The archives of the British Government are gradually being thrown open, and the Indian states also have recently adopted a more liberal policy in this respect. Contemporary historical documents are ample, though they have not yet been worked out as fully or as independently as one could have desired.

It will be hardly any exaggeration to say that Indian history, in a comprehensive sense, has so far been neither written nor even conceived in a proper spirit. A clear grasp of the subject is generally lacking. An attempt has been made above to analyse the different factors that account for this lamentable state of things. We have also tried to indicate the true spirit in which the study of Indian history should be approached, the inherent defects and shortcomings imposed by lack of materials, and the likely dangers and pitfalls which the historian should avoid.

The observations made above would also convey some idea of what the "History of India" means to its readers; what they might legitimately look for, and what they are likely to miss; the proper value they should attach to different aspects, and the profit they may derive from them; the resemblances as well as the differences which it offers to the history of other countries; and lastly, the extent to which the interest of the subject is confined to the particular region and people of whom it treats or concerns a wider range of humanity.

CHAPTER II

SOURCES OF INDIAN HISTORY

It will be abundantly clear from what has been said in the previous chapter that the sources of Indian history differ considerably in its different periods. Broadly speaking, we may distinguish three such periods, viz.: (1) from the most ancient times to the end of the twelfth century A.D.; (2) from the thirteenth to the eighteenth century; and (3) the subsequent period. It will be convenient, therefore, to treat these three periods separately.

1. THE ANCIENT PERIOD

A. *Literary Sources*

The absence of any regular historical chronicle is the leading feature of this period. When we consider the vast mass of contemporary literature and its extremely wide range, the almost utter lack of historical texts certainly appears as a somewhat strange phenomenon. Some people are, therefore, inclined to believe that such literature did exist, and explain its absence by a theory of wholesale destruction. It must be regarded, however, as extremely singular that the agencies of destruction should have singled out this particular branch of literature as their special target. But the strongest argument against the supposed existence of regular historical literature is the absence of any reference to historical texts. We have, therefore. to admit that the literary genius of India, so fertile and active in almost all conceivable branches of study, was not applied to chronicling the records of kings and the rise and fall of states and nations. It is difficult to give a rational explanation of this deficiency. but the fact admits of no doubt.

The deficiency is all the more strange as there are indications that the ancient Indians did not lack in historical sense. This is proved by the carefully preserved lists of teachers in various Vedic texts, as well as in writings of the Buddhists, Jains and other religious sects. That this spirit also extended to the political field is shown not only by the songs and poems in praise of kings and heroes referred to in Vedic literature. but also by the practice of reciting eulogies of kings and royal families on ceremonial occasions. Even so late as the seventh century A.D. Hiuen Tsang noticed that each province in India had its own official for maintaining written records in which were mentioned good and evil events. with calamities and fortunate occurrences. That this practice continued for centuries after Hiuen Tsang is proved by a large number of local chronicles and the preambles in old land-grants which record the genealogies of royal families, sometimes for several generations.

We may thus presume that neither historical sense nor historical material was altogether wanting in ancient India. What was lacking was either the enthusiasm or the ability to weave the scattered raw materials into a critical historical text with a proper literary setting which the people would not willingly let die. In other words, in spite of great intellectual and literary activity, India did not produce a Herodotus or Thucydides, not even a Livy or Tacitus. It has been argued that this was partly due to the peculiar temperament of the people who, to use the words of Hiuen Tsang, "made light of the things of the present world." But this explanation can be hardly regarded as satisfactory when we remember the great progress of the Indians in various branches of secular literature, including law, political science, and the art of administration.

Whatever may be the reason, the fact remains that the only concrete result of historical study in the most ancient period is to be found in long lists of kings preserved in the Purāṇas and the epics. These lists profess to trace the unbroken royal lines from the first human king that ruled down to about the third or fourth century A.D. The earlier part of them is obviously mythical, and the last part is undoubtedly historical; but it is a moot point to decide where the myth ends and reliable tradition begins.

It is interesting to trace the gradual changes in the views of scholars regarding the historical value of these traditional royal lists preserved in the Purāṇas and epics. At first they were rejected wholesale without much ceremony. Later, the accounts of the dynasties ruling in the sixth century B.C. and later were accepted as fairly reliable, as they were partially corroborated by the Buddhist literature and archaeological evidence. Next, the preceding dynasties going back to the time of the Great War described in the *Mahābhārata*, which event is approximately placed in round numbers between 1500 and 1000 B.C., were also regarded by some scholars as furnishing a secure basis for history, though they were loath to accept as correct all the details about names and dates. So far as the account of the royal dynasties before the Great War is concerned, Pargiter was the first to make a bold attempt to coordinate the varying details into a skeleton of political history, and others have since followed in his footsteps. The difficulty of the task is increased by the strongly marked differences in the various traditions, and the conclusions reached by the few scholars who have so far worked in this field show great divergences. The attempt to reconstruct the skeleton of political history before the Great War cannot, therefore, be regarded as yet leading to any satisfactory result. For the period following that (1000-600 B.C.)

we have at least a working hypothesis, and it is not till we come to the beginning of the sixth century B.C. that we can firmly grasp the thread of the dynastic history of Northern India.

The traditions preserved in ancient Indian literature, notably the Purāṇas, thus form the main source of information for the history of the earliest period, and for the period before the sixth century B.C. they constitute our only source. The Buddhist and Jain literatures of the succeeding period form a valuable supplement and corrective to the evidence of the Purāṇas, and isolated references in other literary works, even grammatical texts, have proved to be very important historical data.

For the later period, beginning with the Guptas, we have no texts like the Purāṇas, giving even bare dynastic lists. But although Indian literature practically ignores the history of the long period of one thousand years that follow, it does not altogether cease to be of help. Apart from isolated references scattered in the vast mass of literature of all types, we have two classes of works that contribute directly to our knowledge of history, viz. biographies and local chronicles.

It is fortunate that certain writers took the lives of their royal patrons as the theme of their literary works. Bāṇabhaṭṭa, that great master of Sanskrit prose, wrote the *Harsha-charita* (life of the emperor Harsha), and two poets, Vākpati and Bilhaṇa, described the exploits of Yaśovarman and Vikramāditya (of the later Chālukya dynasty) in two epics, the *Gauḍavaho* and the *Vikramāṅka-deva charita*. We have also a curious poetical work, the *Rāma-charita*, in which the author uses throughout verses of *double entendre*, which, taken one way, describe the story of the *Rāmāyaṇa*, and taken the other way, recount the story of king Rāmapāla of Bengal.

Among other biographical works may be mentioned the *Kumārapāla-charita* of Jayasiṁha, *Kumārapāla-charita* or *Dvyāśraya-kāvya* of Hemachandra, *Hammīrā-kāvya* of Nayachandra, *Nava-sāhasāṅka-charita* of Padmagupta, *Bhojaprabandha* by Ballāla, *Pṛithvīrāja-charita* of Chand Bardai and *Pṛithvīrāja-vijaya* (fragmentary) by an anonymous writer.

These and other works of the same class cannot be regarded as genuine history, although they contain valuable historical information. Their object was the glorification of the king rather than to give a true picture of his life and times, and they were mostly conceived by their authors not as historical texts, but primarily as mediums for showing their literary skill and ingenuity.

Among the local chronicles, the most famous is the *Rājataraṅgiṇī*. It is a history of Kāshmir, written throughout in verse, by Kalhaṇa in A.D. 1149-50. This is the only work in ancient Indian literature that may be regarded as an historical text in the true sense of the word. The author has not only taken great pains to collect his material from the existing chronicles and other sources but, at the beginning of his work, he has laid down a few general principles for writing history which are remarkable as being far in advance of his age. Indeed they may be regarded as anticipating, to a large extent, the critical method of historical research which was not fully developed till the nineteenth century A.D. In view of the lamentable paucity of historical talent in ancient India, it is worth while quoting a few of Kalhaṇa's observations, showing the high level which the Indian intellect had attained even in this much neglected sphere of activity. Regarding the strict impartiality to be observed by an historian Kalhaṇa remarks:

"That virtuous poet alone is worthy of praise who, free from love or hatred, ever restricts his language to the exposition of facts." (I. 7.).

As to the method of collecting data we may quote the following verses among others (I. 14, 15):

"I have examined eleven works of former scholars which contain the chronicles of the kings, as well as the views of the sage Nīla (*Nīlapurāṇa*).

"By the inspection of ordinances (*śāsana*) of former kings relating to religious foundations and grants, laudatory inscriptions (*praśasti-paṭṭa*) as well as written records (*śāstra*), all wearisome error has been set at rest."

In spite of his excellent equipment and high ideals, Kalhaṇa was unable to reconstruct the early history of Kāshmir, for his enthusiasm and industry could not make up for the lack of authentic material. His account of the period before the seventh century A.D. cannot be regarded as trustworthy, and it becomes more and more unreliable as we go back to more ancient periods. Nevertheless his attempt was creditable, and it is refreshing to find that he alone, of all Indian writers, has preserved some accounts of such forgotten Indian rulers as Kanishka. From the seventh century A.D., however, the *Rājataraṅgiṇī* may be regarded as a reliable history of Kāshmir. The author narrates the career of each king in chronological order with a fair amount of detail, showing scrupulous impartiality in his criticism of men and events, and exhibiting soundness of judgment and healthy liberality in his general expression of views. As he gradually comes nearer his own age the history becomes fuller and more and more replete with interesting accounts of men and things. It ceases to be merely a chronicle of dry details and faithfully presents the ebb and flow of national life, the periods of glory and misery, and the greatness and weakness of men and rulers—in short all those minute details which make history a record of intense human interest, faithfully portraying the march of events through which a people works out its own destiny. We close the book with a poignant regret that we do not possess such a history for the whole of India, or many more texts of the same kind dealing with other parts of the country.

Kalhaṇa's example was not lost upon his countrymen and several writers of Kāshmir continued his chronicle. Jonarāja, who died in A.D. 1459, imitated Kalhaṇa's style and brought the historical narrative up to the reign of Zain-ul-Ābidīn. The *Jaina-Rājataraṅgiṇī* by his pupil Śrīvara covers the period A.D. 1459-86. Then came Prājya Bhaṭṭa and his pupil Śuka who carried on the history till a few years after the conquest of Kāshmir by Akbar. These later works are, however, much inferior to the *Rājataraṅgiṇī* both in literary style and in historical accuracy.

Next to Kāshmir, reference may be made to a large number of chronicles of Gujarāt. These include well-known works like *Rās-Mālā, Kīrtikaumudī* of Someśvara, *Sukṛita-saṁkīrtana* of Arisiṁha, *Prabandha-Chintāmaṇi* by Merutuṅga, *Prabandha-kośa* by Rājaśekhara, *Hammīra-mada-mardana* and *Vastupāla-Tejaḥpāla-praśasti* of Jayasiṁha, *Sukṛitakīrti-kallolinī* of Udayaprabha, *Vasanta-vilāsa* of Bālachandra, etc., which are treasure-houses of stories and fables as well as historical anecdotes. The two biographies of Kumārapāla, referred to above, and these chronicles enable us to trace the history of Gujarāt, specially under the Chaulukyas, with fullness of details such as is not possible in the case of any other kingdom in ancient India except Kāshmir.

There were probably local chronicles of Sind which formed the basis of an Arabic history of which we possess a Persian translation, the *Chachnāma*, composed at the beginning of the thirteenth century A.D. It gives a detailed account of the Arab conquest of Sind and briefly refers to its history during the previous century.

We have also local chronicles of Nepāl, which merely contain a list of kings and the duration of their reigns, with only a few details here and there. The earlier portion of these *Vaṁśāvalīs*—as they are called—is purely mythical, but there seems to be an historical basis for the accounts relating to the period commencing from the first century A.D. The list is not, however, carefully compiled. There are wide divergences between the different chronicles, and many details are proved to be wrong by epigraphic evidence. These chronicles were never worked into historical texts by a genius of the type of Kalhaṇa, and although in the absence of other sources they supply the framework for the history of Nepāl, they cannot be regarded as a satisfactory substitute for real and genuine history.

The existence of historical chronicles in Kāshmir, Gujarāt, Sind, and Nepāl supports the presumption that the archives of different states, as a rule, contained such royal chronicles, as stated by Hiuen Tsang. These chronicles, unless raised to the status of a literary work of the type of *Rājataraṅgiṇī*, or included in pretentious or sacred works like the Purāṇas, are not likely to long survive the fortunes of the dynasty whose history they recorded. This probably accounts for their general destruction, though a few have been preserved in outlying places, like Kāshmir, Gujarāt, Nepāl, and Assam (in a later period).

B. *Archaeology*

If we had to depend on literary sources alone we would have known very little indeed of the history of India for the thousand years that elapsed since the fall of the Andhras in the third century A.D. Our knowledge of this period would have been even much less than that of the thousand years preceding it. Fortunately the gap has been filled by the actual remains of this ancient period in the shape of coins, inscriptions, and monuments. They have enabled us to reconstruct an outline of the history of the period which, vague and imperfect though it is, forms the only sure foundation on which the history of India will have to be built up in future.

Indian archaeology is a science of recent growth, and is barely a century old. Its pioneers were a few enterprising European scholars who took a deep interest in the antiquities of India and made an earnest effort to unravel her past. The origin and progress of this fascinating labour of love, which culminated in organized departments of research and exploration, achieving wonderful results, has been reviewed in the next chapter. Here we may merely tabulate these results by way of indicating their bearing on the history of India.

I. *Inscriptions.*—Inscriptions have proved a source of the highest value for the reconstruction of the political history of ancient India. Being engraved on stone and metal they are free from the process of tampering to which books or other documents written on perishable materials are liable. Their value as contemporary documents thus remains unimpeachable. Although not always dated, the character of the script enables us to determine their approximate age. Thus as historical evidence they take precedence over the mass of literature, as the age of most of the texts is uncertain and they all must have undergone considerable modifications in the course of being preserved in copies through hundreds of years.

Apart from these considerations, the nature of many of these inscriptions invests them with a high degree of historical importance. The series of Indian inscriptions opens with the memorable edicts of the great Maurya Emperor Aśoka, engraved on rocks and pillars throughout his vast empire, from beyond the Indus in the west to the Mysore plateau in the south. These are royal proclamations and commandments, mostly in his own words, and convey across twenty-two centuries the life and personality of a great man and a great ruler with a striking vividness to which there is hardly any parallel in the history of the world. It is either the strangest freak of nature or the rare good fortune of India, if not a divine dispensation, that in the midst of an almost wholesale destruction of historical materials of the period, one fragment alone should have been spared, so faithfully reflecting that spiritual greatness which constitutes the glory of Indian civilization and its special characteristic. The records of Aśoka form a class by themselves, and contribute largely to our knowledge of the history of the period and the spirit that animated one of the greatest men that ever sat on a royal throne. No other inscriptions make even a near approach to them in point of interest or historical importance.

One form of alphabet is used in all these records, excepting two groups in the north-west, which are written in an altogether different script. The latter, known as Kharoshṭhī, was obviously derived from Aramaic and, like the Semitic alphabet, was written from right to left. It continued in use in the north-western corner of India for many centuries, but vanished without leaving any trace behind.

The script in which all the other inscriptions of Aśoka were written is known as Brāhmī, and is written from left to right. It is the earliest form of Indian writing known to us, and from it have been derived, by slow evolution through ages, all the Indian characters current today, including Tamil, Telugu, and Kanarese. When the records of Aśoka first came to notice towards the close of the eighteenth century, their script was as much an enigma to all as in the fourteenth century A.D., when the Emperor Fīrūz Tughluk brought a pillar with Aśoka's inscription to Delhi, and made a vain attempt to have it read by the Indian Pundits. The deciphering of the Asokan inscriptions by Prinsep (described in detail in the next chapter) is one of the romances of archaeology comparable to those associated with the discovery of the clue to the hieroglyphics and cuneiform writings. It was accomplished in A.D. 1837, and in course of the next fifty years Indian epigraphy was placed on a firm footing. By the devoted and patient labour of a number of scholars the different types of Indian scripts were thoroughly studied, analysed, and classified, and a scientific basis laid down for Indian palaeography, which has made it possible to corelate them to different ages and localities. Apart from their intrinsic interest as historical records, the Aśokan inscriptions have thus proved of great value as the starting-point of epigraphic and palaeographic studies in India.

The inscriptions of the post-Aśokan period may be broadly

divided into two classes, official and private. The official records are in most cases either *praśastis,* i.e. eulogies of kings written by their court-poets, or land-grants. The most famous example of the former is furnished by the long record of Samudra-gupta engraved on an Aśokan pillar, now in the Allāhābād fort. It describes in great detail the personal qualities and the military achievements of the great Gupta emperor and forms the chief document of his memorable reign. The age of the Imperial Guptas is now justly regarded as the Golden Age of India. But all memories of it, and even the very name of Samudra-gupta—the Indian Napoleon—who laid the foundations of the Gupta empire, were lost to Indian tradition. The Allāhābād *praśasti* has preserved from oblivion the name and fame of this great hero and, along with a number of other inscriptions, forms the main basis of our knowledge of the Gupta period. The Gwalior *praśasti* of Bhoja has similarly thrown a flood of light on the imperial Pratīhāras, another forgotten dynasty of ancient India.

Among other *praśastis,* supplying valuable historical information, may be mentioned that of king Vijayasena of the Sena dynasty of Bengal engraved on a slab of stone found at Deopara. Its nominal object is to record the building of a temple by Vijayasena, but it is almost wholly devoted to a panegyric of the great king, recording his victories and achievements in the most high-flown language. The Aihole inscription of Pulakeśin II, the Chālukya king, belongs to exactly the same type.

By far the largest number of official documents are charters conveying the sale or gift of lands. These are mostly engraved on copper-plates, though in very rare instances they are also found on stone pillars and in temples. These charters define the boundaries of the lands and specify the object and conditions of the grant, often enumerating other interesting details such as the price of land, the mode of its measurement, exhortations to future kings not to confiscate the grants, and quotations from the scriptures threatening severe punishment after death for those who violate the grants in any way.

Interesting though these details are in many ways, they do not contain much that is of historical importance. But by a formal convention, fortunately followed in many if not in all cases, these charters begin with a sort of royal *praśasti* which gives a short account of the donor's family for several generations, and describes in greater detail the life and achievements of the ruling king. These formal and introductory portions in the land-grants have supplied us with invaluable historical material. Sometimes, as in the Chola inscriptions, this introductory part runs to a very great length, and forms a valuable historical document by itself. Very often this portion was wholly or partially stereotyped in the royal archives and used in several grants. Sometimes the portion was independently engraved on copper-plates and these were kept ready in the office, so that when occasion arose, only the details of the grant had to be added to make them formal charters. In short, this historical part had little organic connection with the grant itself, and may be regarded as a *praśasti* prefixed to it.

These *praśastis* were composed by court-poets or other royal officials, and one would naturally hesitate to take them at their face value. There is undoubtedly a great deal of exaggeration in the effusions of the poets. It is customary for them to endow their patron-kings with all the ideal virtues and to represent them as the rulers of the whole world girdled by the four oceans. Such general expressions must be discarded as of no historical value. But greater value attaches to the specific enumerations of campaigns, victories, and conquests; for these documents were public property, and their authors would be justly exposed to ridicule if they had made categorical statements without any basis whatsoever. Of course they were expected to exaggerate the achievements of their masters, but even such exaggeration implies a substratum of fact. A great deal of caution is therefore needed to assess the proper value of the claims made on behalf of a king, and they should be checked by all possible means. Such checks are furnished by the statements made on behalf of the rival kings, and sometimes welcome corroboration is afforded by independent evidence.

In cases where the inscriptions are engraved on rocks or objects not easily portable, their find-spots become of great importance as indicating the territorial jurisdiction of the king. Sometimes the records of vassal chiefs and finds of coins corroborate the claims of territorial conquests. By these and other means it is almost always possible to make legitimate inferences from these documents about the achievements of the kings.

The official documents, however, form only a very small proportion of the inscriptions. By far the larger majority are private records. They cover a wide range, from a short votive inscription of two or three words to pompous poetical compositions glorifying an individual or family. They throw light on various aspects of society even where they do not directly contribute to political history. A good many are engraved on images of gods and religious buildings, recording pious donations. These constitute the chief means of fixing the dates of these images and buildings, and have been of incalculable help in tracing the evolution of art and religion, and determining their general condition in any specified period. Similarly the language and style of the inscriptions have been of immense value to the linguistic and literary history of India. The evidence of the inscriptions, taken in mass, is unerring in these respects. If we analyse, for example, the 1500 or more inscriptions prior to the Gupta age that have so far come to light, we find an overwhelmingly large number—more than 95 per cent—written in Prākṛit and concerned with non-Brahmanical religious sects, mainly Buddhist and Jain. The proportion is almost just the reverse in favour of the Sanskrit language and the Brahmanical religion, if we take the inscriptions of the period subsequent to the Gupta age. Even allowing for all accidental factors, this one fact betokens a sweeping change in the life of the people both in respect of the religious ideas and the medium of literary expression.

These inscriptions also throw important light on political history. Many of them refer to ruling kings otherwise unknown, and some of them even supply dates, either in regnal years or in a specified or unspecified era. This has been a prolific source of the constant addition to our historical knowledge, though where supplementary evidence is lacking we know little more than the royal name, his approximate date and the location of his kingdom. But even such scraps of information, pieced together, have enabled the historian to reconstruct a clear outline of the history of a locality or even of a definite period, of which little was known before.

In a few cases the private records throw more direct light on the political history of India, as they emanate from persons closely connected with a royal family. We have, for example, interesting records of families whose members for generations held high offices like ministers or generals. In others the importance of an individual is indicated by the office he held, or the part he played in the affairs of state. These inscriptions, though issued by or in honour of private individuals, therefore incidentally give us a great deal of information about the kings and political condition of the time.

On the whole it may be said without any hesitation that the epigraphic records of ancient India have been the principal source of our information regarding the political history, and have also proved to be of great value by supplementing literary evidence in regard to the social, religious, and economic condition of India.

2. *Numismatics.*—Next to the inscriptions, coins are the most important source of the history of ancient India. Many thousands of these have come to light. Hoards have been unearthed in different parts of the country—a single hoard sometimes yielding many thousands—and individual specimens have constantly been found on or near the surface of ancient sites. Most of them at first passed into the hands of private individuals, but a number were recovered by scholars or acquired by public institutions. There is no doubt, however, that quite a large proportion was

melted or otherwise lost to antiquarian study, and this deplorable state of things is unfortunately still going on. A systematic study and collection of coins has been possible only in cases of regular archaeological excavations. Not only were many coins, otherwise acquired, lost to us, but no systematic record has been kept of the provenance of those which have survived. This has been a serious handicap to the scientific study of the coinage, as much of the historical importance of a coin is lost if we cannot determine the exact locality of which it formed the currency.

The importance of numismatics for the study of the economic condition of a country is too obvious to need a detailed consideration. Here we shall only indicate how coins have helped us to reconstruct the political history of the various periods.

The earliest coins of India bear only figures, devices, or symbols, but with few exceptions, no legends. These coins were sometimes cast in dies, but more often the symbols were punched on the metallic pieces. Sometimes there are many symbols, punched at different times. They were most probably deliberately stamped by the issuing authority, in order to guarantee their genuineness and value. These authorities might have been kings or states, but also certainly included individual merchants, trade-guilds, city-corporations, and similar bodies, for the idea of a state monopoly of minting coins was yet unknown. In the absence of legends, it is impossible to allot the different coins to these different categories. The meaning of the figures and symbols, once familiar to the people using these coins, is no longer clear to us, though some of them are familiar objects or well-known conventional designs. Various suggestions have been made regarding their significance, but they are highly speculative and rest on no secure foundations. Apart from conveying some vague religious ideas and artistic conventions these coins do not supply any historical information. The rare legends on them refer to the mercantile corporations which issued them.

It is not till after the Greek invasion that we come across coins with the names of kings clearly engraved on them. Excepting, perhaps, a few coins of the time of Alexander, the most important series of such coins were those issued by the Greek rulers of Bactria who ultimately conquered the Punjab and North-Western Frontier. The artistic excellence of these coins has never been surpassed in India, and the portraits of kings and other figures on them show Hellenistic art at its best. These coins of the Graeco-Bactrians set a new fashion and may be said to have revolutionized Indian numismatics. The most important feature added to Indian coins from this time forward was the name, and sometimes even the portrait, of the sovereign who issued them. How greatly it has helped our knowledge of political history will be apparent from the fact that it is from these coins alone that we know of nearly thirty Greek kings and queens who ruled in India. The classical writers have referred to only four or five of them, but not only were the names of the rest unknown to them, but even the very memory of the Greek domination over a corner of India for nearly two centuries was absolutely lost. This remarkable historical episode, interesting alike to Greece and India, came to the knowledge of the world, after nearly two thousand years, by the discovery of those fine series of coins—of gold, silver, and copper—which now adorn many public museums in Europe and India.

The coinage of the Greeks was imitated by the Scythian and Parthian invaders who followed in their footsteps, and although the execution of their coins is far inferior, they are equally important for historical purposes. Here, too, the coins alone have enabled us to reconstruct an outline of their history, and recover the names of quite a large number of their rulers. One branch of the Scythian invaders, who settled permanently in Gujarāt and the Kāthiāwār Peninsula, issued coins which not only gave the name of the ruling king and that of his father, but very often also the date in the well-known Śaka era. This has enabled us to reconstruct the history of the Western Satraps—as these rulers are called—for a period of more than three hundred years. With the exception of a few inscriptions and literary references, which otherwise would have been of little help, the coins have been the sole source of our information regarding the Greeks, the Śakas and the Parthians that entered India after the dissolution of the Mauryan Empire. The Kushāṇas who followed them likewise issued a large number of coins, but the history of this dynasty is also known from other sources.

The coins have also been the principal source of our information regarding the various Indian states—both monarchical and republican—that flourished during the same period. Most of them, like the Mālavas, Yaudheyas, the Mitra rulers of Pañchāla etc., are almost exclusively known from their coins. In other cases, like the Sātavāhanas of the Deccan, the Puranic account is corroborated, corrected, and supplemented by their coins and inscriptions.

The Guptas, who founded the greatest empire in India after the Mauryas, issued a large variety of fine coins. Although we know a great deal of their history from epigraphic records, the coins form an important additional source of information.

With the downfall of the Guptas the numismatic evidence ceases to be an important source of history. Isolated coins, here and there, have no doubt proved to be of great value, but they seldom afford us material information not otherwise available. It is a curious fact that coins of even great emperors like Harsha or ruling dynasties like the Chālukyas, Rāshṭrakūṭas, Pratīhāras and Pālas, not to speak of lesser kings and dynasties, are either unknown or of little significance.

3. *Monuments.*—In addition to coins and inscriptions we have other antiquarian remains, such as buildings or parts thereof, statues of stone or metal, terra cotta, ornamental and decorative fragments, pottery, and various other objects of a miscellaneous character. They are of great importance in tracing the history and evolution of Indian art. The art of a country is generally regarded to be a fair index of its culture, and it throws light on some higher aspects of its civilization which cannot be easily understood from other sources. The remains of Indian monuments have thus considerably helped towards a proper appreciation of the life and spirit of ancient India.

In addition to individual monuments, sometimes we have the vast remains of an ancient city laid bare before us. Some of them, like those of Mohenjo-daro and Harappā, have opened before us an altogether new type of civilization, reaching back to an age of which no memorials in India were known before. This has carried back the antiquity of Indian culture and civilization by several thousands of years and opened up a new vista of its history, character, and association with the outside world. It has also transformed our ideas of the origin of Indian civilization. We can no longer derive from the simple fact of the Aryan migration the complex structure of later Indian civilization, but must look for more than one source which fed the mighty stream. Even in concrete matters our ideas have undergone great changes. As an instance may be cited the origin of the Brāhmī script (used in the Aśokan records) which, as noted above, is the parent-stock from which all Indian alphabets have been derived.

Scholars have almost unanimously held the view that Brāhmī was derived from a foreign source, though they widely differ about its identity. But more than five hundred seals have been discovered at Mohenjo-daro which contain a species of pictorial writing. This has not been deciphered yet, but the probability of the Brāhmī alphabet being derived from it is now being seriously considered. Similarly the deep-rooted conviction that Indian art originated from a foreign source not much earlier than the third century B.C., has been considerably shaken by the discovery at Mohenjo-daro of finely carved stone figures of the third millennium B.C. which would not unfavourably compare with the statues of the classical period in Athens. The archaeological excavation of the Indus valley is still at its infancy, and we may look forward to its continuation as opening up a brilliant chapter of Indian history as yet unknown or even undreamt of.

Coming down to historical times, the systematic excavations of ancient sites like the city of Taxilā or the monastic establishments at Sārnāth (near Benares) have thrown light upon various aspects of life of which there is little or no record in literature. Such excavations, as will be noted in the next chapter, have been few and far between. Still, meagre though they are, compared with the vast extent of the country, these archaeological excavations have enabled us to realize some interesting aspects of Indian civilization which would have been otherwise unknown.

C. *Foreign Accounts*

In addition to literature and archaeological remains we have another interesting source of information in the accounts left by foreign writers. The earliest among them are the two Greek writers Herodotus and Ctesias, both of whom must have derived their information indirectly through Persian sources. Herodotus gives some useful information along with a great deal of fairy tales, but the account of Ctesias largely consists of incredible fables. Far greater interest attaches to the writings of those Greeks who accompanied Alexander to India, and the account of Megasthenes, who lived for some time in the court of Chandragupta Maurya as an ambassador of Seleucus. Though these works are mostly lost, much has been preserved in books, based upon them, written by later authors. These accounts contain a great deal of information that is both interesting and authentic, but they suffer from the defects inherent in the writings of foreigners, ignorant of the language and customs of the country. While great importance naturally attaches to what they recorded from personal observation, we must treat with great reserve their accounts based on others' reports or hearsay evidence. Due allowance must also be made for the necessarily limited circle within which a Greek must have moved in India, and his natural proneness to see everything through Hellenic eyes and distort or exaggerate anything that was strange or unfamiliar to him. It would be foolish to belittle the importance of the classical accounts of India, but it would be equally unwise to put implicit faith in everything contained in them.

Special reference must be made to the classical writers who have elucidated the geography and natural history of India. The earliest of them is the anonymous author of the *Periplus of the Erythraean Sea.* He was a Greek, settled in Egypt, who made a voyage to the Indian coast about A.D. 80 and left a record of its ports, harbours, and merchandise. This short account, full of interesting information, is worth its weight in gold, as it has preserved from oblivion a phase of the trade and maritime activity in ancient India, otherwise unknown. Ptolemy wrote a geographical account of India in the second century A.D. on scientific lines. His data being derived from secondary sources, he has fallen into numerous errors, and his general conception of the shape of India is also faulty in the extreme. Novertheless the attempt was praiseworthy and has supplied valuable information. The same may be said of Pliny's account of Indian animals, plants, and minerals written in the first century A.D. There were also many other writers of a later date.

These classical accounts, most of which have been translated into English by J. W. McCrindle, were generally prompted by a spirit of exploration of unknown lands, and reflect great credit on their authors and the scientific spirit of the age in which they lived. The same spirit was displayed a few centuries later by Arab sailors and merchants, some of whom, like Sulaimān and Al Mas'ūdī, have left brief records of India. The gap in the interval between the two periods is filled by Chinese writers, both chroniclers at home and pilgrims who visited India.

The writings of the Chinese travellers to India form a valuable supplement to the classical accounts. Three of them, Fa-hien (fifth century A.D.), Hiuen Tsang, and I-tsing (seventh century A.D.) are better known than others, and have recorded their experiences in fairly bulky volumes which are happily preserved in their original forms and have been translated into English. All three spent a number of years in India and learnt its language, and the first two travelled widely almost all over the country. In these respects they had an undoubted advantage over the Greek travellers. But unfortunately for the historian of India, these eminent Chinese visitors were all devout Buddhist monks, whose journey to India was merely a pilgrimage to holy lands, and whose outlook was purely religious. Neither Fa-hien nor I-tsing refer to secular matters, except very incidentally, nor do they even mention the name of the king or kings whose dominions were visited by them. Hiuen Tsang is not so circumscribed, but gives some interesting information about his royal patron Harsha-vardhana and other contemporary kings of India. He also briefly refers to the political condition of the kingdoms through which he passed, and devotes an entire chapter to a general account of India. These are, no doubt, very valuable, but they form only a very small part of his extensive records which, like those of Fa-hien and I-tsing, are otherwise devoted to a minute and detailed description of Buddhism in India —its rituals and practices, sanctuaries and memorials, sects and doctrines, scriptures and traditions.

The Chinese travellers have rendered a great service by depicting the state of Buddhism in India. But devout pilgrims as they were, their intense religious faith impaired to a certain extent their rational instincts and power of impartial observation. We must therefore be on our guard against accepting as literally true all their statements, especially those which concern the Buddhist faith in any way, even when based on personal observation. Their judgment on men and things was warped, if not vitiated, by an absolute and implicit faith in the superiority of Buddhism, and the too intimate, if not exclusive, association with men and institutions connected with that religion. Buddhism alone loomed large in their eyes, everything else taking a subordinate and almost an insignificant place. Such an attitude is hardly compatible with recording an account that may be regarded as strictly historical.

From the eighth century A.D. India attracted the attention of the Arab writers. Apart from the account of the Arab merchants and sailors, the Indian borderland finds prominent mention in Arab historical chronicles on account of the political aggrandisement of that militant nation which culminated in the conquest of Sind early in the eighth century A.D. Two and a half centuries later the Ghaznavid Turks followed in the footsteps of the Arabs and carried the banner of Islam far into the interior of India. India now figured prominently in the Muslim chronicles. The best foreign account of India that this age produced was written by Abū Rīhān, better known as Alberuni, a contemporary of Sultan Mahmūd of Ghaznī. While the ruthless conqueror was harrying India by fire and sword, destroying and plundering its cities and temples, the great Arabic scholar engaged himself in studying the culture and civilization of the country. He learned Sanskrit and studied its different branches of literature. The bulky volume which he wrote is in many respects the most rational and comprehensive account of India ever written by a foreigner until modern times. He is singularly free from religious enthusiasm, bordering on fanaticism, and the racial superiority-complex which mark the Muslim writings of the age. He patiently laboured hard to acquire knowledge of Indian society and culture in a laudable spirit of quest for truth, and brought to his task a liberal and rational mind enriched by profound knowledge, remarkable for his age. But from the point of view of Indian history, Alberuni's great work, highly valuable though it is, suffers from two serious defects. In the first place, he says little or nothing of the political condition of India. Secondly, his account rests primarily on his study of Indian literature, and is not based on personal observations. In other words, he saw India, not with his own eyes, but through literary works. Alberuni gives an admirable survey of the mathematics, physics, chemistry, cosmogony, astronomy, astrology, geography, philosophy, religious rites, customs, social ideas, etc., of India, but we feel at almost every step—and he does not conceal the fact—that he is merely reproducing what he read about these things in books written by Indian authors dead and gone long ago, and draws little or no inspiration from the living India of his age.

2. THE MEDIAEVAL PERIOD

(THIRTEENTH TO EIGHTEENTH CENTURY)

Alberuni's work closes a long series of accounts written by foreigners about ancient India. Two centuries later the Muslim Turks established their political supremacy over India, and introduced the art of compiling chronicles recording the political events of the country. The earliest work of this kind, *Tabaqāt-i-Nāsirī* by Minhāj-ud-dīn, composed in the middle of the thirteenth century A.D., traces the history of Muslim rule in India from the very beginning with such fullness of detail as the author could derive from a patient study of all the materials available to him. It was followed by other works at regular intervals among which the following deserve special mention: *Ta'rīkh-i-Fīrūz Shāhī* by Ziyā-ud-dīn Baranī and Shams-i-Sirāj 'Afīf; *Gulshan-i-Ibrāhīmī* by Muhammad Qāsim Firishta; *Āīn-i-Akbarī* and *Akbar-nāma* by Abu'l-Fazl, *Tabaqāt-i-Akbarī* by Nizām-ud-dīn Ahmad, and *Muntakhab-ut-Tawārīkh* by 'Abd-ul-Qādir Budaunī.

There are besides a number of other works dealing with general history as well as provincial states or particular individuals. A fair idea of the nature and extent of these works may be had from that excellent compendium—*The History of India as told by its own Historians*—compiled by Elliot and Dowson, in which an attempt has been made to cover the history of the whole period by extracts (in an English translation) from indigenous historical texts.

The autobiographies of the Mughal emperors Bābur and Jahāngīr, and the biographies of other emperors, kings, and various grandees form a valuable supplement to regular historical works. A part of the official correspondence, both of the Central Government and of the various provinces and subordinate states, has also been preserved.

Official despatches or the letters of military commanders, governors, and diplomatic agents are valuable sources of information, and often give accurate dates and details not available from any other source. Mention may also be made of court diaries and news-reports. These contain reports of the occurrences and sayings at the Public Durbars of Delhi and provincial courts which were taken down by men specially employed for the purpose by subordinate rulers or important officials. These form valuable materials for the reconstruction of the history of the period, and the monumental work *Āīn-i-Akbarī* gives a most detailed and comprehensive picture of the complex administrative machinery set up by the great Mughal emperor. The bardic chronicles of the Rājputs form an important class of historical documents concerning the Hindu states of Rājputāna. It is unnecessary to dwell at length on these familiar sources of history, as they will be reviewed in detail in later parts of this work.

The archaeological evidence of the period, highly valuable from the point of view of the history of art, ceases to be of as much special importance as in the ancient period for the purpose of political history. The coins of the early rulers with their dates and mint-marks, as well as inscriptions, often supply valuable additional information, particularly in respect of provincial history which is not so fully dealt with by the Court historians. But they are at best valuable supplements, and save in rare instances, not the sole or even principal sources of information.

The accounts of foreign travellers are also an important, though supplementary, source for the history of this period. One of the earliest is Marco Polo who visited India and other parts of Asia towards the close of the thirteenth century A.D. He does not, however, tell us much of the political history. The most important in this respect is Ibn Batūta, an African Muhammadan, who spent several years in the court of Muhammad Tughluq. He returned to his native country in A.D. 1349, after twenty-five years of travel, full of adventures, in various parts of Asia. He has left a vivid account of India of his time whose general accuracy there is no reason to dispute. Another important traveller was Nicolo de' Conti, the Venetian, in the fifteenth century. A number of other European travellers in the fifteenth and sixteenth centuries have left interesting information about various parts of India, particularly the powerful kingdom of Vijayanagar. For the Mughal period the voluminous writings of European travellers, including reports of Jesuit missionaries, and official despatches of the Portuguese, French, and English trading settlements, supply a mass of authentic information.

For the second period (A.D. 1200-1800), therefore, the historian of India is no longer hampered by lack of material as in the first or earlier period. He can trace the main outline of the political history with essential details, and has not to piece together fragmentary data from coins and inscriptions by a tedious and laborious process. His principal difficulty is to sift the truth from a mass of data which sometimes contradict one another, and to assess correctly the statements of historians which are not infrequently coloured by passions and prejudices. But these are difficulties which are common to historians of all ages and countries.

3. THE MODERN PERIOD

It is unnecessary to say much on the materials for the history of the modern period, as they present no unusual features. It should be emphasized, however, that state-papers, i.e. contemporary official documents, now take the chief place among these materials, as in the case of European countries. Such state-papers are not altogether wanting for the Mughal period, but they are, comparatively speaking, few in number and play a minor rôle in the construction of the history of the period. From the eighteenth century they increase in volume and importance, and the Peshwa's Daftars may be cited as a striking example. With the establishment of the British ascendancy these state-papers form the most elaborate and valuable source of information. The servants of the East India Company in India had to keep very detailed written records of their transactions and deliberations for the perusal of their masters in England, and this fortunate circumstance has undoubtedly increased the mass of documents which supply abundant historical material of first-rate importance. The correspondence of the various Indian States among themselves and with the British is also very valuable. These materials have been partially lost, but a great deal has been preserved and is now kept in the Imperial Records Office in Delhi and the India Office in London. The Records Office in Delhi has been recently reorganized, and proper arrangements have been made for making the records available to students of history and helping their study by means of classification, indexing, and printing select documents. Numbers of important state papers in Provincial Record Offices, Indian States, and in private possession are also gradually coming to light. These and other materials, to which detailed reference will be made in due course, have considerably facilitated the task of the historian of modern India.

CHAPTER III

GENERAL REVIEW OF ARCHAEOLOGICAL EXPLORATIONS AND EXCAVATIONS

In every country the historian is dependent upon the archaeologist for information about periods to which written records do not go back. This particularly is the case in India, where practically the entire history of the pre-Muslim period is built up on the study of materials recovered by the investigator and excavator during the last century and a half. The splendid achievements of Indian culture throughout the ages were unfortunately not matched by a sense of historical and geographical accuracy, and except for the metrical chronicle of Kāshmir, no other sober history is available for the whole sub-continent. The Muslim period witnessed a marked interest in the recording of contemporary history, and occasionally an exceptional monarch such as Fīrūz Shāh Tughluq (1351-1388) even made an attempt to explore and preserve ancient relics such as the inscribed pillars of Aśoka, but without any tangible result. The study of Indian antiquities was, however, initiated in Bengal soon after the establishment of British power by scholars like Sir William Jones, who founded the Asiatic Society of Bengal in 1784. At first, only linguistic and literary researches occupied the Society's attention. With the turning of the century, a comprehensive survey of the country was started under the orders of the East India Company, and Dr. Buchanan Hamilton was the first explorer who carried out this task first in Mysore and Southern India, and then in North Bengal, Bihār, and Assam, in the second decade of the nineteenth century. His report contains the earliest notices of Indian antiquities, and these are recorded with great accuracy and sound judgment. In Western India the caves of Ajanta, Elephanta, and Kanheri were also discovered and described before the turn of the twenties.

The labours of these pioneers brought to light a number of ancient inscriptions recorded on rocks and pillars, but these were written in a script which no one could read. They thus remained a sealed book to scholars till their mystery was solved by James Prinsep in 1837. Prinsep, who was then Secretary of the Asiatic Society of Bengal, has left an interesting account of this great discovery. It is a romance of archaeology fit to rank by the side of the decipherment of the hieroglyphic and cuneiform scripts. For seven years, we are told, Prinsep spread before him, every morning, the estampages of the inscriptions collected from different parts of India and wistfully gazed at the unknown alphabets which concealed the mystery of India's past. At last the numerous short votive records on the famous *stūpa* at Sānchī gave him the key. How he hit upon it, almost by a lucky chance, may best be told in his own words, as recorded in Volume VI of the *Journal of the Asiatic Society of Bengal* (pp. 460-77, 566-609).

"In laying open a discovery of this nature, some little explanation is generally expected of the means by which it has been attained. Like most other inventions, when once found it appears extremely simple; and as in most others, accident, rather than study, has had the merit of solving the enigma which has so long baffled the learned.

"While arranging and lithographing the numerous scraps of facsimiles, for Plate XXVII [i.e. the Sānchī inscriptions] I was struck at their all terminating with the same two letters, 𑀤𑀸 𑀦𑀁 Coupling this circumstance with their extreme brevity and insulated position, which proved that they could not be fragments of a continuous text, it immediately occurred that they must record either obituary notices, or more probably the offerings and presents of votaries, as is known to be the present custom in the Buddhist temples of *Ava;* where numerous *dhwajas* or flag-staffs, images and small *chaityas* are crowded within the enclosure, surrounding the chief cupola, each bearing the name of the donor. The next point noted was the frequent occurrence of the letter (𑀲), already set down incontestably as *s*, before the final word: now this I had learnt from the *Saurāshṭra* coins, deciphered only a day or two before, to be one sign of the genitive case singular, being the *ssa* of the Pali, or *sya* of the Sanscrit. 'Of so and so the gift,' must then be the form of each brief sentence; and the vowel *ā* and *anuswāra* led to the speedy recognition of the word *dānam* (gift) teaching me the very two letters, *d* and *n*, most different from the known forms, and which had foiled me most in my former attempts. Since 1834 also my acquaintance with ancient alphabets had become so familiar that most of the remaining letters in the present examples could be named at once on re-inspection. In the course of a few minutes I thus became possessed of the whole alphabet, which I tested by applying it to the inscription on the *Delhi* column."

Prinsep then applied, with success, the Sānchī alphabet, as he called it, to the Buddhist group of ancient coins and to other inscriptions, particularly those on the *lāts,* meaning the Aśokan Edict columns, in Upper India, and gave an analysis of the alphabet. Next, by the application of the alphabet to the inscriptions on the celebrated Aśokan pillars at Delhi and Allāhābād, he gave detailed readings and interpretations of these inscriptions. Thus was the master-key of the ancient Brāhmi alphabet discovered.

Prinsep's great discovery ushered in a new era by lifting the veil from the earlier Indian inscriptions, and laid the foundation of research in Indian history and practically every branch of Indian archaeology. Hereafter it became possible to evaluate each discovery and assign it to its proper period by a systematic study of contemporary writings. Scholars like Fergusson, Cunningham, Dr. Bhau Daji, and Dr. Rajendra Lal Mitra handed on the torch lighted by Prinsep, and built up the foundations of our present knowledge of Indian architecture, Indian geography, Indian coins and other branches of Indology during the next generation.

The first official step taken by the Government of India was the appointment of General Alexander Cunningham as Archaeological Surveyor to the Government in 1862. This was due to the initiative of Lord Canning, who for the first time realized that the British Government had a duty towards India in rescuing from oblivion her splendid heritage of the past. The choice of so genuine a lover of Indian antiquities as General Cunningham for this pioneer work of exploration and research was very happy, and the record of his devoted labours for nearly half a century, extending over a vast field, covering almost every branch of knowledge, is in many ways unique. Starting with the data supplied by the Greek historians and the Chinese travellers, he laid the foundations of an exact knowledge of ancient Indian geography by personal investigations and an almost uncanny gift of spotting and identification of ancient sites. His unrivalled knowledge of Indian coins, particularly those of the north-west, laid the foundation of Indian numismatics, which still has to depend upon his published works in certain branches. Many of his speculations and conjectures may not have been confirmed by subsequent research, but this can be excused in a pioneer who covered so much new ground in half a dozen different fields. Such digging as was attempted at places like Bodh Gayā, Bhārhut, Sānchī, Sārnāth, and Taxilā cannot be considered as systematic excavation, but we must remember that the science of archaeology had not then developed anywhere else beyond quarrying for sensational finds.

After Cunningham's retirement followed a period of nearly fifteen years in which no clear archaeological policy was laid down or followed, although Dr. Burgess and his colleagues were able to publish excellent volumes on the results of the Surveys, mostly of Western Indian caves as also in Southern India. Provincial surveys on a very limited scale and without any central direction or support could accomplish little, but in the closing years of the last century, Lord Curzon, the Viceroy of India, ushered in a new era for Indian archaeology. He accepted the encouragement of research and the promotion of archaeological study as a duty and obligation which Government owed to this ancient country and established a Central Department of Archaeology. Thereafter, the course of archaeology has been fairly continuous, though subject to periodic stimulation and depression.

The Department contained several keen and sound Sanskrit scholars of various nationalities, notably Dr. Vogel, Dr. Stein, Dr. Bloch, and afterwards Dr. Spooner, all of whom were very much interested in archaeological exploration; but none of them had the benefit of taking actual part in the work of excavation as Dr. Marshall (afterwards Sir John), the newly appointed Director General of Archaeology, had in Greece before his appointment. His direction and guidance soon proved to be of the greatest benefit to Indian archaeology, and not only did the European officers of the Department hereafter take a share in the work of excavation, but young Indian probationers were enlisted for training as they were eventually to replace scholars from abroad. In the first few years (1903-12) the programme of excavation largely centred round such famous Buddhist sites as Sānchī, Sārnāth, Kāsiā (Kuśinagara) and Sahet Mahet (Śrāvastī). City-sites like Chārsadda (Pushkalāvatī) near Mardan, Bhiṭā near Allāhābād, Basārh (Vaiśālī) near Muzaffarpur, and Rājgir the ancient capital of Magadha, were also touched but not persisted in, although they yielded sufficient finds of great importance for the reconstruction of cultural history. The reason for this, as explained by Sir John Marshall himself, was that the researches of the earlier generation of archaeologists had thrown more light on Buddhist antiquities, and besides there was a greater chance of making some spectacular finds in the Buddhist sites than in the more extensive city-sites where it is difficult to locate spots of special importance. Buddhist sites, generally clustered around lofty *stūpas* and readily recognizable from their configuration, are certainly easier to excavate and there is greater probability of making such sensational finds as, for example, the relics of the Buddha enshrined by Kanishka in the *stūpa* near Peshāwar city. At Sārnāth, the famous lion capital of an Aśokan pillar and the great sculptural wealth of the Gupta empire were among the sensational discoveries made.

The idea of bringing to light the successive cultural periods of Indian history by regular excavations at city-sites was entertained about 1912, when Sir John Marshall took up his work at Taxilā which was to continue for over two decades. At Pāṭaliputra (Patna) Dr. Spooner began in 1913 his examination of the ancient Mauryan capital which was to continue for a number of years, thanks to the liberality of Sir Ratan Tata who provided the entire funds. Unfortunately the latter site, being waterlogged and buried deep under alluvium, did not yield proportionately large results. Strangely enough, some of the most striking finds came from the lower levels exposed in the course of sewage operations and foundations of modern buildings. The excavations at Taxilā, on the other hand, have yielded steadily growing material which has fulfilled the expectations raised by a city-site situated on the main highway from the north-west, forming, as it were, the crucible in which Indian culture was blended with that of other races coming from that direction during the three or four centuries on either side of the Christian era. The most comprehensive operations ever carried out at any single site in India are those at Taxilā, where about a dozen sites have been excavated within an area of some 25 square miles, embracing three separate cities and half a dozen large Buddhist establishments. The earliest city going back to the Mauryan period is that under the Bhir mound, which was superseded by the second and most important city at the site of Sirkap, founded by the Indo-Greek rulers and inhabited during the Indo-Greek and the Śaka periods. The wealth of finds, mainly from the second city, that enriches the museum established on the site makes it the most attractive archaeological collection in the country.

While the lay-out of the Mauryan city was irregular and the construction unimpressive, the second town, with its regularly arranged streets and lanes and well-built houses with spacious rooms and courtyards, is one of the best preserved ancient cities, the relics found being among the most representative and valuable dug out anywhere in India. Among the religious sites at Taxilā the most prominent and extensive is the Dharmarājikā *stūpa,* said to have been founded by the great Aśoka and built over during successive ages and surrounded by scores of smaller *stūpas,* chapels, and large monasteries. Some of the retreats for the Buddhist monks perched on the neighbouring hillocks, such as those at Jaulian, Kalawan, and Mohra Moradu, provide ample evidence of the flourishing state of Buddhism in the palmy days of Taxilā, which came to an end at the close of the fifth century A.D. with the invasions of the Hūṇa hordes.

World War I interfered with the progress of exploration, as it was not possible for the Government to spare funds for scientific research. However, the Royal Asiatic Society of London sanctioned a small grant for the excavation of the great Buddhist site of Nālandā, and this enabled Dr. Spooner to commence work in 1917 which continued unabated for nearly two decades. Besides the complex of *stūpas,* temples, and monasteries brought to light in the course of these excavations, Nālandā has yielded unique bronzes and sculptures of great artistic merit as well as inscriptions which have thrown a flood of light on the history of Northern India and the development of Buddhism in Eastern India. The main building here shows signs of having been enlarged and rebuilt no less than seven times, and some of the monasteries show at least three periods of occupation and reconstruction. Nālandā has been the main centre of archaeological work in Bihār since it was taken up nearly thirty years ago. Rājgir (ancient Rājagṛiha) has also yielded some remarkable finds, notably from the site known as Maniyār Maṭh, but no large-scale examination of this ancient city, one of the earliest historical capitals of India, has yet been attempted.

An epoch-making discovery which changed the course of Indian Archaeology and pushed back Indian antiquities from the Buddhist to prehistoric times was made in 1922-23 when Mr. R. D. Banerji, excavating the ruins of a Buddhist establishment at Mohenjo-daro in Sind, lighted upon certain inscribed seals with pictographic characters which were till then known only from the site of Harappā in the Punjab. The full significance of the discovery was not apparent till two years later, when a comparison of the finds from both the sites convinced Sir John Marshall that they belonged to a prehistoric civilization far earlier than any known so far. Although at first labelled Indo-Sumerian, owing to its obvious affinities with the Sumerian civilization of the third millennium B.C., the newly discovered civilization was subsequently renamed after the Indus Valley, as it was found to be its main habitat. The discoveries stimulated public interest in Indian Archaeology to an unprecedented degree, and the Government of India began to finance liberally schemes of archaeological exploration and research in the different parts of India. For about seven years from 1924-25 the Government grant for exploration gradually rose until it reached the figure of two and a half lakhs which has been the high-water mark in this country. For this the discoveries at Mohenjo-dāro are mainly responsible, and under that name is epitomized the progress of Indian Archaeology during the last two decades.

Preliminary excavations were carried on at a large number of sites in Sind and archaeological explorations were extended even to distant parts of Baluchistān (see Map 2). But these subsequent researches have failed to shed any considerable light on the manner in which this well-developed city civilization of the Indus Valley sprang up, as if from nowhere, and also about its equally inexplicable disappearance without leaving any considerable traces of its survival in the Indus Valley or its surrounding regions. Some seven epochs, either slightly earlier or slightly later than the main stream of culture presented by Harappā and Mohenjo-daro, have been identified, but all of them together do not help to bridge the wide gulf between this chalcolithic civilization and that of the historic period which flourished in the upper and middle Gangetic basin from the middle of the first millennium B.C. This indeed is one of the most important tasks before Indian archaeology, and demands a great deal of patient and systematic work over a number of years. Field research of this type cannot be attempted by compartments but will require an all-India organization with ample resources at its back and co-operation of various regional units.

The initial success of the Archaeological Department of the Government of India induced many of the Indian States to open their own Archaeological Departments. We shall now review the position regarding exploration in each province and important state. In the province of Sind, which leaped into prominence with the Indus Valley discoveries, the record of archaeology is still very meagre, apart from the Indus Valley finds. Besides a few Buddhist *stūpas* and monasteries, mostly assignable to the Gupta period as at Mirpur Khās, none of the remains can be assigned to a period earlier than the Arab invasion in the eighth century. One reason for this must have been the gradual desiccation of the lower Indus Valley. The main interest of the province will therefore vest in the large number of sites of the prehistoric period, scattered over its western half, which have not yet been adequately explored.

In the North-West Frontier Province the great Buddhist sites of Sahr-i-Bahlol, Takht-i-Bahi, and Jamālgarhi have yielded valuable treasures. They fill the local museum at Peshāwar, which is naturally the most important for the Graeco-Buddhist school of Gandhāra. The whole district of Peshāwar teems with mounds which are being fast levelled by cultivators to the great detriment of science.

In the Punjab, Harappā and Taxilā have been the most important centres of archaeological works so far. The province, however, possesses very interesting possibilities of exploration in the earlier phases of culture. The De Terra expedition, which came to study the Ice Age in Kāshmir and the Punjab foot-hills, brought to light important palaeolithic industries in the Soan valley which constitute the earliest relics of the Stone Age in the north. The find of a small isolated site of the Indus period near Rupar in the Sutlej Valley, coupled with the presence of a number of mounds in the submontane region of Ambāla, gives the hope that further interesting discoveries concerning the extension of the Indus Valley culture and its survival may be made in this region.

Kāshmir, the beautiful valley in the lap of the Himālayas, is the only part of India for which, as noted before, an indigenous written history is available for the pre-Muslim period. The task of identification of the many historical places mentioned in Kalhaṇa's Chronicle fell to Sir Aurel Stein, who successfully accomplished it and thereby laid the foundation of his world-wide fame as an explorer and archaeologist. When the Government of Kāshmir opened an Archaeological Department in 1922, it turned its attention to the ancient sites, and eventually some of these were excavated, the result being in most cases a confirmation of Stein's painstaking examination of Kalhaṇa.

The most interesting remains discovered are those of a Buddhist settlement of Kushāṇa period at Harwan (ancient Shaḍahradvana) consisting of a *stūpa* and monasteries on a hill slope with unique terra-cotta plaques ornamenting the walls. Ushkar or Huvishkapura was another early Buddhist site (named after the well-known Kushāṇa emperor) where investigation brought to light an early *stūpa* built in the eighth century. Other sites where excavation was carried out are Parihāspur, Avantipur and the well-known Mārtand, all belonging to the period from sixth to ninth century A.D.

The United Provinces, constituting throughout the historic period "the middle country" (Madhyadeśa) or the heart of the Indian sub-continent, hold the key to the solution of many a problem concerning the development of Indian culture. The vestiges of human occupation from the earliest times to the present day can be recognized here in the shape of mounds representing such famous cities of old as Mathurā, Vārāṇasī, Śrāvastī, Kauśāmbī and Ahichchhatra. Mathurā and its neighbourhood have yielded to the digger the largest number of sculptural treasures, but systematic excavations in the modern sense have not been attempted on a proper scale. The small antiquities from the ancient site of Kauśāmbī, picked up by casual visitors, are more artistic and more numerous than those found anywhere else.

It is by systematic work on the city mounds that Indian archaeology can hope to lay the foundation of a more comprehensive knowledge of Indian antiquities. Such work was commenced at the site of Ahichchhatra in 1941-42 and continued for three seasons, with the object of separating and classifying the different strata of buildings and studying the finds associated with each cultural layer. As a result, the pottery, terra-cottas, and minor antiquities found in the excavation of the ancient cities of Northern India can now be assuredly relegated to definite historic periods such as Maurya, Śuṅga, Kushāṇa, Gupta and Medieval, on the reliable basis of archaeological stratification instead of merely on grounds of style. One great desideratum to which attention has been drawn by critics from abroad is the absence of a properly classified corpus of Indian pottery through the ages. For this, ample material has now been collected from the Ahichchhatra excavation and from other regular excavations, though on a smaller scale, carried out at such sites as Rājghāt (Benares), Mathurā, and one or two sites in the Punjab and north-west. The continental nature of the civilization of North India makes it inevitable that in each of the main periods the standard form adopted by the craftsmen of the central parts should be the guide for other regions, no doubt with local variations. In certain special periods such as the Mauryan, when the Imperial influence radiated from the capital, it has been found that the special black glazed ware must have been centrally manufactured and specimens exported to outlying districts.

Apart from this the characteristic grey ware of the Śuṅga period.

the variety of forms prevalent in Kushāṇa times, and the beautiful decorated pottery of the Guptas can now hardly be mistaken, although they may have been manufactured in places as distant from each other as the Punjab and Bengal. The value of the accurate dating of pottery, which is the most abundant material found in surface explorations, has now been sufficiently realized, and this opens the way to a better approximation of the age of surface remains in the absence of such datable material as coins and inscriptions which are not always forthcoming.

In Bengal archaeological excavation has added a new chapter to the cultural history of the province where relics of the pre-Muhammadan period were almost non-existent on the surface. This was at the great site of Pāhārpur in the Rājshāhi district which took the best part of a decade to excavate and preserve. Here the most remarkable find is the gigantic Buddhist establishment consisting of a towering central temple rising in terraces and surrounded by a vast quadrangle of monastic cells. The plan of the temple showing a grand square cross with projections between the arms, and the scheme of decoration of the walls by rows of terra-cotta plaques interspersed by fine stone images, have thrown a flood of light on the early history of art and architecture in Bengal. Some work has also been attempted at Mahāsthāna, the site of ancient Puṇḍravardhana, and at Bāngarh, ancient Koṭīvarsha, two important cities of North Bengal. The latter work, conducted by the University of Calcutta, constitutes the only attempt made by an Indian University in the field of excavation, which has been thrown open to non-official effort by virtue of an amendment of the Ancient Monument Preservation Act passed by the Central Legislature in 1933. The casual removal of earth for erecting military establishments during World War II has brought to light many remains of ancient structures in the Maināmati Hill near Comilla. A preliminary survey indicates that they are the remnants of Buddhist establishments comparable to those of Pāhārpur, but no systematic excavation has yet taken place in this region.

In the provinces of Assam and Orissa the efforts of archaeologists have so far been confined to the investigation of standing monuments and existing ruins.

The Central Provinces and Central India constitute the richest field for epigraphical discoveries, but no systematic excavation of ancient sites has so far been attempted in the Central Provinces. In Central India good work has been carried on in Gwalior State where the remains of the ancient cities of Vidiśā (Besnagar), Padmāvatī (Padma-Pawaya), and Ujjain have been excavated by the state archaeological department. The great site of Sānchī in Bhopāl has been well excavated by Sir John Marshall. There is a great scope for the detailed investigation of remains, both of the historic and prehistoric periods, particularly in the basin of the Narmadā river which has already yielded remains of palaeolithic and microlithic industries.

In Rājputāna, the late Sir Aurel Stein's examination of the dried bed of Hakrā (ancient Sarasvatī) has brought to light a number of pre-historic sites in the Bikāner and particularly Bahāwalpur States. Systematic excavation in Rājputānạ is confined to Jaipur where the ancient sites of Bairāt, Rairh, and Sāmbhar have yielded a large number of antiquities, including hoards of punch-marked coins and terra-cotta figurines. Bairāṭ has a unique circular temple of the Mauryan times, and Rairh appears to have been a flourishing metallurgical centre and trade mart. The most extensive site in Jaipur is the city of Nagar or Karkotnagar, now represented by extensive mounds recently taken up for excavation which, if carried through, is sure to shed light on the history of the Mālava tribe whose capital it was.

An important undertaking, recently initiated by the Archaeological Department and now taken over by the Ancient History Department of the Deccan College Research Institute, Poona, is the expedition which has investigated the prehistoric remains in Gujarāt. This expedition, undertaken at first with a view to determine the relation of the paleolithic and neolithic remains found in the Sābarmatī valley by Bruce Foote, the pioneer of Indian prehistory, has succeeded in bringing to light at Langhnaj, near Mehsana, Baroda, State, skeleton remains in an advanced stage of calcination in association with microlithic implements. The success of the expedition has induced help from the Tata Trust fund, and the further continuance of the work by a non-official body like the Institute is thus assured. Minor excavations at various ancient sites such as Anhilpur, Pātan, Amreli, and Mul Dwārakā were carried out by the Archaeological Department of the Baroda State.

In the Province of Bombay the prevalence of trap throughout the Mahārāshṭra area accounts for the paucity of stratified accumulations at ancient sites. In portions of the Karnātak district of Bījāpur recent examination of the surface has brought to light the existence of several strata going back to the pre-Mauryan age. Recent work at the ancient city of Kolhāpur has also yielded considerable material of the Sātavāhana and later periods, incidentally throwing light on contacts with Rome.

The most important centres of Sātavāhana power were in the Deccan, and it is there that we must look for further extensive evidence of culture in the Sātavāhana period. The Hyderābād Government has conducted excavations in the ancient capital of Paiṭhan (Pratishṭhāna) and more recently at Kondāpur in the Bidar district. The latter site is a veritable mine of antiquities which include numerous specimens of all types such as terra-cotta and stucco figures, coins and medals numbering several thousand, and pottery. The material discovered here and at the great site of Maski has not yet been adequately studied, and it is essential that it should be properly published if its scientific value is to be enhanced. The Archaeological Department of the Hyderābād State, started in 1915, has recently taken up the programme of archaeological exploration and excavation, and it may be confidently hoped that its work will be commensurate with the great importance of the remains situated in the dominions.

Mysore led the way among Indian States in archaeological investigation by starting a regular department over sixty years ago. At first the activities of the Department were concentrated on a survey of the epigraphic material in which the state abounds, and on which the history of the dynasties that ruled Mysore is almost wholly based. Latterly some attention has been devoted to the excavation of ancient sites of which two have proved to be of very great value. The site of Chandrāvali near Chitaldrug was excavated in 1928 and shows several strata of occupation in which the Sātavāhana period seems to be most important. Brahmagiri, in the northernmost part of Mysore, shows not only the relics of the Mauryan town of Isila, but also those of later historic periods, and, what is more, was founded on earlier settlements of microlithic age.

In the Madras Presidency, the vast number of existing temples and inscriptions have absorbed the main attention of the Archaeological Survey. Although the number of sites of every period are numerous, excavation has so far been attempted only in some of the Buddhist sites in the northern districts and the well-known prehistoric burials at Adichanallur in the extreme south. Of the Buddhist sites the most important are those in the Krishnā valley in which the local rulers of the Ikshvāku dynasty seem to have patronized art in a larger measure than any of their predecessors. Many ancient monuments before the organization of the Archaeological Department, such as the Amarāvatī stūpa in the Guntur district, had already been wellnigh destroyed by villagers and other vandals and their sculptures distributed among different museums, including the British Museum. Recently the discovery of an important site at Nāgārjunikoṇḍa has to some extent made up for the loss. Systematic excavation has brought to light another group of *stūpas* and monasteries, arranged in a characteristic manner, which have yielded a vast number of sculptures and inscriptions. The site is beautifully situated in the Krishnā valley and was anciently known as Śrī-Parvata. A local museum has been built on the spot for housing the sculptures and architectural specimens unearthed. Some work was done recently at the site of Virampattanam, near Pondicherry, the seaport in which, as in many other south Indian sites, evidences of commercial contacts with Rome during the

Imperial period are abundant. The problem of Megalithic burials in South India is vast and complicated, and much damage has already been inflicted by ill-advised digging on the graves associated with stone circles, urn burials, sarcophagi, etc., which occur over extensive areas in Southern India. At Adichanallur a large number of antiquities, including iron swords, daggers, gold and bronze diadems, bronze vessels and animal figures, etc., were found, along with a large amount of red-and-black polished pottery, forming the accompaniments of the burials.

The whole subject has now been assiduously studied and we can expect the results of these studies to throw light on the movement and settlement of different types of people in the Peninsula. The entire field of palaeolithic, neolithic, and megalithic as well as iron age cultures in Southern India is so vast, and transcends in interest investigations relating to the historic periods, that it is likely to form a major preoccupation for several years. The states of Southern India, including Travancore, Cochin, and Pudukottai, have each its own contribution to make to this subject, not to speak of the larger states of Hyderābād and Mysore.

No account of the activities of Indian exploration can be complete without reference to the work carried out in what may be called Greater India. The most brilliant work carried out by the late Sir Aurel Stein constitutes the greatest achievement that can fall to the lot of a single scholar and explorer. Sir Aurel Stein's activities were spread over a very wide field, including Baluchistān, Irān, and the border lands of India. But his most famous explorations were conducted in Chinese Turkistān. In the course of the several expeditions which Sir Aurel Stein carried out for the Government of India, he discovered numerous relics of the ancient civilization which developed in the region. These have been preserved in the dry sandy wastes and show the highly important part which India played in the Far East, and the way in which Indian cultural influences were spread there. The state of preservation of the fresco paintings in the Buddhist temples, wooden, silk, and paper documents, and other perishable objects is remarkable. These objects, recovered from Central Asia, have been carefully brought back and preserved in a special museum erected at New Delhi by the Government of India.

In Burma, which formed part of India till ten years ago, activities were mostly confined to the centres of Prome, Pegu, and Pagan. Excavation has been generally confined to opening up small mounds lying in abundance at these centres, particularly Prome, marking the sites of old *stūpas* or temples. The earliest finds are those at Prome in which Indian influence is very prominent. Although Hīnayāna Buddhism and the Pāli tradition have now acquired a great hold on Burmese Buddhism, it is clear that a large proportion of the earlier colonizers were followers of the Mahāyāna sect and the Brahmanical religion, and it was not till a comparatively later period that the Hīnayāna triumphed over its rivals. Bilingual inscriptions from Prome show the language of the old Pyu inhabitants side by side with Sanskrit. At Pagan excavations have brought to light a number of finds belonging to the eleventh and twelfth centuries, when modern Burmese culture may be said to have originated. At this period Burma was subject to a great deal of influence from India, especially Bengal, in sculpture, painting, terra-cotta, and architecture. It has now been well established that the planning and scheme of decoration of Burmese temples and pagodas is based on Indian prototypes developed in the alluvial plains of Northern India for centuries.

In the Malay Peninsula exploration work has not proceeded on a large scale, but whatever has been done shows a strong Indian influence in the beginning of cultural history. The existence of the great Śrī-Vijaya Kingdom in Indonesia, and its paramount influence over the islands in the Netherlands Indies, has now been clearly established by researches. The great monuments in Java, belonging to the Brāhmanical as well as Buddhist faiths, such as the Barabudur, Chaṇḍi Sewu, and Chaṇḍi Lara-Jongnang amply demonstrate the extent of Indian culture. Lastly, reference may be made to the researches and explorations of the French archaeologists in Indo-China which have thrown a flood of light on Indian colonies of Champā (Annam), Kambuja (Cambodia), and Dvāravatī (Siam), and led to the discovery of such monuments as Angkor Vat and Angkor Thom of world-wide fame.

In Ceylon there is yet a vast field for exploration and excavation, but work so far has been mainly confined to the ancient capitals of Anurādhapura and Polonnaruwa. Originally European scholars were in charge of the work, but a properly trained Ceylonese scholar has now been appointed Archaeological Commissioner, and he is responsible for the excellent work done at the hill site of Mihintale *stūpa* which is reminiscent of Sānchī. Several of the religious sites at Anurādhapura have received attention, but the vast remains of the ancient city have not yet been tackled. A large number of smaller sites in the south of the island have yet to be explored, specially for prehistoric remains in which Ceylon seems to be particularly rich, and a good beginning has been made in this direction by the Director of Museums in Ceylon. Of all countries bordering on India, Ceylon is the most intimately connected with her culture both in the prehistoric and historic periods, and it is but natural that research in both countries should go hand in hand in close co-operation.

Afghānistān has in several periods of its history formed part of India, and some of its most striking remains, as at Hadda, testify to the influence of Buddhism in that country. Some of the most important contributions to early Indian Epigraphy and Numismatics were based on finds made in Afghānistān. Recently a French mission conducted a series of excavations at Begram and other places which have thrown considerable light on its Indian connections.

In conclusion it may be observed that while archaeological exploration has been placed on a fairly strong foundation in this country and much has been achieved so far in bringing to light and interpreting first-rate material for the reconstruction of India's ancient history, a good deal yet remains to be done, and it would require the unabated efforts of generations of properly equipped archaeologists to bring the task to a reasonable state of completeness. While interest in the subject should be progressively widened throughout the length and breadth of this country, it is necessary that proper co-ordination should be established and much more financial support assured. Above all it is essential that a strong centre should foster and guide the activities of workers throughout the country. Indian unity, as exemplified throughout its history, is all the more necessary in the study of India's past, and any compartmental treatment is bound to result in stagnation. Through the immensity and diversity of India there runs a thread of unity which must be kept in view in any attempt to organize work for the systematic investigation of the past, and it is hoped that this consideration will never be lost sight of.

CHAPTER IV

THE GEOLOGICAL BACKGROUND OF INDIAN HISTORY

It is a truism that the course of human history in a region is, in a considerable measure, shaped by its physical and geographical features, which, in turn, in the ultimate, are determined by the geological history the region has passed through in the dim vista of time. Five thousand to ten thousand years ago North India must have offered to the early settlers from Asia, whatever race they belonged to, or from wherever they came, a congenial habitat, in pleasing contrast to the arid and inhospitable steppes of the Aralo-Caspian region, or the rugged mountains of the Irān-Afghānistān-Turkistān plateau. This migration to a quite new physical environment could not but have influenced and largely shaped the trend of history and civilization of the races involved.

Of the three natural physical divisions of India, as we shall see in the sequel, the part which was most suitable for human occupation and to function as the nursery of civilization is the great central tract of the Indo-Gangetic plains. Here were present all factors favourable for life—climate, food-supply, water, and vegetation. This vast expanse of flat alluvial plains of high fertility, watered by a number of perennial rivers, deriving their fertilizing waters from the snows of the Himālayas, must have attracted hordes of migratory peoples in successive waves from many parts of Western and Central Asia. The great alluvial plains of India extending from Sind through northern Rājputāna, Punjab, U.P., Bihār, and Bengal to Assam, an area of over 300,000 square miles, must have offered, as the centuries passed by, an exceedingly delectable home to early man long before the earliest beginnings of recorded history. But the geological beginnings of the sub-continent of India, as we know it today, date back to an antiquity of which it is difficult to give a concept save in terms of astronomical figures of years.

Human history, proto-history, and archaeology begin where the last chapter of our planet's geological history ends. Man's existence on earth dates a long time behind the oldest known records of authentic archaeology, but fragmentary documents of his life in various regions of the earth, of his slow progress in culture and industry, and the relics of his contemporary animals lie buried in the top layers of the earth's crust—the strata of geology which form what has been called its Sub-Recent period. Thus the background of the history of all human races on earth is this zone of strata in the upper crust or shell of the earth's body, laid down in surface deposits, river valleys, deltas, lake-basins, glaciers, etc. In these are preserved traces of the existence of man and of the physical and climatic conditions of the time; they are designated in general as the Pleistocene system, representing the last epoch of the third and latest division of geological time, the Cainozoic Era.

A full account of the Pleistocene under these heads is luckily preserved in India: it is of great value as linking up prehistory with the geological history of a large section of southern Asia. It was this age that saw the completion of the main outlines and relief of the earth as we see it today—its seas and continents, mountains, plateaux, and plains; though climatically the world had yet to witness one of the greatest revolutions, viz. the gradual freezing of the northern regions culminating in what is known as the Ice Age.

INDIA IN THE PLEISTOCENE PERIOD

1. *The Setting of the Stage for Early Man in India*

Pleistocene geological records found in India form an extensive and varied storehouse of materials for the last million years or so, immediately preceding the Recent and Sub-Recent epochs. They carry the human records forward to so late a date as the Neolithic (*circa* 10,000 years B.C). In terms of years the Pleistocene dates back, according to modern estimates, to one million to two million years. The formations enumerated below have an important bearing on man's prehistory as they contain in them numerous documentary relics entombed in the form of his skeletal remains, his artifacts and other proofs of his handiwork, industry, and culture. It is in these that the key to the stages of human evolution might be found.

The principal Pleistocene and Sub-Recent remains in India may be classified as follows:—

(i) Deposits of the Ice Age in India: Glacials of Outer and Middle Himālayas.

(ii) The Indo-Gangetic alluvium of the plains of North India.

(iii) The older alluvium of the peninsular rivers; high-level river terraces of the Himālayan valleys.

(iv Old Lake Deposits (Karewa Series) of the Upper Jhelum Valley in Kāshmir.

(v) Cave Deposits: Human cave-dwellers and their animal contemporaries.

(vi) Laterite Cap of the Peninsula: Loess and soil deposits.

(vii) Changes in the river-systems and drainage of North India.

(viii) The Desert of North India: the growth of desert conditions.

(ix) Late Earth Movements, volcanoes and earthquakes.

Interesting glaciological investigations have been made in the Kāshmir Himālayas and in the Karakoram by a number of explorers and naturalists. The Central and Eastern Himālayas have not received the same attention. It is, however, well known that throughout these mountains grooved and polished rock-surfaces, produced by the scouring action of the glaciers, occur at elevations above 6,000 feet, whereas the present limit of Himālayan glaciers is 13,000 to 15,000 feet. Numerous lakes and rock-basins of Kāshmir, Ladakh, and Kumaon directly owe their origin to the action of glaciers now no longer existing. Four distinct phases of glaciation, separated by three inter-glacial intervals, have been recognized in Kāshmir by their moraines.

Whether India, south of the Himālayas, passed through an Ice Age has been a much-discussed subject. It must be understood, however, that the present zonal distribution of climate being assumed, we cannot look for the presence of ice even on the highlands of South India, because a refrigeration which can produce ice-caps in the latitudes of Europe would not be enough to depress the temperatures in India beyond that of the present temperate zones. But some indirect evidences of considerably lowered temperature are observed in the increased humidity and a succession of cold pluvial periods having affected the distribution of several cold-loving species of animals and plants then living in India. This enables us to explain the occurrence today of some Himālayan temperate flora and fauna in such isolated centres as Mt. Ābū, Pārasnāth, in the Nilgiris and even in the mountains of Ceylon, and their absence throughout the intervening plains of India.

Man was contemporaneous, in N. W. India probably, with the two later glacial advances, as some late discoveries tend to show. De Terra records the presence of implements worked by man in deposits in the outer ranges of Kāshmir and in the Soan valley, belonging approximately to the second Glacial. He correlates the European Chellean and Acheulian with the early Soan cultures and dates this as Mid-Pleistocene.

2. *The Indo-Gangetic Alluvium of the Plains of North India*

As noted above, by early Pleistocene time, the dominant features of India's geography had taken shape, and the country had acquired almost its present form and its leading topography except that the land in front of the newly upheaved Himālayas formed a great longitudinal depression, complementary to the rising mountains, and parallel with them. This trough, at first occupied by salt-water lagoons, gradually freshened, and, receiving constant influx of detritus from the high ground above it, from hundreds of descending streams, began rapidly to be filled by the waste of the Himālayas. This long-continued vigorous sedimentation loading a narrow, slowly sinking belt of country, the deposition of the debris keeping pace with the subsidence, has given rise to the great Indian plains. The continuous upheaving of the mountains must have rejuvenated the streams, multiplying their sediment-depositing power. Thus these plains have come to acquire the simplest geological structure, the alluvial filling a large structural basin in the framework of India.

The greater part of the Indo-Gangetic plains is built up of very late alluvial flood deposits of the rivers of the Indus-Ganges systems, borne down from the Himālayas and deposited at their foot. But most of this terrain became firm and dry enough to be habitable for man only some 5,000-7,000 years ago. Buried beneath this mantle of clay and sand are valuable geological records linking up the Deccan with the Himālaya system. Its geological structure, composition and history therefore possess no great interest though, humanly speaking, it is of the greatest economic as well as historical importance. It has no mineral resources, but its agricultural wealth and fresh underground water stored in the more porous and coarser strata, accessible by ordinary wells and tube-wells, are the highest economic asset of India. Though devoid of records other than those of the yesterday of geological time, these alluvial plains are the stage of the main drama of Indian history since the Aryan occupation.

The area of these plains is 300,000 square miles, covering the most thickly populated and the most fertile part of India. The total thickness of the alluvium consisting of beds of clay, silt, and sand is not ascertained, for the deepest borings (for water down to about 2,000 feet) have not reached the bed-rock. There is a considerable amount of flexure and dislocation at the north margin of the trough, where it passes into the zone of the parallel boundary faults at the foot of the Himālayas. This structural strain explains the well-known seismic instability of this part of India, it being the belt encompassing the epicentres of the majority of the known Indian earthquakes. Many of the river courses of the plains have undergone great alterations. These rivers are bringing enormous loads of silt from the mountains and, depositing it on their beds, raise them to, and even above, the level of the surrounding flat country through which the streams flow in ever-shifting channels. This has been the history of many of the rivers of the plains. The deltas of the large rivers were mostly constructed within prehistoric times, though their surface and outline have undergone material changes during the last few centuries. The Indus and Ganges deltas each cover about forty thousand square miles.

The extensive alluvial tract of Gujarāt on the west coast is of the same age as, though quite unrelated to, the Indo-Gangetic system. Its constitution shows that it is not wholly the work of the rivers, but that in its making the combined agency of river, estuarine and marine coastal depositions has operated.

These ancient alluvial deposits are of value in the study of early and middle Pleistocene as they are characterized by the presence of some of the earliest undoubted traces of man's existence in India, and furnish an easily accessible field to the student of early human culture in India.

The alluvial plains of the Narmadā and Tāpti are remarkable as lying in deep rock-basins at over 500 feet elevation above the present beds of these rivers. Scattered in the clay, sand, and gravel beds are bones of the buffalo, horse, bear, an extinct species of rhinoceros, hippopotamus, elephant, and crocodile. A chipped stone hatchet, fashioned out of quartzite rock, was discovered in 1872, buried in the steep face of a gravel terrace of the Narmadā at a site eight miles north of Gadawāra. This is the earliest prehistoric relic of man discovered in India and is regarded as of the pre-Chellean Age. This fact suggests the settlement of the Narmadā valley by an early palaeolithic race. Another valuable relic, also believed to be of genuine human workmanship, was discovered in a terrace of the upper Godāvari at a level of about twenty-five feet above the present bed of the river. It is a knife fashioned out of an agate flake, 2½ inches long, the sharp cutting edge of which is blunted by long usage. From the association of human remains with large mammalia which differ from the existing Indian fauna in some material respects, the age of these implements can be taken to be Lower Pleistocene. The distance in time of these animals from their present-day descendants gives us some measure of the antiquity of the human settlements on the Narmadā and the Godāvarī.

Various alluvial deposits of the Jumna-Ganges rivers and their tributaries are somewhat newer in age and have been assigned an antiquity intermediate between the Narmadā-Godāvarī beds and the Mid-Pleistocene, from the evidence of fossil-bones and the few artifacts that have been found in them. Lately signs of the existence of palaeolithic man have also been obtained from the valleys of the Tungabhadrā and the Orsang. Recent discoveries since 1935 in the valleys of the Soan (near Rāwalpindi) and in the Sābarmatī of north Gujarāt of interesting suites of stone tools, axes, scrapers, and choppers also throw light on the length of the epoch that intervened between the palaeolithic and the commencement of historic time.

3. *Human Cave-Dwellers of India: Their Animal Contemporaries*

But few caves of archaeological interest exist in India and out of these only one group has received the attention of palaeontologists and been subjected to systematic exploration. The only ones that have been systematically investigated and yielded data on Pleistocene cave life are the group of small caves (Billa Surgam) near Banganapalli in the Kurnool district. From the stalagmitic floor a large assemblage of bones has been dug out, belonging to a mixture of Recent and Sub-Recent species, viz. a monkey, a hyaena, several cats, bear, a small equus, mongoose, bat, squirrel, a shrew, rats, small deer, gazelle, wild boar, along with an extinct type of rhinoceros, wild boar, civet-tiger and giant pangolin. Palaeontologists have assigned to this fauna a horizon near to the Upper Pleistocene top of the Palaeolithic. Among the human implements found in the Billa Surgam caves are numerous bone tools, very few stone tools being so far recorded. These are referred to the middle or upper Palaeolithic.

The Kurnool caves help to present a fragmentary picture of the land life that prevailed in India just prior to the time when man began to domesticate animals for his own use. This life bridges the gap between the end of the Siwalik, a period of maximum development of the higher mammalian species, and the beginning of the Neolithic, when man began to take to pastoral and agricultural pursuits.

Since early Siwalik times there has been a more or less constant intercourse between East Africa, Arabia, Central Asia and India maintained by the migrations of herds of mammals. Pilgrim has stated that the magnificent assemblage of land mammals we witness in the later stages of the Siwaliks was not truly of indigenous Indian origin. According to him it is certain that it received large accessions by migration of the larger quadrupeds from Egypt, Arabia, Central Asia, and even from distant North America by way of land bridges across Alaska, Siberia, and Mongolia.

There seems little doubt that our races of domestic animals are the direct descendants of the post-Siwalik species through the greatly decimated population that inhabited the Kurnool caves and the basins of the Narmadā and the Godāvarī. The Siwalik ancestry of the Indian camel and the buffalo is beyond any doubt, whilst the short-horned and humped cattle of India had as their progenitors the *Bos primigenius* of the Siwalik through *Bos nomadicus* of the Narmadā age. With a varied and abundant animal population as their co-denizens in the fertile and well-watered plains of North India it is no wonder that early man in India was among the first to tame some of the more prized varieties for companionship and domestic service.

4. *Laterite Cap of the Peninsula and Soil Deposits*

Among the geographical, geological, and geophysical factors which have influenced the course of history in India and governed the distribution of large bodies of population over its surface, the peculiar formation, laterite, is of importance. In many ways its influence was the opposite to that of the Indo-Gangetic alluvium, for whereas the country covered under this geological formation invited man's settlement and provided a hospitable base for sustaining life, the laterite rock terrains are generally soilless, comparatively sterile expanses of hard ground, difficult to till, and poor in surface and underground water resources, and drove man to easier conditions of existence.

5. *Changes in the River Systems of North India during the Human Epoch*

The hydrography of North India for a considerable portion of the Pleistocene epoch was profoundly different from what we find today. Few changes in the physical geography of India during early historical times and in Sub-Recent age have been so well proved as the changes in the river-systems of northern India. Following the great geographical revolution of the later Tertiary ages the old drainage lines of northern India have been radically altered and a new drainage system superimposed. The number, volume, and direction of the majority of the units of this drainage bear evidences of these changes, which in some instances, amounted to a complete reversal of the direction of flow of a principal river such as the Ganges.

The drainage pattern of Peninsular India is of great antiquity and has persisted more or less unchanged since the early Gondwana era. On the other hand the northerly drainage of the Deccan, flowing to the shores of the Himālayan Sea (the Tethys) in Gondwana times, was completely disorganized in the beginning of the Tertiary, and subsequently during the late Tertiary and post-Tertiary all its main lines were buried under the 200 mile wide belt of alluvial plains of the north from Sind to Manipur. The present valley system of northern India, one of the youngest hydrographic systems of the world, has inherited nothing from the old, it being an entirely superimposed drainage, with no relations whatever to the old river-courses.

6. *The Great Prehistoric River of Northern India*

Ample evidence is found on the subject of the common ancestry of the Brahmaputra, Ganges, and Indus rivers, their reversal and capture before attaining their present state which has influenced the course of Indian history at many a turn and corner. It was the notable pre-historic river, named the "Siwalik river" by Pilgrim, that flowed from the head of the Sind gulf to the Punjab and thence along the foot of the embryonic Himālaya chains, through Simla and Nainital to Assam. Post-Siwalik earth movements in North-West Punjab brought about a dismemberment of this river system into three subsidiary systems: (1) The present Indus from North-West Hazāra; (2) The five Punjab tributary rivers of the Indus: (3) The rivers belonging to the Ganges system which finally took a south-easterly course.

The severed upper part of the Siwalik River became the modern Ganges, having in course of time captured the transversely running Jumna and converted it into its own affluent. The transverse Himālayan rivers, the Alaknandā, Karnali, Gandak, and Kosi, which are really amongst the oldest water-courses of North India, continued to discharge their waters into this new river, irrespective of its ultimate destination, whether it was the Arabian Sea or Bay of Bengal. During Sub-Recent times some interchange took place between the easterly affluents of the Indus and the westerly tributaries of the Jumna by minor shifting of the water-shed, now to one side now to the other. There are both physical and historical grounds for the belief that the Jumna during early times discharged into the Indus system, through the now neglected bed of the Sarasvatī river of Hindu tradition, its present course to Prayāg being of late acquisition.

The Punjab portion of the present Jhelum, Chenāb, Rāvi, Beās, and Sutlej have originated from the uplift of the topmost stage of the Siwalik system and subsequent to the severance of the Indus from the Ganges. The Potwar plateau-building movements could not but have rejuvenated the small rivulets of southern Punjab, which until now were discharging into the lower Indus; the vigorous head-erosion resulting from this impetus enabled them to capture, bit by bit, that portion of the Siwalik river which crossed the Potwar on its westerly course to the Indus. Ultimately the head waters, joining up with the youthful torrents descending from the mountains, grew in volume till they formed the five important rivers of the province, having their sources in the snows of the Great Himālaya Range. The western portion of the broad but now deserted channel of the main river, after these mutilating operations, has been occupied today by the puny, insignificant stream of the Soan, a river out of all harmony with its great basin in the enormous extent of the fluvialite deposits with which it is choked.

7. *The Deserts of Western India: The Rann of Cutch*

The origin of 40,000 square miles of the Rājputāna desert with its curiously worn and sand-blasted topography is attributed, in the first instance, to a long continued and extreme degree of aridity of the region combined with the sand-drifting action of the south-west monsoon winds, which sweep through Rājputāna for several months of the year without precipitating any part of their contained moisture. A certain proportion of the desert sand is derived from the weathered debris of the rocky prominences of this tract, which are subject to the great diurnal as well as seasonal alterations of temperature characteristic of all arid regions. The daily variation of heat and cold in some parts of Rājputāna often amounts to 100 degrees Fahr. in the course of a few hours. The seasonal alteration is greater. This leads to a mechanical disintegration of the rocks, producing an abundance of loose debris, which there is no chemical or organic action (humus) to convert into soil.

The Rann of Cutch.—Once an inlet of the Arabian Sea and now a saline marshy plain scarcely above sea-level, its sandy metal enclosing deep pockets of millions of tons of pure salt, the Rann of Cutch bears signs of late geological alterations of level caused by earth movements and owes its present condition to the geological process of the Pleistocene age. From November to March, the period of the north-west monsoon, the Rann is a barren tract of dry salt-encrusted mud presenting aspects of inconceivable desolution. During the other half of the year it is flooded by waters of the rivers that are held back owing to the rise of the sea by the south-west monsoon gales. A very little depression of this tract would be enough to convert Kāthiāwār and Cutch into islands. On the other hand, if depression does not take place, the greater part of the surface of the Rann will be gradually raised by the silts brought by the river with each flood, and in course of time converted into an arable tract, above the reach of the sea, a continuation of the alluvial terrain of Gujarāt.

8. *The Meteorological Influence of the Himālaya Mountains*

The Rājputāna desert conditions have thus accentuated with time, the water action of its few streams being too feeble to transport to the sea the growing masses of sand. But that the Indian desert is not of greater extent, or that it shows no tendency to expand in girth is due to the meteorological influence exerted by the Himālaya range. It has protected northern India from the gradual desiccation that has overspread Central Asia from Khorasan in eastern Persia to Mongolia since early historic times, and the desert conditions that inevitably follow in the heart of a continent.

9. *Earthquakes and Volcanoes*

Earthquakes.—The Peninsula of India is a region of great geological stability and is remarkably immune from seismic disturbances of any intensity. But in the extra-peninsular India the recorded earthquakes since even late historic times form a long catalogue of tragedies. It is a well-authenticated generalization that the majority of Indian earthquakes have originated from the great plains of India, or from their peripheral tracts.

Of the great Indian earthquakes recorded in the last two centuries and of which some accounts can be traced, the best known are:

Delhi, 1720; Calcutta, 1737; Eastern Bengal, 1762; Cutch, 1809; Kāshmir, 1885; Bengal, 1885; Assam, 1897 (one of the most disastrous earthquakes recorded in world history); Kangra, 1905; North Bihār, 1934; Western Baluchistān, 1935. The area encompassed by these quakes is the zone of weakness and strain caused by the severe crumpling of the Himālayas within recent times. The structurally disturbed and displaced belt has not yet attained stability of quiescence. It falls within the great earthquake belt which traverses the circumference of the earth east to west, from Japan through the whole breadth of Eurasia across the Atlantic and the North American continent to California.

Volcanoes.—There are no living or active volcanoes anywhere in the Indian region today. A recently extinct volcano lies far on the west border of India in the Nushki desert of Baluchistān—the large extinct crater of Kohi Sultan. The Malay line of living volcanoes—the Sunda Chain—some of the most active volcanoes of the recent age, if prolonged to the north, would connect a few dormant or lately extinct volcanoes belonging to this region. Of these the most important is the now dormant volcano of Barren Island, to the east of the Andaman island group. The last time it was observed to be in eruption was early in the nineteenth century.

10. *Late Earth-Movements and Local Alterations of Level*

Though movements of the mountain-building kind have not visited the peninsular part of India for an immense length of geological time, there have been a few late vertical movements of secular upheaval and depression, some of these of considerable amplitude, involving uplift or sinking of large crust-blocks, while others were of minor or local type. Of these, the later minor alterations of level recorded within the Pleistocene concern us here. Within these times an appreciable elevation of the peninsula, exposing portions of the submerged coastal plains as a shelf or platform round its east as well as west coasts, is the most notable. Such "raised beaches" are found at altitudes varying from a few feet to 150 feet in many places on the Malabar and Coromandel coasts, while marine shells are found at several places some distance inland far above the level of the tides. Marine and estuarine deposits of post-Teritary age are met with on a large scale towards the southern extremity of the Deccan. Besides these evidences of a rather prominent uplift of the peninsula, there are also proofs of minor, more local alterations of level, both elevation and depression. The existence of beds of lignite and peat in the Ganges delta, the submerged forest discovered on the east coast of the island of Bombay and peat deposits near Pondicherry are proofs of slow downward movement. Evidences of upheaval are seen in some coral reefs along the coasts, low-level raised beaches on various parts of the Ghats, and recent marine accumulations above tide level.

The submerged forest of Bombay is nearly twelve feet below low-water mark and thirty feet below high water; here a number of tree stumps are seen with their roots *in situ*, in the old soil. On the Tinnevelly coast a similar forest or fragment of old land surface is seen slightly below high-water mark. At Pondicherry, 240 feet below ground-level, a thick bed of lignite is found, while in the Ganges delta layers of carbonized vegetable debris occur. About twenty miles from the coast of Mekran the sea deepens suddenly to a great hollow. This is thought to be due to the submergence of a cliff formerly lying on the coast. The recent subsidence, in 1819, of the western border of the Rann of Cutch under the sea, accompanied by the elevation of a large tract of land (the *Allahbund*), is the most striking event of its kind recorded in India and was witnessed by the whole population of the country. Here a tract of land, some 2,000 square miles in area, was suddenly depressed to a depth of twelve to fifteen feet, and the whole tract converted into an inland sea. The fort of Sindree, which stood on the shores, the scene of many a battle recorded in history, was also submerged underneath the waters, and only a single turret of that fort remained, for many years, exposed above the sea. As an accompaniment of the same movements, another area of about 600 square miles was simultaneously elevated several feet above the plains, into a mound which was appropriately designated by the people "Allahbund" meaning "built by God." The elevated tract of land known as the Madhupur jungle near Dacca is believed to have upheaved as much as 100 feet in quite recent times. This upheaval caused the deflection of the Brahmaputra river eastward into Sylhet, away from the Ganges valley. Since this change the Brahmaputra has again changed its course to the west.

In the foregoing account of the later geological deposits of India there is everywhere a gradual passage from the Pleistocene to the Sub-Recent and thence to the prehistoric and the Recent. These periods overlap each other much as do the periods of human history, and there is no general agreement as to the exact limits of each.

CHAPTER V

THE GEOGRAPHICAL BACKGROUND OF INDIAN HISTORY

I. PHYSICAL FEATURES

India is a vast country well marked off from the rest of Asia by its mountain wall on the north, north-east, and north-west, and the sea on the remaining sides. Roughly speaking, the territory comprised within it is about 2,500 miles from east to west and 2,000 miles from north to south, with an approximate area of 1,800,000 sq. miles. It has 6,000 miles of land-frontier and 5,000 miles of sea-frontier.

Looking broadly at the physical features of the country we can easily distinguish three main parts, viz. (1) the great mountain wall; (2) the great lowland plain of Hindusthān; and (3) the great Deccan plateau.

1. *The Great Mountain Wall*

The Himālayas which run in a south-east curve all along the northern front of India, and separate it from the plateau of Tibet, include several parallel ranges of lofty mountains, with deep valleys between them. They cover a region about 1,500 miles long and 150 to 200 miles in breadth. The Himālayas contain altogether about 114 peaks of over 20,000 feet, of which 75 exceed 24,000 feet. The best known are Everest or Gaurī Sankar (29,140 feet), the highest mountain in the world, Kānchanjanghā (28,176 feet), Dhaulagiri (26,826 feet), Nanga Parbat (26,620 feet) and Nanda Devi (25,661 feet).

The Hindu Kush mountains which run from the Pāmirs in a south-westerly direction may be regarded as the natural boundary of India in the north-west, though considerable portions of the hilly regions to the south and east are now included in Afghānistān. Further south, the Safed Koh, Sulaimān and Khirthar mountains are now generally regarded as the north-western boundary of India, separating it from the Tableland of Irān. But large stretches of land to the west of this line in modern Afghānistān and Baluchistān, like those to the south and east of the Hindu Kush, were for long both culturally and politically parts of India.

Running roughly southwards from the eastern end of the Himālayas are a series of ranges which form the mountain wall separating India from Burma. In the north are the Patkoi Hills which broaden into the Nāgā Hills and the Manipur Plateau and send out a branch westwards forming the Khāsī, Gāro and Jaintiā hills. South of Manipur are the Lushai and Chin Hills, which narrow into a long single range, the Arakan Yoma, which reaches the sea at Cape Negrais.

These mountainous regions contain some high plateaus and valleys. Beginning from the west we have the plateaus of Baluchistān and Afghānistān which may be regarded as the continuation of the great plateau of Irān.

In these and the neighbouring hilly regions there are many secluded valleys which have been the home of sturdy tribes from time immemorial. They converted their high hills into so many impregnable citadels and maintained their independence even against powerful foes. The detailed accounts which we possess of the brave resistance which these small communities put up against such world-conquerors as Alexander or the Arabs form a brilliant chapter in the heroic annals of India.

Coming next to the Himālayan region we have the famous Kāshmir Plateau, one of the most beautiful in the whole world. The green valley, at an elevation of 6,000 feet, is about 80 miles long and 25 miles broad. It is watered by the Jhelum river and is surrounded by snowy mountains 18,000 feet high. It has been justly regarded as "the earthly paradise."

Further east lies Nepāl, stretching for 500 miles along the Himālayan region proper, which is above 5,000 feet, and the sub-Himālayan region below that height. The latter may again be subdivided into two parts. The part near the Gangetic plain, known as the Terai, is very low and covered with marshes and coarse tall grass. The part near the mountains is covered with forest. Both are damp and unhealthy. The Nepāl valley proper covers a small area round its capital Kātmāndu. It lies between the basins of the Gandak and Kosi and is watered by the Baghmatī river. It is a rich fertile plain surrounded by high hills and although only about 25 miles long and 14 miles wide, nearly a quarter of all the inhabitants of Nepāl live in this valley.

The hilly regions of the east contain the plateau on which Shillong is situated. It juts westward from the main hills and separates the valley of the Brahmaputra on the north from that of the Surmā on the south. The main hill ranges running north to south contain small plains like those of Manipur.

The plateaus mentioned above have been, generally speaking, detached from the currents of life in the country proper. The history of Kāshmir, Nepāl, and Assam forms, therefore, almost isolated chapters in the history of India, and only very rarely comes into contact with it. Afghānistān, being on the main highway between India and the world outside, has however, played a more important part than would otherwise have been the case.

The mountains form an admirable defensive rampart of India

against invasion by land. The Himālayas present a formidable barrier to an army, though small bodies of traders and missionaries can pass over it through difficult routes. The mountains in the north-east, though not an equally effective barrier, have for all practical purposes served India well. They are so steep and so densely forest-covered that to cross them is a task of abnormal difficulty, and no considerable body of foreigners is known to have passed through this route to the interior of the country.

The mountains in the north-west, however, have proved to be more vulnerable. There are several passes across the Hindu Kush and along almost all the chief rivers in this region, viz. the Swāt and the Chitral running south, and the Kābul, the Kurram, the Tochī and the Gomal, running east to the Indus. But by far the most important route is the one that crosses the Hindu Kush through one of its passes, runs along the Kābul valley, and then descends to Peshāwar through the Khyber Pass, a winding and narrow defile about 20 miles long.

Another well-known route runs, beyond the fringe of the Afghān mountains, from Herāt to Kandāhār, and then descends to the Indus valley through the Bolān Pass or the Mulā Pass further south.

The third well-known route from the west followed the coast-line and reached the Indus valley through the narrow gap between the Khirthar range and the sea. But the inhospitable Makrān coast made this route far less frequented than would otherwise have been the case.

The two routes last mentioned were less important as gateways to India than the first. For just beyond the region where they debouch into the Indian plain stretches the great desert of Rājputāna, which bars access to the interior of India. The Khyber route, on the other hand, leads directly across the plains of the Punjab to the interior through the narrow gap between the desert and the mountains. Hence the northern route has been more frequently used by the foreign invaders of India. This explains the strategical position of the Khyber pass as the first line of defence, and that of the narrow plains to the west of the Jumna, above Delhi, as the second.

Thus although the mountains around India have not definitely shut it off from the rest of Asia, they have made even peaceful communication with the neighbouring countries a difficult process. Further, they have proved an almost insurmountable barrier against foreign invasion except through the Khyber Pass, which has been in all ages the gateway of India, and the key of its security from foreign aggression.

The Himālayas have not only served as a great barrier against outside intruders, but have also otherwise contributed to the welfare of India. By protecting her against the cold dry winds from Tibet, and serving as a great screen for the monsoon winds, they have increased the fertility and prosperity of the Indo-Gangetic plains. The numerous rivers fed by the glaciers of the Himālayas have served the same end. Some of these rise behind the Himālayas, in a valley which forms part of the Tableland of Tibet. In the centre of this valley lies the lake Mānasasarovara (Manasarowar), and near it rises the lofty mountain Kailāsa, both famous in Indian mythology. Close to this spot, at a height of 16,000 feet, are the sources of the Indus and the Brahmaputra which run for a considerable distance, respectively, towards the west and the east, before they skirt round the edge of the Himālayas and take a southern bend to enter into the Indian plains. The great Himālayan ranges are thus held "within the arms of the two mighty rivers whose southern bends form the western and eastern limits of the greatest mountain ranges in the world."

2. *The Plain of Hindustān*

Within the mountain-wall described above, and stretching from the Arabian Sea to the Bay of Bengal in a great curve, lies the great plain of Hindustān, nearly 2,000 miles long and 150 to 200 miles broad. It is formed by the basins of the three great rivers, the Indus, the Ganges and the Brahmaputra, and their various affluents and tributaries. Not a hill is to be seen in this vast area. The great rivers all rise in the Himālayas and are supplied perennially from the gradual melting of the snow and the rains on the hills. Many of these rivers wind through small shallow rocky beds in the hills for a considerable distance, but as soon as they reach the plains their course becomes slow over the flat valley, their beds are broadened, and not infrequently these are shifted, often over a considerable distance.

These rivers play a very important part in the life of the people. Carrying sediment from the hills they have formed alluvial delta, often of considerable extent. Their perennial supply of water is an inexhaustible source of irrigation. Their long lazy courses through broad valleys have not only made the lands fertile but have provided good highways of communication. In consequence of all these. highly developed centres of culture and civilization have flourished on the banks of these rivers from remote antiquity.

The two principal river-systems are those of the Indus and the Ganges. The Indus rising in the Tibetan plateau runs west and north-west for nearly 800 miles between the great Karakoram range and the Himālayas. Passing through a tremendous gorge beyond Skarda it is joined by the Gilgit river and turning south cuts its way through the mountains to the Plains. Five rivers, all originating from the Himālayas, and winding through the hills, reach the plains and eventually join to form the Panchanad (five rivers) or Punjab. These are, from west to east, the Jhelum, the Chenāb, the Rāvi, the Beās, and the Sutlej. They have changed their courses even in historic times, and the last two formerly ran in parallel beds for a long distance below their present junction. These five rivers, combined, ultimately join the Indus. The Punjab province, covered by them, is a broad flat alluvial plain.

On leaving the Punjab plain the Indus flows through a narrow rocky gorge into a broad dry alluvial plain bounded by the Plateau of Baluchistān on the west and the great Thar desert in the east. The region of the lower Indus valley—the modern province of Sind—would have been a desert but for this river which irrigates and renders fertile a considerable portion of territory on both sides of it. The Indus is to Sind what the Nile is to Egypt.

The Ganges issues from the Himālayas and has the character of a mountain torrent until it reaches Hardwār. It then runs, first from north-west to south-east, then almost due east, and finally takes a southern course before it reaches the sea. Its most important tributary is the Jumna on the west which, after a long parallel course, joins it near Allāhābād. The tract between the two rivers is called the Ganges-Jumna Doāb. Some of the rivers issuing from the hills of the Central Indian plateau, such as the Chambal, the Kali Sindh, the Betwā and the Ken fall into the Jumna, while the Son, further east, falls into the Ganges. On the north the Ganges is fed by important tributaries issuing from the Himālayas, the chief among which are the Gumti, the Gogra, the Gandak and the Kosi. The Ganges falls into the sea through several mouths. The most important in ancient times was the westernmost called the Bhāgirathī (the Hooghly), on which stand Murshidabad, Hooghly, and Calcutta. We can still trace some of its old beds like the Saraswati which was dried up in the 16th or 17th century. At present the main waters of the Ganges flow through the Padmā, the easternmost mouth.

The mighty Brahmaputra, as noted above, has its source near the eastern base of the Kailāsa mountain. Under its Tibetan name of Tsan-po, it runs east for nearly 700 miles till it bends southwards and enters Indian territory under the name of Dihāng near Sadiya. It is then joined by the Dibāng and the Luhit, and the united stream takes the name of Brahmaputra. In old days it was known as Lauhitya, the trace of which evidently survives in Luhit. The Brahmaputra "rolls in a vast sheet of water, broken by numerous islands" through a narrow valley, about 500 miles long and 50 miles wide, shut in between the Himālayas in the north and the Assam hills in the south. It then passes through the plains of Bengal and joins the easternmost mouth of the Ganges, viz. the Padmā. Before the combined waters of the two fall into the sea, they are joined by other rivers from the eastern watershed between Bengal and Burma through the channels of the Meghnā, another mighty river. As a matter of fact, the last part of the course of these united rivers is now popularly known as Meghnā. The Ganges-Brahmaputra Doāb and the deltas formed by them constitute the rich fertile province of Bengal.

3. *The Plateau*

To the south of the plain of Hindustān lies the great plateau which stretches over the whole of Peninsular India, except the coast-strips, up to its southern extremity. The plateau is divided into two important sections by ranges of mountains, which run across almost its whole breadth from east to west. These are the two parallel lines of hills, the Vindhyas in the north and the Sātpurā mountains, a little to the south, which are continued eastwards as Mahādeo hills and Maikāl range, and pass into Chotā Nāgpur Plateau. The Vindhya and Sātpurā mountains are separated by a narrow valley through which flows the great Narmadā (Narbada) river. These hills with other outlying spurs and ranges constitute what may be called the Central Highlands, a formidable barrier which cuts off Northern India from the Deccan. The portion of the plateau north of the Central belt of mountains is known as the Central Indian plateau, and that to its south, the Deccan plateau.

(*a*) *The Deccan Plateau.*—The surface of the Deccan plateau slopes down from the west to the east. The western edge of the tableland forms a high precipice above the sea and is known as the Western Ghāts, with a narrow plain between it and the sea. On the eastern edge, which is much lower, are the Eastern Ghāts, consisting of groups of low hills separated by wide gaps, through which the great rivers from the north and the west flow down to the coastal plain and then to the sea. As we go southward the hills gradually recede from the sea leaving a coastal plain from 100 to 150 miles wide towards the east. Ultimately they take a sharp bend to the west and join the Western Ghāts at the Nilgiris.

The crest of the Western Ghāts, exceeding 3,000 feet in height, forms a sort of protective barrier to the plateau which is consequently dry. The Western Ghāts are about 1,000 miles in length and throw out many spurs in the east across the Deccan plateau. The plateau is higher in the south, being about 2,000 feet in the region of Mysore and half that height in Hyderābād. The southern point of the plateau is formed by the Nilgiri Hills where the Eastern and Western Ghāts meet. Beyond it are the Cardamom Hills which may be regarded as the continuation of the Western Ghāts.

Two major rivers in the Central Highlands, the Narmadā and the Tāpti, immediately to the north and south of the Sātpurā range, flow from east to west. The rivers in Peninsular India, however, run from west to east. Many of them rise in the Western Ghāts, only a few miles from the western sea-coast, but traverse the whole breadth of the plateau and cut their way through the Eastern Ghāts. These rivers are very different from those of Northern India. Being only fed by the monsoon rains, they become so dry in the hot season that they are hardly navigable even by small boats. In the absence of a constant supply of water they are also less valuable for irrigation purposes.

There are several important river-systems in the peninsula. The valley of the Godāvarī and its tributaries constitutes a large stretch of flat land in the north (in C.P.), but it is narrow in the south and there are dangerous rapids where the river cuts through the Eastern Ghāts. The valley of the Mahānadi also forms a broad plain (the Chattisgarh Plain) in the north-east, growing narrower as it passes through the Orissan hills to the sea.

The Krishnā (Kistna) and its tributaries, of which the chief is the Tungabhadrā, form another important river system which almost divides the Deccan plateau into two sections. This division is emphasized by the high Mysore plateau which lies immediately to the south. In the Mysore plateau rises the Kāverī, another large river, which with its tributaries forms an important river-system in the extreme south.

(b) *The Coastal Region.*—As noted above, there is a coastal plain on each side of the plateau. On the west a narrow low-lying strip stretches from the head of the Gulf of Cambay along the whole coast. Its northern part is now called the Konkan, and its southern the Malabar Coast. As the full force of the monsoon winds strikes against the Western Ghāts the rainfall is heavy in this region and several small and short streams flow across it, but there are no big rivers. In Malabar these rivers form many back-waters along the coast, which facilitate easy communication by boat and favour the growth of a few fine harbours. There are some good harbours also in the northern Konkan.

There is a similar low-lying strip on the east stretching south from the delta of the Ganges. It is much wider than the western strip and its southern part, known as the Coromandel coast, is very broad. Unlike the western strip, again, it is traversed by many big rivers. In addition to the lower courses of the Mahānadi, the Godāvarī, the Krishnā and the Kāverī (Cauvery) mentioned above, a number of smaller streams flow across it. The deltas of these four rivers form an important feature in the economic geography of the eastern coast. The Deccan plateau is also more easily accessible from the eastern coastal plains than from the western, where the steep cliffs of the Ghāts rise abruptly from the plains to a great height. The eastern coast has few natural harbours, but there are open roadsteads having easy communications with the interior.

The two coastal regions running for a thousand miles along the entire lengths of the eastern and western sides of the triangular plateau gradually approach each other as the Peninsula narrows down towards the south, and at last meet at Cape Comorin, the southernmost point of India. There is a small gap, about 20 miles broad, between the Nilgiri and the Cardamom hills, which provides an easy access from the western to the eastern coastal region, i.e. from the Malabar to the Coromandel coast. It is known as the Coimbatore or Pālghāt gap.

To the south-east of Cape Comorin lies the island of Ceylon, which, though not an integral part, has been closely associated with India throughout the course of history. The Gulf of Manar which separates it from India narrows northward to Palk Strait which is so nearly closed in one part by a chain of islands and shoals that the name Adam's Bridge has been given to it. Ceylon is shaped like a mango and its area is a little less than that of Mysore. It is mountainous in the centre, sloping down to flat and broad low-lying coasts all around. There are a few good harbours on the coast and, as in Malabar, there are many backwaters along the seashore.

(c) *The Central Indian Plateau.*—Between the valleys of the Indus and the Ganges lies the vast Thar desert, which stretches almost up to the Aravalli range. The Punjab plain, south of the Sutlej, rises gradually and fades away into this sandy waste, with bare rocky hills and waterless valleys. Beyond the Aravalli is the Central Indian Plateau which slopes gradually from the Central Highlands to the Gangetic plain, in the south, and ends in the east in the hilly and forested region of Chotā Nāgpur, which extends up to the plains of Bengal and Orissa. To the south lies the rich valley of the Narmadā, which rises in the Maikāl range and flowing almost due west, falls into the Gulf of Cambay.

The Vindhyas rise abruptly from the Narmadā valley like a high rocky wall, and seen from the south, look like a regular mountain range with short spurs. But they slope gently to the north, without any steep fall or well-marked spurs, forming the Mālwā plateau, the valleys of Eastern Rājputāna and the tablelands of Bundelkhand and Bāghelkhand. As noted above, all the rivers on this side flow into the Ganges or the Jumna.

The north-eastern outliers of the Vindhyas, such as the Bhanrer and Kaimur ranges, extend almost up to the Ganges south of Benares and then run parallel to this river, leaving only a narrow passage between them, till the Rājmahāl Hills. Here a little beyond the modern Colgong, only a very narrow defile separates the mighty Ganges from the high cliffs of the Rājmahāl range stretching for about 80 miles to the south. A little further to the east, beyond the defile, the Ganges takes a sharp bend to the south and the hills gradually recede from its bank to the west of the wide plains of Bengal. This configuration of the land invested the long narrow passage between Chunār on the west and Teliāgarhi on the east with great strategic importance from the military point of view. This, the only high road between Western and Eastern India, could be effectively commanded by hill forts, and this explains the value of Rohtas, Chunār and, further west, of Kālinjar and Gwālior. Further east, the passes of Shāhābād and Teliāgarhi, separated by a distance of 3½ miles, served as the bottleneck through which every invading army had to pass, and this "gateway" served as an admirable defence for Bengal.

The hills and forests of the Central Indian plateau from Bundelkhand to Chotā Nāgpur include many regions forming comparatively inaccessible retreats. They have given shelter to primitive tribes and enabled comparatively weaker peoples to defy the superior powers of the Indo-Gangetic plain. Thus the Central Indian plateau has profoundly influenced the history of India in many ways.

To the south of the desert and west of the plateau lie the rich lowlands of Gujarāt covered by numerous low hills and watered by the rivers Mahī, Sābarmati, and the lower courses of the Narmadā and the Tāpti. This region includes the characteristic projection, known as the Kāthiāwār Peninsula, and the Rann of Cutch, immediately to the west of it, which is now a great marsh and almost dry in the hot weather (cf. Ch. IV, § VII).

II. INFLUENCE OF GEOGRAPHY UPON HISTORY

Like most other countries in the world the history of India has been profoundly influenced by its geographical features. These have been partly noted above and will be further evident as we gradually proceed with our historical narrative from age to age; but some general broad issues may be discussed here.

In the first place we must note the vast dimensions and the varied physical features of the country. In extent India is almost equal to Europe with the exclusion of Russia. It contains the highest mountain ranges, lofty plateaus, extensive plains only slightly higher than the sea-level, sandy deserts, large rivers, fertile river-valleys and forests of all types and descriptions. Every variety of climate from extreme cold to extreme heat is to be found in the country. All these factors tended to separate India into different local zones, each with a regional spirit of its own. Nevertheless India, being effectively shut off by mountains and seas from the other countries and forming a compact territory, developed as a distinctive political and cultural unit, as compared with the rest of the world. The Indian horizon was a large but limited one, and the common natural boundaries gradually led to a sense of a common motherland. The vision of a fundamental unity always loomed large and coloured the political ideals of the country. This ideal of political unity was rarely realized in actual practice but, as a political theory, it can be traced throughout the long course of Indian history. The cultural unity was, however, more manifest, being inspired by a common language, literature, and religious and social ideals. In spite of seeming diversity there was a large measure of cultural unity, and the goal of political union was never lost sight of. This unity in diversity is the keynote of the tangled history of India, and forms the background against which the seemingly complex developments in the various aspects of Indian civilization must be viewed.[1]

The natural barriers of hills and rivers largely determined the different political (and partly cultural) units into which India was divided. These natural divisions favoured the growth of a local and regional spirit and fostered separatist tendencies. The marked distinction between North India, the Deccan plateau and the peninsular plains to the south and east of the latter, led to the growth of three broad regions which maintained distinctive characteristics and generally played a separate rôle in politics throughout the long course of Indian history. In each of these regions political unity was frequently achieved or attempted with a large measure of success. But the attainment of political unity between any two of these regions, even those to the north and south of the Krishnā, was more difficult, and though there was almost a continuous struggle for achieving it, successful attempts were few and far between. The unity of the Hindustān plains, together with the Central Indian plateau, was rendered more difficult by the very large extent of the country. It was, however, not infrequently realized, at least to a large extent, and the struggle for its achievement was a constant feature of the history of India. But the occasions were, comparatively speaking, rare when a deliberate attempt was made to unite all the regions to the north and south of the Vindhyas.

The political history of India, generally speaking, thus resolves itself into separate histories of the three regions. But the points of contact between them, though infrequent, were not altogether absent, and under powerful dynasties, in all periods of Indian history, a considerable part of each of the three regions was brought under a common sceptre.

The three regions also exhibit similar, though somewhat less prominent, distinctions in cultural history. While the Aryan language and civilization swept over the whole of Northern India obliterating almost all traces of the pre-existing state of things, its success was less phenomenal in the south. Over a considerable part of the Deccan plateau, and all over the South Indian Peninsula to its south and east, the non-Aryan languages still prevail, and some older customs and ideas can yet be traced. On the other hand, these regions were profoundly affected by the civilization of the north. The primitive languages have accepted a considerable Aryan vocabulary, whereas religious and social ideas of the Aryans have almost completely transformed the old order of things.

Within each of the three natural divisions, again, there are sub-divisions caused by physical barriers, which have stood in the way of regional unity and affected the course of history. The great Thar desert, intervening between the plains of the Indus and the valley of the Ganges, has practically converted these two regions into separate units. This has been very unfortunate from the point of view of Indian defence. As noted above, the mountain passes through which foreigners could invade the country all converge on the Indus valley, and the bulk of the North Indian plains being separated from this region by the great desert, the resources of North India, far less the whole of India, could seldom be employed to guard these gateways. Moreover the desert, though effectively checking any aggression from the lower Indus region, permitted the invaders to bypass it through an opening on its north. The narrow plain above Delhi, bounded by the desert, the Jumna and the hills, was the bottleneck through which foreign invaders had to pass from the valley of the Indus to that of the Ganges.

This explains the strategic position of Delhi as an imperial capital and also how it is that the battle-fields of Pānipat, and others near it, have often decided the fate of India. But the foreign invaders had the great advantage of forcing the main gateway and getting a strong foothold in the country, before they had to reckon with the main strength of Indian defence. Illustration of this meets us at almost every step as we go through the history of the foreign conquests of India.

The Thar desert offers a great contrast to the fertile plains around it, but its peoples, though scanty, have imbibed from the soil a sturdy character and love of freedom which sharply distinguish them from their neighbours. The hills and forests have imparted a similar hardihood to the people and supplied means of defence which are lacking in the plains. Besides, these regions, less favoured by nature and more difficult of access, have afforded shelter to the wild primitive tribes who were dispossessed of their hearth and home in the fertile plains by the more civilized conquerors of the land. Thus it is in the desert and the fastnesses of the hills and forests of India that we still meet with the earlier strata of population like the Kols and Bhils who have maintained, almost intact, the primitive characteristics which distinguished them thousands of years ago. To these geographical factors also largely belongs the credit that certain regions have earned by successful struggle for independence against heavy odds. The heroic struggle of the Rājputs and the Marāṭhās, for example, against the imperial powers of Delhi, was probably as much due to the nature of their lands as to the bravery of the people. To a less extent the strategic position of the Teliāgarhi passes explains the frequent rebellion of Bengal against the Central authority of Delhi.

The extensive valley of the Ganges has been divided into several local regions by the large rivers, and the Indus valley, though comparatively smaller, is broadly divided into two by the middle and lower courses of the river. Thus in Northern India the modern provinces of the Punjab, Sind, U.P., Bihār, and Bengal, as well as the desert region of Rājputāna, the plains of Northern Gujarāt, plateaus of Mālwā and Bundelkhand, and the isolated hilly tracts of Choṭā Nāgpur have the roots of their separate entities as distinct units dug deep into the past. No doubt racial and linguistic factors played some part in creating these natural regions, but no one can ignore the very large influence of the geographical factors, including the strategic means of defence afforded by nature.

The Deccan plateau was divided into several distinct regions by the two mighty rivers, the Godāvarī and the Krishṇā, and their tributaries; it was also separated from the coastal plains on the east and the west. The eastern coastal plain was divided by the Orissa hills and the estuaries of the two rivers named above. The region south of the plateau was sharply split into an eastern and western zone by the Nilgiris and Cardamom Hills, and the former was again subdivided, to a certain extent, by the Kāverī river. All these geographical regions had generally speaking developed into separate distinct units and retained their individuality through the ages.

Apart from these broad regional distinctions, even smaller barriers of hills and rivers have tended to keep alive the spirit of local autonomy in well-marked political units created by them. Not only in the vast Hindustān Plains and Central Indian plateau, but even in the comparatively narrower regions of the Deccan plateau and South Indian plains, we find the influence of such regional politics from time immemorial, with a surprising tenacity that has kept up the isolationist spirit even amidst political catastrophes and kaleidoscopic changes of rulers and dynasties. The old kingdoms of Kosala, Magadha, Gauḍa, Vaṅga, Avanti, Lāṭa, and Surāshṭra in the north, and Kaliṅga, Andhra, Mahārāshṭra, Karṇāṭa, Chera, Chola, and Pāṇḍya in the south, among others, seem to possess eternal lives. Empires rose and fell, the whole country passed through a series of foreign invasions, but these states, under different names and various ruling dynasties, continued their individual existence almost throughout the course of history.

The popular view about the lack of political unity in India ignores the vastness of its area and the natural barriers that tend to separate its different regions. When we deplore political disunion in India we really view it on the footing of a comparatively small kingdom like Egypt, Assyria, Babylonia or Irān in the ancient world or a state in mediaeval or modern Europe. But we forget that there was not a single kingdom in any part of the world before the nineteenth century, of a size comparable to that of India, which maintained political unity for a considerable length of time. On the other hand, the important kingdoms of India, such as Magadha, Kosala, Mālava, Chālukya, Chola etc. which, under varying names, have formed its constituent parts since remote antiquity, can well be compared with the single states in Asia and Europe, both in ancient and modern times. As in Asia and Europe, so in India, two or more of these kingdoms have often been politically united, and we have occasionally even mighty empires comprising most of them.

India is almost as large as Europe, excluding Russia, or the whole of Western Asia, and can no more be treated as a single political unit than any of them. The consolidation of large kingdoms was very difficult before modern scientific achievements eliminated the effects of distance and natural barriers, but these were important factors in old days, and operated more or less in the same way all over the world. India, as a consolidated united kingdom, is well within the range of practical politics today, when the whole country is closely knit together by a system of railways, and even two of the remotest regions of India are more familiar to each other than were two neighbouring provinces in the good old days. Now the news of a revolt in the most distant part of India would be conveyed instantly to its political centre, and a large force could reach the scene of disturbance in a few hours or a few days. But things were very different in the days of Aśoka when the peoples of his frontiers such as those of Taxilā (Punjab) and Suvarṇagiri (Mysore) hardly knew each other. If we remember that the emperor would not receive the news of any disaffection in these places in less than a month, and many months would perhaps elapse before his army could reach there, we need hardly wonder that the Maurya empire did not last for more than 137 years.

A considerable part of Indian history is a chronicle of unsuccessful attempts to set up a stable empire over the whole or greater part of India, the impulse to which was partly caused by political ambition, but in part arose or received its strength from a common consciousness of the cultural and geographical unity of India.

The vast extent of the country, and its comparative seclusion from the rest of the world, had other important historical consequences. As noted above, it made India a distinct and self-sufficient geographical unit, almost a little world by itself. An Indian ruler or a military genius had enough scope for his political ambition or martial enterprises within the natural limits of the country, and so the comparatively unknown regions beyond the high hills or seas held out no temptation to him. The distances covered by the campaigns of the most famous military leaders in the ancient world, and the extent of territory conquered by the largest empire-builders in ancient times, could well be comprised within the limits of India. A Chandragupta Maurya or a Samudra-gupta, not to mention lesser names, could quench his inordinate thirst for military glory without crossing the natural boundaries of India. It is only very rarely that rulers like Rājendra Chola overstepped them and carried arms beyond the seas or hills. Thus while foreign conquest is an important feature in the history of Egypt and many ancient kingdoms in Mesopotamia and Irān, it never figured as an important element in Indian polity. As a natural consequence of this, an Indian ruler would scarcely be expected ever to emulate the exploits of Thutmose III, Cyrus, Xerxes, or Alexander, and the vision of a Roman empire extending over three continents would be altogether out of place in Indian history. But at the same time, the conception of a distinct unity, as against the rest of the world, was promoted in India in a manner which was not to be seen in any part of the ancient world of equal magnitude.

The physical features of the country affected the lives and habits of the people. The valleys of the numerous rivers, specially the Indus, the Ganges, and their tributaries, offered easy means of communication and cheap livelihood. Hence their banks were studded with flourishing seats of civilization from very early times. The absence of keen struggle for existence gave opportunities for intellectual pursuits, and the wild beauty of nature favoured a speculative turn of mind and the development of philosophical ideas. But nature's bounty was unfavourable to the growth of physical hardihood or a tendency to scrutinise the mysteries of the physical world leading to a scientific spirit. This at least partly explains why art, literature, and philosophy flourished, but positive sciences made comparatively little progress in India.

The extensive coast-line of India fostered trade and maritime activity and made the Indians hardy mariners. From an early period they navigated the seas, both in the east as well as in the west, and their bold sea-faring exploits carried them to distant and unknown parts of the world.

The very narrow sea-board on the west was shut off from the interior by the precipitous Western Ghāts and hence flourishing sea-ports arose only on its northern and southern extremities. For they had to be sustained by constant supply of industrial products from the interior. As the gap between the Nilgiris and Cardamom Hills in South India offered an easy means of communication between the eastern and western coasts of the peninsula, we find a number of important harbours on the western coast in this neighbourhood.

The eastern sea-board contained important harbours near the mouths of the big rivers viz. the Ganges, Mahānadī, Godāvarī, Krishnā, and Kāverī, as they were important channels of communication with the interior. The Ganges being the only outlet to the sea for the extensive and populous regions in Northern India, the ports at its mouths became flourishing centres of trade.

The trade gave impetus to colonization and Indian colonies were planted even in the most distant regions in the Far East. The maritime activities of India were, however, almost solely devoted to peaceful pursuits. This is mainly due to the vast expanse of the sea on both sides of the peninsula. The direct voyage between the Indian coast and the opposite shore, either of Africa on the west or Indo-China and the East Indies in the east, was long and risky. The Indian rulers having enough scope for military enterprise and imperial ambition in the mainland itself. the dubious chances of success afforded by the sea could scarcely tempt them to devote their energy and resources to building a powerful navy in order to establish an overseas empire.

Only one Indian power, the Cholas, attempted such a bold enterprise after having acquired possession of almost the whole length of the eastern sea-board. But in spite of brilliant success in the beginning, it proved too heavy a burden and had to be abandoned. If India had the advantage, like Greece or Rome, of having a narrow sea with islands and mainland beyond it within easy reach, she might have developed into a naval power as did many of her colonies in Malaya and Indo-China, regions which offered these facilities.

Indian colonization was therefore the result of private individual enterprise, and not due to military conquest or an organized undertaking backed up by the State. No colony was the result of a single mass migration sent forth by an Indian ruler to relieve congestion or to expand his dominions. Sporadic settlements and gradual infiltration by bold Indians, who left home for various reasons and at different times, slowly built up these colonies, and consequently they had no political tie or even intimate association with the mother country. But they proved to be the milestones in the triumphant progress of Indian culture across a vast region. Had these colonies been within easy reach of India she might have built up a colonial empire such as the Greeks and Romans had done. But geographical factors determined the character of Indian colonization. It was to be a means to cultural conquest rather than political aggrandizement, of commercial enterprise rather than economic exploitation.

This brief review has sufficiently demonstrated the profound influence which geography has exercised upon the history of India. It is easy, but not necessary, to dwell upon many other particulars. for these will be evident as we proceed with our historical narrative.

In conclusion we must consider the effect of climate on the history of India. It is generally assumed that the tropical climate has enervated the people of India and mainly accounts for their failure to check the hardy mountaineers from colder regions, less favoured by nature, who were tempted to their country by its wealth and fertility. It has been regarded as an irony of fate that the agreeable climate and the vast plains watered by rivers, which have been the source of India's wealth and happiness, have also proved to be the main causes of her ruin by making their inhabitants fond of ease and luxury, devoted to the ideals and pursuits of peace, and less hardy and persevering than their opponents schooled in the hardship of nature.

On the other hand, it has been pointed out that at least a considerable section of the Indians have been always noted for their prowess and bravery, that the Rājputs, Marāṭhās and Sikhs in modern times have not proved less hardy than any other peoples, and that the defeat of the Indians at the hands of the Western invaders cannot be ascribed solely or even mainly to the influence of climate. The facts of history seem to uphold this contention, as on a careful consideration of the details of the various campaigns, so far known, it would be difficult to maintain that the discomfiture of the Indians is to be attributed exclusively or even mainly to their lack of physical strength.

It is, however, a singular fact worth noting, that in the numerous recorded instances of the foreign invasions from the West, the Indians have almost always been defeated by the new-comers. This can hardly be regarded as a pure accident. Nor can it be explained away by a lack of unity among the defenders, for the invaders did not always possess a numerical superiority over their opponents.

The true explanation seems to lie in India's ignorance of the outside world. The rise of political powers or new political combinations, the evolution of military tactics, and the invention of new military weapons or fresh equipment, even in Central or Western Asia, not to speak of remoter countries, hardly ever interested India, though, as events proved, she fell a constant victim to one or other of them. The details of the defensive campaigns waged by Indian rulers leave no doubt that they were either unaware of the impending danger, and consequently not sufficiently prepared, or were outmatched by the new military formations or weapons to which they were complete strangers. The charge of a compact and well-disciplined cavalry force, held in reserve, has often proved decisive against the mass of elephants and infantry of the Indians, and yet they have never learnt the value of cavalry or the strategic importance of a reserve force. It may be noted as a typical instance that the Indian opponents of Bābur were ignorant of the fire-arms which the latter used with such dreadful effect.

The reason for such ignorance is not merely to be sought in a spirit of isolation fostered by almost insurmountable barriers. It is also partly due to the fact that, for reasons stated above, Indian rulers had no occasion or temptation to carry on campaigns outside India. They lived and fought in their little world, vast enough for their personal ambitions and enterprises, and cared little for what was happening in the outside world.

Unfortunately, the physical barriers which shut off the vision of Indian rulers from the outside world were not strong or powerful enough to keep out all foreign invaders from Indian soil. When some of them did cross the barriers into India, they brought with them new ideas and forces of a progressive world with which India could not cope. But so strongly did the geographical factor operate, that as soon as these foreign invaders settled in India, they imbibed the insular spirit so congenial to her soil, and themselves fell victims to it. So it has been in the past, and so it is destined to be in the future, so long as the political vision of India confines itself within her natural boundaries of hills and seas, and does not look beyond to the world outside.

---

1. It would be wrong to think, as many do, that the conception of the fundamental unity of India is only of recent growth. This idea can be traced to ancient periods by the use of the common name, Bhāratavarsha, for the whole country, and the designation *Bhāratī Santatiḥ* applied to the people of India. Thus we read in the *Vishṇu-Purāṇa* (ii. 3. 1) that "the country lying to the north of the ocean and to the south of Himādri (Himālaya) is called Bhārata-varsha (land of Bharata), for there live the descendants of Bharata (*Bhāratī santatiḥ*)." Similarly the conception of the political unity of India appears from references to "thousand *Yojanas* (leagues) of land that stretch from the Himālayas to the sea as the proper domain of a single universal emperor," and the conventional description in literature and epigraphic records of imperial domains stretching from the Brahmaputra (or Eastern Ocean) to the seven mouths of the Indus (or Western Ocean). As regards cultural unity, the findspots of Aśoka's records prove that one language and one script were used, or at least understood, by common people all over India in the third century B.C. Since then the Sanskrit language and literature have throughout been a common bond of culture in addition to religious and social ideas and institutions.

CHAPTER VI

FLORA AND FAUNA

I. THE FLORA

The vegetation of a country depends on, and to a large extent is determined by, its geographical and climatic features, and India stands in a very favourable position with respect to both these conditions.

"There is no part of the world better marked off by nature as a region by itself than India. It is a region indeed full of contrast in physical features and in climate." The extraordinary varieties in its physical features have been described above. The climate also varies from "torrid to arctic, from almost absolute aridity to a maximum of humidity." It is greatly influenced by the monsoon winds and the distribution and orientation of the mountain ranges and their altitude. The annual rainfall varies prodigiously in different parts of India from 450 inches in the Khāsi Hills of Assam to about three inches in the deserts of Sind and Rājputāna. Its temperature also shows enormous variation with the changes of seasons. At some places during summer months it records 130 degrees or more in the shade and in winter it goes down many degrees below freezing point.

The soils of India, like its climate, comprise almost all the different types found elsewhere in the world. The alluvial soils of Assam, Bengal, the United Provinces, the Punjab, Rājputāna, Sind, Gujarāt, the Godāvarī, Krishnā and Tanjore districts of Madras and the eastern and western coastlands of the Deccan, are important for agricultural crops and have made India essentially an agricultural country. The Deccan trap and the regur or black cotton soils of the greater portion of the Bombay Presidency, Berār, western parts of the Central Provinces and Hyderābād, in the valleys of the Tāptī, Godāvarī, Narmadā, Krishnā and parts of Kāthiāwār, and the western portion of Central India, are very favourable to the cultivation of cotton, jowar (great millet), wheat, linseed and gram. The crystalline and laterite (red) soils of Madras, Mysore, the south-east portion of the Bombay Presidency, the eastern half of Hyderābād, parts of the Central Provinces, Orissa, Chotā Nāgpur, western borderland of Bengal, parts of eastern Rājputāna and the Bundelkhand region of Central India are fertile when dark coloured, and infertile when they are light coloured and sandy.

India's contiguity to bordering countries has been responsible for the migration of a large number of plants from China, Tibet, Siberia, Malaya, Europe and South Africa, and they form the exotic elements of the flora of India. The number of recorded species of flowering plants comes to about 17,000 under 176 families, and there are about 600 ferns and fern allies, 3,000 mosses and 178 liverworts. According to Chatterjee, 38 per cent of the flowering plants of India are exotic.

From their exhaustive and critical studies of the Indian flora Hooker and Thomson observe that "India contains representatives of almost every natural family on the globe...and it contains a more general and complete illustration of the genera of the other parts of the world than any other country whatsoever of the equal or even of considerably larger extent."[1]

India is so extensive and varied a country that for a closer study of its vegetation it has been necessary to divide it into three botanical areas and six provinces. The three areas or regions are: the Himālayan, Eastern, and Western. The Himālayan represents a "rich tropical, temperate and alpine flora with forests of conifers, oaks, rhododendrons, and a profusion of orchids"; the Eastern, "a few conifers, many oaks and palms with a great preponderance of orchids"; and the Western "has only one conifer, no oaks, few palms and comparatively few orchids." The Himālayan flora has in common many European genera; the Eastern, many Chinese and Malayan; and the Western, European, Oriental and African.

These three botanical areas are subdivided into six botanical provinces, based on their climate and physical characters, namely (1) the Eastern Himālaya, (2) the Western Himālaya, (3) the Indus Plain, (4) the Gangetic Plain including the Sunderbans, (5) Malabar, and (6) the Deccan, each characterized by its own flora.

It would be beyond the scope of this chapter to go into details of the vegetation of these provinces, but in order to give an idea of the immensity of India's vegetable wealth a brief enumeration of the principal types of vegetation is given below.

1. *Forest Vegetation: its types*

India is very rich in forests; as a matter of fact forests cover more than one-fifth of its total area. The forests of India supply valuable timber, firewood, essential oils, resin, turpentine, lac, dyeing material, tanning material, myrobalans, sources of paper pulp and other materials of commerce and industry.

According to the variation in climate, altitude and habitat the forest vegetation of India is divided into five types: (1) the Evergreen, (2) the Deciduous, (3) the Dry, (4) the Hill, and (5) the Tidal or Littoral.

The Evergreen.—The dense and luxuriant Evergreen flourishes where the annual rainfall is over 80 inches and contains trees of many important families, such as the Dipterocarpaceae, Guttiferae, Annonaceae, Meliaceae, Burseraceae, Sapotaceae, Euphorbiaceae, and the Palmae. They include many species of great economic value, such as ebony, teak, rosewood, ironwood, bamboos, the jaman, the neem, and tamarind. In the Carnatic Evergreens the families Ebenaceae, Sapotaceae, Capparidaceae, Rhamnaceae and Myrtaceae predominate.

The sea-shores are skirted with coconuts; the villages are surrounded with groves of betelnuts and talipots; cassia, pepper and cardamom flourish wild in the jungles and form staple products of export. Sandalwood is found in the outskirts of Malabar. Nutmeg, coffee, and tea grow in the hill slopes, and cinnamon flourishes in this region. *Artocarpus, calophyllum, cedrela, dalbergia, dipterocarpus*, and others occur in plenty. In Assam forests bamboos, palms, ficus, cycas, ferns, and others grow in abundance.

The Deciduous.—The Deciduous occupies the larger part of the Deccan and is also known as the Monsoon Forests. Trees are large-sized and form very remarkable timbers, such as teak, sāl, padauk, redwood, sandalwood, anjan, species of *Terminalia, Chloroxylon, Swietenia, Diospyros, Acacia, Albizzia,* and others. Of palms, *Phoenix sylvestris* and *Borassus fiabellifer* grow gregariously. The chief bamboos are *Bambusa arundinacea* and *Dendrocalamus strictus;* ferns and their allies are rare in these forests.

The Dry.—The Dry forests are found in the desert regions of Sind, Rājputāna, and the Punjab, and the plants are characterized by thick and fleshy stems and leaves and mostly consist of thickets of shrubs and a few stunted trees; many of them are leafless. The chief families are the Leguminosae, Tamaricaceae, Rhamnaceae, and the characteristic trees are: the *Jhand*, various species of *Tamarix, Capparis, Salvadora, Acacia, Phoenix sylvestris, Zizyphus,* etc.

The Hill.—The Mountain or Hill forests are found in South India above 5,000 feet and in the Himālayas above 3,000 feet altitude. The trees are Evergreen, of which the following are the most conspicuous: oak, picea, deodar, pines, firs, chestnut, walnut, maple, elm, ash, birches, laurels, pyrus, poplar, rhododendron, and species of abies. The prominent families of these forests are the Coniferae, Cupuliferae, Sapindaceae, Lauraceae, Magnoliaceae, Salicaceae and Urticaceae. Indian Bladder-nut and Lilac, *Rosa webbiana, moschata,* and *eglanteria, Parrottia* sp., the mountain ash, the bullace and the common hawthorn are peculiar to the Western Himālayas. Species of magnolia, *musa,* palms, *pandanus*, bamboos, orchids, cycas, and ferns abound in the Eastern Himālayas. Beautiful herbaceous plants like anemone, aconites, violets, primulas and balsams abound. The alpine zones contain species of rhododendron, junipers and associations of dwarfish herbaceous plants, such as species of *Rheum, Arenaria,* and *Saussarea.* Both in the Eastern and Western Himālayas about 4,000 flowering species under

147-160 families, 230-250 ferns and their allies with eight tree ferns have so far been recorded.

The Littoral.—The Littoral forests are found in the deltas of the Ganges, the Mahānadi, and the Indus, and also to some extent in the regions washed by the high tide and salt water. They are rich sources of fuel. The whole of the Sunderbans is named after the Sundri (*Heritiera*) trees. The prominent families of these forests are: Rhizophoraceae, Gramineae, Cyperaceae, Typhaceae, Euphorbiaceae, Verbanaceae and the two palms, namely, *Nipa fruticans and Phoenix paludosa.* In many places Avicennia, Nipa, and Aegialitis form associations; *Suaeda maritima, Acanthus ilicifolius, Sonneratia apetala, Ceriops roxburghiana, Bruguiera gymnorhiza, Aegiceros major,* and others are some of the dominant species of these regions. These forests are popularly known as the Mangrove Forests.

2. *Freshwater Vegetation*

About 160 flowering species form the common water or marsh vegetation of India. The beautiful white, blue, and red water lilies, and their allies, the magnificent white and red lotuses, *Euryale ferox,* a relative of the *Victoria regia,* and *Limnanthemum* with clusters of white flowers lend charm and beauty to the fresh water lakes, pools, ponds, and other inland waters. *Nymphoea alba, Caltha,* and others occur in the lakes of Kāshmir. Species of *Lemna, Wolfia, pistia stratiotes,* water hyacinth (recently introduced), bladderworts, and *Ceratophyllum* are conspicuous free floating aquatic plants, while water-chestnut, *Ipomoea* sp., waterferns, and many others are amphibious. *Vallisneria, Hydrilla, Ottelia, Najas, Chara,* etc., form extensive floor vegetation in shallow water-courses. The Podostemonads are regarded as the most remarkable of India's freshwater flora in the rapid streams of hill slopes.

3. *Cultivated Vegetation*

An account of the vegetation of India will be incomplete without some notice of the large varieties of her cultivated vegetation. As India extends, both horizontally and altitudinally, from the tropical to the temperate zones, cultivated crops of these zones all over the globe are being, or can be, grown successfully in India. Crop vegetation in India, as in other countries, is distinguished into *four* general types, namely: (1) the Hill, (2) the Wet (Monsoon), (3) the Dry (Winter) and (4) the Irrigational.

The total area of cultivable land in India is about 450 million acres, and of these nearly 285 million acres are actually under cultivation. The following is a bare account of the principal crops and their distribution in India. These are classified under *six* major heads, namely: (1) the Cereals, (2) the Pulses, (3) Sugar-cane, (4) Oil seeds, (5) Fibre crops, and (6) Plantation crops.

Cereals.—The cereals comprise rice, wheat, millet, barley, and maize, the first two being the principal cereal crops.

Rice is cultivated in Bengal, Madras, Bihār, the United Provinces, Orissa, the Central Provinces, Assam, Bombay, and Sind, and covers about 70 million acres. *Wheat* is grown in about 35 million acres, and the principal wheat-growing provinces of India are the Punjab, the United Provinces, and the North-West Frontier Province. *Millet* is extensively grown in Madras, Bombay and part of Hyderābād. There are two principal kinds: *jowar* (*Andropogon sorghum*) and *bajra* (*Pennisetum typhoideum*), and the total area under millet cultivation comes to about 63 million acres. *Barley* is grown only over a comparatively small area in the Ganges basin of the United Provinces, Bihār, Peshāwar, and Central Kashmīr. *Maize* in small quantities is cultivated more or less all over India but in large quantities in the United Provinces, Bihār, Nepāl, and the Punjab both in the plains and hills.

Pulses.—This important group includes gram, lentils, peas, arhar, and many species of *Phaseolus*, and the total area under cultivation approximates to 50 million acres of which gram alone occupies between 15-17 million acres. *Gram* is mostly grown in the Punjab, the United Provinces, Bihār, the Central Provinces, Bombay, Hyderābād, and Mysore; *lentils* in the Central Provinces, Madras, and the United Provinces; and *peas* and other pulses in many parts of India.

Sugar-cane.—India is regarded as the original home of sugar-cane and the present area under its cultivation exceeds four million acres. The most important sugar-cane growing provinces are the United Provinces, the Punjab, Madras, Bengal, Bihār, and Bombay.

Oil Seeds.—The importance of oil seeds is very great. Not only do they constitute an essential element in the diet of every Indian, but they are also in great demand for the manufacture of vegetable ghee, perfumeries, varnishes, paints, lubricants, candles soaps, and other similar products of commerce. The principa oil-yielding crops of India are rape and mustard, ground-nuts, linseed, castor-seed, sesamum seed, etc.

The cultivation of *rape* and *mustard* is confined to the northern parts of India, in the United Provinces, Bengal, the Punjab, Bihār, and Orissa over an area of about six million acres. *Ground-nut* is grown over eight million acres chiefly in Madras, Bombay, Hyderābād, the Central Provinces, and Chotā Nāgpur. The area under *linseed* crop is about three and a half million acres distributed over the Central Provinces, Bihār, Orissa, the United Provinces, Bombay, Bengal, Hyderābād, and the Punjab. *Sesamum* is grown in almost all the provinces of India, but mainly in Bombay, Madras, and the Central Provinces. *Castor* oil plants as a principal crop are grown in Madras, Hyderābād, Bombay, and the Central Provinces. *Coconut* oil is derived from the copra of coconuts.

Fibre Crops.—Cotton, jute, and hemp are the principal fibre crops of India. Of these, cotton occupies 25-27 million acres, jute 2.18 million, and hemp 0.6 million acres. *Cotton* is a dry-region crop and is grown in Bombay, the Central Provinces, Berār, the Punjab, Madras, the United Provinces, Bengal, Hyderābād, Baroda, Rājputāna, Sind, and Mysore. *Jute* cultivation is restricted to Bengal, Assam, Bihār, and Orissa. Two varieties of *Hemp*, the Sunn and the Roselle, are grown in Bombay, the Central Provinces, the United Provinces, and Madras, and to a small extent in the North-Western Himālayas and Sind.

Plantation Crops.—The principal plantation crops are: tea, coffee, tobacco, rubber, indigo, opium-poppy, condiments and spices, fruits and vegetables including root crops. The area under *tea* cultivation in India is about 0.82 million acres in the hill slopes of Assam, Bengal, Bihār, Madras, the Punjab, the United Provinces, Cochin, Mysore, and Travancore. *Coffee* cultivation is restricted mainly to Mysore, Madras, Coorg, Cochin, and Travancore, the total area under coffee being about 0.2 million acres. *Tobacco* was first introduced to India in 1508, and the best tobacco is now grown over 1¼ million acres in Bihār, Bengal, Madras, Mysore, Bombay, the Punjab, and Hyderābād. *Rubber* is mainly grown in Travancore, Madras, Coorg, Cochin, and Mysore. *Indigo* cultivation is confined to the Ganges valley, and *Opium-poppy* in Bihār and the United Provinces. *Condiments* and *spices* are grown mostly in South India and Assam over an area of 2 million acres. India's *fruits* and *vegetables*, including root crops, cover an area approximately of 4.5 million acres and include grapes, oranges, apricots, pears, apples, bananas, mangoes, litchis, pine-apples, papaya, guava, water melons, and others. The *coconuts* provide delicious drinks and nutritious food, and are a source of copra and coir.

Before concluding this brief account of Indian vegetation, specific mention should be made of three trees which have figured in Indian vegetable-lore and literature since Vedic times: the banyan (*Ficus bengalensis*), the pipal (*Ficus religiosa*), and the śālmalī (*Bombax malabaricum*). The banyan with its spreading branches and prop roots, the pipal with its wealth of hanging leaves constantly fluttering in the wind, and the towering śālmali, a blaze of scarlet flowers in early spring are distinctive features of the Indian landscape.

2. THE FAUNA

On account of the great diversity of climatic and physical conditions in a vast country like India its animal life is so remarkably varied and abundant that it is beyond the scope of the present chapter to give even a general account of the characteristic features of its fauna. We therefore propose to confine our attention mainly to the vertebrate animals; for though the invertebrates are far greater in number and variety the vertebrates are better known and more beneficial.

1. *The Vertebrates*

Amongst vertebrates, the mammals constitute the highest group and are of special interest as these include man himself. In India, mammals are well represented. Only the duckbill and spiny anteaters and the pouched mammals such as kangaroos and the opossum do not occur in India. Amongst the man-like apes only the hoolock gibbon is found in India. This occurs in large troops in the dense forests of Assam and adjacent areas. The monkeys are represented by a number of species and include the langurs or hanuman monkeys, which have become famous by being connected with the story of the Hindu epic—the *Rāmāyaṇa*. These occur practically over the whole of India. The lemurs in India are represented by the slow loris occurring in the forests of Assam and the slender loris living in the forests of South India.

The various groups of land carnivores are well represented in India. Most of them, particularly the larger ones, constitute the big game for hunting. Amongst these, the Indian lions are at present restricted to the forests of Kāthiāwār peninsula. The tigers are widely distributed throughout India—in the snowy Himālayas, in the evergreen forests and dry open jungles as well as in swamps of the Sunderbans. The panther or the common Indian leopard, the beautiful Himālayan snow leopard, the skin of which is in great demand in the fur trade, and the cheetah or the hunting leopard are the other large carnivores.

The smaller carnivores of the cat-group include, besides the various forms of cats, the civets, the mongooses, and the hyaenas. The other carnivores include the wolves, jackals, wild dogs, foxes, as well as the bears, weasels, and otters.

The hoofed mammals constitute an important group of animals. Because of the immense usefulness of many a member of this group, these play an important part in the economic life of human beings. The hoofed forms are either even-toed or odd-toed. The odd-toed forms are the horse and ass, the rhinoceros and the elephant. Rhinoceros in India is represented at the present day by the single race of one-horned forms, which is now restricted to Assam and the swamps and grassy jungles of low hills in parts of Nepāl. The elephants and the horses are both notable for the part they played in the numerous battles fought on Indian soil in the early days of history. The even-toed forms include the cattle, sheep and goats, deer, gazelle and antelopes, and the boars and pigs. The cattle in India include, besides domestic forms, the bison and the wild buffalo.

The sheep and the goats are chiefly Himālayan. The goats include the Himālayan form—the Asiatic ibex and the Nilgiri wild goat or the South Indian ibex. The several races of deer found in India live in more or less thick jungles. These include the barking-deer, the barasingha or swamp-deer, the sambar, the spotted-deer or chital and the hog-deer. Another race found in the high altitudes of the Himālayas is the hornless dark brown musk-deer. The male of this race bears beneath the skin of the abdomen a gland, the secretion of which is known as musk, reputed for its various uses especially for medicinal purposes. The mouse-deer or the Indian chevrotain is another hornless race of very small size. The black buck, the only representative in India of antelope, has beautiful spirally-twisted horns. The Nilgai is an inhabitant of open forests whereas the four-horned chousingha lives in the forests in the hilly tracts of peninsular India. The chinkara or Indian gazelle lives in the deserts whereas the pigmy-hog occurs in the forests of Eastern Himālayas. Pig-sticking or spearing wild hog from horseback is a favourite sport in India.

The insectivores include tree-shrews, hedgehogs, moles, and shrews. The rodents include the squirrels and marmots, jerboas, rats and mice, porcupines and hares.

The scaly ant-eater or Pangolin is common in India.

The bats include chiefly the large frugivorous flying foxes and the small insectivorous bats.

The whales and dugongs are marine animals and are occasionally found near the Indian coasts. The dolphin and the porpoise occur in the rivers.

The bird life of India has attracted considerable interest due to its remarkable variety and wide range of distribution The distribution of birds in India is not, however, homogeneous. Migration of birds is a well-known fact, but in India the migratory birds are few in number and the few that migrate into the Indian region come from the north only.

The familiar birds which are commonly found around human habitations include the crows, the house *maynā,* and the house sparrow. The crows include the common house crow and the jungle crow. The ravens are larger in size than the jungle crows. The jackdaws and rooks found in Kāshmir and parts of north-west India are winter visitors from the northern region. The jackdaw has a musical and melodious call and it makes a delightful pet. Of the various *maynās* found in India the house *maynā* shares with the crow the distinction of being the most familiar and best known bird.

The magpies are beautifully coloured birds usually living in forests. These birds are very noisy and their call is harsh and unpleasant. Tits are small birds inhabiting chiefly the forests. The babblers and thrushes are gregarious birds feeding on the ground. They are noisy chatterers *par excellence*. Warblers are small birds usually living in open grassy tracts or sandy ground. The red-vented bulbul is a common garden bird throughout India. It is reputed for its cheerful call notes. The well-known Indian robin is the *dayal*, one of the best songsters. The *shama* is another famous singing bird of India. The familiar pleasant call notes of *pee-ou-a* produced by the golden oriole or the mango-bird in the mango season are heard in gardens as well as in forests both at dawn and at sunset. There are many fly-catchers, which are usually small birds. Another familiar bird is the king crow which is frequently found to chase crows. It is a common sight to find this bird perching on telegraph wires beside the railway lines. The weaver birds are noted for the curious flask-shaped nests they make. Tailor birds are well-known for their habit of sewing two leaves together with a piece of grass as a receptacle for their nests. Munias are smaller birds than the robins and are familiar cage birds. Besides the parrots with green plumage and long tails which are well-known as cage birds throughout India, the hill *maynā* is a notable cage bird with wonderful powers of imitating the human voice. Swallows and larks are usually winter visitors. These generally sing while on the wing. The woodpecker is a familiar bird in India. It has a long beak with the repeated strokes of which it removes bark and rotten wood from tree trunks exposing termites, ants, beetles and their larvae on which it feeds. Amongst the barbets which are usually grass green in colour and frugivorous in habit, the most familiar form is the Indian coppersmith found in most Indian gardens and is known by its repeated metallic call like the tap of a small hammer on metal in a monotonous manner for some minutes. Some of the buntings which are common in winter are notorious for causing damage in cornfields. The blue jay or roller is one of the best known Indian birds seen in gardens and orchards. With the end of winter it rolls in the air and with harsh screams declares the advent of the spring.

The kingfisher represents another group of common Indian birds. This has a beautifully coloured plumage. The hornbill is a forest bird with a broad casque over the large curved beak. It is reputed to be the Garuḍa of the Hindus. The hoopoe is found throughout India and is noted for its loud hoots repeated two or three times. The common Indian swifts are famous as producers of edible nests. The nightjars are well-known for their peculiar notes in the earlier and later parts of the night resembling the strokes of a hammer on a plank. They are considered of evil omen.

The cuckoos include several forms and all lay their eggs in the nests of other birds. The call of the common Indian cuckoo is described as *bou-kota-ko*. The hawk cuckoo, commonly known as the brain-fever bird, is reputed for its monotonous call notes in the hot season, each repeated note being higher in the scale. The Indian koel is another familiar bird, frugivorous in habit and commonly found from March to July. Its call consisting of two syllables is familiar to everyone in India. The male is glossy black and the female brown and spotted. Koel lays eggs in the nests of the crows.

The owls are all nocturnal in habit. They feed on various small animals particularly the squirrels, rats, and mice which cause damage to crops and are therefore greatly beneficial to agriculture. It is probably for this reason that the owl is associated with Lakshmī—the goddess of wealth.

Indian birds of prey include the vultures, the different forms of eagle, the various kites, the falcons, the hawks, the sikra, the buzzard, etc., usually birds of larger sizes.

The pigeons, including the Blue Rock pigeon and the doves, are common throughout India whereas the sand grouse is common in open sandy tracts feeding on the ground.

The game birds in India include a variety of forms. Those living on land include the pea and jungle fowls, the pheasants, partridges, quails, etc. The pea fowls are famous for their splendidly coloured plumage and peculiar habit of being noisy at the approach of rain. The red jungle fowl is essentially a forest bird and is regarded as the ancestor of all domesticated poultry. The common quail is well-known as a bird for sport, a favourite delicacy for the table and a cage bird for fighting. The common grey partridges are usually captured with decoy birds and are favourite cage birds. Morning and evening the wild ringing notes of *tit-ee-roo* of these birds are amongst the familiar bird sounds of India.

Of the aquatic game birds the moorhen is widely distributed. Another one is the familiar water cock or Kora. This is often tamed for fighting. Others include the Jacana and the snipes.

Amongst the cranes, the well-known form is the Sarus crane. The gulls are generally found in sea coasts but also occur along with the terns about inland waters. The spotted-billed pelican is purely a water bird seldom seen on land. Other familiar aquatic birds are the common cormorants and the snake birds. The brown dipper is an aquatic bird characteristic of the hill streams of the Himālayas.

Ibises, storks, herons, and spoonbills constitute a well-known group of Indian birds.

Other notable birds living about well-watered regions include the ducks, the pochard, and the grebes. The Brahminy ducks commonly known as chakha and chakhi are found in pairs.

Reptiles.—The crocodiles and the snakes are the most notable animals amongst the reptiles, which also include the lizards, and the tortoises and turtles. The crocodiles which are of particular interest as attacking human beings are represented by the freshwater broad-snouted form known as the mugger and by the estuarine crocodile. Crocodiles are often hunted for their skin which fetches a high price. Besides these, one finds the gharial—a purely fish-eating river crocodile.

The forms of land tortoises in India are few in number. The shells of these are prettily marked. The freshwater tortoises are herbivorous and edible. Of the turtles, the freshwater forms are carnivorous and aggressive. The carapace in these is covered by a soft skin.

The lizards in India are remarkably numerous. These include geckos, chameleons, skinks, monitors. etc. The chameleons are common in the forest region of peninsular India. These are well known for their capacity to change colour. The skin of the monitor or varanus is in great demand and there is a considerable trade in varanus skin.

The snakes in India have attracted much attention because of the large number of deaths amongst human beings and domesticated animals caused by bites of poisonous ones. India is the only country in the world where almost all the forms of known snakes occur. The worm-like subterranean typhlops are the smallest known snakes. The largest living snakes found in India are the pythons and boas. The common non-poisonous snakes are the rat snakes or dhaman, the carpet snakes, the grass snakes, and the water snakes. Amongst the venomous snakes in India the commonest form is the cobra with the hood unmarked or marked either with a single large ocellus or with two ocelli connected together by a curved line. There is also a black variety of cobra. Another deadly poisonous snake is the krait. This includes the banded ones with alternate bands of black and yellow. The large-sized king cobra is known to be extremely fierce and aggressive. The other poisonous snakes in India are the various forms of vipers. These have broad flat heads and are without hoods.

Amongst the snakes two forms deserve special mention. The tree or whip snake is a beautiful slender snake usually of green colour frequently seen in trees, bushes, and creepers twined round the stems. Another one is the beautifully coloured kalnagini. Though its name implies its deadly venomous character, it is in fact a non-poisonous snake and is frequently reared as a favourite pet. The so-called double-headed snake carried by snake charmers has a blunt tail which is occasionally manipulated and furnished with glass eyes to assist in the delusion.

The Batrachians.—The frogs and toads representing the tailless batrachians are common throughout India in ponds, streams, and all damp places. Of the tailed batrachians only the Indian salamander is found in India. The apodous forms include the worm-like burrowers.

Fishes.—India is remarkable for its abundant fish fauna which accounts for the large section of its population depending on fishes as the staple protein diet. The fishes exhibit a considerable diversity in their structure and habits due to the great variety of habitats in which they live. Besides living in inland rivers, streams, ponds, and marshes, they are found in the estuaries as also in the coastal regions and open seas. The marine forms occasionally migrate upward into the estuarine waters and similarly certain fluviatile forms pass down into the estuarine waters. Many fishes behave as larvaecidal agents. Use of such fishes against the growth of mosquito larvae plays an important role in the control of malaria —one of the prevalent diseases in India.

Amongst the cartilaginous fishes, which abound in Indian seas, some of the sharks and rays occasionally ascend large tidal rivers. The high nutritive value of the shark liver oil has opened up an exceedingly important trade in the fishing of sharks. The dried fins of both sharks and rays are exported to China while the flesh of some forms is regarded as a delicacy by certain people, chiefly of the poorer classes.

Amongst the bony fishes the most important are the carp. These are inhabitants of freshwater and many of them, particularly the major carp, bring high prices as edible fishes. Smaller carp are found in rivers and streams in large numbers. The scaleless cat fishes are well represented in India. Amongst the Indian herrings which include several coastal and estuarine fishes, the most important fish is the hilsa, the flesh of which is highly flavoured. Amongst the perch which occur in India in fairly large numbers, the most valuable and largely used food fish is the *bhekti* of Bengal which grows to a weight of 200 pounds. Others, which are reputed as good edible fishes, include the freshwater forms such as nandus, the estuarine or coastal forms such as the mango-fish, the mackerels, pomfrets, tunny, and the mullets. The notopterid chitals represent a well-known group of very compressed fishes. They are highly prized as good edible fishes due to the rich content of fat. Remarkable in India is the occurrence of the air-breathing fishes including the snake-headed fishes, the climbing perch, the scaleless fishes such as singhee and magur and the snake-like cunchia. These are found in every region where there is accumulation of water. There are several forms of flat fish in India. In the hill streams the sucker fishes occur. The globe fishes, pipe fishes, and the sea horses are a few other interesting forms found in the estuarine and coastal regions. Peculiar fishes of the estuaries and mud flats of the coastal region are the mud skippers. The flying fish which inhabit the open seas are common about India.

Lower Chordates.—The lower chordates, including the balanoglossus, the sea-squirt, and the amphioxus are not uncommon in the seas around the coast of India.

2. *The Invertebrates*

The invertebrate group comprising the less-known forms of animal life is in no way less important than the vertebrate one nor less remarkable in variety and numbers. Many invertebrate animals are directly beneficial to man whereas many others are harmful, injurious, and cause extensive damage to life and property. Many invertebrate animals provide articles used for commercial purposes and on these are based various industries of man. The invertebrates constitute an enormously large section of animals and only a few of the more important forms of the different groups are mentioned below in order to complete this sketch of the fauna of India.

The molluscs or shelled animals are well represented in India. They are found in estuaries, in fresh waters, in coastal waters as well as in the open seas around. The bivalved mussels as well as various forms of snails, including the apple snails, are found in ponds. Many gastropods of both shelled and naked varieties and the squids, cuttle fishes, octopus, and nautilus are inhabitants of the seas. The gastropod shells commonly known as cowries are reputed for their use in the past as exchange money. The blowing of chanks or conches is associated with sacred ceremonies and there has developed a good trade in the way of preparing bangles from chank for the women folk of India. The molluscan shells provide materials for road construction and are used in the preparation of lime. The oysters are used as articles of food and provide the source for the development of pearls. The pearl oysters are found in the coastal seas. Pearl fishing was a highly developed industry in ancient India and there is a great possibility of this trade in future.

The arthropods forming the largest group of animals are well represented. Various forms of prawns, shrimps, lobsters, different types of crabs and the numerous small crustaceans occur in fresh waters, in estuaries, on sandy beaches, and in the seas. Amongst insects, in India are found the various forms of ants, wasps, hornets, honey bees, the cockroaches, white ants, numerous forms of butterflies and moths, the glow worms, mosquitoes of different types, locusts, grasshoppers, dragon flies, various forms of beetles, fleas, etc. Some predatory insects such as the praying mantis are beneficial by feeding upon injurious forms. The honey bee is of great benefit as producer of honey and wax. Some of the mosquitoes, certain flies and the fleas, are definitely harmful and injurious and they act as transmitters of diseases and agents in spreading sources of infection. The locusts are the most well known among those which cause extensive damage to crops, whereas the silk moths and the lac insects are but two instances where these produce valuable industrial and commercial materials. In India, where there is an abundance of vegetation, the insects, particularly the butterflies, play an important role in bringing about pollination and the dispersal of seeds. Peripatus—a form intermediate between the segmented animals and the arthropoda—is found in the forests of the hilly tracts of Assam. The centipedes and millipedes are common throughout India. The scorpions and spiders are represented by various forms. In the coastal seas of India the king crab is found in fairly large numbers.

Echinoderms, or the groups of animals including the star fishes, the various urchins, etc., are all marine and found in the seas around the coasts. Of the segmented animals, the earthworms and the leeches of various types, including the large-sized cattle leech, are found all over India. The burrowing segmented form known as the nereis is found in the shallow coastal seas. Sponges occur chiefly in the seas but freshwater sponges are not uncommon in inland waters such as ponds. The coelenterates occur in abundance in the seas surrounding the Indian peninsula. These include the medusae, the jelly fishes, the sea anemones, etc. The skeleton, which is present in many of these, especially of the sea anemones, forms the different types of beautiful coloured corals including the precious red corals. The worms are represented by the round worms and by the flat worms, including the various tape worms. Most of these are parasitic on other animals, especially the vertebrates, and pathogenic, causing diseases. Various wheel animalculae occur in ponds and other freshwater regions. The protozoa or the unicellular animals include a large number of forms. Some of these such as the malarial parasite, the leishmania, the entamoeba, cause serious diseases in human beings and often bring about the death of the victim. Others, such as trypanosoma, babesia, coccidia, cause diseases of domesticated cattle and fowl and thus lead to huge losses of property. There are numerous free-living forms and also many parasitic forms which are however not pathogenic.

1. Introductory Essay to the *Flora Indica*, p. 91.

BOOK TWO

THE PREHISTORIC AGE

CHAPTER VII

PALAEOLITHIC, NEOLITHIC AND COPPER AGES

I. PALAEOLITHIC AGE

We have comparatively very scanty data on Early Man and his environment. Surface finds from the Punjab, Rājputāna, Gujarāt, Central India, Central Provinces, Karnātak, Mysore, South India. Bihār, Assam, and Bengal testify to the widespread existence of man who fashioned rough stone implements mainly of quartzite. These were similar in shape and make to those known to be palaeolithic tools in Europe, but as in a majority of cases their stratigraphic relation was not known, they could not be assigned to a definite geological age. Recent researches have, however, contributed materially to our knowledge of Early Man in three or four provinces of India.

We begin with the Punjab. Except for the fact that it was one of the earliest homes of the Aryans, nothing definite was known about its first settlers, prior to the glacio-archaeologic work of the Yale-Cambridge expedition in 1935.[2] It is now more or less established that Early Man first entered the foothills of the North-West Punjab, the area traversed by the Soan, Haro. and other rivers within the Indus-Jhelum Doāb, and comprised within the Rāwalpindi and Attock districts of the Punjab and Jammu in Kāshmir State, at the end of the First Inter-Glacial Period and the beginning of the Second Ice Age in the south-west Himālayas. Human existence is testified to by the presence of large flakes which are found embedded in fan-shaped boulder gravels of this period (T_1) in the Siwalik foothills and plains in North-West Punjab. Punch. and Jammu.

I. *First Inter-Glacial Age*

Though the earliest implements of man have come from the immediately succeeding stratum, viz. the Boulder Conglomerate zone of the second glacial epoch, it would seem that man had actually inhabited the area almost at the end of the First Inter-Glacial stage. The conditions for existence were not particularly favourable either for mammals or men in the Second Ice Age, to the first phase of which the Boulder Conglomerate stratum is assigned. The climate was not only colder and stormier, but the rainfall was heavier than today, as the deeply stained gravels and implements show. In fact only a few rolled bones of bovoids and proboscideans are found in this deposit.

So far implements have been found in the Boulder Conglomerate at five sites. Three of these—Kallar, Chaomukh, and Malakpur—are in the valley of the Jhelum and its tributaries, the fourth site is near Adial on the Sohan (Soan), and the fifth on the Tawi, a tributary of the Chenāb near Jammu.

All the implements are made of quartzite and are in a worn condition. The upper surface is usually unflaked except for one or two small irregular scars. The under surface, having flat bulbs, but prominent cones, must be the primary flaked surface and has a large plain, unfaceted striking platform at angles varying from 100 degrees to 125 degrees. No retouch is visible except on one find from Kallar. The edges are broken, whether by use or naturally cannot be said.[3]

Typologically as well as stratigraphically this earliest Punjab industry differs from the rest and hence it is called the Pre-Soan industry, to distinguish it from the later industry most of whose sites are on the Soan.

2. *Second Inter-Glacial Age and Early Soan Industry*

The Soan itself has two distinct groups. The early Soan and late Soan. Tools of the former group are found in Terraces T_0 and T_1 and later gravels mostly along the Indus. These have been observed at Khushalgarh, Makhad and Injra and at Gariala on the Haro river south-east of Attock.

Geologically these terraces are assignable to the Second Inter-Glacial Stage. This interval is believed to be very long, when the climate was drier, but owing to continued uplift of the Pir Panjel range, as evidenced by the tilted plains near Chaomukh and Jammu, there was great erosion. This may have destroyed the evidence of the rich contemporary fossil fauna without which man, whose existence is revealed by numerous sites, could not have lived in the area.

Unlike the Pre-Soan tools, the early Soan tools are made from varieties of fine-grained quartzite as well as fine smooth greenish-grey Panjal trap.

Patination and the state of wear divide these tools into three groups, which may be called A, B, C. Group A is the earliest and is heavily patinated, deep brown or purple and much rolled. Group B is deeply patinated like A but unworn, and Group C is less patinated and fairly fresh.

Among all these groups there are pebble tools, scrapers and flakes, the first-named predominating. There is evidence of typologic development towards smaller and neater forms, but it does not synchronize with the stratigraphic evidence.

The pebble tools are all prepared from smooth, rounded rolled pebbles and small boulders. These, when further subdivided, give us (*a*) flat-based, and (*b*) rounded, pebble tools.

True discoidal cores often with a patch of cortex in the centre of one or both surfaces are also found in this group. These cores are similar to the Clactonian and early Levalloisian forms.

There are two kinds of flakes. The first has a high-angled plain platform and, though similar to the Early Soan B, is neater and better and more primarily flaked. In the second kind, much smaller, the angle is low and the platform unfaceted. While there is evidence of use, on these tools there is very little of secondary flaking.

The Soan valley has also yielded other types of tools, probably of the Second Inter-Glacial Age, though they are rolled and occur in the gravels of the Third Glacial phase. These tools comprise hand-axes, cores and flakes, and a couple of crude cleavers. Typologically, very much rolled hand-axes are assigned to the Abbevillian or Lower Acheulian, and the less rolled, with more regular outline and neater step flaking, to the middle Acheulian.

Mention must be made of the few flakes which show typical Acheulian technique with plain platforms and parallel primary flaking, and one or two showing signs of crude retouching.

3. *Third Ice Age and Late Soan Industry*

Between the Early Soan and Late Soan industries intervened the Third Ice Age, and the latter are assigned to this period. During this glaciation which was comparatively less extensive, a vast amount of loessic (wind-borne) silt was deposited over the Potwar, a phenomenon which is attributed to the interaction of several factors: accumulated silt owing to inundation, erosion, mountain glaciation, and violent dust storms. Since the Late Soan tools come from the basal Potwar gravel and loess which is attributed to the Third Ice Age, it is suggested that Early Man had witnessed the beginning of these dust-storms in the Punjab where they are an annual feature in the summer nowadays.

Few fossils have been found in these huge loessic deposits.[4] But it is suggested that vegetation must have been more abundant in plains and the fauna may have been similar to that of the Narmadā valley, where remains of horse, buffalo, straight-tusked elephant, and hippopotamus were discovered in association with Early Palaeolithic tools. However, the Potwar loess (perhaps its upper horizon) has yielded twelve types of fossil invertebrates, molluscs (fresh water and land) and gastropods.

The Late Soan industry[5] is stratigraphically and typologically divisible into two groups. In Late Soan A some specimens are worn. Both pebble tools and flake and core tools occur, but the latter outnumber the former.

Among pebble tools, a form which appears late in Early Soan, viz. a "side scraper"-like implement, made on a roughly oval pebble, with cortexed butt on one side, and flaking along the opposite side, and a wavy straight or convex edge is common.

Three other earlier forms are also found. But a new type is seen in a form where a small ovoid pebble is intentionally broken at an oblique angle to produce a flat base. Two or more flakes are struck upwards from the under-surface on the side that makes an acute angle with the bases. Some specimens exhibit retouch on the edge.

There are many forms of cores. Flakes are of two types: (1) simple, and (2) with retouched edges.

Late Soan B tools are found in a deposit of wind-borne silt above the gravel of the Third Glacial Age. They are fresh and unworn.[6]

Mainly two types of cores occur, one of which was already noticed in Late Soan A.

Flakes again are generally of the Levalloisian type. They are mostly blades or elongated flakes, and a few triangular or oval.

4. *Third Inter-Glacial Age: Chauntra Industry*

So far the only tools met with were pebble tools and flakes. But at a few sites, particularly at Chauntra on the Soan river, some totally different kinds of tools[7] were chiselled out from a gravel which may be of the Third Inter-Glacial Age. This was again a period of stream erosion, as a result of which the river beds were deepened, and lakes emptied. Mountain uplift also must have taken place. However, as in earlier stages, there are few evidences of loessic deposits.

5. *Fourth Ice Age Tools*

Pebble tools and flakes found at Dhok Pathan near Pindi Gheb on the Sil river, a tributary of the Soan, are supposed to be later, possibly of the Fourth Glacial Age. The tools which include pebble tools, cores and unfaceted flakes are "regarded as representing a late, localized industry of peculiar facies, showing marked similarities, in a greatly developed form, to the Early Soan industries of the Indus region."

Early Man thus seems to have inhabited the Punjab from the end of the First Inter-Glacial period onwards right through the succeeding three glacial and two inter-glacial periods. As no human remains have been found along with the implements, it is impossible to say whether the same race witnessed such great climatical changes, and ultimately produced the fine hand-axe and flake industry noticed at Chauntra, or other races came at different periods, or the old and new races lived together.

The evidence detailed before indicates that pebble and flake industries developed together in the same area alongside the Abbevillian-Acheulian hand-axe industries. In the former pebble tools become smaller and neater, and the flakes of Clactonian facies

—crude, unfaceted and devoid of intentional primary flaking—are later associated with neater forms such as Levalloisian type and have regular and convergent primary flaking, faceted platforms, and fine retouching, if any.

The hand-axe industry is for the first time associated with the Soan flake and pebble industry at Chauntra, and here alone it reaches its acme, flowering into a fine late Acheulian type.

On the basis of this contact, for which the evidence is so far slight, De Terra has said that Early Man entered the Punjab together with his hand-axe industry from the south.

After the Punjab comes Rājputāna where stray, mostly surface finds have been made. The few Rājputāna specimens come from Jaipur, Bundi, and Indargarh.[8] These are generally of quartzite, but reddish-brown sandstone accounts for one specimen. Among the tools two types of hand-axes are visible. One is pointed ovate and the other is ovoid. It is roughly chipped and called "Boucher" by Coggin Brown.

Rajputāna leads us to Gujarāt. Here, as elsewhere, only surface finds were made in the last century. But since the discoverer—Bruce Foote—had given good clues together with an excellent study of the stratigraphy of the Sābarmati valley, the task of obtaining stratigraphical evidence was comparatively easy. And it was obtained by the First Gujarāt Pre-historic Expedition.[9] During its survey of the middle reaches of the Sābarmati, a distance of over 100 miles from Hadol in the north to Delwad in the south, five more palaeolithic sites were discovered. Of these the most important were Hadol, Pedhamli, and Ghadhara; of lesser importance Phudera, Aglod, Hirpura, Kot, and Warsora.

The implements are mostly fresh and a few only rolled or semi-rolled, with worn-out edges and flake scars. Typologically they comprise: (1) hand-axes (including sub-types), (2) cleavers, (3) scrapers, (4) flakes, and (5) pebble tools.

No clear evidence of sequence corresponding to the succession of the three or two main phases of the old alluvium, viz. the gravel conglomerate and the reddish silt, is visible in the industry. For the two main typologic features of the industry, which from the predominant tool type has to be called hand-axe industry, are evident in practically all types of tools from the lower stratum. Thus there are:

(*a*) Tools with irregular line, rough 'step' flaking, and pebble cortex at the butt-end or over part of both the surfaces.

(*b*) Tools with regular outline, wavy edges, comparatively smooth "step" flaking and no pebble cortex or the cortex patch at a definite place.

While this is generally true, there are three specimens—two hand-axes, one pear-shaped, and the other very thin, perfectly symmetrical ovate, and an U-shaped cleaver—from the upper part of the reddish silt which are so fine as to suggest a late typologic evolution corresponding to the uppermost phase of the alluvium.

Typologically these three varieties of hand-axes bear close resemblance to (i) the Abbevillian-Early Acheulian, (ii) the Middle Acheulian, and (iii) the Late Acheulian industries of Madras and the Punjab as well as those of Europe, and similar sequences observed in the Nile Valley and the rest of Africa.

A site bearing similar cultural products was discovered by the expedition in the Orsang valley at Bahadarpur. Here the gravel is loose and uncemented and is approximately at a height of twenty-five feet from the present river bed, and underlies deposits of black cotton soil and brownish silt. The top of the gravel yielded a few finds of quartz and quartzite. Unlike the Sābarmati specimens, the majority of the Orsang tools are rolled or semi-rolled and a few only fresh. Typologically these comprise (*a*) hand-axes, ovate, and pear-shaped, (*b*) flakes, one of which is a definite blade, and (*c*) pebble tools.

The Karjan, a tributary of the Orsang and Narmadā, has also given a similar promise of the Old Stone Age culture. Here tools, hand-axes, U-shaped cleavers, of Vaal technique, beautiful discoids and pebble tools of trap have been found.[10]

We next proceed to the Upper Narmadā Valley, where stratigraphical data for the existence of Early Man are available. Unfortunately even now a complete idea of this stone industry cannot be formed, as the specimens found by the Yale-Cambridge Expedition are not fully described. However, the expedition succeeded in establishing the relationship of a middle Pleistocene fauna with an early Palaeolithic industry, a relationship which was so far presumed on the strength of a solitary tool—an ovate hand-axe from a site at Bhutara and fossil mammalian remains. Stratigraphic correlation is also attempted between the Punjab and the Central Indian Pleistocene on geologic and archaeological evidence.[11]

Narmadā Valley has given a glimpse of the various types of industries—Early and Late Soan and the Abbevillian and the Acheulian hand-axe-cleaver. At some localities there is a mixture of the different types, whereas at one locality near Narsinghpur the Late Soan seems to replace the Acheulian culture. De Terra, however, would tentatively suggest that the Narmadā "lower group represents the true Acheulian and early Soan, and the upper group the Late Soan Industry." If this were really so, the two Narmadā gravel groups could be correlated with the Terrace$_1$, Terrace$_2$, Terraces$_{3-4}$ of the Punjab. Whether it was actually so or whether the various industries flourished simultaneously, the gravels belonging to one geologic age, can be determined only by further research and collection of fuller data.

The rest of the evidence in Central India and the Central Provinces consists of surface finds collected in the last century from Saugor, Damoh, Rewah, and Bundelkhand.[12] In this region, which is the meeting-place of the three great geological formations, viz. the quartzite (which has principally developed on the west, in North Gujarāt, and Rājputāna), the sandstone (in Central India), and the trap (which extends from the Mālwa plateau towards the south), tools of all these materials are found. Typologically the tools are similar to those of Rājputāna and North Gujarāt.

Further east a few finds have been reported from Bengal, Bihār, and Orissa, from Paloncha, on the eastern outskirts of the Hyderābād State, and from Hyderābād itself.[13] So far Bengal had given few palaeoliths but recently a large number has been discovered at Kuliana, in Mayurbhanj State (Orissa).[14] The tools are quartzite and include:

(*a*) Pebble tools, some of which resemble crude hand-axes, and others cleavers. There are also choppers, ovate forms and awl-like pointed tools.

(*b*) Core tools, both faces worked.

South of the Vindhyas, after the Narmadā Valley, the next important region is the Konkan coastal strip and the Deccan plateau. Little work was done in the latter, because of its peculiar geological formation. However, fossil fauna of the middle Pleistocene period was found at Mungi and Nandur Madhmeshwar in the Godāvari valley. At the former site an agate flake was noticed in the same stratum. Following up these clues the present writer and his associates have been carrying out a systematic survey of the valley. It has yielded small flakes, blades, and cores of agate, jasper, chalcedony, bloodstone, and trap,[15] but no heavy tools like hand-axes or choppers.

Rude stone implements have been reported from the vicinity of Bombay since 1880. Much of this early work is, however, mere surface collection and not well illustrated. Slight but important is the notice by Todd[16] of Palaeolithic industries in the Salsette Island north of Bombay. Here at Borivli, Kandivli, and other suburbs he discovered tools comprising hand-axes, cleavers, flakes, blades, and microliths. It appears that hand-axes and cleavers were found only at Kandivli. Here no less than six strata were observed. Scrapers, cores, and choppers were found in "Lower Clay" and over its "top," forming the lowest stratum over the rock. Overlying this clay there is a deposit of reddish-brown gravel. In it were found many implements of Chellean and Clactonian type, and on its top, implements of Clactonian type in mint condition, as well as late Acheulian types. The Konkan, with its sequence of industries, thus promises to be one of the key areas for understanding the evolution of Stone Age cultures in Western India.

It is likely that similar early palaeolithic culture flourished in the region lower down, in Southern Konkan and eastwards above the *Ghāts* in the Karnātak area. Foote found an extinct type of rhinoceros and hand-axes in the hard kankar cemented shingle bed of the Bennihalla, a tributary of the Malaprabhā in the Dhārwār district, and also in the shingle bed of the Malaprabhā itself in the Bijāpur district. These tools are large ovate hand-axes and cleavers of quartzite, very much resembling similar tools from the Konkan and the Sābarmatī.

Foote also found a few palaeoliths in the Mysore Karnātak.[17] Some he found "scattered on the pale quartzite shingle bed capping the high ground south-eastward of the town of Kadur" and also at Nyamti, sixteen miles south of Shimoga; others from the laterite debris near the villages of Nidaghatta and Lingadahalli south of Sakrapatna. Two of the latter are of white quartz, all the rest of quartzite. The quartzite specimens are mostly patinated. There are no cleavers, the hand-axes are of oval, ovoid and triangular types. Discs and discoids are also found. No palaeoliths have been reported further south on the Malabar coast.

In contrast to these scanty notices of palaeolithic finds on the west coast of India, the east coast area with the suitable material from the Eastern Ghāts has proved very rich in these finds. Barring the southern extremity, viz. the Tinnevelly district and some gaps from West Godāvari district to Ganjam in the north, palaeoliths have been found from most other districts, viz. Madura, Trichinopoly, North and South Arcot, Chingleput, Chitoor, Cuddapah, Anantpur, Bellary, Nellore, Kurnool, Guntur, and Krishṇā, of the Madras Presidency. Of these North Arcot, Chingleput, Cuddapah, Bellary, and Kurnool districts yielded the largest number.

In the Madura district the finds were collected "from a shingle bed in the alluvium of the Vaigai, on the left bank of the river, immediately north of Madura town"; in the Tanjore district from the "laterite deposit lying to the south-east of Vallam and south-west of Tanjore city"; in the Trichinopoly district "from the laterite forming the plateau east of Ninniyur, forty-five miles north-east of Trichinopoly town"; in the Bellary district "on the surface of the shingle fans lying along the foot of the copper mountain south of Bellary town," also from the Halakundi shingle fans and other sites; in the Cuddapah district from "thin spreads of laterite gravel," in Rayachoti *Tāluk;* in the North Arcot district "in connection with laterite gravels"; in the Chingleput district in the laterite conglomerate at various places; in the Nellore district "mostly washed out of the laterite gravels resting on the gneissic rocks"; in the Maneru valley; in the Kurnool district "in the valley of the Khunder near Roodrar in lateritic gravels"; in the Guntur and Krishnā districts "from the highlevel gravels" at Ippatam and Oostapalli on the Krishnā.

The above review shows that the laterite beds in south-east India are implementiferous. But since Foote had not worked out the stratigraphy completely, nor indicated the typological relation between the finds from the laterite gravel and other gravels and the surface, the value of his large number of finds is mainly typological and not so much cultural.

This want has been to some extent supplied by Cammiade's work in the Kurnool and Krishnaswami's and Paterson's work in the Chingleput district. Cammiade in collaboration with Burkitt has given a correlation of the sequence of industries and stratigraphy with that of climatic changes in south-east India.[18]

According to these authors the tools can be stratigraphically and typologically divided into four main groups which synchronize with two dry and two semi-humid periods, the first two alternating with two pluvial periods. Tools found in the laterite pebble bed in the Bhavnasi gravels at Krishnapuram (78° 73′ and 15° 40′), on the western entrance of the Atmakur-Dornala Pass, "in the derived quartzite pebble bed" on the Rālluvāgu and Yerra-konda-Palem (79° 10-15′ and 15° 40-45′) on the eastern entrance of the same pass, in "the derived laterite" bed on the bank of the Sagileru. at Giddaiur (78° 55′ and 15° 22-23′) near the Nandikanama Pass. and from the upper part of the laterite overlying the gneiss basal bed at Gundla Bhrameshvaram. a little to the south of the Krishnā. constitute the earliest series comprising hand-axes (of quartzite) rather roughly flaked. slightly rolled. and stained with laterite; whereas tools from the superimposed layer of red alluvial clay at Krishnapuram constitute the second series comprising mostly flakes, and a few neatly made hand-axes (of quartzite, sandstone, and chalcedony). Tools of series three and four comprise microlith-like and microliths respectively.

The work of Krishnaswami[19] and Paterson[20] has still further advanced our knowledge of the palaeolithic industries in the Chingleput district. The former discovered tools in the pre-laterite Boulder Conglomerate at Vadamadurai. whereas the two together observed a system of four terraces in the Korttalaiyar Valley, the laterite conglomerate of the Terrace T_2 at Attirampakkam yielding, as it did to Foote. numerous palaeoliths. typologically similar to those from the main detrital laterite overlying the Boulder Conglomerate at Vadamadurai.

The technical stages of two series of tools from the Boulder Conglomerate have been described in European terminology as re-

V.A.—9

presenting the Abbevillian and the earliest Acheulian; that of the tools from the laterite gravel as resembling the middle Acheulian; and that from the layer above laterite as "probably upper Acheulian."

The hand-axes and cleavers from the Attirampakkam laterite are considered to be Late Acheulian or, according to Krishnaswami, Late Acheulian, Micoquian, and Levalloisian. The Madras Museum abounds in collections from other districts: Cuddapah, Nellore, Anantpur, and Kurnool. Of these the collections made by Manley[21] from Nellore and Drummond from Kurnool deserve mention.

From the above review it would appear that practically every part of India except the great Indo-Gangetic plain has given traces of its hoary antiquity. But excepting a few areas, nowhere is the stratigraphical sequence of the Stone Age cultures worked out. Until this is made available, it would be hazardous to opine in what part of India Early Man originated, and what the exact relation[22] is either in time or between the Stone Age cultures above reviewed. The accepted geological antiquity of and the favourable climatic conditions on the eastern coast of South India, and the reported finds from the pre-laterite Boulder Conglomerate at Vadamadurai would, however, give ground for a view that Early Man in India originated in South India, and migrated towards the Punjab at the close of the First Ice Age.

2. THE MESOLITHIC AGE

The cultures which succeeded the Palaeolithic in Europe and certain parts of Africa exhibit certain definite features. On the correlation of these with stratigraphic sequence obtainable at a few sites, two main cultural stages have been recognized: (1) the Transitional or the Mesolithic; (2) the Neolithic. The old glacial conditions had more or less gone and Europe experienced a long dry spell. With the climatic changes the flora and fauna also changed, and most probably a new race of people entered Europe. Culturally, however, this new race was still in the hunting stage. It did not produce food. And above all the implements used were primarily of stone, though bone was also used.

But the nature of these tools is absolutely different. These are extremely small, about an inch or so in length. The technique of making them is also different. Hence they are called microliths or pygmy tools. Except a few Tardenoisian sites in France, and a few in England, most of these implements have been found from the surface, on loessic mounds, or in sandy areas.

Such microliths have been found in practically the whole of India. Foote[23] noticed them from almost all the districts of South India, including Tinnevelly, Hyderābād State, Gujarāt, Kāthiāwār, Central India, Central Provinces, and Chotā Nāgpur, whereas subsequent workers have discovered them in Cutch[24] and the Punjab[25]. But unlike Europe, these were all surface collections. In the absence of startigraphical evidence or other cultural objects from well-conducted excavations it is not possible to assign the microliths in all these areas to a mesolithic period. In some instances microliths appear in dolmens with iron implements; in others with pottery which can be dated to the fourth century B. C. Thus in different regions, according to their geographical situation and cultural development, microliths have been in use as forming composite tools and weapons at widely different periods. These might extend from the mesolithic to historic times.

Small but systematic excavations at the site of Brahmagiri (Chitaldurg district, Mysore) and at Langhnaj (Mehsāna *Tāluk* in Gujarāt) have produced evidence to show that at least at these two sites the microliths might belong to the mesolithic cultural phase.

At Brahmagiri both neoliths and microliths appeared at the five-foot level, but later at eight feet only, microliths were found.[26] So it is suggested that at this site, called Roppa after the nearest village, micro-neolithic culture, comparable to the Compignian of France, flourished. Whether it is so old in point of time cannot be determined, for it yet remains to be proved stratigraphically, as has been shown in Europe, that such cultures are post-Quaternary, and earlier than true Neolithic.

Almost similar is the case with notices of microlithic cultures in the rock-shelters in the Mahādeo Hills at Panchmarhi[27] and at Uchali[28] near Naushahra in the Punjab. At the latter site microliths were found in association with neolithic-like pottery and skeletal remains of *Homo sapiens*, which were in very friable condition. At the former site pottery was found in the first few inches, but below it, a foot deeper, there was no pottery at all. Dr. Hunter who conducted the excavation thought the culture to be pre-Neolithic, whereas on the evidence of paintings on the rock, it is surmised that the culture cannot be older than the second century B.C. It must be said that Major Gordon,[29] whose study of the paintings is indeed scholarly, has not pointed out any stratigraphical or cultural relationship between the paintings and the microliths. It is quite possible that potsherds, which Dr. Hunter found on the surface, belong to the earliest or some phase of the paintings, but that there is no connection between the paintings and microliths,.

Excavations in the loessic mounds at Langhnaj,[30] as well as at Hirpura in Northern Gujarāt, have recently brought to light a rich microlithic culture. Potsherds usually occur up to the first three feet from the surface, along with mircroliths and a few fossilized (calcified) remains of animals. Deeper, up to six to seven feet, only microliths, in association with numerous bone splinters, including a number of large bones of animals (such as ribs, shoulder blades, astragalli, humerus, tibia, teeth, and parts of jaw, fish vertebrae, skeletons of lizards, and other many hitherto unidentified remains) together with seven human skeletons (one intact, and the rest more or less incomplete) have been found.

From the total absence of metals, relative rarity of pottery, and the almost complete calcification of human and animal remains (which is by the way remarkable when compared with similar finds so far made in India from historic and proto-historic sites, and Sub-Recent deposits in the Potwar loess) it is probable that the Gujarāt microlithic culture is of considerable antiquity.

Racially these human skeletons show Hamitic Negroid characteristics, and hence might have been of people akin to those in North-East Africa and also proto-Egyptians. These folk lived on small hillocks and drew their water supply from the hillock-girt inundation lakes. They were primarily hunters and subsisted on such game as the cow, buffalo, wild horse, ox, sheep, goat, rats, fish, and crocodile. They must have used jungle fruits and other forest products, but so far we have not found any remains of these in the shape of stones, etc.

The crouching posture in which the skeletons have been found leaves no doubt that they were deliberately buried, with a definite idea of orientation. Out of seven skeletons four have their head facing the west, and the remaining three, one of which is that of a young woman, have their head facing the east. Large stones—pebbles of quartzite and portions of querns of sandstones—had something to do with the burial ceremony. For these are usually found near the head of the skeletons. The dog also must have played an important part in the life of these people, as so far two almost complete skeletons have been found near the human remains, whereas the rest of the animal remains consist of isolated fragments only.

Whatever the age or ages to which the microliths in India be ultimately assigned as a result of further research, the present collections, particularly those made in Gujarāt, can be typologically classified in the following groups, each having several varieties or sub-divisions:

(i) Rectangular blades.
(ii) Crescent blades. These are primarily one-edged, the back side being made purposely blunt.
(iii) Scrapers. These are mostly thin, flat pieces with one side more sloping than the rest and edged.
(vi) Points.
(v) Cores.

3. THE NEOLITHIC AGE

The neolithic cultural phase in India is so far indicated by one of its main constituents, namely, stone tools. These, unlike those of the earlier cultures, bear unmistakable signs of polish, either all over the tools, or at the butt-end and the working end, or only at the working end. The material is also different. While the palaeolithic man seems to have preferred fine-grained quartzite, the mesolithic chalcedony, and other silicate varieties such as jasper, chert, and bloodstone, the man of this age liked to fashion his tools out of fine-grained dark-green trap, though there are examples of diorite, basalt, slate, chlorite schist, indurated shale, gneiss, sandstone, and quartzite.

How, when and by whom was this culture introduced, and the earlier replaced, cannot be said for want of suitable data. Polished stone implements have a very wide distribution. They have been found in several districts of South India, but particularly Bellary, Mysore and Hyderābād State, Central India, Central Provinces, Bundelkhand, Gujarāt, Kāshmir, West Bengal, Chotā Nāgpur and Orissa. Like the microliths, these tools have also been found in funerary monuments along with iron objects. So they seem to have gone over well into Iron Age and early historic periods.

However, as in the case of microliths, excavations at two or three sites in India have shown that these polished stone implements or drilled hammer stones antedate the Iron Age. The first site is Brahmagiri, mentioned above. Here the neoliths stratigraphically lie below the early Iron Age and historical cultures, and above the microliths.

At Langhnaj, again, a large pierced hammer stone of quartzite with splayed hole from either side, and the front part of a polished celt have been found.[31] The celt has a broad rounded point and smooth, polished, biconvex surfaces; the other end is broken. The splayed holes and the absence of vertical drilling in stone tools, particularly hammer stones, are regarded a characteristic of the Neolithic Age in Europe, while the second implement recalls similar implements of neolithic type from South India and Bengal. Typologically these would be the only neolithic tools from Gujarāt. For the large majority, classified by Foote as neoliths, are really microliths. And if other sites yield results similar to those obtained so far from Langhnaj, then the Gujarāt microlithic culture will have to be assigned to a mesolithic period.

Excavating a megalithic monument at Burzahom in Kāshmir De Terra found neolithic celts below a chalcolithic (?) layer in post-glacial loess associated with hard grey hand-made pottery decorated with incised designs.[32]

The neolithic celts in India which have been so far illustrated[33] may be classified into the following types:

(1) Triangular outline with rounded corners, slightly convex working edge, the sides converging into a pointed but

round butt end (Coggin Brown, Pl. V. 1, 9, 13, 15, 19) polished all over on both sides (Pl. VI. 1, 4, 8, 11, 14; VII. 2, 3, 4).

(2) Cylindrical or elongated oval, convex edge, sides converging into a pointed butt end, biconvex sides, polished all over on both sides (Pl. V. 5, 8, 10; VI. 10, 3).

(3) Broad edge, with rounded corners, sides slightly tapering but ending in a broad convex butt end, surfaces unpolished (Pl. V. 20).

(4) Oval and ovate, one end convex, the other pointed, polished all over (Pl. VII. 5).

(5) Chisel-like triangular, almost straight edged sides converging into a rounded point (Pl. VII. 1; IX. 6).

(6) Long, thin, slight convex edge, tapering sides, but broad straight butt.

(7) Convex edge, slightly tapering sides.

(8) Thin and pointed, rounded sides, broad butt polished all over (Pl. IX. 12).

Hammer stones:

I. Round without any hole.

II. Round or oval (Pl. VI. 7) with a hole in the middle splayed from both sides (Pl. VI. 9; VII. 6).

The above gives a very rough and tentative idea of neolithic tools in India. It needs to be improved by a scientific classification of the collections in the Indian Museum, Calcutta, and Government Museum, Madras, and in the museums at Mysore and Hyderābād.

Much has been said about neolithic culture. According to some scholars the people of this age understood the use of fire, made pottery, cultivated grain and domesticated animals. But as these theories are based on surface finds alone, no definite conclusions are possible until positive evidence is furnished by further excavations. The same remark applies to the views of those who would refer to this age the cinder-mounds, rude drawings in caves, as well as the so-called cup-marks or "small hollowed depressions in the rocks," sometimes regarded as a system of writing.[34] It is highly questionable whether all these really belonged to the Neolithic Age, and hence no detailed account has been given of them.

4. THE COPPER AND BRONZE AGE

When metals began to be used is very difficult to say in the absence of stratigraphic sequence of cultures, and for want of unanimity of opinion on the age of the *Ṛigveda* and later texts which refer to a metal—*ayas*—interpreted either as copper or iron. Until the discovery of the Indus culture (which is treated in detail in Chapter IX) the only evidence for the presumption of a Copper Age in India consisted of surface finds, mostly from the Ganges-Jumnā Doāb. Recently some finds have been made at Kallur in the Hyderābād State and a few copper and bronze weapons, tools, and vessels have been found in dolmens and other sepulchral monuments from Nāgpur, Hyderābād, Madura and Mysore.

In spite of a few stray finds of copper or bronze weapons, tools, and vessels from South India, it would appear that Copper or Bronze Age cultures principally flourished in North India, in the great alluvial plains, stretching from the Arabian Sea to the Bay of Bengal. And it is traces of these that off and on turn up in the Ganges-Jumnā Doāb, the Punjab, and Sind.[35]

The raw materials—copper—for the tools could be had, as has been shown recently by Piggott, from the copper ore deposits in Rājputāna and Chotā Nāgpur, and Singhbhum in Bihār, and Orissa. The finds from several hoards, the largest of which was from Gungeria, consist of tools, weapons and ornaments, such as axes, swords, daggers, harpoons, and rings.

Excluding the solitary socketed axe-edge from the upper levels of Mohenjo-daro, all the axes so far found are "variations of the most primitive form of metal axe, called usually 'the flat axe' or 'blade axe'.' These have been grouped into five classes by Piggott[36] according as they have parallel or tapering sides, straight or rounded butt, straight or convex cutting edge and are shouldered, elongated, etc.

All the swords found in the hoards from the Ganges valley, notably from Fatehgarh, near Farrukhābād, as well as at Kallur in the Hyderābād State, are practically of one type. The hilt and blade are cast in one mould. The blade is leaf-shaped, having a slight but distinct mid-rib. The hilt has antennae.

So far there is a single example of a dagger from an unknown locality. It is of the same type as the sword. The hilt and blade are of one cast; the blade leaf-shaped and ribbed, the hilt has a common butt, with forth-jutting angle.

The harpoons provide a most interesting evolutionary series. Two or three main types are distinguished.

(*a*) The most primitive form has a rough blade with bilateral barbs, slight mid rib, a simple tang with one or more holes below the lowest pair of barbs.

(*b*) More advanced form in which the blade becomes a separate element, the barbs are placed below it, but still resemble in shape those of type *a*.

(*c*) The blade is now leaf-shaped, and the barbs curved, and twice the size of the other examples.

Besides these there are a few copper "riugs," a couple of bent tools, with a "celt-like" flat and "human-figure-like" objects, and stylized lunate axe or lance-heads.[37]

Whence and how did these copper or bronze weapons come to the Ganges valley? A definite answer cannot be given but it is suggested by Heine-Geldern[38] that the prototypes of the simple celt-like axes, as well as the various types of swords, daggers, and harpoons can be traced back, through Irān, to the Caucasus and Danube valley, where these tool types existed at least before 1200 B.C. Hence he is of the opinion that in these stray copper or bronze objects, we have traces of the migration route of the Vedic Aryans Piggott is also inclined to the same opinion, though he would ascribe the harpoons, a product of riverine culture, to a group of food-gathering tribes who, living primarily on fishing, acquired a knowledge of metal working from some centre of higher culture and transformed their characteristic hunting weapons accordingly. How this culture-contact could have taken place has been shown by Heine-Geldern, who thinks that the forepart of the most advanced harpoons of the Ganges valley may have been influenced by the javelin heads from Transcaucasia.

This culture is supposed to be posterior to that of the Indus Valley because in the latter, besides the continuance of the use of stone tools—the blades, etc., resembling larger microliths—the copper tools and weapons are of the simplest type. The harpoons and the sword are so far absent and the flat, broad-edged axe-head is obviously a copy of the Palaeolithic U-shaped cleaver and the Neolithic celt, a fact which can be demonstrated by typological studies, but not yet by stratigraphic sequence of cultures.

5. THE IRON AGE

The only evidence so far for assuming the transition from Copper and Bronze or Stone Age culture to the Iron Age has come from megalithic monuments such as dolmens, cromlechs, cairns, and menhirs. These have a very wide distribution in India.[39] They have been found almost all over South India, Karnātak, the Deccan, Central India, Central Provinces, Orissa, Bihār, Assam, Rājputāna, Gujarāt (very few), and Kāshmir. Only a few have been systematically excavated. This is enough to show that these monuments belong to different periods—from the late pre-historic to historic periods.

The Kāshmir (Burzahom) megalith is assigned to a neolithic period.[40]

The Ranchi monuments,[41] some of which are credited to the Asuras by the present-day Muṇḍas, yielded such a mixed assortment of finds as polished stone tools, carnelian beads, wheel-made pottery, copper and bronze objects, copper and gold ornaments, and even iron slags, that it is impossible to date the monuments to any one age.

The Rājputāna monuments also yielded earthen vessels with

lids, containing partially burnt human bones, skeletons in flexed position, microlith-like flakes, etc.

Monuments south of the Vindhyas, those in the Hyderābād[42] and Mysore States,[43] and in the rest of South India,[44] particularly the monuments examined by Rea at Adittanallur, in the Tāmraparni valley (Tinnevelly district), at Perumbair (Chingleput district), at Kaniyampundi (Coimbatore district) and Perungulam (Malabar), have also produced evidence of a varied stage of cultural development, which must not have been uniform even in peninsular India. Along with beautiful thin-walled red and black pottery of different types, and huge thick-walled ones, are often found microlithic flakes of agate, or crystal, carnelian beads, neolithic celts, and tools and weapons of iron and, at times, of copper or bronze.

If it is difficult in our present limited knowledge, to trace the transition from the Stone or Copper Age to the Iron Age through these megalithic monuments, it is no less difficult to understand the purpose and types of these monuments themselves. Most of these are funerary, connected with the disposal of the dead. But it has also been shown that megalithic monuments in Assam were connected with fertility rites and ancestor worship.[45] Different motives have thus contributed to the raising of these megalithic monuments, To unravel these and weave a cultural pattern out of the separate threads is the great task of Indian archaeology. But unless the monuments are studied scientifically no conclusions as to their true nature, age, and origin[46] can be formulated.[47]

---

1. Das Gupta, H. C., *Bibliography of Prehistoric Indian Antiquities*, 1931.
2. See De Terra, H., and Paterson T.T., *Studies on the Ice Age in India and the Associated Human Cultures*, 1939, pp. 301-10.
3. *Ibid.*, Pl. XXXI. A and Pl. XXXIII.
4. But the reason De Terra and Paterson assign (*op.cit.*, p. 275) viz. "The wind-borne nature of the silt, and its high percentage of lime," which is supposed to be unfavourable to the preservation of bones, does not seem to be correct. For in almost exactly similar soil, a fairly fossilized human skeleton and animal remains have been recently found in Gujarāt. Cf. *NIA*, April 1944, and *Preliminary Report of the Third Gujarāt Expedition*, Poona, 1945.
5. De Terra and Paterson, *op.cit.*, Pl. XXXIX-XLII.
6. *Ibid.*, Pl. XLII.
7. *Ibid.*, Pl. XLIII.
8. Brown, J. Coggin, *Catalogue of Prehistoric Antiquities in the Indian Museum at Calcutta*, 1917.
9. Sankalia, H.D., *Investigations into Prehistoric Archaeology at Gujarāt*, Śrī Pratāpsiṁha Mahārāja Rājyābhisheka Granthamālā, Memoir No. IV, Baroda, 1946.
10. *Ibid.*, Pl. XII.
11. De Terra, *op. cit.*, p. 314. Full details of every layer are not given:
12. Brown, *op.cit.*
13. *Ibid.*, and Foote, *Notes on Ages and Distribution*, 1916.
14. According to the brief summary given by Chattopadhyay, K.P., in *JRASB(L)*, X., pp. 97-8.
15. *BDCRI*, IV. 1-16.
16. *JRAI*, LXIX, pp. 257-72, Pl. XIV.
17. For this and the succeeding paragraphs see Foote, *Notes on Ages and Distribution*, 1916.
18. Cammiade and Burkitt, *Antiquity*, 1930, pp. 327-39.

19. Krishnaswami, V. D., *Prehistoric Man Around Madras* (Indian Academy of Sciences, Madras, 1938).
20. De Terra and Paterson, *op.cit.*, pp. 327-33.
21. See Aiyappan, Manley Collection of Stone Age Tools, *MASI*, No. 68 (1942).
22. For a provisional correlation of the Lower Palaeolithic Cultures all over the world, see Paterson, "Geology and Early Man," *Nature*, 1940, pp. 12, 49, 51.
23. Foote, *op.cit.*
24. Gordon, *JRASBL*, VII, p. 129.
25. De Terra, *op.cit.*, p. 277.
26. Krishna, M.H., *Mysore Archaeological Survey Reports*, 1942, pp. 100-9.
27. Hunter, *Nagpur University Journal*, No. 1, p. 31 and No. 2, p. 127.
28. De Terra, *op.cit.*, pp. 277-8.
29. Gordon, *Art and Letters*, 1936, pp. 35-41.
30. Saṇkalia, *op.cit.*, pp. 64-100, and Sankalia and Karve, *NIA*, VII, 1-6, and *Preliminary Report of the Third Gujarāt Prehistoric Expedition*, Poona, 1945.
31. Sankalia and Karve, *Report of the Third Gujarāt Prehistoric Expedition*, Poona, 1945.
32. De Terra and Paterson, *op.cit.*, pp. 233-4 and Pl. XXIV.
33. The two main works are Brown's *Catalogue*, and Foote's *Notes on Ages, etc.*, and *Catalogue Raisonne*, and *Catalogue Madras Museum*; see also Das Gupta, *Bibliography*, which deals with finds made up to 1930-31. For later notices see annual Reports of the Mysore and Hyderābād Archaeological Departments.
34. Cf. *CHI*, I, 613-4.
35. These notices were first collected and commented by Smith in *IA*, XXXIV, 229 ff. and XXXVI 53 ff.; Brown used these in his *Catalogue* (1917); brought up to date by Das Gupta, *Bibliography* (1931); reclassified by G. N. Mukherjee in *IHQ*, Vol. XI, p. 522; and some items commented by Heine-Geldern (*JISOA*, IV, 87-115) and Piggott ("Prehistoric Copper Hoards in the Ganges Basin," *Antiquity*, 72, December, 1944).
36. Piggott, *op.cit.*
37. Smith, *op.cit.*; *POC*, IV, 1928, pp. 729-34.
38. Heine-Geldern, *op.cit.*
39. Das Gupta, *op.cit.*, for notices up to 1930-31. Later notices are mostly in the Reports of the Mysore (1932 and 1940, 1941, 1942, 1943) and Hyderābād Archaeological Departments (1937-40), *ASI*, and *BDCRI*.
40. De Terra, *op.cit.*, pp. 233-4, Pl. XXIV; and Kak, Ram Chandra, *Ancient Monuments of Kashmir*, p. 111, Pl. XLIII; cf. also *The Progress of Science in India during the Past Twenty-Five Years*, 1938, pp. 309-13.
41. Roy, S.C., *JBORS*, I, 229-53, II, 61-77.
42. Hunt, *JRAI*, LIV, p. 140 ff.
43. *Mysore Arch. Rep.*, *op.cit.* (See note 35 above).
44. Rea, *ASI*, 1902-03; 1904-05, p. 41; 1908-09, p. 92; *ASI* Southern Circle, 1910-11, p. 12, 1913-14, p. 43 and 1914-15, p. 39. *Catalogue of Prehistoric Antiquities from Adichanallur and Perumbair*, 1915, and Richards, *JRAI*, LIV, p. 157 ff.
45. Hutton, *JRAI*, LII, 55 ff. and 242 ff. and LVI, 71.
46. For a tentative classification of megalithic—mostly funerary—monuments, known up to 1923, see Ghurye, *MIA*, VI, 26-57; 100-39; Aiyappan's recent summary in *Proceedings of the Science Congress*, 1945, Presidential Addresses, is useful.
47. The writer is indebted to Rao Bahadur K. N. Dikshit, the Director General of Archaeology in India for having gone through the chapter and making a number of suggestions.

CHAPTER VIII

RACE MOVEMENTS AND PREHISTORIC CULTURE

It is strange (and somewhat difficult of explanation) that skeletal remains of Early Man in India, particularly in the prehistoric and early historical times, should be so scanty. This lack of material has not allowed us to postulate with certainty about racial movements in ancient times, and any appraisement or reconstruction of movements of peoples in India, some four or three or even two thousand years ago, is bound to remain largely hypothetical, and based on or inferred from the present-day situation only. Race is not, of course, synonymous with language; but when a language was becoming characterized as a distinct type in a particular area and among a particular people in prehistoric times, it formed an important cultural expression of that people, and as such a connexion between the two is justified, always bearing in mind the great fact that language is after all but a secondary expression of culture and that it is largely transmissible from people to people.

Racial anthropology, dealing with the physical features of a people, has sought to analyse the various elements which have contributed to build up the population of India, irrespective of what cultural ethnology has to say about languages and cultures. Various views were advanced by diverse anthropologists about the racial elements in the population of India. Until recently, the view that occupied a position of prestige as a sort of official pronouncement on behalf of the Government of India was that put forward by the late Sir Herbert Risley.[1]

This view, adopted in official publications and accepted very largely both in India and outside India without any questioning, divided the people of India, quite arbitrarily, with both insufficient data and immature science (not wholly free, it might also be suspected, from political bias), into seven broad groups, labelled as Mongoloid, Indo-Aryan, Dravidian, Mongolo-Dravidian, Aryo-Dravidian, Scytho-Dravidian, and Turko-Iranian. An Indian anthropologist like the late Rama Prasad Chanda made a more systematized essay based on both anthropometric data and early tradition as preserved in ancient Indian literature towards a determination of the various racial elements in India.[2]

The next advance in this direction was made in 1933 by Dr. J. H. Hutton[3] when a statement as to the race-cum-language-and-culture sequence in India was proposed which took note of the advance made in anthropology and ethnology since 1900. According to this view, we have the advent of the following peoples in India from the outside (no kind of man originated on the soil of India, all her human inhabitants having arrived originally from other lands, but developing within India some of their salient characteristics and then passing on outside India), their names being given in an approximate order of their arrival:

(1) Negritos, brachycephalic Negroids from Africa, the oldest people to have come to India, now surviving in the Andaman Islands (where they have retained their language) and in Malaya; and traces of them seem to occur among the Nāgās in Assam and among certain tribes in South India.

(2) "Proto-Australoids," black, dolichocephalic, platyrrhine, apparently an early offshoot of the Mediterranean race, who came from the east Mediterranean area (Palestine). The Melanesians appear to be in their racial basis of this early Mediterranean Proto-Australoid origin, with modifications from other races both inside and outside India.

(3) Early Mediterraneans, leptorrhine dolichocephals, who brought earlier forms of the Austric speech.

(4) Civilized or Advanced Mediterranean, leptorrhine dolichocephals, who became the "Dravidians" in India.

(5) Armenoids—'a specialized off-shoot from the standard Alpine stock"—brachycephalic—probably came with the Civilized Mediterraneans ("Dravidians") and spoke their language.

(6) Alpines—brachycephalic, leptorrhine: found in Gujarāt and Bengal; earlier than Vedic Aryans, but probably speaking Aryan dialects.

(7) Vedic Aryans, or Nordics, leptorrhine dolichocephals who brought the Vedic Aryan (Sanskrit) speech.

(8) Mongoloids, brachycephals: not important for the greater part of India, as they touched only the northern and eastern fringes.

Finally, the most recent and authoritative view has been put forward by Dr. B. S. Guha, Director of the Anthropological Survey of India.[4] In his newest work,[5] giving a useful résumé of the whole question, Dr. Guha has signalized "six main races with nine sub-types," as follows:

1. The Negrito.
2. The Proto-Australoid.
3. The Mongoloid, consisting of:
   - (i) Palaeo-Mongoloids of (a) long-headed and (b) broad-headed types.
   - (ii) Tibeto-Mongoloids.
4. The Mediterranean, comprising:
   - (i) Palaeo-Mediterranean,

(ii) Mediterranean, and
(iii) the so-called Oriental type.

5. The Western Brachycephals, consisting of:
(i) The Alpinoid,
(ii) The Dinaric, and
(iii) The Armenoid.

6. The Nordic.

Of the above races, (1) the Negrito is all but extinct on the soil of India. A small group of Negritos is still surviving in the Andamans, and traces of the Negrito race have been found among the Kadars and Palayans of Cochin and the Travancore Hills, the Irulas of the Wynad, the Angami Nāgās of Assam and some of the Rājmahāl Hill tribes in Eastern Bihār. The Negritos appear to have been suppressed and absorbed by other races which followed them, particularly the Proto-Australoids (2).

(2) The Proto-Australoids appear to have come from the West, and have become characterized in India. They survive in a good many aboriginal peoples of present-day India, although more or less mingled with other peoples. A branch of the Proto-Australoids passed on to Australia in very ancient times, and the "Austronesian" peoples (Indonesians, Melanesians and Polynesians) have a good deal of the Proto-Australoid element in them. Throughout the greater part of India the Proto-Australoid peoples still live as the lower castes or sections of the Indian people.

(3) Of the various (3) Mongoloid groups, (1) the Palaeo-Mongoloids, sub-divided into two types, (i) (a) with a peculiar head-form resembling dolichocephal, occurring "as the more ancient stratum of the population" and forming "a dominant element in the tribes living in Assam and the Indo-Burmese frontiers" and (i)(b) with round heads, found among the less primitive tribes in Burma and in the Chittagong Hills, appear to represent a less developed group of this race. The (ii) Tibeto-Mongoloids are a more pronounced and advanced Mongoloid type, and they are found in Sikkim and Bhutan, and "must have infiltrated from Tibet in comparatively later times."

(4) The Mediterranean peoples also represent several strains or types, all long-headed. We have in the first instance (i) the Palaeo-Mediterranean type, medium-statured dark-skinned and of slight build: this is found largely in the Kannada, Tamil and Malayalam tracts. (ii) The true Mediterranean or European type, taller and fairer than the Palaeo-Mediterraneans, occurs in the Punjab and Upper Gangetic Valley, and is supposed to represent the civilized pre-Aryan "Dravidian" people of Northern India which became Aryanized in language and contributed largely to the evolution of the Hindu people and culture of North India. (iii) The

third Mediterranean strain, the so-called "Oriental" one, commonly miscalled the Semitic or Jewish, with a pronouncedly longish nose and fair in skin, is found in the Punjab, in Sind, in Rājputana and in Western U.P., and it occurs also not unusually enough in other parts of India.

The various (5) Brachycephal groups really form sub-groups of one single physical type, and they appear (or at least their prototype appears) to have evolved in the Central Asian mountain regions. Brachycephalic peoples, both Alpine and Dinaric, appear to have spread over the greater part of India, the Dinaric type being well-marked in Bengal and Orissa, in Kāthiāwār, and in the Kannada and Tamil countries; and in Coorg it occurs in its purest form. In Gujarāt the Alpinoid brachycephals show a greater predominance. Broad-head elements are found along the West Coast of India, excepting in Malabar; they are not found in the Telugu country. Early brachycephalic groups also established themselves in or passed through the Ganges Valley, as far as the delta, leaving traces or drifts in Central India, Eastern U.P. and Bihār; another line of migration is found along the Himālayas, from Chitral and Gilgit to Western Nepāl. The Parsis of Bombay are a lately arrived brachycephalic group allied to the Armenoids—they present a contrast to the long-headed Iranian Zoroastrians (Gabrs or Guebres) still living in Persia.

Finally, we have the (6) Nordic Aryan-speaking group of India, who gave to India its Aryan speech, and by their organization, imagination and adaptability helped to bring about a great cultural synthesis leading to the foundation of the Hindu civilization of India. These Nordics seem to have been characterised in the Eurasian steppe lands and they entered India some time during the second half of the second millennium B.C.[3] Nordic elements are strong in parts of the North-West Frontier of India, particularly along the upper reaches of the Indus and along its tributaries the Swāt, the Panjkora, the Kunar and the Chitral rivers, and in the south of the Hindu Kush range. In the Punjab and Rājputāna and in the Upper Ganges Valley Nordic elements are present (although more and more mixed with other racial elements as we proceed further to the east), particularly among the higher castes or groups; among certain sections elsewhere in India, the Nordic type predominates, e.g. among the Chitpāvan Brāhmans of the Marāṭhā country. The original Nordic type is supposed to have been tall, fair-skinned, yellow or golden-haired and blue-eyed: such a type seems (from such meagre literary evidence as is available) to have characterized the true Aryans of ancient times, but owing to miscegenation and to climatic conditions the complexion of the body and the colour of the hair and the eye have been modified or eliminated by natural selection to light brown or brown and to black (for the hair and the eyes), although light-eyed people are not uncommon among the Nordic long-heads in India, scattered as they are all over the country.

Dr. B. S. Guha has thus summed up the racial distribution for India as a whole: "It must be clearly understood that no rigid separation is possible as there is considerable overlapping of types. From a broad point of view, however, a Nordic territory in north-western India, mixed with Mediterraneans and Orientals, can be distinguished from a territory in Peninsular India containing the older Palaeo-Mediterranean element. On both sides of this are the domains of the Alpo-Dinarics, mixed no doubt with other types. The primitive darker elements have come in everywhere and, with blood from other strains, chiefly Palaeo-Mediterranean, they constitute the lower stratum of the population. The Mongoloids occupy the submontane regions of the north and the east, but various thrusts from them have gone deeply into the composition of the people."[7]

It has not yet been established that a particular racial type, by the mere fact of some pronounced or subdued racial characteristic which it possesses, must necessarily or inevitably have its mental and emotional outlook or attitude pre-decided. In other words, it cannot be asserted that there must be an ineradicable racial character. But on the other hand the economic *milieu*, and the special training which the mind and the emotions receive in an organized or corporate body of men, create a framework of civilization or ordered life which commonly finds an expression in the language of that body of men: and hence we are more justified in speaking of *language cultures* than of *racial cultures;* and we must also consider that from the beginning of recorded history racial inter-mixture has proceeded apace, leading to a profound modification of any special race-type in its most ancient and pristine form. The six different main types of humanity, with their various ramifications, as discussed above, which have gone to make the people of India, are now included within one or the other of four distinct speech-families: viz., the Austric (Kol or Muṇḍā), the Tibeto-Chinese or Sino-Tibetan, the Dravidian, and the Indo-European (Aryan). Even in some cases the economic *milieu* transcends the diversity of language and language-culture, and tones down very largely, within a given economic area, the more aggressively prominent or more easily noticeable special cultural traits that go with language —religion, social usage, customs, etc. Thus in Chotā Nāgpur, in spite of diversity of language the Dravidian-speaking Oraons and the Austric (Kol)-speaking Muṇḍās are within the fold of a common culture; and in Central Europe, the Indo-European-speaking Germans and Slavs, in spite of their pronounced linguistic diversity although within the same family, and the entirely distinct Finno-

Ugrian-speaking Magyars, share a common type of economic and cultural life. The same observation can be made about the Indo-European-speaking Armenians and Ossetes, the Ural-Altaic-speaking Azarbijanis and the Caucasic Georgians and others in the Caucasus regions.

So, too, for India as a whole, a more or less common type of economic life based on agriculture and taking shape within the limits of India forming a single geographical unit, combined with a large-scale commingling of different races building up a common history, has been responsible for the gradual modification of what doubtless existed in most ancient times as distinct racial types and distinctive language-cultures, and has led to the evolution, as a result of a more or less conscious movement, of a common Indian type and a common Indian culture. In this culture of India, after at least two and a half millennia of close interaction, the original genetic differences in the four language-families obtaining in India from prehistoric times have largely converged towards the evolution of a number of common traits.

It will not be possible at the present moment to make a definite pronouncement about the mental and spiritual environment of the various types of man in their primitive stage when they came into India, although, through a close study of the question, taking all help from anthropology, religiology, linguistics, sociology, prehistoric archaeology, and other human sciences we may make some near enough guesses about their material culture and the contributions they made to the common store-house of Indian life and Indian civilization, both in the material and the mental and emotional sides. In this way we can bring to light the basis on which Indian civilization rests in all its aspects, material, mental, and spiritual, and its genesis will enable us properly to appreciate and understand its subsequent evolution and transformation.

We have to begin with the Negroid or Negrito people of prehistoric India, who were its first human inhabitants. At the present day the Negritos have practically vanished from the soil of India. Originally they would appear to have come from Africa through Arabia and the coast-lands of Irān and Baluchistān. They were in the eolithic stage of culture, and they appear to have been food-gatherers rather than food-producers. In India, the Negritos would appear to have been either killed off by the later immigrants, more advanced than themselves, notably the Proto-Australoids, or absorbed by them. They survive in a few primitive tribes in South India, and traces of the Negrito have been found in the Nāgās of Assam. Beyond India, they passed on to Malaya, where Negrito tribes still survive, and even further into the distant islands of Indonesia, like the Philippines, and into New Guinea. Within the

Indian domain, they are found in a few hundred Andamanese in the Andaman Islands, where they have still kept up their own language. Their settlement in the Andamans shows a certain advance in culture, as they must have crossed the sea in their small dugouts, which testifies to their skill as well as courage and imagination; and they came to be acquainted with the bow and arrow, and the blow-pipe, probably from the Proto-Australoids, unless they invented these themselves. Except in the case of the Andamanese, the Negritos who survive in India and Further India (including Malaya) at the present day speak everywhere debased dialects of their more civilized neighbours. The original Negrito speech of India, whatever it was, seemingly survives in Andamanese, which as a language or dialect group stands isolated. Owing to their very primitive state, the Negritos do not appear to have contributed anything of importance to the civilization of India.

Negrito elements or traits, judging from some racial types depicted in the art of Gupta and post-Gupta India (as in Gupta sculpture and in the Ajaṇṭa frescoes), seem to have survived to a very late period; but now they have been almost wholly eliminated. It has been suggested[8] that the cult of the _ficus_ tree, associated with fertility and with the souls of the dead, and some ideas about the Path of the Dead to Paradise guarded by an avenging demon, which are widespread in Southern Europe, Africa, and Oceania, and partly also India, might well have come from the Negrito people.

Situated as they were, the Negritos were not in a position to influence the languages which came to India subsequently. At least two other linguistic strata covered up Negrito speech—the Austric and the Dravidian, before the Aryan language arrived, so nothing from Negrito speech had much chance of coming into Aryan. But it may be that here and there a word indicative of some object, some element from the flora or the fauna of India, has survived, although in a much altered form, being passed on from the Negrito language through the Proto-Australoid or Dravidian dialects to Indo-Aryan. One such word may be the Bengali and Oriya _bāduḍ_, _bādaḍi_ = "bat": the basic element would seem to be _*bād_, which was extended by the addition of the pleonastic affix—_aḍa_—plus the feminine and diminutive affix-ī from Old Indo-Aryan _ikā;_ and with this _*bād_, otherwise unexplained, may be compared Andamanese _wót-da, wāt-da, wòt, wät_="bat" and the element _pet, wet, met, wed, wät_, in some of the aboriginal languages of Malaya and Indo-China belonging to the Austro-Asiatic branch of the Austric family (some of which are spoken by the Negrito tribes of Malaya); e.g. _tra-pet, sa-pet, ham-pet, sa-met, hamet, ka-wet, ka-wed, gan-ät-, kat_ < _*ka-wat, kawa_ < _*ka-wat, uôt._

The Proto-Australoids, who appear to have come after the Negritos, and that, too, from the West, have furnished one of the basic elements in the population of India. There were, as it would appear, numerous lines of migration of this race from the west and east through India, and the Proto-Australoid type was modified both within and beyond by admixture with other peoples, notably the Negritos and the Mongoloids; and as a result, we have, it would seem, the Kol or Muṇḍā type in India, the Mon-Khmer type in Assam, Burma, and Indo-China, the Nicobarese in the Nicobar Islands, and the Indonesian Melanesian, and Polynesian types in the islands of the Indian Archipelago and those of Melanesia and Polynesia. All these congeries of mixed peoples extending from the extreme north-west of India, throughout the whole of India, Burma, Indo-China and Malay Peninsula into the islands of the Indian Archipelago (Indonesia) and those of Melanesia, Micronesia, and Polynesia—in a word, from Kāshmir to Easter Island—have a Proto-Australoid element; and the languages they speak have been found to possess common traits which warrant their inclusion within a single speech family. The researches of Pater W. Schmidt have established the *Austric Family* of *Languages*, which is found to have two main ramifications—(i) the *Austronesian*, under which come the closely agreeing Indonesian, Melanesian, Micronesian, and Polynesian languages, and (ii) the *Austro-Asiatic*, which embraces the Kol or Muṇḍā speeches of India, Nicobarese, and the Mon-Khmer speeches of India (Assam), Burma, and Indo-China.

As things stand, the original Austric speech, which took different forms under diverse conditions within this vast area over which it spread, would appear to have been brought from the west by the Proto-Australoids; and in its original form (as the ultimate source of both the Austro-Asiatic and Austronesian branches) it could very well have been characterized within India. Outside India, the Proto-Australoids passed on to Australia, where their language and culture took a definite form which was quite isolated and distinct from that of the Austro-Asiatic and Austronesian peoples.

After the Melanesian and Polynesian types in ethnology and language came to be established, it would appear that there were back-washes of immigrations of Melanesians and Polynesians into India, which brought in certain new cultural contributions from these peoples; and these Melanesian and Polynesian immigrants would appear to have now become totally assimilated into the mass of the Indian population. From the Melanesians, the custom of disposal of the dead by exposure, communal houses, head-hunting and a canoe cult appear to have been introduced into India. The introduction of the outrigger canoe and of the coconut into India may have been due to the Polynesians.

The Proto-Australoid's contribution to the primitive culture of India, it has been thought, included the following matters: pottery, which would appear to have been unknown to the Negritos; neolithic development of the palaeolithic culture of the country; the use of the boomerang and of the blowing-gun; and ideas of totemism in religion. Hoe and digging-stick cultivation, followed at least in some parts of the country by terrace cultivation of rice, may have originated on the soil of India in the hands of the Proto-Australoids; and this would appear to have been advanced largely in the extra-Indian lands of south-eastern Asia.

The bases of Proto-Australoid culture—assuming that the language of the Proto-Australoids was the primitive source-speech from which the current Austro-Asiatic and Austronesian languages have descended—can to a certain extent (apart from some prehistoric implements and artifacts[9] which can be ascribed to the Proto-Australoids) be reconstructed through linguistic palaeontology, along lines which have proved to be so successful in the case of the primitive Indo-European cultural *milieu*. Renward Brandstetter has, in his brilliant papers on Indonesian, essayed to reconstruct not only the primitive Indonesian speech (which comes within the Austronesian branch of Austric) but also the natural and mental background of the speakers of Primitive Indonesian.[10] For Austric (if not for Austric as a whole, at least for the Austric speech world of India) a new line of investigation has been started by Jean Przyluski, with full approval and support of Sylvain Levi, Jules Bloch, and others.[11]

In studying certain non-Aryan elements in the Indo-Aryan speech in its different periods—non-Aryan elements which are not Dravidian—Przyluski found out that these belonged to the Austro-Asiatic speeches as they were current in India. At the present day, Austro-Asiatic dialects belonging to the Kol or Muṇḍā group only are spoken on the soil of India, and only one speech of the Mon-Khmer group is current in Assam, viz. Khāsi, while other Mon-Khmer speeches are found in Burma and Indo-China. But from a study of the Austric words found in Indo-Aryan it would appear that dialects allied to both Kol and Mon-Khmer were current in India during the oldest period of contact between Indo-Aryan and Austric, and possibly also speeches more closely connected with Austronesian (Indonesian specially) within the Austric family. However, from these non-Aryan (and non-Dravidian) loans which are from Austric, we can make some guesses as to the nature of the culture-world which the Austric-speaking or Proto-Australoid peoples presented vis-à-vis the Aryan-speaking invaders from the West.

The words from Austric borrowed by Indo-Aryan refer in the first instance to items in the special flora and fauna of India not known to the Aryan-speakers; naturally enough, then, they also refer to culture plants known to the Austric-speakers, and to some of their culture objects and ideas. Thus, the Aryans came into Irān (and possibly also into India) with a knowledge of barley and wheat among cereals: their word for "barley," *yava* in Sanskrit, is of Indo-European origin (= Greek *zea*, I-E **yewa-*), and that for "wheat" (Sanskrit *godhūma*, Persian *gandum* < Iranian **gandhūma*) is of unknown origin. For "rice," the oldest word in Indo-Aryan is *vrīhi*, which has Iranian affinities (e.g. Persian *birinj*, *gurinj*, Old Iranian **vərnəĵa*, Paṣto *wrīže*, whence Greek *oruza*, *briza*) and which may be connected with the Dravidian (Tamil) *arichi* <**arki*, *argi*. But in the New Indo-Aryan languages the common word for "rice" is *chāwal*, *chāwal*, *chāul*, and this would appear to be based on a Middle Indo-Aryan *chāmala* (cf. the Old and Middle Indo-Aryan forms *chāma*, *ā-chāma*) meaning "rice" as well as "food," and this *chāma-la*, in its original sense of "food," might be very well connected with Kol or Muṇḍā root *jom*, "to eat."[12]

Certain common fruits and vegetables may similarly be presumed to have been cultivated by the Austric speakers, as their Sanskrit and other Aryan names are of Austric origin: the banana (Sanskrit *kadalī*, *kandalī*), coconut (*nārīkela*), betel (*tāmbūla*), the brinjal or egg-plant (*vātiṅgaṇa*), the pumpkin (*alābu*), the lime (*nimbuka*), the rose-apple (*jambu*), etc., and also cotton (*karpāsa*, *karpaṭa*) and silk-cotton (*śālmalī*, *śimbalī*). The domestic fowl (*kṛikavāka*, **kurkuṭa* > *kukkuṭa*), the peacock (*mrok* as an expletive in the Atharva-Veda, compare Kol *marak'* "peacock," beside Dravidian *mayil* as in Tamil), the elephant (*mātaṅga*, *gaja*), and some breed of horse or pony (**sāda*, as in Sanskrit *sādin*—"rider") appear to have been known to the pre-Aryan peoples of India speaking Austric. The Austric speakers supplied to Indo-Aryan its common word for "arrow" (*bāṇa*), and for "stick" and "phallus" or "the phallus symbol," both from a word meaning originally "stick," and then "digging-stick for ploughing" (*lakuṭa*, *laguḍa*, *liṅga*: *laũḍā* in NIA—Bihari), and these show two noteworthy aspects of the cultural life of the Austric speakers which had their repercussion on that of the Aryan speakers.[13]

Some of the fundamental bases of Indian civilization on the material side would thus appear to be the gifts of the Austric-speaking Proto-Australoid people: the cultivation of rice, the raising of some important vegetables, the manufacture of sugar from the cane, and the use of the betel vine in life and in ritual; the habit of counting on the basis of twenty (Bengali *kuḍi*, Hindi *koḍī*), and probably also the use of turmeric and vermilion in religious ritual and social life (e.g. in marriage), combined with some notions of future life (survival of the soul after death, and the germs of the idea of transmigration) and some mythological and religious as well as romantic notions and stories appear to have come from the same source. Weaving of cotton cloth was also an Austric or Proto-Australoid invention; and probably the Proto-Australoids were the first people to domesticate and train the elephant.

Certain magico-religious rituals, e.g. the removal of the evil eye by the rite known in Northern India as *nichhāwar* or *baraṇ*, which have a strong place in Hindu society, would seem to be of Austric origin. The idea of taboo would seem to be another trait derived from the mentality of the Proto-Australoids (or Austric speakers) in prehistoric times, when *Ārya* and *Nishāda*—the Aryan and the dark-skinned Austric dwellers in the forests—first met in the Punjab: Sylvain Lévi has drawn our attention to the fact that the Atharva-Veda word *tābuva* was connected with the Polynesian word *tapu* or *tabu* by A. Weber in 1876 and by Barth later on; and it is likely that the word passed on with the Proto-Australoid immigrants into Austronesia, the distant Polynesian islands, while in India it was borrowed in the Atharvaveda. Cosmic and creational myths and ideas as they had originated among the pre-Aryan Austric-speaking peoples of India were adopted into the cosmopolitan or composite Aryan-non-Aryan or Hindu religion and legend, while these made their steady way into the oceanic regions of the Pacific through the islands of Indonesia with the expanding Proto-Australoids. Certain remarkable agreements between the cosmogony of the Polynesians and that of the *Nāsadiya* hymn of the Ṛigveda (X. 129) have to be taken note of in this connexion. The enumeration of the days by the phases of the moon—the *tithis*—which was early adopted by the Hindu people probably simultaneously with its formation and has still been retained in the sacred or religious (ritualistic) calendar of the Hindus, is again an Austric custom which survived in Polynesia: even the old Austric names for two of the phases of the moon, which are still found in the Polynesian group of Austronesian, were adopted in India by Sanskrit (*rākā*="full moon," and *kuhu*="new moon").[14] It has also been suggested that the Sanskrit name of at least one constellation is of Austric origin, viz. *mātṛikā*="the Pleiades," the present-day Polynesian form of which is *matariki*.

The culture-world of India has thus among its material and other ideological bases some fundamental things derived from the Austric speakers, assuming that they were also, in their pure state, Proto-Australoid in race, which became fully characterized on the soil of India. That would be only natural, as this racial element forms one of the most important in the present-day Indian people, as anthropologists tell us, the masses or the lower classes throughout the greater part of India being largely of this stock. The bedrock of Indian civilization is agriculture, and that, in all likelihood in connexion with the cultivation of rice, goes back to the Austric Proto-Australoids of India. The germs of the idea of transmigration which has been so potent a force in Indian thought, religion and life, would probably go back to this source: also some of the fundamental cults and rituals.

In the domain of myth and legend, a number of Austric notions and tales appear to have survived in the myths of the Purāṇas and of the popular Hinduism. The legends of the creation of the world from an egg or eggs, of the *Avatāras* or incarnations of Vishṇu, e.g. that of the tortoise incarnation, of the princess smelling of fish (*matsya-gandhā*), of the Nāgas as serpent spirits of the waters and the underworld, and many more, which do not form part of the Aryan or Indo-European inheritance in Hinduism, and do not seem to have come from the Dravidian world either, can reasonably be expected to have been derived from the Austric or Proto-Australoid world.

All these have been more or less distorted or transformed in the Sanskrit Purāṇas, in the traditions surviving among the Austric-speaking tribes of the present day, or in popular Hindu folklore of today. The use of a rude block of stone as a symbol of the divinity is also Austric—it may also have been Dravidian in addition. Some fairy or folk tales would also go back to the same source. Zoomorphic deities appear also to be survivals from Austric or Proto-Australoid totemism which also was reinforced by the Dravidian cults possessing a similar character (e.g. the *Nāgas* or snake deities, the tortoise, the *makara* or crocodile, the monkey god, Gaṇeśa with his elephant's head, etc.).

It would be too much to try to appraise the stamp of the original Proto-Australoid character upon that of our masses of the present day, but from the character of the present-day Kol or Muṇḍā peoples of Eastern India, and of the peoples like the Oraons whose cultural *milieu* is that of the Kols although they are Dravidian-speakers, we may be allowed to formulate this Austric inheritance. The Austric temperament was pre-eminently gregarious; it was superstitious and to some extent timid, though not cowardly in face of dangers it could understand. Cheerfulness and love of simple music and gaiety came naturally to the Austric temper even in the midst of hard labour: and it was not over-sensitive to physical discomfort. There was a touch of erotic abandon in it, but along with that there was a great respect for convention which put the rein on licence. As a sympathetic student of the aborigines of Chotā Nāgpur, W. G. Archer, has said of the Oraons, who live within the same economic and cultural atmosphere as the Muṇḍās, Santāls, Hos, and other agricultural Kol tribes: "A few notes should be added on Oraon 'character.' To the earliest observers a capacity for cheerful hard work was the most notable character of Oraons; and a sturdy gaiety, an exultation in bodily physique and a sense of fun are still their most obvious qualities. These are linked to a fundamental simplicity—a tendency to see an emotion as an action, and not to complicate it by postponement or cogitation... The final picture is of a kindly simplicity and a smiling energy."[15]

In discussing the Austric or Austro-Asiatic speakers of India and their contribution to the make-up of the Indian people, mention should also be made of the theory of the Hungarian scholar William Hevesy (Hevesy Vilmos, Wilhelm von Hevesy, Guillaume de Hevesy), recently put forward in some books and papers in German and French, combating Pater W. Schmidt's theory of an Austric family of languages divided into two groups, Austronesian and Austro-Asiatic (the latter including the Kol or Muṇḍā languages of India).[16] Hevesy has challenged Pater Schmidt's view that the Muṇḍā or Kol peoples speak dialects which are members of the Austro-Asiatic branch of Austric: he denies the existence of an Austric speech family, and he proposes quite a different affinity for the Kol or Muṇḍā languages, viz., Finno-Ugrian. Hevesy's views were put forward for the first time in 1930, but so far they have met with neither any general or wide acceptance nor a thorough or systematic refutation. According to Hevesy, Muṇḍā or Kol belongs to the Finno-Ugrian speech-group, under which come Magyar or Hungarian, Finn in its various dialects, Esth of Esthonia, Lapp of Lapland, and Vogul, Ostyak, Zyrian, Votyak, Cheremis, Mordvin and Samoyed of Russia and Siberia. Hevesy believes that there was a prehistoric invasion of or immigration into India by Finno-Ugrian or Ugrian tribes from the Eurasian plains to the south of the Ural Mountains, and the Muṇḍās or Kols with their language resulted from a mixture of these Ugrians with the earlier peoples of the country, the Negritos and the Proto-Australoids. Hevesy bases his view on certain points of agreement between the Kol speeches on the one hand and the Finno-Ugrian speeches on the other—points of agreement which have not been admitted by any competent linguistician who is equally at home in Kol and in Finno-Ugrian (and such a person would be exceedingly rare to find). The points of cultural similarity between the Kols and the Finno-Ugrians as proposed by Hevesy are not convincing. There might have been an Ugrian influx into India, in very ancient times, but there is nothing positive to establish it.

The Austric linguistic zone has been conjecturally extended further to the west of India by Jean Przyluski and others, who see in the Sumerian speech of Chaldea a language allied to primitive Austric. Przyluski has even seen an Austric substratum in Indo-Iranian: certain words like Sanskrit *vāla* = Persian *bāl* "hair," Sanskrit *bhishaj*=Avestan *bisaz* "doctor." "healing," as connected with Sanskrit *visha* "poison," etc.. Przyluski explains as being from the Austric, which would appear to have influenced Irānian also.[16a] But this, too, cannot be described as satisfactorily established. We may admit the possibility of Sumerian and Austric being related, for we have to remember that the Proto-Australoids, who are supposed to have been the original speakers of Austric, were a very ancient offshoot of the Mediterranean race, and as such in their trek to India where they became specially characterized they may have left some of their tribes on the way, or some of their kinsmen might earlier have preceded them and had established themselves in Mesopotamia, to become the Sumerians who built up the basic culture of that part of the world. But even then it seems that India was the centre from which the Austric speech spread into the lands and islands of the east and the Pacific; and the theory that there is actually an Austric Family of Languages in its two groups of Austronesian and Austro-Asiatic, as propounded by Pater W. Schmidt, may be said to hold the ground still.

The Austric Proto-Australoids were spread over the greater part of India. In the Indus and Ganges valleys, when the Aryans first met them, they were known as *Nishādas*, and their dark skin and snub noses were held in ridicule by the fair and straight-nosed Aryans. The masses of agricultural Austrics in the North Indian plains from Afghānistān to Eastern Bihār gradually became Aryan-speaking, roughly between *c.* 1500 B.C. (about when the first Aryan invasion or land immigration into India took place) to *c.* 600 B.C., a little before the time of the Buddha: but even in the time of the Buddha, pockets, large or small, of non-Aryan (Austric and Dravidian) speakers still remained throughout this tract. We find, for example, in the Buddhist *Jātakas*, mention of Chaṇḍāla villages where they still employed the Chaṇḍāla tongue, a supposed word from which is given—*giligili*—in the *Chitta-sambhūta Jātaka.* Through the contact of Aryan and Austric, and through large masses of Austric speakers abandoning their native speech, the Aryan speech came to be affected, in phonetics, in vocabulary, in morphology and in syntax. The question of vocabulary, as said before, has been taken up for study, and beginning with the pioneer researches of Jean Przyluski in this field, we are gradually being enabled to find to what extent Austric vocables have found a place in Indo-Aryan in its three stages of Old, Middle, and New Indo-Aryan. Place-names in North India (and undoubtedly also in the Deccan and South India) show Austric elements, thus indicating the presence of Austric speakers in the localities with these names. A name like *Gaṅgā* is in all likelihood of Austric origin, and it appears to have meant just "a river" as in its modern Bengali equivalent *gāng* = "river, channel." Original Austric speakers form a substratum in Burma, Indo-China and South China also, and the Indian *Gaṅgā, gāṅg,* the Indo-Chinese *Khong* as in *Me-khong,* and the South-Chinese *Kiang* < **Kang* < **Ghang* (as in *Yang-tszě-Kiang* and a dozen other river names)—all of these can very well be from the same old Austric word, now lost to most of the Austric tongues.

We may next take into consideration the cultural world of the Dravidian speakers with special reference to its contribution to the formation of the ancient Hindu world. Anthropologists, as noted before, assume at least three varieties or modifications of the Mediterranean race as having come to India, and all of these would appear to have been speakers of Dravidian, at least in India—the Palaeo-Mediterraneans, the Mediterraneans proper, and the so-called "Orientals." They were all long-headed, and they came to India with a fairly high level of civilization. As contrasted with the Proto-Australoids or Austrics, whose culture was mainly a village culture based on agriculture, these Dravidian-speaking Mediterranean peoples (in their various ramifications) in India were responsible for cities and a city culture—for a real *civilization*, in the true sense of the word, including international trade.

The Dravidian speeches of the present day stand apart in a group by themselves, and although structurally they agree with some other speech families (e.g. with the Ural-Altaic family, which includes the Altaic speeches like Mongol, Turki, and Manchú on the one hand and the Ural or Finno-Ugrian speeches like Magyar, Finn, Esth, Lapp, Ostyak, Votyak, Zyrian, Cheremis, Samoyed, etc., on the other, in both Ural-Altaic and Dravidian possessing the same "agglutinative" structure in word-formation), in their roots, words, and affixes they do not agree with any current group of languages. There are fundamental points of difference between Dravidian and all the other speech-families which are current in India—the Austric, the Sino-Tibetan and the Indo-European (Aryan). The Dravidian tongues now form a solid *bloc* in the Deccan and South India to the south of the sixteenth latitude: and between the twenty-fourth and sixteenth latitudes, apart from the massive *bloc* of Telugu in the centre and the east and that of Kannada in the west, there are large Dravidian patches like Gondi, Kui, and Oraon which have been broken up a very great deal by the infiltration of the Aryan dialects.

But there is evidence, both indirect and direct, that in Central India, in North India, and in Western India, and possibly also in Eastern India, Dravidian was at one time fairly widespread. In Baluchistān we have the *bloc* of the Brāhui speech, which is Dravidian; and it is quite conceivable that the Brāhui area is just a surviving fragment of a very wide-spread Dravidian tract which extended from Baluchistān and Sind through Rājputāna and Mālwā into the present-day Marāṭhā country and the Dravidian lands of the south, and which also extended north and north-east in the Punjab and the Ganges valley, and possibly also north-west through Afghānistān into Irān.

Survival of Dravidian vocables in the place-names of Northern India, interpretation of the references to non-Aryan peoples or tribes in Vedic and other ancient Indian literature, the presence of a strong Dravidian element in the Aryan language from the Vedic downwards, the gradual "Dravidization" in spirit of the Aryan language leading to a very large approximation of the Modern or New Indo-Aryan languages to the speech-habits of Dravidian, the Dravidian character of a good deal of the extra-Indo-European elements in Hindu religion, ritual and thought, mythology and legendary history, and the discovery of a Mediterranean type in the people of the Upper Ganges Valley—all these are strong evidences in favour of an assumption that Dravidian speakers were largely to be found in the Punjab and the Upper Ganges Valley also; and toponomy and cultural survivals would point to an extension of the Dravidian speakers further eastward into Bengal, although here the long-headed Austrics and a brachycephalic people seem to have largely intermingled. In the North India plains, more than anywhere else, the Dravidian and Austric peoples appear to have been living side by side: probably there was at first a Dravidian element ruling over the Austric, and this was leading to a cultural and racial fusion.

The want of a solid *bloc* of Dravidian speakers or of Austric speakers in the Punjab and Upper Ganges Valley—the fact of the land being inhabited by peoples of these two different language-cultures—gave to the Aryan speech with its own culture-world its greatest opportunity, so that within a few hundred years after the Aryan language had been established in the Punjab, it could spread as far as eastern Bihār, ousting the earlier pre-Aryan speeches, and gaining greater momentum as its area extended east and south.

We are not absolutely certain that the city-builders of Harappā and Mohènjo-daro in South Punjab and Sind, whom the Aryans doubtless encountered, spoke Dravidian, but there is a balance of probability that they did. This matter cannot be proved or disproved until we find the clue to the script in the hundreds of seals found at Harappā and Mohenjo-daro and other sites. The Rev. H. Heras, S. J. has sought to read Old Tamil in these seals from the South Punjab and Sind; but it is highly improbable that in epigraphs from a culture-age going back to, say, 2500 B.C., there should be found a language which is not much older than A.D. 500. For although the oldest of the *Chen-tamizh* or Old Tamil works in their original form may go back to the centuries round about the time of Christ, the language which is found in them is considerably later. Moreover, we have to take note of the fact that Old Tamil in its phonetics represents a very much decayed form of the primitive Dravidian speech, which—or something like which—can alone be expected to have been in use in the third millennium B.C., the approximate date for the Mohenjo-daro culture. For example, the word *Tamil* itself: *tamiz*, it has been very conclusively established, was pronounced **damiz* in the early centuries of the Christian era, and earlier, in the first half of the first millennium B.C. it was in all likelihood **dramiẓa*, which was adopted into Sanskrit as *Dramiḷa, Dramiḍa, Draviḍa* before the Christian era. All other attempts to read right away, with the help of Sanskrit for instance, the South Punjab and Sind seals need not be taken into serious consideration.

The Aryan invaders or immigrants found in India two groups of peoples, one of which they named the *Dāsas,* and *Dasyus,* and the other *Nishādas.* The Dāsa-Dasyu people evidently had ramifications or extensions in Irān as well: we have in the south-east of the Caspian the *Dahai* people noted by the Greeks, and *Dāha* is but the Iranian modification of *Dāsa;* and in Iranian the word *dahyu* (whence Modern Persian *dih*) was in use, meaning "country" or "the countryside," which would only appear to have been originally a tribal name, the Irānian equivalent of the Indo-Aryan *dasyu,* generalized to mean the "country" only. In India the words *dāsa* and *dasyu* changed their meaning—as names of the enemies of the Aryans offering them resistance, who were frequently enough conquered and enslaved, and these words came respectively to mean "slave" and "robber." The two names appear originally to be related, both being from a root or base *dăs* or *dās:* the words may after all be Aryan or Indo-European in origin—cf. Sanskrit *dāsati* "follows up", and likely equivalents of this Indo-Aryan root occur in other Indo-European languages. We should note similar semantic changes in Europe; how the Slav national appellation *Slavu* (meaning "glorious, noble") came to be transformed into the word *slave* (as in English), and how the Celtic tribal name *Volcae* became **Walx-* or **Walh-* in Germanic, and then came to signify "any foreign people," and gave rise to names like *Wales, Wallachia, Walschand* (= "Italy," in German) and names of peoples like *Welsh* and *Vlach.* The *Dāsa-Dasyu* (= *Daha-Dahyu*) people would appear to have spread from at least Eastern Irān through Afghānistān to North-Western and Western India—Punjab (and probably the Western or Upper Ganges Valley) and Sind—when the Aryans came into India. There is no indication from the Ṛigveda that the Aryans were conscious of entering a new country when they came to India. This was certainly due to the fact that they did not find any appreciable difference in the non-Aryan people they encountered in India from the non-Aryan people they knew in Eastern Irān. It is also equally likely that racial and cultural fusion (including linguistic influencing) had commenced between the Aryan and the Dāsa-Dasyu peoples[16b] outside the soil of India itself—in Irān, in all likelihood. The Vedic speech[16c] already shows a number of words which are non-Aryan words with Dravidian affinities, and shows at least in its phonetics a profound modification on the lines of Dravidian by adopting or developing the cerebral sounds (*ṭ ḍ ṇ l sh*) which are so distinctive of Dravidian.

When the hypothesis of an Aryan invasion and occupation of

India was first proposed some four generations ago, it was believed that the white-skinned, blue-eyed, and golden-haired Aryans, like their kinsmen of Northern Europe, entered India from the plateau of Central Asia, which was then a land of romantic mystery, came to this land of the black-skinned non-Aryans, made an easy and matter-of-course conquest of them, and imposed upon an inferior race or races their superior religion, culture, and language. It was believed that all the better elements in Hindu religion and culture—its deeper philosophy, its finer literature, its more reasonable organization, everything in fact which was great and good and noble in it—came from the Aryans as a superior white race; and whatever was dark and lowly and superstitious in Hindu religion and civilization represented only an expression of the suppressed non-Aryan mentality. This view is now being gradually abandoned. It has been generally admitted, particularly after a study of both the bases of Dravidian and Aryan culture through language and through institutions, that the Dravidians contributed a great many elements of paramount importance in the evolution of Hindu civilization, which is after all (like all other great civilizations) a composite creation, and that in certain matters the Dravidian and Austric contributions are deeper and more extensive than that of the Aryans. The pre-Aryans of Mohenjo-daro and Harappā were certainly in possession of a higher material culture than what the semi-nomadic Aryans could show.

The assumption that the Mohenjo-daro and Harappā people spoke a primitive Dravidian speech accords best with the subsequent trend of Indian history and civilization. From various aspects, a mediterranean origin of the Dravidian people, its religion and civilization, appears to find good support. Reference may be made in this connexion to the city culture of Harappā and the ancient cities of Sind described in the next chapter. On the positive side, the cult of Śiva and the institution of Yoga appear to have been characteristic of the religious life of the people of Sind and South Punjab. The Aryans knew of a Sky Father—*Dyaush Pitā*—and of an Earth Mother—*Pṛithvī Mātā*—but these divinities were vague nature deities, who merely typified the falling of the rain from the sky to help earth to produce corn and fruits. The Kols (e.g. the Santāls) had similarly a Sun god (*Siñ Boṅga*) and a Moon goddess (*Ñinda Chando*) who were the great Father and Mother deities in the Kol pantheon. But the Dravidians had a conception of the forces of Life and of the Universe in the forms of a Great Mother Goddess and her male counterpart a Father God, and this conception, which was more profound, more mystic, more all-embracing and more deeply philosophical as well as more poetic than the simple Aryan idea of a material Sky Father and an equally material Earth Mother, the Dravidians appear to have brought to India from their original homeland in the islands of the Ægean and the tracts of mainland along the Ægean Sea—Greece and Asia Minor. Mā or Kubēlē (Cybele) and Atthis, or Ḥepit and Teshup, the great Asianic Mother Goddess and Father God, the former having as her symbol or vehicle the lion, the latter the bull, form undoubtedly one of the bases on which the Siva-Umā cult of Hindu India grew up.

From linguistics, it can be reasonably assumed that the oldest form of the word *Tamiḷ* or *Draviḍa* (which we can trace) was probably **Dramila* or **Dramiẓa.* We find that the Lycians of Asia Minor, a pre-Indo-European Mediterranean people, called themselves in their inscriptions (written in their own speech in a script allied to the ancient Greek) *Trmmili.* Herodotus has noted that the Lycians originally came from the island of Crete, and that in Crete the pre-Hellenic Asianic people were known by a name which the Greeks wrote as *Termilai.* It would not perhaps be too much to assume that some at least of the Dravidian speakers of India who came ultimately from the Eastern Mediterranean tracts brought with them one of their national or tribal appellations *Termilai—Trmmili—Dramiza,* which became transformed into the modern name *Tamil* by the middle of the first millennium A.D. In South Sind, the Greeks noted a people called *Arabitai:* they might very well have been Dravidian speakers in the fourth century B.C., and the name suggests the one which the Telugus apply to the Tamilians —*Aravaḷu:* and *Arava* is explained scholastically as the Sanskrit word *a-rava* "speechless, voiceless," suggesting the unintelligibility of Tamil as a language for the Telugus. Be that as it may, the culture-world presented by Dravidian (Tamil) linguistic palaeontology gives a fairly high background of civilization, which can be compared with what has been unearthed at Mohenjo-daro and other places, and with such indirect references to non-Aryan (Dravidian) civilization and non-Aryan *milieu* as can be found in the Vedic writings. In 1856, Bishop Caldwell gave the following sketch of the pre-Ayan civilization of the Dravidians from the evidence of the words in use among the early Tamilians[17] (I give the Tamil words within brackets after the English words): The Tamils or Dravidians "had 'kings' (*kō, vēntaṉ, mannaṉ*) who dwelt in 'strong houses' (*koṭṭai, araṇ*) and ruled over small 'districts of country' (*nāṭu*). They had 'minstrels' (*puḷavan*) who recited 'songs' (*cheyyul*) at 'festivals' (*koṇṭāttam, tiraviza*); and they seem to have had alphabetical characters (*ezuttu*) written (*varai*) with a style (*iraku*) on palmyra leaves (*olai*), and a bundle of leaves was called a 'book' (*eṭu*): they acknowledged the existence of God, whom they styled *Kō* or king—a realistic title known to orthodox Hinduism. They created to his honour a 'temple' which they called *Kō-il,* God's house (*kōyil, kōvil*). They had 'laws' and 'customs' (*kaṭṭalai, pazakkam*). but no lawyers or judges. Marriage existed among them.

They were acquainted with the ordinary metals, with the exception of 'tin,' 'lead' and 'zinc,' with the planets which were ordinarily known to the ancients (e.g. *veḷḷi* = 'Venus,' *chevvay* = 'Mars,' *viyāẓam*='Jupiter') with the exception of 'Mercury' and 'Saturn'. They had 'medicines' (*maruntu*), 'hamlets' (*paḷḷi*) and 'towns' (*ūr, peṭṭai*), 'canoes,' 'boats,' and even 'ships' (small 'decked' coasting vessels—*tōṇi, oṭam, vallam; kappaḷ, paṭavu*), no acquaintance with any people beyond the sea, except in Ceylon, which was then, perhaps, accessible on foot at low water; and no word expressive of the geographical idea of 'island' or 'continent.' They were well acquainted with 'agriculture' (*ēr*='plough,' *vēlan-mai* 'agriculture'), and delighted in 'war.' They were armed with 'bows' (*vil*) and 'arrows' (*ampu*), with 'spears' (*vēḷ*) and 'swords' (*vāḷ*). All the ordinary or necessary arts of life, including 'spinning' (*nūl*), 'weaving' (*ney*), and 'dyeing' (*niṟam*) existed among them. They excelled in 'pottery,' as their places of sepulture show." The late Professor P. T. Srinivasa Aiyangar (Iyengar) compiled a remarkable work,[18] in which, on the basis of native Dravidian words in Old Tamil, he has given us a most detailed survey of the type of culture in all its ramifications which obtained among the Primitive Tamil or Dravidian people before they began to come under the influence of the Aryan speech and culture.

Hindu tradition is vaguely conscious of Hindu religious ideas and philosophy, practices and ritual falling under two great categories—*āgama* and *nigama*. *Nigama* stands for the Vedic, i.e. the pure Aryan world of ideas, centring round what has been called the Vedic *karmakāṇḍa*, the practical religion of Vedic inspiration in which the *homa* or fire-sacrifice to the gods of the Vedic world forms the most noteworthy thing. *Āgama* indicates what may be described as the Tantric and Puranic domain of religion and ritual, and it includes *yoga* as a special form of mystico-religious ideology and practice. Pure *Nigama* religion is what we see in the great Vedic sacrifices which are still performed from time to time. Āgamic religion and ritual is largely influenced by the Nigamic or Vedic, but it forms a world apart.

In ordinary Hindu usage, there is a good deal of compromise between the two. Take, for example, the distinctive Hindu ritual of the *pūjā*, by which we mean the worship of an image or a symbol of the divinity by treating the latter, after it has been consecrated, as a living personality, and bringing before it, as before a living being, cooked food, vestments, ornaments, and other offerings which are usable by a man, and showing grateful worship by offering to it flowers, the produce of the earth, and incense, and by waving lights in front of it and playing and singing before it. This is something which is quite different from the Vedic rite of the *homa*, in which a wood fire is lighted on an altar and certain offerings of food in the shape of meat and fat, butter and milk, cakes of barley, and *soma* or spirituous drink, are offered to the gods, who are not at all symbolized by an image, but are supposed to dwell in the sky and to receive these offerings through the fire.

The characteristic offerings in the *pūjā* rite, viz. flowers, leaves fruits, water, etc., are not known to the *homa* rite, except in instances where it has been influenced by the *pūjā*. It has been suggested with good reason that *pūjā* is the pre-Aryan, in all likelihood the Dravidian, form of worship, while the *homa* is the Aryan: and throughout the entire early Vedic literature, the *pūjā* ritual with flowers etc. offered to an image or symbol is unknown. The word *pūjā*, from a root *pūj*, appears, like the thing it connotes, to be of Dravidian origin also. This word or root is not found in any Aryan or Indo-European language outside India. Professor Mark Collins suggested[19] that the Sanskrit word *pūjā* (from which the root *pūj* was deduced later) was nothing but a Dravidian *pū* "flower" plus root **ge* "to do" (palatalized to *je*), which is found in Tamil as *chey*, in Kannada as *ge* and in Telugu as *che: pūjā* < **pū-ge*, **pū-che* was thus a "flower ritual," a "flower service," a *pushpa-karma*, just as *homa* described as *paśu-karma* or religious service entailing the slaughter of an animal. Jarl Charpentier of Sweden derived *pūjā* from a Dravidian root *pusu* meaning "to smear," as the smearing of sandalpaste or blood forms an important item in the *pūjā* ritual. But the use of blood, to be smeared over a piece of stone representing a god or spirit—the blood of a sacrificed animal being later replaced by red paint like the vermilion—would appear more to be an Austric or Proto-Australoid rite than Dravidian.

In any case, the pre-Aryan, and in all likelihood Dravidian, origin of this most noteworthy ritual of a finished Hindu religion, would appear to be quite reasonable to assume. In the present-day texture of Hindu culture and religion the warp appears to be Dravidian and the weft Aryan. *Pūjā* with flowers, leaves, and water was, so far as the first Aryans who came to India were concerned, an alien rite, a local "native" usage, not to be approved, much less adopted, by the Brāhmaṇas and others who claimed to be true Aryans. But "Greece captured her captor". The native or local cults and creeds did not die—on the other hand the exotic *homa* largely became moribund, being kept up artificially among limited groups of Brāhmaṇas and Kshatriyas, and the *pūjā* came to assume its present important place in the religious life of the mixed Hindu people which resulted from the fusion of the Aryan and the non-Aryan. The first conscious attempt to give the *imprimatur* to *pūjā* as a rite, which is to be taken sympathetically, we find in that great work of synthesis in Hindu thought and life, the *Bhagavad-Gītā* of the *Mahābhārata*, which would appear to have been compiled round about the age of Christ; although through certain surreptitious rites like *kākā-bali* or offerings to crows and other birds, something analogous to the *pūjā* was being given a place in the *Gṛihya* or domestic rites of the blue-blooded Aryan householders. The *Gītā* passage (IX.26) runs thus:

patraṁ pushpaṁ phalaṁ toyaṃ yo me bhaktyā prayachchhati,
tad = ahaṁ bhakty-upahṛitam = aśnāmi prayatātmanaḥ:

"If anyone offers me with devotion a leaf, a flower, a fruit, and water, I receive that, offered in devotion by the person whose soul is disciplined."

The context makes it clear that here we have an apology for non-Vedic worship *vis-à-vis* the Vedic fire-sacrifice: this verse, in fact, forms the great charter for the *pūjā* ritual within the *milieu* of Vedic Brahmanism.

The acceptance of pre-Aryan (Dravidian) ritual meant also the acceptance of the conception of the divinity and of the mythological figures of the gods and goddesses which were current among them. In mediaeval and modern Hinduism, certain divinities stand paramount like Śiva and Umā, Vishṇu (specially in his incarnations of Rāma and Kṛishṇa) and Śrī, together with some other gods and goddesses of a secondary character who claim the homage of the people like Hanumant, Gaṇeśa and Śītalā. The popular gods of the Vedic Aryans—Indra, Agni, Varuṇa, Soma, Sūrya, Ushas, Pūshan, Parjanya and the rest—gradually recede into the background, and a group of more puissant and more personal gods, more profound and cosmic and more philosophical in their conception, the Puranic gods of Hinduism headed by Śiva-Umā and Śrī-Vishṇu, become established. As it has been said before, Śiva and Umā are in all likelihood fundamentally of Dravidian origin, and as such, they are the Indian modification—and philosophic sublimation—of the great Mother-Goddess and her consort of the Mediterranean peoples. The name *Śiva* has been explained as being at least partly of Dravidian origin: in Tamil, for instance, *Śivan* (*Chivan*) means red, and the divinity was known to the early Aryans as *Nīla-lohita* "the Red One with blue (throat)" (referring to the legend found in the Purāṇas of later times and unquestionably mentioned in Ṛigveda, (X. 136, vii), of Śiva having drunk up the world poison and preserved it in his throat which became marked with blue for this). *Śambhu*, another common name or epithet of Śiva, has been compared with the Tamil *chempu* or *śembu* meaning "copper," i.e. "the red metal." Śiva and the Vedic Rudra have been identified: it is just likely that the name of the Red God of the Dravidian speakers, the most important divinity in their pantheon, was first rendered into the Aryan speech as **Rudhra*, and then this name was easily identified with an already existing Aryan Storm God, the father of the Maruts or the Storm Winds, whose name *Rudra* in Aryan meant quite a different thing—"the Roarer" (from root *rud*).[20] The name *Umā* recalls *Mā*, the Great Mother of the Asianic and East Mediterranean peoples: and *Durgā*, as one of the common epithets of the Mother Goddess Umā, we can compare with *Trqqas*, a deity mentioned in the Lycian inscriptions of Asia Minor.[21] *Vishṇu* is partly Aryan, a form of the Sun-God, and partly at least the deity is of Dravidian affinity, as a sky-god whose colour was of the blue sky (cf. Tamil, *viṇ* "sky" and the Middle Indo-Aryan or Prākrit form of Vishṇu, which was *viṇhu, veṇhu*).[22] *Śrī* is, to start with, an Aryan divinity, the Indian counterpart of the Goddess connected with the harvest or corn and with wealth, beauty, and well-being, whom we find in the Italic world as *Ceres* among the Latins. But in her association with Vishṇu, as *Gaja-lakshmi* for instance, she is indigenous and pre-Aryan.[23] *Kṛishṇa* (in Prākrit *Kaṇha*, in Tamil *Kaṇṇaṇ*) is a demon opposed to Indra in the Ṛigveda; according to P. T. Srinivasa Aiyangar, he represents, partially at least, a Dravidian God of Youth, who has later been identified with Vishṇu as an incarnation of his.

Another Dravidian God of Youth and youthful powers, of bravery and war, was *Murukaṇ*, who in the composite Puranic mythology became *Kumāra* or *Skanda*, the son of Śiva.[24] *Gaṇeśa*, the elephant-headed demon who was to be appeased at the outset of any function to avert supernatural hindrances, remained such a demon with the Mahāyāna Buddhists, but with the Brahmanical Hindus he was transformed into the benign god who removes obstacles and who typifies wisdom. The very character of the god as having an elephant-head shows his native Indian, i.e. pre-Aryan origin.

The phallic symbol of Śiva, the *liṅga*, appears to be, both in its form and name, of Austric or Proto-Australoid origin. We should remember that the mysterious upright conical stones set up on the ground (like the menhirs in the Celtic areas in Europe) were very much in evidence as cult objects among the Mon-Khmers and the Kols, and these bore a resemblance to the digging stick used among them as a primitive plough; and Jean Przyluski has shown, as it has been noted before, how the words *liṅga, lakuṭa, laguḍa, laṅgula* are of Austric origin. But the figure of Śiva as the great Yogin, seated in yogic meditation. as *Virūpāksha* or "the terrible One." as *Paśupati* or "the Lord of Animals, or Souls," as *Urdhva-liṅga* or "the One with the erect creative force,"—in fact, all the deeper and more philosophical traits in the conception of Śiva appear to have been known among the Mohenjo-daro people, as shown by the very important seal with the figure of a divinity who can only be identified with Śiva of later times.[25] And assuming that the Mohenjo-daro and Harappā people were Dravidian speakers, this would be only another corroboration of the Śiva idea and the Śiva legends being of Dravidian origin: only this symbol of the *Liṅga* in the *gaurī-paṭṭa* or *yoni* being derived to some extent from the Austric menhirs, which survived till recently in the Muṇḍā *sasan-diris* or family burial stones.

Zoomorphic divinities, or lower animals as typifying the forces of nature and supplying symbols or figures for the supernatural or the godhead, appear to have been known to the Aryans only to a limited extent. Thus Indra and other powerful gods have been compared with bulls or rams, and Agni with the horse, and there is also the divine horse named *Dadhikrāvan* in the Veda. But the extent to which zoomorphic deities came into prominence in Puranic Hinduism is something noteworthy, rivalling the ancient Egyptian pantheon in this respect. The submerged totemism of the Proto-Australoids possibly was the oldest and most powerful source of influence for this, and the worship of the Nāgas or serpentine deities and water spirits would appear to have come from the Proto-Australoids. *Garuḍa* as the vehicle bird of Vishṇu is partly a divine eagle—*Suparṇa*—of the Aryans and partly of Dravidian or Mediterranean origin; the name would appear to be Dravidian (cf. Tamil *kaẓu* "kite, eagle"). The sacredness of the ox and the cow may have some Aryan elements in it, but the honour paid to the cow among the Iranian Aryans might be, at its basis, of Dāsa-Dasyu origin, as much as in India.

The great zoomorphic deity of India is of course Hanumant, the so-called Monkey-God. His greatness has no doubt been added to in later times by the Bhakti school of mediaeval Hinduism, which saw in him an ideal devotee of Rāma, God incarnate as the hero of the *Rāmāyaṇa* legend. But in popular belief throughout the greater part of India (in Bengal alone his worship is not so intensely popular), he is something more than a simple *Bhakta* or devotee. He is a fertility deity, who gives children to barren women; and he is the helper at need and remover of obstacles. It seems, as F.E. Pargiter's significant research[26] into the name of Hanumant warrants us in assuming, that there was a great Monkey-God who obtained the worship of the pre-Aryan peoples (namely Dravidians) of India, and whose name was in the Dravidian speech just "the Male Monkey" (in Tamil, *Aṇ-manti*). The Aryan speakers came to know this god, and his name was at first translated into the Aryans' language as *Vṛishā-kapi*. His worship was slowly entering by the back-door among the Aryan speakers through contact with the Dravidians, and this was resented by a certain element among the Aryan people: but others were acquiescing in the introduction of this "native" cult. An echo of this ideological conflict we find in the *Vṛishā-kapi* hymn of the Ṛigveda (X. 86). But *Vṛishā-kapi* became admitted into the newly formed Aryan-non-Aryan pantheon, and his original Dravidian name *Aṇ-manti*, as in Tamil, was then Sanskritized into *Hanumant,* and under this name he is still a powerful deity in popular Hinduism, the sublimation of his character by *Bhakti* adding but fresh lustre to his pristine popularity as a strong helper in need and remover of distress, the rough and ready god of a primitive people.

The extent to which the Aryan religion has been modified by Austric and Dravidian contacts is sufficient indication of the profound influences exerted by the latter in the evolution of the Hindu religion. There has been a widespread racial mixture, as anthropology has indicated. In culture, speaking in the Indian way, one may say that over twelve annas in the rupee is of non-Aryan origin. The bases of Indian economy—food (rice or wheat or millet with pulses or lentils as relish, milk products like *ghee* and curds, vegetables, occasionally a little goat or mutton, and fish and oil of various sorts where milk is not common, as opposed to the Aryan meal of barley cakes and meat and butter), dress (unsewn cotton cloth worn in three pieces as *dhoti* or *sāṛī* i.e. loincloth, *dupaṭṭā* or shawl, and head-cloth or turban, in place of the woollen garments of the Aryans), and dwelling, are pre-Aryan; our way of thinking is un-Aryan—the syntax of the later Indo-Aryan dialects agrees more with that of the Dravidian languages than with that of Vedic and of the extra-Indian Indo-European languages; our counting and computation is largely on the basis of *eight,* which is Dravidian (Mark Collins has explained *ompattu* the Tamil word for "nine" as being really the Aryan *ūna* "one less" plus Tamil *pattu* "ten," and the Telugu *tommiḍi* as really meaning "broken ten" thus suggesting that *eight* was the common number in computation), combined to some extent with counting by *tens,* which is Aryan, and to a slight extent on the basis of *twenty* as the highest number, which is Austric (as Jean Przyluski has shown). Many of our social institutions and conventions (e.g., certain usages regarding prohibited degrees in marriage, and customs like a wife being on familiar terms with her husband's younger brother but regarding his elder brother as her father) and a good many of our wedding and other customs (e.g. the practice known as *strī-āchāra* with its attendant paraphernalia of the various produce of the earth arranged in a winnowing fan, the use of turmeric and vermilion in the wedding ritual, the employment of the coconut and betel-leaf in many of our ceremonies) are of non-Aryan origin. We have a fairly extensive element from the Austric and the Dravidian languages in our Indo-Aryan speech: the number—at least a hundred for Austric, and some four hundred and fifty for Dravidian as given by Kittel in his *Kannaḍa Dictionary*—seems to be on the way to increase the more our knowledge of this matter is deepening and widening. In their phonetics, Indo-Aryan, Austric and Dravidian have converged more or less to a common Indian sound-system. Despite a number of noteworthy differences due to original diversity of race and speech and to climatic and economic conditions, the bases of Indian pre-Aryan (Austric and Dravidian) life and culture, modified by the language and ideology of the Aryans, and later by the ideology of Islam, still remain, and they form a specifically Indian background for a civilization and an outlook that may be described as pan-Indian.

The discovery of Mycenaean artifacts in Greece has proved the truth of what the great explorer of Ægean culture, Sir Arthur Evans, had suspected, that a good deal of the heroic legends of Greece as well as of the legends of their gods and goddesses was of pre-Hellenic, i.e. pre-Indo-European, Ægean or Mediterranean origin, and these were simply Hellenized by being rendered into the Indo-European language of the Greeks as soon as this language became established on its new territory. The stories of the Iliad and the Odyssey and of Œdipus and other heroes were according to this view of Ægean origin, and this has been corroborated, in spirit at least, for some other connected legends. A similar thing appears to have taken place in India. Myths and legends of Gods and Heroes current among the Austrics and Dravidians, long antedating the period of Aryan advent in India (c. 1500 B.C.), appear to have survived the Aryan impact and to have been rendered into the Aryan language in late and garbled, or "improved," versions accommodating themselves to the Aryan God- and Hero-worlds; and it is these myths and legends of gods, kings, and sages which we largely find in the Purāṇas. The Rāma legend looks like a blend of three distinct stories without any historicity put together at different times (the Ayodhyā intrigue and the banishment of Rāma, the abduction of Sītā and her recovery by Rāma, and the episode of the monkey princes), and seems to have grown up in Eastern India, with an Austric background; but later it was re-edited as a national poem within the gorgeous framework of the composite and highly complex Hindu civilization of 2,000 years ago. The Mahābhārata story, on the other hand, which developed in the Midland (present-day Western United Provinces and Eastern Punjab), would appear to embody a good deal of the legends, traditions, and history of the Aryans as well as of the mixed Aryan-non-Aryan peoples, and was created consciously as the national poem of a new Hindu nation of mixed origin welded into one people under Brāhmaṇa guidance. Viewed in this light, the pre-Vedic antiquity of a number of heroic tales and legends and dynastic "histories" as being really pre-Aryan, possibly Dravidian, can be properly understood, as cases of rendering in the Aryans' language of pre-Aryan material.

On the ideological plane, the synthesis of the Aryan and non-Aryan mentalities and attitudes towards life has given rise consciously as well as unconsciously to a common set of ideals which are actively practised, or are subscribed to, by the greater part of Indian humanity, and these ideals are along the following lines: a sense of the unity of all life through its being an expression of an Unseen Reality, which is both immanent and transcendent; a desire for synthesis, to combine apparently disconnected or discordant fragments in life as well as experience in their proper place in an essential unity; a rigid and intransigent adherence to the intellect while seeking to harmonize it in the higher plane with the emotions and with the mystic sense; a recognition of the sorrows of life, leading to a sincere attempt to go to the root causes of these with a view to remove them from the life of the individual, the community, and the whole of humanity; a desire to attain to the Unseen Reality as the solution of all evil and suffering through the ways of knowledge, of mystic realization by discipline, faith, and devotion, and of disinterested service; a sense of the sacredness of all life which is sought to be maintained by passive non-injury (*ahiṁsa*), by intellectual pity (*karuṇa*), and by practical charity and well-doing (*maitrī*); and an acceptance of all spiritual experiences as true and as inevitable, and a tolerance for all of these so long as they do not interfere with the rights of others. A broad toleration which is the result of a wide understanding, and the doctrine of "live and let live"—these characterized, or formed the bedrock of the civilization of India; and this attitude was the result of this civilization being in its origin a complex harmony of composites, where there has not been any consciously active or successful struggle to maintain the racial, linguistic and cultural superiority of one of the component elements over the others.

The speakers of the Austric, Dravidian and Indo-European Aryan tongues, racially Proto Australoids, Mediterraneans, Nordics, Alpines, and Dinarics, made up the Indian people and built up the civilization of India. After this civilization had taken its definite colour and its special orientation, by the middle of the first millennium B.C. another new racial and culture-language element came into India—the Mongoloid Sino-Tibetan speakers—the Kirātas; but they touched only the fringe of India in the north and the north-east and their influence was but local, and not of much significance. According to a Tibetan tradition of very doubtful value, the Tibetans first settled in Tibet during the time of the Buddha. But it was over a thousand years after that, in the seventh century A. D., that they came in active contact with India—an India which was already far advanced in her composite Aryan-non-Aryan culture. The various Sino-Tibetan tribes were in a very primitive and backward condition and they did not have much to give to the Indians, of Austric-Dravidian-Aryan affinities and origin. There is a Mongoloid stratum in the Himālayas and in the tracts immediately to the south, in Assam, in North and East Bengal; and in the evolution of Aryan languages like Gorkhali or Nepāli, Bengali and Assamese, some Sino-Tibetan (Tibeto-Burman) influence has been suggested. The Sino-Tibetan peoples, at least those among them who could benefit by their contact with Indian culture, thoroughly imbibed it and, like the Newārs of Nepāl valley, became fully Indianized. It is only where they are remote from the Aryan-speaking Indians that they are able to maintain their separate identity a little; but their absorption into an Aryan-speaking Indian body-politic is inevitable, whether in Nepāl or in Bengal or in Assam. But in the process of their becoming completely Indianized, they are sure to make at least some temperamental contribution to the Indian populations of the north and the north-east, if not much in the way of the material or spiritual; and it is for the future to disclose what line this Kirāta, this Indo-Mongoloid or Mongoloid contribution to Indian mentality and culture will take.[27]

---

1. *The Census of India*, 1901.
2. *Indo-Aryan Races*, I, Rajshahi, 1916.
3. *The Census of India*, 1931, Vol. I, pp. 424 ff.
4. "Racial affinities of the Peoples of India" in *The Census of India*, 1931, Vol. I, Part III (1935); *An outline of the Racial Ethnology of India*, Calcutta, 1937.
5. *Racial Elements in the Population*, No. 22 of "Oxford Pamphlets on Indian Affairs," Oxford University Press, Bombay, 1944.
6. For a detailed discussion on these points, cf. Ch. X.
7. *Racial Elements in the Population*, p. 26.
8. *The Census of India*, 1931, Report, Part I, p. 443.
9. For these, cf. Ch. VII.
10. Cf. *Mata-Hari* by Renward Brandstetter, Lucerne, 1908. Brandstetter's linguistic papers on Indonesian are available in English translation by C. O. Blagden (*RASB*, London).
11. Some of the important papers in this connection have been translated from French into English by Dr. P.C. Bagchi with additional notes and papers in his *Pre-Aryan and Pre-Dravidian in India* (Calcutta University, 1929).
12. S. K. Chatterji, "Two New Indo-Aryan Etymologies" in the *ZII*, Band 9, Leipzig, 1933-34, pp. 31 ff.
13. P.C. Bagchi, *Pre-Aryan and Pre-Dravidian in India*; J. Przyluski, "Hippokoura et Sātakarni" (*JRAS*, 1929, pp. 274-9; English translation in *JAHRS*, Vol. IV, Part I, 1930); S. K. Chatterji, "Non-Aryan Elements in Indo-Aryan" (*JGIS*, III, 42).
14. P. Mitra, "A Vedic Night of the Moon in Polynesia," *Calcutta Oriental Journal*, Vol. I, July, 1934.
15. W. G. Archer, *The Blue Grove, the Poetry of the Oraons* (London, 1940), p. 19.
16. A résumé of Hevesy's views has been given by Dr. Biren Bonnerjee in *IC*, 1937, pp. 621-32.

16a. J. Przyluski, "Emprunts anaryens en Indo-aryes," *Le Monde Oriental*, Vol. 28 (1934), pp. 140 ff.

16b. For Dāsa-Dasyu, cf. also Ch. XIII.

16c. The Vedic speech would seem to have been written down in a sort of Proto-Brāhmī as an adaptation of the pre-Aryan Harappā and Mohenjo-daro script for the Aryan language in the tenth century B.C., when "Vyāsa," contemporary of the *Mahābhārata* battle, could compile the Veda books from the floating mass of oral religious literature current among the Aryans—and Vyāsa, according to a tradition preserved by Al-Biruni, rediscovered for the Hindus their alphabet. (For different views about the date of the *Mahābhārata* battle, cf. Ch. XIV).

17. *Comparative Grammar of the Dravidian Languages*, third edition (1913), p. 113.
18. *Pre-Aryan Tamil Culture*, Madras, 1930.
19. *Dravidic Studies*, No. III (University of Madras), pp. 59 ff.

20. P. T. Srinivasa Aiyangar (Iyengar), *Life in Ancient India in the Age of the Mantras* (Madras, 1912), p. 125; *Dravidic Studies*, No. III, pp. 61-2.
21. S. K. Chatterji. "Dravidian Origins and the Beginnings of Indian Civilization," (*MR*, Dec. 1924, p. 679).
22. P.T.S. Aiyangar, *op.cit.*, p. 126.
23. *Dravidic Studies*, No. III, p. 62.
24. Cf. also *Pre-Aryan Tamil Culture*.
25. Cf. Ch. IX.
26. *JRAS*, 1913, p. 400.
27. For the Kirātas or Indo-Mongoloids, see Kasten Ronnow in *Le Monde Oriental*, Vol. XXX (1936), pp. 90-169.

CHAPTER IX

THE INDUS VALLEY CIVILIZATION

Until as recently as 1922, early Indian history had little actual remains to offer besides the meagre palaeolithic and neolithic finds, described above (Ch. VII), and the Piprahwa relic was the oldest object of which the date (c. fifth century B.C.) could be approximately determined. The antiquity of Indian history and culture as gleaned from Vedic literature is also not supposed to go beyond the second millennium before Christ. But the archaeological discoveries at Harappā, Mohenjo-daro and other localities (see map No. 2) in the Indus valley have pushed back this limit, at a single stretch, to 3000 B.C., if not to a still remoter period, and India can now lay claim to the honour of being a pioneer of civilization along with Sumer, Akkad, Babylon, Egypt, and Assyria.

The fascinating story of the excavations at various places in the Indus valley has been told above (Ch. III) and we shall now try to reconstruct a picture of the culture and civilization that flourished in this region from the remains found principally at Harappā and Mohenjo-daro.

1. THE TOWN

A visitor to the ruins at Mohenjo-daro (the city of the dead) is struck by the remarkable skill in town-planning and sanitation displayed by the ancients, and, as an English writer has observed, "feels himself surrounded by ruins of some present-day working town in Lancashire." The city was entered from the north and south by the First Street, which is amply wide for both wheeled traffic and pedestrians. East Street, which is the main thoroughfare through the ruins is wider than First Street. The junction of these two is nicknamed "Oxford Circus" by archaeologists.

The city was the creation of careful forethought and planning, as is indicated by the striking regularity of the divisions, the successfully aligned streets, the orientation of all principal streets to the points of the compass, the correspondence of the houses and public buildings with the orientation of thoroughfares, etc. Streets varied from 9 feet to 34 feet in width and ran straight sometimes as far as half a mile. They intersected at right angles dividing the city into square or rectangular blocks. Inside this square or oblong, the area is intersected by a number of narrow lanes crowded with houses. Each lane has a public well, and most of the houses have each a private well and a bath. Nowhere was a building allowed to encroach on a public highway as in Sumer. The angles of the smaller by-ways appear to have been rubbed by pack-animals, and the corners of some buildings were rounded off in order that loads might not be dislodged. The city had an elaborate drainage system consisting of horizontal and vertical drains, street drains, soakpits, etc., which is described later on. The industrial and commercial quarters as well as the lowly abodes of artisans and shopkeepers and the palatial mansions of the rich can easily be distinguished among the ruins. The general impression is that of "a democratic bourgeois economy" as in Crete.

The architecture of Mohenjo-daro, in general, is plain and utilitarian, rather solid than beautiful. There are no sumptuous temples as in Sumer nor monumental tombs as on the Nile. In contrast to Sumer, there is an absence of round columns, recessed doorways, and semi-circular pilasters. The true arch was unknown and the corbelled arch and square or rectangular columns were used instead. The aim in the Indus Valley was to make life comfortable and luxurious rather than refined or artistic.

Harappā is larger in extent than Mohenjo-daro, and had a longer span of life, but presents nearly the same features. Wells at Harappā are rare as compared to Mohenjo-daro.[1a] The most remarkable and largest building at Harappā is the Great Granary, measuring 169 feet by 135 feet, which comprises two similar blocks with an aisle, 23 feet wide, between them. Each block has six halls, alternating regularly with five corridors, and each hall is further partitioned into four narrow divisions. Another discovery at Harappā is the workmen's quarters, which comprise fourteen small houses built in two blocks separated by a long narrow lane. Each house is open on all sides, rectangular, and consists of a courtyard and two rooms.

At the hill sites in the narrow corridor between the Indus and the Kirthar range, excavated by Mr. Majumdar, bricks were never used as at Mohenjo-daro, Harappā, and other sites. Hill-side houses were made of stone at the base up to a height of two to three feet. Mud, reed, and wood were used in building superstructures. No fortifications were discovered at Mohenjo-daro and Harappā; on the outskirts of Ali Murad and Kohtras were found fortified palaces made of stone, which was but rarely used in the plains, not being easily available there. At sites around Lake Manchar, people lived in pile dwellings.

In building walls, pavements, bath-rooms, drains, wells, etc. burnt brick, possibly made from ordinary alluvial soil, was lavishly used. Sun-dried brick was used only for foundations, packing of terraces, etc. Bricks are ordinarily rectangular in shape, well made. and excellently preserved. Even at the lowest levels we find well-made bricks which would be a credit even to a modern brick-maker. Wedge-shaped bricks were invariably used in constructing wells.

and were made in a mould. Sawn bricks were used in bath-rooms to ensure evenness of floor. Curved bricks, which were used for the building of bins lining of wells, have hitherto been found only at Chanhu-daro. None of the bricks have grooves or depressions. Brick kilns have been found at Mohenjo-daro. The colour of the bricks ranges from straw to bright red.

Seven different layers have been recognized in the excavations at Mohenjo-daro. The antiquities in all these levels are homogeneous, the only point of difference being the deterioration of masonry in the later occupation of the cities. Mud mortar was generally used as a cementing material. In drains, where more strength or binding force was required, lime and gypsum mortar were used. The joints in some of the brick-work are so fine that even a thin knife cannot be inserted in them. Occasionally, bitumen was used for water proofing.

Foundations were carried to considerable depths and crude brick was used for infilling. Buildings were erected on artificial mud platforms as a precaution against floods to which ancient Sind was subject.

In most walls bricks were laid in the English Bond method, in alternate headers and stretchers, care being taken to break the joints. A filling of clay or rubble was used between the faces in very thick walls in order to economize bricks. In most cases the vertical alignment of buildings is marvellous, indicating that a plumb bob or a similar instrument was used. This was done by placing each course a little back from the course below or by employing specially moulded bevelled edged bricks. Walls surmounting pavement were wainscotted with bricks laid on edge standing 3 feet above the floor level.

The buildings thus far unearthed in the Indus Valley fall into three main classes: (i) dwelling houses, (ii) larger buildings, and (iii) public baths.

There is much variation in the size of dwelling houses. The smallest have no more than two rooms, while the largest are so vast as to rank almost as palaces. Outside walls of the dwelling houses were severely plain.

Ordinarily there was an entrance from the street side. The houses were quite commodious, divided into well sized rooms, containing wells and bath-rooms, and provided with covered drains connected with street drains. The open court was the basic feature of house planning in the Indus Valley, as in Babylon. The courtyard which was usually paved with bricks laid flat was surrounded by chambers, and doors and windows opened into it. The kitchen was placed in a sheltered corner of the courtyard, and the ground floor contained store rooms, well chambers, bath, etc. Every house had a separate bath-room, placed at the street side, paved with carefully laid burnt bricks, which sloped to a corner containing the drain carrying off waste water. Vertical drain pipes suggest that baths were constructed on the upper storeys also. Doors were possibly made of wood and were placed at the ends of the walls, not in the middle. Ordinary houses very rarely had windows in their outer walls. Possibly perforated lattices were used as windows or ventilators at the top of the wall. Stairways, made of solid masonry, are found in nearly every house. They were built straight and steep, with treads unusually narrow and high. In some cases, the stairways led to the upper storeys which contained the bath and the living and sleeping apartments. Roofs were flat and made of wood. It appears that no latrines were ordinarily provided, or they were situated at the top. Doorless chambers in some houses have variously been taken to be cellars, or cess pits for latrines, or sleeping apartments, or solid foundations as a precaution against floods, or treasure rooms.[2] Practically every house had its own well. and public wells were placed between two houses, with a pavement of burnt brick which sloped down to a drain at one corner. Two wells have a square coping at the top, and two are elliptical in shape. Some form of windlasses appears to have been used for drawing water.

The elaborate drainage system is a unique feature of the Indus Valley Civilization. the like of which has not yet been found in any other city of the same antiquity. Below principal streets and many lanes ran a main drain, 1 to 2 feet deep, covered with brick or stone. and provided with sumps and inspection traps at regular intervals. Individual house drains, each one with its own sump pit, opened into the street drains, which in their turn opened into great culverts emptying into the river. All soak pits and drains were occasionally cleared by workmen. and drains were provided with manholes at intervals for cleaning. This elaborate drainage system, like the town-planning. constitutes a notable point of difference with Sumer, where the inhabitants had, in most cases, vertical pottery drainage shafts beneath their courtyards, but these had no outlet.

As regards larger buildings, some, which were earlier indicated as temples, were later taken to be *khans*. With the possible exception of the building housing the Great Bath. no building has yet been cleared which can definitely be called religious. The great structure near the *Stūpa*, with extra-thick outer walls, has been named the Collegiate Building. and probably housed some high official, the high priest, or a college of priests. A pillared hall, 80 feet square, divided into long corridors interspersed with low benches having even seats, has the chief seat at right angles to the corridors. It may probably have served for a public assembly.

The Great Bath, which has been taken to be a part of a vast hydropathic establishment is "a swimming bath on a scale which would do credit to a modern seaside hotel."[3] The overall dimensions of the building housing it are 180 feet by 108 feet. The actual bathing pool, measuring 39 feet by 23 feet with a depth of 8 feet, is situated in the middle of a quadrangle having verandahs on all sides. At either end, there is a raised platform and a flight of steps, with another platform at the base of each flight of steps. The floor is made of bricks laid on edge, and the walls have been made water-tight by employing specially trimmed brick in gypsum mortar with an inch of damp proof course of bitumen. There is a vaulted culvert, 6 feet 6 inches high, at the south-western corner, which could fill and empty the tank. On three sides at the back of the verandahs are various rooms and galleries. There is a spacious verandah with small rooms at the southern end. There are six entrances to the building containing the bath. It cannot be definitely stated whether the Great Bath was used entirely for secular purposes or for religious ceremonies.

Near the south-west corner of the Great Bath is a *hammam* or hot air bath. It has a number of rectangular platforms of brick about 5 feet high, having a series of vertical chases sunk in their sides. There is another similar building at Mohenjo-daro which shows that the Indus people understood the principle of the hypocaust and had Turkish baths. Another bath-room establishment consisted of two rows of bath-rooms separated by a narrow passage, each bath-room having a stairway, a narrow doorway and carefully paved floor. According to Dr. Mackay, these ablution places were meant for the priests, while the Great Bath was for the general public.

The careful town-planning, adequate water supply, and efficient drainage system presuppose an advanced state of civic authority. Lamp-posts at intervals indicate the existence of street lighting. There was also a watch and ward system for different quarters, and large caravanserais and public store-houses were provided. That the sanitation was well looked after is seen from the rubbish heap consisting of broken pottery, ashes and humus found in deep trenches outside the city. Trees and plants were allowed to grow in the enclosures. The later levels of the city, however, show the decline of civic authority, as buildings were erected in a haphazard manner, there were encroachments upon lanes, and potters were quartered in the city.

2. SOCIAL AND ECONOMIC LIFE

All the skeletons unearthed at Mohenjo-daro belong to the chalcolithic period and may be taken as representative of an urban population. Craniological tests reveal the presence of four racial types at Mohenjo-daro, viz., (i) Proto-Australoid: (ii) Mediterranean; (iii) Mongoloid and (iv) Alpinoid (*ante*. Ch. VIII). The cosmopoli-

PLATE I

Courtest: Archaeological Survey of India

CORBELLED DRAIN, MOHENJO-DARO (See p. 175)

PLATE II

Courtest: Archaeological Survey of India

GREAT BATH, MOHENJO-DARO (See p. 175)

PLATE III

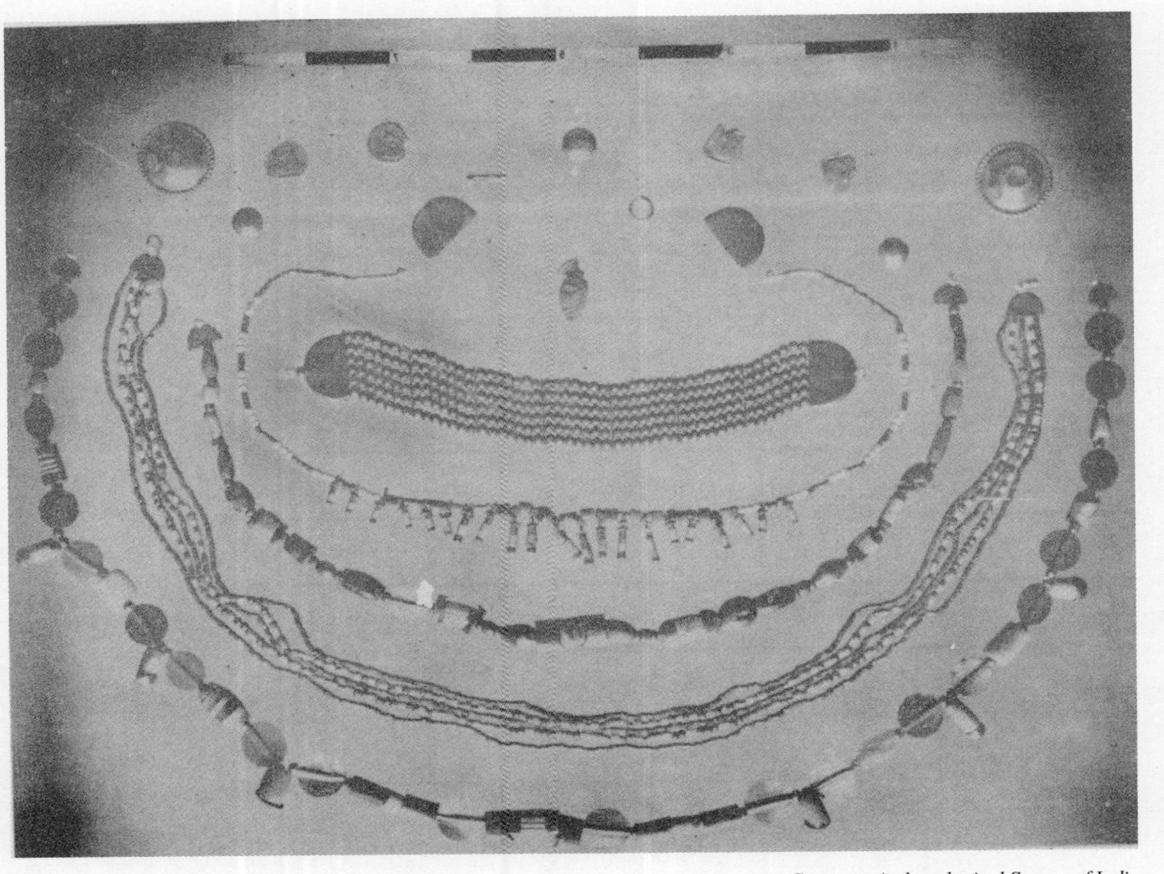

Courtest: Archaeological Survey of India

JEWELLERY—NECKLACES, MOHENJO-DARO (See p. 178)

PLATE IV

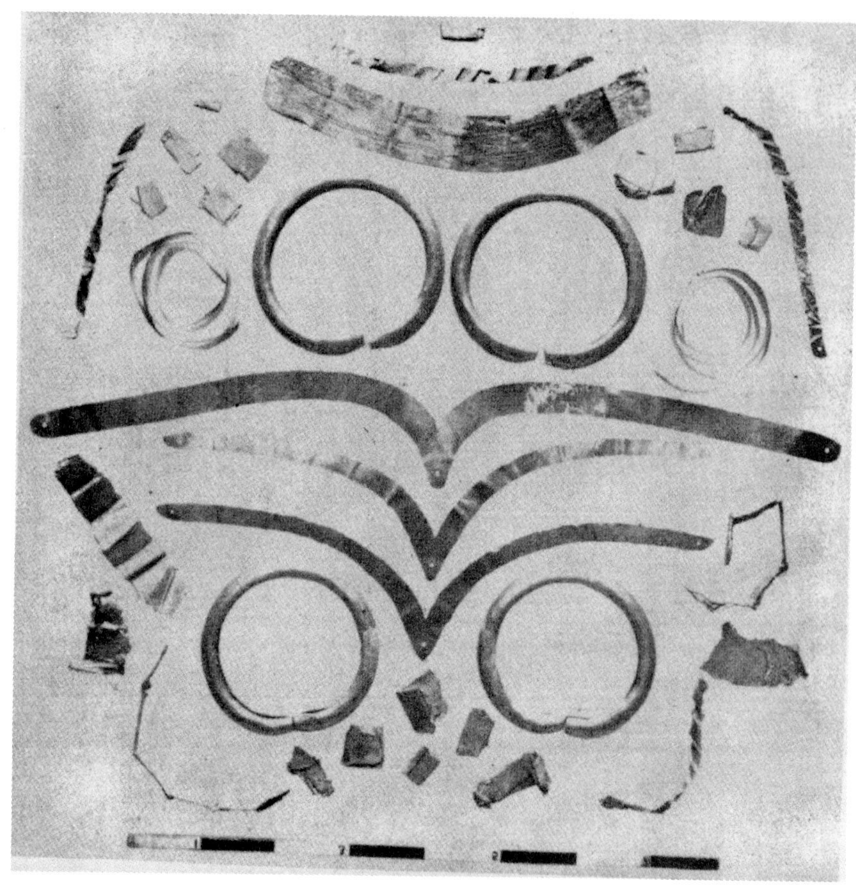

Courtest: Archaeological Survey of India

PERSONAL ORNAMENTS, MOHENJO-DARO (See p. 178)

PLATE V

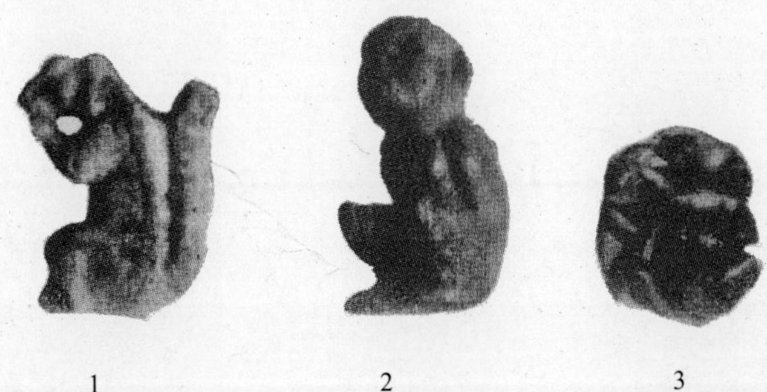

1 2 3

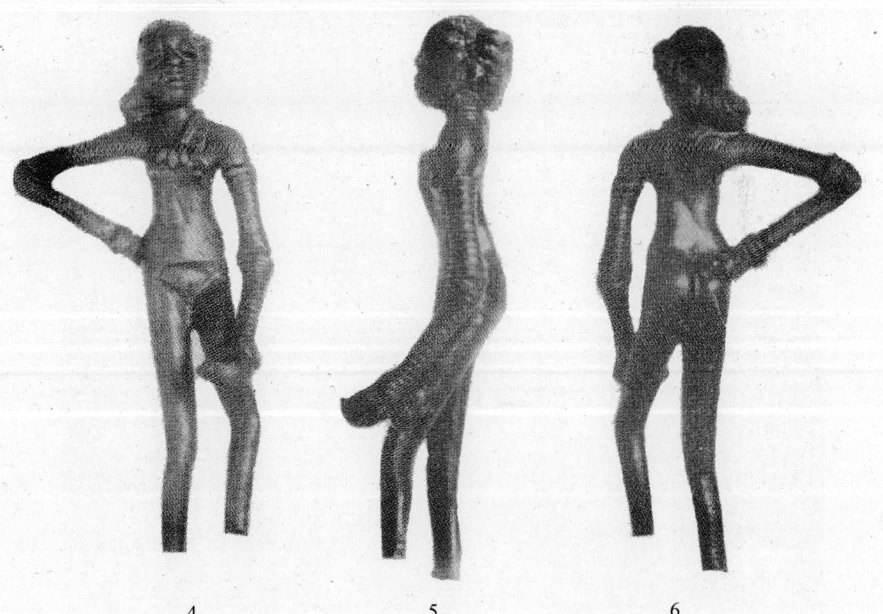

4 5 6

Courtest: Archaeological Survey of India

ARTS AND CRAFTSAIN, MOHENJO-DARO (See p. 175)

1. SQUIRREL IN FAIENCE
2. GLAZED FIGURE OF MONKEY
3. BEAD CARVED WITH THREE MONKEYS

4-6. BRONZE DANCING GIRL

PLATE VI

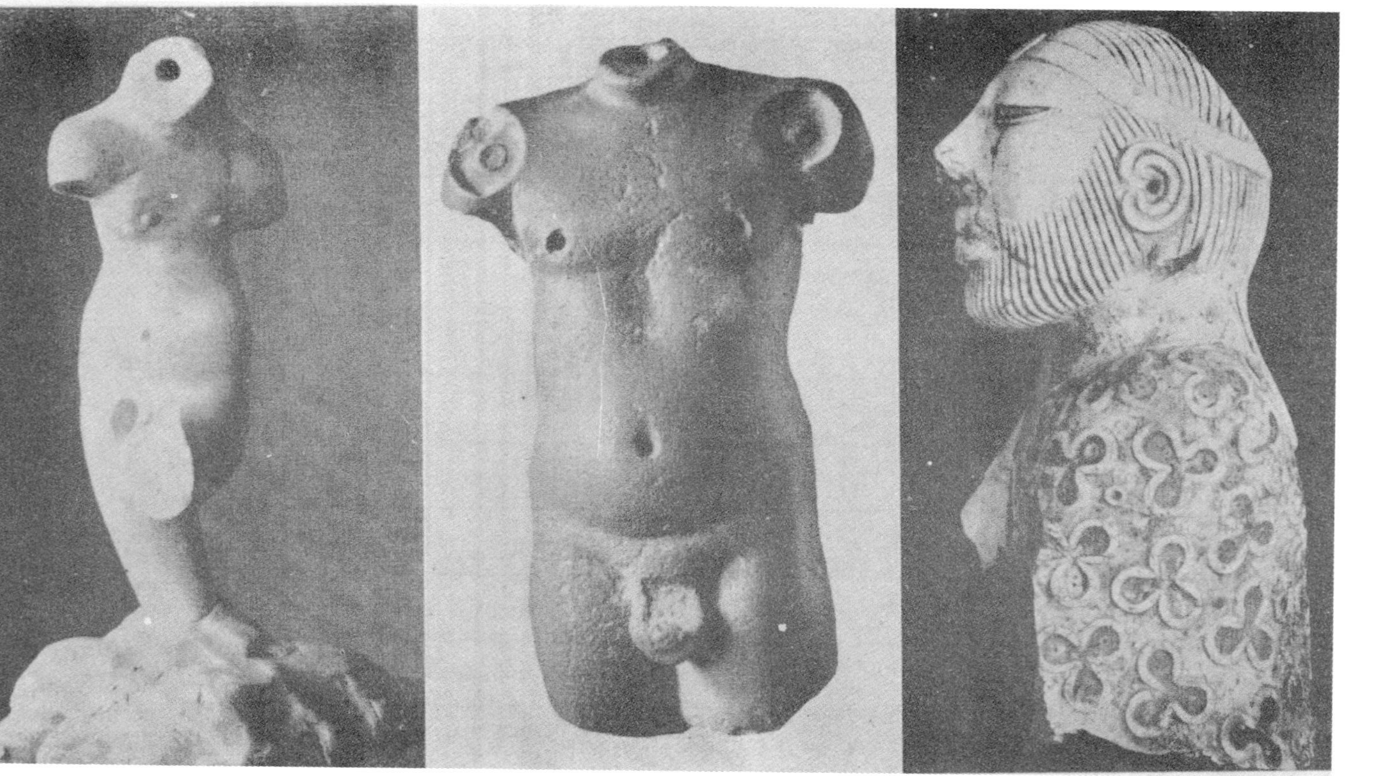

Courtest: *Archaeological Survey of India*

1. GREY STONE STATUE, HARAPPĀ 2. RED STONE STATUE, HARAPPĀ 3. STEATITE MALE HEAD, MOHENJO-DARO

PLATE VII

1 2 3

4 5 6

Courtest: Archaeological Survey of India

ARTS AND CRAFTSAIN, MOHENJO-DARO (See p. 186, 190f)
1-3. UNICORN WITH A STANDARD 4. ŚIVA PAŚUPATI. 5-6 SEALS DEPICTING ŚIVA
7. HORNED ARCHER 8. TRIŚŪLA-HORNED DEITY

PLATE VIII

1. FRACTIONAL BURIAL, MOHENJO-DARO (See p. 193)

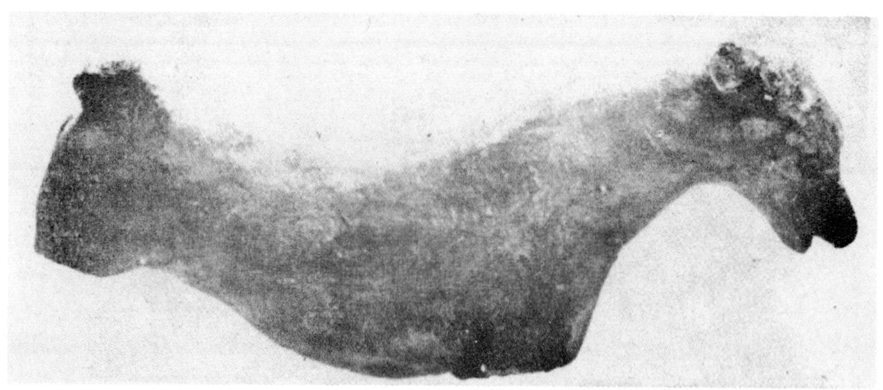

Courtest: Archaeological Survey of India

2. MODEL ANIMAL (HORSE), MOHENJO-DARO (See p. 198)

tan character of the population in a place like Mohenjo-daro with easy land and water communications is quite natural. It was evidently the meeting ground of the people from different parts of Asia. Sculptural representations also speak of the mingling of diverse races.

Only a country capable of producing food on a large scale, and the presence of a river sufficiently large to facilitate transport, irrigation, and trade, can give rise to cities of this size. The large number or saddle querns found in the excavations indicates cultivation on an extensive scale. Though little is yet known about the actual methods of agriculture adopted by the people, the examination of the specimens of wheat and barley found in the ruins shows that they were not of the wild species. The same variety of wheat is cultivated in the Punjab today. The unit of weight indicates that rice was also grown.[4] The date palm was also an article of diet as is shown by the stones found.

Besides wheat, barley, and rice, milk, too, must have been an important item of food, and doubtless vegetables and other fruits besides the date were included in the dietary. Harappā cultivated peas and sesamums.[4a] In addition, animal food was eaten, including beef, mutton, pork, poultry, the flesh of the *gharial*, turtle and tortoise, fresh-river fish and dried fish from the sea, and also shell fish. The half-burnt shells and bones of these animals found in houses, lanes, and streets definitely indicate that they were articles of diet.

Animals were both domesticated and wild. Actual skeletal remains of the Indian humped bull, the buffalo, the sheep, the elephant, the pig, and the camel have been recovered. The Indian humped ox, or "Brāhmani bull," is frequently represented on the seals. It seems to have been a sacred animal, as it is today. Bones of the horse have also been found, but not far below the surface. There is some difference of opinion on the subject, but on the grounds to be subsequently stated, it seems reasonable to suppose that horse was known to the Indus people. The cow was known, and so probably was the lion. Clay models of toys indicate that the Indian bison, the rhinoceros, the tiger, the monkey, the dog, the bear, and the hare were known to the inhabitants. The donkey was known, and among smaller animals may be included the mongoose, the squirrel, the parrot, the peacock, and the domestic fowl. Harappā knew of the domestic cat.

As regards dress, no actual specimens of ancient clothing have been discovered and we have to depend on the indications supplied by figurines and statuary. One alabaster statue shows that two garments were worn. A shawl-like cloth, worn over the left shoulder and under the right arm so as to leave the right arm free, formed the upper garment. The lower garment resembled modern *dhoti* and was worn quite close to the body. Female attire did not differ from that of the male. Garments were of cotton and perhaps of wool, and possibly they were sewn, as would appear from the needles found at the site.

With regard to the various fashions of hair-dressing, we know more about male styles because the head-dresses worn by the female figurines prevent the hair from being seen. It is likely that women had a plait tied with a bow at the end, a favourite way of dressing the hair in modern India. Men wore long hair; this was either parted in the middle and the short locks at the back kept tidy by a woven fillet; or was coiled in a ring on the top of the head, similar side rings concealing the ears, or were carried in a mass to the back; or a plaited lock was carried forward from behind in a large loop which turned in again and was secured by a fillet. Short hair was secured by means of a fillet or was coiled in a knot with hair pins. These fillets were made mostly of gold, silver or copper. Men grew short beards or close-cropped them along with the upper lip, which was sometimes clean shaven.

With the traditional oriental fondness for ornaments, men and women, both rich and poor, decorated themselves with them and all known semi-precious stones and metals were utilized for manufacturing various ornaments. Women wore a fan-shaped head-dress. Small cones of gold, silver, copper, and faience, as also of shell, were worn on the sides of the head. The forehead was decorated with a fillet or a headband. Ear-rings were made of coils of gold, silver, copper, or faience. It is doubtful whether any nose-ornaments were used. There was a variety of necklaces having pendants in the middle with a number of rows of beads of various shapes and materials artistically arranged using spacers and terminals. Finger-rings were plentiful, and bangles and bracelets were commonly used. Materials for bangles and bracelets were gold, silver, copper, bronze, faience, shell, and pottery. Gold and silver bangles were penannular in shape with their hollows filled with a fibrous or a lac core. A bracelet with six strings of globular beads is an excellent specimen of workmanship. Girdles, of which two fine specimens have been found, were worn round the waist. Anklets of the type still used by hill women round the Simla Hills were worn. Various stones such as carnelian, steatite, agate, chalcedony, jasper, etc., were pressed into service in the manufacture of beads which evince fine workmanship and technical skill on the part of the lapidary. Of the various ornaments mentioned above, men wore fillets, necklaces, finger-rings, and armlets. A yellow steatite pectoral was probably the insignia of office of a priest.

We can also form some idea about the toilet and cosmetics of the people. The "vanity case" found at Harappā, with its combination of piercer, ear-scoop, and tweezers, invites comparison with similar finds from Ur, Kish and Khafaje, both types showing the same peculiar construction of the looped head. Toilet jars were made of ivory, metal, pottery, and stone. Small faience vessels having four compartments were used for keeping expensive perfumes or cosmetics. It appears that the ladies at Mohenjo-daro knew of the use of collyrium, face-paint, and other cosmetics. Small cockle shells containing a red ochre rouge, lumps of green earth, white face-paint and black beauty-substance show that the belles in ancient Sind attended to beauty and toilet culture. It is interesting to note that Chanhu-daro finds indicate the use of lip-sticks.[5] Carbonate of lead, a face-paint, may also have been employed as an eye-ointment or hair-wash. Round metal rods in copper and bronze, with both ends rounded and polished, were probably used for applying cosmetics. There were small toilet tables specially designed for women. Other articles on the dressing-table included mirrors, made of bronze, oval in shape, and combs of different shapes made of ivory. Some combs were probably worn in the hair. Razors of various types, made of bronze, served for the toilet of the male.

Various household articles have been found at Mohenjo-daro. These were made of pottery, stone, shell, faience, ivory, and metal. Copper and bronze appear to have replaced stone as the material for household implements. Pottery supplied for the kitchen numerous articles including flesh-rubbers, cake-moulds, dippers, beakers, bowls, goblets, dishes, basins, pans, saucers, ladles, heaters, jar stands, storage jars, etc. Goblets with pointed bases were the customary drinking vessels, which were possibly to be used only once. Querns, palettes, and jar stands figure among articles of stone. Jar covers and ladles were also made of shell. There were needles, awls, axes, saws, sickles, knives, fish hooks, chisels, etc., made of bronze or copper, the first two also in ivory. Blocks of lead were probably used as net-sinkers.

Chairs, bedsteads, and stools were used to decorate the drawing room. Possibly there were wooden beds like *charpais*, and stools were made of wicker work and mats of reeds. There were lamps of copper, shell, and pottery. A pottery candlestick found in the ruins indicates that candles, probably made of wax or tallow with wicks of cotton, played their part in illuminating the houses at Mohenjo-daro.

Marbles, balls, and dice were used for games. Marbles were used as playthings both in Sumer and Egypt. That dicing was a common pastime just as it was in Vedic times is indicated by the large number of dice unearthed. Both cubical and tabular specimens are found, the latter being the commoner. Unlike the oblong pieces in common use in India at present, they are usually cubic in shape like the European dice; but the arrangement of numbers differs from the European system (where the sum of points on any two opposite sides amounts to 7), 1 being opposite to 2, 3 to 4, and

5 to 6. The tabular dice, invariably made of ivory, have three sides marked with numbers 1, 2, 3 and the remaining side is decorated with longitudinal lines. Of the seven pieces found at Harappā, four bear markings like those of Mohenjo-daro; on two are marked 1 opposite to 2, 3 to 4, and 5 to 6; and one has markings like the modern dice (i.e., 1 opposite to 6, 2 to 5, and 3 to 4). Thus there were three different ways of marking dice in the Indus Valley. It is not certain whether the throwing of dice constituted a game in itself. Possibly dice were used in conjunction with board games, as two incomplete specimens of game boards of brick have been found. Some flat models of fish in ivory appear to have been used in some game.

Some representations on amulet seals showing men shooting a wild goat and a large antelope with bows and arrows, and the remains of large antlers of deer and stags indicate that hunting was indulged in. Bull fighting was probably another pastime. There are indications to show that birds were kept as pets, and also for fighting. A certain amount of trapping was also carried on, and fishing was a regular occupation. Clay modelling appears to have been a favourite pastime with children, as is indicated by the large number of crude specimens of childish workmanship.

Specimens of toys are various, interesting, and ingenious. Little clay carts appear to have been the favourite toy with children as would appear from the large number found. Pottery rams, with the fleece indicated by lines of red paint and mounted on two wheels with a hole through the neck for a draw-string were common playthings. The toy carts are particularly interesting as being among the earliest representatives of wheeled vehicles known to us. Usually toys were clay models of men, women, and animals, whistles, rattles, etc. There were also toy birds provided with stock legs, small animals climbing up a pole, and figures with movable arms. The bull with a nodding head worked by a stiff fibre, and a monkey-like animal with movable arms figure among the more ingenious toys. Complex toys like figures moving up and down a string whose progress could be accelerated by manipulating a cord were also manufactured.

Bullock-carts were the chief means of conveyance. In addition to models of carts found at Mohenjo-daro similar to the farm carts in common use at present in Sind and the Punjab, a copper specimen has been found at Harappā, which looks like an *ekkā* of the present day, with a canopy for protection from the sun and rain. It thus appears that the ancients also used the same type of the bullock cart as is found in modern Sind, which was probably drawn by two animals yoked to a pole. Bullock carts with a gabled roof over a wooden frame were also in use.

Weights have been found in large numbers, and range from

large specimens which had to be lifted with a rope to very small ones used by jewellers. Cubical weights seem to be by far the most common. Some small weights of dark grey slate resemble the barrel-shaped weights of Elam and Mesopotamia, and are more accurate and consistent than those of Susa and Iraq. The sequence of ratios is binary in the case of the smaller weights as at Susa, and decimal in the case of larger ones. There is no evidence of a sexagesimal system. The unit weight has the calculated value of .8750 gms, the largest weight being 10970 gms. The most frequently discovered weight is one of 13.64 gms. which stands in the ratio of 16 to the standard unit of weight indicating the dominance of the number 16 in Indian culture.[6] It appears that a strict control was exercised over the maintenance of the proper standard of weight. The poor used ordinary pebbles as weights.

The few specimens of scales used with the weights appear to be of a very ordinary pattern, consisting of a bronze bar with suspended copper pans. Heavy weights must have required much larger beams, which were most probably made of wood. There is no evidence that the steelyard was known.

It is more difficult to form an idea of the measurement of length. A slip of shell, 6.62 inches long, which now preserves nine definite divisions each averaging 0.264 inches, has been taken by Dr. Mackay to be part of a linear measure. As groups of five appear to bear special marks, it seems that the decimal system was known, the measure indicating a decimal scale of 1.32 inches rising probably to a foot of 13.2 inches. Egypt was familiar with the decimal system of linear measure since the Fourth Dynasty, and a purely decimal system is found on Proto-Elamite tablets. Early Sumer used both the decimal and the sexagesimal systems. Probably the decimal system originated independently in the Indus Valley. Harappā ruins have yielded a fragmentary measure, a bronze rod, 1.5 inches long, broken at both ends, bearing four complete divisions accurately marked. It seems to have been based on the standard cubit of 20.62 inches which was widely used in the ancient world. Thus, the Mohenjo-daro and Harappā measures indicate that both the foot and cubit systems were current simultaneously in the Indus Valley.

Of the medicines used by the people we know but little. Pieces of a coal-black substance forming a dark-brown solution of water have been identified with *Śilājit*, which is known to be a specific for dyspepsia, diabetes, diseases of the liver, rheumatism, etc. Several cuttle fish bones have been found stored in pottery. Cuttle bone is internally used as an appetiser, and externally in diseases of ear, eye, throat, and skin. The horns of the deer and antelope (and possibly also of the rhinoceros) were valued for their medicinal qualities. Coral and leaves of the *nim* tree (*azadirachta indica*) were possibly used as medicines. All these specifics are still prescribed in *āyur-*

vedic medicine, and thus the origin of the indigenous medicinal system of India may be traced to the Indus Valley Civilization.

Abundant specimens of weapons, tools, and implements have been discovered. Weapons of war or the chase were axes, spears, daggers, bows, arrows, maces, slings, perhaps catapults, and swords, made generally of copper or bronze. Blade axes resemble the early specimens found at Susa. Spear heads are thin and broad, without the strengthening mid-rib, and with a tang instead of a socket. The daggers and knives are generally long and leaf-shaped, some with a single edge and others with two. Arrow heads are thin, flat pieces of copper with long narrow barbs and no tang. Maces were made of alabaster, sandstone, limestone, or hard green-coloured stone, and the pear-shaped mace, resembling the specimens from Elam, Mesopotamia, and Egypt, was most common. Swords are considerably thickened in the middle, but have blunt points suggesting that they were not used for thrusting. A kind of scale armour prepared from thin domed pieces of copper perforated with two minute holes was worn as for protection, and the shield was probably used for defensive purposes.

Lance heads, chisels, celts, axes, adzes, and saws figure among the tools and implements. Axes are either long and narrow or short and broad: the latter being probably used for cutting wood. A single specimen of a socketed bronze adze-axe is known, which can be compared to some finds in the Caucasus region. The cutting edge of the saw is semi-circular in shape and the toothed edge is wavy. Toothed saws were unknown among other peoples of antiquity.

The people of Mohenjo-daro maintained close contact with the outside world. For the import of various metals, precious stones, and other articles the Indus Valley had connections with Southern and Eastern India, Kāshmir, Mysore, and the Nilgiri Hills, as also with the countries immediately to the West and Central Asia (see below, p. 188). Evidence as to relations with Sumer is overwhelming, and trade contacts were maintained with Egypt and Crete. The representation on a seal of a mastless ship, with a central cabin and a steersman seated at the rudder, indicates that the people of the Indus Valley were acquainted with maritime vessels. The boat has a sharply up-turned prow and stern similar to the archaic representations on Early Minoan seals, cylinders of Sumer, and the Pre-Dynastic pottery of Egypt. Dr. Mackay thinks that the Indus Valley was in touch with Sumer and Elam by the sea route also. Mohenjo-daro thus appears to have been a great inland port carrying on trade with Ur and Kish, probably also with Egypt.

The remains unearthed at Mohenjo-daro demonstrate the existence of different sections of people who may be grouped into four main classes, the learned class, warriors, traders and artisans, and finally manual labourers, corresponding roughly to the four *Varṇas* of the Vedic period.[7] The learned class probably comprised priests and physicians, astrologers, and sorcerers. According to archaeologists there is practically no vestige of the fighting classes; but the existence of "palaces" with ancient foundations, of substantial swords showing that some of the people were well armed, of watchmen's quarters at Mohenjo-daro, and of ancient fort walls at other sites in Sind, points to a class similar to the Kshatriyas, whose duty was to protect the people. A commercial class and various artisans such as the mason, engraver, shell-worker, weaver, gold-smith, etc., formed the third class. Domestic servants and manual labourers like leather-workers basket-makers, peasants, fishermen, etc., belonged to the last class.

3. ARTS, CRAFTS, AND INDUSTRIES

There is very little sign of art for art's sake in the Indus Valley. There is no trace of ornamentation in houses and public buildings. Tools, weapons, vessels, etc., are quite plain and practical, but lack subtle grace. Even the painted pottery has commonplace designs. Specimens of art are to be sought only in figurines, seals, amulets, and other small objects. All figurines are well baked, and some of them are painted in red. The majority of human figures are female, and they are nude except for a narrow girdle round the loins. Animal figures are found in large numbers in pottery; the squirrel and monkeys are made in faience, and a turtle in shell. The short-horned bull is realistically portrayed as on the seals. The mastiff cut from steatite is quite life-like and resembles the English mastiff of today. The small carvings, presumably used as amulets, are most charming: notably little squirrels in faience (Pl. V. 1) not a couple of inches high, sitting up with tails erect and munching something from beneath their fore-paws; little monkeys (Pl. V. 2) with a worried expression, almost identical to what is so noticeable on the faces of their descendants today; and perhaps most delightful of all, a bead carved with three monkeys (Pl. V. 3) sitting round in a circle, clasping one another's waists with their arms. The exquisite bronze figure of an aboriginal dancing girl (Pl. V. 4-6) with her hand on the hip, in an almost impudent posture, is a noteworthy object. Her hands and legs are disproportionately long and she wears bracelets right up to the shoulder. The legs are put slightly forward with the feet beating time to the music. "Though more impressionistic in style than the stone sculptures, this figure, which is cast in one piece, astonishes one by the ease and naturalness of its posture."[8]

Of the seal engravings the best are those of such animals as the humped bull, the buffalo, and the bison, which the artist had an opportunity of studying at first hand. The humped bull is frankly realistic and spirited, and in its portrayal the artist has tempered realism with breadth of treatment and restraint. The buffalo is very effectively shown with a slightly raised head, displaying its great horns in the act of bellowing. The bison with powerful arched shoulders and relatively small hind quarters is quite lifelike. The blue faience tablet, depicting a deity seated cross-legged on a throne with a kneeling devotee on either side and a snake behind; "serves well to illustrate how instructive and illuminating a background this new-found prehistoric art of India is likely to supply to the later art of historic India." The best of the engraved seals are master-pieces of the engraver's art, as vivid in their drawing as they are skilful in execution, which could only have been turned out by people possessed of marked artistic ability and great technical skill.

Statuary is rare, only a few specimens being found. Statues were cut from comparatively soft stones, grey and yellow limestone, alabaster, and steatite. A steatite male head looks like an attempt at portraiture (Pl. VI. 3). The figure is draped in a shawl, decorated with trefoil patterns, which is worn over the left shoulder and under the right arm. The eyes are long, and half closed in a *yoga* attitude. The nose is well formed and of medium size; the mouth is of average size with close-cut moustache and a short beard and whiskers; the ears resemble double shells with a hole in the middle. The hair is parted in the middle, and a plain woven fillet is passed round the head. An armlet is worn on the right hand and holes round the neck suggest a necklace. The noticeable features in all statues are the prominent cheek-bones, the thick, short, sturdy neck, and narrow oblique eyes, in contrast to the Sumerian statues, which have round and full eyes, and full, fleshy lips. The heads are brachycephalic, dolichocephalic and mesaticranial.

Two statuettes from Harappā have revolutionized the current ideas about early Indian art (Pl. VI. 1, 2). In both, there are socket holes in the neck and shoulders for the attachment of head and arms, made in separate pieces in the red-stone torso, the frontal pose is adopted, the shoulders are well backed, and the abdomen slightly prominent. In the opinion of eminent art critics, for pure simplicity and feeling nothing to compare with this masterpiece was produced until the great age of Hellas. The other statuette represents a dancer standing on the right leg with the left leg raised in front, the body above the waist and both arms bent round to the left. The pose is full of movement. The neck is abnormally thick; possibly it may represent Śiva Naṭarāja, or the head may have been that of an animal. The anatomical faithfulness in these statuettes is striking. Specimens of art in lapidary work are found in the remarkably well-made stone beads specially those of clear and clouded agate, red translucent carnelian, etc. An instance of the considerable skill exhibited in the manufacture of stone beads is one that was made of five segments of chalcedony and deep red carnelian, which were cemented together to imitate a bead cut out of a piece of regularly veined stone.

From the discovery of many spindles and spindle whorls in the houses in the Indus Valley it is evident that spinning of cotton and wool was very common. That both the rich and poor practised spinning is indicated by the whorls being made of the expensive faience as also of the cheap pottery and shell. No textiles of any description have been preserved in the Indus Valley owing to the nature of the soil. A close and exhaustive examination, in the Technological Laboratory, of the pieces of cotton which were found attached to a silver vase, shows the specimen to be a variety of the coarser Indian cotton, cultivated in upper India today, and not of the wild species. Some more specimens of woven material adhering to various copper objects have also been found to be mostly cotton, but some were bast fibres. There is no indication from the ruins as to the existence of flax, which is largely grown in India at present and was known in ancient Elam and Egypt. The purple dye on a piece of cotton has been taken to have been produced from the madder plant. Dyers' vats found on the site indicate that dyeing was practised.

The Indus Valley pottery consists chiefly of very fine wheel-made wares, plain pottery being more common than the painted ware or ware with designs. In marked contrast to the delicate thinness of much of the Iranian and Mesopotamian wares, the Indus Valley pottery is heavy and utilitarian.

The clay used was the alluvium from the Indus, tempered with sand generally containing fine particles of mica or lime. Most of the specimens are wheel-turned, very few being hand-made. Pottery, brick, and terracotta were fired in kilns which were circular in shape with arrangements for heating underneath a floor provided with flues.

The plain ware is usually of red clay, with or without a fine red or grey "slip." It includes knobbed ware which is a curious type ornamented with rows of knobs. Imported Indian vases of this type have been found at Tell Asmar. The black-painted ware has a fine coating of red slip on which geometric and animal designs are executed in glossy black paint. Polychrome pottery is rare and mainly comprised of small vases decorated with geometric patterns in red, black, and green, rarely white and yellow.

Incised ware also is rare and the incised decoration was confined to the bases of the pans, always inside, and to the dishes of offering stands. Egg-shell pottery, locally known as *Kagzi*, is of exquisitely delicate workmanship and is absent in Susa and Babylon. Perforated pottery has a large hole at the bottom and small holes all over the wall, and was probably used for straining liquor.

Pottery for household purposes is found in as many shapes and sizes as could be conceived for daily practical use. Straight and angular shapes are the exception, and graceful curves the rule, with the Indus Valley pottery. Miniature vessels, mostly less than half an inch in height, are particularly so marvellously executed as to evoke the admiration of visitors.

Shanhu-daro appears to have been a manufacturing centre of toys, judging from the large number unearthed there. Pottery rattles, gaily decorated, and model pottery carts in various shapes with humped oxen are exceedingly common. Pottery rattles are so substantially made that hardly a broken specimen is found. There is a wide variety in the types of toy cart.

Seals discovered in the various strata constitute one of the most interesting features of the finds. Hitherto over 2,000 seals have been recovered from the various sites. Steatite, faience, ivory, and pottery are the materials used for manufacturing seals.

Stamped seals were invariably made of steatite, which came from Aravalli. Steatite was cut into shape with a saw, after which the boss was cut. The boss was then rounded off after the groove by a knife and finished off with an abrasive. The designs appear to have been cut by a burin. The body was first carved before outlining other parts. Inscriptions were added later. Almost all seals were coated with a smooth glossy glaze. Steatite was hardened by heating.

Seals are of various sizes and shapes, the most popular shape being square or oblong, with a pierced hump at the back for suspension, and a flat face decorated with exquisite designs, generally of animals, and with inscriptions in a pictographic script. The inscriptions on the seals, however, do not seem to have any connection with the figures on them, as the same animal figure is found in company with completely different inscriptions. The Svastika design, which is found in Crete, Cappadocia, Troy, Susa, Musyän, etc., but not in Babylonia or Egypt, appears on particular types of seals and indicates their religious use or significance. Though cylinder seals were universally used in Sumer, only three specimens have so far been found in the Indus Valley, having purely Indian devices.

A number of small steatite tablets recovered from the lowest levels at Harappā, having almost identical legends, are considered as receipts by Dr. Hunter.[9]

There are square or rectangular copper tablets, with an animal or human figure on one side and an inscription on the other, or an inscription on both sides. The figures and signs are carefully cut with a burin. These copper tablets appear to have been amulets.[10] Unlike inscriptions on seals which vary in each case, inscriptions on copper tablets seem to be associated with the animals portrayed on them.

It has generally been assumed that the designs on the Indus Valley seals, like those on the cylinder seals of Babylonia, were of a religious character and showed that the people were animal-worshippers. The commonest animal appears to be the so-called unicorn or antelope, resembling a bull, but without a hump, and a single protruding horn shown in profile. In front of the unicorn is placed a curious object, the lower portion of which is a bowl-like receptacle, with an upper part resembling a cage. Probably both the animal and the object have a ceremonial significance connected with the principal deity of Mohenjo-daro. The other animals are the short-horned bull, the Brāhmani bull, the elephant, the tiger, the rhinoceros, the *gharial* and the antelope. A flat-bottomed low manger or trough appears on some seals, and it is seen only before wild animals. The short-horned bull, the buffalo, and the rhinoceros are very carefully and realistically portrayed. The tiger with an open mouth and protruding tongue sometimes gazes at a tree on whose branches a man is perched. Alongside there appear mythological creatures and composite animals, such as human figures with bull's ears, horns, hoof, and tail; or a horned tiger; or a urus-like animal with additional heads of antelope and short-horned bull; or a most fantastic abortion, a curious human-faced animal partaking of the characteristics of a goat, a bull, a tiger, and an elephant. One circular seal shows six animal heads radiating from a boss.

The uses to which seals were put at Mohenjo-daro are uncertain and have been the subject-matter of various conjectures. The large variations in the inscriptions speak against their use as money. Reversed writing on 99 per cent of these objects becomes inexplicable if they are taken as amulets, and the projecting boss at the back disproves their use for this purpos e. Their use in other countries indicates that they were stamped on some plastic material like clay in order to authenticate property or seal the mouths of jars or doors. Owing to their fragile nature, actual clay impressions have been found of only a few specimens. Terra-cotta sealings were probably used for some specific purpose. Their large number and the fact that they have been found in the houses of the rich and poor alike indicate that the inhabitants attached great importance to them, and probably every citizen carried one on his person. The attempts in some seals to replace the legend after cutting it indicate that after the death of the original owner of the seal, it was taken by another by making appropriate changes in the inscription.[11]

Among semi-precious stones used for ornament, amazon and amethyst came from the south, and lapis lazuli, turquoise, and jadeite from the west. Rājputāna and Kāthiāwār supplied plasma, agate, jasper, and blood-stone. All these were used for manufacturing beads, regard being paid to their colour-scheme, size, and markings. Great technical skill is displayed in the manufacture of beads. The holes in the carnelian beads are well polished and testify to the great skill in boring such hard stones. Some unfinished beads of agate show that they were shaped and smoothed before being bored, for the translucency of the polished stone helped the lapidary in drilling straight. The accuracy of chert weights shows that the people were proficient in the working of flint, agate, gneiss, and other hard stones.

The gold used in the Indus Valley appears to have come from the gold mines at Kolar and in the Anantapur district. Different kinds of beads of gold were variously made by soldering cup-like pieces together or by casting or by beating out and soldering together. Bangles were made of thin sheets of gold with the metal slightly overlapping on the inside. Afghānistān, Armenia, and Persia range among the probable sources of silver. Large globular silver beads were cast or beaten out. Ear-rings were made of silver wire roughly bent round. Silver bracelets were made on core like gold bracelets. Copper and bronze are found side by side to the lowest levels at Mohenjo-daro. Copper may have come from Rājputāna, Baluchistān or Madras. The use of bronze indicates a great advance over contemporary civilizations in metal working. Though thus superior to the Sumerians in possessing the secret of smelting bronze, Indian metal-workers could not rival the beauty and delicacy of the gold and copper objects from Ur. Copper vessels were raised from sheet metal: those of bronze were cast by the *cire perdue* process. Eyes of needles and awls were formed either by drilling holes close together and then breaking the intervening material, or by bending the head over as in some pre-Sargonic needles at Kish. Copper and bronze finger-rings were generally made of coiled wire. Lead was extensively mined in ancient India, and Ajmer may have supplied lead to the Indus Valley. It is significant that the people of the Indus Valley were not conversant with the metallurgy of iron.

Shell is extensively used especially in the making of ornaments and pieces of inlay. Most of the shell might have come from places along the coast of India and the Persian Gulf. Mussel shell was also fairly common and was probably used as a spoon. *Oliva* was worn as an ornament and had some magic value attached to it. Cockle shells were probably used, as in early Sumer, to hold cosmetics. Mother of pearl is conspicuous by its absence, while it was used by the Sumerians for inlay. Shell was apparently available in large quantities. The manufacturers experienced great difficulties in cutting shell. *Columella* was first hollowed out by means of a saw and a hammer, and the tubular piece remaining was sawn into bracelets. Beads of different shapes and pieces for inlay work were made out of the *columella*, and the whole of the shell was utilized. The comparative paucity of ivory objects may possibly be due to the sanctity attached to elephants. The wild elephant, which is totally extinct in North-Western India at present, probably roamed in Sind and the Punjab in the third millennium B.C. At that period the climate of the Indus valley, if we may judge by the flora and fauna, resembled that of the Ganges delta today. Though no true glass has yet been unearthed, the art of glazing appears to have been practised. Vitrified paste and faience were used for glazed work. Faience was extensively manufactured in the Indus Valley and is found at all levels. Ordinary articles of faience are composed of a white or a greyish paste, granular in appearance, coated with a glaze, which has now faded to a light blue or green. Great skill in glazing is exhibited in a pottery bead covered by two coloured glazes, brown and white, which was first taken to have been made of glass.

4. RELIGION

No buildings have so far been discovered in the Indus Valley which may be definitely regarded as temples, and even those doubtfully classed as such have yielded no religious relics. There are no shrines, altars, or any definite cult objects. It is indeed curious that the Indus finds do not include any positive religious material, for religion has always played a dominant part in ancient cultures, and especially in India, where it was the prime factor moulding the lives of people for ages. All that we have to rely on for reconstructing the religion of the people is the testimony of the seals, sealings, figurines, stone images, etc. In spite of the meagreness of the material the light it throws on ancient religion is invaluable. Here we can only refer to a few leading ideas.

The first in point of importance is the cult of the Mother Goddess. A number of figurines of terra-cotta, faience, etc., portray a standing and semi-nude female figure, wearing a girdle or band round her loins, with elaborate head-dress and collar, occasionally with ornamental cheek cones and necklace; sometimes the ear-ornaments are like caps suspended on either side of the head. Some of the figures are smoke-stained, and it is possible that oil, or perhaps incense, was burnt before them in order that the goddess might hearken favourably to a petition.[12] Figurines similar to those in the Indus Valley have been discovered in many countries in Western Asia between Persia and the Ægean, and also round wayside trees and village shrines in South India. These figures are rightly taken to represent the Mother or Nature Goddess. There is no reason to believe that the cult of the Mother Goddess originated in Anatolia or any other particular country because the concepts of the motherhood of God and of the divinity of Nature are quite common among the primitive peoples of the world, and are wide-spread and deep-rooted in India.[12a] The Mother Goddess is represented in every village as the tutelary deity (*grāma devatā*) and is known under various names, such as Mātā, Ambā, Ammā, Kālī, Karālī, etc., sometimes to be dreaded, sometimes warding off evil spirits, imparting fertility, etc. It may be mentioned that the *Ṛigveda* refers to Pṛithvī and Aditi which are akin to the Mother Goddess.

An interesting sealing from Harappā shows a nude female figure, turned upside down, with out-spread legs and a plant issuing from the womb. The reverse side has a man with a sickle-shaped knife in hand and a woman seated on the ground with hands raised in supplication. Obviously this depicts a human sacrifice to the Earth Goddess, portrayed on the obverse with two genii. A similar figure of the Gupta Age has been discovered in the United Provinces with a lotus issuing out of the neck of the goddess. Perhaps the sealing represents a river gushing out of the goddess's womb.[13] The representation of a figure standing in the bifurcated branch of a *pipal* tree also appears to depict the Mother Goddess. To this goddess the worshipper brings a goat, probably for sacrifice, and a number of people standing in the lower register seem to be taking part in the sacrifice. The *Pipal* tree is still held to be sacred in India, but not associated with the cult of the Mother Goddess. The goat sacrifice has survived in the worship of Śakti, another form of the Mother Goddess, in which the sacrifice of animals is the most characteristic feature. It is still uncertain whether the female deity represented by pottery figurines was regarded as a virgin goddess or as the consort of the male god on the seal amulets.

Among the male gods the most remarkable is a three-faced deity wearing a horned head-dress, seated cross-legged on a throne, with *penis erectus*, and surrounded by elephant, tiger, buffalo, and rhinoceros, with deer appearing under the seat. It wears a number of bangles and has a pectoral round the neck, and an inscription of seven letters appears at the top (Pl. VII. 4). This representation has at least three concepts which are usually associated with Śiva viz., that he is (i) *trimukha* (three-faced), (ii) *paśupati* (lord of animals), and (iii) *Yogīśvara* or *Mahāyogī*. The first two aspects are apparent from the seal itself. The deity is sitting cross-legged in a *padmāsana* posture with eyes turned towards the tip of the nose which evidences the Yogīśvara aspect of the deity. It has been suggested by some scholars[14] that this Śiva-cult was borrowed by the Indo-Aryans from the Indus culture but as there is a reference to Śiva in the *Ṛigveda* itself.[14a] Śiva may not be a later intruder in the Hindu pantheon.

Two more seals of Śiva have been found in the course of further excavations (Pl. VII. 5. 6). The deity is always nude save for a cincture round the waist, and has a horned head-dress. In one seal the deity is three-faced and seated on a low dais, while the second has one face in profile; both have a sprig of flowers or leaves rising from the head between the horns. This sprig suggests that the deity so ornamented is a vegetation or fertility god—another link with Śiva, who personifies the reproductive powers of nature. A horned archer dressed in a costume of leaves (Pl. VII. 7) displays the divine hunter aspect of Śiva.

It thus appears that Śiva was one of the principal deities of the people along with the Mother Goddess. His worship was, however, not merely iconic, but also phallic, as would appear from the presence of a large number of conical and cylindrical stones. These conical and cylindrical stones probably symbolize fertility, and are connected with the cult of Śiva as *Liṅgas*. Many scholars find a contemptuous reference in the *Ṛigveda* to phallus worship and regard it as a veiled allusion to the religious customs of the pre-Aryan people of the Indus Valley, but it has been suggested by others that the passage in question simply alludes to sensuous or lustful persons.[15]

Small ring stones suggest that the worship of the *Yoni*, the female symbol of generation, was also prevalent though not to such an extent as *Liṅga* worship. It is, however, possible to take the group of ring stones as pedestals or bases of pillars. Hence until the *liṅga* and one of the ring stones are found in close association, the question of the prevalence of phallic worship cannot be definitely settled. The Vedic religion, it may be observed, was originally aniconic, the worship of icons arising at a later stage.

That animal worship or zoolatry formed part of the religious beliefs of the people is indicated by the representations of animals on seals and sealings, or in terra-cotta, faience, and stone figurines. The animals fall into three groups: (i) mythical animals, e.g. a semi-human, semi-bovine creature, attacking a horned tiger resembling Eabani or Enkidu in Sumerian mythology; or, complex animals, with the heads of different animals attached to a central boss, which may possibly be an attempt to bring together the representations of various deities; (ii) ambiguous animals, which are not completely mythical, like the strange unicorn, accompanied with manger or incense-burner; or animals figuring as officiant genii. The frequency with which the unicorn appears has been taken to indicate that it was the tutelary deity of the city. Lastly there are (iii) actual animals, including the rhinoceros, the bison, the tiger, the elephant, the buffalo, the humped bull or zebra, the short-horned bull, etc. The feeding troughs which appear before some of these have been taken as symbolizing food offerings to beasts which could not be domesticated, indicating the animals as objects of worship. Some of these animals were regarded as the *vāhana* or vehicles of the gods. The bull, for instance, is closely associated with Śiva.

It may be suggested that the limestone statues of animals resting on rectangular plinths represent gods in their animal form. Possibly the unicorn has some connection with the boar incarnation of Vishṇu, which is said to be *eka-śṛiṅga* (one-horned).

Apart from their use as pictographic signs, no birds appear on seals or other amulets. It seems, however, that the dove was looked upon as sacred, as some of the pottery models on little pedestals exactly resemble those found at very early sites in Mesopotamia, where the dove was regarded as sacred to the Mother Goddess.

The worship of tree, fire, and water also seems to have been in vogue. The existence of tree worship is evidenced by the representations on several seals and sealings. The most interesting of these depicts the *triśūla*-horned deity standing nude, with long hair, between two branches of a tree with the half-kneeling figure of a worshipper with long hair, armlets, and horns, behind whom is a composite animal; in the lower register appear seven standing figures, with dresses down to the knees, in procession (Pl. No. VII. 8). The leaves of the tree appear like those of the *pipal*. Some sealings from Harappā show trees enclosed by a wall or a railing. It cannot at present be stated definitely whether tree worship pertained to trees in their natural state or to their indwelling spirits.

Rectangular aisles, separated from each other by long walls, suggest the Vedic sacrificial altar of a rectangular shape (*agniśālā* paved with bricks), in which offerings were made to Fire and other gods.[16]

Though no direct evidence has been found to river worship, the important part played by water in the daily life of the Indus people, as indicated by the elaborate arrangements for bathing and the Great Bath, seems to show that ceremonial ablutions formed a feature of their religion. The Great Bath has been suggested as the temple of the River-God. The crocodile probably represented the river Indus. The cult of the *gharial* survives in Sind even today.

The representations, on some seals, of *Svastika* and the wheel, which are the symbols of the sun, suggest that the sun was not represented anthropomorphically but symbolically. *Svastika* and the cross appear to be religious or magical symbols as in Babylonia and Elam.

From a faience tablet showing a seated deity with a worshipper on either side and a hooded cobra over the head, it appears that some form of *Nāga* worship was practised.

5. FUNERARY CUSTOMS

The evidence with regard to the customs about the disposal of the dead in the ancient Indus Valley is yet far too meagre for any definite conclusions, and though Harappā records more ample material, it relates to a period subsequent to the occupation of Mohenjo-daro.

Three forms of burial have been found at Mohenjo-daro, viz., complete burials, fractional burials, and post-cremation burials. Complete burial means the burial of the whole body, ceremonially performed in various forms, along with the grave furniture, offerings, etc. About 30 skeletons, evidencing complete burials, have been found in different groups. Some of these appear to have been victims of accidental death. All these burials appear, on stratigraphical evidence, to relate to the declining years of Mohenjo-daro.

Fractional burial represents a collection of some bones after the exposure of the body to wild beasts and birds. Five such burials have been found, the best specimen being an urn containing a skull and some fragmentary bones, along with a number of earthenware vessels, and a variety of small objects including balls, beads, shell spoon, bits of ivory, and miniature vessels (Pl. VIII. 1). Human bones are not found in all specimens, probably because after exposure bones were ground to dust before interment.

Post-cremation burials have been inferred from large wide-mouthed urns containing a number of smaller vessels, bones of animals, and of birds or fish, and a variety of small objects, such as beads, bangles, figurines, etc., sometimes mixed with charcoal ashes. These are generally found underneath a floor or a street. Human bones are seldom found, these generally being the bones of lambs, goats, etc., as bones are hardly necessary for post-cremation burials. The uniform character of the urns, quite distinct from the domestic varieties, as also the offerings in the form of objects of special interest to the departed, and the burial of these urns within dwelling houses or in close proximity, leave no doubt as to their being burial urns. These have been discovered at six places in Mohenjo-daro, distributed among strata of all periods.

6. THE INDUS SCRIPT

The Indus script has been characterized by most scholars as pictographic, but save for a small number of signs representing birds, fish, etc., and varieties of the human form, the rest bear more or less a conventional character. Originally pictographic, the signs, as we know them, have become standardized, but not so conventionalized by usage as to have become mere stereotyped summaries like the cuneiform characters of Mesopotamia. During all the centuries of Mohenjo-daro's occupation, the script presents no development in the form of the letters. The script is found in one stage only, so that we cannot trace its genesis from the pictographic to the ideographic or phonetic, or its later development to any of the scripts of India.

The most remarkable features of the Indus script are its clarity and straight rectilinear character, and the extent and variety of its signs. Admirable ingenuity is displayed in modifying the signs by the addition of strokes or accents, and in combining one sign with another in the form of conjuncts. The large number of signs precludes the possibility of the script being alphabetic. It was mainly phonetic, most of the signs apparently standing for open or closed syllables, and the remainder functioning as determinatives or ideograms. Nearly 400 distinct signs have been listed from the script so far.

From the recurrence of certain characters, the facing of the animals and a few other indications, it has rightly been inferred that the direction of writing is from the right to the left, though in a very few inscriptions the direction is from left to right. In legends covering two or more lines the direction is *boustrophedon*.

There are resemblances between some characters in the Indus script and those in the Sumerian, proto-Elamite, Hittite, Egyptian, Cretan, Cypriote, and Chinese scripts. Similarities have also been traced with the script of the Easter Islands, and the Tāntric pictographic alphabets. All these scripts are possibly interrelated, but only up to a certain point. Some scholars even claim the Brāhmī to have been derived from the Indus script.

It is not possible, in the present stage of our knowledge, to determine the language of the script. Some scholars take it to be Sanskrit and others as Dravidian. In their attempts to decipher the script several scholars have taken for granted the identity of the Indus language with one or the other of the known languages or their prototypes.[17] In connection with the resemblances of the Indus signs with other scripts, Rao Bahadur Dikshit observes that the resemblance with Sumerian and proto-Elamite signs presages a close connection, at least in the formative stages; similarities with the Egyptian and Chinese pictographs are superficial, and the Indus script developed independently on Indian soil.[18] With regard to interpreting the script in terms of the Dravidian equivalents, it may be stated that we have nothing to rely on as to the original or the proto-Dravidian language; the language could not have been static during these 5,000 years.[18a] Much more extensive research in Southern India, moreover, will be necessary before definite links can be forged between the later stages of the Indus Valley civilization and the dawn of civilization in Southern India.

The material at our disposal is sufficiently large, but despite earnest attempts by scholars no real light can be thrown on the subject which may find general acceptance. In the absence of a real solution that would stand the test of any and every investigator, all attempts to decipher the script will have merely an academic interest. The Indus Valley had trade relations with Sumer and Elam, and Indus seals have been found at the latter sites. It is likely that some bilingual inscription, turned up by the spade of the archaeologist in Irāq, will give us the right clue to the decipherment of the Indus script.

7. THE ANTIQUITY OF THE CULTURE

Despite its definite individual characteristics, the Indus Valley civilization is not isolated and unique, but has sister civilizations elsewhere, with several outstanding common features, which indicate its contemporaneity with the western city cultures in Mesopotamia. At none of the sites in the Indus Valley has iron been found, which gives us the lower limit of the age of the civilization, as iron was known everywhere in the Middle East in the later half of the second millennium B.C. The civilization that we find in the Indus Valley is still of the chalcolithic age displaying remarkable similarity with the Second Pre-Diluvian Culture of Elam and Mesopotamia, and the proto-historic period of Sumer (c. 2750 B.C.).

Excavation has brought to light seven different layers of buildings at Mohenjo-daro, which have been assigned to three periods, viz. Early, Intermediate, and Late. Earlier layers lie submerged under subsoil water. The phase of the Indus Valley civilization found at Mohenjo-daro and Harappā is known as the "Harappā Culture." Explorations in Sind have brought to light three different "cultures," viz., those of Amri, Jhukar, and Jhangar, the first of which preceded and the last two followed the Harappā culture. Chanhu-daro displayed races of Jhukar and Jhangar cultures in the upper levels.

On the analogies of Troy and Rome, normally a period of one thousand years should be assigned for the occupation of the seven cities of Mohenjo-daro; but as the decay at Mohenjo-daro was much quicker on account of the imminent danger of floods (of which we get evidence), and as the re-occupation of the cities was much more rapid as seen from the uniformity of antiquities in all layers, a period of only 500 years has been assigned for the whole strata. As, however, the civilization is already in a developed stage, roughly a period of 1000 years has been allotted for the antecedent evolution.

The latest settlement of Mohenjo-daro has been attributed to 2750 B.C., so that the occupation of the seven cities ranges between 3250-2750 B.C. This rough dating, however, has been brought down by a few centuries by the find of various Indus Valley objects in datable strata in Sumer and Mesopotamia.

An Indus seal confined to the Late Period at Mohenjo-daro was found at Eshnunna in layers pertaining to 2600-2500 B.C., so that the early period at Mohenjo-daro reaches back to about 2800 B.C. A similar seal, however, has been found at Ur in a tomb which is not older than 2150 B.C.[19] Dr. Frankfort's discovery of cylinder seals of Indian origin at Tell Asmar and of a green steatite vase depicting a Brāhmani bull at Tell Agrab carry back the date of the

Indus Valley civilization to about 2800 B.C. The seals of the Indus Valley type found in Mesopotamia by Dr. Gadd indicate 2800 B.C. as the upper limit of the Harappā culture. Dr. Fabri places the main culture period at Mohenjo-daro between 2800-2500 B.C. on the evidence of a pottery jar with a Sumero-Babylonian inscription found at Mohenjo-daro.[20] A comparison of the plain and painted ware in the Indus Valley with similar specimens at Sumer, Elam, and Egypt shows the Indus Valley civilization to have flourished about 2500 B.C. Ceramic evidence shows that the earliest stage of the Indus Valley civilization is represented at Amri, which may go back to 3000 B.C., followed by the Harappā, Jhukar, and Jhangar cultures.

On a careful consideration of all available material for the age of the Indus civilization, some of which has been indicated above, it appears that the main culture period at Mohenjo-daro or the "Harappā culture" ranged between 2800-2500 B.C. Though it must have had a long history of antecedent development before it reached the stage we meet, no idea of that period can be had, as the lowermost strata cannot be reached at Mohenjo-daro, Harappā, Jhukar, or Chanhu-daro, because of subsoil water. The civilization for all we know may well reach beyond 3500 B.C. The uppermost layers of Chanhu-daro, as suggested by Dr. Mackay, can be assigned to 2300-2200 B.C., whereas the lower strata go back to 2600-2500 B.C. The culture period of the Indus Valley civilization, as revealed by its finds, thus seems to have lasted roughly from c. 2800 to 2200 B.C. The cultures at different sites in the Indus Valley are to be placed between these two extreme dates.

8. AUTHORS OF THE INDUS CIVILIZATION

The only definite material available with regard to the authorship of the Indus Valley civilization is the human skeletons and skulls found among the ruins. As mentioned above, these show that the population of Mohenjo-daro was heterogeneous and comprised at least four different racial types, viz. Proto-Australoid, Mediterranean, Alpinoid, and Mongoloid. The Mohenjo-daro population is, however, generally believed to have mainly consisted of the Mediterranean type, which has been described before (*ante*, p. 145 ff.). The craniological evidence speaks not only of the diverse racial elements, but also of free racial mixture.

No accuracy or scientific precision in this respect can be expected in sculptured pieces, as the artists were not anthropologists. Whatever meagre evidence is supplied by the statuary confirms the craniological evidence as to the existence of different races.

The anthropological and statuary evidence does not aid us in pointing at the authors of the civilization. There has been quite an amount of speculation among scholars and archaeologists with regard to the ascription of the authorship of the Indus civilization to any particular race. Words like Aryan and Dravidian which primarily denote linguistic groups have been indiscriminately used in an ethnic sense in this connection. Thus the authorship has been ascribed to Dravidians, Brāhuis, Sumerians, Paṇis, Asuras, Vrātyas, Vāhīkas, Dāsas, Nāgas, Aryans, etc.[21]

The majority view prefers to hold the authors of the Indus civilization as speakers of "Dravidian" (*ante*, p. 158). So far, however, as the funeral customs are concerned it is impossible to ascribe the Indus Valley culture to the "Dravidians," among whom burial was the prevalent form of interring the dead. Further, excavation in the south has hitherto revealed no traces of the Indus Valley civilization.

The Brāhuis, though speaking a Dravidian language, are of Turko-Iranian origin, and are ethnically quite distinct from the various peoples speaking Dravidian languages in Central and Southern India. There is no definite evidence to support the Brāhui authorship of the Indus culture.

We know nothing definite as to the racial features of the Sumerians. They were, no doubt, in close contact with the Indus Valley in ancient days, and probably formed part of the population at Mohenjo-daro; but there is nothing to credit them with the authorship of the Indus culture.

As regards the Paṇis, Vrātyas, Vāhīkas, Asuras, Dāsas, and Nāgas, we have no material to identify them with any of the known races.

Sir John Marshall has compared the Vedic civilization with that of the Indus Valley and has found that they are quite distinct; and as the entry of the Aryans into India, according to his view of the date of the *Ṛigveda*, is subsequent to 1500 B.C., more than a thousand years after the last vestige of the Indus Valley Civilization disappeared, he cannot think of the Aryans in connection with the Indus Valley civilization.

Now the presumed age of the *Ṛigveda* is really no barrier to the Aryan authorship of the Indus culture (if other evidence proves that hypothesis) for, in the first instance, that age is not known with even an approximate degree of certainty, and secondly, because the *Ṛigveda* can safely be taken to have represented a period long posterior to the advent of the Aryans into India. As to the existence of the Aryans in the Indus Valley at so early a period as the age of the Indus culture, it is held by some, on the evidence of skeletal material, that the Aryans formed part of the diverse population of those days.[22]

Various arguments have been advanced by Sir John Marshall in order to prove that the Indus Valley civilization was quite distinct from, and earlier than, the Vedic civilization. One of his principal arguments, viz., the borrowing of the Śiva cult of Mohenjo-daro by the Vedic Aryans, has been noted above. Among others may be mentioned the absence of the horse and presence of icons. As regards the first, Dr. Mackay takes the model animal illustrated in Pl. VIII. 2 to represent a horse, and has conjectured that the Indus Valley people probably knew the horse at about 2500 B.C. at the latest. The finds of saddles in some of the lowest strata at Mohenjo-daro, and the representation of the horse in the Indus Valley art seem to prove that the horse was known.[23] As to the second, it is true that the Vedic religion was aniconic to a very great extent. But it is not unlikely that the *Ṛigveda* represents an earlier phase of the culture found in the Indus Valley. The use of icons in the Indus Valley, as seen in the phallic cult, probably followed in the wake of Śiva worship in the *Ṛigveda*. Later on, owing to contact with alien or non-Aryan elements, some concepts such as phallic worship, magic and charms, etc., were perhaps incorporated in the comprehensive Hindu religious system. Similarly, the Mother Goddess (Aditi and Pṛithvī in the *Ṛigveda*) and Śiva were developed in the period of the Indus Valley by synthesis and fusion with non-Aryans. There was thus a co-mingling of cultures, Vedic and non-Vedic, and for the authorship of the composite Indus Valley civilization, we need not look to any particular race.

Although Sir John Marshall's view is now generally accepted, some scholars still regard the Vedic civilization as older than that of the Indus Valley. It is impossible, at the present state of our knowledge, to come to any definite conclusion, but it has to be admitted that there is no conclusive evidence against the view that ascribes the authorship of the Indus Valley civilization to the Rigvedic Aryans, and regards it as a logical corollary, a lineal descendant, of the culture described in the *Ṛigveda*. But even then the authorship of the Indus Valley civilization cannot be ascribed to any particular race, as every element in the diverse population contributed its share to the civilization. Even assuming that the Rigvedic civilization was earlier, we must remember that during the period that intervened between it and the Indus Valley civilization, the Vedic religion was incorporating many alien and non-Aryan features such as phallus worship, Nāga worship, magic and spells, etc., and was already tending to become comprehensive, composite and all-embracing, harmonising different constituent elements and catering to the needs of the various strata. It would not, therefore, be correct to ascribe the authorship of the Indus Valley culture to the Aryan or any other particular race. It represents the synthesis of the Aryan and non-Aryan cultures. The utmost that we can say is that the Rigvedic Aryans probably formed an important part of the populace in those days, and contributed their share to the evolution of the Indus Valley civilization.

9. EXTENT, CONNECTIONS, AND SURVIVALS OF THE INDUS CIVILIZATION

The very fact that Mohenjo-daro and Harappā, the first two prehistoric sites excavated in the Indus Valley, although about 400 miles apart, present a homogeneous culture, shows that the civilization was neither local nor regional, nor confined to any restricted area. Subsequent excavations in a large number of other sites have brought to light prehistoric antiquities representing the identical civilization, and these indicate that Mohenjo-daro and Harappā do not mark the extreme limits of its extent. The late Mr. N. G. Majumdar's exploration in Sind revealed various settlements of the Indus Valley civilization in many places in Sind, from the modern Hyderābād, 60 miles north-east of Karāchi in the south, to Gujo, Vijnot, and Jacobābād in the north, forming a long chain of mounds between the present course of the Indus and the foot-hills of the Kirthar range. The annexed map (No. 2) shows that these prehistoric sites follow the old lines of communication between southern and northern Sind through the hill range. Chanhu-daro, over a hundred miles south-east of Mohenjo-daro, and Amri, the same distance down-stream from Mohenjo-daro, are important sites at which the same civilization has been found. On the west bank of the Indus, Lohumjo-daro, Ali Murad, Jhukar, Ghazi Shah, Alor, etc. are the principal sites from which several objects of the Indus culture were recovered. Further west, Sir Aurel Stein's explorations have proved the extension of the Indus Valley civilization to Dabar Kot, Sur Jangal, and Periano Ghundal in Northern Baluchistān and Kulli and Mehi in Southern Baluchistān. According to Stein, Shahi Tump marks the outpost of the Indus Valley civilization.[24]

Terra-cottas recovered at Buxar and at Pāṭaliputra (Patna) indicate the extent of the cultural influence of the Indus Valley eastward.[25] In the Ghāzipur and Benares districts were found pictographs, carnelian beads, and objects exactly similar to those found in the Indus Valley. There are various ancient sites in the United Provinces in the Gangetic basin from which relics of copper civilization have been reported.

Kotla Nihang Khan, near Rupar on the Sutlej in the Ambāla district below the Simla hills, about 220 miles due east of Harappā, also records finds typical of the Indus Valley sites.

Thus the Indus Valley civilization seems to have embraced the whole of Sind and the Punjab, the bulk of Kāthiāwār, a part of the coastal region, the valleys of North-west Frontier province, and a part at least of the Gangetic basin.[26]

The extent of the Indus Valley civilization indicates its connections practically with the whole of Northern India, and in the west, with all the contemporary cultures. Immediately the discoveries in the Indus Valley were published, Sumerologists came forward with affinities of the Indus Valley civilization with Sumer, and at the outset the Indus Valley civilization was designated Indo-Sumerian. But despite its close contact with ancient Sumer, the Indus Valley civilization has peculiarities of its own. It has recently been shown that the similarities between the two cultures have been over-emphasized and the differences overlooked. At any rate there is an overwhelming mass of evidence showing that a flourishing trade, probably through the land routes in Baluchistān, existed between the Indus Valley and Sumer in ancient times. Numerous seals of Indian design and workmanship have been found at various Sumerian and Elamite sites. Importations from Sumer recovered in the Indus Valley, however, are comparatively very few. A white marble seal, an engraved steatite vessel, an etched carnelian bead, a model ram, an adze axe, and small pottery rings used as net-weights have been recorded as probable importations from Sumer, indicating trading intercourse. The most important piece of evidence testifying to the influence of the Indus Valley on Sumer is the fashion of hair-dressing adopted by Sumerian women from the Indus Valley.[27]

For associations with Egypt, however, we have to depend only on indirect connection suggested by certain objects and motifs. No definite object of Egyptian workmanship has been found in the Indus Valley, nor has any Egyptian site recorded an Indus Valley object. Segmented beads and hemispherical terminals of necklaces, bull-legged stools, small model beds with recumbent female figurines, female figurines suckling a child, faceted beads, fly-shaped beads, cord designs, candle stands and mussel-shell-shaped spoons, are among the various objects that link the Indus Valley and Egypt. The borrowings appear to have taken place through Sumer and Elam as intermediaries.

Though Stein's researches clearly show that the population of Baluchistān was far greater than it is now, and that various land routes through Baluchistān were extensively used in ancient times for trade purposes, it appears probable that the Indus Valley people also used sea-routes, despite lack of corroborative evidence.

Before dealing with the survivals of the Indus Valley civilization, we may consider the causes that led to its decay and disappearance. The progressive desiccation of the lower Indus Valley was the main cause of the evacuation of the Indus cities. The growing danger of floods was certainly responsible for the evacuation of Mohenjo-daro. The Indus floods, however, cannot account entirely for the desertion of the Indus settlements, though possibly climatic changes were an important reason. There is a remarkable dearth of means of defence both structural, such as walls, turrets, etc., and mechanical, such as weapons, etc., and it is probable that these rich unguarded cities, with their unwarlike mercantile population, were sacked by invading tribes, some of whom may have been Aryans. The skeletons found at Mohenjo-daro bear out this conjecture. A similar fate overtook the palace of Minos at Crete.

The discovery of the Indus Valley civilization has pushed back the history of India to the period 3000-2500 B.C. if not earlier still. It is generally believed that there is a hiatus in Indian culture of at least 1000 years, up to c. 1500 B.C. when the Aryans set foot in India. It will be shown later (Ch. XIV) that according to the traditional history of the Hindus as recorded in the Purāṇas, ancient history ends with the Mahābhārata war, which was fought in c. 1400 B.C., and goes back to the period immediately after the Flood. As Mohenjo-daro culture is a post-Flood event, we may hold that there is a continuity of historical traditions right from the Mohenjo-daro period down to the Mahābhārata war, and these grow more and more reliable as we come to later times ending in the Gupta Age (fourth century A.D.).

Punch-marked coins, with their symbols reminiscent of the Indus Valley script, and with their standard of weight conforming to the weight system at Mohenjo-daro, constitute an important survival of the Indus Valley dating from before 400 B.C. The die-struck and cast varieties of ancient Indian coins appear to be indebted to the Indus Valley for their form. Some of the motifs, designs, shapes, and forms found in the pottery and terra-cotta objects at Mohenjo-daro and Harappā find their counter-part in the objects discovered in the Punjab and the North-West, belonging to the early centuries before the Christian era. In the field of religious symbols, it may be suggested that the horn-crown on the head of Śiva Paśupati in the Indus Valley has survived as a symbol of great significance in the *nandipada*, and the images of Śiva as Dakshināmūrti and of Buddha as Yogi are due to the influence of the Indus culture.

These instances indicate that there was probably no complete break or hiatus after the Indus Valley civilization.

GENERAL REFERENCES

MACKAY, E.J.H.: *Further Excavations at Mohenjo-daro*. Two vols. Delhi. 1938.
MAJUMDAR, N.G.: *Explorations in Sind*, *MASI*, No. 48. Delhi, 1934.
MARSHALL, SIR JOHN: *Mohenjo-daro and the Indus Civilization*. Three vols. London, 1931.
VATS, M.S.: *Excavations at Harappa*. Two vols. Delhi, 1940.

1. The name Mohenjo-daro has been variously interpreted to mean "the mound of the dead" (*Moh. Ind.*, P. I), "the mound of the confluence" (*JRAS*. 1932. p. 456, fn. I), "the mound of the killed" (*Mahan-jo-Daro*, p. I) or "the mound of Mohan."

1a. *Harappa*. p. 13.

2. *Moh. Ind.*, p. 274 (Mackay), 274, fn. 2 (Marshall): Mariwala, *Ancient Sind*, p. 9.

3. Carleton, *Buried Empires*, p. 151.

4. Childe, *New Light*. p. 209; Dikshit, *Preh. Civ.*, p. 25.

4a. *Harappa*, p. 6.

5. Mackay, *BMFA*. XXXIV. p. 91: cf. *Chan-d.*, p. 235.

6. Cf. *Chan-d.*, pp. 236 ff.
7. Cf. Dikshit, *Preh. Civ.*, pp. 31-2.
8. Carleton, *Buried Empires*, p. 154.
9. *Script*, p. 32.
10. Dr. Hunter regards them as coins or stamped ingots—*JRAS*, 1932, p. 474.
11. Dr. Thomas suggests that the seals served the combined function of seal, amulet, and *ex voto* (*JRAS*, 1932, p. 460), and Dr. Hunter states that they were used for stamping unbaked clay to be carried outside the city with the offerings (*JRAS*, 1932, p. 471).
12. Mackay, *JRSA*, 82, p. 218. Venkateswara refers to these as Dīpalakshmī figures on account of their analogy with later metal figures in South India holding oil in hand (*Cult. Her.*, III, p. 60).
12a. Cf. Ch. VIII, p. 158, for the suggestion that the idea of the Mother Goddess was imported by the Dravidians from the West.
13. Cf. Childe, *New Light*, p. 222.
14. Cf. Ch. X, below, p. 203, and Ch. VIII, above, p. 161.
14a. *RV*, II. I. 6; 33. 9; X. 92. 9; Mookerji, *POC*, VIII, p. 452.
15. Cf. Pusalker, *Prāchyavānī*, I, pp. 29-31.
16. Cf. Viswanatha, *Racial Synthesis in Hindu Culture*, p. 26.
17. For Indus Script, See *Moh. Ind.* (Chs. XXII, XXIII) and articles by Fabri, Heras, Hertz, Hevesy, Hrozny, Hunter, Meriggi, Otto, Petrie, Piccoli, Pran Nath, Ross, Sankarananda, Sastri and Waddell in the Bibliography.
18. *Preh. Civ.*, p. 46.
18a. See *ante*, Ch. VIII. p. 158 ff.
19. Carleton, *Buried Empires*, p. 145.
20. *IC*, III, pp. 663-73; *CS*, VI, p. 435.
21. For different views on the authors of the Indus Culture, see *Moh. Ind.* (pp. 107-12) and articles by Banerji, Banerji-Sastri, Bhandarkar, Cadell, Chanda, Chatterji, Heras, Keith, Law, Mariwalla, Mookerji, Pusalker, Venkateswara, Sankarananda, Sarup, Sastri, Shembavnekar, Sur, and Waddell in the Bibliography.
22. Datta, *Rigvedic Culture of the Prehistoric Indus*, Foreword, p. XXV; Chaudhuri, *CR*, June 1945.
23. Cf. Childe, *New Light*, p. 210.
24. *JRAI*, 64, p. 193.
25. *JBHS*, III, pp. 187-91.
26. It is suggested that the civilization extended southward into the Hyderābād State, the Karnàtak, the Nilgiris, the Tinnevelly district and even as far as Ceylon (*JIH*, XVI, p. 12); but the evidence is far too meagre to justify the inference.
27. Cf. Carleton, *Buried Empires*, p. 161.

BOOK THREE

THE ARYANS IN INDIA

CHAPTER X

THE ARYAN PROBLEM

It was the Florentine merchant Filippo Sassetti who, after five years' stay in Goa (1583-1588), declared for the first time that there existed a definite relation between Sanskrit and some of the principal languages of Europe. But that this relation is due to origin from a common source was suggested only in 1786 by Sir William Jones in his famous address to the Asiatic Society of Bengal. He thus established the common origin of a number of languages such as Greek, Latin, Gothic, Celtic, Sanskrit, Persian, etc., to which the scholars have given the name Indo-European or Indo-Germanic, and therewith laid the foundation of the Science of Comparative Philology. The third and the final step in formulating the Aryan problem was taken by Max Müller, who declared in emphatic terms: "Aryan, in scientific language, is utterly inapplicable to race. It means language and nothing but language; and if we speak of Aryan race at all, we should know that it means no more than X + Aryan speech."[1] This purely linguistic formulation of the problem was, however, never fully accepted by the learned or the laity. On the contrary, a romantic reaction, which identified language with race, set in soon and was given powerful expression by Penka who declared language to be "the organic product of an organism subject to organic laws."[2] The linguistic world of the last century was thus sharply divided into two schools of thought, as old as the Greeks of the classical age, who also were unable to decide whether language is a *phusis* (inborn quality) or merely a *thesis* (acquired habit).[3] Today Müller's school is dominant, no doubt, but Penka's is yet far from discredited, for it is now realized that, though by no means determined by race, yet, as a social phenomenon, a language can assume its particular aspect only within a particular society, and that in those very early times, when the original Indo-European language was gradually taking shape, such a particular society could have been based only on racial affinity, purely cultural bonds being out of the question. In fact, at the beginning, every natural language must have been confined within a not too large racial group—though it by no means follows that there could not have originated more than one language within one racial group at the beginning. It is clear, therefore, that the race-question, if rightly understood, is by no means irrelevant to the Aryan problem. Only it is necessary to remember that the racial group, within which the primitive Indo-European language originated, may have itself adopted a non-Indo-European language in course of its history, or may have altogether passed out of existence. Ours will therefore be a double task: to try to identify anthropologically and locate geographically the primitive racial group within which the basic Indo-European language, as reconstructed by Comparative Philology, had originated.

There being—in spite of Penka and his school[4]—no organic relation between language on the one hand and race and geography on the other, our method cannot but be empirical. And the obviously most important empiric fact about the known Indo-European languages is that quite a large number of them are crowded together within the comparatively small space of Europe, covering practically the whole of that continent, whereas outside Europe, instead of a compact body of idioms of that speech-family are found only scattered members of it, stretching out, as it were, in single file, between the Semitic and the Altaic-Finno-Ugrian linguistic areas, and ending, at least in the age of the earlier *Ṛigveda,* in the region of the Punjab. The geographical distribution of the idioms of the Indo-European speech-family, therefore, does suggest that the original home of the Indo-Europeans is to be sought rather in Europe than in Asia. Moreover, of all the living Indo-European languages of the present day, it is Lithuanian, and not Sanskrit (even if considered a living language) or any of its daughter dialects, that has kept closest to the basic idiom reconstructed by Comparative Philology.

These two fundamental facts make a strong *prima facie* case against the theory that India was the original home of the Aryans. This view, though highly favoured at one time,[5] has not many supporters now, though some Indian scholars still tenaciously cling to it. Their views and arguments have been summarized in the Appendix. The reader will find a refutation of some of them in course of this chapter. But while no definite conclusion about this much-debated problem can yet be reached, it may be reasonably urged that had India been the original home of the Aryans[6] they would have certainly tried fully to Aryanize the whole of this sub-continent before crossing the frontier barriers in quest of adventure.

The fact that the whole of South India and some parts of North India too are to this day non-Aryan in speech is the strongest single argument against the Indian-home hypothesis, especially as the existence of a Dravidian speech-pocket (Brāhui) in Baluchistān clearly suggests that the whole or at least a considerable part of India was originally non-Aryan in speech. The cerebral sounds of Sanskrit which sharply distinguish it from all the other Indo-European speech-families including Irānian, are best explained as the result of Austric and Dravidian influence on the language of the incoming Aryans. Could it be proved that the language of the prehistoric Mohenjo-daro culture was Sanskrit or proto-Sanskrit then indeed it might have been possible to argue that in spite of all the evidence to the contrary India was the original home of the Aryans, for there is no definite proof of the existence of an Aryan race or language outside India previous to the age of the Mohenjo-daro culture. But the Mohenjo-daro seals being still undeciphered, we cannot, for the present, hazard any opinion on this subject.[7]

Many scholars hold the view that the Vedic culture was fundamentally different from that of Mohenjo-daro, and later in date. This question has been discussed above,[8] but special stress may be laid on one point. On the evidence of a well-known plaque discovered at Mohenjo-daro, Sir John Marshall declared that the cult of Śiva-Paśupati (= Rudra) was borrowed by the Vedic Aryans from the Mohenjo-daro culture. Now, it is hardly an accident that precisely this Rudra—and no other deity—is regarded in Vedic cult and religion as an apotropaeic god of aversion—to be feared but not adored.[9] Offerings to all other gods are sacrificed into the fire, but those to Rudra and his servants (Rudriyas) are simply deposited at cross-roads or various forbidding places.[10] Rudra and the Rudriyas are, therefore, in every respect analogous to the *Theoi Apopompaioi* of Greece, the gods of the pre-Hellenic autochthonous population of that country.[11] Should not the Rudra gods, too, be regarded in the same way as gods of the pre-Aryan population of India? But to admit that would be to confess that the Mohenjo-daro people were not Aryans. It is true, as noted above, that Sir John's view is not accepted by all.[12] But if the oldest traceable civilization of India be regarded as of non-Aryan inspiration, the conclusion becomes almost irresistible that the Aryans had come to India from outside.

But why consider the Mohenjo-daro civilization to be the oldest traceable civilization of India? What is there to prove that the Aryan culture of Rigvedic India was not older than the culture represented by the ruins of Mohenjo-daro? Thus arises the great question of the age of the *Ṛigveda*, which, however, in the present context can but be touched in passing on the background of the general problem of the first emergence of the Aryans into the light of history.

From a purely linguistic point of view the *Ṛigveda* in its present form cannot be dated much earlier than 1000 B.C. The language of the *Ṛigveda* is certainly no more different from that of the Avestan *Gāthās* than is Old English from Old High German, and therefore they must be assigned to approximately the same age; and the relation between the language of the *Gāthās* and that of the Old Persian inscriptions of the sixth century B.C. cannot be better visualized than by comparing the former with Gothic and the latter with Old High German. Now, if the inscriptions of the Achaemenid emperors of Irān were composed in Old High German, what would be the date assigned to Ulfilas' Gothic Bible? Surely something like 1000 B.C. This then would be the approximate date of the *Gāthās* of Avesta[13]—with which the *Ṛigveda* in its present form must have been more or less contemporaneous. Thus from general linguistic considerations we get for the Rigvedic language, as known to us, an approximate date of 1000 B.C.[14] Although the culture represented by it must be considerably older, it can hardly be pushed back considerably before 1500 B.C. The Rigvedic language, with its date of about 1000 B.C., therefore, furnishes the *terminus ad quem* and the Mohenjo-daro culture of about 2500 B.C. the *terminus a quo* of the first Aryan invasion of India. In order to ascertain the extra-Indian (as shown above) original home of the Aryans we shall now discuss the earliest datable traces of their eastern tribes (the Indo-Irānians) and then try to follow up the indication of those traces further back.

The earliest indubitable trace of a definitely characterized Indo-Irānian language of the Indo-European family is to be found, as is well known, in the names of the four Vedic gods Mitra, Varuṇa, Indra, and the Nāsatyas (in slightly different forms) occurring in records of treaties, discovered at Boghaz-köi, between the Hittite king Shubbiluliuma and the Mitanni king Mattiuaza of about 1400 B.C.[15] It is very significant that the determinative "god" in the *plural* has been placed before each of the two names Mitra and Varuṇa, for the purpose of this plural determinative could have been only to suggest that the two names formed a *Dvandva* compound—just as in Vedic Sanskrit.[16] Yet it will be wrong to conclude from these names that the language from which they were borrowed was nothing but our Vedic Sanskrit, and to regard the minor differences[17] as due solely to the inadequacy of the Akkadian syllabary used by the Hittites. For the numerals (*aika, tera, panza, satta*), occurring in a manual of chariot-racing composed in the Hittite language by a Mitannian author named Kikkuli, likewise discovered at Boghaz-köi, clearly point to an archaic Indo-Irānian dailect which was not yet fully characterized either as Indo-Aryan or as Irānian.

On the other hand it is equally difficult to accept the view of the writer in the *Cambridge Ancient History* that here we have in the fourteenth century B.C. the undifferentiated Indo-Irānians "who at a later period formed these two important Indo-European stocks."[18] For if the forefathers of the Vedic Aryans were still in Cappadocia in the fourteenth century B.C. on their march towards India, there would be no time left for them to forget all their previous history before giving the final form to the Rigvedic hymns not later than 1000 B.C.: it really cannot be proved that the Vedic Aryans retained any memory of their extra-Indian associations.

excepting perhaps a camouflaged reminiscence of their sojourn in Irān.[19]

But Boghaz-köi is not the only place yielding definite proof of the existence of an archaic Indo-Irānian speech-form about 1400 B.C. The clay tablets with Babylonian cuneiform script discovered at El-Amarna in Egypt[20] have revealed the fact that numerous dynasts with Indo-Irānian-looking names (such as *Artamanya, Arzawiya, Yašdata, Šuttarna,* etc., in which no specifically Indo-Aryan or Irānian feature is perceptible), were ruling in Syria about the same time.[21] Linguistic evidence derived from regions as distant from each other as Cappadocia and Syria, therefore, definitely proves that about 1400 B.C. there existed in those regions archaic Indo-Irānian speech-forms which are undoubtedly older than the oldest Avestan or Sanskrit known to us.

But it is possible perhaps to reach back still farther. About 1760 B.C. Babylon fell into the hands of the Kassites who are known to have used the word "*šuriaš*" to designate the sun.[22] This is the oldest attested word of definitely Indo-Irānian stamp which was perhaps borrowed by the Kassites from the Indo-Irānians before they dispersed from *their* common home, as suggested by Herzfeld.[23] But the evidence of this solitary word of Indo-Irānian origin cannot be regarded as adequate proof of the existence of Indo-Irānians in western Asia already in the eighteenth century B.C. Nor does the joint testimony of this word and the Indo-Irānian names of the Syrian dynasts of the fifteenth century B.C. warrant the assumption that the Indo-Irānians, already as a specifically characterized Indo-European tribe, entered Asia from Europe over the Caucasus, and after occupying Irān pushed on farther to the Punjab, as was held by Hirt.[24] For even though the general movement of the Indo-Europeans in Asia might have been from west to east, yet it should have been quite possible for some Indo-Irānian-speaking tribes to sweep over western Asia in a back-surge of invasion.

This is precisely the view expressed by Eduard Meyer[25] who, on historical grounds, has tried to show that the point from which the Indo-Irānians began to spread eastward into the Punjab and westward into the Mesopotamian world, is to be sought somewhere in the region of the Pāmir plateau.[26] What Eduard Meyer urges against Hirt's theory is worth quoting: "There are, however, very grave difficulties in the way of accepting this theory. Precisely those regions in which according to this theory, these (Indo-Irānian) tribes should have settled down at first—and which in the historical period should have been the theatre of their activities—should then have been so completely evacuated by them that not a single trace of them was left behind. For among the numerous personal and place-names handed down to us from Armenia up to the end of the Assyrian age there is absolutely nothing Indo-European, and even the frontier mountains of Media are inhabited by non-Indo-Irānian tribes: it is quite apparent that the Indo-Irānian Medes have here gradually pushed forward from the east and attained supremacy. On the other hand, although positive proof is wholly lacking, it is quite impossible to assign for the beginnings of the Vedic age—and of the specific Indo-Aryan culture beginning therewith—any date later than 1500 B.C."[27]

This theory of a westward migration of the Indo-Irānians from their common home, so ably presented by Eduard Meyer[28] to explain the apparently simultaneous beginning of Vedic culture in India and the appearance of Aryan princes in Mesopotamia (Mitanni), Syria, and Palestine about the middle of the second millennium B.C., was shared also by Oldenberg[29] and Keith.[30] Johannes Friedrich, too, at least conceded the possibility of a westward movement of a small body of Indo-Irānians.[31] Most emphatic on this point is, however, Wilhelm Brandenstein, who says—without however offering any new argument of his own—"there can be no doubt that also Indians (probably Vedic Indians) have lived in Further Asia."[32] On the whole it is quite clear that the Indo-Irānians advanced not only into India but also spread westward from their common home that was situated probably in the Pāmir region (Meyer) or in Russian Turkestan (Herzfeld). And the dispersal of the Indo-Irānians from their original home should have begun about 2000 B.C., since the Indo-Aryans had become completely Indianized when the Rigvedic culture started on its course as a distinct product of the Indian soil about 1500 B.C. Starting from this we shall now discuss the larger problem of the original home of the Indo-Europeans.

With the possible exception of Luvian, of which we know very little, Hittite is the oldest known Indo-European dialect.[33] Yet, Cappadocia in Asia Minor, the seat of this oldest attested (from about 1900 B.C.)[34] Indo-European language, cannot claim to have been the Indo-European original home; for, as Götze[35] has shown, the pre-Hittite Assyrian commerical colonies of Cappadocia, after an uninterrupted flourishing existence of about one thousand years, came to an abrupt end about 1950 B.C., apparently due to Hittite invasion. The Hittites, therefore, came to Cappadocia from outside, but they could not have come from very far, for the earliest theatre of Indo-European historical activity could not have been too distant from the Indo-European original home.

The date 1950 B.C., practically certain for the Hittite invasion of Asia Minor, is of great importance for Indo-European prehistory, for the Indo-Irānians, too, should have reached their common home (in the Pāmir region or in Russian Turkestan, see *supra*) about that time, since to account for the beginning of the specifically Indian Vedic culture about 1500 B.C. no date much later than 2000 B.C. can be postulated for the occupation of their common home by the Indo-Irānians.

Now if the two oldest known Indo-European tribes, the Hittites and the Indo-Irānians, appear about the same time (*c.* 2000 B.C.) in Cappadocia and Central Asia respectively, then it will be reasonable to conclude that the original home whence both the Hittites and the Indo-Irānians came was more or less equidistant from Cappadocia and Central Asia. Hence follows that neither India nor Central or Western Europe could have been the original Indo-European home.[36]

For our problem it is now of capital importance to enquire from which direction the Hittites entered Asia Minor. On the ground of similarity between prehistoric ceramics of about 2800 B.C. discovered in Eastern Anatolia and Macedonia, Götze concluded that the "Indo-European Hittites" entered Asia Minor from Europe[37] after crossing the straits.[38] But this theory does not, and cannot, explain why in the historical period the Hittites were settled not in Western but in Central and Eastern Asia Minor, and it is not without reason that Eduard Meyer[39] suggested instead that they came from the east.

Of the other Indo-European languages of Asia, special importance, for the Aryan problem, attaches to Tocharian—a late attested (from the fifth to the tenth century A.D.) *Centum* language of Eastern Turkistān,[40] of which the relation with other Indo-European languages and the basic idiom has been fully discussed in a remarkable article by Professor Benveniste.[41] Before the discovery of Tocharian it was possible to maintain—in spite of the fact that the Galataeans (Celts) invaded and occupied Asia Minor in the third century B.C.—that on the whole all the *Centum* languages are to the west and all the *Satem* languages are to the east of the Vistula, and on the basis of this seemingly correct observation Hirt[42] built up his ingenious theory that before their final dispersal the Indo-Europeans should have been settled on both sides of that river, which itself was apparently the main cause of the *Satem-Centum* dialect-split.[43] Now, however, after the discovery of Tocharian, Hirt's theory can no longer be maintained. For Benveniste has shown that Tocharian, which like Hittite had been characterized as a distinct dialect even before the *Satem-Centum* split had taken place, was originally at home far to the east of the Vistula.

Of the Indo-European languages of Europe, Lithuanian, as already stated above, is certainly the most archaic. Organically, as a definitely characterized *Satem*-language, it must be considered of later origin than Hittite and Tocharian, and yet in external appearance (flexions and endings) it looks older than even these. This apparent contradiction can be explained, so far as can be seen, only on one hypothesis: it is necessary to insist that it is a hypothesis pure and simple and nothing more: an Indo-European group bodily came to Lithuania after the *Satem-Centum* dialect split, and there in the backwoods started a long but uneventful national life in practically complete isolation, affording their language little opportunity to change and progress, while to all the other Indo-European-speaking countries came not so much the Indo-Europeans themselves as their languages. In other words, though Schmidt's wave-theory of the spread of dialects should be retained for the other Indo-European dialects, yet, so far as Lithuanian is concerned, we should accept Schleicher's older family-tree theory.[44]

This is frankly speculative, but nevertheless we shall have to accept it, unless we refuse to face the problem. And if we accept it we shall have also to admit that the Indo-European original home could not have been very far removed from Lithuania, for bodily movements of peoples over long distances could not have been possible in those early times excepting over a long period of clash and contact with alien races and speeches, as the result of which the language of the immigrants could not but have been profoundly modified.[45] It is necessary to remember in this connection that the Lithuanian speech-area of mediaeval Europe extended much farther to the east than it does today. And the fact that Lithuanian loan-words in Finnish are more numerous than the Slavic ones in that language clearly suggests that in prehistoric times the Lithuanian speech-area extended much farther still to the east, perhaps separating the Slavs from the Finns, as suggested by Hirt.[46]

The oldest attested Indo-European language of Europe, namely Greek, is frankly an import from outside. As Hall[47] aptly says: "Like Sanskrit, Greek, with all its entirely Indo-European syntax and grammar, has a vast non-Indo-European vocabulary. The reason was the same in both cases. In both lands the invading Wiros (i.e. the Indo-Europeans) found a previously existing non-Aryan race with which they mingled, the Hindus with the Dravidians, the Greeks with the Minoans, and in both cases, while the language of the conqueror prevailed, that of the conquered supplied innumerable names and words to its vocabulary. In both countries the conquered race continued to exist side by side with the conquerors, the dark Dasyus with the fair Aryans, the dark Minoans with the fairer Hellenes." It is generally admitted today that the rulers of Mycenaean Greece of the fourteenth and the thirteenth centuries B.C. were not of Greek stock and did not speak Greek. The first Greek-speaking people of Greece were the Achaians, who appeared on the scene about 1200 B.C. after the decline of the Mycenaean civilization, and adopted Mycenaean culture.[48] The Indo-European speaking tribes should therefore have entered Greece for the first time only about 1200 B.C.[49] But there is nothing to tell us from what region precisely the Greek tribes came.

Thus the most archaic (Lithuanian) as well as the oldest attested (Greek) Indo-European language of Europe fails to make out a definite case for an European original home of the Aryans. The other European languages of the same family need not be discussed for a solution of the Aryan problem from the linguistic point of view, for they are all violent variations of the original Indo-European, particularly Germanic and Celtic. In spite of this inconvenient fact a Germanic home theory has been always very popular with many eminent European scholars for racial reasons. It is argued by them that the interior of the Germanic countries—particularly Scandinavia—cannot be proved to have been ever occupied by an alien race. If yet the Germanic tribes have always spoken an Indo-European tongue—so it is asserted, because it is impossible to prove the contrary—then it will have to be assumed that Indo-European speech came into existence on Germanic soil, and that is to admit that Germany or some Germanic country was the original home of the Aryans.[50] This is in a nutshell the chief argument put forward by protagonists of the Germanic home theory. The inspirer of this school of thought was Penka, who passionately protested against the tendency of ethnologists to accept meekly the findings of philology.[51] Penka's attitude is, however, irrational. The Aryan problem, as formulated by Max Müller, is a purely linguistic one, and it can be connected with ethnology only in the restricted sense explained at the beginning of this chapter. But the primary significance attached to the term "Aryan" by Penka is the physical type represented by the Scandinavians! It is not to be wondered, therefore, that starting with this assumption Penka succeeded in proving, at least to his own satisfaction, that Scandinavia was the cradle-land of the Indo-Europeans.[52]

Modern supporters of Penka's theory have altogether dropped the linguistic argument and tend to concentrate on prehistoric archaeology.[53] Thus the West Baltic coast has been regarded as the home of the Aryans, chiefly on the ground that the oldest and the simplest artifacts of the period following the palaeolithic age, as well as tasteful and technically perfected stone implements, are found there in abundance.[54] But it has been rightly pointed out[55] that in that case the equally numerous and handsome stone artifacts of New Zealand would be an evidence for the high antiquity of Maori culture. Much stress was again laid on the geometric patterns on prehistoric pottery in Central Germany which were regarded as of Indo-European creation. But apart from the validity of this assumption, the discovery of similar patterns on the prehistoric pottery of South Russia, Poland, and Tripolje (Ukraine) which were older than those of Germany negatives the theory of an original Aryan home in Germany.[56]

Indeed, the antiquity of Tripolje pottery, which may be dated in the third millennium B.C., has induced Nehring to formulate the view that Tripolje culture is the culture of the original Indo-Europeans, and in his opinion "the Indo-European original home lay indeed also in South Russia, but extended far beyond to the west."[57] That it could not have comprehended any part of Western Europe is pretty certain, for H. Güntert[58] and F. R. Schröder[59] have shown that Western Europe is one of those areas that were Aryanized last. Pokorny, too, by applying his substratum theory that a later language is always fundamentally modified by the older language over which it spreads,[60] came to the conclusion that "as the original home of the Indo-Europeans before the dispersal of the tribes (c. 2400 B.C.) should be regarded the wide stretches of land between the Weser and the Vistula and beyond these up to White Russia and Volhynia."[61]

The region indicated by Nehring as the Indo-European cradle-land is indeed rather too wide, but from the present-day standpoint of Comparative Philology it would be absurd to think that the original Indo-Europeans "must have lived for long in a severely restricted area," as Giles[62] was inclined to believe. Striking isoglosses [63] clearly show that various movements must have taken place among the different Indo-European tribes before they finally parted company. Brandenstein's researches (see below) are in this regard of capital importance. Nor can it be doubted that the later Indo-Europeans, even before final dispersal, had ceased to be racially homogeneous, and therefore the question whether the Indo-Europeans were blondes or brunettes cannot be regarded as strictly relevant. In recent times the Aryan problem has been hopelessly mixed up with the race question by European scholars of a certain school of thought, who, failing to achieve their object with the help of linguistics and archaeology, have adopted racial anthropology as their chief weapon of battle. Starting with the assumption that blonde hair was the chief characteristic of the Indo-Europeans they have naturally chosen Germany as the Indo-European cradle-land, and adduced as proof, in support of their theory, various facts such as that in Greek mythology Appollo has been called blonde and some prominent Romans (such as Cato the Censor and Sulla) have been described as "red-haired" or "golden-haired" by Plutarch. It hardly needs to be pointed out that red hair was regarded as something unusual and exceptional by the Greeks and Romans, and for that reason only attracted public attention in Greece and Rome. Blonde hair was known also in India. In fact, the grammarian Patañjali[64] declared blonde hair to be one of the essential qualities in a Brāhmaṇa. True Brāhmaṇas, therefore should have been blondes in the pre-Christian era. And yet India, the land of the Brāhmaṇas, has never been claimed as the Indo-European cradle-land by the racial theorists!

The new line of research opened up by Brandenstein[65] is concerned chiefly with applied semasiology. He proceeds chiefly on the assumption that it is possible to draw definite conclusions about the cultural evolution of the primitive Indo-Europeans and their prehistoric seats of settlement from a study of the stocks of words they should have possessed at different stages, and also by examining the changes of meaning undergone by those words. Brandenstein shows first that Indo-Irānian reveals an older stage of semasiological evolution than that reflected in all the other Indo-European dialects put together, and from this he draws the reasonable conclusion that the Indo-Irānians were the earliest to separate from the main body of Indo-Europeans, and that the other tribes continued to live together for some time after their departure. Indo-European of the period previous to the secession of the Indo-Irānians he calls Early Indo-European, and Indo-European of the period posterior to that secession, Late Indo-European. The Early Indo-European vocabulary, in Brandenstein's opinion, reveals a steppe-land at the foot of a mountain-range as the original home which, he thinks, can be no other than the north-western Kirghiz steppe to the south of the Urals. As for Early Indo-European flora, there cannot be found the name of a single plant that is typically European, and the fauna of this period comprised mammals like the elk, otter, wild boar, wolf, fox, bear, etc.

The later Indo-European vocabulary, however, reveals quite a different land and quite different plants and animals. In the place of words associated with dry steppe-land now crop up a number of vocables which clearly suggest swampy tracts, and now appears for the first time also the idea of bridges—suggesting settled residence; on the other hand, words denotative of fauna and flora of this period point to the territory immediately to the east of the Carpathians. Brandenstein therefore concludes that the undivided Indo-Europeans lived originally in what is now the Kirghiz steppe, from where the Indo-Irānian tribes moved eastward, and the other tribes, at a later date, westward. The westward-moving tribes, however, were split up into two groups by the Rokytno swamps, so that some of them struck north to be differentiated later into Nordics, and others advanced into Ukraine and from there farther to the south and the west.

It would be senseless to claim that every detail of the itinerary of the Indo-European tribes chalked out by Brandenstein is, or can be, correct. But it is significant that the results obtained by him by applying his altogether new method should point to approximately the same *locus* as is indicated by the evidence of history, philology, and archaeology. Indo-European pre-history, as reconstructed by Nehring and Brandenstein, is by no means identical, but neither are the two mutually exclusive. The main difference is that Brandenstein takes as an interim home of the west Indo-European tribes practically that very region which in Nehring's view should have been the Indo-European cradle-land.

We shall now conclude this chapter with a brief examination of the evidence of the non-Indo-European language-groups on the Aryan problem. Similarities between Indo-European and Finno-Ugrian language-groups are so striking[66] that they cannot be brushed aside as cases of mere fortuitous coincidence; but on the other hand it would be conceding too much to them to postulate on their evidence an organic relation of distant common origin. The conclusion in any case is irresistible that Indo-European and Finno-Ugrian had influenced each other in very early times. The original seat of the Finno-Ugrians was, however, in Central Russia. And it is significant that from purely ethnographical consideration, too, Flor[67] came to the conclusion that "genetically considered, the Uralians are, in many cases, the zone of origin of numerous Indo-European cultural phenomena."

Some such historical—not organic or genetic—relation between early Indo-European and early Semitic is hard to deny in face of the numerous striking points of similarity (if not identity) pointed out by Möller—similarity in the endings of nominative, accusative, and genitive singular,[68] in certain elements of dual and plural formation,[69] and perhaps also in nominative and accusative singular of the pronominal flexion.[70] He even categorically declared that "the Semites did not radiate from Arabia as is assumed by most Semitists, but came to Arabia from a northern seat either through Asia Minor or over the Irānian plateau."[71]

Möller's theory has indeed not been generally accepted by the scholarly world, but it is no longer possible to deny today that there must have been at least historical contact of some sort between Early Indo-European and Early Semitic. This is important, for if the primitive Indo-Europeans had on the one hand contact with the Finno-Ugrians of Central Russia and on the other with the Semites, then the region that naturally detaches itself as the probable Indo-European cradle-land is no doubt South Russia, specially as Indo-Finnic relations were decidedly more intimate.

The evidence of linguistic palaeontology need not be considered in detail, since Schrader did that with masterly thoroughness in his well-known works;[72] but it is important to remember that the region to which he assigned the Indo-European original home after his epoch-making researches is also South Russia. The argument that has been most persistently levelled against Schrader is the so-called beech-argument: since the beech was known to the Indo-Europeans, it is argued, their original home must have been "to the west of a line drawn from Königsberg in Prussia to the Crimea and continued thence through Asia Minor,"[73] for the beech does not grow to the east of the line. But there is absolutely no certainty that the Indo-European word **bhāgos*, from which the English word "beech" is very probably derived, also signified the thing designated by this English word "beech." Moreover, the word for "beech" seems to have been confined only to the western Indo-Europeans, for there is no trace of it in any eastern dialect if the late Kurdish word *buz*[74] is left out of consideration. In spite of the enormous increase in knowledge since the days of Schrader it would be best, therefore, to adhere to his conclusion that South Russia, more than any other region, can claim to be regarded as the cradle-land of the Aryans (= Indo-Europeans).

---

1. *Collected Works, New Impression*, 1898, Vol. X (The Home of the Aryas), p. 90.
2. *Origines Aricae*, 1883, p. 6.
3. See Plato's *Cratylus* and Christ's *Geschichte der Griechischen Litteratur*, fünfte Auflage von Withelm Schmid, erster Teil, München 1909, p. 639.
4. Penka's own arguments are of only historical interest today and need not be discussed. The chief exponent of Penka's theory of the Germanic home of the Indo-Europeans in modern times was Gustav Kossinna. A brief summary of his theory has been given by Gordon Childe (*The Aryans*, pp. 166 ff.). It may be mentioned that most of the articles on Indo-European origins in the *Hirt-Festschrift* (Heidelberg, 1936) are from Kossinna's school.
5. Given up in Europe since it was discovered that Sanskrit does not give the truest picture of the original Indo-European.
6. In this chapter the word "Aryan" has been used in the sense of "Indo-European."
7. For Mohenjo-daro cf. Ch. IX.
8. Ch. IX, p. 197.
9. In the oldest ritual texts every care is taken not to mention directly the name of this terrible god. He is indirectly referred to as "this god" or "the god whose name contains the word *bhūta* or *paśu*" (i.e., Bhūtapati, Paśupati). The name occurring in a Rigvedic verse (II. 3. I) was purposely pronounced as *Rudriya* (*Ait. Br.*, III, 3. 9-10). From the curious remarks made in *Ait. Br.*, III. 3. 10 it also appears that the reading of *RV*, II. 3. Ic was originally *abhi nah*, etc.: but it was later altered so as not to give Rudra a pretext to rush to the place of sacrifice. Arbman in his dissertation on Rudra. (Uppsala, 1922) has made it probable that in respect of this god the later ritual texts give a more faithful picture of the popular beliefs of the Rigvedic age than the *Rigveda* itself.
10. See Keith. *RPVU*, HOS., Vol. 31, p. 145. Precisely the same was the attitude of the Greeks towards their apotropaeic foreign goddess Hekate (see Nilsson, *Greek Religion*, p. 204).
11. See Jane Ellen Harrison, *Prolegomena to the Study of Greek Religion*, second edition, pp. 8 ff.
12. Cf. Ch. IX, pp. 191, 196 ff.
13. This date of the *Gāthās* and their author Zarathustra has been maintained—against indigenous Irānian tradition—by Ed. Meyer who declared it to be one of the incomprehensible things in history that anyone should consider Zarathustra's patron Vistaspa to have been the same person as the father of Darius I. So also Bartholomae, *Zarathustras Leben und Lehre*, pp. 10-11. For full literature on this point up to 1932 see *Die Iranier in Kulturgeschichte des Alten Orients* (Arthur Christensen), p. 213.
14. Walther Wüst who in recent times has tried most to push back the age of the *Rigveda* admits nevertheless that the Mohenjo-daro culture is not Indo-European and must have passed away before the Aryans occupied India (*WZKM*, XXXIV, pp. 173, 190). Cf. the views of Dr. S. K. Chatterji in Ch. VIII, p. 160 ff.

15. See Jenson, *SPAW*, 1919, pp. 367 ff., Forrer, *ZDMG;* 1922; pp. 254 ff., *CHI*, I, 72; *CAH*, II, 13.
16. See Arthur Christensen, *op. cit.*, p. 209, fn. 6.
17. E.G., Skt. *Indra* but Hit. *In-ta-ra;* Skt. *Varuṇa* but Hit. *U-ru-van-a.* These gods were worshipped not by the indigenous Mitanni people who were non-Indo-European in speech, but by their Aryan rulers known as *Maryanni.* The word *maryanni* may be connected with Rigvedic *marya.*
18. Vol. II, p. 13.
19. See next chapter.
20. See Eduard Meyer, *Geschichte des Altertums*, third edition, Vol. I, § 468.
21. These names have been fully discussed by Mironov in *Acta Orientalia.* Vol. XI, pp. 140 ff. For a helpful criticism of Mironov's equations and etymologies see Keith, *Woolner Comm.* Vol., pp. 137 ff.
22. See Eduard Meyer, *op. cit.*, Vol. I, § 456.
23. *Iran in the Ancient East*, 1941, p. 182.
24. *Die Indogermanen*, Vol. I, p. 118.
25. *Geschichte des Altertums*, II, I, second edition, 1928, p. 35.
26. The same view has been expressed much more emphatically also by Herzfeld (*op. cit.*, pp. 191-2) only with this difference—which is perhaps a necessary corrective to Meyer's theory—that the original Indo-Iranian common home was situated in Russian Turkestan and not in the Pamir region.
27. To admit that Vedic culture began about 1500 B.C. does not of course mean that the Rigvedic language as known to us is to be dated so early. On the contrary it suggests that the Rigvedic language assumed its present form at a considerably later period, probably about 1000 B.C., as suggested above on linguistic grounds.
28. For the first time in *SBA*, 1908, pp. 14 ff,. then again in *KZ* 1909, pp. I ff., and often later; Freiherr von Eickstedt. as quoted by Nehring in his *Studien zur indogermanischen Kultur und Urheimat*, p. 227. considers Kazakstan to have been the common home of the Indo-Irānians; but he does not seem to have taken into consideration the possibility of a back-surge of the eastern Indo-Europeans.
29. *JRAS*, 1909, pp. 1095 ff.
30. *Modi Memorial Volume*, 1930, pp. 81 ff. Some scholars have expressed the view that the Aryans of Mitanni were Indians pure and simple; cf. Jacobi. *JRAS*, 1919, pp. 721 ff., Jensen. SBA, 1919, pp. 467 ff., Sturtevant, *Yale Classical Studies*, I, pp. 215 ff.
31. See Ebert's *Reallexikon der Vorgeschichte*, Vol. I, 1924, p. 137. But Friedrich has adopted a non-committal attitude in this regard in his article "Das erste Auftreten der Indogermanen" in *Hirt-Festschrift*, Vol. II.
32. *Hirt-Festschrift*, Vol. II, p. 37.
33. See my article in *IC*, XI, pp. 147-60, particularly pp. 155-6: cf. also Johannes Friedrich, *Geschichte der Indogermanischen Sprachwissenschaft*, II. 5, p. 42. Nehring's speculations about the *Luvians* (*Studien zur Indogermanischen Kultur und Urheimat*, p. 37) are inconclusive; his assertion that the earliest culture of Troy (c. 3000 B.C.) was certainly Indo-European (*loc. cit.*) seems to be an unproved assumption.
34. Sturtevant, *A Comparative Grammar of the Hittite Language*, p. 29.
35. *Kulturgeschichte des Alten Orients*, dritter Abschnitt, erste Lieferung. 1933, p. 76.
36. Schachermeyr, too, admits that the Hittites probably entered Asia Minor about 2000 B.C. (*Hirt-Festschrift*, Vol. I. p. 234).
37. *Kulturgeschichte des Alten Orients* dritter Abschnitt, erste Lieferung, p. 48.
38. Schachermeyr, *Hirt-Festschrift*. Vol. I. p. 235.
39. *Reich und Kultur der Chetiter*, p. 234.
40. For a pretty complete survey of the problems connected with Tocharian, see Schwentner, *Geschichte der indogermanischen Sprachwissenschaft*, zweiter Teil, fünfter Band, Lieferung 2, Leipzig, 1935.
41. See *Hirt-Festschrift*. Vol. II, pp. 227-40.
42. *Die Indogermanen*, Vol. I, p. 183.
43. The split is caused by the difference in the treatment of certain *k* and *g* sounds. Certain dialects keep these sounds but others change them into sibilants.
44. The theories associated with the names of Schleicher and Schmidt will be found explained in many text-books and need not be discussed here.
45. So also Hirt, *Die Indogermanes*, Vol I. p. 125. Niederle most emphatically asserts that the Lithuanians are still living in their original home on the Baltic (*Manuel de l' Antiquité Slave*, Tome I: Historia, p. 13).

46. *Op. cit.*, p. 121.
47. *Bronze Age Greece*, p. 288.
48. *Op. cit.*, p. 249. Some scholars, however, still maintain that the Mycenaeans were identical with the Achaians and therefore spoke Greek.
49. It is important to remember that the Akaivasha (=Achaians?) are mentioned for the first time in 1229 B.C. in the Egyptian records, and the Danauna (=Hom. Danaians?) in 1192 B.C. (see Gordon Childe, *The Aryans*, pp. 72-73). Meillet seems to have considered the *Akaivasha* of the Egyptians, the Aḫḫijava of the Hittite texts, the *Achai(v)oi* of Homer and the *Achivi* of the Latins to have been one and the same people (*Aperçu d'une Histoire de la Langue Grecque*, third edition, 1930, p. 57). Cf. also Schwyzer, *Griechische Grammatik* Vol. I, p. 46.
50. Practically all that can be said in favour of a Germanic home will be found in the two volumes of the *Hirt-Festschrift*, Heidelberg, 1936.
51. *Origines Aricae*, p. 5.
52. It is curious to note that both Penka (*Op.* cit., p. 56) and Tilak (see his *Arctic Home in the Vedas*), independently of each other, arrived at the conclusion that the original home of the Aryans was situated in the polar region. Penka depended on the evidence of Odyssey X, 81-6, where short nights are spoken of. In the Vedic literature there are indeed passages which may suggest that the Vedic Aryans actually knew of the never-setting polar sun. For instance, *Aitareya Brāhmaṇa*, III. 4.6: *savā esha na kadāchana 'stam eti no 'deti*, etc. But it is quite clear that the author of the *Aitareya Brāhmaṇa* is here only speaking of an astronomical discovery—remarkable for the age—that the sun actually does not "rise" or "set."
53. The racists apart, whose chief preoccupation is to try to prove that the Indo-Europeans were of Nordic stock.
54. Much, *Die Heimat der Indogermanen im Lichte der urgeschichtlichen Forschung*, second edition, 1904.
55. Gordon Childe, *Wiener Beiträge Zur Kulturgeschichte und Linguistik*, Jahrgang IV, *Die Indogermanen und Germanenfrage*, 1936, p. 526.
56. *Hirt-Festschrift*. Vol. I, pp. 19, 24, 37. Rosenberg, *Kulturströmungen in Europa zur Steinzeit, Kopenhagen*, 1931, pp. II ff.
57. So Nehring, *Studien zur indogermanischen Kultur und Urheimat*, pp. 27, 59-61.
58. *Ursprung der Germanen*, p. 120.
59. *Germanentum und Alteuropa*, p. 166.
60. *Substrattheorie und Urheimat der Indogeramanen. Mitteilungen der Anthropologischen Gesellschaft*, LXVI, 1936, pp. 69-91.
61. Quotation by Pittioni, *Wiener Beiträge zur Kulturgeschichte und Linguistik*, Jahrgang IV, 1936. p. 531.
62. *CHI*, I, 66.
63. "Isogloss" means "a linguistic innovation common to two or more groups of the same family of languages."
64. Mahābhāshya *ad* Pāṇini II. 2.6: *gauraḥ śuchyāchāraḥ kapilaḥ piṅgalakeśa ity =enān=api abhyantarān brāhmaṇye guṇān kurvanti.*
65. *Die erste indogermanische Wanderung*. Wien, 1936. Brandenstein's ingenious theory of an early Indo-European home in the Kirghiz steppe and a later Indo-European home in eastern Poland has not been accepted by Nehring (*Studien zur indogermanischen Kultur und Urheimat*, p. 28, fn.) who has promised (*loc. cit.*) to give his reasons for rejecting Brandenstein's theory in a future publication.
66. Hirt. *Die Indogermanen*, Vol. I, p. 72; Nehring, *Studien zur indogermanischen Kultur und Urheimat*, pp. 21-2.
67. *Hirt-Festschrift*, Vol. I. p. 124.
68. *KZ*, Vol. XLII, pp. 175-9.
69. *Vergleichendes indogermanisch-semitisches Wörterbuch*, pp. xiii f.
70. See Albert Schott, *Hirt-Festschrift*, Vol. II, pp. 93-4.
71. *Vergleichendes indogermanisch-semitisches Wörterbuch*, p. xvi.
72. *Sprachvergleichung und Urgeschichte*, second edition, Jena 1890; *Reallexikon der Indogermanischen Altertumskunde*, second edition by Nehring in two vols, Berlin and Leipzig, 1917-1929.
73. So Giles, *CHI*, I. 68. It is difficult to find a single positive argument in favour of Giles' Hungarian home theory.
74. According to Bartholomae (*Indogermanische Forschungen*, Vol. IX, p. 271) this Kurdish word may be connected with "*beech*."

APPENDIX[1]

The theory of the indigenous origin of the Aryans has been advocated by a number of scholars. MM. Ganganath Jha has tried to prove that the original home was the Brahmarshi-deśa.[2] D. S. Triveda suggests that the original home of the Aryans was in the region of the river Devikā in Multān.[3] L. D. Kalla advocates the claims of Kāshmir and the Himālayan region.[4] The various arguments in favour of this view may be summed up as follows:

1. There is no evidence to show that the Vedic Aryans were foreigners or that they migrated into India within traditional memory. Sufficient literary materials are available to indicate with some degree of certainty, that the Vedic Aryans themselves regarded Sapta-Sindhu as their original home (*devakṛita-yoni or devanirmita-deśa*).

Migrating races look back to the land of their origin for centuries. The Parsis in India remember their origin after eight hundred years. The ancient Egyptians and the Phoenicians remembered their respective lands of origin even though they had forgotten their location. The Vedic Aryans, if at all they came from outside, therefore, must have lived in Sapta-Sindhu so many centuries before the Vedic period that they had lost all memory of an original home.[5]

2. The linguistic affinities are not positive proofs of Aryan immigration. The Vedic Sanskrit has the largest number of vocables found in the Aryan languages. These are preserved in the languages of the Sanskritic family in different parts of India even when there has been inter-racial contact for centuries. On the other hand, if the pre-Vedic Aryan language was spoken in different parts of Europe and Asia where the Aryans had settled before coming to India, how is it that only a few vocables are left in the present-day speech of those parts, while the largest number of them is found in the distant places of ultimate settlement and racial admixture in India? On the contrary this disparity can easily be explained if the pre-Vedic was the language of the homeland of Aryans and the other Aryan languages came into existence as a result of the contact between migrating Aryans and non-Aryan elements outside India and Persia.[6]

3. The Vedic literature is the earliest extant record of the Aryan mind. How is it that in the course of their journey to the Sapta-Sindhu the Aryans left no such record elsewhere? This absence of literary records in other countries cannot be explained away by a hypothesis that the Aryans only reached a high stage of cultural evolution in India. But we can satisfactorily explain it if we suppose that the Aryans migrated from India, and the migration being only of the superfluous population of roving tribes without great cultural development, they could not impart the literary and cultural tradition to the counties in which they ultimately settled?[7]

4. The sacrificial rituals had long been established before the compliation of the Saṁhita. Therefore the home of Soma, the Mūjavant or Munjavant hills in the north of the Punjab, indicates the locality from which the sacrificial rituals developed.[8]

5. It is often argued that Lithuanian being the most archaic in the Aryan family of languages, Lithuania is likely to be the original home of the Aryans. But a language remains archaic even when the persons using it are unprogressive; or if they remain in a locality where no fusion is possible with races speaking other languages; or if they develop a highly refined technique for preserving and using archaic forms. The first two conditions are probably responsible for the archaic character of Lithuanian.[9]

6. It is argued that the tiger, a native of the Bengal swamps, is not mentioned in the *Ṛigveda,* but the place of honour is given to the lion. Similarly the elephant, mentioned as the *mṛigahastin,* shows that it was a novelty.[10] These arguments do not carry much weight in view of the fact that the Harappā civilization of the Indus Valley shows little trace of the lion (supposed to be common in the desert of Rājputāna) but is fully conversant with the worship of the tiger and the elephant as indicated by the seals. If in about 3000 B.C. the elephant and the tiger were so well known in the Punjab, it is absurd to suppose that they disappeared so completely as not to be mentioned in the *Ṛigveda* in c. 1500 B.C. The word *mṛiga-hastin* is merely a poetic term and does not imply novelty. In the same way the word *parvatagiri,* used for a mountain in the same *Ṛigveda,* clearly does not mean that mountains were strange to the Vedic peoples. Again it is said that rice is not mentioned in the *Ṛigveda.* Even so, salt is never mentioned in the *Ṛigveda.* Can we conclude that the consumption of salt was unknown in the Rigvedic times? Rice seems to have been unknown in the Harappā civilization also. This only proves that *yava* (barley) and wheat were the staple cereals of North-West India.

7. The geographical data of the *Ṛigveda,* as analysed in Ch. XIII, clearly show that the Punjab and the neighbouring regions constituted the home of the people who composed these hymns. There is no good ground for the belief that they or their ancestors lived in any other country.

---

1. This Appendix is based on a long note on the subject prepared by Prof. S. Srikanta Sāstri and most of the arguments are advanced by Mr. K. M. Munshi in *Glory that was Gurjaradeśa,* I, Section II.
2. *Āchārya Pushpāñjali* (=D. R. Bhandarkar Comm. Vol.), pp. 1-2.
3. *ABORI*, XX. 48 ff.
4. *POC*, VI, 723-4.
5. Munshi, *op. cit.*, 46.
6. *Ibid.*, 81.
7. *Ibid.*, 82.
8. Cf. *KHDS*, II, Part I, pp. 11-16.
9. Munshi, *op. cit.*, 83.
10. *CHI*, I, 81.

CHAPTER XI

INDO-IRĀNIAN RELATIONS

It has been shown in the preceding chapter that the undivided Indo-Irānians, as suggested by their already specifically characterized *Satem* dialect, must have left their original Indo-European home after the Hittites and the proto-Tocharians, but before any other Indo-European tribe. After some wanderings they settled down in what may be called the Indo-Irānian original home which was situated in the Pāmir region (Eduard Meyer) or more probably in the plains of the Oxus and Jaxartes (Ernst Herzfeld). The latter says: "From time immemorial, at least from the third millennium down to the middle of the second, the Aryans inhabited, as an undivided ethnical group, the vast plains of the Oxus and Jaxartes, the land *Erānvēj* of the two rivers Vahvī-Datiyā and Ranhā."[1] It is also quite clear that the Aryan principalities appearing about 1400 B.C. in Mesopotamia and Syria were "the successful creation of a group of *condottieri* and their troops who had detached themselves from the main body, while the wandering tribes passed through eastern Irān towards India."[2]

The undivided Indo-Irānians must have passed a long time in their Central Asian common home, for here grew up a specific Indo-Irānian culture and religion that may be reconstructed, at least partially, by comparing the Veda with the Avesta. Before the occupation of the Irānian plateau by tribes from the Indo-Irānian original home, the high land, to all appearance, was the seat of a culture that was probably matriarchal, and the people worshipped snake-gods like the primitive non-Aryans of India. It is very probable, therefore, that the pre-Aryan cultures of North-West India and Irān were of the same spirit and origin.[3]

This old cultural link between pre-Aryan Irān and pre-Aryan India, instead of being strengthened as a result of the migration of the Aryans into these two countries, as could be normally expected, was to all appearance completely severed, for there is nothing to show that the Vedic Aryans of India maintained an active cultural relation with their brethren in Irān.

In the earliest days the Aryans of India must have been connected with the Aryans of Irān, either as friends or as foes, but "actual historical contact cannot be asserted with any degree of probability."[4] The two peoples turned their backs upon each other as it were, and developed their distinctive civilizations apparently without the least mutual influence, although in language,[5] culture and religion their similarity in the earliest period was little short of identity.

When later in history,[6] under the Achaemenids, Greeks, Bactrians, and Śakas, the Irānians and the Indians were forced to meet as citizens of the same empire, they met as complete strangers, not as cousins of the same family.

Geographical barriers are no doubt to some extent responsible for this apparent mutual oblivion, as also the fact that from the Indo-Irānian common home the pre-Indians and the pre-Irānians expanded in two almost opposite directions. All this, however, cannot explain the complete cessation of cultural contact between Irān and India even as early as the Rigvedic age. The Irānians had retained a distinct memory of the Indo-Irānian common home (Erānvēj) in their mythology, but the Indo-Aryans, who must have developed their distinctively Indian Rigvedic culture about 1500 B.C. at the latest, have nothing to say on this point. It is indeed difficult to get away from the idea that the silence maintained by the earliest Vedic Indians on Irān and the Irānians was at least partly intentional, for some of the geographical names prove beyond doubt that the period of immigration had not been so long as to have completely obliterated all memory of the land they left behind. Thus the names Rasā, Sarasvatī and Bāhlīka, not to speak of others, must have been brought to India from Irān by the Aryans and applied to two Indian rivers and one Indian province.[7] The reticence maintained by the Vedic Aryans about immigration from Indo-Irānia was, therefore, at least partly intentional, for otherwise it would seem that those parts of the *Ṛigveda* in which possible or probable Irānian names occur, were composed already in Irān, as Hillebrandt actually suggested.[8]

Incompatibility of some sort between the earliest Aryans of India and Irān has to be assumed to explain this camouflaged indifference, and it is also clear that this incompatibility was the cause of their divergent movements from their common home and ultimately destroyed the cultural unity between Irān and India of the pre-Aryan days. Seeds of such incompatibility which later developed into mutual hostility can be clearly seen already in the oldest Aryan religion and cult of these two countries. The primitive Indo-European religion recognized only nature-gods (sky, sun, wind, etc.) and a fire-cult.[9] But already the undivided Indo-Irānians knew a soma-cult beside the older fire-cult, and abstract deities[10] beside the older nature-gods. Indo-Irānian society had therefore ceased to be culturally homogeneous even before the forefathers of the Indian and Irānian Aryans parted company, and it is hardly to be doubted that their parting was more the effect than the cause of the cultural contrast revealed in religion. The old Indo-European term **deivo* (= Indo-Irānian **daiva*) was apparently considered inappropriate for the new abstract and ethical deities, and a new term, *Asura*, perhaps borrowed from a higher civilization,[11] came to be used as their designation. Varuṇa was the chief of these ethical deities just as Indra was the chief of the older nature-gods.[12]

The fact that about 1400 B.C., in the well-known treaty-record discovered at Boghaz-köi, the Daiva-gods Indra and Nāsatya appear side by side with the Asura-gods Varuṇa and Mitra, clearly suggests, as Christensen[13] has pointed out, that the antagonism between the worshippers of the *Daiva*-gods and the *Asura*-gods—which is the central feature of early Indo-Irānian history—had not yet broken out. But it was in full blast long before the advent of Zarathustra whose Gāthās should be dated about 1000 B.C. on linguistic grounds, as shown in the preceding chapter.

The antagonism between the worshippers of the new gods and the old must have been one of the main causes of the estrangement and subsequent secession of those Aryans who later conquered India, but their antagonism was not confined to the field of religion alone. Christensen[14] has suggested that the *Asura*-religion was practised by the more cultured and steadier elements of the primitive Indo-Irānian society whose chief occupation was agriculture and cattle-breeding, while the older *Daiva*-religion continued to find favour with the more vigorous but less civilized portions of the people to whom the primitive predatory habits were more congenial: the former were content to remain behind in Irān, but the latter, urged by the spirit of adventure, advanced farther east and at last entered India. But all of those who remained behind were not *Asura*-worshippers, nor all of those who braved the hardships of the forward march into India were adherents of the *Daiva*-religion. The *Daiva*-inscription of Xerxes,[15] discovered in 1935, clearly shows that even so late as the fifth century B.C. *Daiva*-worship had to be forcibly suppressed within the Achaemenian empire. And in India we meet with the curious situation that in the oldest period all the great gods received the title *Asura* as a decorative epithet, though later it came to be used exclusively as a term of abuse. In innumerable passages in the Brāhmaṇas the *Asuras* have been represented as superior to the *Devas* in the arts of civilized life, and both in Vedic[16] and Puranic tradition they are regarded as the elder brothers of the gods. They are as far above the *Dāsas* and *Rākshasas* as the *Devas* themselves.

All things considered, it seems difficult to deny that along with the great horde of *Daiva*-worshipping Aryans came to India also a culturally superior strong minority of *Asura*-worshippers, whose cult and religion was slightly different from that of the former and who were for that reason ceaselessly cursed and condemned by the Vedic Aryans, more out of jealousy, it would seem, than out of contempt. For if the Vedic Aryans intentionally suppressed all reminiscence of the Indo-Irānian original home, as suggested above, would they not also have suppressed the memory of the *Asura*-

worshippers in the same way if they could? But this they could not, because some *Asura*-worshippers were physically present among them.

The earliest Indo-Aryan society, too, like the earliest Indo-Irānian society, was therefore not quite homogeneous culturally. It was predominantly—but not exclusively—*Daivic*, while the contemporary Irānian society was predominantly *Asuric*. After a period of conflict and adaptation there was peace which proved successful to the extent that even the foremost of the *Daiva*-gods, namely Indra, not only came to be regarded as an *Asura* in the oldest parts of the *Ṛigveda*, but was also credited with possessing *māyā*, which was a special property of the Asuras and probably signified "magical power."[17] It is hardly an accident that in Hindu mythology the architect of the gods is an *Asura* whose name is Maya: the rude *Daiva*-worshippers apparently regarded the superior arts and crafts of their rivals as achieved by magic.

In spite of the *Daiva*-bias of the Indians and the *Asura*-bias of the Irānians their culture and religion continued to be essentially the same till the advent of Zarathustra in Irān. Zarathustra's position is more or less analogous to that of the Buddha in India and Orpheus in Greece, both of whom protested effectively against the ceremonial slaughter of animals in the name of religion, but not by far so vehemently as Zarathustra.[18] In his Gāthās Zarathustra condemns in bitter terms the orgiastic festivities at which the *Daiva*-worshippers, inebriated with Soma, offer bloody sacrifices to their gods, extinguishing amidst shouts of revelry the life of the innocent bull.[19] It is clear that the ritual practices against which Zarathustra directed his homilies closely resembled those of the Vedas. A large number of common cult-words such as *haoma* (=*soma*), *zaotar* (=*hotā*), *athravan* (=*atharvan*), *manthra* (=*mantra*), *yazata* (=*yajata*), *yašna* (=*yajña*), *āzūiti* (=*āhūti*), etc., and also the whole sacrificial cult, leave no doubt that Vedic and Avestan ritual are of one and the same origin.[20] Evidently, the Zarathustrian reform could not materially alter the essentially Vedic character of the Soma cult cherished in Irān from ages before his time.

In the field of religion and mythology, however, Zarathustra was more successful. But here, too, the points of similarity are striking enough to prove previous identity. The ceremony of *Upanayana* is practically the same in the Veda and the Avesta, and in both the conventional number of gods is the same, namely thirty-three. Both in the Veda and the Avesta the picture of the gods is primarily that of an heroic Aryan warrior riding in a chariot drawn by powerful steeds. Like the Vedic gods those of the Avesta too hold up the sky to prevent its falling down, and image-worship is equally unknown in the Avesta and the Veda. Varuṇa, like his Avestan opposite number Ahura, assisted by Mitra (Avestan Mithra), is the supreme guardian of moral law, and the conception of cosmic order is represented in both by the same abstract deity, the Vedic Ṛita = Avestan Asa.[21] Even the notorious discrepancy between the Vedic and Avestan Indra will disappear if the history of this god, as reconstructed by Benveniste and Renou,[22] is kept in view. Their ingenious theory may be summarized as follows: In the Indo-Irānian epoch there were two different gods, Indra[23] and Vṛitrahan (*vṛitra* = resistance, *vṛitrahan* = resistance-breaker). Indra was nothing but a concrete personalization of mere physical prowess, known in the legends of most primitive civilizations, but he was too *Daivic* to suit the taste of the stern reformer Zarathustra who did not hesitate to send him to Hades. But the Lord Resistance-breaker, i.e. Vṛioragna, whose function it was to break the resistance put up by evil, continued his glorious career within the Irānian pantheon. Indra and Vṛitrahan were united in the same person only later in the Vedic age. In short, Vedic Indra is the Indo-Irānian Indra (mentioned at Boghaz-köi) *plus* Vṛitrahan, whereas Avestan Indra is the Indo-Irānian Indra *minus* Vṛitrahan. There is no discrepancy, therefore, between Vedic Indra and Avestan Indra if it is remembered that the history of Indra is in reality the history of two different gods who influenced each other in two different ways in Irān and India.

The Nāsatyas who in the Boghaz-köi inscription are mentioned side by side with Indra and Varuṇa also appear in the Avesta, though as a demon[24] like Indra, and even the minor Vedic god Apāṁ-napāt is represented in the Avesta by a god of the same name. To the Vedic Gandharva corresponds the Avestan Gandarəwa, and to the Vedic Kṛiśānu the Avestan Kərəšāni.[25] In the Veda, Yama, the son of Vivasvat, is the ruler of the dead, in the Avesta, Yima, the son of Vīvanhant, is the ruler of paradise.[26] Examples can be multiplied to show that in spite of the Zarathustrian reform, the Irānian religion continued to be much the same as before. On the whole it seems that Zarathustra's reform was not so much a break with the past as a determined and partly successful effort to re-assert the principles of the old Asura religion by ridding it of all *Daivic* contaminations.[27] This is suggested pointedly by the curious fact that not content with consigning to Hades the prominent *Daiva*-gods like Indra, he changed the name also of the chief *Asura*-god Varuṇa into Ahura Mazdāh.[28] That Zarathustra dropped the name while retaining and raising to the highest honour the personality of this god is apparently because in the previous age—at the time of the Boghaz-köi tablets at any rate—he had lived in the corrupt company of the *Daiva*-god Indra. For a similar reason Zarathustra avoided the word *Baga* "god" of Indo-European origin, though it occurs in the pre-Zarathustrian parts of the Avesta and in the Old Persian inscriptions,[29] for an Indo-European word of religious connotation could not but have *Daivic* associations.

So long as it was believed that the Gāthās, because oldest in language, give also the oldest picture of the Aryan civilization of Irān, it was by no means possible to see that the society described in the Veda and the Avesta is essentially the same. But it has now been fully established that the civilization of the Gāthās is a later reformed civilization of Irān, of which a much older phase is reflected in the Yašts, particularly the so-called heathenish Yašts, i.e. the Yašts which have suffered least from Zarathustrian revision.[30] And the culture reflected in these pre-Zarathustrian heathenish Yašts is essentially that of Vedic India. The very Haoma-cult, which is rightly regarded as the chief indicator of Indo-Irānian cultural unity, is not only pre-Zarathustrian but definitely anti-Zarathustrian, and could be retained in the post-Zarathustrian religion of Irān only because the prophet—clearly out of policy—did not specifically mention Soma in prohibiting intoxicating drinks: from this omission it was argued by Avestan theologians that all other intoxicants are impure, but not Haoma.[31] Benveniste has demonstrated that the Persian religion of the Achaemenian age, as described by Herodotus, agrees not at all well with that of the Gāthās, but shows significant points of similarity with the Vedic religion.[32]

The notorious difference in burial customs between Irān and India entirely vanishes on scrutiny. The custom of exposing dead bodies in *dakmas*, which is unknown in India, was not of Persian origin, but a Median custom confined to the Magi. It became the customary funeral rite of Irān only in the Arsacidan age, and is mentioned for the first time in the Vīdevdāt, a product of the Arsacidan period. The Achaemenian monarchs, whose Zarathustrianism cannot be seriously doubted, were placed in elaborate grave-chambers after death, and it is nowhere recorded that the corpse of any one of those mighty emperors had been thrown to birds and beasts.[33]

The ancient Aryan culture of Irān was thus hardly distinguishable from the ancient Aryan culture of India. And that is as it should be, for both were derived from one and the same Indo-Irānian culture.

---

1. *Iran in the Ancient East*, 1941, p. 190.
2. *Op. cit.*, p. 192.
3. *Op. cit.*, pp. II, 177.
4. *Ved. Ind.*, I, p. 505.
5. Linguistic affinity between the earliest Aryans of India and Irān has been discussed by the present writer in *Linguistic Introduction to Sanskrit*, pp. 26-47 and *IC*, VII, pp. 343-59.
6. For the history of later Indo-Irānian relations see *CHI*, I, pp. 323 ff.
7. See *Vedic Index* under these three names. Zimmer was even of opinion that Vedic Rasā directly refers to Irānian Ranhā, i.e. Jaxartes (*AL*, p. 16).
8. *Ved. Myth.*, first ed., Vol. I, pp. 99 ff.; Vol. III, pp. 372-8. Older attempts to read Irānian history and geography in the Veda have been briefly dealt with by Jackson in *CHI*, Vol. I, pp. 322 ff., and more recently by Keith in *Woolner Comm. Vol.* (1940).
9. Cf. the fires of the Prytaneia in Greece, Vestal fire of Rome, Gārhapatya fire of India (Keith, *RPVU*, II, pp. 625-6).

10. Like Vedic *Ṛita* = Av. *Aša* (to be pronounced *arra*, from *arta*).
11. As I have suggested elsewhere (*IC*, VII, p. 339), this term is probably nothing but the personal designation of the tutelary deity of Assyria used as a generic name by the Indo-Irānians who must have come in direct or indirect contact with the Assyrians during the period of Kassite ascendancy, for the Kassites on the one hand borrowed from the Indo-Irānians the word *sūrya* and on the other conquered Assyria. Cf. Thomas, *JRAS*, 1916, pp. 362-6.
12. Varuṇa was originally a nature-god no doubt, since the equation Skt. *Varuṇa* = Gr. *Ouranos* has to be accepted (see Keith, *IC*, III, p. 421). Yet the natural basis of this god had been usurped by *Dyaus pitā* = *Zeus patēr* already in Indo-European times, and as a result he became a pronounced ethical god. Varuṇa's associate Mitra, too, was originally a nature-deity—a sun-god—as I have tried to show before (*IC*, III, p. 63), but he too had to lose his natural basis to the more powerful Sūrya.
13. *Kulturgeschichte des Alten Orients*, p. 211.
14. *Op. cit.*, pp. 211-12.
15. See Sukumar Sen, *Old Persian Inscriptions*, pp. 148-56.
16. See Keith, *RPVU*, II, p. 457.
17. See *IC*, VII, pp. 61-62. Benveniste has shown that the conception of *Māyā*, by means of which Indra and his Irānian opposite number Vṛiθragna could assume different forms at will, dates from the Indo-Irānian epoch (*Vṛtra et Vṛθragna*, pp. 32 ff., 194).
18. Irānian tradition would make Zarathustra more or less a contemporary of Buddha and Orpheus (if, as is generally thought, they were historical persons), but according to Eduard Meyer (*Geschichte des Altertums*, second edition, third volume, p. 110, fn. 3) it is an inexplicable thing that anybody should think so. That Eduard Meyer was right can be hardly doubted, although weighty opinions have been raised against his view. The mention by Assurbanipal about 700 B.C. of Assara Mazaš along with seven good angels and seven bad spirits is a clear indication of acquaintance with the reformed Zarathustrian pantheon (see *CHI*, I, p. 76). It is impossible therefore to suggest that the Kavi Vištāspa mentioned in the Avesta as the patron of the prophet was no other than the father of Darius I (522-486 B.C.), for in that case the Zarathustrian pantheon could not have been known in Assyria in the days of Assurbanipal.
19. See Christensen, *op. cit.*, p. 220.
20. See Hillebrandt, *Rituallitteratur*, § 2.
21. See footnote 10.
22. In *Vṛtra et Vṛθragna*, Paris, 1934.
23. The name of this god is to be derived from Hittite *innar*—"strength."
24. Avestan *Naonhaithya*, to be pronounced *Nōhaithya*.
25. To be pronounced Krišāni.
26. See Macdonell, *VM*, § 5.
27. I expressed a different view in *IC*, VII, p. 338.
28. Darmesteter has aptly said that Ahura Mazdāh is no more different from Varuṇa than Zeus is from Jupiter (*SBE*, IV, p. lii).
29. See Herzfeld, *Altpersische Inschriften*, p. 106.
30. See Christensen, *op. cit.*, pp. 214 ff.
31. *Op. cit.*, p. 229.
32. *The Persian Religion*, Ratanbai Katrak Lectures, Paris 1929, pp. 32 ff.
33. See Herzfeld, *Iran in the Ancient East*, 1941, pp. 216-17.

CHAPTER XII

VEDIC LITERATURE–GENERAL VIEW

Our knowledge of the Indo-Aryans is based on the evidence of Vedic literature, of which the chief constituents are the four collections known as the *Ṛigveda*, *Sāmaveda*, *Yajurveda*, and *Atharvaveda*. Not a single work of the Vedic period can be accurately dated. On linguistic grounds the language of the *Ṛigveda*, the oldest Veda, may be said to be of about 1000 B.C.,[1] but its contents may be—and certainly are in the oldest parts—of much more ancient date, and its latest parts, resembling Atharvanic charms, are as surely of much later origin. This *Ṛigveda* is neither an historical nor an heroic poem, but mainly a collection (*saṁhitā*) of hymns by a number of priestly families, recited or chanted by them with appropriate solemnity at sacrifices to the gods. Naturally it is poor in historical data. The *Sāmaveda* hardly counts at all as an independent text (see below). The Saṁhitās of the *Yajurveda*, if the Brāhmaṇa portions of the schools of the *Black Yajurveda* are left out of account, are nothing but collections of short magic spells used by a certain class of priests at the sacrifices. For the history of the Indian people of the Vedic age the *Atharvaveda* is certainly the most important and interesting of the four Saṁhitās, describing, as it does, the popular beliefs and superstitions of the humble folk, as yet only partly subjugated by Brahmanism.

Next to the Saṁhitās are the Brāhmaṇas, an arid desert of puerile speculations on ritual ceremonies. They mark the lowest ebb of Vedic culture. The Upanishads were at least partially the result of a popular protest against the soulless ritualism of the Brāhmaṇas, as was also the rise of sects like the Vaishṇavas, Jainas, Buddhists, etc. In the Sūtras Brahmanical orthodoxy fought and lost its last battle against these forces of religious liberalism before merging itself in the synthetic national religion of India in the pre-Muhammadan era, i.e. Hinduism. A brief survey of the Saṁhitās, Brāmaṇas, and the Śrauta-sūtras[1a] is given here to indicate the nature and extent of these texts, reserving for later chapters their linguistic and literary valuation.

I. THE SAMHITĀS

I. *Ṛigveda*

Of the various recensions of the *Ṛigveda* known in tradition only one, namely the Śākala recension, consisting of 1,017 hymns of very unequal length, has come down to us apparently complete, and it is this Śākala recension that is meant when one speaks of the

"*Ṛigveda,*" though we have parts of two other recensions of the *Ṛigveda,* namely the Vālakhilya (11 hymns, usually placed in the middle of the eighth Maṇḍala of the Śākala recension) and the Bāshkala (36 hymns in the Aundh edition of the *Ṛigveda,* the so-called Khila-sūktas, most of which are evidently spurious fabrications, inserted at various places in the Śākala text). Why fragments—and only these fragments—of the Vālakhilya and Bāshkala recensions have been handed down to us is quite clear: they had definite, though minor, rôles to play in the ritual (as proved by later ritual texts in the case of some of them), and therefore had to be preserved.[2] Originally the ritual varied not only from school to school but also from family to family,[2a] but later in the Rigvedic age a system of ritual with minor variations, generally recognized by all the principal schools and priestly families, had been built up, for which the texts collected in the Śākala school were accepted *en bloc,* but in which there always remained not a few loop-holes provided by the continually expanding ritual, and these loop-holes had to be stopped with Ṛik-mantras drawn sometimes from other recensions.

Now, if the existing fragments of the non-Śākala recensions of the *Ṛik-Saṁhitā* owe their survival apparently only to the fact that they were utilized in ritual by priests of the Śākala school[3]—and indeed no other plausible reason can be suggested for the anomalous survival of these non-Śākala Ṛik-texts—then the important question arises: should not the preservation of the whole Śākala recension itself be attributed to the same cause? This question has doubtless to be answered in the affirmative.[4] All the hymns accepted into the Saṁhitā must have possessed intrinsic ritual significance at the time of their acceptance.

Later, however, the ritual changed, and not a few of the hymns of the Saṁhitā in consequence lost their proper *viniyoga,* but not their position in the Saṁhitā which had become sacrosanct and therefore unassailable.[4a]

The *Ṛigveda* is not—as it is often represented to be—a book of folk poetry; nor does it mark the beginning of a literary tradition. Bucolic, heroic, and lyrical elements are not entirely absent, but they are sub-merged under a stupendous mass of dry and stereotyped hymnology dating back to the Indo-Irānian era, and held as a close preserve by a number of priestly families whose sole object in cherishing those hymns was to utilize them in their sacrificial cult. Of natural outpourings of heart there is not much to be found in the *Ṛigveda,* for the hymns were part of an elaborate ritual which gradually came to be regarded as capable not only of persuading but also of compelling the gods to do the bidding of the officiating priests. This magico-religious attitude of mind found fullest expression later in the Mīmāṁsā-philosophy in which the gods were retained only in name and the ritual itself came to occupy the place of the gods.

One hymn of three verses[5] and three verses of three other hymns[6] have not been divided in the Padapāṭha by Śākalya, who must have been dead when Yāska wrote[6a] and therefore lived before 600 B.C. This is important, for it shows that hymns and verses could have been added to the *Ṛik-Saṁhitā* even after the date of Śākalya, for it is clear that Śākalya would not have left the hymn and the verses in question undivided if they had formed an integral part of the Saṁhitā in his time. The formation of the *Ṛik-Saṁhitā*, as we know it today, had therefore not been quite complete even so late as the time of Śākalya. On the other hand, there is nothing to tell us when the task of collecting the hymns into a Saṁhitā was started.

Most of the hymns were not composed as such, but were mechanically manufactured out of fragments of a floating anonymous literature,[7] and the process of manufacturing hymns in this manner must have continued for a long time. The fact that there are *Mantras* cited by Pratīkas in the Brāhmaṇas of the *Ṛigveda* which do not occur in our Saṁhitā clearly shows that at the time of these Brāhmaṇas recently adopted or freshly manufactured Ṛik-verses were considered good enough for utilization in ritual, but were yet denied a place in the Saṁhitā.[8] It is impossible to imagine, however, any stage in the development of the *Ṛik-Saṁhitā* at which a demand for new *Mantras* was not present, for the ritual in which they were intended to be used was all the time growing in complexity and expanding in range—and therefore demanding new *Mantras* at every step.[8a] There is indeed much to be said in favour of a ritual tradition advocated by Hillebrandt[9]—which in his opinion was independent of the literary tradition of the *Ṛik-Saṁhitā* known to us, and which contained hymns all of which need not have been included in the latter.[10]

There is at all events no doubt that the texts constituting the Puroruchas, Nividas, and Praishas for the ritual are of pre-Saṁhitā date, and that the Praüga-sūktas, Āprī-sūktas, etc., were composed directly with an eye to application in ritual.[11] All things considered, it seems best to conclude that the hymns constituting the *Ṛik-Saṁhitā*, though certainly not always composed or manufactured directly for the sacrificial ritual, yet owe their inclusion in the Saṁhitā, which guaranteed their preservation, wholly to the fact that at some time or other the ritual offered a place to each of them.

The division of the whole Saṁhitā into ten Maṇḍalas, and the number and arrangement of hymns in these Maṇḍalas, are not at all arbitrary. It is hardly an accident that the number of hymns contained in the first and the last Maṇḍalas is exactly the same, namely one hundred and ninety-one. The kernel of the *Ṛik-Saṁhitā* is, however, constituted by the so-called family-Maṇḍalas, i.e. the six consecutive Maṇḍalas from the second to the seventh, each of which is supposed to have been composed by a particular family of priests. The hymns of these family-Maṇḍalas are often composed of tristichs (*tṛichas*)—evidently because in ritual, as a rule, groups of three verses, and not whole hymns or single verses, are used. The eighth Maṇḍala is known as the Pragātha-maṇḍala, for the verses in mixed metres known as Pragāthas, indispensable for the Udgātṛi-ritual, are drawn mostly from this Maṇḍala. The ninth is most pronouncedly a ritual Maṇḍala, for in it were collected all the hymns addressed to Soma Pavamāna,[12] which were originally included in the other Maṇḍalas. The first Maṇḍala falls naturally into two parts: the first fifty hymns have the Kaṇvas as authors like the eighth Maṇḍala and are arranged according to principles obtaining in that Maṇḍala (see below), but the rest are arranged in the manner of the hymns of the family-Maṇḍalas. The tenth Maṇḍala is manifestly a later addition, often Atharvanic in character—yet not so late that the few Pavamāna-hymns originally belonging to it could not be transferred to the ninth Maṇḍala.[13]

The principle governing the original arrangement of hymns in the family-Maṇḍalas seems to have been determined by three considerations—deity, metre, and the number of verses contained in the hymns concerned.[14] Each family-Maṇḍala opens with a group of hymns dedicated to Agni, immediately followed by another group addressed to Indra.[15] Then follow in each family-Maṇḍala groups of hymns dedicated to various gods, the relative positions of these groups being determined on the whole in the descending order according to the number of hymns contained in each, or, when such groups contain each an equal number of hymns, in the descending order according to the number of verses contained in the first hymn of each group. It follows as a necessary corollary to this rule that if in a family-Maṇḍala several deities have as their shares only one hymn each, then these single hymns should be put at the end of the Maṇḍala and arranged in descending order according to the number of verses contained in each. Within each deity-group the order of hymns is determined chiefly by metre, again in the descending order, the hymns in Jagatī coming first and those in Gāyatrī coming last. These are in brief the laws governing the arrangement of hymns in the family-Maṇḍalas—laws re-discovered in our age by Bergaigne and endorsed by Oldenberg.[16] These laws cannot, of course, be rigorously applied to the text of the *Ṛigveda* as we find it today. Yet, when a re-division of the hymns is made on the plausible grounds suggested by Bergaigne and Oldenberg, it is found that exceptions to these laws are surprisingly few. And it leaves no doubt that the redactors of the family-Maṇḍalas had in mind a comprehensive plan—the advantages of such a plan are obvious—according to which every single hymn in this large collection could occupy only one particular position and no other.

The plan of the eighth Maṇḍala is altogether different. Here the hymns are not arranged primarily according to the deities invoked in them as in the family-Maṇḍalas.[17] The principle followed seems rather to have been primarily to group together all the hymns of each individual author, and then to arrange the hymns of each such group into sub-groups of hymns addressed to particular deities, and that in such a manner that the verse-numbers of the first hymns of these sub-groups would be in a descending order. This peculiarity of the eighth Maṇḍala, together with the fact that most of the hymns in Pragātha metres are found in it, does suggest—but by no means proves—that the eighth Maṇḍala was subjoined at a later date to the kernel constituted by the family-Maṇḍalas.[17a] But there is positive reason to believe that there was a time when the eighth Maṇḍala was actually considered to be the last in the Saṁhitā, for why else should the Vālakhilya-hymns be thrust into the eighth Maṇḍala and not added after the tenth? Also the simple fact that the eighth Maṇḍala is followed by the ninth strongly suggests the same thing, for since the latter consists almost exclusively of Pavamāna-hymns combed out of the other Maṇḍalas, it could have been constituted as a separate collection only after them, and consequently *after* the eighth Maṇḍala also. It should not be forgotten, however, that the ninth Maṇḍala is of a comparatively later date only as a separate collection, but not in contents. Why it was considered necessary to assemble in a separate collection only the hymns addressed to Soma Pavamāna and no other deity is perfectly clear, for while the hymns addressed to other deities were primarily the concern of the Hotṛi-priests, those invoking Soma Pavamāna were originally meant exclusively for the Udgātṛi-priests—who therefore should have taken the initiative in collecting the Pavamāna-hymns in a separate book.[18] And since the Udgātṛi-priests were Sāman-singers and not simply *Mantra*-reciters like the Hotṛi-priests, it is not to be wondered at if the hymns contained in the Udgātṛi-Maṇḍala are arranged, as they actually are, according to metres, the chief concern of the redactors of this Maṇḍala having been apparently to group together hymns composed in the same metre.

From the above survey it will be clear that all attempts to establish a relative chronology of the first nine Maṇḍalas of the *Ṛigveda* cannot but be futile.[19] That the tenth Maṇḍala is later in origin than the first nine is, however, perfectly certain from the evidence of the language.[20] But it is also certain that the whole of the *Ṛik-Saṁhitā*, including the tenth Maṇḍala, had assumed practically the same form in which we find it today already before the other Saṁhitās came into existence.[21]

2. *Sāmaveda*

As regards the *Sāmaveda*[22] it is necessary always to keep in mind that the word *sāman* means "melody," and that the *Sāma-Saṁhitā* is nothing but a collection of melodies. Certain texts are, of course, included in what is known as *Sāmaveda*, but the rôle of these texts in the *Sāmaveda* is altogether secondary—in fact analogous to the part played by musical notes in music. The texts used as musical notes in this Veda are moreover almost wholly drawn from the *Ṛik-Saṁhitā*. According to the figures given in the Aundh edition of the *Sāmaveda*, of the 1,603 verses (not counting the repetitions) of this Veda only 99 (again not counting the repetitions) are not found in the *Ṛik-Saṁhitā*.[23] The literary and historical value of the *Sāmaveda* is, therefore, practically nil, though its importance for the Soma-ritual cannot be overestimated.

The text part of the *Sāmaveda* serving merely the purpose of musical notes, every melody could theoretically be chanted on every verse. Yet this freedom seems never to have been actually taken in the ritual. Rather the ritual demands that particular melodies should be chanted on particular verses. It is the double task of assigning particular melodies to particular verses and particular verses to particular melodies that has rendered so complex the *Sāmaveda* which is, needless to say, a purely ritual Saṁhitā. The complexity of the whole system has become still more enhanced on account of the fact that, on the one hand, the same *sāman* can be chanted on different verses, and on the other, different *sāmans* can be chanted on the same verse. In the language of the ritual texts, the verse on which a *sāman* is chanted is called a *Yoni*, "source." This suggestive term, used already in the Brāhmaṇas, clearly shows that it had become conventional in ancient India to regard the verse as the source of the melody,[24] even though of text and melody one can never be the source of the other. The *Sāmaveda* proper, i.e. the Ārchika, is nothing but a collection of 585 *Yonis*. The Pūrvārchika, together with the Āraṇyaka-Saṁhitā and the Uttarārchika, represents the text-part of the *Sāmaveda*. The Grāmageyagāna, the Araṇyageyagāna, the Ūhagāna and the Ūhyagāna[25] together constitute its song-part.

The Pūrvārchika records only verses (*Yonis*) to each of which corresponds a single *sāman* (melody) named after the seer who is supposed to have discovered it, and these *sāmans* corresponding to the verses of the Pūrvārchika are registered in the Grāmageyagāna and the Araṇyageyagāna. The *Yonis* of the Pūrvārchika are divided into three parts: Nos. 1-114 are verses addressed to Agni; Nos. 115-466 to Indra; and Nos. 467-585 to Soma Pavamāna.

The Uttarārchika, on the other hand, records mostly tristichs (*tṛichas*) or distichs (*pragāthas*)[26] occasionally also complexes of more verses, but never single verses as in the Pūrvārchika. Now, generally the first verse of a Tṛicha of the Uttarārchika is found to occur among the single verses (*Yonis*) of the Pūrvārchika,[27] and when such is the case it is to be understood that the melody belonging to that particular *Yoni* of the Pūrvārchika has to be chanted on the *whole* of the corresponding Tṛicha of the Uttarārchika. In actual chant, however, no verse can retain its original form. Therefore it is not sufficient merely to indicate which verse has to be chanted in which melody. It is necessary further to indicate what modifications a verse will have to undergo when chanted in a particular melody. To indicate the actual forms assumed in chant by the tristichs of the Uttarārchika is the purpose of the Ūhagāna, which thus gives the melodies of the Grāmageyagāna in their final ritual form. The Ūhyagāna does the same for the melodies of the Araṇyageyagāna.[28]

3. *Yajurveda*

The *Yajurveda* is, if possible, even more pronouncedly a ritual Veda, for it is essentially a guide-book[29] for the Adhvaryu-priests who had to do practically everything in the sacrifices excepting reciting the *Mantras* and chanting the melodies.[30] And since variation is more natural in manual work than in recitation and chanting, we actually possess today—not merely in tradition as is mostly the case with the other Saṁhitās—no less than six complete recensions of the *Yajurveda*, of which two (Mādhyandina and Kāṇva)[30a] constitute the White Yajurveda, and the rest (Taittirīya, Kāṭhaka, Maitrāyaṇī and Kapishṭhala) the Black Yajurveda.[31]

The fact that the *Gopatha-Brāhmaṇa* (I. 29) in citing the first words of the different Vedas quotes in the case of the Yajurveda the beginning of the *Vājasaneyi-Saṁhitā*[32] may suggest that the White Yajurveda represents the original tradition of which the Black Yajurveda with all its recensions is a later variation. But the truth should rather be just the opposite, for it is hardly possible that Mantra and Brāhmaṇa, kept separate as in the White Yajurveda tradition, should have got mixed up at a later date. It is generally assumed, therefore, that the Black Yajurveda, with Mantra and Brāhmaṇa mixed up throughout, is older than the White Yajurveda in which the Brāhmaṇa was separated from the Saṁhitā, perhaps in imitation of the Rigvedic model. In the *Taittirīya-Brāhmaṇa*, too, which is merely a continuation of the *Taittirīya-Saṁhitā* (but not necessarily later than it for that reason), and which, too, owes its origin as a separate treatise to the influence of the Rigvedic tradition,[33] Mantra and Brāhmaṇa, have not been separated.[34] It is a peculiar feature of the Taittirīya texts that the Saṁhitā and the

Brāhmaṇa of this school supplement each other in such a way that each seems to presuppose the other.

The relative chronology of the extant versions of the Black Yajurveda has long been an interesting but unsolved problem.[35] Language in this case fails to provide a dependable criterion, for, in spite of inevitable unimportant linguistic peculiarities of each, all of them may be said to speak in the same language.[36] The treatment of the Rigvedic Mantras in the Saṁhitās of the Black Yajurveda is interesting: the *Kāṭhaka* and the *Maitrāyaṇī* in this respect often agree with each other against the *Ṛigveda* and the *Taittirīya*,[37] which should indicate, if Oldenberg's well-known theory is true that slavish conformity to Rigvedic text is a sign of comparative lateness of *Yajurveda-Saṁhitās*,[38] that the Kāṭhaka-Kapishṭhala-Maitrāyaṇī may have been older than the Taittirīya. As regards the Brāhmaṇa-parts of the *Taittirīya-Saṁhitā*, Keith[39] has shown that they are later than the older first five Pañchikās of the *Aitareya-Brāhmaṇa* and older than the *Satapatha-Brāhmaṇa*, but anything more precise about their relative or absolute date eannot be hazarded.

If slavish conformity to the text-tradition of the *Ṛigveda* is indicative of comparative lateness, then the Saṁhitās of the White Yajurveda must be regarded as comparatively late, to judge them by the Rigvedic verses quoted in them, as amply demonstrated by Oldenberg.[40] Moreover the *Vājasaneyi-Saṁhitā* lacks that general uniformity and homogeneity which pervades not only the whole of the *Taittirīya-Saṁhitā* but extends also to the Brahmaṇa and the Araṇyaka of the Taittirīya School. Of the forty odd Adhyāyas of the *Vājasaneyi-Saṁhitā*, it is quite evident that the last twenty-two were added later[41] gradually to a basic text consisting of the first eighteen. As a rule only the formulas found in the first eighteen Adhyāyas occur also in the *Taittirīya-Saṁhitā*, while those of the last twenty-two are met with in the *Taittirīya-Brāhmaṇa*.[42] The next three Adhyāyas (XIX-XXI) give the *Mantras* of the Sautrāmaṇī, a sacrifice performed to expiate the sin of excessive indulgence in Soma, and the following four (XXII-XXV), those of the horse-sacrifice. The remaining fifteen Adhyāyas (XXVI-XL) are expressly called Khila in the ancillary literature.[43]

4. *Atharvaveda*

The *Atharvaveda* is utterly different from the other three Vedas discussed above, for though an effort was made at a comparatively late date to absorb it within the sacred Srauta-literature by furnishing it formally with a Śrauta-sūtra with the significant designation Vaitāna-sūtra,[44] yet it was never accorded full recognition in the ritual of the Soma-cult, and to the last it remained essentially what it was from the start—a prayer-book of the simple folk, haunted by ghosts and exploited by Brāhmins.[45] In its present form the *Atharvaveda* is certainly the latest of the four Saṁhitās, but in contents it is by no means so, for there can be no doubt that Bloomfield[46] was perfectly right in characterizing the *Atharvaveda* as follows: "On the whole the *Atharvaveda* is the bearer of old tradition not only in the line of the popular charms; but also to some extent, albeit slight, its hieratic materials are likely to be the product of independent tradition that has eluded the collectors of the other Vedas, the *Ṛigveda* not excepted." At the same time, however, it is quite clear that the hymns and charms of the *Atharvaveda* were collected in a Saṁhitā and handed down to the present day only because the Brahmanical ritual gradually extended its sway over profane superstition, and by degrees granted a grudging recognition even to frankly magical incantations that were originally doubtless of non-Brahmanical inspiration. This is proved strikingly by the Khila-hymns of the *Atharvaveda*, the so-called Kuntāpa-sūktas, of no particularly sacred character, which, as Bloomfield has amply demonstrated,[47] were nevertheless retained and handed down in tradition, apparently only because they were indispensable for a popular cult that had succeeded in wringing recognition from the circle of sacerdotes.

The Saṁhitā of the *Atharvaveda* is now before us in two recensions,[48] the Śaunakīya recension,[49] and the Paippalāda recension.[50] It is the *Śaunakīya-Saṁhitā* that is usually meant when the *Atharvaveda* is mentioned in ancient or modern literature. But the earliest references seem to have been to some other (probably Paippalāda) recension. Patañjali's statement on Pāṇini V. 2.37 to the effect that the text of the Aṅgirases consists of twenty chapters may apply to both the recensions, since each consists of twenty Kāṇḍas, but the initial verse of the *Atharvaveda* as quoted by Patañjali and also in the *Gopatha-Brāhmaṇa* is not the opening verse of the Śaunakīya recension,[51] but of the Paippalāda text.[52]

Of the twenty Kāṇḍas of the *Atharvaveda*,[53] the last one is manifestly a later addition manufactured almost wholly out of borrowings from the *Ṛigveda* to serve as a manual for the priest called Brāhmaṇāchchhaṁsin who had a definite, though minor, rôle to play at the Soma-sacrifice.[54] Moreover the Kuntāpa-sūktas of this Kāṇḍa are without any Padapāṭha, and nothing parallel to them can be found in the Paippalāda recension—showing that they had been given a place in this late Kāṇḍa of the Saṁhitā at a very late date. In fact, the nineteenth Kāṇḍa ends with a significant prayer which strongly suggests that the Saṁhitā at one time was considered to end with it. But there are reasons to believe that the nineteenth Kāṇḍa itself is a late compilation, for its hymns, though found in the Paippalāda recension, are scattered throughout that text. Both the nineteenth and the twentieth Kāṇḍas have been ignored in the Prātiśākhya of the *Atharvaveda*. The eighteenth

Kāṇḍa, consisting of four funeral hymns, should also be regarded as a later addition, for its contents are absent in the Paippalāda-recension. The seventeenth Kāṇḍa, consisting of only one hymn of purely magical contents, is a curious anomaly, and must be regarded as a late accretion, though partly appearing also in the Paippalāda text. The most interesting of all the Kāṇḍas is the fifteenth, composed not in verse but in typical Brāhmaṇa prose, and devoted to the mystic exaltation of the Vrātya. Probably this Vrātya-kāṇḍa was the first of the additions successively made to the original text of the *Atharvaveda* which has come down to us in two recensions. There is no reason to doubt the antiquity and authenticity of the other Kāṇḍas of the *Atharvaveda*.

2. THE BRAHMAṆAS

The Brāhmaṇas are, if possible, ritual texts of an even more pronounced type than the Saṁhitās, for though the hymns and charms of at least the *Ṛigveda* and the *Atharvaveda* need not all have been of ritual origin, there is no room for any doubt in the case of the Brāhmaṇas that the sole object of their authors was to speculate on and mystify, but hardly to explain, minute details of Brahmanical sacrifices. The duties of the Hotṛi-priests, who had to recite the *Mantras* of the *Ṛigveda* at the sacrifices, have been luxuriantly speculated upon and mystified by the authors of the Brāhmaṇas of the *Ṛigveda*, those of the Udgātṛi-priests in the Brāhmaṇas of the *Sāmaveda*, etc. All that is found in the Brāhmaṇas that is not directly concerned with ritual is, strictly speaking, irrelevant and unnecessary from the view-point of their authors.

The *Aitareya* and the *Kaushītaki* (or *Śāṅkhāyana*) are the Brāhmaṇas of the *Ṛigveda*, and of them the former is older in date and bigger in bulk, but the latter is richer in contents. But the *Aitareya* itself is plainly a composite work, its first five Pañchikās being older than the last three. Similarly, only two Brāhmaṇas of the *Sāmaveda* have been preserved, namely the *Jaiminīya*[55] and the *Tāṇḍya-mahā-Brāhmaṇa*, the latter also known as the *Pañchaviṁśa-Brāhmaṇa* on account of its twentyfive chapters, to which a supplementary chapter was added that somehow came to be regarded as an independent treatise with the singular designation "*Shaḍviṁśa-Brāhmaṇa.*" The *Jaiminīya-Brāhmaṇa* is indeed one of the most interesting works of the later Vedic literature, and rivals in importance the *Śatapatha-Brāhmaṇa*[56] of the *Yajurveda*, for in elucidation of the details of ritual the authors of these two Brāhmaṇas have introduced numerous stories, mostly of an aetiological character, which nevertheless throw welcome light on social conditions. Regarding the relation between the two recensions of the *Śatapatha-Brāhmaṇa*, namely Mādhyandina and Kāṇva, Caland has expressed the opinion that both existed from the very beginning, but later the Kāṇva-recension was influenced by the other.[57]

It is also clear at the same time that neither the Mādhyandina nor the Kāṇva recension of the *Śatapatha-Brāhmaṇa* has been handed down to us in its original redaction, for quotations from the *Satapatha* in early literature are often missing in both the recensions. Moreover, it is certain that the Brāhmaṇa in both its recensions is a composite work. For though Yājñavalkya Vājasaneya is the authority most frequently quoted in the *Śatapatha*, yet in both the recensions there are five Kāṇḍas (Kāṇḍas VI-X in Mādhyandina corresponding to Kāṇḍas VIII-XII in Kāṇva) dealing with the construction of the fire-altar, in which the authority quoted is Śāṇḍilya and Yājñavalkya has not been mentioned at all. It remains still to mention only one of the more important Brāhmaṇas, namely the *Gopatha-Brāhmaṇa* of the *Atharvaveda*, consisting mostly of slightly modified quotations (without acknowledgment) from other sources. It gives the impression of being so late that Bloomfield[58] declared it to be more recent than even the Śrauta-sūtra (Vaitāna) and the Gṛihya-sūtra (Kauśika) of the *Atharvaveda*.

3. THE ŚRAUTA-SŪTRAS

Puerile speculation on the *minutiae* of ritual, so much in evidence in the Brāhmaṇas, developed in the direction of pure speculation in the Āraṇyakas and Upanishads. Winternitz[59] has truly said that "it is often difficult to draw the line between the Āraṇyakas and the Upanishads." Only it is necessary to remember that it is no less difficult to draw the line between the Brāhmaṇas and the Āraṇyakas. Among the Śrauta-sūtras, too, there is at least one text namely the *Baudhāyana Śrautasūtra*, which it is difficult not to regard as a late Brāhmaṇa. Thus a fine line of demarcation between Brāhmaṇa, Āraṇyaka and Śrauta-sūtra is out of the question. Yet it would be correct to say that the speculative spirit developed in the Brāhmaṇas in connection with ritual ceremonies tried to burst its irksome fetters in the Āraṇyakas, and in some of the Upanishads attained the stage of as complete an independence as was ever witnessed by man. The Āraṇyakas and Upanishads,[60] though nominally connected with the Brāhmaṇas, should rather be regarded as the beginning of purely speculative thinking in India. Much more closely connected with the older Vedic literature (Saṁhitās and Brāhmaṇas) are the Śrauta-sūtras, and to a lesser extent, the Gṛihya-sūtras.[61]

The Śrauta-sūtras describe[62] the ritual sacrifices in a language that is both vigorous and prophetic in brevity, but is also utterly unintelligible for that very reason. No greater contrast can be imagined than that between the Brāhmaṇas and the Śrauta-sūtras, though the subject of treatment is the same in both. Both are obscure, but for different reasons: the Brāhmaṇas, because of loose thinking, and the Śrauta-sūtras, because too much is taken to be understood in them. Moreover the Śrauta-sūtras, isolated the common and special features of the sacrifices and cleverly dealt with them as if they were digits of number, and that by itself must be regarded as an intellectual achievement of no mean order.[63] Truly scientific spirit is unmistakably reflected in the Śrauta-sūtras, albeit the subject to which this spirit was applied was still magic pure and simple.[64]

The Śrauta-sūtras of Āśvalāyana and Śāṅkhāyana belong to the *Ṛigveda*, which means that the ritual duties of the Hotṛi-priests have been presented in them in a systematic form. But some of the verses quoted by Pratīka in the *Śāṅkhāyana Śrauta-sūtra* cannot be found in the Śākala-recension of the *Ṛik-saṁhitā*,[65] and so it is surmised that it was affiliated to the Bāshkala-śākhā and not to the Śākala-śākhā of the *Ṛigveda*. As regards the Brāhmaṇas, its affiliation is to the *Kaushītaki* and not the Aitareya-*Brāhmaṇa*. Of its eighteen chapters, the last two, though not necessarily of later origin, were a later addition dealing with the Mahāvrata, a popular festival that was given a Brahmanical complexion at a later date. The *Āśvalāyana Śrauta-sūtra*, on the other hand, is affiliated to the Śākala-śākhā of the *Ṛik-Saṁhitā*, and the *Aitareya-Brāhmaṇa*. Of these two Śrauta-sūtras of the *Ṛigveda*, Śāṅkhāyana's should be the older, for its language in some places is like that of the Brāhmaṇas. The principal Śrauta-sūtras of the *Sāmaveda* are those of *Lāṭyāyaṇa*, and *Drāhyāyaṇa* the first affiliated to the Kauthuma-śākhā and the latter to the Rāṇāyanīya-śākhā. A remarkable feature of the *Lāṭyāyana Śrauta-sūtra* is that the Śūdras, Nishādas, and Vrātyas have not been treated in it as accursed human beings as is generally the case in other Vedic texts.[66]

The *Āpastamba Śrauta-sūtra* of the Black Yajurveda, belonging to the Khāṇḍikīya school of the *Taittirīyas*, is in many respects the most important work of this *genre*, for no other single work gives such an ample (though by no means complete) description of the Vedic sacrifices; but the numerous quotations from other ritual texts found in it suggest that it should not be placed too high in date. The *Satyāshāḍha Śrauta-sūtra* is a particular recension of the *Āpastamba Śrauta-sūtra*. The Āpasthambins seem to have been prejudiced against the Kaṇvas and Kaśyapas, for their Śrauta-sūtra (XIII. 7.5) forbids the giving of presents to them. The oldest and the most archaic of all the known Śrauta-sūtras is certainly the *Baudhāyana Śrauta-sūtra*,[67] also of the Black Yajurveda. In style it still resembles a Brāhmaṇa in most respects, and according to tradition it belongs to the Khāṇḍikīya-school like the *Āpastamba Śrauta-sūtra*. The White Yajurveda is represented in the Śrauta-sūtra literature by the *Kātyāyana Śrauta-sūtra*, of which a striking feature is that three of its Adhyāyas (XXII-XXIV) are devoted to Sāmavedic ritual. Among the teachers cited by name in it are found some of the Black Yajurveda.[68]

Lastly, the Atharvavedins too got their Śrauta-manual in the shape of the *Vaitāna-sūtra*—anomalously enough, for the *Atharvaveda* has, strictly speaking, nothing to do with Śrauta-ritual. But since the Saṁhitā of the Brāhmaṇāchchhaṁsin, one of the priests participating in Soma-sacrifices, came to be appended to the *Atharvaveda*[69] the way was apparently opened thereby for the despised Atharvavedins to make inroad into the protected field of Śrauta-ritual. The result of this novel experiment was the *Vaitāna-sūtra*. But as Bloomfield has observed, "it is not the product of practices in Śrauta-ceremonies which have slowly and gradually developed in a certain high priestly school, but a somewhat conscious product, made at a time, when the Atharvavedins began to feel the need of a distinctive Śrauta-manual to support their claim that the *Atharvaveda* is a canonical Veda of independent and superior character."[70] Strictly speaking, the *Vaitāna-sūtra* is the Śrauta-sūtra only of the twentieth Kāṇḍa of the *Atharvaveda* and not of the whole of it. And since this Kāṇḍa is nothing but the Saṁhitā of the Brāhmaṇāchchhaṁsin, the *Vaitāna-sūtra* may quite appropriately be called the Śrauta-sūtra of the Brāhmaṇāchchhaṁsin. It may be noted that only 18 verses[71] of the twentieth Kāṇḍa of the *Atharvaveda* have not been assigned *viniyoga* in the *Vaitāna-sūtra*.

---

1. See *supra*, p. 203.

1a. The Upanishads and the Gṛihya-sūtras are not being taken into consideration in this chapter, for they are related more intimately to the post-Vedic than to the Vedic literature proper. They will be discussed in later chapters.

2. It was pointed out long ago by Oldenberg (*Prolegomena*, p. 508) that not only the Vālakhilya-hymns, but also the Suparna-hymns, the oldest of the Khila-sūktas, had a definite place in ritual according to tradition. According to the Anuvākānukramaṇī 36, the Bāshkala-Saṁhitā contained 1025 hymns, in its additional eight hymns being included seven Vālakhilyas and the Saṁjñāna (Oldenberg, *Prolegomena*, p. 494). Difference between the three recensions thus lies only in the Khilas.

2a. This is why we have six "family Maṇḍalas" in the *Ṛigveda*. This point has been fully demonstrated by Bergaigne.

3. Strictly speaking, the *Ṛigveda* that we know is the Śaiśirīya redaction of the Śākala recension of the text.

4. All the Vedic scholars, however, excepting Leopold von Schröder, who assigned a place in ritual even to the dialogue-hymns (*Mysterium und Mimus in Ṛigveda*, p. 36), have answered this question in the negative, though not all with equal emphasis.

4a. It has to be remembered, however, that some special kinds of ritual formulas such as the Praisha and Nivid-mantras, though indispensable for ritual from the earliest period, have nowhere been collected in a Saṁhitā.

5. *RV*, I. 190.

6. *RV*, VII. 59, 12; X. 20.I; X. 121. 10.

6a. Because Yāska (VI. 28) when referring to him uses the perfect tense (*chakāra*).

7. This is definitely proved by the material collected in Bloomfield's *Ṛigveda Repetitions*.

8. See on this point particularly Oldenberg, *Prolegomena*, p. 367.

8a. Thus, when as a result of the growing complexity of the Śrauta-ritual an additional assistant of the Hotā (nominally of the Brahman) had to be included among the usual band of priests in the person of the Brāhmanāchchhaṁsin, a new Saṁhitā too had to be created for him which was appended at a very late date to the Atharvaveda, forming its last Kāṇḍa (Oldenberg, *op. cit.*, p. 347; *Das Vaitānasūtra des Atharva-veda*, übersetzt von W. Caland, p. vi).

9. *Bezzenbergers Beiträge*, Vol. VIII, p. 195.
10. Hillebrandt's theory has been criticized—not quite fairly in our opinion—by Oldenberg (*Prolegomena*, p. 519). Variant reading of Ṛik-texts in later ritual literature should not, however, be taken as proof in support of Hillebrandt's theory, for the variations might have been due to intentional alteration of the Ṛik-texts to suit the ritual practices of a later age.
11. See Scheftelowitz, *Die Apokryphen des Ṛgveda*, p. 9.
12. It is not at all right to say—as Winternitz does (*HIL*, I, p. 58)—that the ninth Maṇḍala "contains exclusively hymns which glorify the drink of Soma, and are dedicated to the god Soma." In fact there is not a single hymn in the ninth Maṇḍala dedicated to the god Soma. Such hymns are found only in the other Maṇḍalas—for the simple reason that the Soma-hymns of the ninth Maṇḍala are dedicated solely to Soma Pavamāna and not to Soma.
13. This point has been particularly stressed by Oldenberg, *Prolegomena*, pp. 252-3.
14. Authors' lists given in ancillary literature (Anukramaṇīs), though containing many apparently spurious names, are on the whole quite trustworthy and fully in conformity with the internal data of the hymns. For a different view on this point see Winternitz, *op. cit.*, p. 58.
15. This systematic reversal of the natural order of the gods is not without significance. Indra is undoubtedly the most powerful god in the Vedic religion, but in Vedic ritual Agni may claim the first place—since no sacrifice is possible without fire. This again goes to support the view that the redactors of the *Ṛik-saṁhitā* were guided chiefly by considerations of ritual.
16. *Prolegomena*, p. 192.
17. The eighth Maṇḍala too may be called a family-Maṇḍala, since the authors are mostly of the Kaṇva family, but authors of other families are also frequently mentioned. Nor can it justly claim to be the Pragātha-maṇḍala as it does, for the majority of its hymns are in non-Pragātha metres, and hymns in Pragātha metres are present also in other Maṇḍalas.

17a. That is to say, all the family-Maṇḍalas might have been constituted out of the then existing material in one day or in one minute, but the eighth Maṇḍala, of which the most essential part is manifestly its large number of Pragātha-hymns which originally should have been distributed—not necessarily equally—among all the family-Maṇḍalas (like the Āprī-hymns!), could be constituted only after the family-Maṇḍalas.

18. See Oldenberg *Prolegomena*, p. 250.
19. Attempts galore have, however, been made to achieve the impossible, the last and the most elaborate attempt being Wüst's *Stilgeschichte und Chronologie des Ṛgveda* (Leipzig 1928) in which previous literature on this problem has been fully indicated.
20. Cf. below, Ch. XVI.
21. Oldenberg, *Prolegomena*, p. 328.
22. By "Sāmaveda" is to be understood the Kauthuma-śākhā of this Saṁhitā, with which perhaps the Saṁhitā of the Rāṇāyanīya-śākhā was identical. The *Jaiminīya-Saṁhitā* has been edited by Caland.
23. Readings of this large number of common passages are, however, not identical in both the Vedas. Ludwig, after an elaborate comparison of all these passages (*Der Ṛigveda*, Vol. III, pp. 83 ff.) came to the conclusion that in many passages the *Sāmaveda* has actually retained the original reading and not the *Ṛigveda*. But Ludwig's theory has been severely criticized by Oldenberg (*Prolegomena*, pp. 288 ff.).
24. Much as it was conventional to regard the Padapāṭha as the source of the Saṁhitā-text.
25. The Ūhagāna and Ūhyagāna are not regarded as canonical.
26. By "Pragātha" are meant complexes of two verses of which the second is a Satobṛihatī and the first either a Bṛihatī or a Kakubh (see *Ṛikprātiśākhya*. XVIII. I.), In actual application, however, every Pragātha has to be artificially expanded into a Tṛicha.
27. Quite a number of Tṛichas of the Uttarārchika, however, have nothing to correspond to them in the Pūrvarchika: that is because all of them are chanted uniformly on the Gāyatra-melody composed on the well-known Sāvitrī-mantra (*tat savitur = vareṇyam*, etc.). On the other hand, many Yonis of the Pūrvārchika are without a correspondent verse in the Uttarārchika: this is perhaps because the sacrifices at which the Sāmans concerned were chanted were not Soma-sacrifices (see Caland, *Pañchaviṁśa-Brāhmaṇa*, Translation, Introd., pp. x-xi).

28. The chronological relation between the Pūrvārchika and the Uttarārchika has been always one of the chief problems facing Vedic scholars, but the problem seems insoluble. See on this point particularly Càland, *op. cit.*, pp. xiv ff. and Suryakanta, *Ṛiktantra*, pp. 23 ff. where previous literature on this important problem has been indicated.
29. Yajurveda-texts are by no means guide-books in the sense that any person by studying them can form a picture of the ritual ceremonies dealt with in them. In fact even by studying the relevant portions of the Saṁhitās, Brāhmaṇas, and Sūtras in the light of the commentaries it is not possible to reconstruct fully the duties performed by a single priest at one of the great sacrifices, for all these texts proceed on the assumption that the ritual is already known to the reader in all its details. Only the late Paddhatis may be regarded as guides for the uninitiated, but, of course, they contain much that is not Vedic.
30. Already in the *Ṛigveda* the Adhvaryu is called *suhastya* and *madhupāṇi* (X. 41. 3) in contrast to the Hotṛi who is called *suvāch* (X. 110.7) and *sujihva* (I. 13.8).
30a. Regarding differences of reading between these two. see Caland, *Kāṇva-Śatapatha*, Introd., p. 91.
31. Formerly it used to be tacitly assumed that the Śukla-Yajurveda is so called because Mantra and Brāhmaṇa are not mixed up in it as in the Krishṇa-Yajurveda. But it is more probable that the redactors of the former claimed to have collected in it only the *śuklāni yajūṁshi* "white or pure Yajus" (*Ved. Ind.*. II, p. 183) already mentioned in the *Bṛihadāraṇyakopanishad* VI. 4.33—whence the names "White Yajurveda" and as a contrast, "Black Yajurveda."
32. As pointed out long ago by Max Müller, *HASL*, second edition, 1860, p. 453, and emphasized by Weber, *HIL*, p. 106 fn.
33. See Keith, HOS, XVIII, p. lxxvi. Certain sections of the *Taittirīya-Brāhmaṇa*. such as those on human sacrifice (III. 4) and Nakshatreshṭayaḥ (I.5) are certainly of later origin.
34. The same applies, *mutatis mutandis*, also to the *Taittirīya Āraṇyaka*. "The Sūtras do not recognize any distinction between the *Āraṇyaka*, the *Brāhmaṇa*. or the *Saṁhitā* as regards their Brāhmaṇa portions" (Keith, *ibid.*, p. lxxvi).
35. Schröder in his preface to the *Maitrāyaṇī Saṁhitā* indeed tried to prove the priority of the Kāṭhaka and Maitrāyaṇī recensions. but failed to convince any one.
36. Keith arrived at this conclusion regarding Taittirīya, Maitrāyaṇī, and Kāṭhaka (see *HOS*, XVIII. p. xcvi). As regards the Kapishṭhala, see Oertel, *Zur Kapiṣṭhala-Katha-Saṁhitā*, München, 1934.
37. See Keith, *op. cit.*, p. lxxvii. It should be noted that the Kapishṭhala, which is closely related to the Kāṭhaka, agrees with the latter to differ from the *Rigveda* in 64 cases, and agrees with the *Ṛigveda* to differ from the Kāṭhaka in 45 cases (Oertel, *op. cit.*, pp. 9 ff.).
38. *Prolegomena*. p. 319.
39. *Op. cit.*. p. xcix. This applies, *pari passu*. also to the Brāhmaṇa-parts of the other Saṁhitās of the *Black Yajurveda*.
40. *Prolegomena*, p. 318. Caland also says "there can be no doubt whatever that the White Yajurveda is on the whole younger than the Black Yajurveda" (*Kāṇva Śatapatha*, Introd., p. 92).
41. They are not, of course, for that reason of later *origin*.
42. See Eggeling. *SBE*, XII. p. xxx.
43. For further details about the *Vājasaneyi-Saṁhitā*, with which the Saṁhitā of the Kāṇva-school is practically identical, see Weber, *HIL*, 107 ff.
44. The word *Vaitānika* signifies Śrotriyas maintaining three fires (see Hillebrandt, *Rituallitteratur*, p. 69).
45. Bloomfield's excellent monograph on the *Atharvaveda*—like which unfortunately there is as yet nothing on any one of the other Saṁhitās—offers practically everything that a student of the Vedic literature might wish to know about the *Atharvaveda*. The section on the *Atharvaveda* in this chapter is mainly based on Bloomfield's monograph (published in the *Grundriss*).
46. *Op. cit.*, p. 50.
47. *Op. cit.*. pp. 97-100.
48. For other recensions, see Bloomfield, *op. cit.*, p. 12.
49. Published many times.
50. Edited by Raghu Vira.
51. As pointed out by Weber, *Ind. Stud.*, XIII, p. 433.
52. As surmised already by Bloomfield, *op. cit.*, p. 40.
53. Always the Śaunakīya recension is to be understood unless the Paippalāda is specifically mentioned.
54. See footnote 8a.

55. A complete edition of this important text by Raghu Vira is now appearing from Lahore. The most interesting parts of it were published by Caland in his "Auswahl." For details about it see Caland, *Over en uit het Jaiminīya-Brāhmana*. Some parts of the *Jaiminīya-Brāhmaṇa* were published for the first time by the present writer in his *Collection of Fragments of Lost Brāhmaṇas* (Calcutta, 1935).
56. Of which the Mādhyandina recension was published long ago by Weber and the Kāṇva recension has been published by Caland (the first volume in 1926 and the second in 1940) from Lahore.
57. Caland, *Kāṇva-Śatapatha*, Introd., p. 90.
58. *Op. cit.*, p. 102. Bloomfield's view appears to be the right one but it is opposed by Caland (*Vaitāna Sūtra*, p. iv).
59. *HIL*, I, p. 234.
60. A convenient account of them has been given by Winternitz, *op. cit.* pp. 225 ff.
61. The Dharmasūtras retained only a nominal affiliation to particular Vedic schools.
62. Or rather prescribe, for the style is throughout prescriptive, and not descriptive. This characteristic of the Śrauta-sūtras is shared also by the Gṛihya and Dharma-sūtras. The Brāhmaṇas, however, are truly descriptive.
63. To a lesser extent this method was followed also in the Gṛihya-sūtras.
64. The following brief account of Śrauta-sūtras is mainly based on Hillebrandt, *Rituallitteratur*, § 7.
65. These Pratīkas have been collected by Hillebrandt in his edition of *Śāṅkh. Śr. S.*, Vol. I, p. 628.
66. A Śūdra can be killed at will according to *Ait. Br.*, VII. 29.4.
67. This is the opinion also of Winternitz, *op. cit.*, p. 278.
68. See Weber, *HIL*, p. 139.
69. See footnote 8a above.
70. *Op. cit.*, p. 16.
71. According to the computation of Caland (*Vaitāna-Sūtra*, p. viii).

CHAPTER XIII

ARYAN SETTLEMENTS IN INDIA

I. GEOGRAPHICAL NAMES IN THE ṚIGVEDA

Although it is difficult to arrive at any definite conclusion regarding the original home of the Indo-Aryans, we are in a somewhat better position in respect of their early settlements in northern India and gradual expansion over the whole of this area. For here the evidence of Vedic literature comes to our aid, and fortunately the earliest part of it, the hymns of the *Ṛigveda,* contain abundant geographical data. It is a reasonable presumption that the geographical names which figure prominently or frequently in these hymns indicate regions which were familiar to their authors, and were scenes of the early activities of the Aryans. Names less prominent or frequent might be either outside settlements of the Aryans or the border regions inhabited by non-Aryans. It must be remembered, however, that the *Ṛigveda* is not a geographical manual and its various recensions have not come down to us in a complete form. It would, therefore, be unsafe and hazardous to draw any inference from the silence of the *Ṛigveda.* The non-mention of any locality in the hymns cannot be construed as evidence, one way or the other, unless, of course, it can be proved to be of such importance as to be inexplicable except on the hypothesis of want of knowledge.

In order to ascertain the extent of the Aryan settlements in the period of the *Rigveda,* we should, therefore, consider the references to mountains, rivers, localities, countries, tribes, and kingdoms contained in the hymns. Courses of rivers, especially in the Punjab, have considerably changed in the course of the last three or four millennia. Their names have also varied in different times. There is, therefore, some difference of opinion with regard to the identifications of the rivers mentioned in the Vedic texts. The same is the case regarding the location of the various tribes and countries that figure in the Vedic texts, as their boundaries were subject to constant modifications and they were known by different names in different periods. But in spite of these difficulties it is possible to form a fair idea of the location of quite a large number of them.

As regards mountains, only the Himālaya is directly mentioned in the *Ṛigveda,* Mūjavant, one of its peaks, being referred to as the source of Soma. According to Zimmer, this peak was probably on the south-west of the valley of Kāshmir.

Rivers have all along played an important part in the lives of the Hindus, and even in the Rigvedic age they were esteemed as deities, presumably on account of the immense benefits they conferred on humanity. Out of thirty-one rivers mentioned in the

Vedic texts, about twenty-five names occur in the hymns of the *Ṛigveda* alone. In the celebrated *Nadīstuti* (X. 75), the *Ṛigveda* enumerates several streams most of which belong to the Indus system.

Outside the rivers in the Indus basin, are mentioned Gaṅgā, Yamunā, Sarasvatī, and Sarayu. Gaṅgā does not appear to be a well known or even important stream in the period of the *Ṛigveda*. Yamunā has been mentioned thrice in the *Ṛigveda*, which refers to the great victory of Sudās and the Tṛitsus on the Yamunā in the famous *Dāśarājña*. The Sarasvatī is the river *par excellence* (*Nadītamā, RV*, II 41. 16), and occurs most frequently in the *Ṛigveda*. It seems to have been the holy stream of the Vedic age. In the enumeration of rivers in the *Nadīstuti* (X. 75.5) Sarasvatī comes between the Yamunā and Śutudrī, and is generally identified with the modern Sarsuti, which is lost in the desert at Bhatnair. Roth, Zimmer, Griffith, and Ludwig hold that in many passages of the *Ṛigveda* the Sindhu is meant by the Sarasvatī.[1] It may be observed in this connection that it is possible that the Sarasvatī was as large as the Sutlej in the Vedic age, and actually reached the sea, as the *Ṛigveda* (VI. 61.2, 8; VII. 95.2) describes it as going to the ocean. The Sarasvatī was the first of the Vedic rivers (II.41.16) and its banks witnessed the development of the Vedic sacrifices.

The Dṛishadvatī, which occurs many times along with the Sarasvatī as an important stream, is identified by some with the Ghaggar and by others with the modern Chittang.[2] Between the Sarasvatī and Dṛishadvatī, flowing past Thānesar, was the Āpayā (*RV*, III. 23.4), a small tributary of the Sarasvatī. The Gomatī has been identified by some scholars with the Gomatī, which meets the Ganges to the east of Benares, and this identification may be accepted in so far as the later Saṁhitās and Brāhmaṇas are concerned. The Gomatī of the *Ṛigveda* as mentioned in the *Nadīstuti* is, however, placed between the Kubhā and Krumu. Hence, its identification with the Gomal, a western tributary of the Indus, seems more reasonable. Sarayu, on the eastern bank of which Chitraratha and Arṇa were defeated by the Turvaśa-Yadus, appears to be the modern Sarju in Oudh, as suggested by Zimmer and others.[3] The identifications by Ludwig with the Krumu (Kurram) and by St. Martin with the united course of the Śutudrī (Sutlej) and Vipāś (Beās) are difficult to accept.

Then we pass on to the five streams, viz. the Śutudrī, Vipāś, Parushṇī, Asiknī, and Vitastā, which give the Punjab its name and, united together, flow into the Indus. The *Nadīstuti* omits the Vipāś and inserts the Marudvṛidhā between the Asiknī and Vitastā. The Śutudrī is the most easterly river of the Punjab identified with the modern Sutlej. True to its name, it has considerably changed its course even during historical times. Vipāś, "fetterless," is the modern Beās, which has also changed its course considerably. Its non-mention in the earlier Vedic literature except in two *Ṛigveda*-hymns, coupled with its absence in the *Nadīstuti*-hymn, supports the hypothesis that it was of small importance.

Parushṇī, the modern Rāvi, was an important stream which played a decisive part in the *Dāśarājña* (battle of the ten kings), by rising and drowning the enemies of Sudās. Asiknī, known later as the Chandrabhāgā, is the modern Chenāb in the Punjab. Finally comes Vitastā, the most westerly of these five rivers, known today as Jhelum. Roth and Zimmer consider that the Marudvṛidhā mentioned in the *Nadīstuti* (X. 75.5) denotes the combined waters of the Asiknī (Chenāb) and Vitastā (Jhelum) down to its junction with the Parushṇī (Rāvi), and Chakladar accepts this view.[4] Stein, however, rightly places the Marudvṛidhā in Kāshmir, identifying it with Maruwardwan, a small Kashmirian stream flowing from north to south which joins the Chenāb on its northern bank at Kashtwar. Yāska identifies the Ārjikīyā and Sushomā, mentioned after the Vitastā in the *Nadīstuti*, respectively with the Vipāś and the Sindhu.[6]

Now we turn to the western tributaries of the Indus. The Rasā has been identified with the Jaxartes, a stream in the extreme north-west of the Vedic territory. The Kubhā is the modern Kābul river which flows into the Indus a little above Attock and receives at Prāng the joint flow of its tributaries, the Swāt (Suvāstu) and Gauri. The Krumu or the Kurram and Gomatī or the Gomal are tributaries of the Indus meeting it further south. The Susartu and Śvetyā appear to have been the tributaries of the Indus above the Kubhā, whereas the Mehatnū, Krumu, and Gomatī are the three tributaries below the Kubhā.[7] The Suvāstu, as already stated, is the Swāt, a tributary of the Kubhā, which itself is a tributary of the Indus. The word Suvāstu, signifying "fair dwellings," seems to indicate that there was an Aryan settlement along its banks. Hariyūpīyā, the scene of the defeat of the Vṛichīvants by Abhyāvartin Chāyamāna (*RV*, VI. 27.5) has been taken either as denoting a place or a river. As a place-name Harappā has been suggested as the modern name of Hariyūpīyā.[8] Many other lesser streams have not yet been identified with any degree of certainty, and are not mentioned here.

In conclusion, we must consider also the implication of the term *Saptasindhavaḥ* as used in the *Ṛigveda*. The term means a definite country in *Ṛigveda*, VIII. 24.27, whereas at other places seven streams themselves are intended. According to Max Müller, the seven rivers are the five rivers of the Punjab along with Indus and Sarasvatī. Ludwig, Lassen, and Whitney substitute Kubhā for the Sarasvatī and think that originally the Oxus also must have been one of the seven. Considering that the *Ṛigveda* mentions the Kubhā (Kābul), Gomatī (Gumal), Krumu (Kurram), Suvāstu

(Swāt), etc., which lie to the west of the Indus, it is possible that the Rigvedic people knew of the existence of the Oxus. The reasonable view, however, appears to be to take the seven streams to be the Indus, the five streams of the Punjab and the Sarasvatī.

We may thus conclude that the extent of the country as reflected in the hymns is, Afghānistān, the Punjab, parts of Sind and Rājputāna, the North-West Frontier Province, Kāshmir, and Eastern India up to the Sarayu.

This conclusion is confirmed by another consideration. That the Vedic people had not yet penetrated into the swampy jungles of Bengal may be inferred from the absence of the mention of the tiger in the *Ṛigveda* which assigns the premier place to the lion.[8a]

There is a difference of opinion among scholars as to the part of India where the bulk of the *Ṛigveda* was composed. Max Müller, Weber, Muir, and others held that the Punjab was the main scene of the activity of the *Ṛigveda*, whereas the more recent view put forth by Hopkins and Keith is that it was composed in the country round the Sarasvatī river south of modern Ambāla.[9] Brunnhofer, Hertel, Hüsing, and others, however, argue that the scene of the *Ṛigveda* is laid, not in the Punjab, but in Afghānistān and Irān.[10] These and other theories need not be discussed in detail. Keith has rightly observed that "conclusions can be drawn only with much caution. It is easy to frame and support by plausible evidence various hypotheses, to which the only effective objection is that other hypotheses are equally legitimate, and that the facts are too imperfect to allow of conclusions being drawn."[11]

As the names of the rivers in the *Ṛigveda* show that the Vedic people knew the whole of the Punjab and occupied the best part of it, there is no need to suppose the bulk of the hymns to have been composed either in Irān or in the Ambāla district.

It is a controversial question whether the Vedic tribes in the days of the *Ṛigveda* had reached the ocean and had knowledge of sea navigation. Keith and many other European scholars hold that there is no clear indication in the Rigvedic period that ocean and sea navigation were known.[12] Max Müller, Lassen, Zimmer, and the authors of the *Vedic Index* on the other hand assert that ocean was known to the Rigvedic people.[13] This seems to be the more probable view. The Sarasvatī is stated to have reached the sea (*above*, p. 246), and the hymns X. 136, 5 and 6 seem clearly to refer to the western and eastern oceans. References to the treasures of the ocean and to Bhujyu's story appear to allude to marine navigation. The knowledge of high tide can be inferred from *Ṛigveda*, I.48.3. All these references indubitably prove that the Rigvedic people not only knew the sea, but were mariners and had trade relations with the outside world.

2. THE TRIBES IN THE ṚIGVEDA

The whole of the territory known to the Vedic settlers was divided into a number of tribal principalities ruled normally by kings. The *Dāśarājña* or the battle of the ten kings is an important historical event alluded to in various hymns of the *Ṛigveda,* and as many of the important tribes and personalities figured in this famous battle, it is worth while outlining the conflict. Sudās was a Bharata king of the Tṛitsu family which was settled in the country which later came to be known as Brahmāvarta. At first Viśvāmitra, a scion of the Kuśika family of the Bharatas, was the priest of Sudās, and led him to victorious campaigns on the Vipāś and Sutudrī. Viśvāmitra, however, was dismissed later by Sudās, who appointed Vasishṭha as his priest, probably on account of the superior Brahmanical knowledge of the Vasishṭhas. Thereupon a long and bitter rivalry ensued between the two priests, and in revenge Viśvāmitra led a tribal confederacy of ten kings against the Bharatas, the federation consisting of the five well-known tribes Pūru, Yadu, Turvaśa, Anu, and Druhyu, along with five of little note. viz. Alina, Paktha, Bhalānas, Śiva, and Vishāṇin. In the bloody and decisive struggle on the Parushṇī, the Bharatas emerged victorious, utterly routing the confederacy, of whom the Anu and Druhyu kings were drowned, and Purukutsa of the Pūrus met his death. There was another battle that Sudās had to fight in which the three non-Aryan tribes, Ajas, Śigrus, and Yakshus had united under king Bheda: but these new assailants also met with the same fate and were defeated with great slaughter on the Jumna. The location of these tribes, along with their activities in the period of the *Ṛigveda,* will now be considered in the order of their importance as far as possible.

The Bharatas, who gave their name to the whole country, are the most important of the Rigvedic tribes. They were settled, in the Rigvedic age, in the region between the Sarasvatī and Yamunā The Bharatas appear prominently in the *Ṛigveda* in relationship with Sudās and the Tritsus, and are enemies of the Pūrus. Their princes sacrificed on the Sarasvatī, Drishadvatī, and Āpavā, i.e. Kurukshetra of later times. Their military prowess in the Rigvedic age, displayed in their successful campaigns both against the Aryans on the west and the non-Aryans in the east, is matched by the superiority of their cult and ritual practices which seem to have attained prominence and supremacy in a later period. Viśvāmitra is referred to as a Bharatarshabha and a Kauśika, so that he belonged to the Kuśika family of the Bharatas.

The exact relation of the Tṛitsus and Bharatas cannot be determined and there is a sharp difference of opinion among scholars on this subject. The Tṛitsus occupied the country to the east of the Parushṇī. Both being enemies of the Pūrus, Ludwig's identification of the Bharatas and Tṛitsus appears to be correct. Oldenberg, however, takes the Tṛitsus to be the priests of the Bharatas, thus identifying them with the Vasishṭhas, whereas according to Geldner, the Tṛitsus were the royal family of the Bharatas, which appears to be the most probable view. Zimmer's theory representing the Tṛitsus and Bharatas as enemies is clearly untenable. The Tṛitsus and their kinsfolk the Bharatas were at war with the various tribes on both sides of the Parushṇī and Yamunā, as already stated. In post-Rigvedic times, however, they coalesced with the Pūrus, their erstwhile enemies, to form the Kuru people of later times. The *Ṛigveda* refers to the Sṛiñjayas as being the allies of the Tṛitsus. The Tṛitsus apparently had hereditary kings to rule over them. One of them, Divodāsa, surnamed Atithigva, was a great conqueror, who successfully fought against the Pūrus, Yadus, and Turvaśas on the one hand, and against Śambara, the Dāsa king, the Paṇis, etc., on the other. Sudās, the son of Pijavana, was a descendant of Divodāsa; his exploits in the *Dāśarājña* and against Bheda have been referred to. He was not only a famous warrior, but also a great scholar and composer of hymns.

The Pūrus have been mentioned in the *Ṛigveda* along with Anus, Druhyus, Turvaśas, and Yadus. Though defeated in the *Dāśarājña*, the Pūrus were a very important tribe in the days of the *Ṛigveda*. They were closely connected with the Tṛitsus and the Bharatas, and lived on either side of the Sarasvatī. The unusually large number of kings of the Pūrus suggests the importance of the tribe. The various names indicate the following genealogy of the Pūru kings: Durgaha—Girikshit—Purukutsa—Trasadasyu. Purukutsa is mentioned as a contemporary of Sudās and a conqueror of the Dāsas; a son Trasadasyu is said to have been born to Purukutsa at a time of great distress, probably indicating his death or capture in the famous *Dāśarājña*.[14] The mention of Sudās or Divodāsa and Purukutsa or Trasadasyu in a friendly relation in some passages of the *Ṛigveda* suggests the union of the Tṛitsus, Bharatas, and Pūrus to form the Kurus. The name "Kuru" is not directly mentioned in the *Ṛigveda*, but the amalgamation of these rival tribes in later Vedic period under Kuru is implied by the name Kuruśravaṇa of a king of the Pūru line as shown by his patronymic Trāsadasyava (*RV*, X. 33.4).

Connected with the Kurus were the Krivis, a comparatively unimportant tribe who possibly lived on the Sindhu (Indus) and the Asiknī (Chenāb), and later moved to the east across the Yamunā to the land later known as Pañchāla. The insignificance of the Krivis in later literature as compared with the importance of the Pañchālas is probably due to the fact that the later Kuru-Pañchāla alliance included not only the Bharatas and other tribes but Krivis also. The *Śatapatha Brāhmaṇa* asserts that Krivi was the older name of the Pañchālas (XIII. 5.4.7).

Closely allied with the Tṛitsus was the tribe of the Sṛiñjayas who lived in their neighbourhood, probably in Pañchāla. Hillebrandt locates the Sṛiñjayas to the west of the Indus, and Zimmer, on the upper Indus. As their allies the Tṛitsus were in the Madhyadeśa, the authors of the *Vedic Index* rightly suggest that the Sṛiñjayas may well have been a good deal further east than the Indus. Daivavāta, a king of the Sṛiñjayas, is celebrated as victorious over the Turvaśas and the Vṛichīvants. Daivavāta's sacrificial fire is referred to, and Sāhadevya Somaka is mentioned in this connection. Prastoka, a Sṛiñjaya, has been lauded along with Divodāsa. Turvaśas were the common enemies of the Sṛiñjayas and Bharatas.

The Anus, Druhyus, Yadus, and Turvaśas were the allies of the Pūrus against the Bharatas. These five, according to Zimmer, are the "five peoples" (*Pañchajanāḥ*) of the *Ṛigveda*. The expression "five peoples" occurs under various names in the *Ṛigveda* and later Vedic literature. Who exactly are indicated by the five is not quite certain.[15]

Among the tribes who were hostile to Sudās, the Druhyus, Turvaśās, and Anus lived between the Asiknī and Parushṇī. The names Yadu and Turvaśa normally occur together in the *Ṛigveda*. These two closely allied tribes lived in the southern Punjab and probably further south. Hopkins regards Turvaśa as the name of the Yadu king;[16] but the evidence for this is not conclusive. Zimmer identifies Turvaśas with Vṛichīvants, but the passages merely show that they were allies. The name Turvaśa disappears from later Vedic literature, possibly because they became merged in the Pañchāla people.

The Matsyas in the epic age lived to the west of the Śūrasenas of Mathurā, i.e. in modern Alwar, Bharatpur, and Jaipur, which was probably their home also in the Rigvedic age.[17]

The Ajas, Śigrus, and Yakshus were probably the eastern people. They are generally regarded as non-Aryan, though there is no definite information on this point.

The Pakthas, Bhalānases, Vishāṇins, Alinas, and Śivas were the five frontier tribes. The Pakthas lived in the hills from which the Krumu originates. Zimmer locates them in eastern Afghānistān, identifying them with the modern Pakthun. South of the Pakthas stretched the Bhalānases for whom Zimmer suggests east Kābulistān as original home. The Vishāṇins, so-called probably because their helmets were horn-shaped or ornamented with horns, were, like their allies, a tribe of the north-west, located farther down between the Krumu and the Gomatī. North-east of Kāfiristān has been suggested as the location of the Alinas, who were closely allied with the Pakthas, and were certainly the enemies of Sudās, and not his allies, as thought by Roth. The Śivas lay between the Sindhu and Vitastā in the Vedic period.[18]

Now we turn to the other tribes which have not been directly mentioned as participants in the *Dāśarājña*, or in any of the wars waged by Sudās.

The Chedis, who dwelt probably between the Yamunā and the Vindhyas, had a very powerful king named Kaśu who is said in a Dānastuti (VIII. 5.37-39) to have made a gift of ten kings as slaves to his priest. The Puranic literature represents the Chedis as an offshoot of the Yadus.

The Uśīnaras are mentioned in the *Aitareya Brāhmaṇa* as dwelling in the middle country along with the Vaśas and the Kuru-Pañchālas. There is nothing to support Zimmer's conjecture that the Uśīnaras in the Rigvedic times lived farther to the north-west, and it is reasonable to suppose that in the Rigvedic period also they lived in the middle country.

The Gandhāris, one of the frontier peoples, lived to the extreme north-west of India. The good wool of the sheep of the Gandhāris has been referred to in the Ṛigveda (I. 126. 7). According to Zimmer they were settled in the Vedic times on the south bank of the Kubhā up to its junction with the Indus and for some distance down the east side of the Indus itself.

Ludwig and Weber find in certain Rigvedic passages which mentioned *Pṛithu-Praśvaḥ* (*RV*, VII. 83. 1: meaning "with large ribs," or "with broad axes") a reference to the Pṛithus and Parśus, i.e. the Parthians and the Persians. The meaning and sense in the passages, however, require the word Parśu to be taken as "ribs." In a passage of the *Ṛigveda* (VIII. 6. 46) Yadu is brought into special connection with the Parśus. It cannot, however, be definitely stated that the Parśus were Persians.

The Pārāvatas occurring in several passages of the *Ṛigveda* have been rightly taken as a people on the Yamunā on the strength of the mention of the Sarasvatī in their connection (*RV*, VI. 61. 2) as also of their location there in the *Pañchaviṁśa Brāhmaṇa*. Their location on the northern borders of Gedrosia, as proposed by Hillebrandt and Geldner, does not appear to be correct.

The Kīkaṭas occur in the *Ṛigveda* (III. 53. 14) as a people under Pramaganda's leadership and hostile to the singer. Zimmer, on Yāska's authority, takes these people as non-Aryans and locates them in the country later known as Magadha. Weber accepts the location but takes them to be Aryans, though at variance with the other Aryan tribes.

The Paṇis are often mentioned with the Dāsas and Dasyus as the enemies of the Aryans. Though opulent and rich, the Paṇis never worshipped the gods or rewarded the priests. They have been described as selfish, non-sacrificing, with hostile speech.

greedy like the wolf, niggardly, of cruel speech, Dasyus, Dāsas of inferior status. They were cattle-owners and notorious cattle-lifters, and in some passages definitely figure as demons who withheld the cows or waters of the heavens. Vala, whom Indra pierced when he robbed Paṇi of his cows, appears to be their patron God. Bṛibu is mentioned as one of their kings. The question of the identity of the Paṇis has not yet been settled with any degree of certainty. The words Paṇik or Vaṇik, Paṇya, and Vipaṇi, found in Sanskrit, suggest that the Paṇis were merchants *par excellence* in the Rigvedic age. The Paṇis have been variously identified with an aboriginal non-Aryan people; with Babylonians (on the strength of the word Bekanāṭa); with Parnians, the Dahae and other Irānian tribes; and with non-Aryan caravan traders. They might have been the Aryan sea-traders who spread the Aryan culture to the west.

Derived from the same root (*das*, "lay waste" or "waste away") which originated the word Dasyu, the Dāsas have been described as the enemies of the Vedic people, sometimes of a demoniac character; but many passages speak of them as the human foes of the Aryans. They lived in fortified towns (*āyasīḥ puraḥ*) and were divided into clans (*viśaḥ*). Dāsavarṇa has been alluded to a number of times, and the Dāsas are said to be black-skinned (*kṛishṇatvach*), noseless or flat-nosed (*anās*) and evil-tongued (*mṛidhravāch*), some of these epithets being shared in common with Dasyus. In the *Ṛigveda*, Dāsa is not so reproachful a term as Dasyu. As Dāsa in later literature became a synonym for slave, it can plausibly be said that originally the term was applied to captives in war who were enslaved. Hillebrandt and others identify the Dāsas with the Dahae of Irān,[18a] as they place the scene of activity of the *Ṛigveda* in Arachosia, where they locate the Sarasvatī.

The Dāsas owned considerable wealth, and Ilibiśa, Dhuni, Chumuri, Śambara, Varchin, Pipru, etc., have been mentioned as individual Dāsa kings, some of whom later received demoniac attributes, and were regarded as celestial foes of Indra and other gods. The Kirātas, Kīkaṭas, Chāṇḍālas, Parṇākas, Simyus, etc., were Dāsa tribes who mostly inhabited the Gangetic Valley and fought the Bharatas in their advance to the east and south-east.

Though in many passages the term Dasyu is applied to supernatural enemies, there is no doubt that in several passages the term designates human foes. The main difference between the Dasyus and the Vedic Aryans appears to be religious. The Dasyus were rite-less (*a-karman*), indifferent to the gods (*a-devayu*), without devotion (*a-brahman*), not sacrificing (*a-yajvan*), lawless (*a-vrata*), following strange ordinances (*anyavrata*), reviling the gods (*deva-pīyu*), etc. Some of these epithets have been applied also to the Dāsas, as compared to whom they are less distinctively a people, as no clans (*viśaḥ*) of the Dasyus have been mentioned. Zimmer and Meyer think that the original meaning of the term Dasyu (and Dāsa) was "enemy," which later developed into "hostile country" with the Irānians, while the Indians extended the original signification of "enemy" to include demon foes. That to the Rigvedic bards there was not much difference between the Dāsas and Dasyus would be evident from their sharing some epithets in common, and also from some persons being described both as Dasyu and Dāsa, etc.

The Asuras are generally referred to as enemies of Vedic people and of their gods, but some passages use the term in a good sense. One probable explanation of this has been hinted at before.[19] Another, suggested by Bhandarkar, is that the hymns in which Vedic deities receive the appellation Asura were composed by seers of Asura stock who had embraced the Aryan religion, and the deprecatory passages were composed by Aryan seers antagonistic to the Asuras.[20] The enmity between Aryan and Asura increased in the post-Rigvedic period.

It is indeed difficult to identify the Asuras with any of the ancient people. Sten Konow takes them to be non-human. Banerji Sastri considers the Asuras as immigrants from Assyria, the followers of the Asura cult who preceded the Aryans in India and were the authors of the Indus Valley civilization. Bhandarkar takes the Asuras to be the Assurs or Assyrians and suggests that the *Śatapatha Brāhmaṇa* refers to the Asura settlements in Magadha or South Bihār.

The Rakshas does not indicate any definite tribe; according to the authors of the *Vedic Index* it normally refers to demons in early Vedic literature, and is applied to human foes only metaphorically. The Piśāchas also likewise are not a tribe in Vedic literature though in later literature it is the designation of a tribe.

As a result of the above survey we may briefly indicate the position and extent of the tribal settlements referred to in the *Ṛigeda.* Roughly speaking the extreme north-west was occupied by the Gandhāris, Pakthas, Alinas, Bhalānases, and Vishāṇins, some of whom probably contained non-Aryan elements. In Sind and the Punjab were settled the Śivas, Parśus, Kekayas, Vṛichīvants, Yadus, Anus, Turvaśas, and Druhyus. Further east towards the region of the Madhyadeśa were the settlements of the Tṛitsus, Bharatas, Pūrus, and Sṛiñjayas, the eastern-most part being in the occupation of the Kikaṭas. The Matsyas and Chedis were settled to the south of the Punjab in the region of Rājputāna and Mālwā. It may thus be reasonably concluded that the Aryan settlements during the period of the *Ṛigveda* were practically co-terminous with the extent of the geographical knowledge of the period, as mentioned above.

3. THE PERIOD OF THE LATER SAMHITĀS, BRĀHMAṆAS, UPANISHADS, AND SŪTRAS

1. *Geographical Names*

We may form a fair idea of the Aryan settlements in the post-Rigvedic period, by utilizing the geographical data of the later Vedic texts and following the same line of enquiry as in the last two sections.

The word *Samudra* in later Vedic texts generally, if not invariably, means the sea. The reference in the *Śatapatha Brāhmaṇa* (1. 6. 3. 11) to the eastern and western oceans probably suggests that the Arabian Sea and the Indian Ocean were known to the people of that period.

Trikakud (i.e. having three peaks), as the name of a mountain in the Himālayas, has been identified with modern Trikota. Krauñcha, which occurs only in the *Taittirīya Āraṇyaka* (1. 31. 2), has been identified with that part of the Kailāsa mountain on which Mānasa Sarovara is situated.[21] Maināka is mentioned in the same text as a mountain in the Himālayas. Though not directly mentioned, Vindhya has been definitely alluded to in the *Kaushītaki Upanishad* by the term "southern mountain."

Turning to the rivers, the most striking fact is the disappearance of the Sarasvatī. The place where the river vanished in the desert was known as Vinaśana (Patiala District), and it reappeared at Plaksha Prāsravaṇa at a distance of forty-four days' journey from Vinaśana.

Naturally enough, the rivers further to the east find a prominent mention in this period. Revā, the name of the Narmadā which occurs only in post-Vedic literature, is traced by Weber in the word Revottaras found in the *Śatapatha Brāhmaṇa;* but the interpretation is doubtful. The Sadānīrā has been mentioned in the *Śatapatha Brāhmaṇa* (I. 1. 1. 14 ff.) as the boundary between the Kosalas and Videhas. Some lexicographers have identified it with the Karatoyā, but according to the *Vedic Index,* it is too far east. Weber and Eggeling identify it with the Gandak, and Pargiter with the Rāpti. Though the *Mahābhārata* (Cr. Ed. II. 18. 27), by placing the Sadānīrā between the Gandak and Sarayu, distinguishes between the Sadānīrā and Gandak, the *Vedic Index* pronounces the identification of the two as "probably correct."[22]

The later Vedic texts mention various place-names which can be identified with reasonable certainty. Parichakrā, mentioned in the *Śatapatha Brāhmaṇa* (XIII. 5. 4. 7) as the name of a Pañchāla town where king Kraivya Pañchāla performed his horse-sacrifice, has been identified by Weber with the later Ekachakrā which was near Kāmpila. Āsandīvat is the title of the capital of Janamejaya Pārikshita where the horse for his famous Aśvamedha was bound

(*Śat. Br.*, XIII. 5. 4. 2; *Ait Br*, VIII. 21) It was apparently in the Kurukshetra. It was probably identical with Nāgasāhvaya (Hastināpura) which was abandoned by Nichakshu, a descendant of Parīkshit, on its being washed away by the Ganges, and the capital was removed to Kauśāmbī.[23] Kāmpīla, found in the *Śatapatha Brāhmaṇa*, has been identified with modern Kampil on the old Ganges between Budaun and Farrukhābād. Naimisha forest, mentioned as being clearly of special sanctity, has been identified with Nimsar at a short distance from the Nimsar station of the Oudh and Rohilkhand Railway. The *Taittirīya Āraṇyaka* (V. 1. 1) mentions the Manus as the *Utkara* (heap) of Kurukshetra. This can be identified with the later Marusthala (Maru deserts) as it stood in the relation of *Utkara* to the sacred altar Kurukshetra. The existence of Kauśāmbī which plays an important part in the life of king Udayana Vatsarāja can be inferred from the word Kauśāmbeya in the *Śatapatha Brāhmaṇa* (XII. 2. 2. 13). The town has been identified with modern Kosam on the Yamunā.

The later Vedic literature refers to the three broad divisions—Brahmāvarta or Āryāvarta, Madhyadeśa, and Dakshiṇāpatha. There is also a five-fold division with the enumeration of the residents therein which we come across for the first time in the *Aitareya Brāhmaṇa* (VIII. 14), though it has, in a way, been anticipated by the *Atharvaveda* (XIX. 17. 1. 9). The *Aitareya Brāhmaṇa* divides the whole country into five parts, viz. 1. *Dhruvā Madhyamā Pratishṭhā diś* or Madhyadeśa or middle country, 2. *Prāchīdiś* or the eastern quarter, 3. *Dakshiṇādiś* or the southern quarter, 4. *Pratīchīdiś* or the western quarter, and 5. *Udīchīdiś* or the northern quarter. The extent and limits of these divisions cannot be defined with any degree of plausibility.

2. *The Tribes*

The status, formation, and nomenclature of the various tribes mentioned in the *Ṛigveda* underwent considerable changes during the period under review. Many of the old tribes disappear, pale into insignificance, are merged into others, or are known under new names, and many fresh tribes rise into prominence. The five premier tribes of the Punjab, the Pūrus, Anus, Druhyus, Yadus, and Turvaśas recede into the background. The Pūrus, as already indicated, have along with the Bharatas amalgamated with the Kurus who occupy the territory these two tribes held, and along with their allies, the Pañchālas, are the pre-eminent people in the period. The Bharataṣ as a tribe disappear, but the fame of their kings is not lost to the texts of this period. Bharata Dauḥshanti and Sātrājita are mentioned as famous kings and performers of the Aśvamedha, and Bharata kings are spoken of as winning victories over the. Kāśis and Sātvants and as performing sacrifices on the Gaṅgā and the Yamunā.

The Kurus along with Pañchālas, Vaśas and Uśīnaras occupied the Madhyadeśa. The Kurus do not appear as a people in the *Ṛigveda,* but Kuru forms part of the name of a king, Kuruśravaṇa, mentioned therein. The *Atharvaveda* (XX. 127. 7-10) speaks of the Kuru king Parīkshit in whose reign the Kuru kingdom flourished exceedingly. Reference is made to his descendant Janamejaya who performed an Aśvamedha at Āsandīvat, probably Hastināpura of later days. The Kuru kingdom roughly corresponded to modern Thānesar, Delhi, and the Upper Gangetic Doāb.[24]

The Pañchālas, the close allies of the Kurus as indicated by their joint name, were also a composite tribe. The name does not appear in the *Ṛigveda,* but the *Śatapatha Brahmaṇa* states that the older name for the Pañchālas was Krivi which is found in the *Ṛigveda.* Weber and Geldner suggest that the Pañchālas represent the five tribes of the *Ṛigveda;* but this is not very probable according to the authors of the *Vedic Index.*[25]

We hear very little of the Pañchālas alone apart from the Kurus. Their kings Kraivya and Śoṇa Sātrāsāha are spoken of as having performed the Aśvamedha, and another king Durmukha is said to have conquered the whole earth. One of their kings Pravāhaṇa Jaivali appears as a philosopher king in the Upanishads.

The Vedic texts do not know of north Pañchāla and south Pañchāla which we come across in the *Mahābhārata* and the Purāṇas; evidently the Pañchālas had extended their country by conquests in post-Vedic times. The territory of the Pañchālas roughly corresponded to the Bareilly, Budaun, Farrukhābād, and adjoining districts of the United Provinces.[26]

The Kuru-Pañchālas are the people *par excellence* in the Brāhmaṇa period, and they are referred to as a united nation. At one time the Kuru-Pañchālas are said to have had one king. The mode of sacrifice of the Kuru-Pañchālas is spoken of as the best, and their Brāhmaṇas gained eminence and fame in the period of the Upanishads. The Kuru-Pañchāla kings, the models for others, performed Rājasūyas and set out on their victorious raids in autumn and returned in summer. Speech is said to have been best spoken there, and the Saṁhitās and Brāhmaṇas seem to have taken their definite form among the Kuru-Pañchālas.

We have seen that the Sṛiñjayas were closely allied with the Tṛitsus in the Rigvedic age. The *Śatapatha Brāhmaṇa* (II. 4. 4. 5) supports this view by stating that the Kurus (who were the successors of the Tṛitsus, Bharatas, and Pūrus in post-Rigvedic age) and the Sṛiñjayas had one Purohita. The *Śatapatha Brāhmaṇa* (XII. 9. 3. 1 ff.) further refers to a historical incident relating to this clan. The *Yajurveda Saṁhitās* refer to the Sṛiñjayas having suffered some serious loss due to some ritual error, though what exactly befell them is not mentioned.

Vītahavya, mentioned in the *Ṛigveda* (VI. 15. 2, 3) along with Bharadvāja and as a contemporary of Sudās, may have been a king of the Sṛiñjayas. In the *Atharvaveda* (VI. 137. 1), he appears as connected with Jamadagni and Asita; but this legend has probably little value. The Vītahavyas are said to have come to ruin because they devoured a Brāhmaṇa's cow (*AV*, V. 18. 10-11; 19. 1).

Vaśas and Uśīnaras, as stated earlier, were dwelling in the middle country with the Kuru-Pañchālas. The *Gopatha Brāhmaṇa* which speaks of the Vaśas and Uśīnaras as united (I. 2. 9) regards them as northerners (II. 9). These Uśīnaras according to Weber were the forefathers of the later Kāśis and Videhas.[27] The *Kaushītaki Upanishad* (IV. 1) connects the Vaśas also with the Matsyas. The country of the Vaśas, who later came to be known as Vatsas, was situated round about Kauśāmbī, their capital.

The Śibis were intimately associated with the Uśīnaras. The *Aitareya Brāhmaṇa* (VIII. 23. 10) refers to Amitrātāpana, a king of the Śibis. *Ṛigveda* X. 179 has been ascribed by the *Anukramaṇī* to *Śibi* Auśīnara. Śivapura, which has been identified with Śibipura mentioned in a Shorkot inscription,[28] is referred to by Patañjali (IV. 2. 2) as situated in the northern country. The Śibis inhabited the Shorkot region in Jhang in the Punjab lying between the Irāvatī and the Chandrabhāgā.

Matsyas appear in connection with the Vaśas in the *Kaushītaki Upanishad* and with the Śālvas in the *Gopatha Brāhmaṇa* (I. 2. 9). Their king Dhvasan Dvaitavana, who performed the sacrifice at the lake Dvaitavana, is included in the list of Aśvamedhins in the *Śatapatha Brāhmaṇa* (XIII. 5. 4. 9) According to the *Manusmṛiti* (II. 19; VII. 193) the Matsyas were included in the Brahmarshideśa.

The Śālvas are mentioned in the *Śatapatha Brāhmaṇa* (X. 4. 1. 10). The Mantrapāṭha indicates their location near the Yamunā, and it is not likely that they were in the north-west in Vedic times. The epic associates the Śālvas with the Kuru-Pañchālas, and they occupied probably what is now the modern Alwar state.

The name Ikshvāku occurs but once in the *Ṛigveda* (X. 60. 4) where it denotes a prince. The *Śatapatha Brāhmaṇa* knows Purukutsa as Aikshvāka (XIII. 5. 4. 5), so that some scholars take the Ikshvāku line to have originally been a line of princes of the Kurus, who were on the Sarasvatī in the Vedic period, whereas Ikshvāku is connected with Ayodhyā and the eastern peoples.

Kosala and Videha do not appear in the earlier Vedic literature, being first mentioned in the *Śatapatha Brāhmaṇa* (I. 4. 1. 10 ff.) which relates the story of the spread of the Aryan culture. Videgha

Māthava, the king of the Videhas, accompanied by his priest Gotama Rāhūgaṇa, is spoken of as carrying the sacrificial fire from the bank of the Sarasvatī over Kosala (Oudh) eastwards across the Sadānīrā, and as establishing a settlement which was known as Videha (Tirhut) after the tribal name of Māthava. The story preserves the tradition that the Videhas received their culture from the west, that Kosala was Brahmanized before Videha, that the country as far as the Sadānīrā was conquered in one sweep, and that the progress was checked for a while after which Videha was founded across the river. The later division of Kosala into the northern and southern is not known to the Vedic literature.

Para-Āṭṇāra-Hairaṇyanābha, the Kosala king, is spoken of as the performer of an Aśvamedha (*Śat. Br.*, XIII. 5. 4. 4). The close connection between the Kosalas, Videhas, and Kāśis is indicated by the fact that the three had the same Purohita acting for them (*Śāṅkh. Śr. S.* XVI. 29. 5). It appears, however, that the Kosala-Videhas were allied tribes and that there was some difference and rivalry between these and the Kuru-Pañchālas. The Brahmanism was not as strong in Kosala as among the Kuru-Pañchālas. The Videhas rose into eminence later through their philosopher king Janaka who was a leading patron of the Upanishadic doctrines.

Kāśi, along with Kosala and Videha, came into prominence only in later Vedic age. The Kāśis and Videhas were closely connected on account of their proximity, and Weber suggests that these two together constituted the Uśīnaras.[29] This, however, cannot be accepted, as the Uśīnaras dwelt in the middle country. Kāśi and Kosala are also found together. There is the story of the defeat of Dhṛitarāshṭra, king of Kāśis, by Śatānīka Sātrājita, a Bharata king, resulting in the giving up of the kindling of the sacred fire down to the time of the *Śatapatha Brāhmaṇa* (XIII. 5.4.19). The relations of these eastern people with the Kuru-Pañchālas appear to have been anything but friendly. Political conflict and cultural difference are said to be the probable causes of the rivalry between the two sets.

Still farther off from the old centre of Vedic culture were the Magadhas who make their appearance only in later Vedic literature, and are regarded throughout as of little importance. Magadha corresponds roughly to southern Bihār. The name occurs for the first time in the *Atharvaveda* (V. 22.14), where a wish is expressed that the fever may visit the Gandhāris, the Mūjavants, the Aṅgas and the Magadhas, the first two being northern people and the latter, people of the east. In the Vrātya hymn (*AV*, XV. 2. 1-4) the Māgadhas are associated with the Vrātyas. The *Yajurveda* includes Māgadha in the list of victims at Purushamedha. Zimmer regards Māgadha referred to in the *Atharvaveda* and *Yajurveda* as a member of the mixed caste born of a Vaiśya and Kshatriya. But the fact that the Sūtras and the *Aitareya Āraṇyaka* mention Magadha as a country shows that in the period of the *Yajurveda* and *Atharvaveda*, Māgadha meant a resident of the country and not a member of the mixed caste—an outcaste born of Pratiloma marriage. The authors of the *Vedic Index* account for the fact of Māgadha being a minstrel in later days by assuming Magadha as the home of minstrelsy, bards from which visited more western lands.[30] This class has been taken by later Smṛiti texts as belonging to a separate caste, inventing a story of the inter-marriage of castes for their origin. The dislike of the Magadhas, which may go back to the times of the *Ṛigveda*, was probably due to their not being wholly Brahmanized.

The Aṅgas, unknown to the *Ṛigveda*, are mentioned in the *Atharvaveda* (V. 22) as noted above. There is nothing in the Vedic texts to indicate their location beyond the fact that they were people of the east; but as in later times their settlements were on the rivers Son and the Ganges, it may be presumed that their earliest seat also was in the same region. They have been associated with the Magadhas in some texts. There is no evidence in Vedic literature for Pargiter's view that the Aṅgas and Magadhas were non-Aryan peoples that came overseas to eastern India.[31] Oldenberg, however, thinks that these tribes were the earlier Aryan immigrants. Confirmation for this may be found in the Puranic evidence which speaks of the Ikshvākus and Videhas being of the same stock and as inhabiting the country since Rigvedic times.

The Māgadha is brought into close connection with the Vrātya in the mystical hymn of the *Atharvaveda* where he is celebrated as a type of the supreme power in the universe. The *Yajurveda* includes the Vrātya in the list of victims at Purushamedha (human sacrifice). The Vrātyas were regarded as outcastes, and the *Atharvaveda, Pañchaviṁśa Brāhmaṇa*, and the Sūtras describe a certain rite intended to secure for them admission into the Brāhmaṇa fold. The Vrātyas were a nomadic tribe (*Vrāta*) and neither studied the Vedas, nor ploughed the land, nor traded. Their nomad life is further suggested by their going about in rough wagons, with herds of goats, wearing turbans and wielding a particular kind of bow.

Because the later Dharmasūtras describe the Vrātya as an outsider, a man of mixed origin and of peculiar dress and habits, Roth, Whitney, Bloomfield, Chanda, and others regard the Vrātya as non-Aryan. The early Vedic texts do not support this view. The Vrātyas, though uninitiated, spoke the speech of the initiated. Their speech, though Aryan, had apparently resembled Prakrit rather than Vedic Sankrit, as they softened hard consonants. The Sūtras mention *arhants* and *yaudhas* among the Vrātyas, corresponding respectively to Brāhmaṇas and Kshatriyas in the Brahmanical hierarchy. These particulars, coupled with the fact that they were allowed to become members of the Brāhmaṇa community by performing a specific ritual, evidently show that the Vrātyas were not non-Aryans but were Aryans outside the sphere of Brāhmaṇa culture.

Their location cannot be indicated with certainty. Their life and habits would suggest them to be nomadic western tribes beyond the Sarasvatī. There are, however, certain indications in the Sūtras which definitely connect the Vrātyas with the Māgadha so that the conclusion that some Vrātyas were dwellers in Magadha is irresistible.

Vaṅga, from which Bengal proper receives its designation, is not found in early Vedic literature. The *Aitareya Āraṇyaka* (II.1.1) mentions Vaṅgas, Vagadhas, and Cheras as birds, which probably means that they were non-Aryans speaking languages not intelligible to the Aryans. Vagadha in the text appears to be a misreading for Magadha, as both were neighbours. Vaṅgas were residents of Vaṅga or Eastern Bengal. The name also occurs in the *Baudhāyana Dharma-sūtra.*

The tribes mentioned above occupied the first two of the five divisions, viz. the Middle and Eastern regions, mentioned in the *Aitareya Brāhmaṇa.* In the *Dakshiṇadiś,* or the Southern region, Satvants alone are mentioned in the *Aitareya Brāhmaṇa.* But besides them there were Vidarbhas, Nishadhas, and Kuntis.

The Satvants have been mentioned as the name of a people belonging to the south who were the subjects of the Bhoja kings. These people were subjected to regular raids by the Bharatas, and the *Śatapatha Brāhmaṇa* (XIII. 5.4.21) refers to the defeat of the Satvants by king Bharata who took away their horse prepared for the Aśvamedha. The *Śatapatha Brāhmaṇa* (VIII. 5.4.11)) further indicates that these Satvants lived near Bharata's kingdom, i.e. near the Gaṅgā and Yamunā. They seem to have moved farther south by the time of the *Aitareya Brāhmaṇa* which places them in the southern region beyond the Madhyadeśa, probably beyond the river Chambal (Charmaṇavatī).[32] The Purāṇas corroborate the close relation of the Bhojas and Satvants who have been spoken of as the offshoots of the Yadu family.

Vidarbha is known through its king Bhīma, mentioned in the *Aitareya Brāhmaṇa* (VII. 34) as having received instruction about the substitute for the Soma from Parvata and Nārada. The Vidarbha kingdom was said to be famous for its special breed of hounds, which killed tigers (*Jaim Up. Brā.* II.440). Vidarbha, as is well known, corresponds to modern Berār. Lassen places Vidarbha along the Sātpurā hills to the north-west of Berār.[33] The Upanishads refer to Bhārgava, a sage of Vidarbha, as a contemporary of Āśvalāyana and to Vaidarbhī Kouṇḍinya. Kuṇḍina, the capital of Vidarbha, has been identified with the modern Kauṇḍinyapura on the bank of the Wardhā in the Chāndur *tāluk* of Amraoti.[34]

The *Śatapatha Brāhmaṇa* (III. 3.2.1, 2) mentions the term Naishidha as an epithet of Naḍa, a king of the south. The later form of the name is Naishadha. The Nishadhas, residents of the Nishadha country, were quite distinct from the Nishādas with whom they are often confounded. "Nishāda" was a general term used for a non-Aryan tribe, whereas the Nishadhas, in all probability belonged to the Aryan fold. King Nala of Nishadha is a celebrated figure in the *Mahābhārata* and the Purāṇas. The location of the Nishadha country is not known with certainty, though it may be assumed to be contiguous to Vidarbha.

Under the Pratīchyas or Westerners come the Nīchyas and Apāchyas, as also Bāhīkas and Ambashṭhas. The Nīchya occurs as the designation of certain tribes of the Punjab and Sind. Nothing is known about the Apāchyas. The Bāhikas are spoken of as people of the west of the Punjab in the *Śatapatha Brāhmaṇa* (I.7.3.8) which refers to their calling Agni by the name of Bhava, as distinct from the Prāchyas who called it Śarva. The Ambashṭhas, corresponding to the Abastanoi of Arrian, who were settled on the lower Asiknī in Alexander's time, are referred to in the *Aitareya Brāhmaṇa* (VIII. 21). Their king is stated to have been consecrated with the Aindra Mahābhisheka. They were probably in the Punjab in Vedic times.

Finally we come to the Udīchyas or Northerners, among whom are the Uttarakurus, the Uttaramadras, Mūjavants, Mahāvṛishas, Gandhāris, Bāhlīkas, Keśins, Kekayas, and Kāmbojas.

The Udīchya dialect was celebrated for its purity; hence Brāhmaṇas flocked to the north for purposes of study. The northern dialect resembled that of the Kuru-Pañchāla, and the superiority of the Brāhmaṇas of the north is indicated by the victory of one of their spokesmen over a Kuru-Pañchāla Brāhmaṇa in a debate. The celebrity enjoyed by the north in academic matters is further corroborated by the fact that Taxila became a famous seat of learning, and classical Sanskrit was first developed in Kāshmir.[37]

The Uttarakurus, along with the Uttaramadras, are located beyond the Himālayas. Though regarded as mythical in the epic and later literature, the Uttarakurus still appear as a historical people in the *Aitareya Brāhmaṇa* (VIII. 23) which states that one Jānantapi Atyarāti was anxious to conquer the country of the Uttarakurus, called the land of the gods. Zimmer places the Uttarakurus in Kāshmir to the north of Kurukshetra, and probably they were an offshoot of the Kurus.

The Madra people were divided into two sections, the Uttara (Northern) Madras and the Southern Madras or the Madras proper. The Uttaramadras alone appear in early Vedic literature, and they dwelt, as already stated, beyond the Himālayas, probably in the land of Kāshmir. The mention of Madragāra Śauṅgāyani as an ancient Vedic teacher shows the Madras as experts in Vedic learning.

a fact which is confirmed by the *Śatapatha Brāhmaṇa* which states that sages of Northern India repaired to the Madra country to study the Vedas. The *Bṛihadāraṇyaka Upanishad* refers to Kāpya Patañchala as living among the Madras. The territory of the Southern Madras roughly corresponds to Sialkot and its adjoining districts in the Central Punjab which were known as the Madradeśa as late as the time of Guru Govind Singh.[36] In Buddhist times the Madras dwelt between the Chenāb and Rāvi.

The Mūjavants have been mentioned in the *Atharvaveda* along with the Mahāvṛishas, Gandhāris, and Bāhlīkas as dwelling far away and to whom fever is to be relegated. The *Yajurveda* also speaks of the Mūjavants as a distant people. If the people took their name from Mūjavant, a mountain in the Himālayas, which seems to be quite likely, they were a hill-tribe in the Himālayas.

The Mahāvṛishas appear to be northerners in the vicinity of the other tribes along with whom they are mentioned, though their exact location cannot be ascertained. The *Chhāndogya Upanishad* places king Raikva-parṇa in the Mahāvṛisha country, and the *Jaiminīya Upanishad Brāhmaṇa* mentions Hṛitsvāśaya as the king of the Mahāvṛishas.

The Gandhāris, referred to in the *Ṛigveda,* are mentioned also in the *Atharvaveda* (as already stated) and in the Śrauta Sūtras. They appear apparently as a despised people in the *Atharvaveda.* In later times, however, the angle of vision of the people of the Madhyadeśa changed, and Gandhāra became the famous resort of scholars for instruction in the Vedas and Vidyās. The *Aitareya Brāhmaṇa* (VII. 34) mentions Nagnajit, a king of Gandhāra, among Vedic teachers who propagated the Soma cult, which shows that Gandhāra was not excluded from Vedic Aryans. From the various references to Gandhāra in Indian literature it appears that the boundaries of the country varied at different periods in its history.

The Bāhlīkas, mentioned along with the three foregoing peoples, were a contiguous northern tribe, their name also suggesting "the outsiders." Roth and Weber were inclined to place this tribe in Irān, but there is no need to assume any Irānian influence, for we find that Bāhlīka is the name of a Kuru prince (*Śat. Br.*, XII. 9. 3. 3).[37]

Keśin is the name of a tribe found in the *Śatapatha Brāhmaṇa* (XI. 8. 4. 6) where their king is said to be studying how to avert a bad omen at the sacrifices. They were probably a branch of the Pañchālas.[38]

The *Śatapatha Brāhmaṇa* (X. 6. I. 2) and the *Chhāndogya Upanishad* (V. 11. 4) mention Aśvapati, king of the Kekayas, as a man of learning who instructed a number of Brāhmaṇas. The Kekayas in later days were settled in the north-west between the

Sindhu and the Vitastā, and probably occupied the same territory in the Vedic age. According to the Puranic tradition the Kekayas were descended from Anu,[39] which is confirmed by the fact that the Anus of the *Ṛigveda* dwelt in the same territory in which we find the Kekayas.

The earliest mention of Kāmboja occurs in the *Vaṁśa Brāhmaṇa* of the *Sāmaveda* where a teacher Kāmboja Aupamanyava is referred to. The sage Upamanyu, mentioned in the *Ṛigveda* (I. 102. 9), is in all probability the father of this Kāmboja teacher. From the fact that Kāmboja Aupamanyava is stated to be a pupil of Madragāra, Zimmer infers that the Kāmbojas and the Madras were close neighbours in north-western India. The speech of the Kāmbojas is referred to by Yāska as differing from other Aryans, and Grierson sees in this reference the Irānian affinities of the Kāmbojas;[40] but the fact that Kāmboja teachers were reputed for their Vedic learning shows them to have been Vedic Aryans, so that Kāmboja was an Aryan settlement. Later on Kāmbojas settled to the north-west of the Indus, and were the Kambujiyas of the old Persian inscriptions.

There is some difference of opinion as to the location of the Kāmbojas. Rhys Davids places them to the extreme north-west of India, S. K. Aiyangar and P. N. Banerji in a country near Sind, Raychaudhuri in the Rāwalpindi and Peshāwar districts, Smith along the mountains of Tibet or Hindu Kush, and Eliot in Tibet or its border.[41] The latest attempt at locating the Kāmbojas is by Jayachandra who, after discussing the problems afresh, identifies Kāmboja with Badakhshān and the Pāmirs, and Motichandra has further supported the identification.[42]

There are various other minor tribes mentioned in Vedic texts, but we know very little of them.[43]

Finally, we come to the semi-Aryan, non-Aryan and barbarous tribes. The *Aitareya Brāhmaṇa* mentioned the Andhras, Puṇḍras, Śabaras, Pulindas and Mūtibas as being Dasyus, i.e. outcastes living on the borders of the Aryan settlements. These people are said to be born of the fifty eldest sons of Viśvāmitra through their father's curse on their refusal to accept the adoption of Śunaḥśepa. They were thus outside the Aryan fold. The Andhras, Śabaras and Pulindas are known from the *Mahābhārata* to have been tribes of the Deccan.

The Andhras originally lived between the Krishnā and the Godāvarī.[44] Andhras in modern times are the Telugu-speaking people of the Deccan.

The Puṇḍras, whose name occurs also in the Sūtras, have been located in Bengal and Bihār by the *Mahābhārata*. They were situated in North Bengal and gave their name to their capital town Puṇḍravardhana. The Puṇḍras are probably the ancestors of the Puros, an aboriginal caste in Bengal.[45]

The exact location of the Śabaras is not known. They can be identified with the Suari of Pliny and the Sabarae of Ptolemy and are probably ancestors of the Savaralu or Sauras of the Vizagapatam hills, the Savaris of the Gwalior territory and the savages on the frontiers of Orissa.[46]

The name of Pulindas does not appear in the parallel list given in the *Śāṅkhāyana Śrauta-sūtra.* They are found along with the Andhras at the time of Aśoka. Their capital, according to the *Mahābhārata,* probably lay to the south-east of the Bhilsa region.

The territory of the Mūtibas has not yet been located. Raychaudhuri thinks it not altogether improbable that the Mūchipas, a variant of Mūtibas, are the people who appear in the *Mārkaṇḍeya Purāṇa* under the designation of Mushika, and locates the latter on the banks of the river Musi on which Hyderābād now stands.[47]

The name Mlechchha, found in the *Śatapatha Brāhmaṇa,* is used in the sense of a barbarian in speech who uses *"he'lavo"* for *"he'rayah."* This shows that these barbarians were Aryan speakers who employed a Prākṛit form of speech.

The Nishāda mentioned in the later Saṁhitās and Brāhmaṇas appears to be, not the name of any particular tribe, but the generic term for non-Aryan tribes who were not under Aryan control. Nishādas have been distinguished from the other four Varṇas. Weber considered the Nishādas to be settled aborigines. The Smṛitis explain the Nishādas as the off-spring of a Brāhmaṇa father and a Śūdra mother. The epics represent the Nishādas as having their settlements in the Vindhya and Sātpurā ranges, and it seems that during the post-Ṛigvedic period also they inhabited mountainous tracts.

The *Ṛigveda* repeatedly refers to the attacks on the aborigines. They are called *Kṛishṇa-tvach* (black skins) metaphorically. Kuyavāch (evil speaking), a demon slain by Indra, probably personifies the barbarian opponents. Mṛidhravāch (speaking insultingly) is also similarly used for denoting barbarians in the *Ṛigveda.* If Balbūtha, called a Dāsa, were the son of an aboriginal mother or an aboriginal himself, his reference as giving gifts to the singer indicates the establishment of friendly relations between the Aryans and Dāsas.

The above review of the Aryan settlements would make it clear that the period of the later Saṁhitās, Brāhmaṇas, Upanishads, and Sūtras is characterized by a spirit of adventure and expansion, and the advancing Aryans were spreading in every direction, colonizing the east, south, and north. The Gangetic Doāb was completely occupied by the Aryans and the adventurous Bharatas and Videghas led expeditions along the Yamunā, the Sarasvatī, and the Sadānīrā. Towards the east Kosala, Videha, Magadha, and Aṅga came under Aryan occupation during this period. In the north and the north-west, we come across the Uttarakurus and the Uttaramadras, Bāhlīkas, Mahāvṛishas, and Mūjavants, showing the expansion along Kāshmir and the Himalayas. Towards the south the Vindhya appears for the first time in the *Kaushītaki Upanishad* (II. 8), and the Kuntis and Vītahavyas seem to have penetrated further south, and the Narmadā and Vidarbha also were within the Aryan fold.

The disappearance of the Sarasvatī referred to in the *Pañchaviṁśa Brāhmaṇa* (XXV. 10. 6) is an important geographical landmark in this period. The main centre of the life of the period is Kurukshetra in the country of the Kuru-Pañchālas, bounded by the Khāṇḍava on the south, Tūrghna on the north, and Parīṇāh on the west. It is noteworthy that the sphere of civilization is gradually shifting eastward and its localization in the region to the east of the land of five rivers is an accomplished fact. The Punjab and the West not only recede in importance, but the tribes of the west are looked upon with disapproval in the *Śatapatha* and *Aitareya Brāhmaṇas*. There has been a change and regrouping of tribes of the Rigvedic period, and many new tribes emerge during this period. The Bharatas do not occupy the premier position, but are merged in the Kurus who, with their allies the Pañchālas, are the tribe *par excellence*. With Vaśas and Uśīnaras, the Kuru-Pañchālas occupy the Madhyadeśa. The Uttarakurus and the Uttaramadras lay to the north beyond the Himālayas, and Satvats to the south. To the east Kosala, Videha, Magadha, and Aṅga rise into prominence. The Andhras, Puṇḍras, Mūtibas, Pulindas, and Śabaras, as also the Nishādas, are the outcast tribes which were not fully Brahmanized.

The territory comprised within the sphere of Aryan influence down to the period of the Upanishads may thus be roughly described as the whole of India to the north of the Narmadā, and some regions even to the south of that river.

GENERAL REFERENCES

MACDONELL, A.A., and KEITH, A.B.: *Vedic Index*. Two vols. London, 1912
OLDENBERG, H.: *Buddha* (Eng. Translation by W. Hoey). London, 1882.
ZIMMER, H.: *Altindisches Leben* Berlin. 1879.

1. Hillebrandt (*Ved. Myth.*, I, pp. 99 ff; III, pp. 372 ff.) thinks that it is Arghandab in a few places.
2. Macdonell, *History of Sanskrit Literature*, p. 142; Keith, *CHI*, I, p. 80.
3. *AL*, p. 17; Chakladar, *MR*, Jan. 1930, p. 41; Raychaudhuri, *Ind. Antiquities*, p. 51.
4. *Zur Litteratur und Geschichte des Weda*, pp. 138 ff.; *AL*, pp. 11, 12; *MR*, Jan. 1930, p. 41.
5. *JRAS*, 1917, pp. 93-6; Raychaudhuri, *Ind. Antiquities*, p. 51.
6. *Nirukta*, VI. 26; IX. 26.
7. Law, *Rivers*, p. 10.
8. Ray, *JBORS*, March, 1928.

8a. For arguments against this view, cf. Ch. X, Appendix, p. 217.

9. *Cf. Ved. Ind.*, I, p. 468; *CHI*, I, p. 79 n.1, Hopkins, *JAOS*, 19; pp. 19-28; Keith, *CHI*, I, p. 79; Winternitz, *HIL*, I, p. 63; Pischel and Geldner, *Ved. Stud.*, II, p. 218; III, p. 152.

10. Brunnhofer, *Arische Urzeit*, 1910; Hertel, *Indo-Germ. Forchung*, 41, p. 188; Hüsing, *MAGW*, xlvi; Hillebrandt, *Ved. Myth.* I, pp. 98 ff.; Childe, *Aryans*, p. 32; Winternitz, *HIL*, I, pp. 63-4.
11. *CHI*, I, pp. 78-9.
12. *CHI*, I, p. 79.
13. *SBE*, XXXII, pp. 61 ff.; *In'ische Alterthumskunde*, I, p. 883; *AL*, pp. 22 ff., *Ved. Ind.*, II, p. 432.
14. *RV*. IV. 42. 8, 9 and Sāyaṇa's Commentary.
15. The *Ait. Br.* takes the five to be gods, men, gandharvas, and apsarases, snakes, and the fathers, whereas Yāska thinks that gandharvas, fathers, gods, asuras, and rākshasas are meant. Aupamanyavas and Sāyaṇa hold that the four varṇas and the Nishādas made up the five. Roth and Geldner take the expression to indicate the people of the whole earth.
16. *JAOS*, 15, pp. 258 ff.
17. Cf. Dutt, *Aryanisation of India*, p. 104.
18. *Banerji Sastri*, *JBORS*, 12, p. 253.
18a. The Dāsas and Dasyus have been fully discussed above in Ch. VIII, p. 159.
19. See Ch. XI, p.
20. *Some Aspects of Ancient Indian Culture*, p. 34.
21. Dey, *GD*, p. 104.
22. *Ved. Ind.*, II, p. 422.
23. Raychaudhuri, *PHAI*, p. 20.
24. *Ibid.*
25. *Ved. Ind.*, I, p. 469.
26. Raychaudhuri, *PHAI*, p. 59.
27. *Ind. Stud.*, I, pp. 212-3.
28. *EI*, 1921, p. 16; Majumdar, *CAG*, p. 669.
29. *Ind. Stud.*, I, pp. 212-3.
30. *Ved. Ind.*, II, p. 117.
31. *JRAS*, 1908, p. 852.
32. Raychaudhuri, *PHAI*, p. 76.
33. Cf. Law, *Tribes*, p. 100.
34. Raychaudhuri, *PHAI*, p. 74.
35. Franke, *Pali und Sanskrit*, pp. 88, 89.
36. Raychaudhuri, *PHAI*, p. 54.
37. Vāhlīka and Vālhīka appear as variants of Bāhlīka. The *Mahābhārata* and the Purāṇas locate the tribe in the neighbourhood of Gandhāra and Punjab.
38. Bhandarkar identifies the Keśis with the Kassis or Kassites (*Some Aspects of Ancient Indian Culture*, p. 3).
39. Pargiter, *AIHT*, pp. 109, 264.
40. *JRAS*, 1911, pp. 801-2.
41. Cf. Law, *Tribes*, pp. 2-3.
42. *JUPHAS*, XVI, pp. 43-6.
43. Such e.g., are the Ruśamas, Śviknas, Sparśus, Kāraskaras. Śaphālas, etc.
44. *ZDMG*, 56, pp. 657 ff.
45. Bhandarkar, *ABORI*, XII, pp. 104, 105.
46. Raychaudhuri, *PHAI*, p. 79; Dutt, *Aryanisation of India*, p. 69.
47. *PHAI*, p. 80.

BOOK FOUR

HISTORICAL TRADITIONS

CHAPTER XIV

TRADITIONAL HISTORY FROM THE EARLIEST TIME TO THE ACCESSION OF PARĪKSHIT

1. SOURCES OF INFORMATION

Our sources for the traditional history from the earliest times to the accession of Parikshit are mainly the Purāṇas, though the *Mahābhārata* and the *Rāmāyaṇa* occasionally give dynastic lists and deal with traditional accounts. General observations on the Purāṇas and the Epics will be found in the next volume. Here it is intended to give only a brief introductory note dealing with the historical value of the Purāṇas.

The Purāṇas, in their present recension, can hardly be placed earlier than the Gupta period. Thus they received their final form more than 2,000 years after the earliest events related by them. Besides this distance in time, the traditional account, contained in the Purāṇas, is vitiated by exaggeration, mythological details, pronounced religious bias, and the divergences in the texts of the different Purāṇas. These have been subjected to various modifications, revisions, etc. at different periods and no "definite" text of the Purāṇas is available. In spite of these obvious defects the Puranic account may not be regarded as wholly unreliable. It is likely that the royal genealogies and ancient ballads of kings and heroes were preserved from very early times by the Sūtas. It is expressly laid down in the *Vāyu Purāṇa* (I. 31-2) that "the Sūta's special duty, as perceived by good men of old, was to preserve the genealogies of gods, *ṛishis* (sages), and most glorious kings, and the traditions of great men." These accounts probably formed the basis of the original Purāṇa, from which the genealogical texts of the existing purāṇas were ultimately derived. Pargiter holds, on the basis of Indian tradition, that this original Purāṇa was composed more or less about the same time when the Vedic texts received their final form.[1] Although this view may be justly questioned, the existence of a Purāṇa text at a very early age is not improbable.

In any case there is hardly any doubt that the royal genealogies in the Purāṇas embody many genuine historical traditions of great antiquity which have not been otherwise preserved. It has also been pointed out by Pargiter that the Puranic account is corroborated in many respects by Vedic texts, which contain contemporary historical data. A comparative study of the Purāṇas and the Vedic texts shows that the former, though reduced to writing at a comparatively late period, embody the earliest traditional history, and much of their material is old and valuable.

When we find Puranic accounts corroborated by the Vedic evidence, it is but legitimate to take their testimony as valid even in matters on which the *Ṛigveda* is silent.

That the kernel of both the *Rāmāyaṇa* and the *Mahābhārata* embodies historical facts is also now generally accepted.[1a] The epic details, embellishments, exaggerations and flights of fancy, evident in the *Rāmāyaṇa* and the *Mahābhārata*, have been kept distinct from the Puranic account of traditional history in this chapter. Besides their central story, the *Rāmāyaṇa* and the *Mahābhārata* contain some dynastic lists and accounts. The Great Epic itself implies that it was composed after the Purāṇas. The genealogical accounts in the *Mahābhārata* are peculiar in that they are partly in prose and partly in verse, and do not appear to be ancient. The *Rāmāyaṇa* genealogy of the solar dynasty runs counter to the Puranic genealogy; but as the latter has been corroborated by other authorities, the Puranic genealogy is to be accepted in preference to that in the *Rāmāyaṇa*.

2. CHRONOLOGICAL SCHEME OF TRADITIONAL HISTORY ACCORDING TO THE PURĀṆAS

The Bhārata War is the central landmark in Indian traditional history, and the fixing of the date of that event will give us a starting point in settling dates of events occurring before and after it. We shall, therefore, first of all, try in brief to determine the date of the Bhārata War.

According to the Aihole inscription of Pulakeśin II (seventh century A.D.) the Bhārata War took place in 3102 B.C., which is the starting point of the Kaliyuga era according to the astronomical tradition represented by Āryabhaṭa[1b]. But Fleet has pointed out that the reckoning was not founded in Vedic times; it was first started about 3.500 years after the time for purposes of calculation, and was not known to astronomers before Āryabhaṭa.[2] Another school of Hindu astronomers and historians, represented by Vṛiddha-Garga. Varāhamihira and Kalhana, places the Bhārata War 653 years after the Kaliyuga era, i.e. in 2449 B.C.[3] These two schools thus present conflicting views, and as they are based on a hypothetical reckoning of a late date, we can hardly attach much importance to them.

Astronomical references in the *Mahābhārata* itself about the position of the *Nakshatras* and planets have been utilized for determining the date of the war. But, the same data have yielded various divergent results.[4] As a matter of fact. the statements in the Epic are conflicting and self-contradictory. so that in order to arrive at some conclusion it is necessary to reject certain statements or their implications as later interpolations or mere exaggerations. No satisfactory and acceptable result can be arrived at from these data.

On the basis of the Puranic tradition about the number of kings that flourished in different dynasties between king Adhisīmakṛishṇa (great-grandson of Janamejaya) and the coronation of Mahāpadma Nanda, Pargiter places the Bhārata War in c. 950 B.C. According to him 26 reigns intervened between these kings, and allowing a period of 18 years per reign, and taking the accession of Mahāpadma in 382 B.C., the period of Adhisīmakṛishṇa would be (26×18+382=) 850 B.C. And adding a hundred years for the reigns of intermediate kings between Yudhishṭhira and Adhisīmakṛishṇa Pargiter arrives at (850+100=) 950 B.C. as the date of the Bhārata War.[5]

Pargiter's date is contradicted by the statement in the Purāṇas and the *Mahābhārata* that between the birth of Parīkshit and the coronation of Mahāpadma, there elapsed a period of 1,015 (or 1,050) years.[6] This brings the date of the Bhārata War to (1015+382=) 1397 B.C. Though the number of kings mentioned in the Purāṇas during this period does not appear to be correct, as it gives an abnormally high average regnal period per generation, the figure mentioning the period (viz. 1015 or 1050) seems to represent a fairly reliable tradition, especially as the date it gives for the Bhārata War (c. 1400 B.C.) is corroborated by a consideration of the Vaṁśāvalī list of teachers. We may, therefore, take c. 1400 B.C. as the provisional date for the Bhārata War, and the event must have taken place between this date and 1000 B.C. in round numbers.

Now working backwards from the earlier date, the age of Manu Vaivasvata, who flourished, according to the genealogies prepared on the basis of traditional accounts, 95 generations before the Bhārata War, can be put as (95×18+1400=) 3110 B.C., taking one generation to average 18 years (as we have to deal with very long genealogies extending over 90 generations, we would be erring on the side of caution if we assumed 18 years as the average reign). This date, viz. 3110 B.C., curiously enough, approaches 3102 B.C. which has been taken as the beginning of the hypothetical Kali age for astronomical calculations. There is no doubt that the date 3102 B.C. signifies some important and epoch-making event in the traditional history of India. If it denotes the period of the beginning of the rule by Manu Vaivasvata, that means that it stands for the date of the Great Flood recorded in the *Śatapatha Brāhmaṇa* and other accounts, at which Manu was the saviour of humanity. The devastating Flood undoubtedly was the most important landmark in the history of the ancient world, and common flood legends suggest that the same event has been described in Indian, Hebrew, and Babylonian accounts. The Flood in Mesopotamia is generally held to have occurred about 3100 B.C.[6a] The Flood in India probably also occurred at the same time, and the date 3102 B.C., supposed to be the beginning of the Kali era, may, therefore, commemorate this event.

The year 3102 B.C. thus represents the age of Manu, the first traditional king in India. Yayāti, who is fifth in descent from Manu and figures also in the *Ṛigveda*, thus flourished (18×5=) 90 years after Manu or in (3100—90=) 3010 B.C. Māndhātṛi, coming after twenty generations, has to be placed in (3100–20×18=) 2740 B.C. The period of Arjuna Kārtavīrya, Viśvāmitra, Jamadagni, Paraśurāma, and Hariśchandra can be put between (3100—31×18)=) 2542 B.C., and (3100–33×18=) 2506 B.C. or roughly between 2550 and 2500 B.C. Sagara of Ayodhyā and Dushyanta and Bharata of Hastināpura flourished between (3100-41×18=) 2362 B.C. and 3100—44 ×18=) 2308 B.C. or roughly between 2350 and 2300 B.C. Rāma flourished 65 generations after Manu, i.e. in (3100—65×18=) 1930 B.C. or roughly in 1950 B.C. and the famous Dāśarājña war which occurred about three or four generations after Rāma, in c. 1900 B.C. These dates will, of course, have to be lowered by 400 years if the Bhāratā War is placed in c. 1000 B.C.

3. PRE-FLOOD TRADITIONS AND THE DAWN OF HISTORY

Like the dynastic lists in Sumer and Egypt, the Indian lists also record pre-diluvian dynasties, though as may naturally be expected in such accounts, there is a large mixture of myths and legends. They begin with the mythical king, Manu Svāyambhuva, who is said to have been born of Brahmā, and had from Śatarūpā, the half-female form of his body, two sons, Priyavrata and Uttānapāda, and three daughters. These daughters are the themes of very elaborate legends which connect them with the gods, sages, sacrifices, etc. Svāyambhuva Manu, also known as Virāj, was the lord of the first Manu cycle.

The *Vāyu Purāṇa* mentions Ānanda as a Brahmā (supreme ruler) who was a predecessor of Manu Svāyambhuva. This Ānanda is said to have established the *Varṇas* (castes), formulated their duties, and also established the institution of marriage; but these fell into abeyance in a short time and were revived by Manu Svāyambhuva.[7] Manu Svāyambhuva's capital lay on the bank of the river Sarasvatī. He is said to have subdued all enemies and became the first king of the earth. Manu Svārochisha, the second Manu, was the son of Svāyambhuva's daughter Ākūti. Priyavrata, the eldest son of Manu Svāyambhuva, is said to be the first of the Kshatriyas. Three of his sons renounced the world in child-hood in order to perform penance, and became Manus in the next Manvantaras. These were Uttama, Tāmasa, and Raivata, respectively the third, fourth, and fifth Manus.

Uttānapāda, the second son of Svāyambhuva Manu, had three sons, Dhruva, Kīrtivat, and Uttama. The story of the celebrated boy devotee Dhruva, who on account of the insult offered him by his step-mother, the favourite queen of Uttānapāda, left the world for penance and secured boons from the Lord Vishṇu, is well-known to every devout Hindu. Dhruva was succeeded by Prāchīnagarbha. Chākshusha in this line was the sixth Manu. His grandson Vena was a very wicked and tyrannous king. There was a general rebellion against him and he was deposed and killed. His son Pṛithu, celebrated as the first consecrated king, from whom the earth received its name Pṛithvī, was enthroned his successor. He levelled the whole earth, clearing it of ups and downs, and encouraged cultivation, cattle-breeding, commerce, and building of cities and villages. The oath that he had to swear would compare favourably with the oath any constitutional sovereign of England has to take.[8] Fifth in descent from Pṛithu was Daksha, whose daughter's grandson, Manu Vaivasvata, saved humanity from the deluge which occurred at this time.

4. THE FLOOD AND MANU VAIVASVATA (c. 3100 B.C.)

The earliest and the shortest Indian account describing the flood is found in the *Śatapatha Brāhmaṇa,* and there are later embellished versions in the *Mahābhārata* and the Purāṇas.[9] According to the *Śatapatha Brāhmaṇa,* when Manu was washing his hands in the morning, a small fish came into his hands along with the water. The fish sought protection from Manu, saying, "Rear me, I will save thee." The reason stated was that the small fish was liable to be devoured by the larger, and it required protection till it grew up. It asked to be kept in a jar, and later on, when it outgrew that, in a pond, and finally in the sea. Manu acted accordingly. The fish forewarned Manu of the forthcoming flood, and advised him to prepare a ship and enter into it when the flood came. The flood began to rise at the appointed hour, and Manu entered the ship. The fish then swam up to him; he tied the rope of the ship to its horn, and thus passed swiftly to the yonder northern mountain. There, Manu was directed to ascend the mountain after fastening the ship to a tree and disembark after the water had subsided. Accordingly, he gradually descended, and hence the slope of the northern mountain is called *Manoravataraṇam* or Manu's descent. The waters swept away all the three heavens, and Manu alone was saved.

Manu Vaivasvata is said to be the originator of the human race, and all the dynasties mentioned in the Purāṇas spring from him. He framed rules and laws of government, and collected a sixth of the produce of the land as a tax to meet administrative expenses.

Manu is stated to have been the father of nine valiant sons, besides the eldest, who is represented to have had a dual personality as the male Ila and female Ilā. There is a great divergence in the names of the nine sons and their order in the different accounts. According to the collated text, suggested by Pargiter,[10] the names are: Ikshvāku, Nābhāga, Dhṛishṭa, Śaryāti, Narishyanta, Prāṁśu, Nābhāgodishṭa (or Nabhānedishṭha); Karūsha, and Pṛishadhra. Of these sons only four are important as being the originators of important lines. Ikshvāku, the eldest, had his capital at Ayodhyā, and his son Vikukshi founded the Aikshvāka (or the Solar) line. The location of the Nābhāgas, descended from Nābhāga, is uncertain. They probably reigned in the midlands of the Gangetic Doāb, and included Rathītara from whom came the Rathītaras who were Kshatriyan Brāhmaṇas. The Nābhāga dynasty played practically no part in traditional history, and probably disappeared under the early Aila conquests. From Dhṛishṭa came the Dhārshṭaka Kshatriyas who probably ruled over Vāhīka in the Punjab. Nothing further is known about them. Their social position is interesting to the student of social history as they are sometimes called Brāhmaṇas, sometimes Kshatriyas and sometimes even Vaiśyas, indicating the fluidity of castes at this period in our history. Śaryāti was the founder of the Śāryātas who ruled in Ānarta. The Śāryātas were one of the earliest Aryan tribes to come in contact with Gujarāt, which received its ancient name from Ānarta, the son of Śaryāti. There is much confusion about the genealogy of Narishyanta, some accounts stating the Śakas to be his descendants. Nothing is known about the descendants of Prāṁśu. Nābhāgodishṭa settled in north Bihār, and established the Vaiśāla dynasty which ruled at Vaiśālī identified with Basārh[11] (Muzaffarpur district). From Karūsha came the Karūshas, the determined fighters, who occupied the Karūsha country—the region round the modern Rewah and eastwards to the river Son. Pṛishadhra was excluded from any share of the earth because he killed his *guru's* (preceptor's) cow.

From Ilā, as the female, who married Budha, was born Purūravas, the originator of the Aila (or the Lunar) dynasty. From the Ailas sprang various dynasties such as the Kānyakubjas, Yādavas (Haihayas, Andhakas, Vṛishṇis), Turvasus, Druhyus, Ānavas, Pañchālas, Bārhadrathas, Chedis, etc.

From Ilā transformed into a Kimpurusha named Sudyumna, sprang the Saudyumnas—his three sons Utkala, Gaya, and Vinatāśva, who respectively ruled over the Utkala country, Gayā, and the eastern regions including the northern Kurus. The Saudyumna kingdoms were annexed by the Ānavas and Kānyakubjas.

The early disappearance of the dynastic lists of the kingdoms established by Karūsha, Nābhāga, Dhṛishṭa, Narishyanta, Prāṁśu, and Pṛishadhra seems to be due to the victorious campaigns led by Purūravas, Nahusha and Yayāti of the Lunar dynasty, who displaced all these kingdoms and expanded the Paurava realm.

5. THE YAYĀTI PERIOD
(c. 3000-2750 B.C.)

1. *The Lunar Dynasty*

Purūravas Aila, Ilā's son through Budha or Soma, was the progenitor of the celebrated Lunar dynasty. Though the seat of the government of the Ailas and the scene of their later activities have been placed at Pratishṭhāna[12] by the Purāṇas, the origin of the Ailas, according to these texts, seems to be connected with the Himālayan region.

Purūravas is said to have ruled over the seven islands and performed a hundred Aśvamedhas. The story of Purūravas and Urvaśī is too well known to be dealt with here.[12a] However, towards the end of his reign, Purūravas is said have been intoxicated with power and declared war on the Brāhmaṇas, robbed them of their jewels, and coveted the golden sacrificial floor of the Naimisha sages, who were performing sacrifice. The sages in revolt killed him and installed his eldest son Āyu on the throne. Purūravas was the contemporary of Ikshvāku of the Solar dynasty. The Aila kingdom developed quickly under Purūravas. Being checked in their expansion to the north by the powerful kingdom of Ayodhyā and to the south by the war-like Karūshas, the Ailas extended their sway eastward and north-westward into the Gangetic Doāb and Mālwā and Eastern Rājputāna. The expanded realm was divided among Purūrava's two sons, Āyu and Amāvasu.

Āyu continued the main line at Pratishṭhāna, and Amāvasu, to whose share fell the northern territories in the mid-Gangetic Doāb, founded the Kānyakubja dynasty. Āyu was friendly towards the Ṛishis and Brāhmaṇas. His marriage with Prabhā, the daughter of a Dānava king Svarbhānu, indicates that he held catholic views and was a conciliator between Āryas and Dānavas. Āyu had five sons, only two of whom were important. The eldest, Nahusha, succeeded Āyu in the main line at Pratishṭhāna, while the second, Khshatravṛiddha, established himself at Kāśī in the east.

Nahusha was a famous king, a great conqueror, the first man to establish a theatre on the earth. The *Mahābhārata* story of his securing the kingdom of Indra, and of his subsequent fall therefrom on account of his arrogance and ill-treatment of Agastya, runs counter to many well-established synchronisms and is obviously a later invention.[13] His son and successor Yayāti is mentioned in the Purāṇas and the *Mahābhārata* as a *Samrāṭ* (emperor) and a great conqueror who extended his kingdom far and wide. He reduced all Madhyadeśa west of Ayodhyā and Kānyakubja and north-west as far as the Sarasvatī. He also brought under his sway countries towards the south, south-east, and west of his territory. The Purāṇas and the *Mahābhārata* give a detailed account of Yayāti's marriage with

Devayānī, daughter of Uśanas-Śukra, the great Bhārgava *ṛishi*, and Śarmishṭhā, daughter of king Vṛishaparvan of the Asuras. Yayāti's marriage with Devayānī being the *pratiloma* marriage, reprehensible according to later customary law, some excuses have been invented in justification of it.

Yayāti had five sons. Devayānī bore two, Yadu and Turvasu, and Śarmishṭhā three, Anu, Druhyu, and Pūru. Yayāti divided the kingdom among his five sons, placing the youngest son Pūru to continue the main line, ruling over Madhyadeśa, the southern half of the Ganges-Jumna Doāb, with its capital at Pratishṭhāna. The main Lunar line hereafter came to be known as Pūru Vaṁśa or the Pauravas after Pūru. There is a great divergence in the Purāṇas regarding the territories assigned by Yayāti to his sons. Pargiter's collated text[14] suggests that Yadu, the eldest son, was given territories towards the south-west embracing the country watered by the rivers Charmaṇvatī (Chambal), Vetravatī (Betwā) and Śuktimatī (Ken). Turvasu got the south-east territory (round Rewah). To Druhyu was assigned the west, i.e. the country west of the Yamunā and north of the Chambal. Anu received the north, i.e. the northern portion of the Ganges-Jumna Doāb.

By the time of Pūru, the Ailas had thus established seven kingdoms,, viz. Pratishṭhāna, Yādava, Turvasu, Ānava, Druhyu (i.e. the kingdoms of the five sons of Yayāti), and the kingdoms of Kānyakubja and Kāśī. Pūru, though the youngest, got the ancestral kingdom of Pratishṭhāna through obedience to his father. He was succeeded by his son Janamejaya.

The Kānyakubjas and Kāśis, the subsections of the Lunar dynasty, are not noted for any remarkable achievements or personalities during the period under review. Yadu, the eldest son of Yayāti, founded the Yādavas, the first Lunar dynasty to rise into prominence. They first destroyed the Rākshasa power in Gujarāt-Kāthiāwār, who overthrew the Śāryātas there. Only Kroshṭṛi and Sahasrajit, among Yadu's sons, are important, for with them the Yādavas branched off respectively into the Yādavas and Haihayas.

Yādava Chitraratha, about twelfth in descent from Yadu, was the contemporary of the Paurava king Matināra. Gaurī, the daughter of Matināra, was married to Yuvanāśva II of the Solar dynasty of Ayodhyā, and their son Māndhātṛi, king of Ayodhyā, married Bindumatī, the daughter of Śaśabindu, son of Chitraratha. Both Chitraratha and Śaśabindu were great kings. The Yādavas first developed a great kingdom under Śaśabindhu, which included the territories of the Pauravas and Turvasus on the east and the Druhyus on the north.

2. *The Solar Dynasty*

Now we turn to the Solar dynasty which comprises the three

lines of Ayodhyā, Videha, and Vaiśāla, and the Śāryātas. These are the only branches that are important out of the lines produced by the nine sons of Manu.

Ikshvāku, the eldest of Manu's sons, was the first king of Ayodhyā, and Manu gave him Madhyadeśa. According to the Purāṇas, Ikshvāku had a hundred sons of whom Vikukshi the eldest, Nimi and Daṇḍa were most famous. Vikukshi, also named Śaśāda, succeeded Ikshvāku in the Ayodhyā kingdom, and Nimi founded the Videha line. The Daṇḍaka forest is said to have been named after Daṇḍa or Daṇḍaka, the third son of Ikshvāku.

Parañjaya or Purañjaya, the son of Vikukshi, received the appellation Kakutstha on account of his being borne away by Indra, in the form of a bull, on his head (*kakud*) on the battlefield. Śrāvasta, the son of Yuvanāśva and sixth in descent from Kakutstha, is said to have founded Śrāvastī[16] which later became the capital of north Kosala. Of his grandson Kuvalāśva, a wild legend is current explaining how he received the alternative name Dhundhumāra. Kuvalāśva is said to have marched against an Asura, Rākshasa or Daitya named Dhundhu near a shallow sand-filled sea in the Rājputāna desert in order to rescue a sage named Uttaṅka. He destroyed the subterranean quarters of the Asura and put an end to his fiery home. This legend probably suggests that Kuvalāśva subjugated the Asuras and aboriginals to the west and in the southern parts of Rājputāna and spread Aryan culture in those lands. Dr. Law sees a reference to a natural phenomenon in this legend. He conjectures that the subterranean retreat of the Asura was really a small volcanic pit near the western sea-coast causing occasional earthquakes, and emitting smoke, ashes, and fire. Kuvalāśva, by digging up the earth, first brought on volcanic eruptions destroying the army in flames and smoke; but later on a subterranean water channel rushed into the volcanic pit and extinguished it for ever.[16] According to Pargiter this legend alludes to a shallow sand-filled sea in Rājputāna which formed the limit of Aryan advance towards the south[17]. Kuvalāśva's eighth descendant was Yuvanāśva II, also known as Saudyumni. A grotesque legend is told about the birth of a son to the king himself out of his left rib as a result of his drinking the holy sacrificial water intended for his queen. The child was nursed by Indra with the nectar exhaled from his thumb, whence it came to be known as Māndhātṛi.

The other branches of the Solar dynasty may be briefly referred to. The Videhas sprang from Ikshvāku's son Nimi, also known as Videha. Nimi dwelt in a town named Jayanta and the capital was Mithilā, said to have been named after his son Mithi. The Videha line of kings came to be known as Janakas on account of this Mithi Janaka.

The Vaiśālas, though descended from Nābhānedishṭha (or Dhṛishṭa, son of Nābhāga and grandson of Manu), came to be called such retrospectively from the name of king Viśāla who founded Viśālā or Vaiśālī as his capital. Bhalandana and Vatsaprī are named as the first two kings. Bhalandana, who was a great sacrificer and a valiant and universal conqueror, is said to have become a Vaiśya.

The Śāryātas originated from Śaryāti, the son of Manu, and played but an unimportant rôle in traditional history. Śaryāti, who is said to have offered his daughter Sukanyā in marriage to Chyavana of the Bhṛigu family, was succeeded by his son Ānarta. The Śāryāta dynasty was short-lived and was destroyed by the Puṇyajana Rākshasas. The history of the Saudyumnas has been referred to above (p. 278).

3. *Brāhmaṇa families*

Brāhmaṇa families also play important rôles in traditional history, and we may take note of contemporary Brāhmaṇa families in the different periods of traditional history. The Brāhmaṇa families claim descent from eight mythical *ṛishis* (sages), called mind-born sons of Brahmā. There are also other fabulous accounts which seek to explain their names on the basis of etymology inventing fanciful stories. Out of the eight Brāhmaṇa families, i.e. Bhṛigu, Aṅgiras, Marīchi, Atri, Vasishṭha, Pulastya, Pulaha, and Kratu, the last three did not produce true Brāhmaṇa stocks. Pulastya was the progenitor of the Rākshasas, Vānaras, Kinnaras and Yakshas. From Pulaha came Kimpurushas, Piśāchas, goblins, lions, tigers and other animals. Kratu, according to most accounts, had no wife or child, and remained celibate, but some accounts make the Vālakhilyas his offspring. The remaining five, however, were not assigned equal antiquity. The Bhārgavas, Vasishṭhas, and probably Aṅgirasas, appear to have been the earliest Brāhmaṇa families. The Atris and Kaśyapas (from Marīchi) originated later.

The Bhṛigus or Bhārgavas claim descent from the primeval *ṛishi* Bhṛigu. Chyavana and Śukra are the earliest Bhṛigus mentioned in the Purāṇas. Śukra was connected with the Daityas, Dānavas, and Asuras as their *guru*, and was the rival of Bṛihaspati, the *guru* of the Devas. Śukra's daughter Devayānī married Yayāti, the Pūru king, and bore him Yadu and Turvasu.

The Vasishṭhas in Puranic accounts claim to have a mysterious origin, being descended from Mitrāvaruṇa in the present Manvantara. Some accounts make the first Vasishṭha one of the ten mind-born sons of Brahmā in the Svāyambhuva Manvantara.

The Vasishṭhas have been connected as hereditary priests with the kings of Ayodhyā from the earliest times. The Purāṇas mention a Vasishṭha in connection with Ikshvāku and his sons Vikukshi-Śaśāda and Nimi.

Though the Atri clan was an ancient one vying in antiquity with the earliest Brāhmaṇa families, the earliest individual member of the Atri family to be referred to in traditional history is Prabhākara, who is said to have married the ten daughters of Bhadrāśva, (or Raudrāśva) an early Paurava king. From Prabhākara's ten sons descended the best Ātreya *Gotras*.

Marīchi's son Kaśyapa, the progenitor of the Kaśyapas, is made a Prajāpati or identified with Kaśyapa, the creator of all beings and the father of the gods and Asuras.

Besides these ancient families, there were other Brāhmaṇa stocks such as Viśvāmitras and Jamadagnis, which did not claim primeval antiquity, and which emerged in traditional history at a later period.

6. THE MĀNDHĀTṚI PERIOD (c. 2750-2550 B.C.)

I. *The Solar Dynasty*

We now turn to the next period, the central figure in which is Māndhātṛi, son of Yuvanāśva, of the Ikshvāku family. The Yādava empire under Śaśabindu (p. 280) was rivalled by the Ayodhyā kingdom under Māndhātṛi (p. 281), a famous king, a *chakravartin* and a *samrāṭ*. According to the Puranic accounts, Māndhātṛi Yauvanāśva, an Aikshvāka, was a great *chakravartin*. He was the son of Yuvanāśva, and Gaurī, the daughter of Matināra of the Pauravas. He was considered the fifth *avatāra* (incarnation) of Vishṇu. He was a great sacrificer and is said to have performed a hundred Aśvamedhas and Rājasūyas. His gifts and charities are eulogized and songs praising him have been handed down from very ancient times. He is mentioned as a king of very wide sway, magnanimous and giver of cows. Māndhatṛi married Bindumatī, daughter of Śaśabindu of the Yādavas. He had three sons, Purukutsa, Ambarīsha, and Muchukunda. His sister (daughter or granddaughter) Kāverī married Jahnu of the Kānyakubjas.

The account of his birth from his father's side and being called Māndhātṛi because of what Indra said at the prince's birth (*māṁ dhātā*, i.e. the child will suck me), invented evidently to explain his name, is a late fabrication fashioned with great ingenuity. Māndhātṛi is said to have obtained half the throne of Indra and conquered the whole earth in one day. He extended his sway over the neighbouring Paurava and Kānyakubja realms, and also conquered the Druhyus and the Ānavas in the north-west. He probably spared the Yādavas who were related to him, but conquered the Haihayas in the Deccan. Māndhātṛi was succeeded by his eldest son Purukutsa.

Purukutsa continued the conquest of his father. The Nāgas induced Purukutsa to destroy the Mauneya Gandharvas who had despoiled them. They gave him their princess Narmadā, and he rescued them from the Gandharvas. This shows the extension of the Aryan culture towards the river Narmadā and the land of the Nāgas who were probably aborigines or primitive peoples.

Muchukunda, the third son of Māndhātṛi, was a famous king. The fable connecting him with Kālayavana and Kṛishṇa is an anachronism.[18] He built and fortified a town on the Narmadā between Pāripātra and Ṛiksha mountains. Muchukunda's supremacy, however, did not last long, and the Haihaya king Mahishmant conquered that town and named it Māhishmatī. The Ayodhyā kingdom declined after Purukutsa, and some of the kingdoms of the Lunar dynasty again rose into prominence.

2. *The Lunar Dynasty*

The Paurava realm appears to have lain prostrate at the time of Māndhātṛi, for he is said to have sacrificed on the Yamunā, and crossing the Paurava kingdom he conquered the Druhyu king, who was pushed from Rājputāna to the borders of the Punjab by the Yādava king Śaśabindu. It was probably Śaśabindu, the Yādava king, who conquered the Paurava realm, and the Haihaya king Bhadraśreṇya traversed it to reach Benares. There arose no king of eminence among the Pauravas for generations after Yayāti and Pūru, so that the kingdom dwindled down, and the neighbouring kings absorbed parts of it till the Paurava kings were reduced to mere kings in name, and probably lived out in exile, as would appear from the account of Dushyanta who was with Turvasu Marutta, son of Karandhama.

The Kānyakubja kingdom appears to have been overrun by king Māndhātri in course of his conquest of the Druhyus. The suzerainty of Ayodhyā over Kānyakubja was, however, short-lived, and Jahnu brought Kānyakubja into local prominence. Jahnu married the grand-daughter of Yauvanāśva (i.e. Māndhātṛi).

The Haihayas (of the Yādava branch of the Lunar dynasty) continued to prosper in their region south of Mālwā, and as noted above, Mahishmant (one of their kings) founded the town Māhishmatī. His successor, king Bhadraśreṇya, was an aggressive monarch who conquered the Paurava realm. He also extended his sway eastwards into the Kāśi territories, conquered the kingdom, occupied Benares and reigned there. There Benares king Haryaśva tried to recover it, but was killed by the Haihayas and his son Sudeva also was overpowered. Later, Benares is said to have come under the possession of Kshemaka Rākshasa from whom it was subsequently recovered by Durdama of the Haihayas. The occupation by Rākshasas indicates the devastation of the country by war resulting in its occupation by the rude tribes from the forest.

The Ānavas also grew in power. King Mahāmanas, seventh in descent from Anu, extended the sway of the Ānavas towards the east and the Punjab; and the bifurcation of the Ānavas under his two sons Uśīnara and Titikshu shows the extent of his conquests.

Uśīnara established a kingdom on the eastern border of the Punjab, which was divided among his five sons. Śibi succeeded to the throne at Multān; from Nṛiga, who established a separate kingdom in the present Montgomery district and the northern parts of Bikaner, sprang the Yaudheyas; Nava was the originator of the kings of Navarāshṭra; rulers of the city of Kṛimila came from Kṛimi; and Suvrata started the Ambashṭhas, probably in the eastern Punjab. Śibi Auśīnara, however, was the most prominent among Uśīnara's sons, and the Śibis sprang from him. Śibi conquered practically the whole of the Punjab except the north-west corner, and established through his sons four kingdoms of (i) the Vṛishadarbhas, also known as Śibis, in the home territories of Multān, (ii) the Sauvīras in Sind, (iii) the Kekayas in the modern districts of Gujarāt and Shāhpur between the Jhelum and the Chenāb, and (iv) the Madrakas, with their capital at Sākala (modern Siālkot), in the Lahore division of the Punjab and the Jammu province in Kāshmir.

Titikshu moved eastward and crossing Videha and Vaiśālī came down to the east and founded a new kingdom in east Bihār where ruled the Saudyumnas. This new kingdom was known as the "Kingdom in the East," which later developed into the five kingdoms of Aṅga, Vaṅga, Kaliṅga, Puṇḍra, and Suhma, divided among Bali's five sons.

Lastly we come to the Druhyus. As the result of the successful campaigns of Saśabindu, Yuvanāśva, Māndhātṛi, and Śibi, the Druhyus were pushed back from Rājputāna and were cornered into the north-western portion of the Punjab. Māndhātṛi killed their king Aṅgāra, and the Druhyu settlements in the Punjab came to be known as Gāndhāra after the name of one of Aṅgāra's successors. After a time, being over-populated, the Druhyus crossed the borders of India and founded many principalities in the Mlechchha territories in the north, and probably carried the Aryan culture beyond the frontiers of India.

7. THE PARAŚURĀMA PERIOD (c. 2550-2350 B.C.)

The whole of the age which has been designated the Paraśurāma period comprising about twelve generations (till the rise of king Sagara of Ayodhyā of the Solar dynasty) was dominated by the Haihayas and the Bhṛigus in turn. There is practically nothing worth recording in the Paurava line during this period which shows a great break till the time of Dushyanta who came after Sagara.

1. *The Bhṛigus*

The Bhṛigu-vaṁśa or the Bhārgavas, the family to which Paraśurāma belonged, dwelt in Ānarta (Gujarāt). After the Śāryātas perished and Western India was dominated by the Haihayas, the Bhṛigus became associated with the Haihayas. King Kṛitavīrya of the Haihayas is said to have bestowed great wealth on the Bhārgavas who were his priests. On refusal of the Bhārgavas to return it, Kṛitavīrya's descendants ill-treated them and used violence against them so that they fled into Kānyakubja in the Madhyadeśa for safety. Chief among the Bhṛigus was Ṛichīka, son of Ūrva, a famous *Ṛishi* skilled in archery, who cherished great wrath towards the Haihayas. In order to wreak vengeance on the wicked Haihayas, the Bhārgavas engaged themselves in collecting arms and sought marital alliances with the Kshatriya ruling families. Ṛichīka sought in marriage Satyavatī, the daughter of king Gādhi of Kānyakubja. The king did not approve of the match and evaded it by demanding an almost impossible price in the form of a thousand black-eared horses. Ṛichīka, however, fulfilled the condition and married Satyavatī. Jamadagni, the celebrated Bhṛigu sage, was born of this marriage. He was thus Viśvāmitra's sister's son.

Jamadagni became skilled in archery and arms and made an alliance with the ruling family of Ayodhyā by marrying Reṇukā, daughter of Reṇu, a junior king in the line. Jamadagni was not a militant *Ṛishi* but followed peaceful avocations.

When the Haihaya king Kārtavīrya came to his hermitage with his army, Jamadagni treated him with right royal hospitality through the help of his celebrated divine Kāmadhenu (wish-giving cow). On Jamadagni's refusal to part with the cow, Kārtavīrya forcibly seized her; but the Yavanas, produced from her body, defeated Kārtavīrya. Subsequently, Kārtavīrya destroyed the hermitage and carried away the sacred cow.

Four or five sons were born to Jamadagni, of whom Rāma (or Paraśurāma), though the youngest, was the greatest among the Bhṛigus. The Purāṇas represent Paraśurāma as an incarnation of Vishṇu. He is said to have been born during the period of interval beween the *Tretā* and *Dvāpara Yugas*. The *Mahābhārata*, however, refers to him as an incarnation only in two late passages.[19] Paraśurāma is represented as a very great warrior, skilled in all weapons, especially in archery. The *Paraśu* (battle axe) was his special weapon, on account of which he came to be called Paraśurāma in distinction from Rāma Dāśarathi. The slaughter of the Kshatriyas twenty-one times, and ridding the earth of the Kshatriyas are said to be the principal feats of Paraśurāma.

The Bhṛigu-Haihaya conflict started after Kārtavīrya (Arjuna or Sahasrārjuna) raided Jamadagni's hermitage in the absence of Rāma, molested the old sage and forcibly took away the sacred cow (as already stated). In revenge, Rāma lopped off Arjuna's arms and slaughtered him like an ordinary animal. Thereupon, on the advice of Jamadagni, Rāma set out on a pilgrimage for the expiation of the sin of killing Arjuna. During the absence of Paraśurāma, Arjuna's sons slew Jamadagni when he was in deep meditation. This enraged Rāma to the extreme, and he declared a vendetta not only against the Haihayas, but against the Kshatriyas in general, and is said to have rid the earth of the Kshatriyas twenty-one times. At regular intervals after the birth of fresh Kshatriyas, Rāma restarted his campaign and slew all of them. Rāma filled a number of lakes at Kurukshetra with the blood of the Kshatriyas. As the result of these raids, some Kshatriyas fled to the mountains or hid themselves among the women-folk. Only Ṛikshavān of the Pauravas, Sarvakarmā of Ayodhyā, Bṛihadratha of Magadha, Chitraratha of Aṅga, and Vatsa of Kāśi are said to have escaped from Rāma's slaughter.[20] All this, indeed, is an exaggeration. It appears that on the strength of the matrimonial alliances of the Bhārgavas with the ruling families of Kānyakubja and Ayodhyā, and also of the growing discontent due to the devastating raids and consequent unpopularity of the Haihayas, Rāma organized a confederacy of various kingdoms including Vaiśālī, Videha, Kāśi, Kānyakubja and Ayodhyā which fought the Haihayas on various battlefields. These are probably referred to by the annihilation of the Kshatriyas twenty-one times. As the result of his all-round attack from all fronts, the Haihayas, for a time at least, must have suffered a serious setback.

Rāma is said to have retired to the forest for penance in order to atone for his sins after each slaughter. Finally, to rid himself of the sin, he donated the whole earth to Kaśyapa. To free the earth from any possible future attacks from Rāma, Kaśyapa banished him from the earth which now belonged to him. Rāma then wrested from the sea the west coast and colonized it. The whole of the west coast from Bhṛigukachchha (Broach) down to Cape Comorin retains association with Paraśurāma.

According to the genealogical tables, Paraśurāma is several generations prior to the period of Rāma (son of Daśaratha) and the Pāṇḍavas; yet he has been brought into connection with these heroes in the *Rāmāyaṇa* and the *Mahābhārata.* Thus he is said to have appeared before Rāma after his marriage with Sītā, advised Balarāma and Kṛishṇa with regard to a suitable site for safety against the raids of Jarāsandha, to have been the preceptor of Bhīshma, Droṇa, and Karṇa, to have fought against Bhīshma, to have advised Duryodhana not to fight the Pāṇḍavas, etc. These are clearly instances of anachronism as the result of the anxiety of the writers of the Epics to establish contact of their heroes with the great Bhārgava. In order to get over these obvious anachronisms a theory was promulgated, at a later date, that Paraśurāma was *chirañjiva* (immortal).

2. *The Haihayas*

After the death of Purukutsa, the kingdom of Ayodhyā lost its paramountcy in Upper India and the Haihaya branch of the Yādavas gradually began to extend its sway from the west, penetrating to the east and north, as noted above (pp. 284 ff.). Reference has already been made to Kṛitavīrya and his son Arjuna, a great monarch, *samrāt,* and *chakravartin* who, during his long reign, extended the Haihaya sway far and wide and raised the Haihaya power to great eminence. Arjuna is known by his patronymic Kārtavīrya and also as Sahasrārjuna (thousand-armed). The thousand arms ascribed to Arjuna were possibly his fleet of a thousand ships. Arjuna propitiated Dattātreya, a sage regarded as an incarnation of Nārāyaṇa, and started his career of conquest which at once carried the Haihaya empire to great prominence and supremacy. He fought the Karkoṭaka Nāgas who occupied Anūpa (territories near the mouth of the Narmadā), captured Māhishmatī and made it his capital. Kārtavīrya also defected Rāvaṇa who invaded his territories, brought him captive and subsequently released him. He appears to have led his victorious campaigns from the mouth of the Narmadā to as far north as the Himālayas, since in one of his raids he is said to have come across the hermitage of Āpava Vasishṭha in the Himālayas and burnt it, as a consequence of which he was cursed. Arjuna is said to have conquered the whole earth, and performed a number of sacrifices.

Arjuna's conflict with Jamadagni and Rāma, to which we have already referred, occurred towards the end of his long and prosperous reign.

Barring his relations with Āpava Vasishṭha and Jamadagni, which show Arjuna in an unfavourable light as inimical to the Brāhmaṇas, he is always the subject of high praise and encomium in epic works. He is described as an ideal monarch unparalleled in penance, charities, learning, and virtues, who conquered the whole world and ruled it with perfect justice. It is only his connection with the Bhṛigus that has been responsible for painting the ideal monarch in the blackest colours. His victories show that he carried the banner of Aryan conquest far and wide, and that Māhishmatī on the Narmadā was an outpost of the Aryan colonies of those days.

Mr. Karandikar, after a thorough study of the Purāṇas, has suggested quite a different interpretation of the Sahasrārjuna episode.[21] According to him, the Bhṛigus were great navigators and expert mariners who controlled the maritime trade between India and the western world, and occupied the coastal line on the Arabian Sea. They amassed a great fortune through their trade with foreign countries. The reason of the Bhṛigu-Haiḥaya conflict was that Arjuna did not wish that the Bhṛigus, who were agents of the foreigners, should thrive at the cost of the people. He wanted to keep the trade and commerce of the Indian people under the control of an Aryan state, for the Bhṛigus were more self-seekers than patriots. Arjuna sought the help of the Atris, who were equally expert ship-builders, and who built for him a fleet of a thousand ships or a ship with a thousand oars (making Arjuna Saharsabāhu, i.e. thousand-armed). Karkoṭaka Nāga, Rāvaṇa and others who were defeated by Arjuna were seeking some opportunity to wreak vengeance on him. Arjuna's effort at getting control of the sea-trade was an eyesore to the Bhṛigus, and further fuel was added by Arjuna's demanding back the wealth he had bestowed on the Bhrigus. Paraśurāma led the opposition with the aid of the parties defeated by Arjuna, killed him, and destroyed the Haihaya power. The annihilation of the Kshatriyas twenty-one times is interpreted as the destruction of the population in the Narmadā region a number of times in order to wipe out the memory of the popular king Arjuna. On the devastated Haihaya realm Paraśurāma founded new cities, and colonized some tracts in the west coast, founding Śūrpāraka which became the centre of trade. The result of Paraśurāma's activities was to divert the trade from the hands of the Aryans in the north to the Dravidians in the south.

Whatever we might think of the above interpretation there is no doubt that as the result of the Bhrigu-Haihaya conflict the Haihayas received a great setback. But they soon recovered from their reverses, and again extended their power in Northern India. Arjuna had many sons of whom the chief was Jayadhvaja who reigned in Avantī. Śūrasena, another son, appears to have been associated with Mathurā, while Śūra, the third son, probably was connected with Surāshṭra. Jayadhvaja's son Tālajaṅgha had many sons, of whom the chief was Vītihotra. The Purāṇas state that the Haihayas formed five groups, viz. Vītihotras, Śāryātas, Bhojas, Avantis, and Kuṇḍikeras all of whom were collectively called Tālajaṅghas.[22] Of these, Vītihotra and Tuṇḍikera or Kuṇḍikera were in the Vindhyan range; the Śāryātas were in Western India, Bhojas near the Aravalli hills, and Avantis in Mālwā. They carried their raids not only against the kingdoms of the Madhyadeśa but even against Kānyakubja, Kosala, and Kāśi. The Kānyakubja kingdom appears to have succumbed to these raids. The Haihayas killed Haryaśva of Kāśi in a battle in the Ganges-Jumna Doāb, but met with reverses later on, and the Vītihotra prince on the Benares throne had to seek refuge with a Bhārgava sage. After this, the Haihaya dynasty practically came to an end, and the king became a Brāhmaṇa.

The kingdom of Ayodhyā, considerably weakened after Māndhātṛi and Purukutsa, was attacked by the Haihayas with the co-operation of the hardy and semi-barbarous tribes (called Śakas, Yavanas, Kambojas, Pāradas, and Pahlavas) from the north-west. This co-operation indicates that the intervening kingdoms between

Ayodhyā and the frontier countries were overthrown by the Haihayas. Bāhu (or Asita according to the *Rāmāyaṇa*), king of Ayodhyā, had to leave the throne and seek refuge in the forest where he died near the hermitage of Aurva Bhārgava. His queen gave birth to a son in the forest who was named Sagara and was educated by Aurva Bhārgava. As we shall presently relate, Sagara was the greatest king of the Solar dynasty during this period and recovered his lost kingdom with the help of the Bhārgavas. Vaiśālī and Vidiśā also were attacked by the Haihayas and Vidiśā probably was under Haihaya occupation. Tradition, however, suggests that the Haihaya conquests towards the east were checked by the Vaiśāla kings.

The Haihayas thus were engaged in making continual raids and over-throwing kingdoms; they, however, did not found any kingdoms in the countries overrun by them which lay devastated and fell an easy prey to the attacks by wild tribes.

3. *Other Lunar Dynasties*

The Yādavas: Contemporaneous with king Sagara of Ayodhyā was Vidarbha of the Yādavas, who sought peace with the Ayodhyā king, advancing south-westward, by offering his daughter Keśinī in marriage to the latter. King Vidarbha then retired towards the Deccan into the country named after him, leaving the whole of northern India to acknowledge the suzerainty of Sagara. After Sagara's death, the Yādavas of Vidarbha extended their authority northward over the Haihaya country. The three sons of Vidarbha founded three sub-lines. Kratha or Bhīma, the eldest, continued the main line. The second son Kaiśika became king of Chedi and founded the Chedi line.[23] The location of the territories of the youngest son Lomapāda has not been given.

The Ānavas: The Ānava kingdom in the east founded by Titikshu appears to have been considerably expanded by the time of king Bali of the Ānavas, a contemporary of Sagara, and was subsequently divided among his five sons, Aṅga, Vaṅga, Kaliṅga, Puṇḍra, and Suhma, who were begotten by the sage Dīrghatamas Māmateya on queen Sudeshṇā at Bali's request. The capital of Aṅga was Mālinī, four miles west of Bhāgalpur. Separated from Magadha by the river Champā, Aṅga comprised the modern districts of Bhāgalpur and Monghyr. Vaṅga was further east corresponding to the modern Dacca and Chittagong Divisions. Puṇḍra was Northern Bengal. Suhma comprised the Burdwān Division, and Kaliṅga, the sea-coast of Orissa including the Northern Circārs.

Kānyakubja: A few generations after Jahnu, came Kuśika the originator of the Kuśikas. Kuśika's son from Paurukutsī, Purukutsa's descendant in about the sixth degree, was Gādhi. Gādhi is described as an incarnation of Indra, which probably means that he had an alternative title such as Indra or one of his synonyms. Gādhi's daughter Satyavatī, as already stated, was given in marriage to the Bhṛigu sage Ṛichīka Aurva. Through Ṛichīka's favour, Gādhi had a son Viśvaratha or Viśvāmitra who is a prominent figure in ancient legends. Convinced of the superiority of the spiritual power of Brahmanism by being worsted in his attempts to deprive Vasishṭha of his sacred cow, he resolved on attaining Brahmanism, and set out for austerities after renouncing his kingdom. Eventually, he succeeded in winning recognition as a Brāhmaṇa or Brahmarshi even from Vasishṭha. Then, Viśvāmitra is said to have championed the cause of Satyavrata Triśaṅku in opposition to Vasishṭha, and raised Triśaṅku to divine celebrity. Further, Viśvāmitra is said to have harassed Hariśchandra, Triśaṅku's son, in order to test Vasishṭha's praise of him as unrivalled in virtues. Viśvāmitra, again, is said to have slain Śakti and other Vasishṭhas through Saudāsas, i.e. descendants of Sudās. Then Viśvāmitra is spoken of as having adopted Śunaḥśepa as a son whom he saved from being offered as a substitute victim for Hariśchandra's son Rohita. Viśvāmitra further appears in connection with Rāma of Ayodhyā, and also as father of Śakuntalā who was married to Paurava Dushyanta and gave birth to the celebrated emperor Bharata. The Purāṇas further show that the rivalry between Viśvāmitra and Vasishṭha is not only endless but hereditary.

It appears that the Purāṇas combine the various accounts of different Viśvāmitras and roll them into one. For instance, Viśvāmitra, the father of Śakuntalā, Viśvāmitra, the contemporary of Rāma, and Viśvāmitra, the contemporary of Hariśchandra, Jamadagni, Śunaḥśepa and of Sudās, Kavaśa Ailūsha and the Dāśarājña were quite distinct personalities. The heroes of different episodes, relating to widely distant ages, have been unified into a single personality in the Purāṇas, and this has caused a good deal of chronological confusion and genealogical chaos.

Viśvāmitra, the Kānyakubja king, was related to Jamadagni and Paraśurāma. It is therefore likely that the Kānyakubja kingdom helped the confederacy raised by Paraśurāma against the Haihayas. Viśvāmitra ruled for some time, and as the result of his discomfiture at the hands of Vasishṭha, relinquished his kingdom and left for austerities in a forest leaving his family in a hermitage near Ayodhyā. Viśvāmitra saved Sunaḥśepa, son of Ajīgarta, who was being sacrificed as a substitute for Rohita, son of Hariśchandra, and adopted him, after renaming him Devarāta. Viśvāmitra's sons did not accept Devarāta's headship, and so Viśvāmitra cursed them to become Mlechchhas such as Andhras, Puṇḍras, and Śabaras. Ashṭaka probably succeeded Viśvāmitra on the Kānyakubja throne.

Kāśī: Pratardana (the son of Divodāsa) or his son Vatsa extended his sway further, and annexed the country around Kauśāmbi which came to be named the Vatsa country. Vatsa's son Alarka regained the capital Vārāṇasī from the Rākshasas who had occupied the city since the days of Bhadraśreṇya and re-established it as the Kāśi capital. Alarka had a long and prosperous reign.

4. *The Solar Dynasty*

Ayodhyā: After the rise of the realm to great heights in the reigns of Māndhātṛi, Purukutsa, and Trasadasyu, the empire appears to have remained, if at all, merely in name, and we do not meet with any important king till we come to Trayyāruṇa, Satyavrata-Triśaṅku, and Hariśchandra. Satyavrata--Triśaṅku is the subject of numerous fantastic tales in the Purāṇas[24] Being expelled by his father at the instance of his family priest on account of some excesses, the prince is said to have led the life of a Chaṇḍāla wandering in the woods on the banks of the Ganges for twelve years. Trayyāruṇa died in the meanwhile, but Triśaṅku was not recalled. There was a great famine lasting for nine years during the time of Triśaṅku's exile. While in the forest, Triśaṅku supported the family of Viśvāmitra which was starving, when Viśvāmitra, after renouncing the kingdom, had gone to the forest to perform penance. Viśvāmitra learnt of the generosity of the prince after his return, and in gratitude, as also in order to defeat his antagonist Vasishṭha, got Triśaṅku installed on the Ayodhyā throne. Triśaṅku was succeeded by Hariśchandra, the embodiment of truth. He was a *samrāṭ* and is said to have performed the Rājasūya. The story of Hariśchandra, whose truthfulness was put to very severe tests by Viśvāmitra, is well known. Hariśchandra's son Rohita is said to have built Rohitapura.[25] Rohita's younger son Champa built Champāpurī near Bhāgalpur in east Bihār. Sixth in descent from Hariśchandra was Bāhu. Sagara, so named because he was born with the poison which his step-mother administered to his mother, was born posthumously to Bāhu in the hermitage of the sage Aurva. Sagara was taught archery by the sage Aurva, who specially instructed him in the celebrated Āgneyāstra. The foreign tribes, who came in the train of the Haihayas (*ante*, p, 289 ff.) and settled down in Ayodhyā, were called Kshatriyas. They respected Brāhmaṇas, observed Brahmanic rites and rituals, and retained Vasishṭha as their priest. They remained in possession of Ayodhyā for over twenty years till Sagara attained maturity.

Sagara had to pass through Madhyadeśa and Central India to lead an expedition against the Haihayas. After destroying them Sagara led his conquering hordes against their hardy outlandish allies, the Śakas, Yavanas, Kambojas, etc. He would have completely crushed them but for the intercession of his priest Vasishṭha with whom they sought refuge. Sagara then let them off after imposing on them certain signs of symbolical defeat and disgrace; the Śakas were made to shave only half their heads, Kambojas to have their heads completely shaved, Pāradas were forbidden to shave or trim the hair of their heads, and Pahlavas to shave their beards, thus rendering them unfit for Vedic ceremonials.[26] The story seeks to interpret, in the manner of the Purāṇas, the peculiar customs of these peoples who were becoming Kshatriyas under the priestly guidance of the Vasishṭhas. Sagara's name is connected with the ocean (*sāgara*) in a fantastic legend which states that the ocean became Sagara's son.[27]

Sagara subjected all contemporary powers and was the emperor of the whole of the north. The only important kingdoms to survive Sagara's onslaughts appear to be Videha, Vaiśālī and Ānava in the east, the Vidarbhas and the Yādava branch on the river Chambal in the south, Kāśi in the Madhyadeśa and Turvasus in the hilly tracts of Rewah. Sagara's eldest son Asamañjas, being cruel to the citizens, was discarded, and the latter's son Aṁśumant succeeded him.

Vaiśālī: Karandhama, king of Vaiśālī, is said to have been besieged by a confederacy of kings whom at last he defeated. He also rescued his son Avīkshit, who was captured by the king of Vidiśā (probably a Haihaya chieftain) and his allies after a great conflict, and dealt them a severe blow. Marutta, one of the sixteen universal monarchs of antiquity, was born to Avīkshit from Viśālā, daughter of the Vidiśā king. Marutta was a ceaseless and tireless performer of sacrifices. He had thousands of vessels, sacrificial utensils, etc., made of gold. Despite his great valour, Marutta had immense troubles from the Nāgas. He was determined to exterminate them completely by setting fire to their habitations, though they took refuge with his father; but, when the Nāgas restored to life the *Ṛishis* killed by them by means of herbs and by sucking out the poison. he let them off. According to Pargiter, these enemies were really the Haihayas, and Marutta deserves credit for ending the Haihaya aggressions permanently in the east.[28]

5. *Brāhmaṇa Families*

As noted above, the Bhṛigus or Bhārgavas practically dominated the whole epoch, and Ṛichika, Jamadagni, Paraśurāma, and Agni Aurva were the prominent Bhārgavas.

Ayāsya is the first Aṅgiras mentioned in traditional history, and he officiated as a priest at the sacrificial ceremony of offering Śunaḥśepa as a victim in the reign of Hariśchandra of Ayodhyā. The Aṅgirasas are found in connection with the Vaiśāla kings as their hereditary priests. Uśija Aṅgiras was the priest of Karandhama and Avīkshit, and two of his sons, Bṛihaspati and Saṁvarta officiated for Marutta Āvīkshita. Uchathya, the eldest son of Uśija, had by his wife Mamatā a son named Dīrghatamas, who was born blind.

Dīrghatamas was expelled for gross misconduct and set adrift in the Ganges, where after floating some distance downstream, he was rescued by king Bali of the Eastern Ānavas. At Bali's desire, he begot five sons on Bali's queen, as mentioned above (p. 290). Dīrghatamas is later said to have regained his sight. Towards the end of his life, Dīrghatamas consecrated king Bharata of the Pauravas. Bṛihaspati had a son Bharadvāja, who moved to Kāśi and became priest to king Divodāsa. His son Vitatha was adopted by Bharata and he continued the Paurava line.

Datta Ātreya, who was propitiated by Haihaya Arjuna, was the only prominent figure among the Atris.

Devarāj Vasishṭha was a priest of the Ayodhyā kings during the reigns of Trayyāruṇa and Satyavrata. His descendant officiated for the foreign Śakas, Yavanas, etc. and later became priest to Sagara. Another Vasishṭha was Āpava, in the Himālayas, whose hermitage was burnt by Haihaya Arjuna.

Kaśyapa, who officiated as priest at the sacrifice of Rāma Jāmadagnya and to whom the latter donated the whole earth, is the earliest Kaśyapa mentioned in traditional history. He is later said to have expelled Rāma from the earth as noted above (p. 287).

The only historical figure among the Agastyas is the Agastya who married Lopāmudrā and was a contemporary of Alarka, grandson of Pratardana of Kāśi.

With the wars of Paraśurāma and Sagara described above, the Kṛitayuga, according to the Purāṇas, came to an end. As the result of these wars, the old kingdoms of the Pauravas, Kānyakubjas, Druhyus, and Ānavas in the Punjab gradually disappear. The Yādavas recede into the Deccan, while the Haihayas are completely routed. The eastern kingdom of Vaiśālī, Videha, Ayodhyā, Kāśi and the Ānavas in Bengal continue to exist during the next period.

8. THE RĀMACHANDRA PERIOD (c. 2350-1950 B.C.)

1. *The Solar Dynasty*

There was some setback to Ayodhyā after Sagara's death. Sagara was succeeded by his grandson Aṁśumant. The dynasty again rose to prominence under Aṁśumant's second successor Bhagīratha, and the latter's third successor Ambarīsha Nābhāgi. Bhagīratha is included in the list of sixteen famous kings and is celebrated as a *chakravartin* and a *samrāṭ*, as also one who gained fame by his gifts of cattle. He was a devotee of Śiva. He is reputed to have brought down the sacred river Ganges (which is known as Bhāgīrathī after him)[29] from the heavens, through the power of his penance, in order to liberate his ancestors cursed by Kapila. The fable perhaps indicates that Bhagīratha was the originator of the worship of the Ganges, or more plausibly, it may have some reference to the canals dug by him from the Himālayas. Ambarīsha was a powerful monarch and in his reign Ayodhyā rose into prominence. The legends about his connection with the Bhāgavata cult and the Dvādaśī vow are later creations. His third successor was Ṛituparṇa who figures in the well-known Nala episode.[30] Ṛituparṇa's son Sudāsa has been identified with the Vedic Sudās of the *Dāśarājña* by some scholars; but beyond mere similarity of names, there is nothing in support of this identification. Around Sudāsa's son Mitrasaha has grown a cluster of wild and fantastic legends, invented perhaps to explain his second name Kalmāshapāda. The king is said to have served human flesh through mistake to his preceptor Vasishṭha who doomed the king to become a Rākshasa; but on realizing that the king was not at fault, the sage limited the duration of his curse to only twelve years. The king, in his turn, prepared to curse his *guru*, but at the intercession of his queen, threw the *mantra*-charmed water over his own feet, because throwing it on the ground would have rendered the earth barren for years. But the charmed water turned his feet into stone, which led to his being called Kalmāshapāda.[31] After Kalmāshapāda resumed his natural state, he had, on account of a curse, to raise issue from his wife by a *Niyoga* or levirate union with Vasishṭha. Aśmaka, the son of the union, founded the city Paudanya.[32] Aśmaka had a son named Mūlaka, who later came to be called Nārīkavacha because it is said he sought protection among the women-folk through fear of Paraśurāma. But Paraśurāma flourished generations before Aśmaka, and the story has no chronological value. Probably it refers to the disturbed state of the kingdom after the days of Kalmāshapāda when his successors were weaklings, and during this period, when the Bharatas and Pañchālas were at the height of their power, the Ayodhyā kings appear to have suffered reverses as the result of which Mūlaka was to be brought up in secret. It appears that there was a bifurcation in the Ayodhyā line for some six or seven generations after Kalmāshapāda's time. The two lines, however, were united in a single monarchy under Khaṭvāṅga, also known as Dilīpa II. He was a great *samrāṭ* and a *chakravartin*, and is said to have helped the gods in their fight against the Asuras. He was a great devotee of Vishṇu, and had a son named Raghu. The Ikshvāku dynasty came to be called Raghuvaṁśa on account of this celebrated Raghu. He conquered the whole earth and performed the Viśvajit sacrifice. Being an ideal monarch, Raghu has been called the first king of Ayodhyā. Raghu was succeeded by his son Aja, the consort of the Vidarbha princess Indumatī, to whom was born Daśaratha. Daśaratha was a valiant and all-conquering monarch who led his victorious campaigns throughout the length and breadth of North India, and spread the Aryan culture far and wide. The Yādava contemporary of Daśaratha was Madhu who had consolidated the Yādava kingdom, and the contemporary Pauravas held at least four states in the Ganges-Jumna Doāb, with the north Pañchāla branch specially prominent. The Kosala kingdom at the time of Daśaratha was bounded on the east by Videha, Vaiśālī and Aṅga; the Vatsa country which formed part of Kāśi lay to its south; it was bounded on the west by the Paurava principalities of north and south Pañchāla, the main Hastinapura realm, and one more Paurava kingdom between north Pañchāla and Kosala. The region south from the Jumna up to Gujarāt and beyond the Vindhya and the Satpura mountains was under Yādava domination with the emperor Madhu at the helm.

Besides his three principal queens, viz. Kausalyā, Sumitrā and Kaikeyī, Daśaratha had a number of other wives. Daśaratha had married Kaikeyī on the stipulation that the son born of her was to succeed him. He had a daughter Śāntā whom he gave in adoption to the Aṅga king Lomapāda. Being without an heir for a long time, Daśaratha performed Putrakāmeshṭi (rite for securing male issue) on the advice of Vasishṭha under the guidance of Ṛishyaśṛiṅga, who was married to Śāntā. As a result, four sons were born to Daśaratha, viz. Rāma to Kausalyā, Bharata to Kaikeyī and Lakshmaṇa and Śatrughna to Sumitrā. Rāma and Lakshmaṇa obtained instruction in the science of archery from Viśvāmitra and they helped him in the performance of a sacrifice by vanquishing the horde of Rākshasas that disturbed him. Then Viśvāmitra took the princes to Mithilā, where Rāma fulfilled the conditions and was married to Sītā. It is later on when Daśaratha proposed to instal Rāma as crown prince that the main story of Rāma, as recorded in the *Rāmāyaṇa*, may be said to begin.[33]

The story of Rāma is particularly important as it brings South India definitely into view for the first time. Various have been the theories and interpretations about the *Rāmāyaṇa*, and the text of the epic has been subjected to interpolations and additions in every stage of its career. But despite its accretions, mythological and fabulous legends, etc., the text can be made to yield historical facts. When preparations were made to instal Rāma, the eldest son, as heir apparent, palace intrigues set in, and his step-mother Kaikeyī secured through Daśaratha the banishment of Rāma along with Sītā and Lakshmaṇa to the Daṇḍaka forest for fourteen years. Daṇḍaka in these days was a great impenetrable forest save for a few patches here and there occupied by Aryan adventurers. Rāma first went to Prayāga and from there south-west to the region of Bhopāl, whence he proceeded south across the Narmadā and then probably to the Chhattisgarh district, where he dwelt for ten years. Thereafter he went south to the middle of the Godāvari in the province called Janasthāna, which was a colony of the Rākshasas, who had intercourse with their kingdom in Ceylon. The Rākshasas ill-treated the *Munis* (sages) and Rāma espoused the latters' cause and killed a number of Rākshasas. In revenge Rāvaṇa, the Rākshasa king, carried away Sītā to Ceylon. Rāma proceeded south in quest of Sītā, came to lake Pampā and Ṛishyamūka Parvata, where he made friends with Sugrīva, the king of the Vānaras, who was expelled by his brother Vālin. Rāma killed Vālin and reinstated Sugrīva on the throne. With the aid of the Vānara army and chiefs, Rāma invaded Ceylon, defeated the Rākshasas, killed Rāvaṇa and recovered Sīta. He placed Bibhīshaṇa, younger brother of Rāvaṇa, on the throne in Ceylon and returned to Ayodhyā.

Bharata acted as regent during Rāma's exile. Rāma was crowned after his return to Ayodhyā, and reigned prosperously for many years.

The story of Rāma, divested of its miraculous, fabulous, incredible and mythological elements, clearly indicates that he was a great king who spread Aryan ideas and institutions into regions far and wide. "Rāma's rule" is still proverbial for the Golden Age.

Rāma's younger brothers ruled over different provinces. Lakshmaṇa had two sons, Aṅgada and Chandraketu, and they were assigned two countries in Kārapatha-deśa near the Himālayas, with their respective capitals at Aṅgadiyā and Chandrachakrā. Bharata apparently got the Kekaya kingdom which was the province of his mother, and also Sindhu, i.e. Upper Sind. His two sons, Taksha and Pushkara, conquered Gāndhāra from the Gandharvas, and founded respectively Takshaśilā and Pushkarāvatī.[34] Śatrughna fought the Sātvata-Yādavas on the west of the Jumna and killed Mādhava Lavaṇa, son of Madhu. He established his capital at Madhupurī or Madhurā re-naming it as Mathurā, and his son Subāhu reigned there. Rāma had two sons, Kuśa and Lava, born of Sītā in the hermitage of Vālmīki after Rāma had deserted her in deference to public opinion. Kuśa succeeded Rāma in the Ayodhyā kingdom, while Lava got the northern portion of Kosala with Śrāvastī as capital.

These collateral kingdoms, however, appear to have come to an end soon. The two Gāndhāra states are not mentioned any further, and probably were amalgamated by the neighbouring Druhyus. Śatrughna's sons were expelled from Mathurā by the Yādava king Bhīma Sātvata, and Mathurā became a Yādava principality. No further account is given of the territories of Lakshmaṇa's sons nor of Lava's kingdom. Ayodhyā sinks into insignificance hereafter in traditional history, the chief rôles being played only by the Pauravas and the Yādavas.

Videha: Sīradhvaja, the father of Sītā, was one of the most celebrated of the Janakas. King Sudhanvan of Sāṅkishya demanded the hand of Sītā in marriage from Sīradhvaja, but the latter killed Sudhanvan in a fierce battle and installed his own brother Kuśadhvaja on the Sāṅkishya throne. Sīradhvaja's daughters, Sītā and Urmilā were married respectively to Rāma and Lakshmaṇa, sons of Daśaratha, and Kuśadhvaja's daughters Māṇḍavī and Śrutakīrti, respectively to Bharata and Śatrughna.

Vaiśālī: Marutta's son Narishyanta is said to have performed a grand sacrifice, and he was a great donor. His son Dama was a great warrior who won a Dasarna princess after defeating rival kings in a Svayaṁvara. A few generations after Dama came Tṛiṇabindu, who is said to have ruled during the third quarter of the Tretā Age. Tṛiṇabindu married Alambushā and had a son Viśāla and a daughter Ilavilā. Ilavilā was given in marriage to Pulastya, and their son was Viśravas Ailavila. Viśāla is credited with the foundation of the capital Viśālā, and so this kingdom came to be called Vaiśālī (a name hitherto used in anticipation). Pramati or Sumati, the last name in the list, was a contemporary of Daśaratha.

2. *The Lunar Dynasty*

Pauravas: Dushyanta, the Paurava hero, appears to have flourished about a couple of generations subsequent to king Sagara of Ayodhyā. Dushyanta was adopted as heir by the Turvasu king Marutta who had no son, so that the Turvasu line merged into the Pauravas. The central power of the Ikshvākus became weak after Sagara's death, and Dushyanta took that opportunity of recovering his ancestral kingdom. Dushyanta also revived the dynasty and hence is styled its Vaṁśakara. He married Viśvāmitra's daughter Śakuntalā who was brought up in the hermitage of one Kaṇva of the Kaśyapa family, and his son was the celebrated prince Bharata.

Bharata, also known as Damana or Sarvadamana, performed a number of sacrifices on the Ganges and the Jumna with the aid of Dīrghatamas Māmateya. He also sacrificed on the Sarasvatī. He was a great conqueror and *samrāṭ* with a wide sway. He extended his dominions northward and his territories stretched from the Sarasvatī to the Ganges. The Paurava dynasty came to be called Bharatas after the time of Bharata. It was probably during Bharata's regime that the headquarters of the state were shifted from Pratishṭhāna to the city, called later Hastināpura, after his successor Hastin. According to some accounts, Bharata gave his name to our country which was henceforth called Bhāratavarsha. Bharata was disappointed in his sons and killed them. He propitiated the Maruts in order to obtain an heir and they gave him Bṛihaspati's son Bharadvāja as an adopted son. Bharadvāja's son Vitatha, however, succeeded Bharata. Hastin, the fifth successor from Bharata, had two sons Ajamīḍha and Dvimīḍha under whom the Paurava realm extended and fresh kingdoms were founded. Ajamīḍha, the elder, continued the main line at Hastināpura and Dvimīḍha founded the Dvimīḍha dynasty in the modern district of Bareilly. Ajamīḍha had three sons, viz. Ṛiksha, Nīla, and Bṛihadvasu. On Ajamīḍha's death, the main Paurava realm was divided among these sons, Riksha succeeding his father at Hastināpura in the main line, which remained the Paurava line, and Nīla and Bṛihadvasu founded what later came to be known respectively as the north Pañchāla and south Pañchāla dynasties.[35]

The country came to be known as Pañchāla from the "five" sons of Bhṛimyaśva (the sixth successor from Ajamīḍha) who were jocosely nicknamed "capable" (*pañcha alam*). The Pañchālas, thus, were a branch of the Bharatas. The name suggests an amalgamation of five tribes, and there has been some speculation as to which particular tribes went to form the Pañchālas. The Pañchāla kingdom was divided between the five sons of Bhṛimyaśva, each of them receiving a small principality. Mudgala, the eldest, founded an important branch. Vadhryaśva, the grandson of Mudgala, extended the kingdom, and his son Divodāsa further augmented it. Pargiter and other scholars identify this Divodāsa and his descendant Somadatta-Sudāsa with their Vedic namesakes, the latter of whom was the chief participant in the celebrated battle of ten kings.[36]

Yādavas: Kratha-Bhīma continued the main Yādava line of Vidarbha, and Kaiśika, his younger brother, was the progenitor of the Chedis. The most important king of Vidarbha was Bhīmaratha, father of the celebrated Damayantī, who was married to Nala of Nishadha. Madhu, who came about ten generations after Bhīmaratha, appears to have consolidated the small Yādava principalities into which the Yādavas were divided before him. Madhu's son Lavaṇa was killed by Śatrughna, who installed his own son Subāhu in Mathurā. But Subāhu was ousted by Bhīma Sātvata, son of Satvat, who was Madhu's fifth successor.

Eastern Ānavas: We do not know any particulars about the kings in the Aṅga genealogy till we come to Lomapāda, who is placed seventh in the genealogical list. Lomapāda was a well-known archer and a great friend of king Daśaratha of Ayodhyā, the father of Rāma. Lomapāda was childless and adopted Śāntā, the daughter of king Daśaratha. Śāntā was married to Ṛishyaśṛiṅga who performed the Putrakāmeshṭi sacrifice for Lomapāda as the result of which Lomapāda got a son nāmed Chaturaṅga. Lomapāda's great-grandson Champa gave the name Champā to the Aṅga capital, which was till then known as Mālinī.

Kāśi: King Alarka, who finally drove the Rākshasas from Benares and re-established his capital there, is said to have been born to Ṛitudhvaja (another name of Vatsa) from Madālasā. Alarka was a spiritually-minded king and relinquished the kingdom in favour of his brother when the latter invaded it. Alarka was succeeded by his son Sannati.

3. *Brāhmaṇa Families*

Among the Bhārgavas during this period, appears Vālmīki of the *Rāmāyaṇa*, who was called Prāchetasa.

The father of Śakuntalā was an important Viśvāmitra in this period, and another appears as the contemporary and rival of Vasishṭha, the priest of Mitrasaha-Kalmāshapāda.

9. THE KṚISHṆA PERIOD (*c.* 1950-1400 B.C.)

With the coronation of Rāma as king of Ayodhyā after the destruction of the Rākshasas began the Dvāpara age which ended with the Bhārata War. During this period it is only the Pañchālas, Pauravas, and Yādavas that prominently figure in traditional history, while Ayodhyā and others sink into the background.

1. *Pañchālas*

The North Pañchāla power rose into prominence during the reign of Sudāsa who made extensive conquests. He defeated the Paurava king Saṁvaraṇa and conquered his kingdom. Sudāsa was succeeded by his son Sahadeva and grandson Somaka, but the fortunes of the Pañchālas waned after the time of Sudāsa. Saṁvaraṇa, the Paurava king, had recovered his territory probably from Somaka, and later, king Ugrāyudha of the Dvimīḍhas killed the North Pañchāla king (probably the grand-father of Pṛishata) and annexed his realm. Pṛishata, the exiled North Pañchāla claimant, sought refuge in Kāmpilya of South Pañchāla. Ugrāyudha then attacked the Pauravas after Śantanu's death, but was defeated and killed by Bhīshma, who restored Pṛishata to his ancestral kingdom of Ahichchhatra. Drupada succeeded his father Pṛishata in North Pañchāla. Droṇa, a fellow student, whom Drupada had insulted, defeated the latter with the aid of the young Pāṇḍu and Kuru princes who were his disciples. Out of both the North and South Pañchālas which he thus conquered, Droṇa kept North Pañchāla for himself and gave South Pañchāla to Drupada. The Somakas and Sṛiñjayas, the remnants of the Pañchālas, appear to have joined Drupada as they accompanied him in the great Bhārata War. Drupada performed penance in order to get a son who would avenge his defeat by Droṇa and kill him, and Dhṛishṭadyumna was born as the result. The Pañchālas played a very important part in the age of the Bhārata War. The Pāṇḍavas married Draupadī, the Pañchāla princess, daughter of Drupada, and the Pañchālas were the staunch supporters of the Pāṇḍavas.

Brahmadatta seems to have been an important king among the South Pañchālas. Tradition connects him with the revision and rearrangement of Vedic and exegetical texts. He fixed the Kramapāṭha of the *Ṛigveda* and of the *Atharvaveda*, and his minister Kaṇḍarīka of the *Sāmaveda*. Brahmadatta's great-grandson Janamejaya Durbuddhi, the last king, was a tyrant and was killed by Ugrāyudha of the Dvimīḍhas, and the dynasty came to an end.

2. *Pauravas*

As noted above, the Pañchāla king Sudāsa overthrew Saṁvaraṇa, the Paurava king. The latter fled to Sind and then recovered his kingdom through Vasishṭha's help.[37] Saṁvaraṇa had by Tapatī a son named Kuru, who was a renowned king raising the Paurava realm to great eminence. Kuru is said to have sacrificed at Prayāga which indicates that he extended his sway up to that place after subduing the intervening South Pañchāla territory. Kurukshetra and Kurujāṅgala, the cultivated and uncultivated portions, respectively. of Kuru's territory, have been regarded by Pargiter as being named after this Kuru.[38] Kuru was celebrated for his righteous rule, and Kurukshetra was regarded as a religious place. He was so much esteemed that his successors were called Kurus or Kauravas after him, the term sometimes being applied also to the people of the realm.

There is some confusion in the Puranic texts with regard to Kuru's immediate successors. The collated text[39] suggests that Kuru had three sons, Parīkshit, the eldest, Jahnu, and Sudhanvan. Parīkshit had Janamejaya as his son, and the latter's sons were Śrutasena, Ugrasena, and Bhīmasena; but nothing further is said about them. The accounts then pass on to Jahnu's son Suratha and his descendants, who thus appear to have continued the main Paurava (or Kuru) line. The succession of Jahnu's son Suratha on the main line indicates that Janamejaya's branch lost the sovereignty. A story is told how Janamejaya lost his throne.[40] Janamejaya injured the sage Gārgya's son and was cursed by Gārgya. Indrota Daivāpa Śaunaka performed a horse-sacrifice for him, which absolved him of his sin, but he could not recover his sovereignty and hence his three sons do not appear in the accounts.

The line of Sudhanvan, the youngest son of Kuru, bifurcated into the Chedi and the Magadha branches, founded by his fourth successor Vasu. The kingdom held by the main Paurava line appears to have declined, and there was no ruler in this line to revive the Kaurava fortunes till the time of Pratīpa, who was a famous ruler. Pratīpa had three sons, Devāpi, Bāhlīka, and Śantanu. The eldest Devāpi was a leper, and hence could not become a ruler. The second Bāhlīka resigned in favour of Śantanu, who thus succeeded Pratīpa. The epic gives various legends about Śantanu. Śantanu married Gaṅgā, and Bhīshma was born to them. Bhīshma, whose original name was Devavrata, vowed to remain celibate all his life and renounced his right to the throne in favour of his younger brothers in order to enable his father to marry Satyavatī. Bhīshma is a celebrated figure in the galaxy of Indian heroes. He was a great warrior, an able administrator and well versed in politics, science of war, etc. Ugrāyudha of the Dvimīḍhas attacked the Kauravas but, as noted above, Bhīshma killed him and reinstated Pṛishata, the son of the late ruler of North Pañchālas, whom Ugrāyudha had driven out.

To Śantanu were born Chitrāṅgada and Vichitravīrya from Satyavatī. Chitrāṅgada was killed while fighting against the Gandharvas and Vichitravīrya succeeded him on the throne. But Vichitravīrya died young without leaving any issue, and the queen of Vichitravīrya had through *Niyoga* (levirate) two sons from Vyāsa, viz. Dhṛitarāshṭra and Pāṇḍu. Dhṛitarāshṭra, the elder, being born blind, Pāṇḍu was crowned king of Hastināpura while the veteran Bhīshma looked to the affairs of state. Dhṛitarāshṭra married Gāndhārī, and had by her a hundred sons, chief of whom were Duryodhana, Duḥśāsana, etc. Pāṇḍu married Kuntī or Pṛithā, daughter of Kuntibhoja and an aunt of Kṛishṇa, and Mādrī, sister of Śalya, the Vāhīka king. After his marriage with Mādrī, Pāṇḍu started on his campaign of conquest. He vanquished the Daśarṇas, the kings of Mithilā, Kāśi, Suhma, and Puṇḍra and extended the Kuru dominions.[41] While engaged in hunting, Pāṇḍu killed a sage in the form of deer and was cursed. In repentance, Pāṇḍu left his kingdom and went along with his wives to the Himālayas for performing penance. There Kuntī gave birth to Yudhishṭhira, Bhīma, and Arjuna who are, in reality, said to be respectively the sons of Yama, Vāyu, and Indra; and Mādrī, to the twins Nakula and Sahadeva from the Aśvins. Pāṇḍu died in the hermitage, and Mādrī, burnt herself along with him on his funeral pyre. Thereafter, Kuntī returned to Hastināpura along with the five sons. Dhṛitarāshṭra assumed the reins of government in the meanwhile and appointed Yudhishṭhira, the first-born among the Kuru family, as the crown prince. Though the sons of both Dhṛitarāshṭra and Pāṇḍu were Kauravas, the term was restricted to the sons of Dhṛitarāshṭra, and Pāṇḍu's sons were called Pāṇḍavas.

Chedi and Magadha: Vasu, the fourth successor of Sudhanvan, conquered the Chedi kingdom from the Yādavas and founded a dynasty there, whence he obtained the epithet Chaidyoparichara (overcomer of Chaidyas). His capital Śuktimatī lay on the river Śuktimatī (the Ken). Vasu was a *samrāṭ* and a *chakravartin* and extended his sway over adjoining Magadha, and possibly over Matsya also. He had five sons, among whom he divided his territory, establishing them in separate kingdoms. Magadha came as the share of his eldest son Bṛihadratha. Kuśa was given Kausambī, Yadu had Karūsha, and Pratyagraha got Chedi. Probably the last son got Matsya which adjoined Chedi in the north-west.

With Bṛihadratha establishing himself in Magadha, with Girivraja as his capital, and founding the famous Bārhadratha dynasty, Magadha becomes a prominent factor in traditional history. Jarāsandha in the Bārhadratha line was a very powerful king, and under him Magadha rose to great prominence. He extended his territories as far away as Mathurā, where Kaṁsa, the Yādava king, who was his son-in-law, accepted his suzerainty. Kaṁsa tyrannized over his people and was killed by Kṛishṇa who placed Ugrasena on the Mathurā throne. Enraged at this, Jarāsandha led many a campaign against Kṛishṇa and the Bhojas of Mathurā, defeating them several times. Though the Yādavas could withstand Jarāsandha for a time, they decided to migrate in a body south-westward as they were afraid of a complete rout at his hands. They then established themselves in the west coast with their head-quarters at Dvārakā under Kṛishṇa. Jarāsandha was killed by Bhīma, the Pāṇḍava, and his son Sahadeva became an ally of the Pāṇḍavas.

3. *Yādavas*

The large Yādava kingdom ruled over by Bhīma Sātvata was divided among his four sons, Bhajamāna, Devāvṛidha, Andhaka, and Vṛishṇi. Bhajamāna's descendants appear to have attained no distinction. Devāvṛidha was connected with the river Parṇāśa (Banās in West Mālwā), and his descendants were the Bhojas of Mārttikāvata, apparently in Śālva country around Mount Abu. Andhaka, who reigned at Mathurā, had four sons, but only Kukura and Bhajamāna are important. From Kukura were descended the Kukuras who formed the main dynasty down to Kaṁsa. Bhajamāna's descendants were known as Andhakas, and they ruled somewhere near Mathūrā. An important king in the line was Kṛitavarmā, the son of Hṛidika, who fought on the side of Duryodhana and was one of the three on the Kauravas' side who survived the Bhārata War. Thereafter, he went to Dvārakā and later was killed by Sātyaki in the fateful fratricidal struggle that brought the downfall of the Yādavas. Vṛishṇi had at least four sons, the eldest and the youngest having the same name Anamitra. From them arose numerous families. From Anamitra or Sumitra, the eldest, was born Nighna, and his sons Prasena and Satrājit succeeded him. Satrājit is a well-known figure in the Syamantaka legend connected with Kṛishṇa, and was the father of Satyabhāmā, one of the eight principal queens of Kṛishṇa. Devamīḍhusha in the line married an Ikshvāku princess named Aśmakī and a son named Śūra was born to him. From Śūra and his queen, a Bhoja princess named Mārīshā, were born ten sons and five daughters including Vasudeva who was the eldest, and Pṛitha, Śrutadevā, and Śrutaśravā. Pṛithā was adopted by the old king Kuntibhoja from whom she came to be known as Kuntī. She married the Paurava prince Pāṇḍu, and was the mother of elder Pāṇḍavas. Śrutadevā married a Kārūsha king named Vṛiddhaśarmā. Śrutaśravā was given to the Chedi king Damaghosha, and Śiśupāla was born to them. Vasudeva married the seven daughters (Devakī, etc.) of king Devaka of the

Kukuras, and Balarāma and Kṛishṇa were the sons of Vasudeva. Vasudeva's daughter Subhadrā married Arjuna, the Pāṇḍava, to whom Abhimanyu was born from her. Abhimanyu's son was Parīkshit who occupied the Hastināpura throne after the Bhārata War. The descendants of Anamitra, the youngest son of Vṛishṇi by Mādrī, are called Śainyas through his son Śini. Sātyaki and Yuyudhāna were born in this family.

Āhuka among the Kukuras had, by a Kāśi princess, Devaka, Ugrasena, and other sons. Devaka had four sons and seven daughters (Devakī, etc.). Kṛishṇa was born of Devakī. Ugrasena had nine sons and five daughters, Kaṁsa being the eldest. Kaṁsa usurped the throne after imprisoning his father. Vasudeva was his minister. Kaṁsa killed seven children of his cousin Devakī, relying on a prediction that her eighth issue was destined to be his slayer. Kṛishṇa and Balarāma were brought up in Gokula and Vṛindāvana. Kṛishṇa killed Kaṁsa and reinstated Ugrasena on the Mathurā kingdom as already stated.

Kṛishṇa being the central figure in this epoch, we shall briefly deal with his life and historicity.[42] Kṛishṇa was born in the prison cell at Mathurā, but immediately after birth was removed to Gokula on the other side of the Jumna with the aid of the prison warders and others who were dissatisfied with the tyrant Kaṁsa. He was brought up in Gokula as the child of Nanda and Yaśodā, whose daughter was substituted for Kṛishṇa and was later killed by Kaṁsa. As a child, Kṛishṇa appears to have been endowed with extraordinary gifts and passed through many adventures. His childhood was spent in Gokula and various incidents connected with his youth are recorded in the Purāṇas and other texts. The incidents are presented in the garb of myths and miracles, but there may be a real basis for some of them. A few years after Kṛishṇa's birth, the cowherds left Gokula on account of an onrush of ferocious wolves and settled in Vṛindāvana, where Kṛishṇa subjugated Kāliya, a Nāga chief, and ordered him to leave the place with his tribe. In Vṛindāvana, in place of the usual Indrayajña, Kṛishṇa established the practice of worshipping nature. Kṛishṇa's extraordinary exploits, widespread popularity, and great fame reached the ears of Kaṁsa, and he planned to kill, through his wrestlers, the Vṛishṇi princes Kṛishṇa and Balarāma, after inviting them to Mathurā to visit his court and attend a wrestling bout. Kṛishṇa and Balarāma, however, killed the prize fighters. Kṛishṇa then slew the tyrant Kaṁsa himself, and re-instated Ugrasena on the Mathurā throne. Thereafter, Kṛishṇa and Balarāma left for Kāśi for their education, but had to return soon on account of the invasion of Mathurā by Jarāsandha, the Magadha king, who was enraged at Kāṁsa's death, the latter being his son-in-law. Jarāsandha's invasions were resisted for some time, but finally the Yādavas decided to leave Mathurā in a body and settled in Dvārakā on the west coast.

Kṛishṇa appears for the first time in the *Mahābhārata* story at the Svayaṁvara of Draupadī. He was a friend and counsellor of the Pāṇḍavas, and his sister Subhadrā was married to Arjuna. King Jarāsandha of Magadha was killed by Bhīma under Kṛishṇa's directions. At the *rājasūya* performed by the Pāṇḍavas, Kṛishṇa was offered the first worship. This enraged the Chedi king Śiśupāla who heaped vile abuse upon Kṛishṇa and was killed by him. After the period of the Pāṇḍavas' exile was over, Kṛishṇa acted as their emissary of peace to Duryodhana, but all his efforts at conciliation proved futile. In the great Bhārata War, Kṛishṇa offered his personal help as a charioteer to Arjuna, while his army joined the Kauravas. Kṛishṇa helped the Pāṇḍavas a number of times during the great war. In fact it was mainly, if not solely, due to the important part played by Kṛishṇa in the great war that the Pāṇḍavas emerged victorious.

Kṛishṇa returned to Dvārakā after Yudhishṭhira was installed on the Hastināpura throne. He revived the stillborn child of Abhimanyu's widow Uttarā, later known as Parīkshit. The last meeting of Kṛishṇa and the Pāṇḍavas was at the latter's Aśvamedha. Towards the close of Kṛishṇa's life there was a fratricidal struggle among the Yādavas in which practically the entire Yādava males were destroyed. Then Kṛishṇa sent a messenger to Hastināpura inviting Arjuna to come to Dvārakā and look after the women and children, and asking them to accompany Arjuna, Kṛishṇa retired to the forest. Arjuna came to Dvārakā, took with him the remnants of the Yadu family, and installed Vajra, the only surviving grandson of Kṛishṇa, on the throne of Mathurā. Kṛishṇa, when in deep meditation, was hit by the arrow of a hunter who mistook him for a deer. Thus passed away one of the grandest figures in ancient India. There is now a generāl consensus of opinion in favour of the historicity of Kṛishṇa. Many also hold the view that Vāsudeva, the Yādava hero, the cowherd boy Kṛishṇa in Gokula, the counsellor of the Pāṇḍavas, and the great philosopher of the *Bhagavadgītā*, or in short Kṛishṇa of the Purāṇas and Kṛishṇa of the *Mahābhārata* were one and the same person.[43] The deification of Vāsudeva Kṛishṇa as an incarnation of Vishṇu must be dated before the period of the *Mahābhāshya* (i.e. second century B.C.).

4. *Eastern Ānavas*

Under the suzerainty of Jarāsandha, king of Magadha, Aṅga came to be ruled for some time by Karṇa, who was a faithful ally of the Kauravas, and one of the principal actors in the Great Epic of India. Among the galaxy of epic heroes Karṇa occupies a very high position, and his real worth has not been fully appreciated as he is looked at with prejudice on account of his becoming a staunch supporter of Duryodhana. Ill-luck seems to have pursued Karṇa from his very birth, when he was deserted by his mother Kuntī, as he was born, when she was still a maiden, from the Sun God. He was thus in reality the eldest of the Pāṇḍavas, but being brought up by a Sūta, he met with slights and insults at every stage in his life. His so-called low birth came in the way of his being ranked as fit to compete with Arjuna. Duryodhana at once crowned him the king of Aṅga, and thus began a cordial friendship which made Karṇa the strongest supporter of the Kauravas, whose every cause he championed with thorough wholeheartedness. Karṇa met with his end not because he was beaten, nor on account of his being inferior to Arjuna in any way, but he was the victim of his own greatness, and destiny was always against him. He is indeed a unique hero who should be admired for his magnanimity, unflinching devotion to the cause he championed, valour, skill, and truthfulness. Vṛishasena was the eldest of the sons of Karṇa; but along with his five brothers, he was killed in the Bhārata War.

5. *The Solar Dynasty*

After Rāma's time, Ayodhyā plays no important part in traditional history. Kuśa, Rāma's son, who became the ruler of south Kosala with his capital at Kuśasthalī, appears to have extended the Aryan culture in the Vindhya regions. The story of Kuśa's marriage with a Nāga princess shows how he spread the Vedic culture among the aborigines. The next important figure after Kuśa is Hiraṇyanābha Kausalya who is described as a disciple of Jaimini from whom he learnt the science of Yoga. The last Solar king of the pre-Bhārata War period was Bṛihadbala who led the Ayodhyā forces against the Pāṇḍavas. Though Bhīma conquered him before the Rājasūya, Bṛihadbala was subsequently subjugated by Karṇa and hence he fought at the head of the Kaurava forces. Bṛihadbala was killed by Abhimanyu in the Kurukshetra war.

10. THE BHĀRATA WAR (c. 1400 B.C.)

1. *Kauravas and Pāṇḍavas*[44]

All the young Kuru princes received training in arms from Kṛipa and Droṇa, where Aśvatthāman and Karṇa were their study-mates. Bhīma and Duryodhana specialized in club-fighting and wrestling, Nakula and Sahadeva in fencing, Yudhishṭhira in chariot fighting, and Aśvatthāman in magic arts. Arjuna was not only the best archer but excelled all in every respect. But Karṇa was Arjuna's equal in archery. On completion of their training, Droṇa demanded as his fees the defeat and capture of the Pañchāla king Drupada who had insulted him as his co-student. The Kuru princes marched against Drupada and vanquished him. Droṇa made peace with Drupada by leaving South Pañchāla to him and taking North

Pañchāla for himself. Dhṛitarāshṭra's sons, through jealousy, set on foot various plots in order to destroy their cousins, but the Pāṇḍavas escaped unhurt through all these traps. After their safe escape from the lac house at Vāraṇāvata, the Pāṇḍavas started on a journey in the guise of Brāhmaṇas. They came to Kāmpilya, and on Arjuna's successfully accomplishing the feat imposed as a test in the *Svayaṁvara* of princess Draupadī of Pañchāla, daughter of king Drupada, she became the common wife of the five Pāṇḍava brothers. Hearing of the successes of the Pāṇḍavas, Dhṛitarāshṭra called them back to Hastināpura and gave them the Khāṇḍava-Prastha desert. The Pāṇḍavas founded Indraprastha and made it their capital. Owing to breach of a self-imposed rule, Arjuna went on a voluntary pilgrimage for twelve years during which he contracted marital alliance with Chitrāṅgadā, princess of Manipur, and Subhadrā, the Yādava princess, sister of Kṛishṇa. The Pāṇḍavas burnt down the whole of Khāṇḍava jungle, saving the life of Maya Asura, who in gratitude erected for them a wonderful assembly hall. Then Yudhishṭhira decided to perform a Rājasūya sacrifice as the emblem of sovereignty. As a preliminary to the sacrifice, the other four Pāṇḍava brothers set out on conquering the whole earth. King Jarāsandha of Magadha was their greatest opponent and challenger, and under the advice and guidance of Kṛishṇa, Bhīma killed Jarāsandha in a duel. Jarāsandha's son Sahadeva was installed on the Magadha throne and he became an ally of the Pāṇḍavas. Bhīma, Arjuna, Nakula, and Sahadeva led campaigns respectively towards the east, north, west, and south. The descriptions of these conquests throw much light upon the countries and peoples of the days of the *Mahābhārata*, though at places there are myth and anachronism. Numerous kings including the Kauravas were invited to the Rājasūya, and Kṛishṇa was offered the first worship therein. The Chedi king Śiśupāla objected, and in the quarrel that followed, was killed by Kṛishṇa. It was after the Rājasūya when Duryodhana was inspecting the *Sabhā* or Assembly Hall built by Maya that the seeds of the Bhārata War were deeply sown. The rapid rise of the Pāṇḍavas was an eyesore to the Kauravas and they hit upon a plan to oust them from their kingdom. Taking advantage of the Kshatriya code of conduct that one should not refuse, when invited for a duel or for a gambling-match, Duryodhana called on Yudhishṭhira for a game of dice, in which the latter staked everything including Draupadī, and lost it. The denuding of Draupadī occurred after this game of dice. From hot words, the princes were coming to blows, but old Dhṛitarāshṭra let off the Pāṇḍavas. Soon afterwards the second game of dice was played in which the stake was that the loser should spend twelve years in the forest, and the thirteenth *incognito*. The Pāṇḍavas lost this game also, and had to leave for the forest. Draupadī accompanied them. During the thirteenth year, Pāṇḍavas stayed in the Matsya country in disguise. There they helped the Matsya king Virāṭa against the attack of the Kauravas. Virāṭa's daughter Uttarā was married to Abhimanyu, the son of Arjuna. After completing the full period, seeing that war was inevitable, each party tried to enlist as many sympathisers as possible. Kṛishṇa himself sided with the Pāṇḍavas but his forces fought on the side of the Kauravas. Śalya was won over by Duryodhana. Drupada's priest was sent to the Kauravas on behalf of the Pāṇḍavas for negotiations, and finally Kṛishṇa himself went as an ambassador of peace. But Duryodhana was adamant and refused to part with even a particle of earth. Thus began the Great War which may be regarded as the greatest event in the prehistoric age of India and forms the theme of the Great Epic *Mahābhārata*.

2. *Bhārata War*

The epic gives a long list of princes on each side. The Kauravas had eleven divisions under them as against the seven of the Pāṇḍavas. Towards the east, out of the old Magadhan empire, only western Magadha ruled by Jarāsandha's son Sahadeva was on the Pāṇḍava side. All the rest, viz. eastern Magadha, Videha, Aṅga. Vaṅga, and Kaliṅga, which were under Karṇa, joined the Kaurava forces. The Kirātas under Bhagadatta, ruler of Prāgjyotisha, also were under the banner of the Kauravas, so that practically the whole east supported them. In Madhyadeśa, the rulers of Vatsa, Kāśi, Chedi, Karūsha, Daśārṇa. and Pañchāla figured among the supporters of the Pāṇḍavas, while Bṛihadbala, king of the Kosalas. went to the opposite camp. The Yādavas were divided in their allegiance. Kṛishṇa was the non-combatant adviser of the Pāṇḍavas and Balarāma remained neutral. Yuyudhāna and Sātyaki, among the Vṛishṇis and Yādavas, came to the Pāṇḍavas, while Nīla of Māhishmatī, Vinda and Anuvinda of Avanti, Kṛitavarman of the Bhoja-Andhaka-Vṛishṇis, Vidarbha, Nishāda, and Śālva supported the Kaurava forces. In the Punjab and the north-west, Jayadratha of Sindhu-Sauvīra who was the brother-in-law of the Kauravas, Śakuni of Gāndhāra, Suśarmā of Trigarta, Kekaya, Śibi. Śalya of Madra (related to the Pāṇḍavas), Vāhlīka, Kshudraka, Mālava. Śritāyu of the Ambashṭhas, and Sudakshiṇa of the Kambojas, were in the Kaurava army; only Abhisāra, which formed the south-western part of Kāshmir is said to have joined the Pāṇḍavas. Thus, the Pāṇḍavas' supporters were Pañchālas, Matsya, Chedi, Karūsha, Western Magadha, Kāśi and south-western Yādavas. Under the Kauravas came practically the whole of eastern India, the whole of north-west, Kosala, Vatsa, and Śūrasena in the Madhyadeśa, and Māhishmatī, Avanti, and Śālva in the west. In short, broadly speaking the Madhyadeśa and Gujarāt stood for Pāṇḍavas and the rest, viz. east, north-west, and western India, opposed them. The Pāṇḍava army encamped near Upaplavya, the capital of the Matsyas; and the Kaurava forces were gathered near Hastināpura. Last minute efforts were made for an amicable settlement, but the negotiations proved futile, and the great battle was fought on the famous field of Kurukshetra.

Dhṛishṭadyumna, son of Drupada, was appointed the Commander-in-Chief of the Pāṇḍavas and Bhīshma led the Kauravas. The two hosts were bound to follow certain rules of war traditional among the Kshatriyas. Only opponents of equal birth and armed with the same kind of weapons were to fight each other. None was to fight without first challenging his opponent. Those engaged in personal combat with another, and those who surrendered, as well as the fugitives and non-combatants were to be spared. The venerable Bhīshma commanded the Kaurava forces during the first ten days of war. It was only through the arrows discharged by Arjuna against Bhīshma under the cover of Śikhaṇḍin (whom Bhīshma did not fight, Śikhaṇḍin being originally a woman) that on the tenth day Bhīshma fell down headlong from his chariot. Droṇa was consecrated the next commander, and he carried on the fight till the fifteenth day. Abhimanyu was killed on the thirteenth day and Ghaṭotkacha, the demon son of Bhīma, on the fourteenth. Drupada and Virāṭa were killed by Droṇa on the fifteenth day, and finally that evening Dhṛishṭadyumna killed Droṇa, while in deep sorrow on hearing the false news of the death of his son Aśvatthāman. Karṇa was the next commander. His turn lasted only for two days during which Bhīma tore open Duḥśāsana's breast. Karṇa was killed by Arjuna. Śalya became the commander on the eighteenth or the last day of the battle. He was killed Yudhishṭhira by about mid-day, while Sahadeva killed Śakuni. The entire host of the Kauravas was thus completely annihilated and Duryodhana fled to a pond where the Pāṇḍavas challenged him. In the club-fight against Bhīma Duryodhana's thighs were smashed and he dropped down bleeding. Duryodhana appointed Aśvatthāman as the last commander who, with the help of the other two survivors from among the Kaurava heroes, viz. Kṛipa and Kṛitavarman, stealthily entered into the Pāṇḍava camp at night and slaughtered the surviving Pāṇḍava princes and Dhṛishṭadyumna while asleep. With the death of Duryodhana perished all the male members of his large family except his old and blind father. The Pāṇḍavas emerged victorious, but besides the five Pāṇḍava brothers, Sāṭyaki was the sole survivor on their side. Thus the victory, though complete, was won at a very high cost.

The Kuru line being extinct with the death of the hundred sons of Dhṛitarāshṭra, Yudhishṭhira became king of the Kurus and ruled at Hastināpura. Later on Yudhishṭhira performed a horse-sacrifice on Vyāsa's advice in order to purge himself of all sins. Arjuna was placed in charge of the horse and the sacrifice was completed with due ceremonial. Dhṛitarāshṭra retired to forest with Gāndhārī after a few years and was consumed in a forest conflagration. Yudhishṭhira, however, did not reign long. Some years after the Bhārata War, the Vṛishṇis and Yādavas of Gujarāt perished in fratricidal strife and Kṛishṇa died. Arjuna was sent to bring the survivors of the Yādavas, but on his way back he was attacked and defeated by the Ābhīras. Arjuna returned to Hastināpura with Kṛishṇa's grandson Vajra, and placed him at the head of the people who followed him from Dvārakā. Thereafter Yudhishṭhira abdicated and retired to the forest along with his brothers, placing Parīkshit, Arjuna's grandson, on the throne.

The accession of Parīkshit marks the beginning of the Kali Age, as the Dvāpara Age is said to have closed with the Bhārata War. In the Puranic accounts also "the past" ended, and "the future" began, at the close of the Bhārata War which was an epoch-making event in the annals of the country. The dynasties of the Kali Age in the Purāṇas begin with the accession of Parīkshit, though some begin their accounts after Adhisīmakṛishṇa, fourth in descent from Parīkshit.[45]

The traditional accounts do not state how the family feud in the Kuru family was turned into an all-India affair, so that every ruling dynasty of any note during the period, howsoever far from Kurukshetra, is represented as having participated in the war. The non-mention of the Bhārata War in later Vedic Literature does not necessarily disprove its historicity. For one thing, it was a purely political contest, and hence naturally did not interest the authors of the *Brāhmaṇas*.[46] An *argumentum ex silentio* is seldom conclusive. Again the Pāṇḍus, according to traditions, were not a body of strangers, but were scions of the Kuru family. The very significance of the term Pāṇḍavas, as distinct from the Kauravas, was forgotten soon after the war, and the term Kurus alone survived. Though the *Mahābhārata*, in its present form, is a late production, the kernel of the story takes us back to the period between 1400 and 1000 B.C. when, as noted above, the battle was probably fought. The *Āśvalāyana Gṛihya-sūtra* (III. 4. 4) refers to the Bhārata and Mahābhārata, and *Śāṅkhāyana Śrauta-sūtra* (XV. 16), to the disastrous war of the Kauravas. Pāṇini refers to the heroes of the Bhārata War as already objects of worship. All these clearly prove the antiquity of the story of the *Mahābhārata*.

II. COMPARATIVE VALUE OF THE VEDAS AND THE PURĀṆAS AS SOURCES OF TRADITIONAL HISTORY

There is a difference of opinion among scholars as to the comparative value of the Vedic texts and the Purāṇas in regard to the historical data supplied by them. Keith is excessively sceptical about the historical value of the Purāṇas and is doubtful regarding the historicity of any event which is not explicitly mentioned in the *Ṛigveda.* Pargiter goes to the other extreme and gives more weight to the Puranic tradition than to the Vedic evidence, which he styles as the tradition of the Brāhmaṇas who possessed no historical sense. The so-called Kshatriya tradition, however, is hardly an unpolluted source of history. Priority of date and comparative freedom from textual corruption are doubtless two strong points in favour of Vedic texts. The evidence of the Purāṇas, on the other hand, cannot be ruled out altogether, because despite a good deal of what is untrustworthy in them, they alone contain something like a continuous historical narrative, and it is absurd to suppose that the elaborate royal genealogies were all merely figments of imagination or a tissue of falsehoods.

But the theory which pronounces the Purāṇas as representing Kshatriya tradition as distinct from, and superior to, the Brāhmaṇa tradition contained in the Vedic texts, does not appear to be correct. The theory is mainly based on two assumptions: (1) that the heroes of the legends and stories in the Purāṇas are Kshatriya kings who mostly do not figure in Vedic literature, and (2) the transmission of their history was entrusted to Sūtas of Kshatriya origin. There is hardly any foundation for these beliefs. The Sūta was not a non-Brāhmaṇa but a venerable sage. As regards the so-called Kshatriya traditions, there have never been in India two such watertight compartments as the Brāhmaṇa tradition and the Kshatriya tradition. Even in the works distinctly assigned to Kshatriya tradition by Pargiter, we find the glorification of the Brāhmaṇas, and the so-called Brahmanic literature abounds in Kshatriya legends. The Purāṇas themselves assign a comparatively small portion to genealogical accounts, the genuine Kshatriya tradition according to Pargiter; their main bulk deals with Vedic and Brahmanic lore. Moreover, the Purāṇas follow the Vedic religion and take pride in styling themselves as the "fifth Veda." The earliest reference to the Purāṇas, as observed by Keith, is for a point of Brahmanical lore and not for a point of genealogy or history.[47] Again, even according to Pargiter, the Purāṇas, as we have them now, are undeniably a Brahmanic compilation; so no part of it can be distinguished as Brahmanic or Kshatriya tradition.[48] It would perhaps be more correct to say that these are not two distinct sets of tradition. but both are Brahmanical traditions, though produced under different environments and with different aims and objects.

Moreover, it may be observed that there is no irreconcilable contradiction or conflict between the Vedic texts and the Purāṇas. The *Ṛigveda*, as we have it, is a Kuru-Pañchāla product; naturally, therefore, the kings belonging to those clans play prominent rôles in it, and others find but incidental mention. Kings, who are mentioned in the Vedic texts but are not found in the Puranic traditions, were possibly princes and chieftains of smaller dynasties, not preserved in the dynastic lists in the Purāṇas. There is also the possibility of the same person being referred to under different names in the two sets of traditional accounts. Some of the kings mentioned in the *Ṛigveda* can be fitted in the gaps in the Puranic lists. The *Ṛigveda*, no doubt, offers the proper corrective to the Puranic lists, but, when we find Puranic accounts to be corroborated by the Vedic evidence, it is legitimate to take their testimony as valid even in matters on which the *Ṛigveda* is silent. The proper procedure for the writing of traditional history is to take into account the joint testimony of the Vedic and Puranic texts wherever available, and to try to bring harmony into the apparently conflicting texts. The evidence of the Purāṇas in these matters needs very careful consideration.

A critical examination of the Puranic texts and Vedic literature reveals the fact that the Puranic genealogies in some cases refer to the same persons figuring in the Vedic literature. The Puranic data about some of the royal dynasties, kings, and Brāhmaṇa families find confirmation in Vedic literature, and there is no basis for the view that there are hardly any points of contact between the Vedic and Puranic traditions. Here we shall briefly refer to the important persons who appear in both Vedic literature and the Purāṇas.

The *Ṛigveda* mentions Yayāti as an ancient sacrificer and a son of Nahusha, and he is also known as a seer of some hymns. But his connection with the Lunar dynasty or with Pūru, Anu, Druhyu, Yadu, and Turvasu, as told in the Purāṇas and *Mahābhārata,* is not found in the Vedic texts, and hence Macdonell and Keith condemn the epic tradition as "inaccurate."[49]

The names of the above five sons of Yayāti, however, occur in the *Ṛigveda* as those of ancient tribes. The word Yadu occurs several times in the *Ṛigveda* as the name of a king and his tribe. He is closely associated with Turvaśa and once with Druhyu, Anu, and Pūru. The *Mahābhārata* and the Purāṇas indicate this association by making Turvasu the full brother of Yadu, and Anu, Druhyu and Pūru, his step-brothers. The *Ṛigveda* also indicates the close connection of Yadu and Turvaśa with north-western India. The five tribes Yadus, Turvaśas, Anus, Druhyus, and Pūrus represent, according to one view, the Vedic Pañchajanas. The *Ṛigveda* or Vedic literature does not corroborate the Puranic relationship of Yayāti, son of Nahusha, with these five princes, though Yayāti, the son of Nahusha, as noted already, is well known to Vedic texts. The Pūrus appear in the *Ṛigveda* as the enemies of Sudās and they dwelt on the Sarasvatī. It appears from the *Ṛigveda* that the Pūrus had sometimes friendly and sometimes inimical relations with the Tṛitsus to whom Sudās belonged. There is nothing to show any connection between Vedic Pūru or Purukutsa and Puranic Pūru, son of Yayāti.

The Solar king Māndhātṛi appears to have been referred to as Māndhātṛi Yauvanāśva in the *Gopatha Brāhmaṇa,* the identity being further strengthened by the fact of both being the sons of Yuvanāśva.[50]

The interpretation of the famous *Dāśarājña* (battle of ten kings) of the *Ṛigveda* in traditional history supplies us with many interesting and important synchronisms, and the importance of the problem demands treatment at some length.

We have already seen that Mudgala, the eldest of the five Pañchālas, was the founder of the main branch of the north Pañchālas, and among his descendants were Vadhryaśva, Divodāsa, Mitrayu, Maitreya Soma, Sṛiñjaya, Chyavana Pañchajana, and Sudāsa or Somadatta. There is no consistency among the different texts with regard to these names, Sudāsa being in some Purāṇas replaced by Somadatta. Despite these difficulties, Pargiter and other scholars identify Divodāsa and Sudāsa in these lists with their namesakes in the Ṛigveda and see in the account of Saṁvaraṇa in the *Mahābhārata*[51] the reference to the battle of ten kings in the *Ṛigveda* which resulted in the defeat of the Pūru king.

Pargiter points out that Mudgala, Vadhryaśva, Divodāsa, and Sṛiñjaya are mentioned in the *Ṛigveda* hymns. Chyavana is probably meant in one hymn and his other name Pañchajana is no doubt a misreading of Pijavana. Sudāsa is called Sudās Paijavana. The *Aitareya Brāhmaṇa* says that Sahadeva was descended from Sṛiñjaya, and one hymn (*RV*, IV. 15. 7-10) says that Somaka was his son. The hymns agree with the genealogies in all these particulars. Chyavana was a great warrior and his son Sudāsa extended his dominions. They probably conquered the Dvimīḍha dynasty and the south Pañchālas, as there appear to be gaps in the genealogical lists of these dynasties at this period.[52]

According to Pargiter, "Sudās drove the Paurava king Saṁvaraṇa of Hastināpurā out, defeating him on the Jumna. His conquests stirred up a confederacy of the neighbouring kings to resist him—Pūru (Saṁvaraṇa), the Yādava (the Yādava king of Mathurā), the Śivas (Śivis, who were Ānavas), Druhyus (of Gāndhāra), Matsyas (west of Śūrasena), Turvaśa (the Turvasu prince, apparently in Rewa) and other smaller states. Sudās defeated them in a great battle near the Parushṇī (Ravi), and Pūru (Saṁvaraṇa) took refuge in a fortress near the Sindhu (Indus) many years."[53]

It may be stated at the outset that despite many differences between the Vedic account on the one hand and that given in the *Mahābhārata* on the other, it is undisputed that the heroes of the *Dāśarājña* flourished at the period which has been assigned to Sudāsa-Somadatta of the north Pañchāla line and to Saṁvaraṇa and Kuru of the Paurava line. Dr. Pradhan has arrived at the same conclusion of the identity of Vedic Sudās with the Pañchāla Sudāsa after independent enquiry starting on different synchronisms.[54] It has also been shown that Kuru and Saṁvaraṇa were contemporaries of Tura Kāvasheya whose father Kavasha Ailūsha figured in the *Dāśarajña*.[55] The discrepancies that we notice in the Vedic account and the accounts in the Purāṇas and the *Mahābhārata* only show that traditional history, though based on a kernel of historical facts, is not only not infallible but inaccurate at times, and its credibility requires to be tested in the light of contemporary Vedic evidence. The details of the *Dāśarājña* as given in the *Ṛigveda* no doubt are a first-hand contemporary account. The accounts in traditional history were pieced together out of the remnants of ancient tales, legends, etc. at a later date when memories of actual events were but faint and inaccurate.

Now, apart from the fact that the geographical boundaries do not concur in the Vedic and Puranic accounts (as will be shown presently), it will be seen that there are many particulars that apparently speak against the proposed identification. In the first place, though the *Ṛigveda* mentions Mudgala and Sṛiñjaya, it does not indicate any relationship between them and Sudās. Secondly, the Rigvedic Sudās is distinctly called the son of Pijavana whereas the Puranic Sudāsa had Chyavana-Pañchajana for his father. Yāska, *Mahābhārata* and Manu know Pijavana to be the father of Sudās, and hence the Purāṇas cannot be said to have mistaken Pañchajana for Pijavana as suggested by Pargiter.[56] It seems that the title Pañchajana has been given to Sudāsa in his capacity as the leader of the five tribes. Further discrepancies are found in the non-mention in the *Ṛigveda* of the important tribes of the period according to the Purāṇas such as the Sātvatas, the Bhojas, the Videhas, the Ikshvākus, etc., either among the allies or among the adversaries of Sudās. Among the tribes mentioned in the *Ṛigveda* as participating in the *Dāśarājña*, Turvaśas, according to traditional history, had long ceased to exist, having merged in the Pauravas. The Tṛitsus, who were the principal helpers of Sudās according to the *Ṛigveda*, are not to be found at all in the Puranic tradition. Matsyas, one of the opponents of Sudās in the *Ṛigveda*, emerge in traditional history only nine generations after Sudāsa. The Pūru adversary of Sudās has been named Purukutsa in the *Ṛigveda* whereas according to traditional history he comes to be Saṁvaraṇa of the Pauravas. It is further curious that the *Mahābhārata* does not mention Sudāsa by name at all, but refers to him only as Pāñchālya (a king of the Pañchālas). The scene of the battle has not been mentioned in the *Mahābhārata* or the Puranic texts. The *Ṛigveda* represents the battle to have been fought on the banks of the Parushṇī. This location of the conflict, however, seems to be most difficult, if not quite impossible, if we consider the territories occupied by the different members of the confederacy at the period, according to traditional history. The Druhyus were occupying Gāndhāra at the time, and it is difficult to see how they could be interested in or affected by the conflicts of people far away from them. The Turvaśās, as already stated, did not exist at the time; and even if they did exist, as suggested by Pargiter, it is difficult to comprehend how they marched off over 500 miles from the Karūsha country to participate in the exploits of a remote king. The geographical knowledge of the period of the *Ṛigveda* (as seen in Ch. XIII) did not extend much beyond the Ganges and Jumna or Sarayu to the east, and only up to the Vindhyas in the south; but the period of Sudāsa in traditional history, which comes after that of Daśaratha and Rāma, indicates knowledge of practically the whole of India. The truth underlying these discrepancies between the Vedic and the Puranic and *Mahābhārata* accounts seems to be that the Puranic tradition "is patching up its genealogical fabric from whatever shreds of floating knowledge it comes across without any means of checking."[57] This does not certainly mean that the Vedic and the Puranic Sudāsa were quite distinct personalities. When we take into consideration that the Vedic and traditional accounts agree admirably with regard to the chronology of the period of the conflict, it appears certain that the similarity of names is not a mere coincidence. There are serious discrepancies, no doubt, when we come to the locations and political environments of the different participants in the conflict. But the mistake is due to the lack of definite knowledge on the part of chroniclers of traditional history. It may also be observed that the *Mahābhārata* account simply refers to the driving out of the Paurava king Saṁvaraṇa from his kingdom by the king of the Pañchālas. At the distance of time between the *Dāśarājña* and the composition of the *Mahābhārata*, the chroniclers remembered only the utter rout of the Paurava king at the hands of a Pañchāla king.

Another important problem is the identity of Janamejaya Pārīkshita mentioned in the Vedic texts and in the Purāṇas and the *Mahābhārata*. The Purāṇas and the *Mahābhārata* refer to two Janamejaya Pārīkshitas, one an ancestor of the Pāṇḍavas (being grandson of Kuru), and the second, a successor of the Pāṇḍavas (grandson of Arjuna).

On account the similarity of patronymic as also of the names of his brothers, the earlier Janamejaya is confused with the later Janamejaya and there has been transference of tradition.

The *Aitareya* and the *Śatapatha Brāhmaṇa* enumerate Janamejaya as the performer of the Aśvamedha sacrifice.[58] The very fact that Bhīshma narrates the story of Janamejaya's Aśvamedha to Yudhishṭhira as an ancient legend clearly shows that the Aśvamedha referred to was performed by the ancestor of the Pāṇḍavas, and proves that a Janamejaya Pārīkshita before the Pāṇḍavas' time was a real person and not a shadowy figure as Dr. Raychaudhuri would have us believe.[59] The descendant of the Pāṇḍavas is credited with the performance of the *Sarpasatra* and not an Aśvamedha. The Aśvamedha started by the later Janamejaya was not completed.[60] The Brāhmaṇas further mention Tura Kāvasheya as the priest who anointed Janamejaya with Aindra Mahābhisheka, and Tura Kāvasheya can be proved to be contemporaneous with Janamejaya the ancestor of the Pāṇḍavas. Kavasha Ailūsha, father or grandfather of Tura, was drowned in the *Dāśarājña*, so that he was a senior contemporary of Kuru, son of Saṁvaraṇa, who lived during the *Dāśarājña* period.[61] Janamejaya, who was the grandson of Kuru, was thus contemporaneous with Tura. This sacrifice, with Tura Kāvasheya as priest, was performed for celebrating the attainment of imperial status by Janamejaya and not for atonement of any sin. The *Śatapatha Brāhmaṇa* refers to another sacrifice performed by Janamejaya Pārīkshita with the aid of Indrota Daivāpa Śaunaka for ridding himself of a grievous sin which is described as *Brahmahatyā* (killing of a Brāhmaṇa).[62] The Purāṇas and the *Mahābhārata* do not associate Janamejaya, the descendant of the Pāṇḍavas, with any guilt. That the ancestor was the person alluded to is clear from the fact that the story of the sin of Janamejaya is told by Bhīshma, and therein Janamejaya is accused of unwittingly killing a Brāhmaṇa.[63] This also proves that Indrota Daivāpa Śaunaka flourished generations before the Bhārata War. The *Harivaṁśa* refers to Janamejaya's killing the son of Gārgya for insulting him, as the result of which Gārgya cursed him.[64] The Aśvamedha performed by Indrota Daivāpa Śaunaka was to purge Janamejaya of this sin. The incident of the chariot of Yayāti related in the same story, which states that the chariot continued in the Paurava line till the period of Janamejaya, and after him was transferred to Vasu Chaidyoparichara, eighth descendant from Kuru, clearly shows that the reference in the story is to the ancestor of the Pāṇḍavas. The chariot then passed on to the Magadhas and came to Kṛishṇa after Jarāsandha was killed.[65] All these preceded Janamejaya Pārīkshita, the descendant of the Pāṇḍavas, and hence the allusions clearly refer to the ancestor of the Pāṇḍavas. The *Harivaṁśa* clearly indicates that the Aśvamedha story relates to the earlier Janamejaya by making Janamejaya (the descendant of the Pāṇḍavas) the auditor of the story which is told by Vaiśampāyana, who adds that there were two Janamejaya Pārīkshitas among the Pauravas.[66]

The references in the Vedic texts thus clearly prove the existence of a Janamejaya Pārīkshita who was an ancestor of the Pāṇḍavas, and the grandson of Kuru. The peace and plenty in the Kuru realm, alluded to in the *Atharvaveda*[67] and in the Brāhmaṇas, came as the result of Kuru's extensive conquests, and his son

Parīkshit and grandson Janamejaya continued the good work started by Kuru. Janamejaya's heinous crime, however, deprived him and his successors of their kingdom which passed on to the younger branch (as already stated) and the Pārīkshitas suffered extinction. The *Bṛihadāraṇyaka Upanishad* refers to the vanished glory of the Pārīkshitas and enquiries as to their state in the next world.[68] To that the reply is given that they must have attained the state to which performers of Aśvamedha sacrifices are eligible.

These and other co-ordinations of the incidents and persons mentioned in traditional history and the Vedic texts clearly show that the two traditions are neither independent nor contradictory; that the traditional history has its basis in facts and is not the product of imagination; that traditional history has mostly preserved ancient tradition; and that when supported by Vedic texts its evidence is unimpeachable. No excuse is therefore needed for the somewhat long historical account, given above, on the basis of Epic and Puranic tradition. It has been customary for the writers of Indian history to confine themselves, so far as the political history of the period is concerned, to the few isolated facts gleaned from the Vedic texts. But we must not forget that "the Vedic literature confines itself to religious subjects and notices political and secular occurrences only incidentally so far as they had a bearing on the religious subjects." As Pargiter has very pertinently observed: "Ancient Indian history has been fashioned out of compositions, which are purely religious and priestly, which notoriously do not deal with history, and which totally lack the historical sense. The extraordinary nature of such history may be perceived, if it were suggested that European history should be constructed merely out of theological literature. What would raise a smile if applied to Europe has been soberly accepted when applied to India."[68a]

The force of these remarks is undeniable and no student of Indian history should ignore the legendary element in the Purāṇas and Epics. It is necessary to remember that, for reasons stated above, we cannot accept those traditions as genuine historical facts so long or so far as they are not corroborated by contemporary texts or other reasonable evidence. Until then we can treat them only as *traditional* history. But such traditional history has its value, and is in any case a necessary preliminary step for the discovery of genuine history.

12. THE EXPANSION OF THE ARYANS AND ARYAN CULTURE

In one respect, however, it seems difficult to accept the traditional account without a great deal of reserve. This is the geographical background of the Aryan conquest of India as described in the Purāṇas.

The Purāṇas say nothing about the original home of the Aryans. The scene of traditional history opens in India, with the division of the territory, comprising the whole of North India extending in the east up to Orissa, among the ten sons of Manu, the king and the common ancestor of the ruling families in India (*ante,* p. 278).

From this starting point, the traditional history enables us to trace the progress of Aryan advance during the four Ages—Kṛita, Tretā, Dvāpara, and Kali. Kings Sagara, Rāma, and Kṛishṇa are said to have flourished respectively at the end of the Kṛita, Tretā, and Dvāpara Ages, so that the Kṛita Age covers roughly 40 generations, Tretā 25 generations, and Dvāpara 30 generations (cf. App. II). The Kali Age set in after the Bhārata War.

By the end of the Kṛita Age, we find the Aryans in occupation of the whole of North India including Sind and Kandahār in the west, and Bihār and West Bengal in the east. In the south, Gujarāt, Kāthiāwār, the Western Coast south of Bombay and Berār were colonized by the Aryans, and their southern limits had extended beyond the Vindhya and the Narmadā down to the Tāpti and the Sātpurās.

While Paraśurāma is generally associated with the creation of Śūrpāraka near Bombay, a stanza in the *Mahābhārata* shows that it was colonized earlier by Jamadagni.[69] Paraśurāma is credited with the Aryanization of the whole of the western coast of Bombay, especially the Konkan, the Karhāṭa, the Tulava, and the Kerala. The traditions, at any rate, indicate the important rôle played by the Bhārgavas in the colonization of the Deccan.

The Aryan occupation during the Tretā Age extended further east and south, embracing, in addition to the territories occupied in the Kṛita Age, Orissa, Assam, Chhotā Nāgpur, Central Provinces, and some parts further south. The southern territories of Janasthāna, Kishkindhā, and also Laṅkā came under the sphere of Aryan influence during the days of Rāma.

By the time of the Bhārata War (c. 1400 B.C.) which marked the close of the Dvāpara Age, the Aryans had expanded over the whole of India, and even beyond its frontiers in the west.

This traditional account of the Aryan expansion is, however, in conflict with the evidence of the Vedic texts. As has already been shown in Ch. XIII, there are good grounds to suppose that by the time the *Ṛigveda* was composed, the Aryans had not penetrated much further into the interior beyond the frontiers of the Punjab and Rājputāna. If we remember that the *Ṛigveda* did not probably receive its final form long before the end of the so-called Dvāpara Age, its testimony is decidedly fatal to the geographical views assumed in the Purāṇas.

But the Rigvedic evidence does not stand alone. We have an account of the spread of the Aryan culture in the Brāhmaṇa period in the story of Videgha Māthava (*ante*, p. 258-59). This, as well as the fact that Kosala and Videha do not appear in the earlier Vedic literature, but are mentioned for the first time in the *Śatapatha Brāhmaṇa*, and the contemptuous references in the *Atharvaveda* and the Sūtras indicate that Magadha and Vaṅga were then outside the pale of Aryan culture. All these leave no doubt about the general correctness of the assumption that the Aryans had not advanced beyond the middle region of Northern India till after the end of the age represented by the Vedic Saṁhitās, i.e. at a time when most, if not all, the traditional royal dynasties dealt with in this chapter had ceased to exist.

It is worthy of note that even the Smṛiti texts quote verses defining Āryāvarta or the land of the Āryas as co-extensive with Northern India. As to the expansion of the Aryan culture to the Deccan and South India, the evidence of Pāṇini's *Ashṭādhyāyī* and Kātyāyana's Vārtikas on Pāṇini, seems to be fairly conclusive. The only country in the Deccan south of the Narmadā mentioned by Pāṇini is Aśmaka, whereas Kātyāyana knows Pṇāḍya, Chola, and Kerala. This shows that the Aryans came into contact with these South Indiaṇ peoples during the time intervening between Pāṇini and Kātyāyana, i.e. some time between the sixth and fourth centuries B.C.[69a] Yet the Purāṇas and the *Rāmāyaṇa* would have us believe that the whole of South India, including Ceylon, was colonized by the Aryans or brought under their sphere of influence by the time of Rāmachandra in the Tretā Age!

It is impossible to rely upon the traditional account as recorded in the Epics and Puranic texts, at least in respect of those particulars which are so flatly contradicted by the evidence of earlier texts—an evidence which is all the more valuable as it is based upon incidental notices not likely to be fabricated in order to serve any preconceived notion. Whatever we might think therefore of the kings and dynasties mentioned in the traditional account, we can hardly accept, without demur, the location of their principalities as described in the Epics and the Purāṇas.

It might be argued that many of the royal dynasties mentioned in the traditional account were not Aryans. This is not unlikely, for evidence is gradually accumulating (*cf.* Chs. VIII, IX) that a fairly developed culture and powerful kingdoms flourished in India before the Aryans. But such a theory goes definitely against the traditional account which represents all ruling families, described above, as descended from the common ancestor Manu.[70]

At the same time the existence of non-Aryans may be easily inferred. For besides the descendants of Manu who established dynasties all over India, traditional history mentions Rākshasas, Vānaras, Asuras, Daityas, Dānavas, Nāgas, Nishādas, Dasyus, Dāsas. Pulindas, Śakas, Yavanas, Kambojas, Pāradas, Pahlavas, etc. who appear to have been outside the Aryan fold. The Rākshasas were aborigines who were hostile to the Brāhmaṇas, while Vānaras, another aboriginal tribe, were allied to the Brāhmaṇas. Asuras, Daityas, Dānavas, and Nāgas denoted peoples of different cultures in various stages of civilization ranging from the rude, aboriginal, uncivilized tribes to the semi-civilized races, offering strong resistance to the spread of Aryan culture. There appear to have been three stages in the description of the hostile tribes of Asuras, Dānavas, Daityas, and Rākshasas in Puranic accounts. Originally, these denoted human beings, but as they were generally the enemies of the Aryans, these names came to mean alien and hated, hostile or savage men. Later on, these names became terms of opprobrium and abuse which led to the attribution of evil character to these peoples. Even certain Aryan kings were termed Dānavas or Asuras due to their evil character. Finally, these terms came to be associated with demoniac beings and were used synonymously with demons. The Nāgas appear to be partially civilized people. The Nishādas, Dāsas, Dasyus, Pulindas, and Kirātas were mostly aboriginal, rude, savage tribes in a very primitive stage of civilization. All these tribes lived in hilly tracts, and some of them were cannibals. The Nishādas, also known as Mlechchhas, were according to ancient traditional views a mixed race of Aryan origin born from a Brāhmaṇa male and a Śudra female.[71] They are associated with the hills of Central India and the Vindhyan tracts. They had also settlements in the Vatsabhūmi and, further east, near Allāhābād. The Pulindas, Śabaras, Mūtibas, etc. were the aboriginal tribes of the south. The Pulindas were connected with the north also. The Kirātas had settlements in Assam and Nepāl. The Śakas, Yavanas, Kambojas, Pāradas, Pahlavas, etc. were foreign tribes from the west, but they were evidently absorbed among the Kshatriyas. Pāṇḍya, Chola, and Kerala dynasties in the south claimed descent from the Lunar Turvasus.

But whatever we might think of the geographical and ethnical background of the traditional account, it perhaps reflects more accurately the method and process of Aryan colonization in India. One distinguishing feature of the Aryan expansion, as described in it, deserves special mention. The Aryans extended their sway and colonized fresh lands not by conquest alone with the aid of big armies. The colonization was also effected by small bands of adventurous Brāhmaṇas and Kshatriyas from different Aryan kingdoms, who went to new countries and, after clearing the jungles and making the tracts habitable, set up hermitages and residences there. The territories surrounding the Aryan-occupied Madhyadeśa, the Vindhyas and Vidarbha, were colonized in this fashion. The Aryans colonized under the leadership of Kshatriya tribes, and new settlements were named after these tribes. The speed of Aryan expansion was necessarily slow where they received opposition from the aborigines or semi-Aryans or non-Aryans, as in the case of their eastward progress.

Rāma of Ayodhyā is made to play a very important part in the expansion of Aryan culture in the south. It was probably on account of the signal service attributed to him in colonizing the Deccan, and spreading the Aryan religion far in the south and rendering it free from the harassment of aggressive and semi-barbarous tribes, that he has been included among the incarnations of the god Vishṇu. This expansion of Aryan culture in the south was the result of the hearty co-operation of the Brāhmaṇa and the Kshatriya in carrying the banner of Aryanization. The Brāhmaṇa missionaries who accompanied the Kshatriya conquerors, introduced the essentials of Aryan culture and tradition to the masses, converted the principal figures, and paved the way for social and cultural contact by allowing high-born Aryans to marry with non-Aryans. Agastya, the pioneer among the *Ṛishis* to erect a hermitage in the trans-Vindhyan regions, preceded Rāma by generations; but he paved the way for later adventurers. The story of Agastya reveals the important part played by the Brāhmaṇas in the spread of Aryan civilization over southern India. The ancient *Ṛishis* undertook missionary enterprise and helped in the propagation and diffusion of the Aryan culture by their active efforts, often at considerable risk to their lives. They moved in large numbers to distant lands, and performed sacrifices and observed religious rites in their new settlements. Their genuine missionary spirit, coupled with their peaceful character, not using any force nor resorting to retaliation despite provocation, helped in creating a favourable atmosphere for the reception of the Aryan religion. The *Ṛishis* mixed with the aborigines and civilized them. The Aryan spirit was kept alive by the Brāhmaṇa, not by the Kshatriya; but, "without the protection of the chief, the Brāhmaṇa was powerless; and it was not the Brāhmaṇa's peaceful penetration, but the military exploits of the chief that enthralled the popular imagination."[72] Rāma's expedition, as described in the *Rāmāyaṇa*, did not put the non-Aryans of the south under the political subjugation of the Aryans, but it brought the southern territories of the Vānaras and Rākshasas as protectorates under the sphere of Aryan influence,[73] and was mainly responsible for bringing these peoples under Aryan influence.

The contribution of the Yādavas in carrying the banner of Aryan culture over large tracts of land in the south-west and in Rājputāna, Gujarāt, Mālwā, and the Deccan, which came under their occupation, needs special mention. It was due to the activities of the Yādavas that these regions were brought under the Aryan way of life. The peculiar feature in the career of the Yādavas is the considerable mixture they had with the non-Aryans, though they trace their descent from Purūravas through Yadu. This fact coupled with the possible looseness in the observance of the Aryan *Dharma* led the Epics and Purāṇas to call the Yādava branches Asuras, and to class them with the tribes of the extreme north-west and west among the Nīchyas and Apāchyas. The fact that they mixed freely with the Non-Aryans, with whom they had marital relations and some of whose customs they incorporated, facilitated the Aryanization of the so-called outsiders, and thus spread Aryan culture far and wide. Kṛishṇa of the Yādavas, well known as a politician, warrior, and religious teacher, was a national hero, who was regarded as an incarnation of Vishṇu. He held liberal and catholic views and his doctrines helped in the spread of Aryan ideas among the so-called Śūdras.

Whatever we might think of the historicity of Rāma and Kṛishṇa, as depicted in the above accounts, they may not unreasonably be regarded as true types of Aryan heroes who were pioneers in the spread of Aryan culture and colonization all over India.

GENERAL REFERENCES

KIRFEL, W.: *Das Purāṇa Pañcalakṣana*. Bonn, 1927.
PARGITER, F. E.: *Ancient Indian Historical Tradition*. London, 1922.
RANGACHARYA, V.: *Pre-Musalman India*, vol. II. "Vedic India," Part I. Madras, 1937.

1. *AIHT*, pp. 30, 54.
1a. Some, however, do not attach any historical value to the story of the *Rāmāyaṇa* cf. e.g. Ch. VIII, above, p. 168..
1b. *EI*, VI, pp. 11, 12.
2. *JRAS*, 1911, pp. 479 ff., 675 ff.
3. *Bṛihat-Saṁhitā*, XIII. 3; *Rājataraṅgiṇī*. I. 48 56.
4. Rai, *PIHC*, IV. p. 115 (3140 B.C.); Triveda, *JIH*. XVI. iii (3137 B.C.); Vaidya, *HSL*, IV. pp. 4-8 (3102 B.C.); Abhyankar, *ABORI*, XXV. pp. 116-36 (3000 B.C.); Sen Gupta, *JRASB(L)*, III. 101 ff.; IV. 393 f. (2449 B.C.); Karandikar, *POC* XII. Summaries Part II, pp. 6-8 (1931 B.C.); Deb, *JASB*, XXI.. pp. 211-20 (1400 B.C.); Daftary, *POC*, XII. Summaries Part II, pp. 8-12 (1197 B.C.); Pradhan, *CAI*, pp. 262-9 (1151 B.C.).
5. *AIHT*, pp. 179-83.
6. Cf. *AIHT*, p. 179; *DKA*, pp. 13-22; 67-9; 58, 74.
6a. Woolley, *Ur of the Chaldees* (Pelican), pp. 23-4.
7. *Vāyu P.*, 21. 28; 8. 160-7; 57. 39-41, 56.
8. *Mbh*, XII. 59. 106-8.
9. *Śat. Br.* I. 8. 1. 1-6; cf. *SBE*, XII. pp. 216-8, *Mbh* (Cr. Ed.) III. 185; *Matsya*, P., 1. 11-34; 2. 1-19; *Bhāgavata P.*, VIII. 24 ff., IX. 1 ff.
10. *AIHT*, p. 84, n. 2.
11. *JRAS*, 1902, pp. 267-8; Majumdar, *CAG*, pp. 507-8; Dey, *GD*, p. 17.
12. Pratishṭhāna has been identified with Pihan, a village near Prayāga (Allāhābād)—Jayachandra, *BIR*, pp. 128-9.
12a. For the Rigvedic hymn on the subject, cf. Ch. XVI.
13. *Mbh* (Cr. Ed.), III. 176-8; (Bom. Ed.), XIII. 99-100.
14. *AIHT*, p. 259, fn. 7.
15. Śrāvastī has been identified with modern Sahet Mahet on the Rāpti in the district of Gonda in Oudh (Dey, *GD*, p. 189). Cf. also Majumdar, *CAG*, p. 469.
16. *Tribes in Ancient India*, p. 121.
17. *AIHT*, pp. 260-1.
18. *Padma P.*, VI. 189. 73; 273. 51-70; *Brahma P.*, 196. 16-197. 5; *Vishṇu P.*, V. 23. 26-24. 5; *Hari*, II. 57. 43-63.
19. *Mbh*, XII. 339. 84, 103-4; cf. Sukthankar, *ABORI*, XVIII. p. 48.
20. *Mbh*, XII. 49. 76-83.
21. In the *Navā Kāḷ* (Marāṭhī Daily of Bombay) in the year 1932-3.
22. *Matsya P.*, 43. 48-9; *Vāyu P.*, 94.51-2; Kirfel, *PPL*, p. 420.50.

23. Chedi comprised the land between the Chambal and the Ken on the southern bank of the Jumna corresponding to modern Bundelkhand. Cf. Dey, *GD*, p. 48; Majumdar, *CAG*, p. 725.
24. Kirfel, *PPL*, pp. 317-23.
25. Rohitapura has been identified with Rohtās in the district of Shāhābād in Bihar. Dey, *GD*, p. 170.
26. *Vāyu* P., 88. 140-1.
27. *Vāyu P.*, 88. 144-63; *Brahma* P.. 8. 52-71.
28. *AIHT*, p. 268.
29. The name Bhāgīrathī is applied to the stream which originates from Gangotrī and Gomukha, and joining Bhilaṅgana at Tehri meets Alakanandā, the main stream of the Ganges, at Devaprayāga. Jayachandra, *BIR*, p. 150.
30. For the Nala episode, cf. *Mbh* (Cr. Ed.), III. 50-78.
31. *Mbh* (Cr. Ed.), I. 166-73 gives another account.
32. Paudanya (Potana in *Mbh*, Cr. Ed., I. 168. 25) is the Potana or Potali of the *Jātakas* (Raychaudhuri, *PHAI*, p. 121). It has been identified with Paithan or Pratishṭhāna on the north bank of the Godāvari, 28 miles to the south of Aurangābād—Dey, *GD*, pp. 157, 159.
33. For the account of Rāma we have mainly relied on the *Rāmāyaṇa*.
34. Ancient settlements of Takshaśilā are found near the Bhir mound near Shāhdheri which lies 20 miles north-west of Rāwalpindi (Marshall—*Guide to Taxila*). Pushkarāvatī may be identified with Chārsadda near the confluence of the Kubhā and Suvāstu, 17 miles north-west of Peshāwar.
35. North Pañchāla, called Ahichchhatra, comprised the modern Rohilkhand district in the U.P., and had its capital at Ahichchatra identified with modern Rāmnagar (Dey, *GD*, p. 2). South Pañchāla, which incorporated the old kingdom of Kānyakubja, consisted of the districts of Āgrā and Cawnpore with its capitals at Mākandī and Kāmpilya (modern Kampil, 28 miles east of Fatehgarh—Dey, *GD*, p. 88).
36. The problem of the *Dāśarājña* (battle of ten kings) has been discussed in section II of this chapter.
37. *Mbh* (Cr. Ed.), I, 89. 31-43.
38. *AIHT*, pp. 76, 281.
39. *AIHT*, p. 113, fn. 9.
40. *Hari*, I. 30. 10-14; *Vāyu P.*, 93. 21-26; *Brahma P.*, 12. 9-15; *Brahmāṇḍa P.*, III. 68. 20-26; also *Mbh*, XII. 150-52; cf. *Arthaśāstra*, Mysore, 1919, p. II.
41. *Mbh* (Cr. Ed.), I, 105. 7-22.
42. The life of Kṛishṇa has been reconstructed on the basis of the old and authentic Purāṇas, the *Harivaṁśa* and the *Mahābhārata*.—See Munshi, *Glory that was Gurjaradeśa*, I. pp. 120-24.
43. Cf. Munshi, *Glory that was Gurjaradeśa*, I, pp. 111-27.
44. The account of the Kauravas and the Pāṇḍavas has been based on the *Mahābhārata*. In spite of epic embellishments, the kernel of the story may be regarded as historical.
45. Similarly some Purāṇas begin the "future" about a century after the Bhārata War. (Pargiter, *AIHT*, pp. 51-4.)
46. *AIHT*, pp. 283-4.
47. *JRAS*, 1914, p. 1027.
48. *JRAS*, 1913, p. 889.
49. *Ved. Ind.* II. p. 187.
50. *Gopatha Brāhmaṇa*, I.2. 10 ff; *Ved. Ind.*, II.p. 133.
51. *Mbh* (Cr. Ed.), I. 89. 31-43.
52. *AIHT*, p. 120.
53. *AIHT*, p. 281.
54. *CAI*, pp. 83-98.
55. *BV*, II. pp. 72-76.
56. *Nirukta*, II. 24, 25; *Mbh*, XII. 60. 39; *Manu*, VII. 41; Pargiter, *AIHT*, p. 120.
57. Ghurye, *POC*, IX. p. 950.
58. *Ait. Br.*, VII. 27; VIII. 21; *Śat. Br.*, XI. 5. 5. 13; XIII. 5. 4. 1-4.
59. *Mbh*, XII. 150. 2; *PHAI*, p. 12.
60. *Hari*, III. 2.5-6, 28-9; 5.11-7.
61. Cf. *BV*, II. pp. 72-6.
62. *Śat.* Br., XIII. 5. 4. 1 ff.
63. *Mbh*, XII. 150. 3.
64. *Hari*, I. 30.
65. *Hari*, I. 30. 6-16.
66. Cf. *Hari*, I. 32. 100-1, 105.
67. *AV*, XX. 127. 7-10.

68. *Bṛih. Up*, III. 3.
68a. *AIHT*, p. v.
69. *Mbh* (Cr. Ed.), III. 86. 9.
69a. Cf. D. R. Bhandarkar—*Carmichael Lectures*, 1918, pp. 6-7.
70. Pargiter, however, infers from the traditional account that the kings belonged to three different stocks or races of which the Ailas were the Aryans, the Saudyumna stock, the Muṇḍā race and its branch the Mon-Khmer folk in the east, and the Mānva stock (i.e. the remaining descendants of Manu), the Dravidians (*AIHT*, p. 295). Traditional history associates the Ailas or the Lunar dynasty with the Himālayas. Pargiter, therefore, interprets the traditional accounts as stating that the Aryans came into India from the Himālayan regions (*ibid.*, pp. 297 ff.). But the term Aryan is not confined to the Ailas alone; it comprises all the so-called stocks enumerated by Pargiter. There is absolutely no differentiation between the Solar and the Lunar dynasties as regards status or dignity.
71. *Manu*, X. 8.
72. Kennedy, *JRAS*, 1915, p. 516.
73. Cf. Viswanatha, *International Law in Ancient India*, pp. 25, 45; *Racial synthesis in Hindu Culture*, p. 9.

CHAPTER XV

FROM THE ACCESSION OF PARĪKSHIT TO THE END OF THE BĀRHADRATHA DYNASTY

The Purāṇas have preserved a list of the kingdoms that flourished at the end of the Bhārata War and continued till they were all absorbed by the great Nanda empire of Magadha in the fourth century B.C. In addition to the kingdom of Magadha, ruled at first by the Bārhadrathas, and then by other dynasties, the Puranic list refers to the Pauravas, Aikshvākus, Pañchālas, Kāśis, Haihayas, Kaliṅgas, Aśmakas, Maithilas, Śūrasenas and Vītihotras. The area embracing these states comprised the eastern part of North India, the middle country, and some parts towards its west; but the countries further west and north-west have not been referred to. Of the various dynasties mentioned, the Purāṇas deal in some detail only with the Pauravas, Aikshvākus and the dynasties of Magadha, but give merely the number of kings in the case of other contemporary dynasties. The detailed history of the period recorded in the Purāṇas is thus confined more or less to the region now represented by the United Provinces and South Bihār.[1]

1. THE PAURAVAS

The first Paurava king after the Bhārata War was Parīkshit, son of Abhimanyu, and grandson of Arjuna. Parīkshit was well-versed in the science of duties of kings and was endowed with noble qualities. The story of the conquests of Parīkshit or of the prosperity of the Kuru kingdom during his reign, recorded respectively in the Purāṇas and *Atharvaveda*, seems to relate to an earlier king of that name.

The Kuru kingdom over which Parīkshit ruled extended from the Sarasvatī to the Gaṅgā according to epic tradition. It corresponded to modern Thānesvar, Delhi, and the upper Gangetic *Doāb*.[2] The Kaliyuga era is said to have started in the reign of Parīkshit after the death of Kṛishṇa, and Parīkshit is reported to have chased away the Kali out of his kingdom, which merely indicates his excellent and benign rule. It is said that one day when lost in a forest, while hunting, Parīkshit met a sage and asked him the way. The sage was observing a vow of silence and did not reply. Being angry Parīkshit placed a dead snake round the sage's neck and went away. The sage's son cursed Parīkshit, and foretold that within a week the king would be bitten to death by Takshaka, king of the snakes. Despite the king's elaborate precautions, the curse had its effect and Parīkshit died of snake bite on the appointed day.

This mythical story seems to suggest a genuine historical fact. The rise of the Nāgas in Gāndhāra has already been referred to. It appears that taking advantage of the weakened condition of the Pauravas as the result of the Bhārata War, Takshaka, king of the Nāgas, marched against Hastināpura and king Parīkshit evidently died in his attempt to check their attacks.

Parīkshit's son Janamejaya was a minor when he was installed king. To avenge his father's death Janamejaya invaded Takshaśilā and slaughtered countless Nāgas. It was only through the intercession of Āstika that Janamejaya stopped this slaughter. Takshaka appears to have escaped safely. The conquest of Taxilā in the extreme north-west indicates that the intervening Madra or Central Punjab also was under the control of Janamejaya. The slaughter of innumerable Nāgas has been mythologized into the *Sarpasatra* (snake-sacrifice) of Janamejaya where serpents fell as oblations into the sacred fire through the spell of the *Mantras*.[3] Janamejaya was a powerful and strong monarch and he re-established the Kuru dominion. After conquering Taxilā and uprooting the Nāgas, Janamejaya appears to have made Taxilā his headquarters for some time. The story of the *Mahābhārata* was recited to Janamejaya at Taxilā by Vaiśampāyana.[4] Aśvapati of Kekaya was a contemporary of Parīkshit and Janamejaya. When Janamejaya subjugated Gāndhāra, Aśvapati Kekaya, whose territory lay to the east of Gāndhāra, probably accepted Janamejaya's suzerainty. Aśvapati was famous for his good government and philosophical knowledge. It is not definitely known whether Aśvapati was a title or a personal name, but it seems to be more likely that it was the title of the rulers of Kekaya.

Kakshasena, a brother of Janamejaya, seems to have established a separate kingdom. From the references in the *Pañchaviṁśa Brāhmaṇa* which states that Dṛiti, apparently priest of king Abhipratāriṇ, son of Kakshasena, performed a sacrifice in Khāṇḍava, in which lay Indra-prastha,[5] it appears that the junior branch resided at Indraprastha. A further reference to the "Abhipratāriṇas" (i.e. descendants of Abhipratārin) in the same text as "the mightiest of all their relations"[6] suggests that the junior branch excelled the other branches of the Kurus. The Kuru kings at Indraprastha continued to rule there long after the destruction of Hastināpura and the migration of the senior branch to Kauśāmbī.[7]

Janamejaya was succeeded by his son Śatānīka, who married a princess from Videha. To Śatānīka was born Aśvamedhadatta who was succeeded by his son Adhisīmakṛishṇa. None of these descendants have been definitely referred to in the Vedic texts and the exact relationship of some Kurus mentioned in the Vedic texts is not clear. It appears that Śatānīka was the contemporary of Ugrasena Janaka of Videha, and Aśvamedhadatta of Pravāhaṇa Jaivāli of the Pañchālas, both of whom were philosopher kings.[8] In the reign of Adhisīmakṛishṇa, when Divākara was ruling in Ayodhya and Senājit in Magadha, the Purāṇas are said to have been recited for the first time in the twelve-year sacrifice in the Naimishāraṇya forest on the river Gomatī in Ayodhyā. Śaunaka officiated as the head sacrificer and to him were recited the *Mahābhārata* and the Purāṇas as handed down by the Sūtas.[9] Thus there seems to have been a collection and edition of the traditional accounts for the first time, on the occasion of the Naimisha sacrifice. The lists of dynasties and kings that subsequently ruled were recorded in the future tense as if they were prophecies. The *Matsya* and *Vāyu* begin their "future kings" after the time of Adhisīmakṛishṇa.

During the reign of Nichakshu, the son and successor of Adhisīmakṛishṇa, the Kuru kingdom appears to have passed through severe calamities. The capital Hastināpura was washed away by the Ganges.[10] The devastation of crops in the Kuru country by locusts (or hail-storms), mentioned in the *Chhāndogya Upanishad*,[11] is also possibly to be referred to this period. The famine brought on by locusts was probably followed by heavy downpour flooding the country. Consequently not only Hastināpura but the whole of the northern *Doāb* was seriously affected. The Kuru people evacuated and migrated in a body over 300 miles down-stream and settled in Vatsabhūmi, with Kauśāmbī, (modern Kosam on the Yamunā near Allāhābād) as their capital. This wholesale migration, according to Pargiter, was due to the pressure from the Punjab.[12] But the explanation given in traditional accounts, coupled with the locust menace, satisfactorily accounts for the migration. The Vatsas, it may be recalled, were under the Paurava king of Kāśi,[13] and sided with the Pāṇḍavas in the Bhārata War.

The history of the Paurava kings of Kauśāmbī is obscure. The Purāṇas give only a list of twenty-three kings after Nichakshu, up to Kshemaka, the last in the line. Among them Śatānīka and his son Udayana are interesting and important figures. Śatānīka, also styled Parantapa, is said to have attacked Champā, the capital of Aṅga, during the reign of Dadhivāhana.[14] Udayana succeeded his father on the Vatsa throne. According to Buddhist accounts, Udayana was born on the same day as the Buddha. Whether we accept it or not, there are good grounds to believe that Udayana was contemporaneous with the Buddha and also with Pradyota Mahāsena of Avanti and Ajātaśatru of Magadha. His history will, therefore, be more appropriately dealt with in the next volume.

2. THE KOSALAS

The Puraṇas give a list of 31 Ikshvāku kings of Kosala beginning with Brihadbala who was killed in the Bhārata War. His sixth descendant Divākara was a contemporary of the Paurava king

Adhisīmarkṛishṇa. This Puranic list serves as a typical instance of the confusion brought about by jumbling together different historical traditions at a late date. For this genealogical list of the Ikshvāku kings of Kosala includes the names of Śākya, Śuddhodana, his son Siddhārtha and the latter's son Rāhula, immediately before Prasenajit, who is known from Buddhist sources as the son of Mahākosala and a contemporary of the Buddha. Without, therefore, relying much on this inaccurate and incomplete list we may glean a few interesting facts about Kosala from the Buddhist literature.

It appears from the Buddhist account that the Kosala kings had their capitals at Sāketa and Śrāvastī in addition to Ayodhyā. Ayodhyā was probably the earliest capital followed by Sāketa, and Śrāvastī was the last. Ayodhyā was a town on the river Sarayū. Sāketa is often taken to be identical with Ayodhyā, but the separate mention of both as existing in Buddha's time suggests that they were possibly adjoining cities like London and Westminster.[15] Śrāvastī (in Pāli Sāvatthī) has been identified with Sāhet-Māhet, on the south bank of the Rāpti on the borders of the Gonda and Bahraich districts of the United Provinces. In Buddha's time, Ayodhyā had sunk into comparative insignificance but the other two figured among the six great cities of India. The Buddhist works mention some kings of Kosala whose names are not found in the dynastic lists.[16]

We learn from the Buddhist accounts that there were frequent wars between the neighbouring kingdoms of Kosala and Kāśi and there was continued rivalry for supremacy between them. It appears, however, that sometimes friendly relations prevailed between Kāśi and Kosala and there were matrimonial alliances, and probably the countries at times were under a common ruler who came at the head either by conquest or by inheritance.[17] The Vedic texts indicate the close association of these two states by the phrase Kāśi-Kosala. In their struggle for supremacy sometimes Kāśi and sometimes Kosala emerged victorious. Though the Kāśis appear to have succeeded in the beginning, the final victory went to the Kosalas. The results of these contests, as recorded in the Buddhist literature, can be grouped in four successive stages as has been suggested by Dr. Law.[18]

The canonical legend in which Brahmadatta, the powerful king of Kāśi, in his campaigns of conquests, defeated the weak Kosalan king Dighiti, marks the first stage in the Kāśi-Kosala struggle. Brahmadatta then ordered the execution of Dighiti and his queen who were captured in the Kāśi realm living in disguise. Then the Kosala prince Dighāyu gained confidence of king Brahmadatta, was raised to the position of a general, and was reinstated on the Kosalan throne on account of his generosity in not killing Brahmadatta in revenge. In the second stage, illustrated in the *Rājovāda Jātaka*, both Kāśi and Kosala appear as equally powerful realms flourishing side by side, respectively under Brahmadatta and Mallika. The Kāśi ruler followed the religious principle of conquest of wrath by kindness, whereas the Kosala king adhered to the strong administrative principle of treating hard with hardness and soft with softness. The *Mahāsīlava Jātaka* brings out the third stage, in which the Kosala king took advantage of the good nature and religious tendencies of the Kāśi king and invaded the neighbouring kingdom.

The final stage marks the total absorption of the Kāśi kingdom under the Kosala king Mahākosala, who has been mentioned as the sovereign of both Kāśi and Kosala. From the fact that the Buddhist records do not refer to contests between Kosala and any other tribe or state, it would appear that the gradual absorption of the clans and tribes in the northern part of Kosala was effected without any important battle, campaign, or siege.[19] The contact of Kosala with Kāśi, however, as we have seen, resulted in a struggle lasting for generations with varying fortunes till Kāśi was completely subjugated by the Kosala king Kaṁsa, who appears to have been a predecessor of Mahākosala or the great Kosala. Mahākosala was the father and immediate predecessor of Prasenajit (in Pāli Pasenadi). Dr. Raychaudhuri is inclined to identify Hiraṇyanābha mentioned in later Vedic texts with Mahākosala.[20] Mahākosala gave his daughter Kosaladevī in marriage to the Magadhan king Bimbisāra. The fateful sequel of this marriage will be described in the next volume.

3. MAGADHA

We have already seen in the last chapter that the Bārhadratha dynasty ruled in Magadha at the time of the Bhārata War, and that Jarāsandha, the first great emperor of Magadha before that war, was succeeded by his son Sahadeva, who became an ally of the Pāṇḍavas, and was killed in the war. After Sahadeva, his son Somādhi became king at Girivraja, at the foot of which Rājagṛiha, the ancient capital of Magadha, grew up. The old site of Rājagṛiha corresponds to modern Rājgir in the Patna district. Senājit, the sixth successor of Somādhi, was a contemporary of the Paurava Adhisīmakṛishṇa and Kosala Divākara. Ripuñjaya, the twenty-first in descent from Somādhi, is stated to have been the last king of the Bārhadratha dynasty. Ripuñjaya is said to have been killed by his minister Pulika (variants: Su°- Mu°- or Punika, Pulaka) who then installed his son Pradyota on the throne. The Pradyota dynasty, according to the Purāṇas, lasted for five generations covering a period of 138 years, and was supplanted by Śiśunāga who, after placing his son to rule over Kāśi, fixed his capital at Girivraja (or Rājagṛiha).[21] Bimbisāra and Ajātaśatru appear in the Puranic lists as fifth and sixth in descent from Śiśunāga, who founded a new royal dynasty, called the Śaiśunāga.

But the Purāṇas have distorted history, and most of the above statements regarding the events following the death of Purañjaya are contradicted not only by the testimony of other Sanskrit sources and Buddhist accounts, but by the Puraṇas themselves. Here, as in the case of Kosala, genuine historical facts have been wrongly jumbled together, and it appears that the independent lists of the dynasties of Pradyota, Śiśunāga and Bimbisāra have been placed in a false sequence and supplied with imaginary connecting links.

That the Pradyotas ruled at Avanti would be evident from the statement in the *Matsya Purāṇa* itself,[22] and we have no reliable evidence that there was any Pradyota dynasty of Magadha. The first Pradyota was a contemporary of Bimbisāra of Magadha according to Pāli accounts, and a co-ordination of the Purāṇas with other Sanskrit literature also supports the same conclusion; but the Purāṇas separate Pradyota and Bimbisāra by about ten generations. If Śiśunāga destroyed the fame of the Pradyotas, he must come about four or five generations after Chaṇḍa Pradyota, the first king of the Pradyota dynasty. Śisunāga has been placed as the progenitor of the Bimbisāra family by the Purāṇas, whereas the Pāli accounts rightly place him four or five generations after Pradyota (and hence also Bimbisāra, his contemporary) and make him the founder of a dynasty that succeeded the dynasty of Bimbisāra.

The Purāṇas themselves in a way indicate the posteriority of Śiśunāga to Bimbisāra as they include Vārāṇasī in Śiśunāga's dominions,[23] because Bimbisāra and Ajātaśatru were the first to establish Magadha domination in Kāśī. The hostility between Avanti and Magadha, again, is to be met with for the first time in Ajātaśatru's reign. There is no trace of it during the period of Bimbisāra, and hence Śiśunāga who supplanted the Pradyotas must come after Bimbisāra and Ajātaśatru. The probable reason for placing Śiśunāga before the Bimbisāra-Ajātaśatru group appears to be that Śiśunāga had his capital at Rājagṛiha, and as Udāyin was credited in the Puranic accounts with the removal of the capital to Pātaliputra,[24] it was thought by the ill-informed Puranic chroniclers of a late date that Śiśunāga came before Udāyin. But the statement in the *Mālālaṅkāravatthu* that Rājagṛiha lost its rank as a royal city from the time of Śiśunāga indicates that Śiśunāga flourished after the palmy days of Rājagṛiha, i.e. the period of Bimbisāra and Ajātaśatru. Śiśunāga probably chose the old capital Rājagṛiha as his headquarters in order to meet the attacks from Avanti on that part of Magadha.

We may thus hold that the Bārhadratha dynasty in Magadha ended with Ripuñjaya who was probably killed by his minister, and was succeeded by Bimbisāra. The history of this famous king who laid the foundations of the greatness of Magadha will be related in the next volume.

4. OTHER KINGDOMS

In addition to the three important kingdoms of Magadha, Kosala, and Vatsa, mentioned above, several others flourished during the period following the great Bhārata War. But their history is little known, and we have to rest content with a few casual notices, gleaned from different sources. Beginning from the west we have the Pañchāla kingdom, the total number of whose rulers from the Bhārata War up to Mahāpadma Nanda is given as twenty-seven in the Purāṇas though no names are mentioned.

Parichakrā, Kāmpilya (or Kāmpīla) and Ahichchhatra are the important cities in Pañchāla that have been mentioned in the Vedic and Puranic texts. Reference has already been made to the first two cities. Ahichchhatra has been identified with a ruined site of the same name near modern Rāmnagar in the Bareilly district. The city was still considerable in extent when visited by the Chinese pilgrim Hiuen Tsang in the seventh century.

Reference has already been made to the division of the Pañchāla into north and south during the reign of king Drupada. A Jātaka story seems to suggest that a Chedi prince went to the north and formed the Uttara Pañchāla kingdom with colonists from the Pañchāla and Chedi countries.[25] The *Aitareya Brāhmaṇa* (VIII. 23) represents Durmukha as a universal monarch who made extensive conquests in every direction and was anointed by Bṛihaduktha.

Probably the Durmukha (Dummukha) of the Brahmanical and Buddhist accounts is identical with Dvimukha of Pañchāla, who, according to Jain tradition, was a Pratyeka-Buddha. Some accounts associate the name of Brahmadatta, legendary king, with Pañchāla.

We have next the kingdom of Śūrasena with its capital at Mathurā on the Yamunā. Śūrasena (modern Muttra district including some of the territory still further south) before the period of the Bhārata War was under the occupation of the scions of the Yadu family. The Purāṇas mention twenty-three Śūrasenas after the Bhārata War up to the period of Nanda, but no dynastic lists are available.

To the south of Śūrasena lay Avanti. Avanti roughly corresponds to central Mālwā, Nimār and the adjoining parts of the Central Provinces.[26] The capital of the state was also known as Avanti or Ujjayinī, identified with modern Ujjain on the Siprā, a tributary of the Chambal. Ujjayinī was a very important city in ancient India both politically and commercially, and it is rather strange that the rulers of so famous a city have not been directly mentioned in the Puranic accounts. It is probable, however, that the twenty-eight (according to some Purāṇas twenty-four) Haihayas (the descendants of Yadu) who are said to have ruled after the Bhārata War were really the rulers of Avanti. For it may be recalled that the Avantis were one of the five branches of the Haihayas.[27] According to some scholars the twenty Vītihotras who are mentioned in the Purāṇas as having ruled after the Bhārata War, were kings of Avanti.[27a] But no definite information is available regarding the history of Avanti after Vinda and Anuvinda, who flourished at the time of the Bhārata War. When we next hear of Avanti, more than five centuries later, it was under the Pradyotas, as has been related above.

Special importance attaches to the kingdom of Videha as it was a great centre of culture and learning. The Videha dynasty, or the race of the Janakas according to Puranic accounts, ended with Kṛiti, who has been identified with Kṛitakshaṇa, son of Bahulāśva, the ruler at the time of the Bhārata War.[28] But as we find mention of Janakas of Videha even after the period of Yudhishṭhira, the identification of the last of the Janakas does not seem to be correct as is rightly pointed out by Raychaudhuri.[29] Kṛiti may reasonably be identified with Karāla (Janaka) the Vaideha, mentioned in the *Arthaśāstra,* who is said to have perished along with his kingdom and relatives on account of his violation of a Brāhmaṇa maiden.[30] This story is confirmed in the Buddhist accounts, which make Kaḷāra the last of the line.

The great king Janaka of Videha, and the sage Yājñavalkya, from whom he learnt *Brahmavidyā* (spiritual knowledge), are famous names in Indian history, but their chronology is uncertain and there might have been more than one pair bearing these names. It appears from the *Mahābhārata* that one Janaka was ruling over Videha at the time of Janamejaya, son of Parīkshit, and Śvetaketu, son of Uddālaka, a prominent figure in Janaka's court, attended Janamejaya's snake sacrifice.[31] The philosopher king Janaka of the Upanishads was a contemporary of Yājñavalkya and Aśvapati, king of the Kekayas, but unfortunately both Yājñavalkya and Aśvapati are also family names, just like Janaka, so that no chronological deductions can be drawn from this synchronism. Dr. Raychaudhuri places the Vedic Janaka, whom he takes to be the father of Sītā, after the date of Janamejaya Pārīkshita, the descendant of the Pāṇḍavas.[32] This identification goes against many well-established synchronism in traditional history and fails to account for the period of Rāma and the subsequent Ikshvākus in the scheme of history.

There is, however, no doubt that one pair of Janaka, the philosopher king, and Yājñavalkya flourished after the period of the Bhārata War, as Śatānīka, the successor of Janamejaya, is said to be the disciple of this Yājñavalkya who was himself a disciple of Vaiśampāyana. Ugrasena may probably be the personal name of this Janaka, though this name does not occur in dynastic lists.[33] It may be noted that the fame of the Janakas of Videha, both before and after the Bhārata War, rests more on their patronage of learning, culture, philosophy, and spiritual attainments than on their martial exploits or sacrifices. Kings of Videha usually maintained friendly relations with neighbouring states and formed matrimonial alliances with different contemporary ruling families.

The degeneracy in character of the last monarch, as already stated, brought the Videha dynasty to an end, and the overthrow of the monarchy was followed by the rise of a republic. This political revolution in Videha is one of the important events during this period. In Buddha's time the Videhas, along with the Lichchhavis of Vaiśāli and other clans, formed a powerful confederation known as the Vajjis. The Kāśi people apparently had a hand in the overthrow of the Videhan monarchy, as frequent struggles between Kāśi and Videha have been referred to in an earlier period. Perhaps a junior branch of the royal family of Kāśi established itself in Videha.[34] The Purāṇas mention twenty-eight Maithilas as having ruled after the Bhārata War. They were probably rulers of Videha.

The traditional accounts contain no information about the kingdom of Kāśi after the Bhārata War beyond mentioning that there were twenty-four Kāśi kings down to the period of the Nandas. The Kāśis, being contiguous to the Kosalas and Videhas, naturally had some connections with these states. The later Vedic texts mention Kāśi-Kosala and Kāśi-Videha together, stating also that sometimes these had the same king and a common *Purohita,* which indicates the close contact that subsisted between these three states, Kāsi, Kosala, and Videha.[35]

The ill-feeling and rivalry between Kāśi and Kosala which is indicated by Buddhist texts has already been referred to in connection with the Kosalas. The *Assaka Jātaka* testifies to the extension of the Kāśi suzerainty to Potali in the kingdom of Assaka in Southern India. Kāśi, the capital of the state, was the premier city in all India, extending over twelve leagues as compared to seven leagues which was the extent of Mithilā and Indraprastha.[36] On account of the importance of the city of Kāśi or Benares, it was the coveted prize of the neighbouring states. According to the Puranic account, during different periods in its history, Kāśi came under the sway of three successive suzerain powers of Northern India—the Pauravas of Vatsa, the Ikshvākus of Kosala and the kings of Magadha.[37] In the interval between the decline of Vatsa and the rise of Kosala, Kāśi appears to have enjoyed independence under its famous king, Brahmadatta, who conquered Kosala, possibly about a century and a half before Buddha's time.

To the east of Magadha lay Aṅga. It has already been stated (p. 325) that Śatānīka, the father of Udayana of Kauśāmbī, attacked Champā, the capital of Dadhivāhana, king of Aṅga who, according to Puranic accounts, was the son of Aṅga. The Jain tradition represents Dadhivāhana's daughter Chandanā or Chandrabālā as the first female to embrace Jainism shortly after Mahāvīra's death. In the confusion consequent on Śatānika's invasion of Champā, Chandanā fell into the hands of a robber, but she is said to have maintained the vows of the order throughout. Aṅga seems to have been on terms of hostility all along with its neighbouring state of Magadha, and at one time included parts of Magadha, as would appear from the mention of Rājagṛiha as a city of Aṅga. The Aṅga suzerainty would also be evident from the defeat of king Bhaṭṭīya of Magadha by king Brahmadatta of Aṅga. But the Aṅga kingdom lost its independence when Bimbisāra, son of Bhaṭṭiya, avenged his father's defeat and killed the Aṅga king Brahmadatta, annexed the capital Champā, and continued there as viceroy till he left for Rājagṛiha on his father's death.[38] Bimbisāra later converted Aṅga into a separate province and appointed his son Ajātaśatru (Kunika) as governor with headquarters at Champā.

The existence of several other kingdoms during this period is known to us, but we know hardly anything about them. The Purāṇas refer to thirty-two rulers of Kaliṅga, and twenty-five of the Aśmaka kingdom, but do not give any other details. There were also the kingdoms of Gandhāra and Kāmboja in the west, but they do not come into prominence until somewhat later. There were probably other kingdoms of which we do not even know the names.

On the whole, the history of India, during the period of 400 or 800 years following the Bhārata War, according as we place that event in 100 or 1400 B.C., is only known to us in vague outline. All that we can say definitely is that Northern India was divided into a large number of states and, so far as our knowledge goes, no paramount power arose within this long period which could effectively exercise its supremacy over all or even a large number of them. We can dimly discern the struggles for supremacy, and even the ideal of imperialism so strongly stressed in the *Mahābhārata* was by no means absent, but we do not note any substantial progress towards the political unification of India.

---

1. The omission of the states in the Punjab and the north-west is significant, and probably indicates that these states were seriously affected by the disorganization consequent on the Bhārata War. We find the wild tribe of the Nāgas, who were probably inhabiting Gandhāra, suddenly rising to power and taking possession of Takshaśilā. They also invaded the Paurava kingdom, which had become feeble, and reached up to Hastināpura where they killed the Paurava king Parīkshit.
2. *PHAI*, p. 20.
3. The *Sarpasatra* mentioned in the *Pañchaviṁśa Brāhmaṇa* at which one Janamejaya is said to have officiated as a priest is quite distinct from the *Sarpasatra* instituted by king Janamejaya, as it was for securing preservation and well-being of the serpents, whereas the epic *Sarpasatra* was for the destruction of the serpents (*Pañch. Br.*, XXV. 15. 3; *Ved. Ind.*, I, 274). Raychaudhuri regards the epic account of the *Sarpasatra* as having no historical basis, but accepts the conquest of Taxilā by Janamejaya as a historical fact (*PHAI*, 30-31). But the Brāhmana passages on which he relies for support (*Ait. Br.*, VIII, 21; *Śat. Br.*,

XIII. 5.4. 1-3) relate to the universal conquests of Janamejaya, the predecessor of the Pāṇḍavas, and are stated in connection with his horse-sacrifice. Janamejaya, the descendant of the Pāṇḍavas, also started a horse-sacrifice, but it was not completed on account of some technical difficulties (*Hari*, III. 2. 5-6, 28-29; 5, 11-17), and hence Janamejaya who is said to have performed horse-sacrifices must certainly be his ancestor.

4. *Mbh*, XVIII. 5. 34.
5. *Pañch. Br.*, XXV. 3. 6, XIV, 1. 12.
6. *Pañch. Br.*, II. 9. 4.
7. Raychaudhuri, *PHAI*, p. 38. According to Pargiter, "the principalities on the Sarasvatī and at Indraprastha disappeared, and Hastināpura remained the outpost of the Hindu kingdoms of North India" (*AIHT*, p. 285).
8. Pargiter, *AIHT*, pp. 328, 330.
9. Pargiter, *DKA*, pp. 1, 4, 9-10, 15.
10. *DKA*, p. 5.
11. *Chhāndogya* Up., I. 10. 1: "*Matachīhateshu Kurushu...*"
12. *AIHT*, p. 285.
13. Pargiter, *AIHT*, pp. 269-70.
14. *JASB*, 1914, p. 321.
15. Rhys Davids, *Buddhist India*, p. 39.
16. Such as Sāgaradeva, Bharata, Aṅgirasa, Ruchi, Suruchi, Pratāpa, Mahāpratāpa, Sudarśana, Mahāsammata, Muchala, Kalyāṇa, Śatadhanu, Makhadeva, Sādhina.
17. Law, *Tribes*, p. 127.
18. *Ibid.*, pp. 125-7.
19. *CHI*, I, p. 180.
20. *PHAI*, p. 89..
21. Pargiter, *DKA*, pp. 18-22.
22. *Matsya P.*, 272. 1: *Bṛihadratheshvatīteshu Vītihotreshv = Avantishu; Pulakaḥ svāminaṁ hatvā svaputramabhishekshyati.*
23. Cf. *Matsya P.*, 272. 6; *Vārāṇasyāṁ sutaṁ sthāpya.*
24. Cf. *Matsya P.*, 272. 6; *Vāyu P.*, 99. 319.
25. Law, *Tribes*, p. 32.
26. Raychaudhuri, *PHAI*, p. 122.
27. Cf. *Matsya P.*, 43. 48-9.
27a. *JBORS*. 1915, p. 10.
28. *AIHT*, pp. 96, 149, 330.
29. *PHAI*, p. 69.
30. *Arthaśāstra*, Mysore Ed., 1919, p. 11.
31. *Mbh* (Cr. Ed.), I. 48. 7; cf. III. 132. 16, 19; also III. 135. 21-3.
32. *PHAI*, p. 47.
33. *Mbh* (Cr. Ed.), III. 134. 1.
34. *PHAI*, pp. 71-2.
35. *Śāṅkhāyana ŚS*, xvi, 29. 5; *Baudhāyana ŚS*, XXI, 3; *Gopatha Br.*, i, 2. 9; Law, *Tribes*, p. 127.
36. Cf. Jātaka Nos. 515 (Sambhava), 489 (Suruchi) and 545 (Vidhurapaṇḍita).
37. *CHI*, I, p. 316.
38. Hardy, *Manual of Buddhism*, p. 163 n.

BOOK FIVE

THE AGE OF THE RIK-SAMHITA

CHAPTER XVI

LANGUAGE AND LITERATURE

THE language of the *Ṛigveda* is the oldest known Indo-Aryan language. In several respects,[1] it is true, its specific characterization has gone further than that of the oldest forms of Irānian speech known to us. But that does not warrant the assumption that the Rigvedic language is later than Gāthic Avestan. For the innovations differentiating the language of the *Ṛigveda* from that of the Avesta are for the most part not such as may be expected to develop in course of normal and gradual evolution, but are rather suggestive of a violent deflection from the natural course. Thus the normal and natural tendency of all the known Indo-European languages has been to spirantize the occlusives either through an overdose (as in Germanic) or through an underdose (as in Celtic) of expended expiratory energy; but the language of the *Ṛigveda*, instead of spirantizing the Indo-Irānian occlusives, has on the contrary occluded a number of Indo-Irānian spirants, eliminated some, and retained only the surd sibilants. The appearance of a whole series of cerebrals, unknown in any other Indo-European dialect, points, likewise, rather to violent deflection than to gradual evolution. Similar violent deflection from the normal course of evolution cannot, however, be pointed out in Irānian. It would, therefore, be wrong to consider the innovations of both Avestan and Sanskrit in the same light, or to draw any conclusion as to their relative chronology from a comparison of those innovations.

Regarded from this point of view, it would moreover seem that the whole problem of Indo-European phonetics requires restatement and reconsideration. It has been always tacitly assumed that Sanskrit, which possesses so few spirants, gives the truest picture of Indo-European consonantism; but that is, at the best, an unproved hypothesis. What is an incontestable fact is that a strong spirantizing tendency was present already in the basic Indo-European language, and that this tendency, already in the later Indo-European epoch, caused the emergence of a whole new series of palatals out of the velars.

Moreover, in all the better known Indo-European dialects of the historical age, the number of spirants is much larger than in Sanskrit. And when we add to all this the further consideration that in actual pronunciation the true occlusive—which is in each case an ideal norm between the results of the expenditure of too much and too little expiratory energy—is hardly ever heard in any language then perhaps it would seem obvious and necessary to consider the imposing system of occlusives registered by Sanskrit grammarians not as a faithful picture of the original state of things in the basic Indo-European, but as the result of later variation.

It is not too much to suggest that also the sonant aspirates, which are found in no other Indo-European dialect, are but the Indian version of Indo-European sonant spirants. It appears, therefore, that not only the Indo-European vowel-system has been fundamentally transformed in Sanskrit, as is universally recognized to-day, but also that, at least in one respect, namely in respect of spirants, Sanskrit consonantism has innovated no less. And this holds good for the oldest recorded form of Sanskrit, namely the language of the *Ṛigveda.*

The Rigvedic language is hieratic, and therefore to some extent exclusive and artificial; but it is on that account by no means an instrument of mere suggestion without any power of direct and forceful expression, as is the case, in a great measure, with Classical Sanskrit. On the contrary in pithiness it excels even the Latin of the Classical Age. That is largely because the Rigvedic poets strove throughout to present a complete idea, though not always a complete sentence, in every verse-foot (*pāda*). *Pādas* of this kind, usually of eight to twelve syllables, were naturally not easy to construct, and, therefore, ready-made *Pādas* have often been repeated in the *Ṛigveda* with or without any material variation, though not so indiscriminately as were the Homeric verse-fragments in the *Iliad.*[2]

The verb generally used in the *Ṛigveda* to express the art of versification is *taksh,* which literally means "to hew." Just as a carpenter, by applying the art of his trade, constructs beautiful pieces of furniture, so does the poet—*kāru* (literally: "manual worker")—manufacture beautiful verses and hymns with which to win the favour of the gods, either for himself, or more frequently, for his patron. Such hymns were regarded directly as gifts of gods (*devattạ*). It is clear that verse-making had already become a recognized profession in the Rigvedic age, and also that this profession had become a monopoly of the priestly classes. In the hands of the professional verse-makers Rigvedic poetry attained an amazing degree of technical perfection, but true poetry could not and did not flourish in the Rigvedic atmosphere, surcharged as it was with a spirit of bargaining between gods and men. Poetry of a high order springs either from absolute self-surrender, or from absolute individualism. But the spirit of Rigvedic poetry always oscillates between these two extremes, without ever attaining the highest altitude of either. Barring the all-pervading element of ritualism that has deadened its life, Rigvedic poetry therefore strikes the reader as intensely human, though not as actually sublime. With these few preliminary remarks about Rigvedic language and literature, we shall now proceed to a more detailed analysis of both.

1. LANGUAGE

In its phonetic structure the Rigvedic language shows practically the same sounds as the Classical Sanskrit, the only notable exceptions being *ḷ* and *ḷh*, which take the place of intervocalic *ḍ* and *ḍh* in the *Ṛigveda*. But the frequency of the sounds is not the same in the *Ṛigveda* and in Classical Sanskrit. The relative frequency of *r* and *l* in Rigvedic and later language is highly interesting. In the older language, *l* is of rare occurrence, but it extends its sphere more and more at the expense of *r*, and it is well known that in the Prākritic stage some dialects of eastern India had completely eliminated *r*. It is also well known on the other hand that in ancient Irānian every Indo-European *l* had become an *r*. During the intervening period, of which roughly the first half is covered by changing and living Sanskrit,[3] *r* lost more and more ground to *l*. In the later portions of the *Ṛigveda*, *l* is eight times as frequent as in the older parts, and in the *Atharvaveda* it is seven times as frequent as in the *Ṛigveda*.[4] Thus it is clear that increase of *l* in frequency went hand in hand with the progress of the Aryans towards the east. In a passage often repeated in the Brāhmaṇas it is said that the Asuras suffered defeat at the hands of the gods because they mispronounced the word *arayaḥ* as *alayaḥ*.[5] This would suggest that in the later Vedic age, when the word *asura* had lost its original meaning and became a general term of opprobrium, the propensity of the easterners to pronounce *l* for *r* was noticed and frowned upon by the orthodox Aryans. Or it may mean that the Asuras referred to were none but those of the incoming Aryan tribes who, being of a particular group with its particular phonetic laws, not only retained unchanged the Indo-European *l*, but also made it the representative of Indo-European *r*.[6] In short, the behaviour of *l* and *r* in the *Ṛigveda* suggests as clearly that the invading Aryans were not quite homogeneous in speech as the increase of *l* at the expense of *r* suggests increasing eastern influence on the Vedic language.

That the Rigvedic language was not quite homogeneous is proved also by its lack of uniformity in regard to Fortunatov's law. According to this law, Indo-European *l*, when followed by dental occlusive or *s*, disappears after cerebralizing the following sound, whereas Indo-European *r* under similar circumstances remains. Thus in Skt. *jaṭhara-*, the *-ṭh-* is derived from Indo-European *-lth-* (cf. Gothic *kilthei*), and in Skt. *bhāshate*, the *-sh-* is derived from Indo-European *-ls-* (cf. Lithuanian *balsas*); but in Skt. *vart- vars-*, the *r* in the sound-group *-rt-* and *-rs-* (both of Indo-European antiquity, cf. Lat. *verto*, Gr. *ersē*)has not disappeared. These and other similar examples seem to prove Fortunatov's law; but there are exceptions. Indo-European *l* + dental has clearly developed into *-rt-* in Skt. *jartu-* which is a side-form of *jaṭhara-*, and is, like it, connected with Goth. *kilthei*, and in Skt. *karshū*, which is connected with Greek *tèlson*, the *l* of the Indo-European consonant group *-ls-* has not disappeared as Fortunatov's law would have it, but has become *r*. De-occludization of some occlusives in the *Ṛigveda* shows that this characteristic of the Prākrit dialects was latent also in the oldest Sanskṛit. Thus we find *h* for *dh* in the verbal ending *-hi* for *-dhi*, in *hita* from *dha-*, in *gṛiha* from **gṛidha*, etc., *h* for *bh* in grah-, a side-form of *grabh-*; *h* for *gh* in *hanti* (cf. *ghnanti*), *in arh-*, a side-form of *argh-*, in *dah-* from *dhagh-*, etc.

Apart from these significant details which seem to challenge the claim of the Rigvedic language to have been a homogeneous one, there are others which definitely prove that to some extent it was also artificial. Thus it can hardly be an accident that in the Atri-Maṇḍala (fifth) there is not a single infinitive form in *-tu;* the Kāṇvas, the reputed authors of the first and the eighth Maṇḍalas, seem to have intentionally avoided using infinitive forms in *-tum* and *-tavai;* the Vasishṭhas, the authors of the seventh Maṇḍala, show a similar aversion to absolutives in *-tvā* and *-tvāya*. Moreover, perfect forms like *yamátur* (VI. 67 1) and *skambhathur* (VI. 72. 2), without reduplication, must be regarded as purely artificial momentary formations like the non-reduplicating second person dual perfect *takshathur* (X. 39. 4), formed perhaps in imitation of the third person plural preterite *takshur* (II. 19. 8), which in that case must have been mistaken for a perfect-form as Wackernagel[7] has suggested. This also proves in a striking manner that the language of the earlier Maṇḍalas was already in danger of being misunderstood when the hymns of the tenth Maṇḍala were being composed.

Intentional imitation of the earlier parts of the *Ṛigveda* in the later parts is clearly proved in the case of the group of hymns X. 20-26, the author of which "has emphasized his dependence on earlier tradition by prefixing to his own group the opening words of the first hymn of the first book."[8] At any rate, parts of the earlier *Ṛigveda* must have become part of the ritual tradition at the time of the author of the hymn X. 181, for he mentions the fact that the Rathantara-sāman is chanted to a couplet composed by Vasishṭha (VII. 32. 22-23) and the Bṛihat-sāman on another composed by Bharadvāja (VI. 46. 1-2).

On the whole, however, the language of the first nine Maṇḍalas must be regarded as homogeneous, in spite of traces of previous dialectal differences, particularly in the treatment of *r* and *l*, and of faint suggestions of particular mannerisms of different composer-families. With the tenth Maṇḍala it is a different story. The language has here definitely changed. The difference in language between the earlier Maṇḍalas and the tenth would have appeared in its true proportions if the texts concerned had been written down at the time they were composed and handed down to us in that written form.

The fact, however, is that the text-tradition of the *Ṛigveda* was stabilized at a comparatively late date, and fixed in writing at a much later epoch. The result has been not unlike what would have happened if the works of Chaucer and Shakespeare were put in writing and printed for the first time in the twentieth century: in short the text of the *Ṛigveda* as handed down to us is, in various details, not only different from what it actually was, but to some extent also screens the differences that mark off the languages of the earlier Maṇḍalas from that of the tenth.[8a] The evidence of the metres, which, *inter alia,* demand a heavy penultimate in verse-feet of ten or eleven syllables but a light one in those of eight or twelve,[9] clearly proves that the actual pronunciation of the word *pāvaka* must have been *pavāka* in the Rigvedic age, but the fact has been completely suppressed in the traditional text. Similarly, on the evidence of the metres, the word *chhardis* seems to have been without an *r* in the *Ṛigveda,* and very probably the redactors of the *Ṛik-saṁhitā* in some passages intentionally altered *chhadis* into *chhardis* for reasons that cannot now be ascertained.[10]

Apart from these and other sporadical instances of misrepresentation,[11] the text of the *Ṛigveda* has in various respects undergone a fundamental rehandling that has to no small degree altered its original character. In the original text, there was hardly ever *sandhi* between the end of a verse-foot and the beginning of another, as is clearly indicated by the evidence of metres, but the final redactors have systematically joined them in *sandhi* wherever possible,[11a] though they did not apply their misguided zeal to cases of non-*sandhi* within the verse-foot. The application of *abhinihita-sandhi* (absorption of an initial *a-* into a final *-e* or *-o*) is in this regard highly interesting. Whether within a verse-foot or between two verse-feet, the *abhinihita-sandhi* in almost all its instances has to be dissolved in reading. But the fact is that this *sandhi* is found in the written text regularly between two verse-feet (i.e. where it should not have taken place at all), but within the verse-foot its occurrence is irregular and facultative, seemingly without any principle. Similar, though not quite the same, is the case also with the other kinds of vowel-*sandhi* in the *Ṛigveda,* such as *kshaipra* (i.e. the change of a preceding vowel into the corresponding semi-vowel before a dissimilar vowel) and *Praślishṭa* (i.e. coalition of two similar vowels into a long one), for they too have to be dissolved in reading, often within the verse-foot and practically always between two verse-feet. But semi-vowels which are not the result of *kshaipra-sandhi* have also to be very often dissolved (*iyādipūraṇa*).

The evidence of metre shows, moreover, that not seldom a short vowel has to be inserted in reading between a consonant and an *r* immediately preceding or following it in the same word (thus *indra* has often to be read *indara*). This inserted vowel sometimes reveals flexional forms which otherwise would never have been discovered. Thus apparently the stems in *-i*, *-u*, *ṛi* take the endings *-yoḥ*, *voḥ*, and *-roḥ* respectively in genitive and locative dual as in the classical language, but readings restored with the help of the metre clearly show that the normal ending in the Rigvedic age was dissyllabic in each case: the traditional text has adopted these monosyllabic endings, evidently under the influence of the later language.[12] The case of long *ṛī* is rather peculiar. As a rule it is found in the written text only in those forms which are palpably similar to other forms with other long vowels; thus *pitṛīn* is written with long *ṛī* because palpably similar forms such as *munīn* or *sādhūn* show a long vowel. Otherwise the short *ṛi* in the *Ṛigveda* represents also the long *ṛī*. Thus in *dṛiḍha* the short *ri* stands for long *ri* that is demanded both by grammar and orthoepy. Frank cases of *Prākritism* are *jyotis* from *dyut-*, *ushṭānām*[13] for *ushṭrāṇām*, *śithira* for *śrithira*, *sūre duhitā* (I. 34. 5) for *sūrc duhitā* (VII. 69. 4), etc. On the other hand, words like *nīḍa* (*from* **ni-zd-a*), *dūḷabha* (from **duz-dabh-a*), *shoḍaśa* (from **shash-daśa*), etc., could have been formed only at a pre-Vedic stage of the language.

Such a pre-Vedic stage is suggested also by forms of the so-called *flexion forte* of a number of *i*-stems and *u*-stems, found only in the *Ṛigveda* and certainly of Indo-European antiquity.[14] Vowels of dissyllabic value are a precious relic of Indo-European antiquity, the commonest case being the ending *-ām* in the genitive plural which has often to be read as *-aām*. The use of a verb-form in the singular number when the subject is a plurality of neuter things was the normal rule in the original Indo-European of which ample evidence is found in other Indo-European dialects, but in the *Ṛigveda* we have only one sure instance of this usage, namely *dhṛishṇave dhīyate dhanā* (I. 81. 3).

The verbal system revealed by the *Ṛigveda* is infinitely more complex than that of Classical Sanskrit, and yet what we find is a drastically simplified form of what it was in the basic Indo-European language. Thus the original thematic ending *-o* in the first person singular has been preserved only in thirteen subjunctive forms,[15] but in other subjunctive forms of the first person singular it was extended by *-ni* that came to be associated with it already in the Indo-Irānian epoch. The active ending in the first person plural seems to have been *-mes* in the original Indo-European on the evidence of Greek and other languages, but the ancient Irānian dialects know only *-masi*;[16] in the *Rigveda* both *-masi* and *-mas* occur side by side, the former being more than five times as frequent as the latter; in the *Atharvaveda* *-mas* becomes commoner than *-masi*, and in the classical language *-masi* disappears altogether. The augment has retained in the *Ṛigveda* its original character of an independent preverb, and as such is very frequently dispensed with when the past sense is clear from the context. The forms thus obtained are either of the indicative or of the injunctive mood, almost equal in number in the *Ṛigveda*, the injunctive forms being in about one-third of their occurrences governed by the prohibitive particle *mā*.[17] In the classical language the augment can be dropped only when in construction with this prohibitive particle. The perfect is not necessarily a tense of the past as in Classical Sanskrit, but is merely suggestive of the fullest amplitude of action. It is pronouncedly suggestive of past action only when preceded by adverbs like *purā* "formerly," but it can also be governed by particles like *nūnam* "now."

On the whole the Rigvedic verb expresses more the modes and aspects of action than the time of occurrence, if the augment, which was not an integral part of the verb, is left out of consideration. The subjunctive mood is in full bloom in the *Ṛigveda*, but it was completely eliminated from the classical language. On the other hand, the optative, though not so popular as the subjunctive in the *Ṛigveda*, has been retained throughout. The future tense which was in origin a desiderative present was in the *Ṛigveda* still in the process of changing its rôle. It is still in its beginnings, and the *Ṛigveda* forms a future stem only from fifteen roots.

The language of the tenth Maṇḍala represents a distinctly later stage of the Rigvedic language.[18] Hiatus, which is frequent in the earlier *Ṛigveda*, is already in process of elimination here. Stressed *i u* cannot in *sandhi* be changed into *y v* in the earlier parts, but in the tenth Maṇḍala they can. The ending *-āsas* in nominative plural is half as frequent as *-ās* in the *Ṛigveda* taken as a whole, but its number of occurrences is disproportionately small in the tenth Maṇḍala. Absolutives in *-tvāya* occur only here. The stem *rai-* is inflected in one way in the first nine Maṇḍalas, and in another in the tenth,[19] and in the inflexion of *dyau-*, too, the distribution of strong and weak forms is much more regular in the earlier Maṇḍalas. The Prākritic verbal stem *kuru-* appears only in the tenth Maṇḍala for the earlier *kṛiṇu-*. Many words appear for the first time in the tenth Maṇḍala or are shared by it only with the interpolated parts of other Maṇḍalas. The old locative form *pṛitsu*, adjectives like *girvaṇas* and *vicharshaṇi*, and the substantive *vīti* do not occur at all in the tenth Maṇḍala, though in the earlier Maṇḍalas they are quite common. The particle *sīm*, which is unknown in the *Atharvaveda*, occurs fifty times in the first nine Maṇḍalas but only once in the tenth. Words like *ājya, kāla, lohita, vijaya*, etc., occur for the first time in the tenth Maṇḍala, as also the root *labh-*. Words shared with the tenth Maṇḍala only by the interpolated parts of other Maṇḍalas, the Vālakhilyas, and unmistakably late hymns are *loka* (for earlier *uloka* which is a haplology for *uruloka*), *mogha*, *visarga*, *gup-* (a back-formation from *gopa*), etc. And words which occur mostly, though not exclusively, in the tenth Maṇḍala and these parts, are *sarva*, *bhagavant*, *prāṇa*, *hṛidaya*, etc. The archaic particle ī of pronominal origin, for which the Padapāṭha throughout wrongly reads *īm*, does not occur at all in the tenth Maṇḍala, and the particle *īm*, which is only less archaic than *ī*, occurs in it only about half a dozen times.[20] Of forms like *dakshi*, *adukshat*, etc.,[21] which are the results of the action of a pre-Vedic phonetic law,[22] only one, namely *dudukshan*, occurs in the tenth Maṇḍala. It is unnecessary to dilate any further on the language of the *Ṛigveda*.

2. LITERATURE

The Rigvedic literature is not less colourful. The earliest attempt to classify Vedic hymns systematically according to contents is to be found in Yāska's *Nirukta* (VII. 1-2). Stating first that the stanzas are either indirectly addressed (*paroksha*), directly addressed (*pratyaksha*), or are self-invocations (*ādhyātmikī*), Yāska proceeds to specify the characteristics and cite instances of the various types of hymns. There are, to begin with, hymns in pure praise of the deity without any prayer, as, for instance the Indra-hymn I. 32, bearing unmistakable characteristics of a popular ballad:[23]

1. The heroic deeds of Indra shall I proclaim, the deeds
that the thunder-wielder performed first.
He slew the dragon, freed the waters, slit the bowels
of the hills.
2. He slew the dragon resting on the hill.
Tvashṭā had forged for him the shining thunder,
And the waters springing forth rushed towards the ocean,
like cows lowing (at the sight of their calves).
8. Like a broken reed there he lay.
Over him flowed the waters gladdening hearts;
Those whom Vṛitra held beleaguered by his body—
at their feet now he lay.
11. As Dāsa-wives stayed the waters guarded by the dragon,
like the cows restrained by the Paṇis:
the watery pit which was sealed,—that he opened by
slaying Vṛitra, and released the waters.
15. Indra is the monarch of all that move and rest.
the thunder-wielder is monarch of tame and horned
animals:
He indeed is ruler of all the peoples;
like a felly round the spokes of a wheel he protects all.

Mantras of the second type, according to Yāska, are those in which the poet prays for favours without praising the deity. It is significant that Yāska cannot cite a single *Mantra* of this type out of the *Ṛigveda,* but adds that they are plentiful in the Yajurveda. Oaths and imprecations constitute the third type according to Yāska, and he cites as instance *Ṛigveda* VII. 104. 15: "May I die to-day if I am a sorcerer or if I have tried to take a man's life by sorcery, but may he, too, who falsely called me a sorcerer, bewail the death of ten grown up sons." Fourthly, according to Yāska's classification, there are hymns containing objective descriptions of particular states, and, significantly enough, he cites as a specimen the cosmogonical hymn X. 129: "Then there was neither death nor immortality, etc." In the fifth category are included by Yāska the *Mantras* expressive of apprehension, such as X. 95. 14: "The benevolent god may fly forth to-day and never return."[24] Lastly, according to Yāska, there are hymns of which the purpose is to administer censure or praise, and as an illustration he cites that unique hymn, namely X. 117:

1. Hunger was certainly not meant as a means of death by the
   gods. For also him who has eaten his fill, death befalls
   in various forms;
   The wealth of the liberal is never exhausted,
   But the stingy person never finds a friend.
2. He who though possessing food, to the broken and begging
   destitute, approaching him, refuses a morsel,
   And hardens his heart against him even though he had served
   him before,
   he too, likewise, never finds a friend.
3. He indeed is a patron who gives to the beggar,
   longing for food, wandering and thin,
   Who then readily responds to his call to arms,
   and also thenceforward becomes his friend.
4. He is no friend who does not give to the friend
   —to the comrade asking for food;
   Let him turn away from him, with him there is no shelter,
   rather seek shelter with a generous stranger.
5. Let the wealthier person be generous to the applicant;
   let him take a longer view;
   For life rolls on like the wheels of a chariot,
   wealth comes now to one, now to other.
6. The food earned by the fool is in vain,
   truly say I that it is death to him;
   He feeds no comrade nor a friend; he eats alone and also
   bears the burden of his sins alone.
7. Only when ploughing does the plough-share produce food;
   only by walking can a distance be covered;

A Brāhmaṇa who can speak is preferable to one who cannot,
A liberal friend should be better than an illiberal one.

The hymn is packed with noble sentiments, and its every word is charged with vigour. Yet it should not be forgotten that the hectoring eloquence of this energetic priest was probably directed mainly to the purpose of frightening the wealthy into ceding a part of their wealth to the Brāhmaṇas especially, and not to the poor of every class, for of genuine sympathy for the poor there is not much in the *Ṛigveda*.

Yāska's brief and purely formal classification of the contents of the *Mantra*-texts is, however, anything but satisfactory. It is true that the main body of the hymns contains praises or prayers or both. But from the literary point of view they should best be regarded as lyrical poems adapted to the purpose of ritual. Of these the hymns addressed to Heaven's daughter Aurora (Ushas) are perhaps the oldest and certainly the most beautiful. They have something of the lyric beauty and love of nature of Shelley and Wordsworth, and one cannot help feeling that they were inspired by the sight of the sunrise over the snowclad peaks of the Himālayas. A few stanzas of the first hymn to Ushas (I. 48) will suffice to reveal the spirit of simple adoration in which the goddess was invoked by the *Ṛishis:*

1. Light us up with happiness, O Ushas, daughter of heaven,
with great lustre, O radiant one, with wealth, O bountiful goddess.

5. Like a fair maiden comes Ushas, gladdening (all),
she comes awakening four-footed beasts, and makes the birds rise into the air.

9. O Ushas, shine with shimmering radiance, O daughter of heaven, bringing us ample happiness, as you shew your light upon the daily sacrifice.

10. The breath and life of the whole world is in you,
O noble one, as you shine forth;
as such, O resplendent one with towering chariot,
give ear to our cry, O bestower of various gifts.

11. O Ushas, win then (for us) the prize that is admired among human folk.
With that, hasten to the sacrifices of your worshippers,
the sacrificers who are chanting your praises.

14. Whoever were the *Ṛishis* of old that invoked you
for protection and support, O noble one,
Yet accept our hymns and bestow on us a gift in token
of your satisfaction, O Ushas, with brilliant lustre.

Here it is simplicity and not greed that is begging of the goddess gifts and more gifts. But it cannot escape even the most superficial reader that in hymns such as this the means that the poets have in view for attaining their object is simply to please the deity by flattering songs and ritual sacrifices. There is no suggestion as yet of a belief in the existence of a supreme justice from which flow all punishment and reward. In the hymns to Varuṇa, however, this sentiment is already in the horizon: The hymn to this god by Kūrma Gārtsamada (II. 28), for example, opens in the usual flattering tone:

1. May this (hymn) addressed to Aditi's son who is wise and
 self-supreme excel all the existing (hymns) in greatness;
 The god whom it is exceedingly pleasant to worship,—
 of that affluent Varuṇa do I beg glorious fame.

But the tone soon changes, and adulation turns into admiration for god-created cosmic harmony:

4. Aditi's son unleashed them (i.e. the rivers) and
 started them on various paths,
 the rivers course along in obedience to Varuṇa's ordinance;
 Never released are they, nor ever tired,
 like birds they swiftly fly in never-ending course
 (*lit.* round the earth).
5. Loosen the bond of sin like a girdle, O Varuṇa;
 We shall fully conform to the rule of equity you have ordained.
 May not the thread snap while I am still weaving my prayer-song,
 may not the measuring-rod break out of season.
6. Avert terror from me, O Varuṇa,
 be kind to me, as a righteous ruler.
 Release me from anguish, as a calf from the rope;
 not even for a moment can I live away from you.
7. Do not strike us, Varuṇa, with the weapons which, in your search,
 O Asura, destroy those who commit sin.
 May we not have to bid adieu to light;
 loosen the hold of the envious on us, so that we may live.

That virtue is its own reward, and, as a spiritual quality, is incommensurable in terms of material advantage, does not seem to have been realized by the Rigvedic poets. The spirit of the people that peeps through the thick veil of ritual pedantry is one of gladness, aspiring ever for more, never knowing rest or contentment. Absence of evil is not what they pray for most. Their supreme desire is to triumph over poverty and resistance. Their chief god is Indra who does not possess a single spiritual trait. But their minds are fresh, and, therefore, deeply impressed by the violence of natural phenomena. Atri's hymn (V. 83) to Parjanya (the storm-god) is perhaps the most striking example:

2. He strikes down the trees, he strikes also the Rakshasas,
   the whole world is afraid of (Parjanya) carrying mighty arms.
Even the sinless quake before the bull-like god,
   when Parjanya, thundering, strikes the evil-doers.
3. Like the charioteer lashing forward his horses by the whip
   does he announce the messengers of rain,
Lion's roars from a distance are heard,
   When Parjanya renders rainy the sky.
4. Winds blow fast and lightnings flash,
   plants shoot up and heaven swells;
Quickening showers fall for all
   when Parjanya gladdens the earth with his seed.
7. Roar and thunder, sow the seed,
   come flying hither in squelching car;
Turn downward the skin unbound,
   so that be levelled high lands and low.

Hymns of this type are unique in world literature, for nowhere else can the deification of natural phenomena be so clearly perceived.

Martial spirit is well reflected in hymn VI. 75, though, evidently, it is not a real war-song, but rather a magical incantation supposed to secure victory in battle:

1. Like a thunder-cloud becomes his face,
   when the mailed warrior plunges into the thick of battle.
Be victorious without being injured in body,
   may the strength of the armour protect you.
2. By the bow we'll win the cattle, by the bow the battle,
   by the bow shall we win the mighty struggles.
The bow destroys the enemy,
   by the bow shall we conquer the regions.
3. As if to whisper the string nears the ear,
   holding in embrace its dear friend (the bow);
Stretched on the bow it lisps like a girl,
   this string, that helps on to victory.

The din of battle is always in the background of the Rigvedic stage, but the poets, being for the most part priests, failed to give anything like a true picture of it. Yet, sometimes, the priests themselves were present on the battle-field. The Bhārata-army succeeded in crossing the rivers Vipāś and Śutudrī only when Viśvāmitra by his eloquence persuaded them to lower their level. The colloquy between the priest and the rivers (III. 33) is quite interesting. Says Viśvāmitra:

3. To the most motherly stream have I come,
   the broad and propitious Vipāś have we reached;
One the other licks like the mother-cow her calf,
   as in the same bed they follow their course.

Not to be taken in so easily, the rivers ask suspiciously:

4. Swollen thus with a flood of milk
do we flow along the god-created bed;
Our course, once in flow, can not be stopped:
with what object does the sage invoke us?

And Viśvāmitra comes pat with his request:

5. Stop in your course a moment, O true ones,
listen to my Soma-sweet speech;
An ardent prayer to you I address;
seeking help Kuśika's son invokes you.

The rivers at last agree and express their consent with the words:

10. We shall do as you say, O poet,
since in cart and chariot you have come from afar;
To you shall I stoop as the mother swelling (with milk to her child),
like a maid her lover shall I obey you.

The most famous and interesting of the dialogue-hymns contained in the *Ṛigveda* is the one (X. 95) in which the mortal Purūravas tries but fails to persuade the nymph Urvaśī to continue to live with him. The lure of paradise is too much for the fickle female. She leaves her mortal lover, and her last words (verse 15) are cruel and cynical, though not unsympathetic:

Purūravas, do not die, do not perish (?)
Let not the cruel wolves devour you;
The friendship of woman is never indeed firm,
for they are hyenas in heart.

These dialogue-hymns may be regarded as dramas in embryo (not necessarily for the stage). In most cases they are obscure. But there is nothing to justify the theory[25] that the verses were once connected by prose narrative now lost. The dialogue-hymns, though in most cases clearly of secular origin, must have been utilized in some sort of ritual drama, for otherwise it is difficult to explain their inclusion in the Saṁhitā.

Though Rigvedic poetry is predominantly lyrical, the Sāṁhitā contains not a single hymn that may be called a love-poem. In the *Atharvaveda*, too, we have only love-charms. This is difficult to explain, specially when so many different types of hymns of non-religious origin are included in the *Ṛigveda*. One of them is the well-known and oft-quoted satirical frog-hymn (VII. 103):

1. Hibernating throughout the year
like Brāhmiṇs observing a vow,
Animated by the divine Parjanya
the frogs are now croaking loudly.
2. When heavenly showers fall on them,
lying in a pond like shrivelled skins,

Like the lowing of cows for their calves,
sound the voices of frogs in unison.
3. When showers fall on longing creatures
and slake their thirst at the start of the rainy season,
With rapture in the voice, like the son his father,
they greet each other without cessation.
5. One repeats the word of another,
like students echoing the voice of the teacher;
Together they form a chorus,
when at rain-fall loudly they croak.

Another remarkable hymn of non-religious origin is the merry song by Śiśu Āṅgirasa (IX. 112) with the refrain "flow O Soma for Indra's sake".

1. Diverse indeed are our aims,
different are the tasks of men,
The builder seeks for cracks, leeches for the sick,
and priests are greedy for sacrifices.
2. With seasoned timber of ancient trees
and the feathers of birds,
The goldsmith seeks those who possess gold,
ready with his furnaces and precious gems.
3. A bard I am, my father a leech,
and my mother is a grinder of corn;
Diverse in means, but all wishing wealth,
equally we strive for cattle.

The fourth and concluding verse is coarse in expression, foreshadowing verses of the same brand in the *Atharvaveda*. This hymn is of particular importance also for the light which it throws upon the caste-system in the Rigvedic age, for it shows clearly that professions were not yet determined by birth. But there was already a fully developed class-system dating from the Indo-Irānian epoch, as is unavoidable in every society that has outgrown the savage state; and inevitably the professions in the Rigvedic class-system already showed a distinct tendency to become hereditary.

Dāsa princes like Śambara, Dhuni, Chumuri, Pipru, and Varchin have been actually mentioned by the Rigvedic poets, but it is significant that, as a rule, Indra himself has been made to combat them on his own initiative and not in course of rendering merely routine assistance to Aryan chiefs.[26] For it shows that even in the heyday of Rigvedic culture there was no longer a living memory of the first encounters with the aboriginal races.[27] At the time of the Battle of the Ten Kings (*dāśarājña*), however, which is the central event of the history of the period (*ante*, p. 250) when the Aryan tribes began to feel themselves secure enough to indulge in the luxury of fighting each other, Indra is invoked only to render aid, but not to lead the onslaught. This significant difference in the treatment of previous and contemporary events would seem to suggest that the priestly poets of the Rigvedic age were not without a semblance of historical sense.

On the other hand, the hymns, which in the absence of anything better are taken to be historical poems, namely the *Dānastuṭis* (psalms in praise of munificence), are generally made-to-order pedestrian compositions without any historical data of real value. Generally they are sets of three to five verses appended to a hymn of the usual type. Only one hymn (I: 126) is entirely a *Dānastuti*, and that one is perhaps the worst in the *Ṛigveda:*

1. No bad hymns am I offering by exerting my intellect
   In praise of Bhavya ruling on the Indus,
   Who assigned to me a thousand sacrifices,
   The incomparable king desirous of fame.
2. A hundred gold pieces from the fame-seeking king
   Together with a hundred horses as a present have I received,
   I, Kakshivant, obtained also a hundred cows from my master,
   Who exalted thereby his fame immortal up to heaven.
3. Dark horses given by Svanaya, and
   Ten chariots carrying slave-girls fell to my share;
   Followed a herd of sixty thousand cows,
   All this as sacrificial fee did Kakshivant receive at the end of the session.
4. Forty ruddy horses of the set of ten chariots
   Are heading the column of a thousand cows;
   Fiery steeds decorated with pearls
   Have the Kakshivants and Pajras received.
5. After the first gift, I received
   Three chariots and eight cows capable of nourishing even a rich patron
   For you, my good relations, who, as clan-fellows,
   Driving in chariots, hankered for fame.[28]

This dismal hymn ends with two more verses notable only for their extreme obscenity. It is in these *Dānastutis* that Brahmanical greed appears in its worst aspect in the *Ṛigveda.*

Scarcely less debased than the *Dānastutis* are the Āprī-hymns,[29] manufactured artificially for employment in animal-sacrifice. Every priestly family has its own Āprī-hymn, and all of them (ten altogether) are constructed in the same pattern. Eleven different deities and deity-groups in as many different verses have been invoked in each Āprī-hymn in the same order. Only in regard to the second deity there is evident uncertainty, for in four Āprī-hymns it is Tanūnapāt, in four other Narāśaṁsa, and in the first two Āprī-hymns we find as second deity both Tanūnapāt and Narāśaṁsa, each with a verse for himself. Moreover at the end of the second Āprī-hymn, there is a special verse invoking Indra. Thus the first Aprī-hymn consists of twelve, the second of thirteen and each of the rest of eleven verses. The Āprī-hymns, though of no literary value, are of immense importance for the history of Vedic religion. They prove conclusively that also in the oldest period, as at later epochs, ritual had never been fully standardized. There is no reason to doubt that these hymns were actually used at animal-sacrifices as tradition maintains. But there is nothing in the Āprī-hymns to suggest that in the Rigvedic period the animals sacrificed were regarded as substitutes for the sacrificers themselves as was the case in later ritual.[29a]

The funeral hymns too seem to have been composed specially for ritual purposes, but they contain truly noble sentiments. As cremation and burial were both in vogue, we have both burial and cremation hymns. But the character of the respective hymns leaves scarcely any doubt that burial was the earlier custom. It is significant that the deceased, if a man, still holds a bow in his hand, which the priest takes away from him at the time of burial with the words (X. 18. 9):

The bow I take from the hand of the deceased
for our power and glory and strength:
Even there where you lie may we as good heroes
repulse all the attacks of the foes.

The martial spirit of the Vedic Aryans finds truest expression in this verse. Even at the moment of death the thought supreme in their minds is that of war. Twice in the *Ṛigveda* man has been called *mṛityubandhu* "regarding death as a relation." The Rigvedic Indians were passionately fond of life, but they were not afraid of death. A gentler but more sophisticated spirit is revealed by the cremation-hymn X. 16:

1. Do not burn him, Agni, do not scorch him either,
do not tear asunder his skin or body;
When you have devoured him, O Jātavedas,
then do you send him on to the Fathers.
2. When you have devoured him, O Jātavedas,
then do you give him over to the Fathers;
When he reaches the other world of the dead,
then may he obey the will of the gods.
3. Let the eye go to the sun, let the breath go to the wind;
to heaven or to earth according to their desert;
Or to waters go, if that is your lot,
or set you up in the plants with your limbs.

The last verse is of special interest for various reasons. Pantheism of a primitive variety is discernible in the first line. The second line suggests the idea of retribution though as yet far short of the philosophical doctrine of *Karma*. Belief in a life after death is also revealed in this verse, but there is no suggestion as yet of belief in hell or rebirth. The first occurs only in the *Atharvaveda*, and the second clearly appears for the first time in the Upanishads.

Quite a number of philosophical hymns are contained in the *Ṛigveda*, and they have been often discussed and translated.[30] An important point to note in this connection is, however, that the terms *māyā* and *rūpa*—on which hinges the whole of later Vedānta philosophy—have been used already in the *Ṛigveda* precisely in their Vedānta sense.[31] "*Rūpa*" in the *Ṛigveda* never signifies real form, but only the transient and deceptive *appearance;* and "*māyā*" in most passages has been used to signify only that occult power by means of which the deceptive appearance can be assumed or discarded.[32] If the doctrine of *māyā* and *rūpa* is the essence of Vedānta (end of Veda), then it may as well be called Vedādi (beginning of Veda).

Nowhere in ancient literature have the gods been more concretely conceived as in the *Ṛigveda*, but the same *Ṛigveda* also reveals the fact that already there were some who would believe in the existence even of Indra, the most concrete of the Vedic pantheon. Quite in the strain of "O God, if there be a God," a poet in the *Ṛigveda* makes this astonishing remark (VIII. 100. 3):

> Chant the hymn, striving for strength,
> unto Indra the truthful, if indeed he exists.
> One says to other, "Indra does not exist,
> who has him seen? whom shall I praise?"

But in the next verse is heard already the voice of Kṛishṇa in the *Bhagavadgītā*. For Indra replies:

> Here am I, look at Me, O singer,
> all beings I excel in greatness;
> Behests of the cosmic order magnify Me,
> for I rend the worlds when I am bent on rending them.

The Rigvedic conception of concrete gods will be dealt with more fully in Chapter XVIII.

---

1. As, for example, the rise of the cerebral series and the levelling of short diphthongs.
2. Gilbert Murray says of the *Iliad:* "We often find, too, that descriptive phrases are not used so accurately to fit the thing described. They are caught up ready made from a store of such things: perpetual epithets, front halves of lines, back halves of lines, whole lines, if need be, and long formulae. The stores of the poets were full and brimming. A bard need only put in his hand and choose out a well-sounding phrase. Even the similes are ready-made." (*The Rise of the Greek Epic*, second ed., p. 258). All this may be maintained, *mutatis mutandis*, also of Rigvedic poetry.
3. In the days of Pāṇini, whom I place in the fifth century B.C., Sanskrit was still a living language of some sort. But in the days of the grammarian Patañjali it must have become more or less like Latin in mediaeval Italy. In any case, Sanskrit had ceased to be a living language long before the days of Aśoka. Cf. Keith. *HSL*, pp. 8-17.
4. See Wackernagel, *Altindische Grammatik*, I, § 191c.
5. I take this to be the meaning of the well-known passage; *te'surā helayo helayo iti parābabhūvuḥ*.
6. Cf. Wackernagel, *op. cit.*, I § 192c and § 193a.

7. *Ibid.*, p. xv. See however Macdonell, *Vedic Grammar*, § 482e.
8. *CHI*, I, p. 77.
8a. Thus in *sandhi* the final -*n* has been throughout reduplicated after a short vowel when the following word begins with a vowel. But in the older parts the reduplication fits in with the metre only in those cases in which the final -*n* had been originally followed by a consonant. (See my *Linguistic Introduction to Sanskrit*, p. 57.)
9. See *Ṛikprātiśākhya*, XVII. 39.
10. If *chhardis* is etymologically connected with Engl. *shield*, as it is supposed to be, then of course the *r*-form must be regarded as original. But this etymology is anything but certain.
11. It must be clearly understood that the written text, everywhere and in every case, truly represents the text as it was *when it was finally fixed*. It is misleading only in the sense that it does not everywhere give the text in its original form. See Oldenberg, *Prolegomena*, p. 372, fn. 2.
11a. For the few instances of non-*sandhi* between Pādānta and Pādādi in the written text though *sandhi* was possible, see *Ṛikprātiśakhya*, II. 60 ff.
12. See Wackernagel, op. *cit.*, III, § 22b.
13. The form in which the word has been handed down is *ushṭrānām*. Non-cerebralization of *n* however shows that in actual pronunciation it was *ushṭānām*.
14. See my *Linguistic Introduction to Sanskrit*, pp. 131-2.
15. See Macdonell. *Vedic Grammar*, p. 314, fn. 2.
16. See Thumb, *Handbuch des Sanskrit*, § 425 Anm.
17. Macdonell, *ibid.*, § 413b.
18. On this point see particularly Oldenberg, *Prolegomena*, pp. 268-70.
19. See Wackernagel, *op. cit.*, III, p. 214.
20. *Ibid.*, p. 519.
21. Collected in *Rikprātiśākhya*, IV. 98. These archaic forms, too, have been throughout misrepresented in the Padapāṭha.
22. See my *Linguistic Introduction to Sanskrit*, p. 45.
23. Without trying to be literal, I have tried in these translations to convey the sense of the original as accurately as possible.
24. So this much-discussed, but still obscure, verse has been translated by Lakshman Sarup, *The Nighaṇṭu and The Nirukta*, English trans., p. 114.
25. Suggested by Oldenberg, *ZDMG*, XXXIX, pp. 52 ff.
26. At least one Dāsa chief, however, namely Balbūtha, had adopted Aryan culture and even patronized Brāhmana singers (see *Ṛigveda*, VIII. 46. 32).
27. This is a fresh argument in favour of dating the first Aryan invasion of India earlier and not later than the middle of the second millennium B.C.
28. The fifth stanza is obscure; only a literal translation has been attempted.
29. A brief account of the Āprī-hymns has been given by Max Müller, *HASL*, second edition, revised, pp. 463-7.
29a. In later Vedic ritual, the animal sacrificed is throughout regarded as a surrogate victim which the initiated person has to immolate in order to obtain release from his vow.
30. See Winternitz, *HIL*, I, pp. 97 ff.
31. It is curious that this fact has not yet been properly emphasized by any modern investigator.
32. Also in the Avesta the word *māyā* has a similar meaning, but the point has yet to be properly investigated.

CHAPTER XVII

POLITICAL AND LEGAL INSTITUTIONS

I. POLITICAL INSTITUTIONS

As a general rule, monarchy was the system of government prevailing in this age. The term *Rājan,* king or chieftain, is of frequent occurrence in the *Ṛigveda.* The country which the Vedic Aryans occupied was split up into numerous tribal principalities. One passage of the *Ṛigveda* (I. 126. 1) speaks of a king living on the bank of the Sindhu, and another (VIII. 21. 18) refers to a king Chitra and other nobles as residing in the neighbourhood of the river Sarasvatī. Ten kings are described as having fought in the historic battle against Sudās (*ante,* p. 250). In the *Dānastutis* and elsewhere, a very large number of rājās are also mentioned. These passages leave no doubt that the form of government was normally monarchical, the tribe as a political unit being under a single ruler. This, of course, is to be expected from the patriarchal organization of Aryan society and from the state of constant warfare with their neighbours (aboriginal and not rarely Aryan), which was a normal feature of the life of the Vedic Aryans.

But in the *Ṛigveda* we come across terms which in later times were undoubtedly applied to non-monarchical constitutions. Thus we have references to the *gaṇa* with the *gaṇapati* or *jyeshṭha* (elder) at its head. The last probably corresponds to the *jeṭṭhaka* of the Pāli texts, and it is not impossible that there were even in this early period, the germs of the republican states of the type we meet with in early Buddhist times[1] (cf. vol. II, ch. I).

The passages cited above also show that, generally speaking, the kingdoms were small in extent and were units of a single tribe. Whether the confederacy of the Five Tribes who attacked Sudās actually involved a system of political organization or some sort of political collaboration cannot be definitely determined. But it is not altogether unlikely. One passage in *Ṛigveda* (VIII. 5. 38) speaks of king Kaśu making a gift of ten kings to a *Ṛishi* (sage) and other passages (II. 41. 5; V. 62. 6) represent Mitra and Varuṇa as occupying a spacious palace with a thousand pillars and a thousand gates. Even allowing for poetic exaggeration, the description postulates the existence of a royal palace of imposing proportions, and necessarily presupposes a fairly large kingdom that could boast of a capital capable of accommodating a palace of such dimensions. We have again to admit that the size of some kingdoms at least was large enough to enable the rulers to command that affluence which is so often described in the *Dānastutis.*[2] The presents conferred by the kings on their priests were gorgeous, ample, and varied. They consisted of cows numbering thousands at times, of horses, chariots, blocks of gold, dresses and beautifully attired female slaves. Hence the wealth possessed at least by some of these rulers was considerable.

Further, it is interesting to note that we meet with the expression *Samrāṭ*, which meant an "emperor" in later days, and also the idea of a universal monarch (*viśvasya bhuvanasya rājā*).[3]

In any case, the king occupied a position of high dignity and supremacy which was emphasized by a formal consecration and laudatory hymns. He wore a gorgeous robe, and his palace, whatever its dimensions, undoubtedly surpassed in grandeur the common dwellings of the people. On the whole the *Ṛigveda* leaves no doubt that the king was no longer merely a leader of a primitive tribe, but occupied a position of pre-eminence which was deliberately distinguished in all possible ways from the rest of the people.

The lines of kingly succession that we can trace in the *RV* raise the presumption of hereditary kingship as the normal system, but there is clear evidence that when the situation demanded it, *viśaḥ* (settlements) who constituted the *rāshṭra* (national unit) could select a worthy monarch of their own choice from among the members of the royal family or of the nobility (the *rājanyas*). Geldner[4] holds that passages like X. 124.8 that are generally cited to establish the selection of a king by the settlements merely indicate their formal sanction of a *fait accompli*. But the very fact of this formal sanction presupposes that the right of selection was exercised by the subjects some time earlier.

Two assemblies called *sabhā* and *samiti* formed an essential feature of the government. The term *sabhā* is often mentioned in the *Ṛigveda* (VI. 28. 6; VIII. 4. 9, etc.), and denotes both "the people in conclave" and the "hall" which was the venue of their meeting. Since, however, the *sabhā* was used for the game of dice (X. 34. 6), it is clear that even non-political business could be transacted at the hall or by the people who constituted the *sabhā*. That it was a gathering of the elect, i.e. of Brāhmaṇas and the rich patrons, when it was convened for administrative purposes, is clear from the term *Sabheya*, "worthy of the assembly," as applied to a Brāhmaṇa (II. 24. 13). The *samiti* in the sense of an "Assembly" of the Vedic tribe is mentioned in the *Ṛigveda* (I. 98. 8; IX. 92. 6, etc.). According to Ludwig,[5] the *samiti* was a more comprehensive conference including not only all the common people (*viśaḥ*) but also Brāhmaṇas and rich patrons (*maghavan*). Although it is difficult to distinguish between a *sabhā* and a *samiti*, we can provisionally arrive at some tentative conclusions. It appears that the *samiti* was an august assembly of a larger group of the people for the discharge of tribal (i.e. political) business and was presided over by the king. The *sabhā*, a more select body, was less popular and political in character than the *samiti*. Although the functions and powers of *sabhā* and *samiti* cannot be exactly defined, numerous passages referring to them clearly indicate that both these Assemblies exercised considerable authority and must have acted as healthy checks on the power of the king. Great importance was attached, not only to concord between the king and the Assembly, but also to a spirit of harmony among the members of the Assembly. The last hymn of the *Ṛigveda* invokes such unity in solemn and beautiful language:

"Assemble, speak together; let your minds be all of one accord"

* * * *

"The place is common, common the assembly, common the mind, so be their thoughts united."

* * * *

"One and the same be your resolve, and be your minds of one accord

"United be the thoughts of all that may happily agree."

The royal authority was also materially curbed by the power and prestige of the *Purohita*, who accompanied the king to battle (p. 348) and helped him with prayers and spells, and the influence of the priesthood generally, to which the *Dānastutis* bear indirect testimony. The cases of Vasishṭha and Viśvāmitra are noteworthy in this connection. Special reference may also be made to the following verses (*RV*, IV. 50. 7-9):

(7) That king, indeed, overpowers all opposing forces with his valour and might who maintains Bṛihaspati (the Brāhmaṇa priest) well attended, and praises and honours him as (a deity) deserving the first share (of the homage due);

(8) He (that king) verily abides. well established in his own place; to him, the holy food flows for ever; to him the *viśaḥ* bow down of their own accord, the king with whom the Brāhmaṇa takes precedence.

(9) Irresistible, he wins the riches of his enemies and his kinsmen; the king who affords protection to the Brāhmaṇa desiring help—him the gods help.

There is hardly any material difference between the power of the Brāhmaṇa (Bṛihaspati) over the king as described in this passage and the power of the *Purohita* over a king, which is associated in our minds with the later stages of political history when the caste system was fully developed.

The immigrant Aryans had necessarily to carry on bitter and prolonged fights with the indigenous people called the *Dāsas* or *Dasyus*. But there was no attempt at the extermination of the conquered foes. The process of amalgamation of the invaders with the conquered aborigines took the form of intermarriage and the absorption of the latter into the fourth (and occasionally into the third) *varṇa* or social class. The translation of the word *dāsa* by "slave" has led to the misconception that the conquered aborigines, both male and female, "were enslaved."[6] *Dāsa* does mean a "life-long servant," but the horrors associated with the term "slavery" are not to be thought of in this connection. Similarly the so-called female slaves (*dāsīs*), captured or received as gifts by kings, were life-long servants assigned generally to the harems of kings in later times. There is, however, no recorded instances in the *RV* or later literature of the harsh or cruel treatment of a *dāsa* or *dāsī*, which is generally associated with slavery.

The protection of the people was the sacred duty of the king. In return he expected and received loyal obedience from his subjects. The word *bali* occurs several times in the *RV* in the sense of a tribute or offering to a god (I. 70. 9; V. 1. 10, etc.). In the sense of a tribute to the king it is met with in the compound *bali-hṛit*, "paying tribute" (VII. 6. 5; X. 173. 6). The tributes were probably received in kind from the subjects. Whether these were voluntary or involuntary, and thus amounted to a kind of indirect taxation, is a debatable point. The truth seems to be that the tribesmen who were led to victory and safety by their ruler voluntarily showered presents on their leader; and that these became more or less regular and periodical in times of peace and to that extent less voluntary. There seems to be little doubt, however, that the hostile tribes defeated in battle were forced to pay some kind of *bali* or tribute to the victor. There thus seems to be in existence taxation, both of the voluntary and involuntary type, in the days of the *Ṛigveda*. If in a simile in *RV*, I. 65. 4 the king is described as "devouring the people," it is not to be understood in the sense of "oppression of the people" but rather his "living on them." The king was not the owner of the land. Even when the *Dānastutis* speak of generous gifts by the kings to the priests, they are normally articles of personal property rather than land.

The king was pre-eminently the war-lord and *RV* gives us some idea of the mode of warfare. The king and his nobles (the *rājanya* or Kshatriya class) fought from chariots, and the common people on foot. The knowledge of battle arrays of different types may be inferred from the use of certain terms such as *śardha. vrāta*, *gaṇa*, etc. which probably denoted different military units. As in later days, we hear of martial music and banners in connection with battle. The principal weapon was the bow and arrow. The arrows were tipped with points of metal or poisoned horn. Other weapons were lances, spears, axes, swords, and sling-stones. The use of (leather?) guards to save the hands and arms from the friction of the bow-string, as also a coat-of-mail and helmet, characterized the equipment of a warrior. Horse-riding was known. It is difficult to agree with the scholars who hold that no mention is made of the use of cavalry in war. As to the actual mode of warfare, all we can infer from passages like *RV*, II. 12. 8 is that a body of foot-soldiers marched along with the charioteers, the two together constituting the army. If Sāyaṇa's interpretation of X. 142. 4 is accepted, then besides ordinary wars of defence and conquest, raids into neighbouring territory were frequent and normal for winning booty which the king shared with the people. Ramparts or forts (*pur*), which were either of stone or metal (*āyasī pur*), and sometimes consisted of an enclosure protected by a palisade consisting only of a hedge of thorn or a row of stakes, were used as places of refuge against attack in times of war. The method of laying siege in *RV* days was probably by setting fire to the surrounding palisades or walls (VII. 5. 3). But mention is also made of *pur charishṇu* (*lit.* moving fort) which may be a sort of engine for assaulting strongholds. Reference has been made above pp. 348) to hymns breathing a martial spirit.

2. ADMINISTRATIVE ORGANIZATION

The "Five Peoples" (*pañcha janāḥ*) was perhaps a comprehensive term for the Vedic Aryans (*ante*, p. 251). These five peoples were split up into numerous tribes, the tribe being the political unit (as mentioned above). The *Viś* (a term the various senses[7] of which have puzzled many scholars) played a vital part in the political organization.

In a political sense, the members of a tribal unit were the *viśaḥ* constituting the *rāshṭra* (or tribal kingdom). Below the *viś* came the *grāma* or village, which was the basic administrative unit. Reference is also sometimes made to *jana*, another unit whose precise nature is not known.[8] The administrative organization was essentially rural in conception. The *grāma* was practically self-contained, and had for purposes of defence a fortified enclosure (*pur*) on an eminence. These enclosures, as mentioned above, were made of stone (sometimes probably also of iron) and had many walls. Towns with wooden walls or palisades and ditches all round were undoubtedly known, but played practically no part in the economic life of the people. They figured only in the defensive warfare of the Vedic Aryans and were occupied (it seems) during emergencies by the warrior-class.

The *grāma* was probably made up of little knots of houses of the several branches of one family (*Kula*). The part played by the *Kula* in the administrative organization is perhaps indicated by the description (X. 179. 2-3) of a *Kulapā* (guardian of the family), forming the entourage of a *vrājapati* (probably the same as the *grāmaṇī*) and fighting under his banner. The *grāmaṇī* exercised, it seems, both civil and military functions. The *Senānī*, whose military authority in times of war is undeniable, probably discharged civil functions in times of peace, ranking higher than the *grāmaṇī*. In the description of the *Dāśarājña* fight (VII. 18. 11) Sudās is said to have overthrown "the twenty-one tribes (*janān*) of the kings or folk of the two Vaikarṇas." It is probable that they were a joint people, the *Kuru-Kṛivis*. It is doubtful, however, whether this aggregate of twenty-one *janas* represented a political and administrative organization higher than a *jana*.

Of the various functionaries of the king, the most important appear to be the *Purohita* and the *Senānī* referred to above. The king probably appointed a large number of priests to perform the sacrifices and other sacred rites. There are also references to spies (*spaśa*) who were apparently engaged by him, as in later days, to secure information about the kingdom and the people. We also hear of *dūtas* or messengers who were undoubtedly the principal means of communication between the different states. The king had no doubt other officers, but we have no detailed knowledge of them.

3. LAW AND LEGAL INSTITUTIONS

The regular word for law or custom in the *RV* (I. 22. 18; 164. 43, 50; III. 3. 1; 17. 1; 60. 6; V. 26. 6; 63. 7; 72. 2, etc.) is *Dharman*, but there are very few data as regards the administration of justice or the code of law followed. We can only infer from later practice that the king administered justice with the assistance of legal advisers including the *Purohita*.

Theft, burglary, highway robbery, and cheating (chiefly at gambling) are among the crimes recorded, cattle-lifting at night being a very frequent one. Marriage of brother and sister was looked upon as incest. Tying the criminal to a stake was a common form of punishment. The epithet *śatadāya*, i.e. "one, the price of whose blood was one hundred (coins)" shows that the system of wergeld (*Vairadeya*) or blood-money was probably in force. Whereas death was one of the punishments for theft in later times, it was not so in the Rigvedic age. The aim seems rather to have been the satisfaction of the person wronged.

Geldner[9] suggests that a heated *paraśu* (axe) used as an ordeal is referred to in *RV*, III. 53. 22, and Ludwig[10] thinks that *RV*, I. 158. 4 ff., refer to Dīrghatamas having been subjected to the fire and water ordeals. These are quite plausible suggestions, though no definite conclusions are possible.

Ṛiṇa (debt) is frequently mentioned in the *RV* though in a metaphorical sense in the majority of passages where it occurs. Indebtedness seems to be a fairly well-known condition. There was a special term *ṛiṇam saṁ-nī* for paying off a debt. The loan (*ṛiṇa*) thus was the only contract known and that, chiefly, at gambling. A

debtor was punished with a period of servitude to the creditor and was bound by the creditor to a post (*dru-pada*) to bring pressure on him for payment. Some kind of reference to a rate of interest or instalment of principal may be traced in one passage, but this is not certain. The interest was presumably paid in kind. The hymn disapproves of the practice.
right of a father to adopt is clearly recognized, though a *Vasishṭha*

The land was probably owned by individuals and families, and the proprietorship was vested in the father, as head of the family. It is not certain whether the sons had any share in the land of the family during their father's lifetime. If there were several sons, they could easily secure new allotments, if necessary, because as fresh land could be easily obtained, the problem was not, in any sense, an acute one.

The individual ownership of land is, however, a debatable point. The *RV* supplies the following data. A piece of ploughland is indicated in the *RV* by the words *urvarā* and *kshetra* (I. 127. 6; IV. 41. 6; V. 33. 4; VI. 25. 4; X. 30. 3; 142. 3, etc.). A passage (I. 110. 5) shows that fields were carefully measured from which it follows that individual ownership in land for cultivation was recognized. The same conclusion follows from VIII. 91. 5 in which Apālā refers to her father's field *urvarā* as a personal possession. This conclusion agrees well with the use of epithets like *urvarā-sā, urvarā-jit, kshetrā-sā* "winning fields," and the mention of fields in the same context as children (IV. 41. 6).

Nothing definite can be averred as to whether a grown-up son continued to stay with his father, his wife becoming a member of the father's household, or whether he established a house of his own. Variations in local custom probably explain discrepant statements in this connection. Similarly, we do not know whether the son was granted a special plot of land after marriage, or whether he acquired it only after his father's death. But we must not form an exaggerated estimate of the control of the father over a son, no longer a minor, because *RV*. I. 70. 10 suggests that the sons might divide their father's property in his old age, and X. 85. 46 gives a hint that the aged father-in-law passed under the control of his son's wife. The suggestion that separate holdings existed as early as the Rigvedic days is confirmed by the name of the deity *kshetrasya pati* (Lord of the Field) to be understood as the god presiding over each field.

---

1. This view has been put forward by Dr. H. C. Raychaudhuri, *Advanced History of India* (Macmillan & Co.), p. 29.
2. For *Dānastutis*, cf. Ch. XVI.
3. *Advanced History of India*, p. 29.
4. *Ved. Stud.*, II, 303.
5. *Translation of the Rigveda*, III, pp. 253-6.
6. *CHI*, I, p. 85.

7. (1) In a geographical sense, the term means "settlement or colonies," and a group of these settlements or colonies probably made up the *jana* (people) (cf. the next footnote). (2) Politically the *viśaḥ* were the subjects who constituted the *rāshṭra* and who, foregathering in a formal assembly, could in an emergency unseat an incapable ruler or set the seal of approval on the coronation of a worthy one. (3) In a socio-religious sense, the *viśaḥ* represented the third class of Aryan society engaged in agriculture and commerce. (4) No wonder that in some passages, it should have the fourth or general sense of "people."
8. Sometimes *Viś*, *jana* and even *grāma* are used almost synonymously, But *grāma* was normally a smaller unit than the *viś* or *jana*. The relation between these two is not quite clear. Dr. H. C. Raychaudhuri observes as follows: "In some Vedic passages there is a clear contrast between the two, and Irānian analogies seem to suggest that the Viś is a sub-division of a *jana*, if tre latter may be taken as a parallel to the Irānian *Zaniu*. It is also to be noted that the Bhāratas are referred to as a single *jana*, but when the word *Viś* is used in reference to them, we have the plural *Viśaḥ* possibly pointing to the existence of plurality of such units" (*Advanced History*, p. 29).
9. *Ved. Stud.*, II, 159.
10. *Translation of the Ṛigveda*, IV, 44.

CHAPTER XVIII

RELIGION AND PHILOSOPHY

As has already been indicated above (Ch. XII), the different parts of the *Ṛigveda-Saṁhitā* were composed at different times, and it should be regarded, not as a single text by one author, but rather as a whole literature accumulating for centuries, a library, as it were, in the making for years. Nay, although the hymns of the *Ṛigveda* represent, in the main, the product of that period of intellectual activity when the Aryans found their way into India from their original home, it is not beyond the realm of probability that some of them were composed, or at least existed in the minds of the Aryan poets, even before they entered India. It is thus possible that a few stanzas or even hymns are reminiscent of the meteorological and astronomical conditions that obtained thousands of years ago, somewhere outside India. No wonder then, that we should find in the *Ṛigveda* thoughts, beliefs, and practices that one would associate with the most primitive grades of society and with an unsophisticated age, side by side with an elaborate sacrificial technique and advanced metaphysical speculation indicating the deepest apprehension of the godhead and its relation to man. The view, therefore, that the state of religious belief in the *RV* is a product of priestly effort and amounts to wholesale syncretism is as wrong as the one that it presents us with nothing else but a naïve outpouring of the primitive religious consciousness.

I. MYTHOLOGY

1. *Origin*

Let us therefore draw up a clear picture of the religious conceptions and philosophical thoughts revealed in poetic garb in the *RV*, in the order of their evolution, as far as possible, before attempting to label, define or classify them. The *RV* poets were deeply affected by the apparently mysterious working of the awe-inspiring forces of nature. Their hymns reflect in places that primitive attitude of mind which looks upon all nature as a living presence, or an aggregate of animated entities. The luminaries who follow a fixed course across the sky are the *devas* (*lit.*, the shining ones) or gods. Naturally the sense of the dependence of human welfare on the powers of nature, the unexplained mysteries of whose working invests them with almost a "supernatural" or divine character, finds its expression in various forms of worship.

At the same time, the attempt of the human mind, more poetic than scientific, to account for the various forces and phenomena of nature with which man is confronted, leads to the rise of myths. When the imagination interprets a natural event as the action of a personified being resembling a human agent, a myth is born. The creative fancy of the Rigvedic poets goes on adding new touches to the picture, so that a natural phenomenon ultimately appears as a drama of human passions and not as an unintelligible and chaotic happening. The stage of anthropomorphism is thus reached. Although Rigvedic mythology is not as primitive as some scholars once believed it to be, in no other literary monument of the world do we come across this primitive phase of the evolution of religious beliefs which reveals to us the very process of personification by which natural phenomena developed into gods. The myths that have grown up around a deity are in many cases transparent enough to keep the physical basis almost in full view all the time. The name of the god often hides but little. Nevertheless, in cases where such a clear view of the original nature of a god is not possible, the etymological equations of comparative mythology have not proved to be the reliable guides that they were once supposed to be.

The closely allied mythology of the Irānians is illuminating at times, but mythological affinities are not as numerous as one would be led to expect from the striking linguistic affinity of the oldest form of the *Avesta* with the Rigvedic dialect in vocabulary, metre, syntax, diction, and general poetic spirit, the reason being the considerable overhauling of mythological conceptions in Irān by the religious reform of Zarathustra (*ante*, p. 226). The *Ṛigveda* is a monument of Indo-European mythology and, in this respect, is equalled in importance only by Greek mythology. The Rigvedic mythology thus forms a connecting link between the later Indian phase of religious beliefs and the Indo-Irānian as well as the earliest Indo-European phase.

We now turn to the lines of mythological evolution within the *Ṛigveda*. In the hymns to the Dawn, the Sun and the Fire, among others, we are face to face with the corresponding physical phenomena exercising directly their beneficent powers. The process of personification next makes gradual progress, and the personified phenomenon is deified, and thus emerge the concrete figures of Ushas, Sūrya, and Agni with whom the poet holds, as it were, direct communion. We are not so fortunate in the case of the greatest figures of the Rigvedic pantheon, namely Varuṇa and Indra, regarding whose physical basis no certain conclusions have yet been arrived at. But in the case of a large number of Rigvedic gods, we are able to trace the original forces or events in Nature. Where the personification does not dominate the conception, the name of the deity is identical with that of the natural phenomenon, as in the case of Ushas and Sūrya. Where the names differ, the personification has evidently advanced to the stage of anthropomorphism and apotheosis. The number of gods is now on the increase, the increase being due either to some striking attribute abstracted from the concrete personality of a deity and founding the conception of a new deity which develops independently, as in the case of Savitṛi, or to an abstraction (like Viśvakarman) taking up a concrete form later through association with some cosmic function or natural power.

2. *The Nature and Classification of Gods*

Although the divine rank thus got swollen, there is no fixed order of seniority among the gods, as in a pantheon, in the strict sense of the term. For too many functions, powers, and offices are held in common by two or more deities. There is a sort of communism or democracy among them, though it is not thoroughgoing or consistent, and for this "the belief in individual gods alternately regarded as the highest" (i.e. Henotheism or Kathenotheism as Max Müller has named it) is responsible. The particular deity that the poet happens to be invoking monopolizes, for the time being, all the attributes. The god is addressed for the moment as if he were the greatest and even the only god. Almost in the same breath, however, (in the very next stanza or hymn) this mighty god is described as dependent on others.

In fact, the joint exercise of various powers, functions, and notable deeds by two or more or all the gods is almost a favourite theme in the *Ṛigveda* hymnology. In a thoroughly impartial spirit, the mutual co-operation, interdependence, and subordination of the various deities in pairs or larger groups is often described. There is hardly a god in the *Ṛigveda* so insignificant as not to receive homage from others not excluding the highest. "Henotheism," in the strict sense of the term, is not to be thought of because the divine host of the *Ṛigveda* is not a pantheon (technically speaking) with an acknowledged overlord. Various explanations have been offered to account for this apparently inconsistent evaluation of divine ranks and dignities in the *Ṛigveda*. It has been urged, for example, that the inconsistency may be due to the partiality of a particular *Ṛishi* or Vedic *Śākhā* to a particular god. But the force of this argument is considerably weakened by the large number or Rigvedic repetitions and (on the whole) their even distribution throughout the text. As Bloomfield observes, "no theory as to the character and origin of the *Ṛigveda* can pass by these facts. They mark the entire *mantra*-literature as in a sense epigonal and they forbid pungent theories about profound differences between the family books, their authors, and their geographical provenance."[1]

It has also been contended, as Macdonell[1a] points out, that "in the frequent hymns addressed to the *Viśvedevas* or All-gods, all the deities, even the lesser ones, are praised in succession, and that as the great mass of the Vedic hymns was composed for the ritual of the Soma-offering, which included the worship of almost the entire pantheon, the technical priest could not but know the exact relative position of each god in that ritual." This explanation rests on the unwarranted assumption that the ritualists of a later age, when sacrificial technique was enormously developed, had to, and could, preserve very scrupulously the mythological values of Rigvedic poetry.

Another approach to the problem of introducing order and system into this apparent chaos has been through classification. There is, first of all, the traditional classification hinted at in *RV*, I. 139. 11 and followed by Yāska, giving us a triple division of the Vedic gods corresponding to the three orders, namely, terrestrial (*pṛithivīsthāna*), aerial or intermediate (*antarikshasthāna* or *madhyamasthāna*) and celestial (*dyusthāna*). Pṛithivī, Agni, Soma, Bṛihaspati, and the rivers belong to the first order; Indra, Apāṁnapāt, Rudra, Vāyu-Vāta, Parjanya, Āpaḥ, and Mātariśvan to the second; and Dyaus, Varuṇa, Mitra, Sūrya, Savitṛi, Pūshan, Vishṇu, the Ādityas, Ushas, and the Aśvins to the third. This classification is founded on the natural basis which the deities represent, and is thus the most practical and least open to objection (comparatively speaking). *RV*, X. 158. 1, which invokes Sūrya, Vāta, and Agni for protection from heaven, air, and earth respectively is apparently the lead followed by the predecessors of Yāska whose views are quoted in the *Nirukta*, and who hold that there are only three representative deities, Sūrya in heaven, Vāyu or Indra in air and Agni on earth, each of these having various appellations according to differences of function.

The division is overlapping and not very clear-cut, as Tvashṭṛi and Pṛithivī are assigned to all the three spheres, Agni and Ushas to the terrestrial as well as the aerial spheres, and Varuṇa, Yama and Savitri to the aerial as well as the celestial ones. Another and a less satisfactory division is the historical one, into Indo-European, Indo-Irānian, and Indian deities, based on the age of the mythological creation. But the data as regards the dates and periods of many gods is insufficient and the available accounts of Germanic, Slavonic, and Celtic mythologies are defective. A division into prehistoric, transparent, translucent, opaque, and abstract or symbolic gods, based on the stages of personification which the deities represent, introduces the subjective element, owing to want of finality regarding etymologies and interpretations, and involves difficulties as regards clear lines of demarcation. A classification according to relative greatness may derive support from *RV*, I. 27. 13. But the difficulties of determining relative greatness are almost insuperable (VIII. 30. I contradicting I. 27. 13) and only a few tentative conclusions are possible. For example, Indra, the mighty warrior, and Varuṇa, the supreme moral ruler, stand out pre-eminent above the rest. Agni and Soma—the two ritual deities—should come next, but Indra, Agni, and Soma are the three most popular deities judging by the frequency of the hymns addressed to them. The statistical standard provided by the number of hymns dedicated to the gods and the frequency of the mention of their names is also not a sure guide.

Before we sum up the general features of Rigvedic religion, we shall pass under review the class-characteristics of the gods of the Rigvedic pantheon, and the individual characteristics of the more important among them. The gods are usually stated to be thirty-three in number, divided into three groups corresponding to the three divisions of the Universe as mentioned above. The gods are described as born, though not all simultaneously, and yet they are immortal. This immortality is either taken for granted or is a gift from Agni and Savitṛi, or is the result of the drinking of the Soma. In appearance they are human, the parts of their bodies (such as their arms or tongue) being identified poetically with the phenomena of nature, such as rays or flames. They travel through the air in cars drawn generally by steeds and occasionally by other animals. The food of men, such as milk, grain, and flesh, becomes the food of the gods when offered in the sacrifice, and is partaken of by them either on the grass kept ready for their reception at the place of the sacrifice or in the heaven where the god of fire carries it to them. The exhilarating juice of the Soma plant constituted the favourite drink of the gods. On the whole, the gods are benevolent, the only one with malevolent traits being Rudra. Splendour, strength, knowledge, possession, and truth are their common attributes. As a matter of fact, they have so few individual or distinctive traits, that a riddle hymn like VIII. 29 is possible, wherein each stanza describes a deity by its characteristic marks, leaving its name to be guessed. The identification of one deity with another and the invocation of deities in twos, threes, or even in whole groups has helped to add to this vagueness of outline. The gods subdue the forces of evil and regulate the order of nature, which they themselves follow and enforce on mortals. They reward the righteous and punish the sinful.

3. *The Celestial Gods*

We now turn to the individual deities and give a brief survey of their noteworthy characteristics in the order of the spheres to which they belong. The oldest among the gods of heaven, going back to the Indo-European period, and identical with the Greek Zeus, is Dyaus, a personification of the sky, a personification which, however, did not advance beyond the idea of paternity. He is called a ruddy bull bellowing downwards, a poetic description, probably, of the colour of lightning, the fertilizing power of rain and the thunder of heaven. The image of the beautiful star-studded sky of the night is obviously called up when Dyaus is once compared with a black steed bedecked with pearls. Dyaus is generally paired with Pṛithivī, the earth, in the compound Dyāvāpṛithivī, the Universal Parents, who are celebrated in six hymns.

The comparatively small number of hymns addressed to Varuṇa hardly does justice to his importance in the *RV*. The personification has so far advanced that his physical basis remains obscure. It has been suggested that the word *varuṇa-s* is probably the same as the Greek word *Ouranos* (sky) though phonetic difficulties make the identification uncertain. Varuṇa is the upholder of the physical and moral order symbolized in ṛita with which he is more intimately connected than any other god. The Varuṇa hymns which are predominantly ethical and devout in tone give us the most exalted poetry in the *Ṛigveda*.[2] He is a king and a universal monarch having a golden abode in heaven which is lofty and firm, and has a thousand columns and doors. He wears glistening garments. He has spies whom none can deceive. He is predominantly called the Asura, who rules by means of his *māyā* which means "occult power" (applicable in a good sense to gods, and in a bad sense to demons). By this power he sends forth dawns and makes the sun (who is also described as his eye) traverse the sky. He supports heaven, earth, and air. He, with Mitra, is most frequently invoked as a bestower of rain. He regulates the seasons. Neither god nor mortal may violate his ordinances. Varuṇa's special connection with the waters is unmistakable. He is a regulator of the waters and causes the rivers to flow. If the ocean does not overflow, although the rivers constantly pour into it, it is due to the *māyā* of Varuṇa. He is above all the *dhṛitavrata,* the upholder of ordinances such as the fixed paths of the luminaries across the sky. He stands out pre-eminently as the moral governor among all the deities. The fetters (*pāśas*) with which he binds sinners are characteristic of him in this capacity. In every hymn to Varuṇa, there is a prayer for forgiveness of sin.

There is uncertainty regarding the physical basis of the idea of Varuṇa. The view generally held is that it is the encompassing sky. This original conception, it is supposed, goes back at least to the Indo-Irānian period since *Ahura Mazdāh* (the wise spirit) of the *Avesta* agrees with the Asura Varuṇa in character, though not in name. In the opinion of the present writer, Varuṇa in the *RV* is pre-eminently the All-Pervader, the All-Encompasser, the All-Enveloper—an aspect fully agreeing with his name which appears to be derived from the root *vṛi* ("to cover" or "encompass"). This All-Encompassing character is in keeping with his lordship over the twin spheres of light and darkness, of Night as well as Day, and with his position as supreme ruler (*samrāj*) of the physical and moral world and as the custodian of *ṛita*. This *ṛita*, which like a wheel circumscribes the universe, regulates it, and keeps it in place, is Varuṇa's *pāśa* and has for its physical basis the belt of the zodiac from which no luminary (*deva*) may deviate and the penalty for transgression whereof is ensnarement by the shackles of *non-ṛita* or darkness and death. This is one side of the All-Encompassing character of Varuṇa. Another and a more important side (unfortunately missed by most scholars) is Varuṇa's overlordship of the Waters (*āpaḥ*) which are far more intimately connected with him in the *Ṛigveda* than is generally supposed. The researches of Warren[3] and of Tilak[4] establishing the cosmic character of these Waters have not received the attention they deserve. They may be summed up as follows:

(1) The Waters are both terrestrial and celestial. The attributes of the latter in the *Ṛigveda* cannot all be satisfactorily accounted for on the hypothesis that they are rain-waters. (2) The release of the Waters and the breaking forth of the dawn or the emergence of light are described as simultaneous events (I. 164. 51). (3) In fact, the movement of the Waters and the spreading forth of the rays of light originate from the same source and follow the same path (of *ṛita*) simultaneously. (4) These Waters are described as moved upwards by Indra when set free for movement, simultaneously with the luminaries, after the killing of Vṛitra (II. 15. 6; I. 80. 5; I. 32. 12, etc.). Their downward movement is, of course, described, as in VIII. 69. 11 where the seven rivers are said to flow into the jaws of Varuṇa as into a surging abyss or ocean. (5) The Universe is said to have consisted of nothing but undifferentiated Waters in the beginning (X. 82. 6; 129. 3). These Waters are coeval with the universe (X. 30. 10). (6) The cosmic circulation of the celestial waters and the simultaneity of the free flow of the Waters and the rising of the Dawn are stated unambiguously in the *Avesta* (Vendīdād XXI. 4-5; Yasht VI. 2, 3; etc.). (7) This theory of the cosmic circulation of the Waters is not peculiar only to Indo-Irānian mythology, but is found in Greek and Egyptian mythologies also. In other words, the celestial waters or watery vapours which pervaded the regions above, below, and around the earth were supposed by the Rigvedic poets to be the stuff out of which the universe was created,[5] and were, like the ether of modern scientists, the medium of the transmission of the light of the luminaries.

A completely satisfactory explanation of the Rigvedic account of Varuṇa as the All-Pervader follows from his rulership of these Cosmic Waters. If Varuṇa in later mythology sank to the position of an Indian Neptune, it was among other causes also due to the original sense of the *Apaḥ* (Waters) as "Cosmic Waters" in the *Ṛigveda* being lost sight of.

Mitra is so closely associated with Varuṇa, that only one hymn (III. 59) is addressed to him alone separately and his individual character cannot be definitely established. His distinctly peculiar epithet is *Yātayaj- jana,* the "bestirrer of the people," because he marshals people into activity as the great Āditya. Mithra is a sun-god, the guardian of faithfulness, in the *Avesta,* and Rigvedic evidence points to Mitra as a solar deity in the aspect of a benevolent power of nature as suggested by the name Mitra which originally meant "an ally."

Sūrya is the most concrete of the Solar deities, the name (which designates the orb of the Sun as well as the god) showing that his character as a luminary was always present to the mind of the poets. As the all-seeing god, he is often called the eye of Mitra, Varuṇa, Agni, and other gods. The dawns produce Sūrya and he is to be the son of the goddess Aditi and of Dyaus. He is a ruddy bird or eagle that flies through space. He is cognate with the Avestic *hvare,* "sun," who has swift horses and who is the eye of Ahura Mazda.

Savitṛi is pre-eminently a golden deity. His eyes, arms, hands, and tongue are golden; so are his car and its pole. He diffuses golden splendour. He removes evil dreams and drives away demons and sorcerers. In the famous Gāyatrī stanza (III. 62. 10), which has remained the sacred morning prayer of the Hindus for more than two thousand years, he is invoked to confer his splendour on, and stimulate the thoughts of, the worshipper. When Savitrī is said to shine with the rays of the sun, to urge the sun or to announce men as sinless to the sun, he is evidently distinguished from Sūrya, as in *RV,* VII. 63. But there is a large number of passages where it is difficult to distinguish between the two. The poets love to play on the name of the god, derived as it is from *sū,* to stimulate. It is to be noted that he is connected with evening as well as with the morning time.

Pūshan is a god with a very vague personality, the anthropomorphic details being very few. He has a beard and braided hair. His chariot is drawn by goats and he carries a golden spear, an awl, and a goad. His favourite food is *Karambha* ("gruel"). He is connected with marriage in the wedding hymn (X. 85). He acts as the envoy of Sūrya with his golden aerial ships, and as a charioteer drives downward the golden wheel of the sun. He is a guardian of the roads, the deliverer, *par excellence,* from danger, and takes care of cattle. *Āghṛiṇi* ("shining") is an exclusive epithet of his. Very probably, he was originally a solar deity standing for the beneficent power of the sun manifested chiefly in its pastoral aspect.

The only prominent anthropomorphic trait, nay, the main characteristic of the nature of Vishṇu—a minor deity in the *RV*—is his three steps which give him the exclusive epithets *uru-gāya* ("wide-going") and *uru-krama* ("wide-stepping"). Two of his steps are visible, but the third or highest is invisible, far beyond the flight of birds, and is like an eye fixed in heaven, shining brightly down. Since he is described as setting in motion, like a revolving wheel, his ninety steeds (days) with their four names (seasons, an evident allusion to the three hundred and sixty days of the solar year), Vishṇu probably is a personification of the activity of the sun, whose passage through the three divisions of the universe, namely, earth, air, and heaven, is referred to in his three steps. Indra is the only deity most closely associated with him.

The word *aditi* is primarily a noun meaning "non-binding," "bondlessness," from *diti* "binding," derived from the root *dā* "to bind." Hence as a goddess, Aditi is naturally invoked to release her worshipper from bondage. This original meaning of unpersonified "freedom" seems to survive in a few passages of the *RV*. Now the Ādityas are several times described as *aditeḥ putrāḥ* ("sons of Aditi"), and this expression may have meant in the pre-Vedic age simply "sons of freedom" (like *sahasaḥ putrāḥ*="sons of strength") and probably described a prominent quality of Varuṇa and the other Ādityas. Macdonell[6] wonders, "But how are we to account for so early a personification of such an abstract idea, and in particular for Aditi becoming the mother of the Ādityas?" The explanation probably is as follows: Aditi is also unmistakably connected with light in the *RV*. Varuṇa—the Āditya—is connected prominently and almost exclusively with *ṛita;* so is Aditi. This *ṛita* has for its physical basis the belt of the Zodiac (as mentioned above). Now the *devas,* the lights of heaven, seemed to the ancients to recover their freedom from the clutches of darkness and to restart on their bright career from a fixed point in the east, lying on the belt of the Zodiac or the Ṛita. This point in all probability was Aditi. No wonder, the luminaries suddenly emerging thus into freedom and light (emerging in other words into life itself) from this fixed point (Aditi) received the epithet "sons of Aditi." Diti was the exactly opposite point on the path of the Zodiac in the west, where the lights went out. It will not be necessary on this theory to suppose[7] that the name of Diti as a goddess was merely an anthithesis to that of Aditi, formed from the latter to express a positive sense, as *sura,* "god," was later (by false etymology) evolved from *asura* "demon." It is to be noted in this connection that none of the wind or storm gods are called Ādityas. The latter are all gods of light. Six Ādityas are enumerated once (II. 27. 1), the number being stated as seven and even eight in the last books of the *RV*. Among the Ādityas, Varuṇa, Mitra, and Aryaman are Indo-Irānian in origin, while Bhaga, Daksha, and Aṁśa seem to be deified abstractions. The sun is probably the seventh Āditya, and Mārtaṇḍa the eighth, whom Aditi casts off and brings back (X. 72. 8, 9), is very likely the setting sun.

In the case of Ushas, the goddess of Dawn, the personification is slight, the poet never losing sight of the beautiful physical phenomena behind the deity. Gaily attired like a dancer with a garment of light, she rises in the east and exhibits her graces. She is ever-youthful, being born again and again, though ancient. Her association with the sun is naturally very close. He is her lover, but as she precedes him, she is also said to be his mother. She is the sister of the night. She is also associated with Agni. As already noted above (p. 346) the Dawn-hymns are among the most poetic of the *RV*.

From the point of view of the number of hymns addressed to them and also otherwise, the twin deities, known as the Aśvins, are the most important after Indra, Agni, and Soma. They are matutinal deities, their connection with light being well established. Except in two or three passages, they are assumed everywhere as inseparable. Their paths are said to be golden. *Dasrā* (wondrous) and *nāsatyā* are their most peculiar and frequent epithets. They are particularly associated with honey (*madhu*), which they desire, drink, carry on their car, and dispense to the bees and mortals. They are also fond of Soma. Their golden car, fashioned by the Ṛibhus, is sometimes drawn by one or more buffaloes or by a single ass (*rāsabha*). Their sister is probably the Dawn. They are associated with Sūryā who is either the sun conceived as a female or the daughter of Sūrya. They are the two husbands of Sūryā whom they carry in their car. They are above all succouring divinities, the deliverers and rescuers, *par excellence*, from distress. They are divine physicians with several legends of miraculous cures to their credit.

Their physical basis has been a puzzle from the days of Yāska till to-day. The Aśvins probably date from the Indo-European period, in character if not in name. Some think that they represent the morning twilight—half-light and half-dark. The Aśvins, who are sons of Dyaus (*divo napātā* = Lettic *dēwa deli* = Lithuanian *dēwo sunelei*), who ride through the sky with their steeds, and have a sister, greatly resemble the two Lettic God's sons, who come riding on their steeds to woo the daughter of the sun, either for themselves or for the moon, and the Twin Horsemen of Greek mythology, the sons of Zeus and the brothers of Helen. The name of Sūryā, *sūryasya duhitā*, corresponds to the Lettic *saules meita*. The succouring activity of the Aśvins finds a parallel in the feats of the Lettic God's sons as well as in those of the Greek Dioskouroi, particularly in their character as rescuers from the ocean, delivering the daughter of the sun or the sun himself. Another plausible theory is that which considers the Aśvins as the morning and evening stars. The astronomical fact that the latter are not two but one is no serious objection, as the identity of the two stars was recognized long after the physical basis of the Aśvins was forgotten. The invariable separation of the two stars, whereas the Aśvins appear both together in the morning, is an objection that can be explained, if we remember that the Aśvins are spoken of separately in a passage or two, and that the Aśvins are invoked sometimes in the morning and evening, though sunset plays but little part in Vedic worship. Weber's opinion[8] that the Aśvins represent the two bright stars Castor and Pollux constituting the twin constellation of the Gemini receives striking support from the theories of Tilak advanced in his *Orion* and *The Arctic Home in the Vedas.* If, as Tilak says,[9] the sacrifice or the year once commenced with Aditi at the vernal equinox in or near Punarvasu, i.e. in the twin constellation of the Gemini, and if we are to assume that there are reminiscences in the *Ṛigveda* of the year-long day and night of the Arctic regions, then the twin Stars, Castor and Pollux, represented by the Aśvins, would herald the Arctic Dawn appearing after the long Arctic night or at the beginning of the year. But as the Arctic theory is far from being accepted by scholars, the morning and evening star theory remains the most plausible theory advanced so far.

4. *The Atmospheric Gods*

Indra, the favourite national god of the *Ṛigveda,* has the largest number of hymns, nearly 250, i.e. about one-fourth of the total number or hymns in the *RV,* addressed to him.[9a] He has more myths woven around him and a more developed anthropomorphism on the physical side than any other god. He is not a purely Indian creation and his name is pre-Indian (a demon in the Avesta).[9b] The cosmic aspect of his nature as the liberator of the Waters is older than the martial one, which seems to have developed to the detriment of the former aspect. His physical proportions and powers are stupendous, almost cosmic. His arms bear the *Vajra,* his exclusive weapon, though he also carries a hook and wields the bow and arrow. He is a car-warrior (*Ratheshṭha*), whose golden car is drawn by two steeds. He is more addicted to Soma, which stimulates him to battle, than any other god, the epithet *somapā* "Soma-drinker," being characteristic of him. His father is Dyaus according to some passages, Tvashṭṛi according to others. Agni is his twin brother, most often conjoined with him as a dual divinity. The Maruts are his principal and constant allies, the epithet *marutvant* being peculiar to him. The essential myth, forming the basis of his nature and repeated frequently and with variations, is the Vṛitra myth. Accompanied by the Maruts and exhilarated by Soma, he attacks Vṛitra, often called the *Ahi* (serpent). He smashes Vṛitra who encompasses the Waters, and so deserves the exclusive epithet *apsu-jit* "conquering in the Waters." In this struggle, which is constantly renewed, he also pierces the mountains and releases the pent-up waters, like imprisoned cows. The demons, whom Indra throws down, dwell on the *parvata* or *giri* (mountain or cloud,) and an *adri* (rock) is said to encompass the Waters. The clouds containing the Waters are figured as fortresses (*pura*) of the aerial demons, described either as autumnal or as made of iron or stone, and as 90, 99 or 100 in number. He is, therefore, characteristically called the fort-destroyer (*pūrbhid*) but his exclusive and chief epithet is "Vṛitra-slayer" (*Vṛitra-han*).

The release of the Waters is simultaneous with the winning of light, sun, and dawn. Independently of the Vṛitra fight also, he is said to have found the light, the dawn or the sun, and made a path for the latter. The cows mentioned with the sun and dawn must be understood to be the morning beams. The gaining of Soma is also associated with the winning of the cows and the sun and with the Vṛitra fight. His connection with the thunderstorm is indicated when he is said to have created the lightnings of heaven and directed the flow of the Waters downwards.

The cosmic actions usually attributed to all the gods are attributed to him also. His particular achievement is that he settled the quaking mountains and plains.

As the destroyer of demons he is naturally the favourite god of battle invoked more often than any other god by warriors. He protects the "Aryan Colour" and subjects the blackskins—the Dasyus. He is so generous to his worshippers that *maghavan* "bountiful" is almost an exclusive epithet of his.

Besides the Vṛitra-myth, other minor stories are also related of him, such as "shattering the car of Ushas and stopping the steeds of the sun". Some of the stories have an historical element also, as when he is said to have aided Sudās.

Indra, with his physical superiority, his excesses in eating and drinking and his cruelty in killing his own father Tvashṭṛi, forms a marked contrast to Varuṇa, the upholder of moral order.

The true character of Indra can be understood by ascertaining that of Vṛitra, his opponent. The indigenous commentators and a number of scholars look upon Vṛitra as the demon of drought, confining the waters within the clouds. A more reasonable view is that[10] he was originally a frost and winter demon from whose grasp the waters have to be wrenched free every year, that thunderstorm and rain are not the only natural basis of the Vṛitra myth, and that the geographical and climatic environments in the later home of the Vedic Indians only helped so to revise the original myth as to render very plausible the interpretation of the mythological figure of Indra as the god of the thunderstorm. In support of this view may be stated the following facts:

(1) Thunderstorms or rains are hardly mentioned in the Indra-Vṛitra myth and the clouds play quite a minor part in it. (2) As the waters released by Indra are described as running like horses in a race, rain-water could not be meant, as it does not flow horizontally nor could races be imagined as run vertically. (3) As the *Vajra* is described as made of ore, it is not certain that it means a thunderbolt. (4) If Indra is the god of the thunderstorm, then the god Parjanya will be a superfluous figure. (5) The parallels in Indo-European mythologies suggest that the description of the Vṛitra fight originated not in India but in a country where the hideous winter lies on land and water, and that the Vṛitra myth came with the Aryans from Kāshmir or the north-western countries into the Punjab. (6) As the midday libation is specially reserved for Indra and the Maruts, Indra very probably represents mythologically the sun at the zenith. In all probability, therefore, Indra was originally a god of light.

We pass over the minor atmospheric gods like Trita Āptya, Apāṁ Napāt, Mātariśvan, Ahi Budhnya, and Aja Ekapād, and turn to Rudra who, though a subordinate deity in the *RV*, is interesting from the point of view of later mythology. He has braided hair and a brown complexion. He wears golden ornaments and a glorious necklace (*nishka*). He is the father of the Maruts whom he brought forth from the shining udder of Pṛiśni. He is fierce like a terrible beast and is called a bull as well as the ruddy boar of heaven. He is exalted and mightiest of the mighty. He is the lord (*Īśāna*) and father of the world. He is easily invoked and auspicious (*śiva*), but in many passages is looked upon as malevolent. He is implored to save his worshippers from his bolt which destroys cows and men. Dread of his wrath and shafts is frequently expressed. The beneficent side of his character, however, comes out in other passages. His two exclusive epithets *jalāsha* (cooling) and *jalāsha-bheshaja* (possessing cooling remedies) suggest his healing powers. He is the great physician. The physical basis is not certain. It is suggested that the storm in its destructive aspect may explain the malevolent side of his nature, while the fertilizing and purifying function of the thunderstorm may well be the basis of his healing and beneficent powers (see also pp. 161-2, 207).

The Maruts—the storm-gods—form an important group of deities (*gaṇa, śardhas*), numbering thrice sixty or thrice seven. They are the sons of Rudra and Pṛiśni, the cow (representing the mottled storm cloud?), also of Vāyu, and are sometimes described as self-born. They are all brothers of equal age, having the same birthplace and abode. They are golden, ruddy, and self-luminous and are associated with *vidyut*, particularly having the epithet lightning-spread (*ṛishṭi-vidyut*); the cars on which they ride gleam with lightning. Among their personal decorations, such as helmets, mantles, garlands etc., armlets and anklets are peculiar. They make a loud noise, represented by thunder and the roaring of the winds, and as such are pre-eminently the singers of heaven, their songs inspiring Indra. Their chief function is to shed rain which is figuratively called either milk, honey, or *ghī*, and which is connected with the thunderstorm. At the same time they produce light and make a path for the sun. They are the constant allies of Indra, in whose company they are addressed as "priests," their songs representing hymns of praise. Indra achieves all his exploits in their company. Like Rudra, they are invoked to avert lightning, the arrow and the bolt from the worshippers, and also to bring healing remedies.

Vāyu and Vāta (wind) are almost interchangeable terms; when distinguished, the former is chiefly the god, the latter the element. The name "Parjanya" means literally "rain-cloud" which, when personified, becomes an udder, a water-skin or a pail. Parjanya is also described as a bull that quickens the plants and the earth.[11]

As regards Āpaḥ (the waters), the personification is only incipient. They are mothers, wives, and goddesses who bestow boons. They are celestial as well as terrestrial, and the view has been mentioned above (in connection with Varuṇa) that the celestial waters were probably looked upon as an ether-like medium on which the luminaries made their fixed journeys along the Zodiac (*ṛita*), and that the blocking of them by Vṛitra was supposed to prevent the rise and movements of these luminaries, thus causing long darkness. As the waters are invoked as *āpo* in the *Avesta*, their deification is pre-Vedic.

5. *The Terrestrial Gods*

Agni, a personification of the sacrificial fire, presents in its conception the household life of the Vedic Aryans, and is second in importance only to Indra whose conception presents their external life of struggle and conquest. The anthropomorphism of the physical appearance of Agni is naturally very slight. He is butter-backed, and flame-haired, and eats the oblations with his tongue. Wood or *ghī* is his food, and melted butter his beverage, though he is invited also to drink the Soma with other gods. He is nourished three times a day. Although he is invoked to partake of the sacrificial offerings himself, he is more prominently the mouth by which the gods eat the sacrifice. His splendour is naturally his most prominent quality. He shines by day and night. He is called "smoke-bannered" (*dhūma-ketu*) and is said to be supporting the sky with his smoke as with a post. He is a charioteer of the sacrifice and brings the gods in his golden lightning car. He is said to be the son of heaven (Dyaus) and also of heaven and earth. Indra, with whom he is more closely associated than with any other god, is called his twin brother.

There are various myths about his births, forms, and abodes. He is daily produced from the two kindling-sticks (*araṇīs*), which are called his parents or mothers, and therefore he is ever young, though ancient. He is called the "son of strength," probably because of the strength required to kindle the fire, the ten fingers (called maidens) being exercised in the process. Agni's origin in the aerial waters is often referred to. As the Son of Waters (*Apāṁ napāt*) he has become a separate deity. He is also said to be born in the highest heaven and was brought down from heaven by Mātariśvan (the Indian Prometheus). This is his third origin—the celestial one. The three-fold nature of Agni is a favourite topic with *RV* poets; his heads, bodies, stations, splendours and births are each threefold. He is the earliest representative of the famous Indian trinity, and yet sometimes he is called *dvi-janman* ("having two births") from the point of view of a two-fold division of the universe into heaven and earth.

His connection with domestic life is a special feature. He is the only *gṛihapati* (master of the house), the *atithi* (guest"), and a kinsman of men. He is the *dūta* ("messenger"), *par excellence*, appointed by gods and men to be an oblation-bearer.

As the central figure of the sacrifice, he is called variously *ṛitvij, vipra, purohita, adhvaryu* and *brahman* and is thus the divine counterpart of the earthly priesthood. He is pre-eminently "omniscient" or "one who knows all created beings" (*jātavedas*). The funeral hymn (X. 14) distinguishes between the *havya-vāhana* form of Agni (the conveyor of offerings) and the *kravyād* form of Agni, that burns the dead body on the funeral pyre.

Even in the Indo-European period, the sacrificial fire was a well-known institution, as offering gifts to the gods by casting them into fire was customary among the Italians and Greeks. In the Indo-Irānian period a vast ritual had already developed around the sacrificial fire which is personified and worshipped as a beneficent god.

Rigvedic mythology is dominated by two all-pervading figures, the Sun and the Fire. There are but few deities in the Rigvedic pantheon that cannot be explained (though this may not be necessary) as manifestations of either the one or the other. Now the sun is regarded as a form of Agni (VII. 2. 1) and Agni is said to be born as the rising sun in the morning. This ultimate unity underlying the divine diversity may provide a solution of many a puzzle in Rigvedic mythology.

Bṛihaspati, also called Brahmaṇaspati (lord of prayer), has but few physical features, and these are the usual ones ascribed to all other gods. Like Agni, he is both a domestic priest and a *brahman* priest and the generator of all prayers. He is identified with as well as distinguished from Agni. Being often invoked with Indra (some of whose epithets like *maghavan* and *vajrin* he shares), he is drawn into the Indra myth of the release of the cows. Thus he has no homogeneous character, combining in himself, as he does, martial as well as priestly elements. As the divine *brahman* priest, he seems to have been the prototype of Brahman, the chief of the later Hindu triad. On the other hand, as the lord and creator of *brahman,* which played an important part in the later ritual and finally became the supreme principle in Vedānta philosophy, the god is very interesting from the point of view of the later religious and philosophical development of India.

Next in importance to Indra and Agni comes Soma, because the Soma sacrifice was the centre of the Rigvedic ritual. As the Soma plant and its juice were ever present before the Rigvedic poets, the anthropomorphism is less developed than that of Indra or Varuṇa. The weapons of Soma such as the bow, his car, and his team are described. An entire book—the ninth—is devoted to Soma (the deity and the plant) and the preparation of the Soma juice. The *aṁśu* (ṣhoot or stalk) is pounded between stones called *adri.* The pressed juice, in the act of passing through the filter of sheep's wool, is called *pavamāna* (or *punāna*) "flowing clear." The juice thus purified and as yet unmixed is called *śukra* or *śuchi* (bright), also *śuddha* (pure). This filtered Soma next flows into jars (*kalaśa*) or vats (*droṇa*) where it is mixed (technically "cleansed") with water and milk to sweeten it. The Soma has three kinds of admixture (*āśir*), with milk (*go*), sour milk (*dadhi*) or barley (*yava*). The admixture is poetically described as a bright robe. Soma is thus pressed three times a day; the morning libation is the first drink of Indra, the midday one belongs to him exclusively, while the evening pressing is for the Ṛibhus. The admixture of Soma brings him into a special relation with the Waters, who are called his "mothers" or "sisters." Soma is also the lord of streams.

The exhilarating power of Soma is appreciated. It is a divine drink conferring immortality on gods and men. It is called *amṛita,* the "draught of immortality." Soma has curative powers also. As a deity, Soma is a wise seer, a poet, who stimulates thought and inspires hymns. The fact that Soma invigorates Indra in his fight with Vṛitra is repeated so often that Indra's exploits and cosmic actions come to be attributed to him.

Like the corresponding *Haoma* in the *Avesta,* Soma grows on the mountains, but his true origin is said to be in heaven, from which he was brought to earth by an eagle. Soma is a king; the lord of plants or lord of the wood (*vanaspati*). In a few of the latest hymns of the *RV,* Soma is mystically identified with the moon.

The preparation and offering of the Soma was a feature of Indo-Irānian worship. There are numerous similarities between the Soma and the Haoma (Avestan) cults. The belief in an intoxicating beverage of the gods, a kind of honey or mead, may probably go back even to the Indo-European period.

Among the remaining terrestrial deities, Pṛithivī is so closely associated with Dyaus, that generally they are celebrated conjointly, Dyaus being never lauded alone in any hymn, while Pṛithivī alone is invoked only in one short hymn of three stanzas (V. 84). The personification is so slight that the attributes are mainly those of the physical earth. Certain rivers are also lauded, the most important among them being the Sarasvatī in whose case the personification has made greater progress than in the case of the other rivers like the Sindhu (Indus) and the sister streams of the Punjab, namely Vipāś (Beās) and Śutudrī (Sutlej).

The progress of religious thought in the *RV* is discernible in the transition from the concrete to the abstract and in the rise of abstract deities, the earlier and the larger class of which originated from epithets applicable to one or more of the older deities, like Tvashṭṛi, Prajāpati, etc. A smaller class consists of personifications of abstract nouns like Manyu (wrath), Śraddhā (faith), etc. Goddesses play a very unimportant rôle, the only notable exception being that of Ushas. Dual divinities like Mitrā-Varuṇā and Dyāvā-pṛithivī (dual compounds with each member in the dual) are a special characteristic. Groups of deities, like the Maruts (a large group associated with Indra, Agni, and Soma), the Ādityas (a small one, with Varuṇa as chief), and the Vasus have been already mentioned. An all-embracing group is that of the Viśvedevas (the All-gods). A few divinities there are of the tutelary order, like Vāstoshpati (lord of the dwelling), Kshetrasya-pati (lord of the field), and Sītā (the furrow).

Various features of the earth's surface such as mountains, besides rivers and waters and plants, and artificial objects like sacrificial implements and weapons are also deified, in addition to the great phenomena of nature.

The Demons, often mentioned, are either the aerial foes of the gods like Dāsas or Dasyus (Asuras occur in the later parts of the *RV* only) or constitute a lower class of terrestrial goblins, commonly called Rākshasas or a species designated by the term *yātu* or *Yātudhāna*. Magical practices are dealt with in about a dozen hymns in the tenth Maṇḍala which treat of augury or spells against poisonous vermin, diseases, a child-killing demon, enemies in general, and rival wives. Incantations to preserve life, to bring on sleep, and to procure offspring are found in X. 58-60; VII. 55, and X. 183 respectively, while the well-known Frog-hymn (VII. 103) (*ante*, p. 349) is supposed to envisage frogs as magical bringers of rain.

The first four out of the so-called funeral hymns (X. 14-8) (*ante*, p. 352) are addressed to deities who control life after death.

Some of the significant aspects of Rigvedic mythology may now be summed up thus:

(1) The principal phenomena of Nature, conceived as alive and represented in anthropomorphic (not rarely in theriomorphic) shape, were the objects of worship. (2) The so-called simple primitive side of Nature-Worship may be supposed to be reflected in the adoration of plants, trees, and mountains. (3) A great god like Indra is sometimes conceived as a bull, or the Sun as a horse, but *totemism* in the sense of the actual direct worship of animals, or the belief in an animal ancestor, is not to be thought of. Vṛitra (the drought-demon), for example, is conceived as a snake, but the snake receives no worship. (4) Whether fetishism is to be read into a reference to an image of Indra, and whether the worship of idols or images of gods was known to the *Ṛigveda*, are points on which no certain conclusions can be reached.

2. SACRIFICE

It is hardly any wonder that the humanized gods of the *Ṛigveda* should share some human weaknesses and be susceptible to flattery and gifts. A full meal was certain to win divine favour. Thank-offerings were known. Though the feeling of dependence was there, and though the surrender of one's property and possessions became ultimately the mark of deep affection for God, it was the definite hope and expectation of rewards that chiefly inspired the offering of prayers and oblations in the *Ṛigveda*. But who was to carry the offerings from earth to the gods in heaven? Very naturally the fire, with its towering flames and ever-rising smoke, already deified as Agni (as Atar by the Irānians), was thought of as an intermediary and messenger and as a bearer of oblational offerings from men to gods. The sacrificial fire is, in fact, an Indo-European institution, as the Romans, the Greeks, and the Irānians also had the custom of offering gifts to the gods in fire. In the Indo-Irānian period already an elaborate ritual, in the keeping of the priestly class, is found developed around the sacrificial fire.

In the *Ṛigveda*, the sacrifice is yet only a means of influencing the gods in favour of the offerer, and it is doubtful whether in this age the conception of gods as subject to control by the worshipper, if he only knew the correct means, was developed, and whether the selection of the horse as a sacrifice was motivated by the belief that thereby the swift steed—the sun—regained strength and favoured the worshipper. As regards the more mystic view of the sacrifice as a sacrament, the common meal of the priests on the sacrificial victim may only be looked upon as a bare hint in that direction, because though the priests believed that this meal brought them into a special relationship with the god who by sharing it with them acquired in part the same nature as themselves, it is doubtful whether they deemed themselves to be consuming the victim. It may be noted in this connection that union or companionship with the gods (I. 125. 5) or with the sun is vouchsafed to those who give liberally or those who are generous with the sacrificial fees.

If we remember that the *Ṛigveda-Saṁhitā* is composed of earlier and later portions, it will be easy to understand how, on the one hand, a large number of the hymns arose independently of all sacrificial ritual, although many of these were used later on for sacrificial purposes, and how, on the other hand, many other hymns were from the first intended for nothing but sacrificial songs and litanies. Two varieties of this sacrificial cult are to be noted in the main, as follows:

(1) Certain hymns and verses of the *RV* were used as benedictions and prayers at birth, marriage, and other occasions of daily life, at funerals and ancestor-worship, as well as at ceremonies for ensuring the fertility of the cattle and the growth of the fruits of the field. These ceremonies, called *gṛihya karmāṇi,* were, as a rule, associated with sacrifices of the simplest type, viz. burnt offerings (i.e. offerings of milk, grain, *ghī,* or flesh thrown into the fire). At these, the householder himself (who was assisted, if necessary, by one single priest, the Brahman) officiated as the sacrificial priest and the single fire of the domestic hearth served as the altar. These simple sacrifices which every one, rich or poor, performed according to his means, consisted chiefly of prayers (the first stage of the Vedic religion). In addition to these and a few incantations in the tenth Maṇḍala which represent popular religion consisting of spells to defeat rivals, to prevent and cure diseases and to repel noxious animals, we have (2) the grand sacrifices, especially in connection with the Soma-cult relating to Indra, which could only be undertaken by aristocratic and wealthy men (*maghavan*), and especially by the kings. An extensive sacrificial area with three altars for the three sacred fires, and a multitude of priests headed by four chief priests who received liberal payment (*dakshiṇā*) for the joint performance of numerous elaborate and intricate rites and ceremonies on behalf of the *yajamāna* (sacrificer) who did very little himself, characterized these Śrauta sacrifices. The hymns of the *RV* are much occupied with the Soma ritual. Animal sacrifices are indicated by the *āpri-sūktas,* and the horse-sacrifice (*aśvamedha*) was undoubtedly performed. The Purusha-Sūkta, does not describe an actual human sacrifice, but merely preserves, in all probability, the memory of it, as it was performed in prehistoric times, because the Śunaḥśepa hymns of the *Ṛigveda* (I. 24-30 and IX. 3) are not exactly related to the Śunaḥsepa legend of the *Aitareya Brāhmaṇa*

which is probably reminiscent of human sacrifice in pre-historic times.

3. PHILOSOPHY

It has been generally held that the Rigvedic religion is essentially a polytheistic one, taking on a pantheistic colouring only in a few of its latest hymns. Yet a deeply abstract philosophizing crops up unexpectedly in some hymns as a reminder of the long journey made from primitive polytheism to systematic philosophy, through the stages of naturalistic polytheism, monotheism, and monism.

The plurality of gods could not satisfy the intellect of the Rigvedic seers. One god was therefore identified with another, or gods were invoked in pairs or conjointly in groups of three or more. Systematization took the form of the classification of the gods into different categories or of the amalgamation of them all into one comprehensive group of the "All-gods." This systematization was but a step forward towards the more logical monotheism. There cannot be more than one supreme and unlimited Being. The appearance of what Max Müller calls henotheism is due to this unconscious urge towards monotheism imperfectly moulding polytheistic tendencies and thus presenting an inconsistent picture. When "individual gods are alternately regarded as highest," a large number of attributes, personal characteristics, and functions become common to all the gods, the merging of all these qualities into one divine figure becomes easy, and thus polytheistic anthropomorphism evolves into a kind of spiritual monotheism.

But the *Ṛigveda* betrays discontent even with this monotheistic development and the single supreme anthropomorphic deity that should follow from it. *RV*, I. 164.4 asks "Who has seen the first-born, when the boneless one bore the one with bones? Where is the life, the blood, the self of this *bhūmi* (universe)? Has anyone approached the knowing one to ask this question?" As if in answer to this question, verse 46 of the same hymn affirms that the central principle was the sexless *sat* (the "real") which, though one, was called by various names, Indra, Mitra, Varuṇa, Agni, Yama, Mātariśvan, etc. Thus, in some of the late hymns of the *Ṛigveda,* which designate indifferently the Supreme or Absolute as "He" or "It," is reflected the usual vacillation between monotheism and monism met with in all philosophies. In the opinion of the present writer, the transition from monotheism to monism was effected smoothly and almost unconsciously, owing to the growing influence of the conception of *Ṛita.* As mentioned above, the primary sense of *Ṛita,* appearing alongside of, and yet clearly distinguished from, its secondary sense or senses, is the physical one. *Ṛita* is the path of the Zodiac within which the apparent motions of the *devas* (luminaries) are confined and which is dotted by the *nakshatras*. No wonder that the *devas* are said to be born in *Ṛita* and governed by it. *Ṛita* next comes to denote very naturally the cosmic order or law prevailing in nature. In the moral world, the word designates "order" through the meanings "truth" and "right," and in the religious world "the order" takes the form of sacrifice or rite. The way to the later conception of the Absolute, which is impersonal and is designated by the neuter terms *sat* or *brahman*, has been paved by this abstract conception of *Ṛita*, which looks like the earliest crude precursor of the Absolute of the later Vedānta.

The problem of the origin and nature of the world-stuff is a philosophical one, and is not neglected by the Rigvedic poets. *RV*, X. 190 tells us that from heat *(tapas)* were produced *ṛita* and *satya;* then night, the ocean, and *saṁvatsara* (year) were produced in succession... *RV*, X. 72. 2 says that *sat* was produced from *asat*. From the mythological point of view, each one of the gods in turn is said to be the creator of the universe, the universe being sometimes looked upon as the finished product of the carpenter's and joiner's skill. For example *RV*, X. 31. 7 asks "What was the wood, which the tree, out of which they fashioned heaven and earth?" *RV*, X. 121 takes up the problem of creation on a monotheistic level and tells us that Hiraṇyagarbha arose from the great waters, pervading the Universe, and thus created the world out of eternally pre-existing matter. But X. 129—the well-known Nāsadīya hymn —describes creation from the highest monistic level. "In the beginning, there was no 'Non-existent,' because this creation arose therefrom, nor the 'Existent,' because its usual manifestations—the firmament or the heaven beyond it—were not then. The One breathed by itself, breathless, and there was nothing beyond it. There was no death then; how could there be anything immortal then? There was no light which could give us distinctions like night or day." Thus is suggested the highest philosophical truth that we cannot characterize the Absolute because of the inadequacy of our categories. *Tapas* is the warming up of being into existence, whereby is developed from the Absolute the implication of the primary antithesis, namely the opposition of ego and non-ego. The hymn further tells us that Desire (*Kāma*), the germ of the mind betraying self-consciousness, is the bond binding the existent to the non-existent. The doubt expressed at the end as to whether anyone knows the truth about creation is a beautiful expression of the ignorance of the wise. This hymn rises to the breath-taking heights of monism and leaves behind the dualistic metaphysics of the hymn to Viśvakarman (X. 82) wherein we are told that the Waters contained the primordial germ—the floating world-egg from which arises Viśvakarman, the first-born of the universe—the creator and maker of the world. The Nāsadīya hymn, in the terminology of modern philosophy, makes nature and spirit both aspects of the One, the Absolute, which is neither the self nor the non-self.

The word *māyā* in the *RV* generally denotes "occult power" applicable in a good sense to gods and in a bad sense to demons, and may be rendered by the English word "craft", having a similar double application. But, as noted above (p. 353), in X. 54. 2 it is used in the sense of "illusion" or "show," thus forestalling later Vedānta philosophy. It may be safely affirmed, however, that the Rigvedic tendency is towards a naïve realism, not monistic idealism, towards which the general spirit of Indian thought was soon to drift. If X. 72. 2 says that the "existent" was produced from the "non-existent," all that is meant is that the manifest arose from out of the non-manifest. If being or non-being is postulated as the first principle, it is strictly from the point of view of the world of experience.

Instead of the five elements of later philosophy, the *RV* postulates only water as the primordial element or matter, from which the others gradually evolve. In the Purusha-Sūkta (X. 90) the body of the Purusha is said to be the original material, as it were, out of which the world is made. The gods are the agents of creation, the act of creation is a sacrifice, and the Purusha is the victim. Although anthropomorphism, pushed to the last limit, is responsible for the greatness of God and the unity of world and God, being described in terms of the gigantic dimensions of the Purusha, the hymn X. 90 is a sort of crude allegory of the theory of creation from the One Absolute found in X. 129. Only, here the Supreme reality becomes the active Purusha—the begetter as well as the begotten: "From the Purusha Virāṭ was born, and from Virāṭ again the Purusha," (X. 90. 5).

4. ETHICAL AND SPIRITUAL THOUGHT

As the Rigvedic Aryans were full of the *joie de vivre*, they were not particularly interested in the life after death; much less had they any special doctrines about it. We can therefore glean only a few notices of the life beyond, that are scattered throughout the *Ṛigveda*.

Two separate pathways along which all moving creatures travel, namely the path of the Fathers and that of the gods and mortals, are spoken of in X. 88. 15, and it is supposed that there is a reference here to the way to the other world. Companionship with the Sun and the gods and immortality are highly prized goals (X. 107. 2; I. 125. 5). After his death, a man is supposed to enter the kingdom of Yama (who and his sister Yamī were primeval twins). Yama was the first of the mortals who died and discovered the way to the realm over which he rules and which is the destination of the subsequent dead. The spirits of the departed ones are supposed to go through *ishṭāpūrta* to this paradise, where Yama and the Fathers live in the midst of the joys of immortality, and the spirits are material enough to enjoy such pleasures as the drinking of Soma, milk, honey, and *surā*, as also music. This is hardly surprising, as the goal of all human endeavour is to become like gods. This heaven is reached through sacrifices and worship of the gods. The spirit is endowed with a shining form in heaven (X. 14. 8).

Hell is represented as a place of punishment for evil-doers (*avratas*). This is characterized as low and dark (X. 152. 4), as a kind of pit (IX. 73. 8). There is, however, no sordid picture of hell and its terrors. In our search for any reference, implicit or explicit, to rebirth or transmigration, we come across only a few doubtful passages. According to *RV*, 1. 164. 30, "the soul (*jīvaḥ*) of the dead one moves in its own power, the immortal one having a common origin with the mortal one (the body)." But this translation is not certain. The reference in *RV*, X. 15. 2 to Pitṛis who reside in the earth-region or in the dwellings of men need not imply belief in the soul as a ghost revisiting the haunts of men, but may only be the germ of the idea of the acceptance of the funeral (*Śrāddha*) offerings by them which became so famous at a later time. *RV*, X. 16. 3 exhorts the soul of the dead to go over to heaven or earth, to the waters or to the plants, along with all its physical parts. But is this going over a rebirth? In X. 58 the departing spirit of a dying person is called back from Yama, from heaven, earth, the quarters, the sea, the waters, the sun, the dawn or the mountains, i.e. from wheresoever it may have gone to. So we may conclude that only the germs of the conception of rebirth were there, and these developed either naturally, or through the influence of ideas current among the original tribes with whom the Aryans came into contact.

RV, VII. 86. 6 and 88. 5, 6 clearly show that the consciousness of sin (*anṛita, āgas, enas*) was recognized. Sin resulted from the violation of *ṛita* or "order" in the moral sphere (i.e. of "truth" and "right") as well as in the religious one (i.e. of sacrifice or rite), or of the commands of God. In the unalterable law of good or bad effects, flowing from good or bad conduct, are to be found the first germs of the law of *Karman* (that most outstanding characteristic of Indian thought)—binding on gods and mortals alike. Offering prayers and performing rites, living in short in perfect harmony with the will of God—this was the ideal moral life according to the *RV*. Man owes some duties to his fellow-beings also (X. 117). *RV*, V. 85. 7 tells us that an offence against a friend, neighbour, or comrade, or even a stranger is a sin (*āgas*). Adultery, witchcraft, gambling, drinking, senselessness, and self-deception are ranked as deviations from the moral life. The view, therefore, that the so-called uncertainty of the fate of the evil after death is a vagueness characteristic of the comparative indifference to morals, and that if gods are extolled as true it is not an assertion of ascertained truth, is wrong.

On the whole a very optimistic outlook on life is revealed in the hymns of the *RV*. Not that the Rigvedic Aryans do not desire immortality (*amṛitatva*) or the company of the gods in heaven. As we have seen above, there are many hymns and stanzas which raise questions and posit answers, all inspired by the eternal quest of the human heart for a solution of life's problems. These hymns betray a metaphysical streak and a flair for cutting the Gordian knot of philosophy—seeds which were to blossom later into the wild yet beautiful garden of the Upanishads. But the joys and pleasures of this world interest them deeply. Thus the *Ṛigveda* is full of prayers for long life, freedom from disease, heroic progeny, wealth, power, abundance of food and drink, the defeat of rivals, etc. There is no trace of pessimism in the thoughts of the Rigvedic sages. Whether life was a reality or illusion, substance or shadow, they want to enjoy it to the full. They do not seem to subscribe to the doctrine that life is a misery, which can only be ended by eradicating desire or *vāsanā*, the cause of the ever-recurring cycle of births and deaths—a doctrine developed later by the Buddhists and found in the Vedānta. The religious thought, therefore, betrays a practical streak. The worship of the powers of Nature is sincere but utilitarian, and *do ut des* is quite openly the theory of all sacrifice and homage.

GENERAL REFERENCES

Macdonell, A. A.: *Vedic Mythology* (Strassburg, 1897).

1. *Ṛigveda Repetitions*, Preface, p. xviii.
1a. *VM*, p. 16.
2. Cf. Ch. XVI, p. 343. For a beautiful hymn in the *Atharva-Veda*, cf. Ch. XX. pp. 417-8.
3. *Paradise Found* (Tenth Edition, 1893) Part V, Ch. V, pp. 250-60.
4. *The Arctic Home in the Vedas*, p. 233-96.
5. *RV*, X. 121. 1 and 3 ff. See also *Śat. Br.*, XI. 1. 6. 1; *Ait. Br.*, I. 1; and *Manu-smṛiti*, 1. 9.
6. *VM*, p. 122.
7. *VM*, p. 123.
8. *Ind. Stud.*, 5. 234.
9. *Orion*, p. 205.
9a. For some specimens, cf. Ch. XVI, pp. 344 ff.
9b. Cf. Ch. XI, p. 227.
10. Zimmerman, *A Second Selection of Hymns from the Ṛigveda* (Second Edition 1922), Appendix IV, pp. CI ff.
11. Cf. the hymn to Parjanya quoted in Ch. XVI, pp. 347.

CHAPTER XIX

SOCIAL AND ECONOMIC CONDITIONS

I. SOCIAL CONDITION

1. *Family Life*

THE foundation of social life was the patriarchal family. In *Ṛigveda* (I. 24. 12-15 and V. 2. 7), where we find the rudiments of the Śunaḥśepa story, a kind of absolute control by parents over children is suggested. That family discipline was strict is illustrated by the case of Ṛijrāśva who was deprived of his sight as a punishment by his father (I. 116. 16). Similarly in *RV*, X. 34. 4 we are told how the insolvent gambler is disowned by his parents and brothers, in front of his creditor. This does not mean that the relation between the parents and children was not generally one of warm affection; for a father is looked upon as the type of all that is good and kind. The wedding hymn (X. 35) indicates that the newly-married wife rules over (or wins by her love?) her brothers-in-law and even over her husband's parents although she herself entertains a feeling of respect for them. This is clear evidence of joint family life. That under certain circumstances this joint family included the wife's mother is suggested by X. 34. 3 where the gambler complains that "his mother-in-law hates him." After the death of the father, the eldest son took charge of the family.

A notable feature of the etiquette of the Rigvedic age was the great store set on hospitality. The frequent epithet of Agni, viz., *Atithi*, the beloved guest in human abodes, takes for granted the affection and respect generally shown to a guest. No wonder that in later literature detailed descriptions of the merits of hospitality should occur, and that hospitality to a guest should be elevated to the rank of a religious duty, as one of the five great daily sacrifices (*pañcha-mahāyajñas*).

2. *The Caste System*

The elaborate institution known as the Caste System among the Hindus in India may almost be said to be without a parallel in the world, although there is hardly a country where classes or orders of society or grades of social distinction of some kind or other are not met with. A common origin, name, tutelary deity, occupation, and ceremonies generally distinguish one homogeneous caste-group from another, but to-day caste is rigidly fixed by birth, and exclusive *commensality* and *connubium* between the members of a caste-group to the exclusion of all others are its fundamental and outstanding characteristics. Further, the conception of impurity communicable to a higher caste by contact with a lower one underlies this fissiparous tendency, and has resulted in the untouchability of the so-called Śūdra, who by popular error is almost indentified with the *pañchama,* or one outside the framework of the *Chāturvarṇya.* Again, in place of the four original *varṇas* or class-groups, there are today thousands of caste divisions and sub-divisions and the number is still growing. This unique development of an ordinary social phenomenon naturally invests its history with a special importance.

The extent to which caste had been developed in the age of the *Ṛigveda Saṁhitā* has formed a subject of keen controversy among scholars.[1] The uncertainty regarding the exact interpretation of the basic words and phrases in the *Ṛigveda,* and the relative chronology of the various relevant passages scattered throughout that Veda, make it difficult to arrive at any conclusion that is likely to meet with general acceptance. We shall, therefore, state first of all in detail the most widely accepted version—in a sense, almost the recognized version—of the development of caste in the *Ṛigveda,* contenting ourselves with only a brief statement of divergent views. Much confusion will be avoided, if we keep in view the fact, generally agreed to, that the development of caste has been a progressive one, and that we should not expect in the *Ṛigveda Saṁhitā* the picture of the Caste System which is presented even in the *Yajurveda Saṁhitās.*

There are various speculations in later Brahmanical literature regarding the origin of castes. The most common is that which represents the Brāhmaṇas, Kshatriyas, Vaiśyas, and Śūdras to have been created respectively from the head, breast or arms, the thighs, and the feet of the Creator. An echo of this is found in a hymn of the *RV* (X. 90), the famous Purusha-sūkta, which describes the mythical legend of the sacrifice of a primeval giant called Purusha, the ideal "Man" or World-Spirit. The relevant passage has been translated thus:[2]

"When (the gods) divided Purusha, into how many parts did they cut him up? What was his mouth? What arms (had he)? What (two objects) are said (to have been) his thighs and feet? The Brāhmaṇa was his mouth; the Rājanya was made his arms; the being (called) the Vaiśya, he was his thighs; the Śūdra sprang from his feet."

This passage refers to the first three Castes not as sprung from, but as identical with, the mouth, arms and the thighs of the Creator. But in spite of this difference many regard this hymn of the *RV* as the earliest exposition of the later Brahmanical view, and regard the essential features of the Caste System as existing even in the earliest Aryan society in India.

This theory has been challenged by many scholars whose views may be briefly stated as follows:

The evidence of the Purusha-sūkta, an admittedly late hymn, is not valid for the bulk of the *Ṛigveda,* which was produced by the as yet un-Brahmanized tribes of Vedic Indians living in the Indus region and the Punjab. The Caste System was developed only later, when a section of these Vedic tribes migrated farther east. The term *Varṇa* (*lit.,* Aryan colour) is used in the *Rigveda* of all the three highest castes of later times, being contrasted only with Dāsa (the *dasyu-varṇa* or "aboriginal colour"). The terms "Rājanya," "Vaiśya" and "Śūdra" occur only in the Purusha-sūkta, the term "Brāhmaṇa," also, being rare in the *Ṛigveda.* The term "Kshatriya," of which "Rājanya" is an earlier variant, occurs but seldom in the *Ṛigveda.* The term "Brahman" denotes "a priest by profession" only in some passages, while in others it denotes any person who was distinguished by genius or virtue, or one who, for some reason, was deemed specially receptive of the divine inspiration.

The transition from the casteless, though classified, society of the bulk of the *Ṛigveda* to the elaborate Caste System of the *Yajurveda* is to be traced to the complication of life resulting from the further migration of the Vedic Aryans from the Punjab to the east. The necessity of carrying on a ceaseless fight with, and the conquest of, the aborigines called for an organization of the conquering people by the merger or fusion of petty tribes into centralized kingdoms. Thus emerged the powerful monarch, while the lesser tribal princes, deprived of their royal rank, sank to the position of nobles. The monarchy, moreover, needed now a standing armed force, prepared to meet all eventualities, such as resisting the sudden incursions of native or other Aryan tribes and quelling revolts on the part of the subdued aborigines. This standing army was naturally recruited from the ranks of the nobility of tribal princes and the chief armed retainers of the king. This is the genesis of the warrior class. At the same time, the "people" of the Aryan masses, secure in the protection afforded by the warrior class, ceased to take interest in military matters and settled down to a peaceful life devoted to agriculture, pastoral pursuits, trade, and industry. They constituted the third class, the *Viś,* later called "Vaiśyas."

Side by side also grew a distinct community of priests. In the earlier period, not only the householder but even the petty prince could offer sacrifice to the gods for himself and his people, the ritual being very simple. But when the size of the kingdom grew and military and administrative affairs kept the hands not only of the king but also of the warrior class full, while, at the same time, the ritual tended to become more complicated and elaborate, the need was keenly felt of a hieratic order, composed of the more intellectual elements among the non-fighters who could dedicate themselves, undisturbed by the distractions of war or peace, to the faithful and exact performance of the highly developed ritual, and to the preservation (by word of mouth) of the traditional formulae and sacred hymnology of the Aryans, a heritage in part at least from almost prehistoric times.

As regards the fourth class, the Śūdra is mentioned for the first and only time in the "Purusha-sūkta." But *dasyu* and *dāsa* are known to the *Rigveda,* both as aborigines independent of Aryan control and as conquered slaves. The latter may reasonably be supposed to represent the Sūdras of the later texts. But not all the defeated aborigines could be absorbed as slaves in the royal household or in the houses of individual owners. There must have been whole villages of the aborigines, though under Aryan control. The term "Śūdra" was evidently applied to the inhabitants of these villages as well as to the wild hill tribes which lived by hunting and fishing and acknowledged the overlordship of their Aryan neighbours. In course of time it included even *dasyu-varṇa* (or dark-skinned) people who remained beyond the pale of the Aryan state and who were virtually excluded from the religious and ritual cult of the Aryans. The development of the Caste System in a rigid form, with strictly hereditary and mutually exclusive caste-groups, did not take place till the time when the Vedic Aryans had settled down in the Middle Country and were already Brahmanized enough to look upon the inhabitants of the North-West—the home of the *Rigveda*—as uncivilized Vrātyas because they did not follow the strict Caste System.

The view summed up above may be regarded as the one now generally accepted by scholars. According to this recognized version, in the earliest society represented by the bulk of the *Ṛigveda*, there were probably different classes and professions, but none, not even the priestly and the warrior classes, were hereditary; the warriors were drawn from the people at large, and any person with the requisite qualifications could officiate as a priest.

This view is not, however, accepted by some whose arguments may be briefly stated thus: (1) The main, if not the earliest part of the *Ṛigveda* was, in all probability, composed not in the Punjab but in the east, in the country later known as the Madhyadeśa or Brahmāvarta. So the argument based on the non-Brahmanical character of the Vrātyas of the Indus and the Punjab becomes pointless. (2) The term Brāhmaṇa, "son of a Brahman or priest," suggests that the priesthood was normally hereditary. There is no definite instance of a person other than a priest exercising priestly functions. Nor was this feasible, as the priesthood, even in the *Ṛigveda*, distinguishes within its fold a vast number of sub-groups of specialists and experts. (3) The power of the Purohita over the king in the *Rigveda*, derivable from the fact that the correct performance of the sacrifice demanded the services of a hereditary priest, is nearly as great as in the post-Rigvedic age. (4) The *Ṛigveda* knows of a ruling class—the Kshatriya—who, as a class of nobles, are appropriately named in the Purusha-sūkta as "Rājanya" or "men of kingly family." As kingship was normally hereditary, the Kshatriyas were also in all probability a hereditary body. The Śūdras were admittedly a separate group; so all the elements of the Caste System were in existence in the age of the *Ṛigveda.* (5) There are glimpses in the *Ṛigveda* of a threefold (VIII. 35. 16-18) or fourfold (I. 113. 6) division of the people, corresponding to the well-known three upper or all the four divisions of the Caste System. (6) The existence of similar classes among the Irānians, namely priests, warriors, agriculturists, and artisans, makes it very probable that by the time of the *Ṛigveda* the four classes had developed into hereditary caste-groups, owing to the contact of the *Ārya-varṇa* Aryans with the dark-skinned aborigines, and the necessity this imposed on Aryan society of reorganizing its whole structure.

Although there is great force in some of these objections, it must be conceded that they are not strong enough to upset the recognized version. The existence of the four classes in Avestan literature certainly argues for the existence of somewhat similar classes in Rigvedic society, but much stronger positive evidence is necessary to establish that these classes were hereditary.

Further, the term Brāhmaṇa, son of a priest, occurs very rarely, and the word Brahmaputra, in the same sense, is found only once. This, when contrasted with the numerous references to Brahman, seems to indicate that there was no idea of a hereditary priesthood in the earlier Vedic period.

On the whole, it is difficult not to agree with the views, propounded long ago by Muir, that the Brāhmaṇas (far less the Kshatriyas or Vaiśyas) did not constitute an exclusive caste or race, and that the prerogatives of composing hymns and officiating at the services of the gods were not regarded, in the age of the *Ṛigveda*, as entirely confined to men of priestly families.[3] The same thing was equally, or perhaps more, true of the minor professions, as the hymn, quoted above on p. 350, refers to the father, mother and the son following three different vocations in life, viz. those of a poet, a grinder of corn, and a physician. The heredity of occupation was, therefore, not yet a recognized principle, far less an established fact. The utmost that can be said is that there were recognized professions like priesthood, or distinctions of nobility, and these had in many cases a tendency to become hereditary, but, as in other countries or societies, their ranks might have been recruited from all sections of the community. Of the other essential features of the Caste System viz., prohibition of interdining and intermarriage, no such restriction is even remotely hinted at in the hymns of the *Ṛigveda.*

3. *Marriage and the Position of Women*

The frequent mention of unmarried girls like Ghoshā, who grew up in the houses of their parents (I. 117. 7; X. 39. 3; 40. 5), the references to the ornaments worn by maidens at festival occasions in order to win lovers (I. 123. 11; VII. 2. 5), to a youth's courtship of the maiden he loves (I. 115. 2), to the lover's gifts (I. 117. 18), to their mutual love (I. 167. 3; IX. 32. 5, etc.) and to the spell (VII. 55. 5. 8) by which a lover hopes to lull the whole household to sleep while he visits his beloved—all this evidence speaks in favour of the custom of girls normally marrying long after they had reached puberty. Some of the passages mentioned above, but not all, may refer to the *hetaera* class as existing in Vedic society. The marriage ceremony also supports this view, as it is presumed to be immediately followed by consummation (X. 85. 29 ff.).

The restrictions on the field of choice in marriage were few. Marriage connections with the *dasyu-varṇa* people, with whom the Aryans came into conflict in India, were probably prohibited. Among Aryans only the marriages of brother and sister (X. 10), and of father and daughter were banned.

There seems to have been considerable freedom on the part of young persons concerned in the selection of a wife or husband, as they generally married at a mature age. There is no clear evidence that the consent of the parent or brother was essential. The latter appeared on the scene after the parties concerned had come to an understanding, and their participation as well as that of the "wooer" (*vara*) in the formal "wooing" was a mere formality, though it was an essential preliminary to the marriage ceremony.

The uncomplimentary references to some sons-in-law (VIII. 2. 20; I. 109. 2) suggest that in some cases a bride-price was paid by a not very desirable son-in-law. Similarly when girls had some physical defect, dowries, it seems, had to be given (VI. 28. 5; X. 27. 12). When Vimada carried off Purumitra's daughter against his will, but probably with the consent of the daughter (I. 112. 19; 116. 1; etc.), we have an admixture of those elements which led to the formulation, later, of the Gāndharva and Rākshasa forms of marriage.

A hymn in *RV* (X. 85)—which may be called the wedding hymn—gives us some idea of the oldest marriage ritual. The bridegroom and party proceed to the bride's house (X. 17. 1), where the well-adorned bride remains ready (IV. 58. 9) to join the marriage-feast. The guests are entertained with the flesh of cows killed on the occasion (X. 85. 13). The ceremony proper now commences. The bridegroom grasps the hand of the bride and leads her round the fire (X. 85. 36, 38). These two acts constitute the essence of the marriage and the bridegroom is now the husband who takes her by the hand (*hasta-grābha:* X. 18. 8). The bridegroom next takes the bride home in a car, in a wedding procession (X. 85. 7. 8. 10. 24-27. 42). Then follows the consummation which is signified chiefly by the purification of the bride's garment (X. 85. 28-30. 35).

Perfect harmony and happiness are prayed for in conjugal life, which (it is hoped) will be long enough to bless the couple with sons and grandsons (VIII. 31. 5-9: X. 34. 11; 85. 18. 19. 42 ff.). X. 85. 46 describes the newly married wife as taking up a most respected position as the mistress of her new household, wielding authority over the husband's father, brother, and unmarried sisters. This verse envisages the case (very probably) of the marriage of the eldest son in the family, when the old father has retired from active life. The authority exercised must have been more or less the rule of love. The wife participated regularly in the sacrificial offerings of her husband.

The fulfilment of the desire for offspring, and male offspring in particular, was the chief aim of marriage. Abundance of sons is constantly prayed for along with cattle and land, but no desire for daughters is expressed. This desire for a son is natural in a patriarchal organization of society. The son alone could perform the funeral rites for the father and continue the line. Sonlessness was as much deplored as poverty (III. 16. 5). The adoption of sons was recognized, though not favoured (VII. 4. 7. 8).

There is very little evidence of the prevalence of the custom of *Satī* or widow-burning in the *Ṛigveda,* though we may detect a semblance or reminiscence of this ancient custom in X. 18. 8, where the widow is asked to descend from the funeral pyre of her dead husband on which she was first made to lie. The only safe conclusion would be that the practice, even if known, was not widely prevalent, or at best was confined to the Rājanya class, if Indo-Germanic parallels are a correct guide. *Ṛigveda,* X. 40. 2 and X. 18. 7, 8 point to the practice of requiring a childless widow to cohabit with her brother-in-law until the birth of a son. This *niyoga* is a kind of short-term levirate. These passages (and I. 124.7 also which mentions a *gartā-ruḥ*) are clear evidence that the remarriage of widows was permitted in certain circumstances, though there is no clear or definite reference to it in *RV.*

The *Ṛigveda* certainly permits polygamy (I. 62. 11; 71. 1; 104. 3; 105. 8; 112. 19; 186. 7; VI. 53. 4; VII. 18. 2; 26. 3; X. 43. 1 101. 11, etc.), though monogamy may have been the rule (I. 124. 7; IV. 3. 2; X. 71. 4). Whether monogamy developed from polygamy in the Rigvedic age as Zimmer[4] thinks, or whether polygamy is secondary as Weber[5] believes, cannot be decided. Probably polygamy, though allowed, was practically confined to the Rājanya class. Polyandry is not referred to anywhere in the *Ṛigveda*. The few passages in the wedding hymn (X. 85. 37, 38) in which "husbands" (plural) are spoken of in connection with a single wife can be explained on a mythological basis. Female morality maintained a high standard, the same degree of fidelity not being expected from the husbands.

There are few doubtful references to lovers and love-making (I. 134. 3; VIII. 17. 7). A *raha-sūḥ*, "bearing in secret" is mentioned in II. 29. 1. A protégé of Indra is referred to as the "castaway" (*parāvṛji or parāvṛikta*), presumably as the offspring of illegitimate love. It is difficult to accept the view of Pischel and Geldner[6] that Ushas is the characteristic *hetaera*, nor are hetaerae referred to when women are described as going to the *samana*, though the dancer (*nṛitu*) may have belonged to that class. The so-called incestuous intercourse between father and daughter in the story of Prajāpati (X. 61. 5-7), and between brother and sister in the dialogue between Yama and Yamī (X. 10) can be satisfactorily explained (in the opinion of the present writer) on a mythological or astronomical basis.

Women had to be under the protection of some guardian or other; for example, in the care of their fathers until marriage, of their husbands after marriage, and of their brothers if not married; still they enjoyed much freedom. They did not always remain indoors, but moved about freely; they publicly attended feasts and dances, and there are references to "fair ladies flocking to festive gatherings."

4. *Education*

In the *Ṛigveda*, there is no explicit reference to the ceremony of *Upanayana* or Initiation (*lit.*, the drawing near or leading forth of a boy for study under the teacher) which is regarded as of such great importance in later ages. But all primitive people have some kind of ceremony, signifying the formal admission of an adult youth to membership of tribe, and we may infer from the closely parallel Indo-Irānian ceremony of Navjot that the elements of this ceremony probably existed in the Rigvedic age and even earlier.

The Frog hymn (VII. 103) quoted above, on p. 349, gives us a glimpse of the educational system (if system it can be called) of the Rigvedic age. The fifth verse gives a picture of the earliest Vedic school by the comparison of the croaking of the frogs to the chorus of voices heard when a teacher recites the Veda, section by section (*parvan*), and the pupils repeat his words after him. The first verse of the hymn suggests through a simile that this concerted school-recitation sprang into life suddenly, at a stated time (the opening of the monsoon?), because frogs raising their (rain-inspired) voices at the opening of the monsoon after lying low for (the rest of) the year are compared to Brāhmaṇas, conforming to their fixed annual routine (*vrata*). Evidently the entire instruction was orally given. Debates are also referred to (X. 71). The word *"Brahmachārin"* in the technical sense of a "religious student" is found in X. 109. 5. The father was not rarely also a teacher, his son taking lessons from him along with a few neighbouring students. That the sharpening of the intellect, as well as the development of character, in the *Brahmachārin* was aimed at, is seen from the celebrated Gāyatrī verse (III. 62. 10) which prays to Savitṛi for a stimulation (a whetting) of the intellect.

While there is no doubt that the instruction was orally imparted, it is a very debatable point whether the art of writing was known at all in this age. It is a well-known fact that no actual specimens of alphabets have been discovered in India which can be definitely dated before the fourth century B.C. Consequently most of the scholars are of opinion that the art of writing was unknown in ancient India. Bühler sought to prove that the Indian merchants learnt this art in Western Asia and introduced it in their country some time about the eighth century B.C. This view, which regards the most ancient alphabet of India (the Brāhmī alphabet of Aśoka's inscriptions) as derived from the North Semitic types of the ninth century B.C., now holds the field. But the discovery of the numerous seals at Mohenjo-daro, with pictographic writing (Ch. IX, p. 195) has put an altogether new complexion on the whole question. It is now believed by many that the Indus script formed the parent-source from which the oldest Brāhmī alphabets have been derived. Some are even of opinion that when the *Ṛigveda* was finally arranged in its present form it was written in a script which formed an intermediate stage between the Indus script and the Aśokan alphabet. If we accept the old theory of Bühler, we have to presume that the vast Vedic literature was composed and preserved by oral transmission alone—a stupendous feat of memory which appears to be almost miraculous. On the other hand, if we believe that these voluminous texts were committed in those old days to writing, we are faced with the problem of writing materials, of which we definitely know nothing. The whole thing is shrouded in mystery which cannot be solved until more definite facts come to light.

5. *Amusements and Entertainments*

Music, both vocal and instrumental, was well known. The Frog-hymn (VII. 103. 7-8) refers to the musical chanting of Brāhmanas engaged in the extraction of the Soma juice. Different vocal sounds are carefully analysed in that hymn and elsewhere. Singing is often mentioned as adapted to different ends, such as "chanting," "reciting," "hymning," etc. Among instruments we find reference to the *vīṇā* (lute or string-instrument), *vāṇa* (flute or wind-instrument), and the drum. The dancing of maidens is mentioned. Probably, men also danced, as is implied in a simile in X. 76. 6. The dialogue-hymns of the *Ṛigveda* have been the fruitful source of many theories regarding the earliest form of the drama (*ante*, p. 349). One theory is that they are relics of old mysteries from Indo-European times. Dr. Keith[7] holds that dramatic spectacles, religious in character, were known in the Rigvedic age. The chariot-race was a favourite sport and source of entertainment, and the race in general is the source of numerous similes and metaphors in the *Ṛigveda*. The fascination exercised by gambling and the ruin caused by addiction to it, is often referred to and is actually the subject-matter of a hymn (X. 34).

6. *Food and Drink*

Milk and its products, chiefly *ghṛita* (*ghī* or clarified butter), formed the principal ingredient of food. Grain (*yava*) was parched or ground into flour with a mill-stone and then mixed with milk or butter, and finally made into cakes. Vegetables and fruits were eaten in large quantities.

Meat also formed a part of the dietary. The flesh of the ox, the sheep, and the goat was normally eaten, after being roasted on spits or cooked in earthenware or metal pots. Probably meat was eaten, as a rule, only on occasions of sacrifice, though such occasions were by no means rare, the domestic and the grand sacrifices being the order of the day. This explains why horse-flesh was eaten only at the horse-sacrifice to gain the strength and swiftness of the horse. The cow receives the epithet *aghnyā* (not to be killed) in the *Ṛigveda*, and is otherwise a very valued possession. It is difficult to reconcile this with the eating of beef, but we may get some explanation if we remember the following: (1) Firstly, it was the flesh of the ox rather than of the cow that was eaten; a distinction definitely made. (ii) The flesh of the cow was (if at all) eaten at the sacrifices only, and it is well known that one sacrifices one's dearest possession to please the gods. (iii) Even in the *Ṛigveda*, only *Vaśās* (barren cows) were sacrificed. For example, Agni is called in VIII. 43. 11 as *vaśānna*. The expression *"atithinīr gāḥ"* (cows fit for guests) in X. 68. 3 implies the same distinction.

Milk, drunk warm as it came from the cow, was a favourite drink. Though the Soma juice, in *Ṛigveda*, appears exclusively as a sacrificial drink (as "Haoma," it was prepared and similarly celebrated in the Indo-Irānian period), it must have been a very popular inebriating drink in the original home of the Aryans. It had three kinds of admixture, with milk, sour milk, and *yava*. In the Rigvedic period, *surā* was the popular drink, extremely intoxicating as compared to the Soma which, though mildly inebriating, was an invigorating beverage. *Surā* was probably distilled from grain. It is condemned as "leading people to crime and godlessness." *Madhu*, though often used to denote "Soma" or milk or any sweet food or drink, has also the sense of "honey" in the *Ṛigveda*.

7. *Dress and Decoration*

The dress (*vasana* or *vastra*) consisted of two garments according to the strictly Rigvedic evidence, namely the *vāsas* (or "lower garment" in a narrow sense) and the *adhivāsa* (an "over-garment" or an "upper garment"), though in the days of the later *Saṁhitās*, the *nīvi* (or under-garment) came to be used in addition. The Maruts wear deer-skins, and a *muni* (X. 136. 2) is clad in skins or soiled garments.

The *atka* (a "garment") appears to be described as woven and well-fitting, though the real meaning is doubtful. Woollen clothing was in vogue. A sort of mantle or cloak (*drāpi*) is often mentioned. A kind of embroidered garment (*peśas*) seems to have been used by female dancers (I. 92. 4, 5; II. 3. 6, etc.). A special garment was worn by the bride at the marriage ceremony; it was later given to a Brāhmaṇa and is called *vādhūya*. The Maruts are described as wearing mantles adorned with gold. There was a general fashion for dressing well as may be inferred from words like *suvāsas* (well-clad) and *suvasana*, and there were garments of different colours too. There is no clear evidence of any differentiation between male and female dress.

Several ornaments are mentioned in *Ṛigveda*. The *Karṇaśobhana* was "an ornament for the ear," apparently for the use of men (VIII. 78. 3) and that it may have been a gold ornament is suggested by I. 122. 14 which refers to a deity as gold-eared (*hiraṇyakarṇa*). The *Kurīra* (X. 85. 8) was some kind of head-ornament worn by females, specially brides. The same may be said of *nyochanī* (X. 85. 6), a bride's ornament. *Khādi* was a kind of ring, worn as an armlet or an anklet (I. 166. 9; VII. 56. 13). *Nishka* was a gold ornament worn on the neck, and we shall presently see that it must have been of a size suitable for its use also as a sort of currency. *Maṇi* was some kind of jewel (whether "pearl" or "diamond" is not certain) worn round the neck (I. 122. 14). *Rukma* was an ornament worn on the breast (II. 34. 2, 8). Garlands were often worn by men desiring to appear to advantage (IV. 38. 6; V. 53. 4. etc.). One hymn (X. 184. 3) refers to the Aśvins as "lotus-wreathed."

The hair were kept combed and oiled. The use of the word "*opaśa*" indicates that plaits were worn by women in dressing the hair. There are undoubted references to the custom of wearing the hair in braids or plaits. A maiden had her hair made in four plaits (X. 114. 3). It seems from the descriptions of Rudra and Pūshan that men also wore their hair plaited or braided, and the Vasishṭhas were noted for wearing their hair in a plait or coil on the right (VII. 33. 1). The beard and moustache are mentioned, but shaving is referred to (X. 142. 4). Most probably *Kshura* means "razor" in the *Ṛigveda.*

8. *Knowledge of Medicine and Sanitation*

The physician is often mentioned with respect for his skill. Miraculous cures are ascribed to the twin-gods, the Aśvins, who are the great healers of diseases and experts in the surgical art. Among diseases *Yakshma* is frequently mentioned (I. 122. 9; X. 85. 31; 97. 11, 12; 137. 4; 163. 1-6). It denotes "illness" in general, and probably "consumption" in particular, rendering the body emaciated. IX. 112. 1 speaks of a physician wanting to cure a fracture in a way which seems to indicate that the practice of medicine was already a profession. The entire hymn X. 97 is addressed to the *Oshadhis* (the plants) with special reference to their curative powers. So herbs and plants figured prominently in the materia medica of this period. Prayers for long life are pretty frequent. The legends illustrating the reputed healing powers of the Aśvins give us an idea of the general ailments and bodily mishaps. They are divine physicians who restore eye-sight and cure the blind, sick, and maimed (VIII. 18. 8; 22. 10; I. 116. 16; X. 39. 3). They rejuvenate the sage Chyavana (I. 116. 10) and revive the sage Rebha when drowned and given up as dead. They give a cooling and refreshing draught to Atri Saptavadhrī when suffering from suffocation. They cure Parāvṛij of blindness and lameness, and when the leg of Viśpalā is cut off in battle, they replace it with an iron one. The last instance proves that a kind of primitive surgery was practised.

2. ECONOMIC CONDITION

1. *Agriculture and Cattle*

Agriculture made real headway during the Rigvedic age, although the practice of ploughing can be traced to Indo-Irānian times. The operation of tilling the soil meant (as now) the cutting of furrows in the field with the wooden ploughshare drawn by bulls, the sowing of seeds in the furrows thus made, the cutting of the corn with the sickle, the laying of the bundles of corn on the threshing-floor, threshing, and finally sifting and winnowing. Irrigation was known, and helped cultivation. The exact nature of the grain which was thus grown cannot be ascertained. It was called *Yava* and may have been "barley" as it was understood to be in the later Saṁhitās. Rice was not cultivated until a later period.

The Rigvedic Aryans were primarily a pastoral people and naturally cows and bullocks were their most valued possession. These constituted the chief form of wealth and the only original *dakshiṇā* (sacrificial fee). The word "*dakshiṇā*" in fact is an adjective meaning "right," or "valuable," with an ellipse of *go* (cow), because the sacrificial fee was a cow placed "on the right side" of the singer to be rewarded. Similarly one of the words for "fight" was *gavishṭi* "a search for cows." The name of *Aghnyā* ("not to be killed"), applied several times to the cow, shows that the cow was coming to be regarded as a sacred animal. This feeling of sanctity of the cow can be traced even to Indo-Irānian times. Cows were kept in stalls during the night and in the heat of the day. They were allowed to roam freely in the pastures at other times, and were milked three times every day. The cow returning from the pasture-land in the evening and licking her calf fastened by a rope was one of the most gladdening sights, and the lowing of the milch-kine the most musical sound to the Rigvedic Aryans. There are even special terms like "*sva-sara*" for the time of the grazing of the cows in the morning, and *saṁ-gava,* for the time when the grazing cows are driven home together for the milking. The *Ṛigveda* is aware of the dangers to which the grazing cows were liable, such as being lost, falling into pits, breaking limbs, and being stolen. The ears of cattle were marked, probably to indicate ownership. Bulls and oxen were regularly used for ploughing and drawing carts. That the cow should give warm or cooked milk was a standing wonder. That the dark or red cow could give shining milk was little short of a miracle! (VIII. 93. 13).

2. *Trade and Commerce*

There are clear references in the hymns (I. 56. 2) to trading in distant lands for profit. The prayers and oblations offered for "gaining a hundred treasures" (III. 18. 3) are also probably those of merchants seeking divine aid for success in trade. Apart from trade with foreign countries, or alien tribes, there must have been quite an extensive inland trade, but no definite details are available. Haggling in the market was, however, well-known.

The exchange of commodities on the principle of barter seems to have been in vogue, but cow had already come to be regarded as a unit of value (IV. 24. 10). There might have been other recognized units of value. Great importance attaches to one such unit called *nishka.* It meant originally a gold ornament of the shape of a necklace or a necklet (V. 19. 3). When, however, in I. 126. 2 the poet celebrates the receipt of a hundred *nishkas* with a hundred horses, as a gift, he could hardly be referring to a hundred necklets. So it probably came to be used as a sort of currency even during the Rigvedic age.

Booty in battle was one of the sources of wealth to the State, and consisted chiefly of flocks and herds. In individual economy, dowry and bride-price played no small part. Movable property could change hands by gift or sale which amounted to barter. Land was not an article of commerce, and does not seem to have presented any problems in connection with the transfer of immovable property in the case of the family or of the individual. The population being scanty and scattered over wide areas, fresh land could be easily obtained, if needed by a family which had grown to a very large size with several sons. The rivers of the North-West are referred to as yielding gold.

Whether any sea-borne trade was carried on during this age is a much disputed question, as already noted above (p. 248). The view that the Rigvedic Indians took part in ocean-shipping is opposed on the following grounds: (1) The *nau* (boat or ship) was, in the majority of cases, merely a boat or "dug-out" for crossing rivers, and there may have been large boats in use for crossing the broad rivers of the Punjab. These boats were so simple in their construction that only the paddle or oar (*aritra*) needed for propelling them is mentioned. There is no mention of masts or sails, of rudder or anchor. Thus the Vedic Indian was not much of a navigator. (2) Metaphors used by a people familiar with the ocean are lacking in the *Ṛigveda*. (3) The numerous mouths of the Indus are ignored, although that river was the convenient natural outlet to the sea. Against these arguments must be set down the following facts: (1) The *Rigveda* mentions men who go to the ocean (*samudra*) eager for gain (I. 56. 2; IV. 55. 6) and *samudra* cannot be explained away in these passages as standing for the very broad and wide stream of the lower Indus. (2) There are some allusions to a trade more extensive than that implied by boats for crossing rivers. (3) Verses I. 116. 3 ff. tell us that the Aśvins rescued Bhujyu in the ocean with a ship of a hundred oars (*śatāritra*). A ship of this type could be needed only for a sea-voyage. (4) X. 136. 5 refers to "eastern and western oceans." These passages, in the opinion of the present writer, clearly indicate that sea-trade was carried on during this age.

3. *Occupations and Industries*

Some of the important professions and vocations of this period have been incidentally referred to above. The Brāhmaṇas or the priestly class dedicated themselves to the highly specialized occupation or profession of officiating at the sacrifices and preserving the sacred hymnology of the Aryans by conducting Vedic classes. The Kshatriya or Rājanya class had taken to the fighting profession. Members of the third—the Vaiśya—class naturally took to agriculture, cattle-breeding and other pastoral pursuits, and the various arts, crafts, and industries. The lowest, the Śūdra class, was engaged in service of all kinds. But, as noted above, the classes were not irrevocably bound up with specific occupations. Many Rājanyas are found among the poets of the *Ṛigveda*, and members of the three higher classes were not rarely promiscuously engaged in cattle-breeding, during times of peace, and in fighting, during times of war. Money-lending was practised chiefly by the Vaiśyas, but also occasionally by Brāhmaṇas.

It appears from the large number of similes and metaphors drawn from the art of fashioning chariots for war and race, and carts for agriculture and transport, that carpentry was an honoured profession, the carpenter being also a wheelwright and joiner. He did all sorts of work in wood, and even carved work of a finer type was not beyond his skill (X. 86. 5; I. 161. 9; III. 60. 2). The worker in metal smelted ore in the furnace using the wing of a bird as a bellows to fan the flames. Household utensils like kettles were made of metal (*ayas*). What metal the *ayas* was is uncertain. It may have been either copper, bronze, or iron, if we suppose that the word is consistently used in the same sense; but it is also possible that it is used in more senses than one. Its colour is to be inferred from the epithets used with it, such as "reddish." As the use of copper precedes that of iron in the development of civilization, *ayas* may have indicated "copper" or its alloy "bronze"; but this is by no means certain, and iron may have been known. Earthenware and wooden vessels were used for purposes of eating and drinking, along with those of metal. The art of the tanner (*charmamnā* in VIII. 5. 38) and the use of hide are well known. Ox-hide was used to manufacture bowstrings, thongs (to fasten parts of the chariots), reins and the lash of the whip (VI. 75. 11; I. 121. 9; VI. 47. 26; 46. 14; 53. 9, etc.). It was also placed above the boards on which the Soma was pressed with the stones. It is not unlikely that skin bags were also made with it (X. 106. 10). Among the home and cottage industries may be mentioned sewing, the plaiting of mats from grass or reeds, and the spinning and weaving of cloth, chiefly done by women. Among the other professions may be mentioned those of the dancer, both male and female, barber (*Vaptṛi*) and vintner. It is noteworthy that those who practised these professions were not looked upon as inferiors in the age of the *Ṛigveda*.

Hunting as a sport and profession was known and must have been practised by the Rājanya class, chiefly with the aid of practised professionals. Nets and pitfalls were the normal instruments of capture, and the bow and arrow was also employed. Birds were caught in nets, and antelopes (*ṛiśya*) in pits. There are some obscure references to the capture of boars and buffaloes (*gaura*). The lion was caught in traps. The *Ṛigveda* is an important source of our knowledge of hunting in early times. The butcher's profession was also probably known, as the services of a Śamitṛi (in the sense of "one who cuts up") were probably needed at animal sacrifices (I. 162. 9; II. 3. 10; III. 4. 10, etc.).

There is no distinct reference to the specific occupation of slaves. They probably assisted their Aryan masters who did not think it beneath their dignity to practise all the arts and crafts needed by society.

4. *House-Building and Means of Transport*

Although it is suggested that some kind of a distinction between villages and towns is indicated in I. 44. 10 and 114. 1, city-life is not much in evidence. The village was a group of houses, built near each other for purposes of safety, and was surrounded by some kind of a hedge as a protective barrier against enemies and wild beasts. It is difficult to determine the exact sense in the *Ṛigveda* of *pur* which later meant a town. It seems to have been an earthwork fortification, protected by a palisade or stone wall. The frequent mention of the capture or destruction of such strongholds indicates that they were numerous and scattered all over the country, and that they could be easily erected like the stockades made by primitive tribes all over the world. The *pur* or earth-work fortification may either have been part of the village or just outside it, to be resorted to in times of emergency. It was called autumnal, probably because the emergency arose generally in autumn, when raids from neighbouring tribes became possible at the end of the monsoon, or the emergency was in the shape of a flooding of the plains owing to the rising of rivers in autumn.

Houses were made of wood, the beams (*vaṁśa*) being made of bamboo (also *vaṁśa*). The so-called strongholds or forts probably had a series of concentric walls.

The conception of Pūshan as the guardian of the pathways gives occasion for the numerous references of all kinds of transport and means of communication such as carts (*anas*) and chariots (*ratha*) on land and ships on the sea. The Aśvins are credited with ships (or conveyances) moving through the air (*antariksha*), which come uncannily near the modern conception of airships.

The chariots and carts were drawn by oxen, mules, or horses. The chariots of the rich were drawn by two and sometimes even four horses. Riding on horseback was also much in vogue. Names of various parts of chariots occur very frequently in the *RV* hymns, and indicate a considerable improvement in their construction over the primitive types. Travelling was fairly common. Prayers are offered to the gods (VII. 35. 15) to "give broad paths to travel,"—paths that should be straight in direction and thornless (X. 85. 23). A solemn prayer to Indra for the safety of the journey (III. 53. 17-20) gives many interesting details of a cart driven by oxen in which the journey was made.

The references to artificial waterways such as *kulyā* in III. 45. 3 and "*khanitrimā āpaḥ*" in VII. 49. 2 make it certain that some kind of an irrigation system was known. Wells artificially made are contrasted with springs. Such wells were covered, and are described as unfailing and full of water. The water was raised by a wheel to which a strap with a pail attached to it was fastened. These wells could be used for irrigation purposes, when the water was led off into broad channels (*RV*, I. 55. 8; X. 101. 6, 7; 102. 11; VIII. 69. 12; 72. 10).

---

1. There is a voluminous literature on the origin and antiquity of the Caste System in India, to some of which reference will be made in the bibliography. For the views mentioned in this section see *CHI*, I, pp. 92 ff.; Muir, *Original Sanskrit Texts*, Vol. I; N. K. Dutt, *Origin and Growth of Caste in India*. In an article entitled: "Were Castes formulated in the Age of the Ṛigveda" in *BDCRI*, II, 34 ff., the present writer has sought to prove that the formulation of castes, if not the Caste System, was already a *fait accompli* in the age of the *Ṛtgveda*.
2. Muir, *op. cit.*, p. 10.
3. *Op. cit.*, pp. 263-4, 280.
4. *AL*, p. 323.
5. *Ind. Stud.*, V, p. 222.
6. *Ved. Stud.*, I, pp. xxv, 196, 275, 299, 309; II, pp. 120, 154, 179, etc.
7. *SD*, p. 16.

BOOK SIX

THE AGE OF THE LATER SAMHITAS

CHAPTER XX

LANGUAGE AND LITERATURE

1. LANGUAGE OF THE SAMHITĀS

1. *Sāmaveda*

A language ceases to change only after death, and so the language of the *Ṛigveda,* even though hieratic and therefore to some extent artificial, did change in so far as it was a form of living speech at the same time. The earliest traceable stage in its course of change is that marked by the variant readings of the *Mantras* of the *Ṛigveda* contained in the *Sāmaveda.* In many cases these *Sāmaveda*-variants show forms which, however, seem to be archaic in comparison with the corresponding forms in the parallel *Ṛik-mantras,* and therefore it was argued, particularly by Ludwig,[1] that, at least in some cases, the Samavedic readings should be regarded as retaining the original text. But the question is, whether these apparently archaic forms were not the result of conscious efforts on the part of the redactors of the *Sāmaveda* to strike an archaic effect.[2] Almost all such forms in Samavedic parallel passages occur elsewhere also in the *Ṛigveda,* and none of them needs to have been derived from a pre-Rigvedic stage of the language. Without entirely denying the possibility of an original reading having been retained in some cases only in the *Sāmaveda,* it is only fair to conclude therefore that there is no compelling reason to consider the Samavedic text-tradition as superior to that of the *Ṛigveda,* specially as, even according to Ludwig's notion, the instances of older forms are more numerous in the text of the *Ṛigveda.*

Moreover, the older forms in the passages of the *Ṛigveda* are on the whole not at all such as might have been planted in the text with a view to artificially producing an archaic effect, though that may be held of some of the older forms appearing in the Samavedic readings. Thus *vakshatu* in *SV*, II. 9. 1. 16. 3 (= No. 1809) is indeed of older stock than *yachchhatu* in the parallel passage *RV*, VIII. 34. 2. But it would be wrong to conclude therefrom that the *Sāmaveda* in this case represents the older and perhaps the original reading, for such a view of the situation cannot but lead to the absurd position of considering all the Rigvedic passages containing forms like *vakshatu* to be older than all the Rigvedic passages containing forms like *yachchhatu*. In fact, the sporadical occurrence of particular late forms cannot prove the lateness of the texts containing them, be those texts Rigvedic or Samavedic, for early and late forms of nearly all categories have been used side by side in every period of the age of the Saṁhitās. A real change in the linguistic habits of the speakers concerned can be postulated only when the instances of variation point to a general tendency. Such general tendencies can, however, be clearly perceived in the variant readings of the *Sāmaveda,* and they point invariably to a later stage of development. Thus the archaic genitive singular feminine form *avyaḥ* has been in all cases changed into *avyāḥ* in the Samavedic variants. The enclitic particle *īm* of pronominal origin which was visibly going out of use already in the Rigvedic language, occurs also in some passages of the *Sāmaveda,* but it is significant that in some others the reading has been so altered as to eliminate it; thus *abhīm ṛitasya* of *RV* appears as *abhy ṛitasya* in *SV, payasem* as *payased, utem (=uta īm)* as *ūtim.* Similarly, there is a pronounced tendency in the Samavedic variants to eliminate dissyllabic vowels as a result of which Rigvedic *akshār* and *prāḥ* had to become *aksharat* and *paprāḥ* in the *Sāmaveda.* The archaic absolutive ending *-tvī* occurs only in two of the *Ṛik*-verses repeated in the *Sāmaveda,* but in both this *-tvī* has been changed into *-tvā.* Accented *i* does not in *Sandhi* change into *y* (in spite of graphic forms) in the first nine Maṇḍalas of the *Ṛigveda,* but it does in the *Sāmaveda.* In consequence, *ví aśema devāhitam* (*RV,* I. 89. 8) had to become *vy àśemahi devāhitam* (*SV.* II. 9. 3. 9. 2. = No. 1874) in which the loss of a vowel through *Sandhi* had to be made up for by replacing *aśema* through later *aśemahi* that does not at all occur in the *Ṛigveda.*[4]

2. *Yajurveda*

Next to the Saṁhitās of the *Ṛigveda* and the *Sāmaveda* are to be ranked, from the linguistic point of view, in chronological order, the Mantra-portions of the *Black Yajurveda,* which in their turn are clearly older than the *Vājasaneyi-Saṁhitā* which should perhaps be dated earlier than the *Atharvaveda.*[5] Regarding the language of the Mantra-portions of the *Taittirīya-Saṁhitā,* Keith has shown[6] that it represents a stage intermediate between the Rigvedic language and the language of the Brāhmaṇas, though resembling the former much more closely than the latter. The same may be said also of the language of the other three Saṁhitās of the *Black Yajurveda,* for linguistically the Mantra-portions of all the four schools are really homogeneous, and therefore must be assigned to approximately the same age. Without making proper distinction between Mantra and Brāhmaṇa portions, Schroeder tried to prove the superior age of the *Maitrāyaṇī Saṁhitā* on linguistic grounds,[7] but his arguments are unconvincing. The fact that the root *stigh-* of Indo-European antiquity occurs in Indian literature only in the *Maitrāyaṇī-Saṁhitā* cannot of course prove the antiquity of the *Maitrāyaṇī-Saṁhitā* itself. Nor can the other peculiarities of the language of the *Maitrāyaṇī* and the *Kāṭhaka* pointed out by Schroeder be accepted as proof of greater antiquity. The root *khyā-* appears in the curious form *kśā-* in *Maitrāyaṇī, Kāṭhaka* and *Kapishṭhala,* but that is no sign of antiquity as Schroeder was inclined to believe. It simply shows that in the dialects represented by these texts the semi-vowel *y* in *khyā-* became spirantic in pronunciation, and as such it points rather to a comparatively later age. Similarly, these three show the form *plāyate* for Taittirīya *prāyate* which is certainly older. The periphrastic verb-forms *utsādayām akar, prajanayām akar* and *pāvayāṁ kuryāt,* specifically mentioned by Pāṇini[8] as characteristic of the Vedic language, actually occur in the *Maitrāyaṇī,* but cannot prove it to be older than the *Taittirīya,* for the formation is not a primary one, as Keith[9] has justly pointed out. In microscopic details little differences can no doubt be observed in the four known Saṁhitās of the *Black Yajurveda,* but the general structure of their language is absolutely the same.[10] Equally extreme rarity of narrative perfects in all the Saṁhitās of the *Black Yajurveda*[11] is not only an additional proof of their essential contemporaneity, but also assigns them chronologically to the oldest period of the Vedic prose. In fact, in this respect the language of the *Black Yajurveda* is distinctly more faithful to the Indo-European basic idiom than the language of the *Ṛigveda* itself, for the narrative perfect, certainly not of Indo-European origin, is much more in evidence in the latter.[12]

The Mantra portions of the *Taittirīya-Saṁhitā,* that are independent of the *Ṛigveda,* mark a stage of distinct advance towards the normal language of the Brāhmaṇas. Thus *-ebhiḥ* for *-aiḥ, -ā* for *-ena, -āsaḥ* for *-āḥ* and *-ā* for *āni* are steadily diminishing in the Mantra-portions (and completely disappear from the Brāhmaṇa parts).[13] Similarly, the verb in the independent Mantra-parts of the *Taittirīya-Saṁhitā* shows a definite tendency to eliminate the Rigvedic endings *-masi, -thana* and *-tana.* The future is a rarity in the *Ṛigveda,* but it is common in the *Taittirīya* and there is perhaps even an instance of periphrastic future (*luṭ*), namely *anvāgantā.*[13a] While the later gerundives in *-tavya* and *-anīya* do not yet occur in the Taittirīya-mantras, the older ones in *-āyya* and *-tva* have almost completely disappeared in them. Lastly may be mentioned as occurring in Taittirīya-mantra the much discussed but still unexplained verb-forms *dhvanayit* and *ajayit.*[14] As for the *Vājasaneyi-Saṁhitā* of the White Yajurveda, even its oldest parts (Adhyāyas I-XVIII) are certainly later than the Mantra-portions of the *Taittirīya.* In the treatment of Rigvedic Mantras it shows much less independence than the Black Yajurveda and conforms much more to the Rigvedic text-tradition. As a result, the Kāṇva school of the Vājasaneyins has adopted the peculiarly Rigvedic sound *ḷ* for intervocalic *ḍ* also in its own Saṁhitā. In language, the *Vājasaneyi-Saṁhitā* does not differ from the Brāhmaṇas.[14a]

3. *Atharvaveda*

A linguistic appraisal of the *Atharvaveda* is unusually difficult, for very old things have been described in it sometimes in very late language, but at the same time it also offers forms that would be regarded as archaic even in the *Ṛigveda*. This can perhaps be best explained on the assumption that though no less old than the *Ṛigveda* in contents, the *Atharvaveda* was codified and canonized so late that the redactors considered it necessary to re-dress it in an artificial garb of hieratic solemnity. At any rate, it is clear that the redactors of the *Atharvaveda* had inherited a long tradition of Mantra literature of which all the parts seemed to them to be equally old, and which, therefore, they used indiscriminately in dressing up the Atharvan text. The basic language of the *Atharvaveda* is, however, not too unlike, say, the Sanskrit of the grammarian Patañjali, and is on the whole not difficult to understand, excepting where the text consists of purely magical incantations, which the authors, as is everywhere the case with similar compositions, intentionally tried to make obscure.

About one-seventh of the material of the first nineteen of the twenty Kāṇḍas of the *Atharvaveda* is drawn from the *Ṛigveda*, and in these Kāṇḍas Ṛik-mantras often appear with significant variants. The twentieth Kāṇḍa, the Saṁhitā of the Brāhmaṇāchchhaṁsin as we have called it, consists, however, wholly of Mantras drawn from the *Ṛigveda* which appear here without a single variant reading, and among them are contained also Mantras from Vālakhilya-hymns,[15] as, for instance, the first two of the four verses of *AV*, XX. 51 are identical with Vāl. I. 1-2, and the second two with Vāl. II. 1-2.[16] However interesting in other respects, the twentieth Kāṇḍa is therefore quite valueless from the linguistic point of view. Linguistically interesting and important are only those Ṛik-mantras (drawn mostly from the tenth Maṇḍala) which are scattered in the other Kāṇḍas, for in them a general trend towards the later language is distinctly perceptible.[17] Thus the later absolutive ending *-tvā* often replaces Rigvedic *-tvāya* or *-tvī* (e.g. *hitvā* for Rigvedic *hitvāya* and *bhūtvā* for Rigvedic *bhūtvī*). Forms of instrumental plural in *-ebhiḥ* and *-aiḥ* are equally current in the *Ṛigveda*, but in the *Atharvaveda*, against 263 cases of *-aiḥ* there are only 53 of *-ebhiḥ*.[18] The root *grabh-* becomes *grah-* in the *Atharvaveda* when followed by suffixal *-ṇ-*, thus producing forms such as *gṛihṇāmi* (for Rigvedic *gṛibhṇāmi*) that are the only forms current in later Sanskrit. The word *syona* is always trisyllabic in the *Ṛigveda*, but in the *Atharvaveda* it is in most cases dissyllabic as in the later language. The Rigvedic form *panthāḥ* in nominative plural gives way in the *Atharvaveda* to the classical form *panthānaḥ* on the analogy of *adhvānaḥ* (from *adhvan*), and it is remarkable that in *AV*, XIV. 1. 34a (=*RV*, X. 85. 23*a*) *panthāḥ* has been replaced by *panthānaḥ* even to the detriment of metre.[19] But it is not in the variants of Ṛik-mantras alone that the late character of the language of the *Atharvaveda* is revealed. The vocative singular masculine of stems in *-vāṁs* always ends with *-vaḥ* in the *Ṛigveda* (e.g., *chikitvaḥ* from *chikitvāṁs-*), but in the *Atharvaveda* it already assumes the classical form in *-van* (e.g., *chikitvan*); and the vocative singular masculine of *vant*-stems is almost always in *-vaḥ* in the *Ṛigveda*, but in the independent passages of the *Atharvaveda* it is always in *-van*,[20] as in later literature. As instances of Atharvavedic innovations in verbal flexion may be mentioned that in the *Ṛigveda* the subjunctive middle ending in the second person singular is *-ase*, (e.g. *vardhāse*), but in the *Atharvaveda* it is *-asai* (e.g., *nayāsai*) as also in the Brāhmaṇas; similarly the parallel ending in the third person singular is *-ate* in the *Ṛigveda* excepting in one form, but in the *Atharvaveda* and later it is exclusively *-atai* (e.g., *śrayāte* in *RV*, but *śrayātai* in *AV*).[21] The only instance of periphrastic perfect in the Mantra-texts[22] is *gamayāṁ chakāra* in *AV*, XVIII. 2. 27, and the earliest occurrence of periphrastic future[23] is to be found perhaps in the form *anvāganta*[23a] in *AV*, VI. 123. 1-2. And again it is the *Atharvaveda* and no other Mantra-text that contains gerundives in *-tavya* and *-anīya*, e.g., *hiṁsitavya* (*AV*, V. 18. 6) and *āmantraṇīya* (*AV*, VIII. 10. 7).[24]

These are the more important features of the Atharvavedic language that stamp it definitely as the latest of the Mantra-texts linguistically, and the metrical and non-metrical parts of the *Atharvaveda* are composed in apparently the same language.[25] At the same time, however, some of the words specially characteristic of the *Atharvaveda*, such as *hvayāmi*, *sarva* (as compared with *viśva*), *rajju*, etc., are of prehistoric origin[26] and therefore would seem to argue for it a very high antiquity.

2. THE SAMHITĀ LITERATURE

1. *Atharvaveda*

From the view-point of contents, there can be no doubt that the typically Atharvanic charms and incantations are the product of a primitive culture not far removed from the dawn of human civilization. Mantras of this type are not altogether wanting in the *Ṛigveda*, but, being essentially a Śrauta Mantrapāṭha for priests whose chief concern was the cultivation of Soma ritual it could not include many of them, since the whole Soma ritual was strictly hieratic. The Mantras of the *Atharvaveda* on the other hand were meant for application at the humbler Gṛihya sacrifices of the common people evolved round the plain and simple primitive fire-cult. But the priestly classes, in course of time, got the control of the originally non-

Brahmanical Gṛihya sacrifices, and, naturally, also compiled a Mantrapaṭha for these. This Gṛihya Mantrapāṭha is the *Atharvaveda.*

The Śrauta Mantrapāṭha, i.e., the *Ṛigveda,* was compiled by the priests for the priests, and partly for their social superiors, the princes and potentates. The tone of the *Ṛigveda,* therefore, even where the Mantras are not directly addressed to the gods, is mainly one of begging and persuading. But the tone of the *Atharvaveda* is altogether different. Here the Brāhmaṇa priest is addressing his social inferiors from whom he need not turn off the shady side of his character. Thus in the hymn on the "Brāhmaṇa's wife" (*Brahmajāyā*) the priest has demanded a remarkable privilege for his class (*AV*, V. 17. 8):

> Even though there were ten non-Brāhmaṇa previous husbands of a woman,
>
> The Brāhmaṇa alone becomes her husband if he seizes her hand.[27]

It is significant that the verses immediately preceding and following this verse occur also in the *Paippalāda-Saṁhitā,* and seven of the verses of this hymn constitute the Rigvedic original (X. 109) of which it is an expanded version. But this particular verse, planted in the hymn to serve an obvious purpose, occurs neither in the *Ṛigveda* nor in the *Paippalāda.* The point has been still further emphasized in the following verse (*AV*, V. 17. 9):

> The Brāhmaṇa indeed is the husband, neither the Rājanya, nor the Vaiśya.
>
> This the sun goes on proclaiming to the five tribes of men.

The burden of the other verses of this notorious hymn is, however, not the Brāhmaṇa's preposterous claim to other men's wives, but threats and curses on those who would dare to molest the Brāhmaṇa's wife, e.g. (verse 12):—

> Not on his couch reclines a wife bringing a hundred (as dowry?)
>
> In whose kingdom the Brāhmaṇa's wife is restrained through ignorance.

Not only the Brāhmaṇa's wife, but also his property was sought to be protected by a similar appeal to people's superstition.[28] Thus in the next hymn (*AV*, V. 18) we are told (vv. 9-10):—

> Brāhmaṇas have sharp arrows and missiles,
> the volley they hurl is not in vain;
> Pursuing with fervour and with fury
> they cast him down from afar.
> They that ruled a thousand
> and were ten thousands,—
> Those Vaitahavyas were defeated
> for having devoured a Brāhmaṇa's cow.

But the trick becomes ridiculous when it is suggested in all seriousness as a way of averting the ill omen of a twinning animal, that one of the twin calves should be made over to a Brāhmaṇa (*AV*, III. 28. 2). Most amusing, however, is the long hymn (*AV*, XII. 4) in fierce denunciation of those who fail to bestow on Brāhmaṇas their barren cows.

The Brāhmaṇa's supposed privileges have thus been shamelessly asserted in the *Atharvaveda*, and of his obligations there is hardly any mention. Thus in *AV*, III. 58 the Brāhmaṇa, it is true, is praying for glory instead of wealth, but he cannot help adding: "so that I may be dear to the bestower of *Dakshiṇā* (sacrificial fee)." To the Brāhmaṇas of the *Atharvaveda* it was evidently more important to be dear to the bestower of *Dakshiṇā* than to be dear to the gods. Nor were the Mantras of the *Atharvaveda* primarily meant for those sacrificial sessions (*sattras*) at which there was neither *Yajamāna* nor *Dakshiṇā*.

The community in which the Atharvan priest ordinarily moved was no doubt the society of the poor and ignorant villagers, to meet the demands of whose primitive superstitions was his principal professional business. But as even the highest and the mighty in the land were not above those superstitions, the Atharvan gained access even to the rulers of the country, and in fact came to be recognized as the king's *alter ego* in the rôle of his Purohita. How the Atharvan alone of the various types of priests came to occupy this enviable position is quite clear. While the other priests were adepts in the higher Śrauta-ritual of which the solemn ceremonies were performed only at intervals or on special occasions, the Atharvan had to advise the king on trivial events of his daily life, such as a cough (*AV*, VI. 105), sleep (*AV*, IV. 5), nightmare (*AV*, VI. 45), etc., and therefore had to be constantly in attendance on him.[22] Who else in these circumstances could be the king's chief adviser? Moreover, were not the king's victories due to the effective prayers of his Purohita? A king's Purohita actually says in the *Atharvaveda* (III. 19):—

1. Sharpened is this prayer of mine,
   sharpened is my manly strength:
   Sharp and imperishable be their rule
   whose victorious Purohita I am.

4. Sharper than the axe,
   and sharper than the flame,
   Sharper than the thunder of Indra
   are those whose Purohita I am.

Since an Atharvan priest was by custom the king's Purohita it is but natural that an elaborate hymn of coronation at which, also according to later ritual, the Purohita was the chief functionary—should be included in the *Atharvaveda* (IV. 8):—

1. Being sets milk in beings,
   he has become the lord of beings;
   Death attends his coronation,
   let this king accept this royalty.
2. Stride forward, do not falter (?)
   stern corrector, rival-slayer.
   Approach, O benefactor of friends,
   may you be blessed by the gods.

The hymn also refers to the custom of treading on a tiger-skin at coronation:—

4. As a tiger on tiger-skin
   stride unto the great quarters;
   Let all the people and heavenly waters
   rich in milk desire you.

There is also a similar hymn intended for recital at the election of a king (*AV*, III. 4):—

1. To you has come the kingdom, with splendour rise forward;
   as lord of the people, sole king, rule;
   Let all the quarters call you, O king,
   may all wait on you and pay you homage.
2. Let the people choose you for kingship,
   let these five divine quarters (choose you);
   Rest at the summit and pinnacle of your kingdom,
   and from there share out riches to us.

That the king had sometimes to be elected, though kingship was generally hereditary, is clearly suggested by the last verse. The exact form of government, however, cannot be ascertained from the Mantras of the *Atharvaveda*. But that the people were happy and proud of their motherland is perfectly clear from the splendid Bhūmi-sūkta (*AV*, XII. 1) which might have been the national anthem of Vedic India[30]:—

1. Truth supreme and right formidable, consecration and penance, holiness and sacrifice are sustaining the earth;
   May she, the mistress of all that was and will be, the earth, make for us extensive space.
2. (She who ordains) freedom from restraint among men,
   whose are the hills and streams equally numerous (?)
   Who bears herbs of various virtues—
   may she, the earth, spread and prosper for us.
3. On whom are the ocean and the river and the waters,
   on whom have sprung food and the peoples,
   On whom quickens this that breathes and stirs—
   may that earth grant us cattle and also food.

8. She who in the beginning was water in the ocean,
whom the sages followed (?) by means of occult power,
The earth, whose deathless heart, encompassed in truth,
rests in highest heaven—
may she confer glory and strength on our excellent state.
11. Let your hills and snowy mountains
and your forest be pleasant, O earth!
On the earth, brown, black, red, and multiform,
firm and extended, by Indra defended,
I have stood unconquered, unsmitten, uninjured.
12. What is your middle, O earth, what your navel,
what refreshments arose out of your body,
Instal us in them and be towards us gracious;
Earth is the mother, and I am her son;
Parjanya is the father, may he grant us plenty.
45. May the earth bearing peoples of various speeches
and of customs varying according to their homes,
Grant me wealth in a thousand streams
like a steadfast and unresisting milch-cow.
56. What villages, what forests,
what assemblies are on the earth,
What congregations and councils,
there may we speak in praise of you.[31]

The hymn runs up to sixty-three verses, and at the end, the poet, dissolving in rapture and gratitude, pours out his heart in these simple words:—

63. O mother earth, settle me down
and kindly make me well-established:
In concord with heaven, O sage,
settle me in splendour and glory.

A number of Hymns of the *Atharvaveda* are on the borderline of magic and politics.[32] As example may be cited *AV*, VII. 12:—

1. May the assembly and the council[32a] protect me,
the two daughters of Prajāpati in agreement;
May he whom I meet seek to help me,
may I speak pleasantly at the meeting, O fathers:
3. Of these seated here together
I take away splendour and discernment;
Of this whole gathering, O Indra,
make me the possessor of fortune.

Of the same type, but much more elevated in tone, is the oft-quoted and justly celebrated charm for securing concord (*AV*. III. 30):—

1. Like in heart, of like intent
non-hostile do I make you;
One another you should love,
as the cow loves her new-born calf.

2. May the son do the father's will
 and be of one mind with his mother,
May wife to husband honeyed words
 and peaceful always speak.

3. May not brother his brother hate,
 or sister her own sister;
In full accord, with duty same,
 should they speak words gently.

6. Same be your drink and common your food,
 to the same yoke together I bind you,
Worship Agni together in harmony
 like spokes round the nave of a wheel.

Far more numerous are, however, the charms of a homelier sort. "House and home, field and river, grain and rain, cattle and horses, trading and gambling, journeying and returning, serpents and vermin, furnish the special themes for these prayers and charms."[33] Thus *AV*, I. 13 is a charm to conciliate the goddess of lightning:—

1. Homage be to your lightning, homage to your thunder,
 Homage to your bolt which you hurl at the wicked.
2. Homage to you, child of stream, from which you gather heat;
 Take pity on our bodies, and to our children be kind.

Protection against fire is supposed to be achieved by means of the charm (*AV*, III. 21) which begins thus:—

Fires that are in the waters,
 in Vṛitra, in man, and in stones,
Who have entered the plants and the trees.
 to those fires be this oblation.

Abundance of grain is secured by means of the charm *AV*, III. 24:—

4. As a fountain of a hundred jets,
 of a thousand jets, unexhausted,
So is this our grain
 of a thousand jets, unexhausted.
5. Collect, O with hundred hands,
 pile, O with thousand hands;
Bring about the amplitude here
 of what was and will be done.

This charm was applied evidently at the time of gathering corn. The charm for sowing seed is *AV*, VI. 142:—

1. Shoot up and multiply by your own strength, O barley,
 Fill (?) all the vessels, may not heavenly thunder destroy you.
2. Where we appeal to you, the divine barley that listens to us,
 There shoot up like the sky, be unexhausted like the ocean.

3. Unexhausted are your attendants (?), unexhausted be your heaps,
Unexhausted those who give you, and also those whom you consume.

Very curious are the so-called Mṛigāra-sūktas (*AV. IV.* 23-29), the first and last verses of each of which occur also in the *Black Yajurveda*[34] in connection with a Mṛigāreshṭi, of which these are obviously a further elaboration. Each of these hymns (they cannot be called magical charms, though they are used as such) is addressed to a separate deity, and every verse of each of them ends with the refrain: "let him (or do ye) free us from distress." Rudra has been invoked in a long hymn (XI. 2), and as is usual in prayers to this god, has not been asked to confer boons, but only not to injure. The various names applied to the god in this hymn naturally call to mind the Śatarudriya.[34a]

Least savoury of the magic charms of the *Atharvaveda* are those of witchcraft (*abhichāra*) and the like which constitute the Aṅgiras part of the Saṁhitā. The purpose of some is defensive, but the majority of them are offensive in purpose and directed against human enemies. Evil spirits are firstly called upon to come out in the open and proclaim their real character, for, as soon as they do that, they lose their dangerous power of doing injury. The metal most effective against the demons is lead, which therefore plays a prominent part in these hymns.

Low and primitive morality speaks in these hymns. But there are also hymns pregnant with noble sentiments. For instance, the famous hymn[35] to Varuṇa (*AV*, IV. 16):—

1. The mighty lord on high our deeds, as if at hand, espies;
The gods know all men do, though men would fain their acts disguise.

2. Whoever stands, whoever moves, or steals from place to place,
Or hides him in his secret cell—the gods his movements trace.
Wherever two together plot, and deem they are alone,
King Varuṇa is there, a third, and all their schemes are known.

3. This earth is his, to him belong these vast and boundless skies;
Both seas within him rest, and yet in that small pool he lies.

4. Whoever far beyond the sky should think his way to wing,
He could not there elude the grasp of Varuṇa the king.
His spies, descending from the skies, glide all this world around;
Their thousand eyes all-scanning sweep to earth's remotest bound.

5. Whate'er exists in heaven and earth, what'er beyond the skies,
Before the eyes of Varuṇa, the king, unfolded lies.

The ceaseless winkings all he counts of every mortal's eyes,
He wields this universal frame as gamester throws his dice.

Atharvavedic poetry has reached its peak in this hymn. But to gain a true view of the *Atharvaveda,* the other side of the picture should not only not be ignored, but should rather be kept more in mind. Thus there are two imprecations (VII. 95. 96) directed against the kidneys of an enemy. The purpose of the hymn VII. 70 is to frustrate the enemy's sacrifice, as is disclosed by its very first verse:—

Whatever that one offers with mind, speech, sacrifice, oblation and Yajus—
That offering of his let Nirṛiti in concord with death destroy before it has taken place.

Most typical of the hymns of this *genre* are perhaps those with the refrain "he who hates us, whom we hate" (e.g., *AV,* II. 19-23). Along with charms for victory, longevity, cure from fever, etc., we find also charms for winning the heart of a maid, e.g., *AV,* II. 30:--

1. As the wind shakes the grass
So I shake your mind,
So that you may desire me,
That you may not go away.

4. What was within, be that out,
What was out, be within;
Of the maids of every sort
Seize the mind, O herb:

That magical charms of this sort were not applied exclusively in connection with extra-conjugal love is, however, clear from a similar charm (VII. 37) put in the mouth of a newly married bride who admonishes her groom with these words (accompanied by corresponding act):—

With my garment produced by Manu do I surround you.
So that you be mine alone, and never even discourse of other women.

This tyrannical passion has been aptly likened by another poet in the *Atharvaveda* (III. 25. 2) to "an arrow, winged with longing, barbed with love, and whose shaft is unswerving desire" (Bloomfield).

Quite a number of medicinal charms are included in the *Atharvaveda.* The chief malady that was sought to be treated magically is *takman* (this term does not occur outside of the *Atharvaveda*). From the symptoms described it is almost certain that it was nothing but malarial fever. The plant Kushṭha is mentioned as potent in fighting *takman,* but whether as medicine, or as amulet, is not quite clear. It is interesting to note that in one hymn (V. 22) *takman* has been asked to seize the Śūdrā and the Dāsī or to go away to the Mūjavants or "to the Valhikas further beyond," and in the last verse the author says quite maliciously that he is sending *takman* to the Gandhāris, Aṅgas and Magadhas "like one sending a treasure to a person." That the *Atharvaveda* should contain charms against snake-bite is quite obvious. One of them (V. 13) deserves special mention not only as marking perhaps the lowest bathos of Atharvavedic witchcraft but also on account of the word *tābuva* occurring in its tenth verse:—

Not *tābuva*, not *tābuva*, yes you are *tābuva*; ...
The poison is made sapless by *tābuva*.[36]

The word *tābuva* of this verse was connected with "taboo" by Weber, though not without hesitation, and in the same hesitating manner the etymological equation *tābuva* = "taboo" continues to be accepted or rejected to the present day.[36a]

Of isolated typical hymns of the *Atharvaveda*, mention should be made of the one (XI. 5) in mystic exaltation of the *Brahmachārin*, from which it is quite clear that the institution of *Brahmacharya* as described in the later Gṛihya-sūtras was fully established already in the age of the *Atharvaveda*.[37] Similar mystic exaltation, in typical Brāhmaṇa-prose, of the Vrātya (i.e., new convert to Brahmanism) is the theme of the entire fifteenth Kāṇḍa, in the fifth Paryāya of which Rudra under various designations (Śarva, Bhava, Īśāna, Paśupati, Mahādeva) has been mentioned as guarding the various quarters for the Vrātya. Remarriage of widows[38] is taken for granted (vv. 27-28) in the long hymn (*AV*, IX. 5) on the expiatory power of the offering of Pañchaudana (i.e., a goat and five rice-dishes). The two hymns, V. 20 and 21, are the most important battle-charms in the *Atharvaveda*, and they might have been used also directly as battle-songs. Regarding the apocryphal Kuntāpa-sūktas, it should be noted that Parikshit, probably of the Kuru-dynasty, has been mentioned in the first of them[39] as a king in whose kingdom the people were prosperous. From the literary point of view the most interesting is the seventh Kuntāpa which is nothing but a Vedic nursery-song with the refrain: "not there is that, O maid, where you think."

2. *Yajurveda*

As for the *Yajurveda*, the Saṁhitā portion appears in an extended form in the latest of the *Yajurveda-Saṁhitās*, viz., the *Vājasaneyi-Saṁhitā*, of which only the earlier parts, in practically the same form and language,[40] but not necessarily in the same order, appear in the Saṁhitās of the *Black Yajurveda*.[41] From the view-point of literature and contents, therefore, a survey of the *Vājasaneyi-Saṁhitā*, as given by Winternitz,[42] suffices for the Mantra-parts of the whole *Yajurveda*. A fresh survey of the same literature need not be attempted here, especially as the ultimate literary value of the Yajus-mantras is nil. Yet it may be mentioned in passing that in the Śatarudriya section (Adhyāya XVI) of the *Vāja-*

saneyi-Saṁhitā the terrible god has been invoked under various designations, the result, no doubt, of the aversion to uttering directly his real name that can be perceived already in the *Atharvaveda*. The most interesting, however, is the section on Purushamedha (Adhyāya XXX), where, in the language of ritual symbolism, the various then existing classes and castes have been mentioned, which, according to Weber,[43] point to a period of unrest and turmoil.

3. THE BRĀHMAṆAS

1. *Language*

The Brāhmaṇa literature is vast and varied, but also dry and repulsive, excepting where, leaving their proper subject which is mystical and puerile speculation on ritual practices, the Brāhmaṇa authors cite illustrative examples from social life, invent aetiological myths to serve as the basic principle to all imaginable concrete facts, or simply narrate mythological or semi-historical stories, sometimes in the form of ballads.[44] The prolixity of the Brāhmaṇa-authors is sickening, and yet the texts are not at all perspicuous, in spite of their huge bulk in some cases. But the language with its even rhythm is not without a beauty of its own, strangely like that of the early canonical texts in Pāli. The *Śatapatha-Brāhmaṇa* and the *Jaiminīya-Brāhmaṇa*, however, show a fully developed literary style. This is important, for it is much more difficult to develop a literary style in free prose than in verse, and is possible only after considerable literary culture.

The Brāhmana texts, together with the prose parts of the *Atharvaveda* and the *Yajurveda*, are perhaps "the only genuine prose works which the Sanskrit, as a popular language, has produced."[45] Broadly speaking, the language of the Brāhmaṇas is homogeneous. At the same time, however, every one of the older Brāhmaṇa texts has its own minute linguistic peculiarities. Pāṇini's grammar offers a unique criterion by which to judge them. It cannot be proved that Pāṇini was acquainted with the Saṁhitā or the Brāhmaṇas of the *White Yajurveda*,[46] though he certainly knew all the other Saṁhitā-texts known to us, as well as the *Aitareya-Brāhmaṇa*.[47] Now, to explain this curious fact it cannot be reasonably argued—as is often done—that though the *White Yajurveda* was considerably older, yet Pāṇini had no personal knowledge of it for the good reason that it was produced in eastern India; for Pāṇini certainly knew the *Taittirīya-Saṁhitā*, a product of the south, and the *Maitrāyaṇī-Saṁhitā*, a product of the west, though he himself was at home in the north. His apparent ignorance of the *White Yajurveda* therefore must be regarded as a proof of the latter's comparatively late origin. But it also proves that for a composite picture of the language[48] of the Brāhmanas one may confidently appeal to Pāṇini. For details, however, which prove the older Brāhmaṇas to be much older than Pāṇini, special studies are necessary.

Nothing is more characteristic of Brāhmaṇa prose than the substitution of the ending *-ai* for *-āḥ*, both in ablative and genitive singular of feminine stems (e.g., *bhūmyai* for *bhūmyāḥ*). Forms in this anomalous *-ai* occur already in the prose parts of the *Atharvaveda;* but oftener in the Mantras of the *Yajurveda*, and very frequently in the Brāhmaṇas. In the *Jaiminīya-Brāhmaṇa*, this *-ai* has even completely supplanted the usual *-āḥ*,[49] but it does not occur at all in the *Śatapatha-Brāhmaṇa* of the Kāṇva--recension.[50] The *an*-stems are very often endingless in locative singular in the *Ṛigveda*, and not a few times also in the *Atharvaveda*, but in Brāhmaṇa prose *ahan* and *ātman*[51] are the only two endingless locatives in living use.[52] In its verbal system, too, the language of the Brāhmaṇas is in many respects sharply distinguished from that of the Mantra-texts. The loss of augment is here restricted practically to prohibitive constructions with *mā*, as in the classical language,[53] and the so-called injunctive too is found in Brāhmaṇa prose hardly ever except after this prohibitive *mā*.[54] The subjunctive finds its place, not in narrative, but in direct speech.[54a] Faint traces of gerunds in *-am* can be found already in the *Ṛigveda*,[55] but they are quite common in the Brāhmaṇas,[56] and past active participles in *-tavant*, quite unknown in the *Ṛigveda*, but quite common in the later language, begin to appear furtively in them.[57] The suffix *-uka* with the meaning of a present participle is a marked characteristic of the language of the Brāhmaṇas,[58] as also the infinitive in *-toḥ* in construction with *īśvara*.[59] The use of *rūpam kṛi-* in the sense of "to become" is a peculiar feature of *Brāhmaṇa* syntax.[60]

In the use of the tenses of the past the Brāhmaṇas show much more precision than the *Ṛigveda*. The aorist is rarely used in them outside of direct speech, and in narration the tense of the past used in the Brāhmaṇas is normally the imperfect, but not unoften also the perfect.[61] The perfects with a heavy reduplication have regularly a present meaning, but other perfects are used as often or oftener also in narrative past,[61a] and the frequency of this narrative perfect is rightly regarded as a sign of comparative lateness of the texts concerned.[62] Pāṇini's rules about the tenses of the past are not applicable to Brāhmaṇa prose, but it is curious to note that of the few narrative perfects occurring in the Brāhmaṇa-portions of the *Taittirīya-Saṁhitā* not a single one has been used to relate personal experience—so that in this respect at least they are fully in accord with Paninean grammar.[63] The periphrastic perfect with *kṛi-* as auxiliary, of which the earliest occurrence in the *Atharvaveda* has been noted above, is fairly common in the Brāhmaṇas, but that with *as-* is extremely rare, and no form with *bhū* can be quoted at all.[64] In this respect, too, the language of the Brāhmaṇas is in essential agreement with Pāṇini who permits only *kṛi-*, though already Kātyāyana and Patañjali twisted the meaning of the relevant Sūtra of Pāṇini so as to include also *bhū-* and *as-*.[65] On the whole, the language of the Brāhmaṇas is more precise in expression than that of the Mantra-texts, and as a living and forceful form of speech it is infinitely superior to the monstrous prose of the classical writers.[66]

2. *Literature*

The literaure of which this language is the vehicle is, however, arid and dismal, and could have been the product of only a very primitive intelligence. And yet it was in the age of the later Brāhmaṇas that the older Upanishads were composed, and Pāṇini's peerless grammar—perhaps the highest product of ancient Indian scientific thought[6] —was written. It is clear that the intellect and mentality revealed by the extensive Brāhmaṇa texts was the monopoly of the cabalistic priests of the later Vedic age, and not a characteristic of the enlightened sections of the people. As "literature" the Brāhmaṇas, digressive portions apart, may prove to be of interest only to students of abnormal psychology.[68] At the risk of a little exaggeration it may perhaps be maintained that all that is noble and beautiful in Hinduism was foreshadowed already by the *Ṛigveda*, and all that is filthy and repulsive in it, by the Brāhmaṇas. The morality of the Brāhmaṇa texts is no higher than that of primitive medicine-men. Thus in connection with the Mahāvrata sacrifice most immoral and obscene acts are enjoined to be performed in the presence of pious spectators.[69] The grasping greed of the Brāhmin, so much in evidence already in the *Atharvaveda*, has passed all bounds in the Brāhmaṇas. Here the Brāhmin coolly claims that in every dispute between a Brāhmin and a non-Brāhmin the judgment should be given in favour of the Brāhmin.[70] With a cheerful disregard of other people's interest a Brāhmaṇa author has declared that a murder is no murder if the victim is not a Brāhmin![71] And another declares with the same cool confidence that the Śūdra is *yathākāmavadhya*, i.e., one who can be killed at will.[72]

Scarcely less repulsive than this mentality of the Brāhmaṇa authors is their sickening prolixity. Lack of logic they tried to compensate for by repeating *ad nauseam* the same insipid thought. Hence the inordinate bulk of some of the Brāhmaṇa texts. But when no reasonable limit is set to a book, it is bound to take in much that is irrelevant, and it is these irrelevant portions of the Brāhmaṇas that are of interest from the view-point of literature. The true stuff of the Brāhmaṇas is dismal. If in the ritual it is required to move a cup an inch from east to west, the Śrauta-sūtras will simply state that and nothing more. But a Brāhmaṇa is almost sure to spin out a whole paragraph in "elucidation" of this act that may very well be as follows: "The cup should be moved from east to west, because the sun moves from east to west. He who moves the cup from east to west moves, therefore, also the sun, and thus conquers the world of heaven. It is moved an inch, because an inch is the twelfth part of a foot. And the foot is a metre. The Jagatī-metre has twelve syllables. In that he moves the cup an inch which is the twelfth part of a foot; he therefore moves the metres." This sounds strange no doubt. But, all the same, this is the stuff of which the Brāhmaṇas are made. Everything else that is found in the Brāhmaṇas is, strictly speaking, irrelevant.[73]

In these irrelevant portions, however, may be found pieces of truly literary composition, though never of a high order. They are of various *genres*. Firstly, there are the Gāthās or narrative verses, composed in a language more archaic than the average language of the Brāhmaṇas, but less so than that of the Saṁhitās.[74] Then there are interesting legends like that of the Great Flood,[75] but most of them are frankly aetiological. Quite a number of beautiful stories are contained in the Brāhmaṇas in which the gods indulge in pranks with the mortals much in the fashion of their Olympian compeers.[76] It is very characteristic of the Brāhmaṇa authors that sin is generally regarded by them as a *physical* defilement.[77] But genuine devotion to truth is not wanting. Thus when Aruṇa Aupaveśi in his old age was asked by his relations to establish ritual fires and become an Āhitāgni, he shuddered in horror and replied that he doesn't dare, for an Āhitāgni has to control his speech and can never speak an untruth, since "worship, above all, is truthfulness."[78] That by truth the Brāhmaṇa authors meant more than mere accuracy in speech is clearly suggested by the story of a dispute between mind and speech that was settled by Prajāpati in favour of mind on the ground that speech is the messenger and imitator of the mind.[79] As regards speech concrete, the Brāhmaṇas clearly state that the speech of the country of the Kuru-Pañchālas is the best.[80] And abstract speech (*nāman*) has been connected with form (*rūpa*) in a Brāhmaṇa text[81] quite in the manner of later philosophy. The daily performance of the five *Mahāyajñas* (offerings to gods, to beings, to the Fathers, the study of the Veda, and charity), the corner-stone of orthodox Hindu sociology, has been enjoined for the first time in a Brāhmaṇa text.[81a] The doctrine of reward and retribution after death for good and evil done during lifetime is also mentioned clearly in the Brāhmaṇa texts,[82] but the doctrine of rebirth is conspicuous by its absence, though the possibility of re-death in the world of the Fathers has been recognized already,[83] and further that during sleep life temporarily separates from the body.[84]

If treatment of women is a criterion of civilization, then the civilization of the Brāhmaṇa texts can expect only an adverse verdict from posterity. In the Ṛigvedic age, the newly married wife used to be greeted with the words: "you should address the assembly as a commander,"[85] but the Brāhmaṇa authors, after identifying the woman with Nirṛiti (i.e. evil),[86] declare that "the woman, the Śūdra, the dog, and the crow are falsehood (*Anṛita*)."[87] Marriage by purchase must have been common—if not the rule—in the age of the Brāhmaṇas, for in deprecation of a faithless wife a Brāhmaṇa text says: "she commits an act of falsehood who though purchased by her husband goes about with others."[88] There was no question of women freely addressing assemblies in this age, for the same text[89] lays down that women should not attend meetings. In every respect the culture of the priestly classes was at its lowest ebb in the age of the Brāhmaṇas. But it was still alive, though confined within a small coterie. The Upanishadic seers vitalized it again, but gave it an altogether different form.

4. THE ĀRAṆYAKAS

The Āraṇyakas ("Forest-texts"), the concluding portions or appendices to, the Brāhmaṇas are so called (it is generally supposed) because their contents are of so secret and uncanny a nature that they would spell danger if taught to the uninitiated, and had therefore to be learnt in the forest and not in the village. They are concerned neither with the performance nor with any explanation of the sacrifice, but with its mysticism and symbolism. They form a natural transition to the Upanishads, the oldest of which are either included in or appended to the Āraṇyakas, the line of demarcation being not always easy to draw. The Āraṇyakas, and Upanishads by themselves, and not the system of philosophy based on them, were originally called "Vedānta" (literally, the concluding portions of the Veda)—a title applicable to them in more senses than one as follows:—

(1) From the point of view of relative literary chronology, they stand at the end of the Veda. (2) As the most obstruse and mystical of the Śruti works, they were naturally taught to the pupil towards the close of the period of his apprenticeship with his *Guru*. (3) They formed the end of the daily Vedic-recital.

As component (and concluding) parts of the Brāhmaṇas, the Āraṇyakas (and some Upanishads) are found attached to as many Śākhās (Vedic schools) as the Brāhmaṇas belong to The *Aitareya Āraṇyaka* is appended to the *Aitareya Brāhmaṇa* of the *RV*. It consists of five books which are looked upon and designated as five separate Āraṇyakas. The first deals with the Soma sacrifice from the ritual point of view. The second is intermixed with theosophical speculations on Prāṇa and Purusha, and is Upanishadic in character, the last four chapters actually forming the *Aitareya Upanishad*. The third book contains allegorical and mystical meanings of the Saṁhitā, Pada, and Krama texts (Pāṭhas). The last two books contain miscellaneous matter, such as Mahānāmnī verses and details about the Nishkevalya Śastra, to be recited in the Mahāvrata, and are attributed to Āśvalāyana and Śaunaka—two Sūtra authors. The *Śāṅkhāyana or Kaushītaki Āraṇyaka* is the concluding portion of the *Kaushītaki Brāhmaṇa* of the *RV* and agrees very closely with the *Aitareya Āraṇyaka* in its contents. It consists of fifteen chapters of which 3 to 6 constitute the long and important *Kaushītaki Upanishad*. In the *Black Yajurveda*, the *Taittirīya Āraṇyaka* is only a continuation of the *Taittirīya Brāhmaṇa*. It consists of ten chapters or prapāṭhakas (commonly called Araṇas), 7 to 9 constituting the important *Taittirīya Upanishad*. The tenth chapter called *Mahānārāyaṇa Upanishad* is a very late addition to the *Āraṇyaka*. In the *White Yajurveda* the fourteenth book of the *Śatapatha Brāhmaṇa* is *in name only* an *Āraṇyaka*— the *Bṛihadāraṇyaka*—the last six chapters of which constitute the celebrated *Upanishad* of that name and the major part of the so-called *Āraṇyaka*.

For the *Sāmaveda*, the only Āraṇyakas are the first Āraṇyaka-like section of the *Chhāndogya Upanishad*, which belongs probably to the *Tāṇḍya-Mahā-Brāhmaṇa* and the *Jaiminīya Upanishad Brāhmaṇa* which is nothing but an *Āraṇyaka* of the Jaiminīya or Talavakāra school of the *SV* and comprises the well-known *Kena* (or *Talavakāra*) *Upanishad*.

It is not necessary to discuss here the contents of the Āraṇyakas, as the principal ideas contained in them will be dealt with in the chapter on religion and philosophy (Ch. XXII).

---

1. *Der Rigveda*, Band III, p. 92.
2. See Oldenberg, *Prolegomena*, p. 274.
3. *Ibid.*, pp. 92-3.
4. For further instance of evidently intentional alteration of Rigvedic passages in the direction of later forms in the *Sāmaveda*, see Oldenberg, *op. cit.*, pp. 277-81.
5. See Keith, *HOS*. XVIII, p. clxv.
6. *Op. cit.*, pp. cxl ff.
7. See his *Maitrāyaṇī Saṁhitā*, Vol. I, pp. xiv-xviii and Vol. II, pp. viii-x.
8. III, 1. 42.
9. *Op. cit.*, p. xcv.
10. *Ibid.*, p. xcvi.
11. *Ibid.*, p. xcvii.
12. See Wackernagel, *Altindische Grammatik*, Vol. I, p. xxxi.
13. See Keith, *op. cit.*, pp. cxl ff.
13a. This form, probably with the same function, occurs also in the *Atharvaveda* (see below).
14. See Whitney, §§ 1048, 904b.
14a. The Mantra portions of the *Yajurveda* are devoid of literary value, and therefore will not be discussed further in this chapter. For social and political history, however, these portions are very important and in that connection they will be discussed in other chapters.
15. The ten Kuntāpa-sūktas (regarded as Khilas) placed towards the end of the twentieth Kāṇḍa are curiously analogous to the Vālakhilya-hymns of the

Rigveda, also placed towards the end of what was originally perhaps the final Maṇḍala of the Ṛigveda.

16. A curious fact that seems to have escaped notice so far is that the last hymn of the *Atharvaveda* (XX, 143) consists of *RV*, IV. 44 (seven verses) followed by *RV*, IV. 57. 3 and *RV*, VIII. 57. 3 (= Vāl. IX. 3). Does it show that when the twentieth Kāṇḍa was put together the genuine *Ṛik-saṁhitā* was supposed to conclude with the Vālakhilya verse *RV*, VIII. 57. 3 which the final redactors of the Atharvaveda wanted to put at the end of their Saṁhitā also? If this is conceded, then it will be possible to argue further that the twentieth Kāṇḍa of the *Atharvaveda* was constituted not long after the composition of the *Aitareya Brāhmaṇa*, which, as pointed out above, knows only eight Vālakhilyas. Why the penultimate verse also, like the final one, should be the third verse of a fifty-seventh hymn of the *Ṛigveda* is difficult to say. At any rate, this numerical identity can be hardly fortuitous. It is striking to note that originally it might have been easily the last verse of the fourth Maṇḍala of the *Ṛigveda*, though in the present text it is the third verse of the penultimate hymn of that Maṇḍala. Thus the final verse of the *Atharvaveda* was probably also the final verse of the original *Ṛik-Saṁhitā*, and the penultimate verse of the *Atharvaveda* might have been the last verse of its first half. Was it the intention of the final redactors of the *Atharvaveda* in putting these two verses at the end to emphasize in their usual mystical manner that their work was now doubly complete?
17. See Oldenberg, *Prolegomena*, pp. 320 ff.
18. Wackernagel, *Altindische Gxammatik*, Vol. III, § 52a.
19. *Op. cit.*, p. 308.
20. See *Ibid.*, pp. 258, 301.
21. See Macdonell, *Vedic Grammar*, p. 322.
22. Macdonell, *op. cit.*, § 496.
23. Macdonell, *op. cit.*, § 540.
23a. The same form occurs also in *Taitt. Saṁ*, V. 7. 7. 1, but there too it is not quite clear whether it has been used actually as a periphrastic future.
24. *Op. cit.*, § 581a-b.
25. A complete list of the non-metrical passages of the *Atharvaveda* has been given by Lanman, *HOS*, Vol. VIII, p. 1011.
26. See Bloomfield, *The Atharvaveda*, p. 47.
27. In rendering passages of the *Atharvaveda* I have, as far as possible, followed Whitney's translation, though it is wooden and purely etymological; for whatever it may be in other respects, it is at least literally correct.
28. Compare in this connection also *AV*, XII, 5. 3 ff.
29. It is probably due to this exalted office of king's Purohita that the Atharvan priest, under the designation "Brahman," became the supreme supervisor also at the great Śrauta-sacrifices of his noble patron, in consequence of which the *Atharvaveda* itself came to be known as the Brahmaveda. Various scholars have expressed various opinions as to the inter-relation between, or the identity of. the Atharvan, the Brahman, and the Purohita (see specially Bloomfield, *op. cit.*, § 34, and *Vedic Index* under "Purohita" and "Brahman). The theory suggested here seems, however, to offer the best explanation.
30. The grandeur and beauty of this hymn has been completely destroyed by Whitney in his etymological translation.
31. This verse contains important terms of indefinite political connotation. I have provisionally accepted them here in the following senses: *sabhā* = assembly, *saṁgrāma* = congregation (Whitney: host), *samiti* = council.
32. See Bloomfield, *op. cit.*, § 54.
32a. *Sabhā* and *Samiti*, for the constitutional importance of which cf. pp. 357, 433.
33. *Op. cit.*, § 57.
34. See Whitney-Lanman's preface to IV. 23; Bloomfield, *op. cit.*, p. 82.
34a. *Taittirīya-Saṁhitā*, IV. 5; *Vājasaneyi-Saṁhitā*, XVI.
35. The translation given here is taken from Muir's metrical rendering of the hymn which reproduces the spirit and meaning of the original much more accurately than Whitney's wooden and etymological translation.
36a. See above, Ch. VIII. pp. 153.
verse is the positive counterpart of *ned* (*na id*).
36a. See above, Ch. VIII, pp. 153.
37. It is characteristic of Atharvavedic loose thinking that in v. 18 of this hymn *Brahmacharya* has been recommended not only for women, but also for animals.
38. The *Ṛigveda* recognizes levirate, but remarrige of widows is not directly mentioned in it. Cf. Ch. XIX. p. 390.
39. See *Vedic Index* under "Parikshit."

40. The linguistic differences discussed earlier in this chapter are not important enough to make out a case for distinct dialect for any one of the Saṁhitās of the Yajurveda.
41. See *supra*, Ch. XII.
42. *HIL*, I, pp. 171-87.
43. *HIL*, pp. 110-11.
44. Perhaps the best exposition of the Brāhmaṇa literature will be found in *La doctrine du sacrifice dans les Brāhmaṇas* by Lévi and *Die Weltanschauung der Brāhmaṇa-texte* by Oldenberg.
45. Eggeling, *SBE*, XII, p. xxv.
46. See Paul Thieme, *Pāṇini and the Veda*, pp. 73-6, where previous literature on this problem has been indicated.
47. See Liebich's genial monograph *Pāṇini, ein Beitrag zur Kenntnis der indischen Literatur und Grammatik.*
48. But not for syntax.
49. Wackernagel, *Altindische Grammatik*, Vol. III, § 15d.
50. The Kāṇva-Śatapatha in this regard thus differs not only from the Mādhyandina-Śatapatha, but also from all the other Brāhmaṇas. See Caland, Introd. to *Kāṇva-Śat.*, p. 65.
51. Again it is interesting to note regarding the *Śatapatha-Brāhmaṇa*, that the locative singular of *n*-stems "has nearly always the -*i* in the Kāṇva-recension, but is formed by the Mādhyandinas nearly always without case sign." Caland, *op. cit.*, p. 38.
52. Wackernagel, *op. cit.*, Vol. III, § 145d.
53. Whitney, § 587b.
54. Whitney, § 563.
54a. See Keith, *HOS*, XXV, p. 87.
55. Whitney, § 995a.
56. On this -*am* see particularly Renou, *Mémoire de la Société Linguistique de Paris*, tome XXIII, 1935, pp. 359-92.
57. Whitney, § 969.
58. Whitney, § 1180.
59. Whitney, § 984c.
60. Whitney, § 268a. This need not be surprising, for the original meaning of *rūpa* was "assumed form" as in the *Ṛigveda*. The literal meaning of *rūpam kṛi* was thus "to assume a changed form," i.e. "to become."
61. See Delbrück, *Altindische Tempuslehre*, p. 128.
61a. The different values of the perfect in Vedic literature have been thoroughly discussed by Renou in his *La Valeur du Parfait*, Paris, 1925.
62. See Keith, *HOS*, XXV, p. 86.
63. See Keith, *HOS*, XVIII, p. cliv, fn. 1.
64. See Whitney, § 1073.
65. See Liebich, *op. cit.*, p. 80.
66. See also Keith, *HOS*, XVIII, p. clvii.
67. It should not be forgotten that until the nineteenth century Europe could not produce in the field of grammar and philology anything that can bear comparison with Pāṇini's *Ashṭādhyāī*.
68. I cannot but agree on this point with Leopold von Schröder (*Indiens Literatur und Cultur*, p. 114).
69. See Keith, *RPVU*, p. 351. It should not be forgotten, however, that the Mahāvrata was originally a popular folk-festival over which the Brāhmins merely threw a mantle of ritual sanctity.
70. *Taittirīya-Saṁhitā* II. 5. 11. 9.
71. *Śatapatha-Brāhmaṇa*, XIII. 3. 5. 3.
72. *Aitareya-Brāhmaṇa*, VII. 29. 4. It should not be forgotten however that in the orthodox Mīmāṁsā-school of interpretation such passages are taken to be mere rhetorical exaggerations (*Arthavāda*). That they really are exaggerated statements and must not be taken literally is quite obvious, though, strangely enough, most of the non-Indian scholars have taken even such statements to be literally true. Passages of like import are quite common also in the *Manusmṛiti*, but nobody has ever suggested that in the Śuṅga period the treatment prescribed by Manu was actually meted out to the Śūdras. There is no reason to doubt that the Brāhmaṇa-passages, like those about Brāhmins and Śūdras referred to here, were mere *Arthavādas* from the very beginning. But since the mind of a man can be measured also by the exaggerations he is in the habit of making, these *Arthavāda*-passages cannot be ignored in estimating the moral outlook of the Brāhmaṇa authors.

73. The relevant portions, though devoid of literary value, are not without interest for social history. Thus from our hypothetical Brāhmana-passage it is possible to infer that the Brāhmaṇa authors thought that the sun moves from east to west, and that they knew that a Jagatī-pāda consists of twelve syllables.
74. The most famous narrative in Gāthās is the Śunaḥśepa-legend in the *Aitareya-Brāhmaṇa*, VII, 13-18. As it is not possible to do justice to the truly literary compositions contained in the Brāhmaṇas within the space available here, only a few of their salient features will be indicated. For a fuller account, see Winternitz, *op. cit.*, pp. 187 ff.
75. *Śatapatha-Brāhmaṇa*, I, 8. 1.
76. See, for instance, the story of Śaryāta Mānava and his daughter Sukanyā in the *Śatapatha-Brāhmaṇa*, IV. 1. 5. 2. This story appears also in the *Jaiminīya-Brāhmaṇa*, See Caland, *Auswahl*, pp. 251-2, and my *Collection of Fragments of Lost Brāhmaṇas*, pp. 25-29.
77. See Keith, *RPVU*, p. 245.
78. *Śatapatha-Brāhmana*, II. 2. 2. 20.
79. *Taittirīya-Saṁhitā*, II. 5. 11. 4; *Śatapatha-Brāhmaṇas*, I. 4. 5. 8-11.
80. See *Ved. Ind.*, II., p. 279.
81. *Taittirīya-Brāhmaṇa*, II. 2. 7. 1.
81a. *Śatapatha-Brāhmaṇa*, XI, 5. 6. 1 ff.
82. See Keith, *RPVU*, p. 474.
83. *Op. cit.*, pp. 572-3.
84. *Śatapatha-Brāhmaṇa*, III. 2. 2. 23.
85. *RV*, X. 85. 26: *vaśinī tvaṁ vidatham āvadāsi.*
86. *Maitrāyaṇī-Saṁhitā*, I. 10. 11.
87. *Śatapatha-Brāhmaṇa*, XIV. 1. 1. 31.
88. *Maitrāyaṇī-Saṁhitā*, *loc. cit.*
89. *Op. cit.*, IV. 7. 4: *tasmāt pumāṁsaḥ sabhāṁ yānti. na striyaḥ.*

CHAPTER XXI

POLITICAL AND LEGAL INSTITUTIONS

1. POLITICAL THEORY

The lack of a spirit of inquiry into the *rationale* of social and political institutions is generally regarded as a singular characteristic of oriental civilization including the Indian. Thus an eminent scholar[1] writes: "To the early Eastern mind, the fact that a thing existed was sufficient of itself to show its right to be. Thus was effectually excluded all possibility of inquiries as to the relative perfection, or justification for the existence of, *de facto* social and political institutions." But this view is not wholly accurate. For the dim beginnings of speculation regarding the origin of kingship, the *raison d'être* of the state, the status and relation of different classes in society and the justification of the same, together with other cognate problems, can be clearly traced in the literature even of the early period with which we are dealing. Unfortunately, as this literature, our only source of information, is wholly sacerdotal in character, the theories and speculations are presented in a theological and metaphysical environment. It is, however, important to note, that instead of passively accepting whatever existed in state or society, there was an active effort to trace the origin of institutions and offer an explanation of how things came to be what they were. It is a reasonable presumption that if the secular literature of the period had been preserved, we would have come across more rational theories based on logically grounded belief rather than on faith or dogma.

The political theories are sometimes discussed in connection with the gods, whose thoughts and activities are, however, so much akin to those of men, that no great stretch of imagination is required to interpret the views as equally, or really, applying to human affairs. This is best illustrated by the fundamental question of the origin of kingship. This definitely forms a subject of speculation in the literature of this period, and the Brāhmaṇa texts anticipate writers on polity of a later period by clearly formulating the question, "how is it that the king who is one rules over so many subjects." There are various replies to this question, and it is interesting to note that they form the germs of the more elaborately propounded views of later times. The first in point of importance is the view put forth in the *Aitareya Brāhmaṇa* (I. 1. 14). It is said that the "gods and demons fought with one another, but the gods were defeated. The gods said: 'It is because we have no king that the demons defeat us, so let us elect a king.' They elected a king and through his help obtained complete victory over the demons." As Dr. Beni Prasad has very rightly observed,[2] "here the kingship originates in military necessity and derives its validity from consent." Though appearing under the thin disguise of divine affairs, there can be hardly any doubt that it is a very rational view of the origin of kingship which prevailed among a class of political thinkers of the period.

A somewhat similar view appears in another garb in the same *Aitareya Brāhmaṇa* (VIII. 4. 12). The story is told with reference to Indra's kingship. "The gods headed by Prajāpati said to one another, 'this one is among the gods the most vigorous, the most strong, the most valiant, the most perfect who carries out best any work (to be done). Let us instal him in the kingship." Here, again, the kingship originates in election and common consent, based on the possession of the highest qualities by the chosen candidate.

But side by side with these rational views we find also the theory of the divine origin of kingship, which figures so prominently in later political literature. The germ of this has been traced by some scholars[3] even in the *Ṛigveda* (IV. 42), in the hymn attributed to the Pūru king Trasadasyu, who exclaims, "I am Indra, I am Varuṇa," and again, "on me (the gods) bestow those principal energies (that are) characteristic of the Asuras." But this may be explained as an expression of personal vanity rather than the formulation of a political theory. In the later Saṁhitās and the Brāhmaṇas, however, the divinity of the king is put forth as a general doctrine. The king is declared to have gained identity with Prajāpati by virtue of the Vājapeya and Rājasūya sacrifices.[4] The *Śatapatha Brāhmaṇa* (V. 3. 3. 12) definitely declares: "He the Rājanya is the visible representative of Prajāpati (the lord of creatures): hence while being one, he rules over many." The *Taittirīya Brāhmaṇa* (II. 2. 10. 1-2) tells the story how Indra, originally the most inferior among the gods, was created their king by Prajāpati, and received from him both the royal symbol and lustre. This is another illustration of the application of secular ideas to the realm of gods. But although the king is raised to the rank of God, the human origin is not lost sight of, and he is never regarded as divine by virtue of hereditary descent.[5]

Reference may be made in this connection to a short passage in *Śatapatha Brāhmaṇa* (XI. 1. 6. 24): 'Whenever there is drought, then the stronger seizes the weaker, for the waters are the law." Although somewhat enigmatic and mystical, it seems to foreshadow the later theory of the "state of nature" resulting in anarchy and confusion, which led to the foundation of state and monarchy.[6]

The beginnings of these political speculations were evidently inspired by the rapid increase, in number as well as in size, of the

Aryan kingdoms in India, and the consequent growth of the power and majesty of the ruling chiefs who had mostly outgrown the stage of tribal leaders and become territorial monarchs. As we have seen above (p. 265-6) the Aryans had, during this period, spread over nearly the whole of Northern India and established a large number of states. If the Puranic traditions, recorded in Ch. XIV, have any value, we must hold that there was a keen struggle for supremacy among these states, and some of them at any rate occasionally became very powerful by annexing neighbouring kingdoms. But even apart from Puranic traditions we have the evidence of the Vedic texts testifying to the amalgamation of early Rigvedic tribes into more powerful political units. The Pūrus and the Bharatas became united under the name Kuru; the Turvaśas and the Krivis became the Pañchālas; and lastly there are clear hints about the amalgamation of these two into a Kuru-Pañchāla group.

Besides, the descriptions of the Aśvamedha and Rājasūya sacrifices in the texts of this period show that ambitious kings strove to be all-powerful by extending their sway over neighbouring kingdoms, and seem to imply the existence of fairly large kingdoms. Keith,[7] however, is of the opinion that although some of the tribal kingdoms of the Rigvedic days had probably grown in size through amalgamation and expansion, there were no great kingdoms even in this period and no empire as such. The fact that kings are often described in the *Atharvaveda* as fighting with their cousins (*bhrātṛivyas*) or with their non-Aryan enemies, has been taken to confirm this view. This is, however, hardly conclusive. On the other hand the *Aitareya Brāhmaṇa* tells us that kings in the east were called *samrāṭs* (emperors?), those in the south *bhojas*, those in the north *virāṭs* and those in the famous middle country (eastern Punjab and western U.P.) merely *rājans*, and that titles like *ekarāṭ* and *sārvabhauma* could be claimed by a king who had conquered the kings in all the four directions. These specific references to imperialism, the flamboyant accounts of the imperial grandeur of kings who performed the Aśvamedha or the ceremony of royal consecration, and the titles like "conquerors of the whole earth" assumed by them on these occasions, indicate the existence of large kingdoms and occasionally also of empires, even if we make full allowance for obvious poetic exaggerations. There is a fairly long list in the *Aitareya Brāhmaṇa* of kings who had received the royal consecration at the Rājasūya, and in a general way the list agrees with that in the *Śatapatha Brāhmaṇa* of those who had performed the horse-sacrifice. The very multiplicity of these "imperial" monarchs, each one of whom strides forth in the ceremony as a conqueror in all the four directions, perhaps shows that the performance of the Rājasūya not unseldom represented royal aspirations rather than actual conquests. Some of the details of the Rājasūya ceremony are, however, worth noting as embodying the religio-political theory of those days: The king is dressed in rich royal robes and is anointed formally by the priests. He then sets his foot on a tiger's skin which is symbolic of his having become as powerful as the tiger. He next carries out a mimic cattle-raid, takes up formally the bow and arrow and takes a step in each of the four directions--a step symbolic of his conquest of that quarter. He then plays, formally, a game of dice in which it is pre-arranged that he commands the winning throw and becomes a victor.

As the *Śatapatha* (XII. 9. 3. 3) and *Aitareya* (VIII. 12. 17) *Brāhmaṇas* speak of a *daśa-purushaṁ rājyaṁ* (a kingdom of ten generations) and as royal descent can be traced in several other cases, the monarchy may be said to be normally hereditary. The term *rājaputra,* which can be interpreted as "king's son" in the majority of its occurrences in the texts of this period, bears testimony to the same fact. Occasionally, however, a king was selected by the people though the choice was probably restricted to the royal family or at best to members of the noble clans. The election of kings is clearly referred to in certain passages[8] (*AV*, I. 9; III. 4; IV. 22), but they are interpreted by Geldner[9] as indicating the purely formal approval of the king's occupation of the throne by the subjects (*viś*) rather than a selection, in all seriousness, of the king by the cantons (*viś*). Nevertheless it is certain that in emergencies, people had the power of selecting one member of the royal family in preference to another who was incompetent (Ch. XVII, pp. 356-7)

But whatever we might think of the election of kings as a means of popular control over them, there is no doubt that the people continued to play an important part in politics. Thus particular stress is laid on the necessity of concord between the king and his electors in a passage in the *Atharvaveda* (III. 4) which, by the way, s a clear testimony of the prevalence of the system of election of the kings. Besides, it is held by some scholars that an essential part of the coronation ceremony was a solemn oath taken by the king to the effect that if he opposed the people, he might lose all the merit he had accumulated in his life.[10] But it is doubtful whether the question here is of opposing (*lit.*, oppressing) the people or the priest by whom the oath was administered.[11]

There are hymns in the Saṁhitās and Brāhmaṇas to celebrate not only the coronation of kings but also the return of exiled kings. This implies that the people had the power to punish kings, if an emergency arose, by banishing them. Then in the *Tāṇḍya Brāhmaṇa* (VI. 6. 5) a sacrifice is mentioned whereby the officiating Brāhmaṇa could help the Vaiśyas (the subjects) to destroy the king. Royal power was, it is true, gradually consolidating itself, but even a long and unbroken descent could not save a king from the wrath of his subjects. For example, the Sṛiñjayas expelled their king Dushṭaritu Pauṁsāyana from the kingdom, in spite of his ten generations of royal descent.

The popular control in the affairs of states was exercised, as in the Rigvedic period, through the two popular Assemblies, *sabhā* and *samiti* (*ante*, Ch. XVII, p. 356). These are also referred to in the later Saṁhitās and Brāhmaṇas in terms which indicate an effective exercise of authority not only in the general administration but also over the person of the king. Thus we find a fervent prayer put in the mouth of the king: "May the *samiti* and the *sabhā*, the two daughters of Prajāpati, concurrently aid me."[11] It is significant to note that this passage describes the popular Assemblies as issues of the same Prajāpati, from whom the king, according to the theory of his divinity, derives all his power and authority (*ante*, p. 430). Thus both monarchy and the popular assemblies are placed on the same footing as divine institutions according to *Śatapatha Brāhmaṇa*. Other passages[12] in the literature of this period also indicate that the king took particular care to be in the good grace of the assemblies and the loss of their favour and support was regarded as a dire calamity for him.

We have no detailed knowledge of the working of the *Sabhā* but may glean a few particulars about it from isolated references. This term also denoted the "assembly-hall" which was used for serious political work as well as for dicing, social intercourse, debates, and entertainment. When the assembly (*sabhā*) met, a sacrifice was offered in the assembly-hall on behalf of the assembly, the fire used being called *Sabhya*. The *Maitrāyaṇī Saṁhitā* (IV. 7. 4) tells us that women did not attend the *sabhā*, which is but expected as women did not take part in political activity. The same Saṁhitā mentions *sabhā* in the sense of the court house of the village-judge—the Grāmya-vādin—who is referred to in all the Saṁhitās of the *Yajurveda*. From the use of the terms *sabhāsad* and *sabhāchara* in the very probable senses of "assessor" and "member of the law-court" respectively, it appears that the *sabhā* met more often for the administration of justice than for political discussion. A *sabhā-pati*, "lord of the assembly," is mentioned in the Saṁhitās of the *Yajurveda*, and the *Taittirīya Brāhmaṇa* (III. 7. 4. 6) speaks of a *sabhā-pāla* probably in the sense of "a guardian of an assembly-hall." The *sabhā* thus appears to be an active institution housed in a place where legal rather than political business was more often transacted, and which also served as the venue of social gatherings and games. It is difficult to distinguish clearly between the functions of the *sabhā* and the *samiti* from the available evidence. All that can be said is that discussion and decision on policies of all kinds as well as legislation constituted the main business of the *samiti*, which was a larger body, whereas judicial work, which could also be transacted by the *samiti*, fell chiefly within the purview of the *sabhā*, though the latter had the right to discuss political matters also.

In spite of the popular assemblies, the king's power was on the increase. This was no doubt due to the growth of large territorial states and the evolution of an official hierarchy in place of the old nobility by birth. The king's main function was the protection of the state and the people, and it was recognized that this required firmness and vigour on his part. In the absence of any authoritative principles of international law, hostility, tacit or avowed, was the normal relation between states, and the king had necessarily to be a great war-lord, endowed with ample military resources. These requisites of kingly office are reflected in a hymn of the *Atharvaveda* (VI. 87-8) which addresses a new king as follows:

"Here be you firm as a mountain and may you not come down. Be you firm here like Indra; remain you here and hold the realm.

"Firm is the heaven, firm is the earth, firm is the universe, firm are the mountains, let the king of the people be firm.

"Vanquish you firmly, without falling, the enemies, and those behaving like enemies crush you under your feet. All the quarters unanimously honour you, and for firmness the assembly here creates you."[13]

This evolution of kingly power, out of sheer political necessity, made further progress by the enunciation of his divinity. The *Śatapatha Brāhmaṇa*, a strong exponent of this theory, upholds the doctrine that by performing certain rites in the Rājasūya sacrifice the king becomes not only exempt from punishment but also the lord of the law.[14] But these extreme theoretical assumptions were hardly applicable to real life. The actual instances of expulsion of the king, referred to above, belie these canonical statements. Besides, one fundamental principle which characterizes the political thought of the Hindus is the conception of *Dharma* or Sacred Law which sustains the universe and to which both the king and all sections of the community owe allegiance. The sages, not the king, had the power to interpret this law which was included in the Sacred Canon, and it was the clearly recognized duty of the king to abide by, and give effect to it. The moral and spiritual sanctions behind this Sacred Law were a sufficiently powerful motive, more than we can possibly imagine today, for restraining the wilful exercise of authority by the king. The *Bṛihadāraṇyaka Upanishad*, which forms a part of the *Śatapatha Brāhmaṇa*, clearly enunciates this great principle, though it was more elaborated at a later age. In assessing the true character—beneficent or otherwise—of kingly rule in this age, we must take note of the high intellectual qualifications of the kings. Though Kshatriyas, they were as well-versed as, if not more than, the Brāhmaṇas in the Vedas and Upanishads. They took great interest in philosophical discussions. They not only patronized learning, but were themselves teachers and had even Brāhmaṇa disciples, although it was not normal for a Brāhmaṇa to learn from a Kshatriya. Such highly cultured kings must have generally proved benevolent rulers. A memorable piece of advice given to a king as recorded in the *White Yajurveda* (X. 27) is well worth quoting here. The priest exhorts the king at the coronation in these words: "As a ruler, from this day onwards, judge the strong and the weak impartially and fairly. Strive unceasingly to do good to the people and above all, protect the country from all calamities." There is evidence to show that in this period, the position of the Kshatriyas in general and that of the king in particular had gone up in relation to the Brāhmaṇas, in the social scales of the caste-system. A passage in the *Aitareya Brāhmaṇa* (VII. 29) describes the relationship of each of the remaining three castes to the Rājanya who is taken as the norm (See below, Ch. XXIII).

2. ADMINISTRATIVE ORGANIZATION

Frequent references to a large body of royal officials indicate the development of the administrative system during this period. Among the officers that form the *entourage* of a king at the royal consecration, figure a *Senānī*, a *Grāmaṇī*, and a *Bhāgadugha* (collector of taxes or distributor of food?). The *Grāmaṇī*—the head of a village, corresponding to the modern village *patel*—is referred to in the *Taittirīya Brāhmaṇa* as belonging to the Vaiśya caste. There were probably grades of *Grāmaṇīs*, according to the size of the *grāma*. He was the main channel of royal authority, being entrusted with local administration; but his powers were probably more civil than military.

In addition to the above three officials, lists of members of the *entourage* at the Rājasūya, as given in the *Taittirīya* texts, include several others who were not merely courtiers but also public functionaries, and this gives us a general idea of the various administrative departments. There is above all the Purohita who was something like an Archbishop and also a counsellor of the king. Next comes the Sūta. The Sūta, which literally means a "Charioteer," raises a curious question. Was he merely the "coachman" by appointment to His Majesty? This appears improbable from the very important rôle the Sūta plays as a herald or minstrel in the propagation and popularization of heroic and epic poetry in later times. It is not unlikely that, originally a charioteer, the Sūta was an employee to whom naturally fell the task of relieving the boredom of the king or warrior, whom he drove on long marches and great distances, by entertaining and encouraging him with stories and especially heroic legends. This fits in very well with the important part that charioteers are supposed to play, chiefly in wars, but not rarely also in peace. They had a facile tongue and a fund of stories and worldly wisdom. One need but remember the vital part played by the charioteer in the *Bhagavadgītā*.

After the Sūta, we find mention of two other officials, viz., the Saṁgrahītṛi, the treasurer, and the Akshāvāpa, the Superintendent of dicing. Whatever our views regarding gambling, we must remember that dicing was (like racing today) a royal sport, and that there must have been a department of dicing in those days. This is confirmed by the symbolic ceremony of "dicing" as forming part of the Rājasūya. This list is supplemented by the *Śatapatha Brāhmaṇa* which includes the Kshattṛi (the Chamberlain?), Gonikartaṇa (Govikartana), the Huntsman, and Pālāgala, the Courier. The *Maitrāyaṇī Saṁhitā* mentions the Takshan or "carpenter" and the Rathakāra or "chariot-maker."

Reference is also made to the Sthapati. He was either the chief judge, as we shall have occasion to mention later, or the local chief of a part of the kingdom, because we come across a Nishāda-Sthapati in the Sūtras, who may have been the ruler of some frontier aboriginal tribe.

The officers mentioned, above, with the exception of the last, are called *ratnins* or "Jewels." The name is derived from an important rite of the Rājasūya ceremony, called Ratna-havis or Jewel-offering, in course of which the king on successive days had to make offerings to the gods in the houses of these officials.[15] This fact leaves no doubt of the high status and the great importance of these royal functionaries. Yet the Brāhmaṇa texts emphasize the point that some of them were inferior to both Brāhmaṇas and Kshatriyas, and immediately after the Jewel-offering ceremony, the king had to perform two rites for expiating the sin committed by putting these unworthy persons of low classes or castes in contact with the sacrifice (*Śat. Br.* V. 3. 2. 2). This curious procedure proves beyond doubt that a new type of nobility, that of royal service, had emerged by the side, if not in place, of the old nobility by birth.[16] It is an indirect testimony to the growth of a solid hierarchy of officials and the efficient organization of the machinery of administration.

Isolated references give us some idea of the great power and influence of this official nobility. Thus the Sūta and the Grāmaṇī are designated king-makers (*rāja-kṛit*),[17] while a list of eight persons, said to be *Vīras* (chief supporters or defenders) of the king, comprise, in addition to his queen, son, and brother, the Purohita, the Sūta, the Grāmaṇī, the Kshattṛi, and the Saṁgrahītṛi.[18]

The descriptions of the Rājasūya (royal consecration) in the later Saṁhitās and Brāhmaṇas depict the king as the "Protector" of the people in general and of the Brāhmaṇas in particular. In return for this protection the king is allowed to live on the (income of the) Viś (the subjects).[19] For discharging this duty efficiently, the king had to fight not only in defence of his realm but also to conduct offensive war, which was generally undertaken in the season of dew (i.e. at the end of the monsoon) and in which he had to "sack cities." He led the fighting host to battle in person, with the Senānī (army-leader) working under his direction, and had the right to a share of the booty of war after a victory. The Purohita ensured the king's safety and victory in battle by his prayers, spells, and charms, and this is in keeping with the rôle of the Purohita in peace as the regular adviser of the king.

For the maintenance of the machinery of administration which protected the people in war and peace, the king had the right to receive contributions and loyal service from his subjects. Though in origin these may have been voluntary they soon assumed the form of tribute (*Bali*), a kind of taxation that seems to have been meant in the reference to "the share of village, horses and kine" in the *Atharvaveda* (IV. 22. 2). The very frequent description, in the texts of this age, of the king as the "devourer of the people," is perhaps not to be understood in the sense of a "fleecing of the people" by the king, but as indicating that the royal household and the king's retinue were maintained by the contributions of the people in the form of food-grains and other necessaries of life (*ante*, Ch. XVII, pp. 359-60).

The incidence of taxation, however, did not fall equitably upon all classes of people. As the members of the royal family, the nobility and the Kshatriya class generally assisted the king in war, it is but natural that this right of maintenance should also be claimed by them. The Brāhmaṇas also claimed to be exempt from the normal exercise of royal authority, particularly in respect of taxation. In the Rājasūya ceremony the priest tells the assembled people: "This man is your king, Soma is the king of us Brāhmaṇas."[20] This passage is then applied to justify the Brāhmaṇa's exemption from taxation. How far this exemption was carried in actual practice it is difficult to say. But it appears that on the whole, the main burden of the taxation fell on the "people," who pursued peaceful occupations, such as agriculture, cattle-keeping, the arts, crafts, industries, and trade. The texts often describe the "people" as forming the backbone of royal power.

3. LAW AND LEGAL INSTITUTIONS

The *Śatapatha Brāhmaṇa* (V. 4. 4. 7) tells us that the king wields the rod of punishment (*Daṇḍa*), but is not subject to it. He himself, as a rule, appears to have administered criminal justice. That he was assisted by assessors is probable, though not certain. At any rate, in his absence, he could delegate his jurisdiction to a royal officer, because the *Kāṭhaka Saṁhitā* (XXVII. 4) mentions the Rājanya as an overseer (*adhyaksha*) when a Śūdra is punished. Among the crimes enumerated or otherwise recognized are, theft, robbery, adultery, incest, abduction, the killing of an embryo, the killing of a man, the slaying of a Brāhmaṇa (which alone amounts to murder proper and is expiable by the performance of an Aśvamedha), drinking intoxicating liquor, and treachery, punishable by death. Petty offences in the village seem to have been left to the Grāmyavādin or "village judge" for disposal. The view[21] that there was increase of crime during this age because Rudra is hailed as the protector of thieves does not appear to be correct.

It is curious that even a minor bodily defect such as the possession of bad nails, or the violation of a purely conventional practice was looked upon as a crime. But we should remember that the implicit belief in rebirth, and the fixed notion that for every defect or mishap in this life a person himself is responsible through actions committed either in this life or in a past one, can explain a number of anomalies in the judicial or social code of the Hindus. This is often forgotten when the charge of an inhuman and brutal outlook is preferred against their legal and social structure. That the sense of justice was high is seen from the record of long discussions over a case where a child is accidentally run over and killed by the king and the Purohita driving in a chariot. The matter is referred for arbitration to the Ikshvākus who gave the judgment that an expiation was due. Private vengeance was also permitted to serve the ends of justice, though the crudities of such a procedure were held in considerable check by the system of *Vairadeya* "wergeld"—"the money (in the form of a hundred cows, for example) to be paid for killing a man as a compensation to his relatives."

For evidence, eye-witnesses were more important than informers. Ordeals were also probably looked upon as valid tests of innocence or guilt. The *Chhāndogya Upanishad* (VI. 16. 1-2), while explaining how "Truth has the power of saving a man even from death," says: "When an alleged thief is brought handcuffed to the place of trial he is asked to catch hold of a heated axe. If he has not committed the theft, he covers himself with the glory of truth, does not burn his fingers, and is set free as an innocent person, but if he is guilty he is burnt on the spot."

The punishments for crime were rather severe. If a thief was caught red-handed, death or the cutting off of hands was the penalty; in milder cases, binding to posts and the return of stolen goods sufficed as punishment.

As regards civil law our knowledge is mainly confined to the ownership of land, succession, and partition of property. Individual property or individual ownership in land for the purposes of cultivation is recognized. This individual tenure of land turned out to be (in actual practice and fact, if not in legal theory) tenure by a family, rather than by an individual. In this sense must be understood "the conquests of fields" so often referred to in the Saṁhitās. Communal property in the sense of "ownership by a community" or "communal cultivation" is, however, unknown. It is but natural that a family should live together, with undivided shares in the land. With settlement and peaceful occupation of the country, inheritance of landed property must have been in force even earlier than the age of the Sūtras, which state them clearly for the first time. The word "*Dāya*" has already come to mean in this age "inheritance" in the sense of "a father's property which is to be divided among his sons either during his life or after his death." In a legal sense, the property of the family is the property of the head of the house, usually the father. The *Taittirīya Saṁhitā* (III. 1. 9. 4) has the famous episode of Manu's division of property among his sons. Nābhānedishṭha was excluded from the inheritance, but as a compensation was taught how to appease the Aṅgirasas and secure cows from them. An important aspect of this account is that the property divided was movable property and not land, and that cattle rather than land was the foundation of wealth, because cattle could be and were used individually, whereas land could not be freely disposed of. In the *Aitareya Brāhmaṇa* version of the story, the sons are said to have made the division, leaving to Nābhānedishṭha only the care of their aged father. Does this suggest that the sons were legally owners with their father? The evidence however seems to be in favour of the rule of *patria potestas,* whereby the father owned the property. The sons, when grown up, might claim the property and induce the father to divide it, but this cannot amount to the doctrine that every child on birth had a legal share in the property. The legend of Śunaḥśepa points to the developed *patria protestas* of the father. As regards the division, preference was shown to the elder son if it took place after the death of the father; during his lifetime, the preference was usually shown to the elder son but not rarely to another (*Pañchaviṁśa Brāhmaṇa,* XVI. 4. 4). Women were excluded from inheritance or partition. Neither they nor the Śūdras had any right to property. There is not much information available regarding the legal relations of husband and wife after marriage. The husband in all probability claimed the wife's dowry and earnings, if any. The *Śatapatha Brāhmaṇa* (IV. 4. 2. 13) says that women own neither themselves nor an inheritance.

Original acquisition of chattels was brought about by taking possession of them when found on one's own land or on unoccupied land, provided no one else claimed earlier ownership of them. They could be transferred by gift and barter or sale. The only contracts known were those in regard to the business of money-lending. The *Dāsas* and *Dāsīs* did most of the labour for which ordinary workers would have to be hired. The artisans and skilled workers of the village received fixed remuneration from the villagers and not payment for each separate piece of work.

As regards civil procedure, voluntary arbitration appears to be the earlier form of judicial procedure, in which the plaintiff (the (*praśnin*), the defendant (*abhi-praśnin*) and the arbitrator or judge (*praśna-vivāka*) figured, as the three appear in the list of victims at the Purushamedha in the *Vājasaneyi Saṁhitā* (XXX. 10). It is uncertain whether assessors were called in. The *jñātṛi* is very probably a technical legal term for a witness in civil transactions. Ordeals were but rarely used for deciding civil disputes, but their use as an evidence in civil law is proved by the case of Vatsa who demonstrated his purity of descent by walking through fire without sustaining any injury. The oath, though not mentioned as an independent instrument of evidence, must have formed part of the ordeal declaration when there was an occasion for it.

Finally we may discuss the legal aspect of the question of the ownership of the land *vis-à-vis* the king, as far as it is reflected in the texts of this age. Land was originally acquired when it was occupied by Aryan tribesmen among whom the apportionment must have taken place later. When the tribal chief assumed the status of a king he controlled all transactions regarding land. When the *Śatapatha Brāhmaṇa* (VII. 1. 1. 8) tells us that the Kshatriya gives a settlement to a man with the consent of the people, it implies that separate holdings existed. The conception of the absolute royal ownership of all land does not seem to have arisen during this age. "Grants" of land only implied transfer of privileges regarding revenue but no ownership. Similarly when the king granted to his favourites his royal prerogatives over villages, the "grant" is to be understood as the transfer of privileges in fiscal matters. That a gift of land in the sense of "the conferring of ownership" was looked upon as unconstitutional may be inferred from a story in the *Śatapatha* (XIII. 7. 1-15) and *Aitareya* (VIII. 21. 8) *Brāhmaṇas* that when king Viśvakarman offered the earth (probably a piece of land) to his officiating priest, the earth refused to be given. Such gifts of land probably constituted a violation of customary law. The king certainly had the power to expel a Brāhmaṇa or Vaiśya (there is no mention of the Kshatriya) from his land, but this power drew its sanction not from his ownership of the land but from his sovereignty, and was recognized only as a royal prerogative.

GENERAL REFERENCES

DR. U. GHOSHAL, *A History of Hindu Political Theories* (1923).
DR. BENI PRASAD, *Theory of Government in Ancient India* (1927).

---

1. Willoughby, *Political Theories of the Ancient World*, p. 14.
2. *Op. cit.*, p. 15.

3. Ghoshal, *op. cit.*, p. 27.
Śat. Br., V. 1. 3. 4.; 1. 4. 2.; 2. 1. 11.; 2.1.24.; 2. 2. 14-15; 2. 5. 3.; 3. 4. 23.; 4. 3. 27.; *Taitt. Saṁ.*, 1. 8. 16.
5. *Śat. Br.*, V. 3. 3. 12. Ghoshal, *op. cit.*, p. 33.
6. Ghoshal, *op. cit.*, pp. 41-2.
7. *CHI*, I, p. 130.
8. One of these is quoted in Ch. XX, p. 410.
9. *Ved. Stud.*, 2, 303.
10. Beni Prasad, *op. cit.*, p. 17. Jayaswal, *Hindu Polity*, II, 27-8.
10a. *POC*, VIII, 502.
11. *Śat. Br.*, IV. 1. 4. 1-6.; Cf. also *AV*, VII. 12, quoted in Ch. XX, pp. 411-12.
12. *AV*, VI. 88. 3.; VII. 12.
13. For other hymns of this nature cf. Ch. XX, p. 410.
14. *Śat. Br.*, V. 4. 4. 7.; 3. 3. 9. Ghoshal, *op. cit.*, p. 40. Dr. Beni Prasad, however, thinks that "the lordship of the law" here means the "lordship of justice" (*op. cit.*, p. 19).
15. The ceremony is described with slightly varying lists of officials in *Śat. Br.*, V. 3. 1.; *Taitt. Saṁ.*, I. 8. 9.; *Taitt. Br.*, I. 7. 3.
16. Dr. Ghoshal thinks that the official nobility took the place of the old nobility of birth (*op. cit.*, p. 39).
17. *Śat. Br.*, III. 4. 1. 7.; XIII. 2. 2. 18.
18. *Pañchaviṁśa* Br., XIX. 4.
19. *Ait. Br.*, VIII. 12. 17.
20. *Śat Br.*, V. 3. 12., 4. 2. 3.
21. *CHI*, I, p. 135.

CHAPTER XXII

RELIGION AND PHILOSOPHY

1. THE ATHARVAVEDA

For our survey of the evolution of religion and philosophical thought in the post-Rigvedic age we may begin with the *Atharvaveda* as it has preserved an aspect of primitive religious ideas which are not to be found in the other Vedic texts.

The oldest name of the AV in Vedic literature is *Atharvāṅgirasaḥ*, that is, "the Atharvans and the Aṅgirasaḥ." The two words denote two different species of magic formulae: *atharvan* is "holy magic bringing happiness" and *aṅgiras* is "hostile or black magic." The former includes among others formulae for the healing of diseases, while the latter includes curses against enemies, rivals, malicious magicians, etc. These two kinds of magic formulae then form the chief contents of the *AV*,[1] but these ancient magic songs which were originally popular poetry appear in the *Saṁhitā* in a Brahmanized form because of the priestly outlook of the compilers, which betrays itself in the similes and epithets. The gods are the same as in the *RV*, Agni, Indra, etc. But their characters have become quite colourless, all being invoked as "demon-destroyers", and their natural basis is utterly forgotten. The theosophical and cosmogonic speculations of the *AV* indicate a later stage of development than that in the *RV*. It contains more theosophic matter than any other Saṁhitā. The philosophical terminology is of an advanced type, and the pantheistic thought is practically the same as in the Upanishads. There is, of course, a magical twist given to the philosophical hymns. For example, *AV*, IV. 19. 6 employs the conception of *asat*, "the non-existent," as a spell to destroy enemies, demons, magicians, etc.

Above all, the principal aim of the *Atharvaveda* is to *appease* (the demons), to *bless* (friends), and to *curse*, and as such it did not find much favour with the priesthood, who excluded it from the sacred triad—the threefold lore. This was, however, a later development. At their origin, magic and cult both have an identical aim—the control of the transcendental world. They have this essential unity of purpose. There soon comes a time, however, when the priest who pays homage to the gods parts company with the magician who is in league with the demons. It is a remarkable fact, however, that in spite of this aversion to the Veda of magic, the ritual texts which describe the great sacrifices do incorporate exorcism-formulas and magic rites[2] whereby the prest can destroy "the enemy whom he hates and who hates him," and the law-book of Manu (XI. 33) sanctions the use of exorcism against enemies.

As Dr. Winternitz[3] points out, "many of these magic songs, like the magic rites pertaining to them, belong to a sphere of conceptions which, spread over the whole earth, ever recur with the most surprising similarity in the most varying peoples of all countries. Among the Indians of North America, among the Negro races of Africa, among Malays and Mongols, among the ancient Greeks and Romans, and frequently still among the peasantry of the present-day Europe, we find again exactly the same views, the same strange leaps of thought in the magic songs and magic rites, as have come down to us in the *Atharvaveda* of ancient India. There are, then, numerous verses in the *Atharvaveda*, which, according to their character and often also their contents, differ just as little from the magic formulas of the American-Indian medicine-men and Tartar Shamans as from the Merseburg magic maxims, which belong to the sparse remains of the oldest German poetry." The *AV* then is unique among the texts of this age—the Saṁhitās and Brāhmaṇas—as an important source of information regarding popular religious belief, not so far modified by priestly religion as to be unrecognizable in its original form.

Occasionally, we come across hymns like IV. 16, which look like a patchwork of old and new material. The first half of IV. 16 describes the power of the Almighty, the omniscience of God, in language of such impressive beauty, that as a piece of literary art it has hardly any equal in the whole of Vedic literature,[4] and yet the second part is an exorcism-formula against liars. This is a case (not rare) in the *AV* where a fragment of older poetry breathing genuine religious fervour has been dressed up as a magic formula.

There are hymns of a philosophical import in the *AV* though they are inspired more by practical considerations than by a longing for the Ultimate Reality. The hymns definitely presuppose a high level of metaphysical thought. There is some exaggeration in the opinion of Winternitz,[5] that there is in these hymns more of the mystery-mongering so characteristic of the magician than the search for truth that distinguishes a philosopher, and that they do not represent even a transitional stage between the creative thought of the philosophical hymns of the *RV* and the philosophy of the Upanishads. The idea of a supreme God like Prajāpati, as the creator and preserver of the Universe, and that of an impersonal creative principle (which form the two chief doctrines of the Upanishads), and some technical terms such as "*brahman*," "*tapas*," "*asat*," are met with in the *Atharvaveda*. The conception of Rudra-Śiva in the *AV* certainly represents a transitional stage between the conception of Rudra in the *RV* and the systematic philosophy of Śaivism in the *Śvetāśvatara Upanishad*. Original or otherwise, profound philosophical ideas do crop up now and then in the *AV*. *Kāla* or Time as the First Cause of all existence (XIX. 53. 5, 6) is a truly philosophical notion, but round it are woven metaphors that give a mystic turn to the great idea (XIX. 53). Similarly *Prāṇa* (Breath) and *Kāma* (Love) are described as First Causes in XI. 4 and IX. 2 respectively. The Rohita hymns (XIII. 1-4) contain a sublime glorification of the "Red One" (the genius of the sun) as a cosmogonic power. Alongside of this are found mystical fancies such as the exaltation of the sun as a primeval principle under the guise of a *Brahmachārin*, and the glorification of the Ox, the Bull, the Cow, and the Vrātya, each being alternately looked upon as the Highest Being, in XI. 5; IV. 11, IX. 4, X. 10 and XV respectively. *AV*, X. 2 is but an imitation of the philosophical hymn X. 121 of the *RV* and treats of the realization of *Brahman* in man, from the physical aspect. *AV*, XI. 8 suggests the idea of *Brahman* as the First Cause of all existence and of the oneness of man with the world-soul. Reference has already been made above (p. 414) to the long hymn (XII. 1) to Mother Earth which is acclaimed as one of the most beautiful productions of the religious poetry of ancient India. Though classified as a cosmogonic hymn, there is not much philosophy in it, but a relieving feature is that it contains no trace of mysticism and thus rises to the sublime heights of religious poetry.

It must be admitted that the *Atharvaveda* religion, being thus more popular than priestly, formed a transitional stage to the idolatries and superstitions of the ignorant masses, rather than to the sublimated pantheism of the Upanishads and further that it led to magic being confused with mysticism.

It is generally held that the religion of the *AV* is only an amalgam of Aryan and non-Aryan ideals achieved after the advance of the Aryans into India. According to this view[6] the Vedic Aryans, as they advanced into India, came across uncivilized tribes worshipping snakes, serpents, stocks, and stones, but instead of destroying these barbarian neighbours or allowing themselves to be swamped by them, the Aryans absorbed them. This spirit of acccommodation naturally elevated the religion of the primitive tribes but degraded the Vedic religion by introducing into it sorcery and witchcraft. In the opinion of the present writer, this view is not wholly correct. Magic and religious cults, having an identical aim in the beginning, namely, the control of the transcendental world, have parted company in the *AV* exactly as they have done in the religions of most peoples in the world, though there is no denying that such a process of separation was considerably helped by the Aryan contact with the natives of India, who had their own worship of spirits and stars, trees and mountains, and other superstitions.

2. THE SĀMAVEDA AND THE YAJURVEDA SAMHITĀS AND THE BRĀHMAṆAS

With the *Sāmaveda* and *Yajurveda* we enter a new world, as it were. The atmosphere is pervaded now by the smoke of the sacrifice and the incense of the ritual. The sacrifice dominates everything. These two Saṁhitās have been compiled strictly from the point of view of their use at the sacrifice. They are, indeed, nothing more than text-books—song-book and prayer-book—for the practical use of two of the four principal priests, the Udgātṛi and Adhvaryu. No account of the religion of this period can be understood in its proper perspective unless we follow the broad lines along which the institution of the sacrifice developed in this age.

The simple ceremonial of the domestic ritual which any individual, rich or poor, priest or layman, could perform in his own home may be reasonably supposed to be the starting point of the sacrificial cult. The single fire of the domestic hearth was the altar at which burnt offerings were presented, to the accompaniment of appropriate prayers. There were daily and periodical sacrifices, such as the morning and evening offerings, the New and Full-moon sacrifices and the four monthly or seasonal sacrifices. This domestic fire was also the blazing divine witness, propitiated by suitable oblational offerings accompanied by appropriate prayers, to a number of domestic ceremonies that endowed with religious sanctity various events in the life of a family, such as birth, marriage, other occasions of daily life, funeral, ancestor-worship, house-building, cattle-feeding, and farming. The domestic fire was also the centre of magic rites which were calculated to avert diseases and unpropitious omens, as also the centre of exorcisms and rites for love-magic, etc. A very large number of the songs and spells of the *Atharvaveda* naturally fit in, most admirably, into the framework of these domestic rites, as a substantial part of these partakes of the nature of magic rites. In these, what may be called the domestic varieties of the sacrificial cult, the householder himself generally officiated as the sacrificial priest, but he might call in the "Brahman," *if* he needed assistance.

But even in the age of the *Ṛigveda*, as noted above (p. 380), the cult of the Grand Sacrifices, especially the Soma-sacrifices, was gradually developing by the side of the cult of the domestic rites, described above. They were, however, so elaborately developed and systematized during the period under review that the *Sāmaveda* and *Yajurveda Saṁhitās* have been compiled solely for use at these Grand Sacrifices. A regular science of sacrifice has now been evolved and forms the sole topic of the Brāhmaṇa texts. Three sacred fires instead of one were necessary for these Grand Sacrifices, and altars for these were erected on a vast sacrificial place set up according to rules and to the accompaniment of an elaborate ritual. A formidable array of priests, divided into four groups headed by four chief priests, was required for the correct performance of the extremely complicated ritual and elaborate ceremonial which were the *sine qua non* of the Grand Sacrifices. The *Yajamāna* (sacrificer) had practically nothing to do but to give liberal fees to these priests. These Grand Sacrifices were called "Śrauta" or "based on Śruti," in the sense that the description of their theory and practice was also embodied in the Śruti literature, i.e. the Saṁhitās and Brāhmaṇas, whereas the domestic (*Gṛihya*) sacrifices referred to above were called Smārta (based on Smṛiti or "memory") in the sense, that they are described *only* in the Gṛihya-sūtras which fall into Smṛiti literature which has no divine sanction and is authoritative only in so far as it embodies the tradition derived from ancient sages.

The titles and functions of the heads of the four groups of priests are: (1) The Hotṛi or "Invoker" who was to praise the gods and invoke them to the sacrifice and whose duty it was to form the canon (*śastra*) for each particular rite of the Soma sacrifice by selecting, from the hymns of the *Ṛigveda*, the verses applicable to it and to recite them; (2) the Udgātṛi or "Chanter" who sings chants (*sāman*), accompanying appropriately the various stages of the preparation and presentation of the sacrifices, especially the Soma sacrifices; (3) the Adhvaryu or "Performer," who executes all the sacrificial acts, muttering simultaneously the prose prayers and the sacrificial formulae (*yajus*); (4) the Brahman or "High Priest" who as the general superintendent vigilantly guards against any error or deviation from the correct performance of the sacrifice and protects the sacrifice from danger by repeating sacred formulae by way of expiating for any error done. The Brahman has to be well versed in all the Vedas, but the Hotṛi has to be conversant only with the *Ṛigveda*. from which he takes the *Yājyās* (sacrificial verses) and the *anuvākyās* (invitatory verses). Similarly the Udgātṛi has to be well versed in the *Sāmaveda Saṁhitā* only, to master the melodies and the song-verses with which they are connected, and to sing the *stotras*, consisting of song-stanzas, i.e. stanzas or *ṛichaḥ* which are made to bear certain melodies or *sāmans*. Finally, the Adhvaryu priest has to be proficient only in the Saṁhitās of *Yajurveda* as he mutters the prose formulae and prayers called *Yajus* and the verses (*ṛichaḥ*) collected in it for his use.

Like the two Saṁhitās mentioned above, the Brāhmaṇas also treat of the sacrificial liturgy. The age represented by them all is an age of forms, concerned more with the externals of religion than its spirit. Mechanical sacerdotalism is the religion now. Symbolic significance is attached to even the smallest minutiae of ceremonies that are purely external (*ante*, p. 423). Every prayer that accompanies a rite asks for some worldly gain.

Nevertheless there is an interesting substratum of popular religion, underlying this intricate and elaborate ritual of the sacrifice. The Rājasūya or the ceremony of royal consecration must have had once an appeal to the festive instincts of the people. The Vājapeya is characterized by a chariot race which must have been originally the main element and which must have always made a great hit with the people. The ritual of the Mahāvrata, which is probably a reminiscence of a very popular primitive celebration of the winter solstice, plays a notable part in the Gavāmayana, the year-long Sattra. The horse-sacrifice is fundamentally the elaboration of a simple rite of sympathetic magic. Above all, however, the building of the altar for the sacred fire is the one rite which, though a simple one in ancient times, has been so worked over by the priests that it reflects in a mystic sense almost a new conception of the unity of the universe and the mode of its preservation. The Brāhmaṇas record, as an ancient practice no longer current, the slaying of a man during the building rite in order to secure the permanence of the structure. The only plausible explanation of the disproportionate importance and treatment claimed by this rite is the one given by Eggeling[7] that the building of the fire-altar symbolizes the reconstruction of the Universe in the shape of Prajāpati, the full significance of which will be explained later.

There is no longer the spontaneity or simplicity of religious feeling that is associated in a large measure with the sacrifice in the age of the *Ṛigveda*. Although the theory of the sacrifice is superficially "I give thee (O God) that thou mayest give," there is so little faith in it, that sympathetic magic dominates the entire sacrificial system. The priest has arrogated to himself such powers in this regard, that he could ruin (if he pleased) even the patron for whom he officiates by deliberately committing errors. The efficacy of the ritual depended on the correct pronunciation of the *mantras* recited, because it was their sound rather than their meaning that was credited with power. The *viniyoga* or liturgical application of the *RV* hymns to the details of the sacrifice had no relation to their meaning. So ludicrously theoretical was the development of the sacrificial cult that the list of sacrificial victims in the *Yajurveda* texts includes human beings as well.

As the sacrifice is the only power that counts and could bend even the gods to the will of the sacrificer, the old gods are not of much consequence now. As a result some of the minor deities of the *Ṛigveda* have either disappeared or exist in name only. Prajāpati (as "Lord of creatures") is the main subject of theosophical speculation in the Brāhmaṇas, but he is not "a god of the people" as Rudra is. This is indicated by the number of litanies addressed to the latter in the Yajurvedic Saṁhitās, and the attention devoted to him in the *Aitareya, Kaushītaki* and *Śatapatha Brāhmaṇas.* Rudra as Bhūtapati is a dread figure, who (we are told in *Aitareya Br.*) usurped the dominion of Prajāpati over all cattle, when the latter committed incest with his daughter. He appears at the sacrifice in black raiment and claims the sacrificial victim. This Rudra is (in all probability) not merely a development of the Rigvedic Rudra, but an adaptation of him by amalgamation with a popular god, an aboriginal god of vegetation, closely connected with pastoral life. He is thus the "great god" (*mahādeva*) and has already received the appellation "Śiva" (the "Auspicious One") which became later his chief name. Next to Rudra comes Vishṇu, constantly identified with the all-important sacrifice and therefore rising to a high position. Probably he was prominent enough to claim the undivided allegiance of some localities while Ṛudra was worshipped in others. Nārāyaṇa and Vishṇu are brought into relation in the *Taittirīya Araṇyaka.* In other respects, there is little change in the Rigvedic pantheon. Gandharvas, Apsarases, Nāgas, etc., are raised to a semi-divine rank. Snake-worship (borrowed probably from the aborigines) and the mechanical motif of the "Devāsura" battles make their appearance now. Monotheism is being advocated. "Brahman," from meaning the "prayer-verses and formulae" in the Veda, containing secret magic power by which man seeks to bend divine beings to his will, came next to mean the *trayī vidyā* or "a collection of these prayers and formulae in the three Vedas"; then "the first created thing," because the *trayī* was supposed to be of divine origin and because the superhuman (nay superdivine) sacrifice was contained in and therefore derived from the *trayī;* and finally (in this period) came to signify the "creative principle"—the cause of all existence. Such an evolution of meaning was possible because, in this age, the divine origin and authority of the Vedas is accepted without question. In the Purushasūkta (RV, X. 90) the act of creation is treated as a sacrifice completely offered (*sarva-hut*) from which the three Vedas arose. The *Śatapatha Brāhmaṇa* (XI. 5. 8. 1 ff.) version of this doctrine is that the Self-existent breathed out the Vedas. The so-called authors of the Vedas are just inspired seers *(Ṛishis)* to whom the divine revelation was communicated. The doctrine that *śabda* or "articulate sound" is eternal has thus an important correlation to the fact that the Vedas were transmitted by word of mouth, from teacher to pupil in unbroken succession through untold generations. The Vedic tradition, considered sacred and infallible, must necessarily embody the truth, the whole truth, and nothing but the truth. But the early Vedic texts are not always consistent. This enabled later the votaries of the most diverse doctrines to quote texts from the Vedas in their support, and although philosophy became scholastic as a result, one advantage was that a reliable basis—the unfailing intuition of the most ancient inspired seers—was available to the Indian thinkers.

There are many creation-legends in the Brāhmaṇas which are a strange admixture of metaphysical thought with disconnected explanations of sacrificial rules. The majority of them generally begin with the narration that Prajāpati practised austerities through self-torture and mortification as a preparation for the task of creation, but there are passages in the Brāhmaṇas where Prajāpati himself is looked upon as created and where the starting point of creation is either the primeval waters or Brahman or the Non-existent. Desire is the germ of existence, the motive power of all creation.

That life is a duty and a responsibility is the central ethical teaching of the Brāhmaṇas. Man is born with certain *ṛiṇas* or debts which he must discharge in his life. He has a debt to pay to the gods, to the *Ṛishis,* to the manes, to men, and to the lower creatures. And he discharges these debts, if he worships the gods, studies the Veda, performs funeral ceremonies, is hospitable to guests, and offers oblations to the *bhūtas.* Thus, there is no lack of high moral sense and noble sentiments. Selflessness must characterize all our actions. The Brāhmaṇas have a remarkable sacrifice—the *Sarvamedha*—wherein everything is to be sacrificed to attain the freedom of the spirit. Prayer and good works constitute godliness, which is the first requisite of a good life. Truthfulness in utterance and action is the foundation of moral life. There are hints in the Brāhmaṇas that excessive ritualism was bringing on a reaction. For example, knowledge rather than sacrificial gifts or asceticism is valued in the *Śatapatha Brāhmaṇa* (X. 5. 4. 16), although asceticism is also held up as a great ideal elsewhere (*Taittirīya Brāhmaṇa,* III. 12. 3). The theory that confession implying repentance somewhat mitigates the guilt is seen in the *Śatapatha Brāhmaṇa.* Inner purity was insisted on, as much as external purity. Truth, performance of *dharma* (duty), respect for parents, love of fellow-beings, and abstinence from theft, adultery, and murder were the *sine qua non* of a good life.

The description of heaven in the *RV* is only elaborated in the other Saṁhitās and Brāhmaṇas. The essentials are the same. The *Atharvaveda* tells us how the dead man is conducted upwards by the Maruts with gentle breezes fanning him until he recovers his complete body and meets the Fathers who reside in the company of Yama. The idea that the dead in heaven are nourished by the piety of the relatives on earth is also found in the *AV.* Such nourishment may either be buried with the dead, so that the grains of corn and sesame, so buried, may turn into wish-cows in heaven, or the nourishment may be conveyed through subsequent offerings. This is indeed the germ of the later Śrāddha idea. The *Ṛigveda* conception of *nirṛiti* as a place of darkness in which the luminaries are lost has been developed by the *Atharvaveda* into a *naraka-loka* ("hell") which is the abode of female goblins and a place of utter darkness. The *Śatapatha,* the *Jaiminīya* and *Kaushītaki Brāhmaṇas* add their own touches to this horrid picture of hell. The two paths—one of the Devas and the other of the Pitṛis—are naturally mentioned, as they have been already foreshadowed in the *RV*. The theory of metempsychosis does not appear to have been very clearly formulated in the Saṁhitās and Brāhmaṇas, though the doctrine that the agony of death is to be endured not once only but repeatedly as one may die repeated deaths in the next world, prepares us for the very important part that the theory plays in the Upanishads where the conception of repeated deaths is merely transferred from the next world to the present. The idea of reward and punishment, after death, in exact correspondence to the good and bad deeds of a person in this life, has gained a firm hold in this period. The attainment of immortality and the company of the gods in the heaven—a highly ennobled form of earthly life perpetuated in surroundings of bliss—is the deeply cherished aim of, and incentive to, the practice of piety and good works in this life.

This is a considerable advance over the view of the *Ṛigveda.* There, immortality in the abodes of the blessed—the region of milk and honey—is assured to knowledge and virtue, whereas not much thought is given to the fate of the sinner who is apparently condemned to the complete obliteration of his personal existence. Now, however, the wicked are described as being born again in the next world (along with the good) suffering the punishment which their misdeeds bring upon them. That "man is the architect of his own fate" becomes a perfect truth according to this theory. And the supreme merit of philosophical thought in this period is the development of the doctrine that reward and punishment are not eternal. This is but a logical development. How could the limited good or evil that men can do in the brief span of a single life on earth bring on endless pleasure or pain in the next world? Hence follows the theory that penance and atonement can purify and absolve the soul from guilt and exhaust the period of suffering. The Brāhmaṇa doctrine, that whatever food a man consumes in this world in return consumes him in the next world (*Śatapatha,* XII. 9. 1. 1) is but the transfer from the physical to the moral plane of the law that action and reaction are equal and opposite. Similarly, the enjoyment of the rewards, which is in exact measure to the good deeds performed, must some time come to an end. Thus there is the prospect of rebirth again for both the pious and the wicked. So arises the wonderful conception of a beginningless and endless circuit of birth and death; the so-called *saṁsāra* or "bondage of life and death," culminating in that unique conception of ultimate happiness which is much higher than that of a life in heaven. It is a conception of freedom from *saṁsāra,* which is the true *moksha* (release) or absolution. First desire and then its fulfilment is a vicious circle, and the only escape from it is desirelessness induced by true knowledge. This, however, is the main doctrine of the Upanishads and is only adumbrated in this period. For example, when the *Śatapatha Br.* asks the seeker for truth to meditate upon the Self, made up of intelligence and endowed with a body of spirit, a form of light, and an ethereal nature, the doctrine has a speculative but none the less ritual background. Similarly, the building of the fire-altar is (as mentioned above) symbolical of the reconstruction of the Universe, in the shape of Prajāpati. If we now bear in mind the two sets of mystical equations: (1) Prajāpati = Agni = divine counter-part of the human sacrificer; and (2) Prajāpati = Time = Death (in the final analysis), we can understand that the human sacrificer becomes Death (in a mystic sense) and thus raises himself above death to everlasting bliss. In this process the true nature of Prajāpati and of the sacrificer is revealed as Intelligence. This same doctrine reappears in another form in the Upanishads as we shall see later.

3. THE ĀRAṆYAKAS

The excessive ritualism of the Brāhmaṇas produced a natural reaction. The Āraṇyaka texts are themselves virtually an admission that the correct performance of a compulsory ritual, that had developed to enormous proportions in the Brāhmaṇa period, could not be expected from all, young and old, from residents of villages and towns as well as from those who resided in the forest. There were again some parts of the sacrificial lore which were of an occult and mystical nature and which could be imparted to the initiated only in the privacy of the forest. The Āraṇyakas do not lay down rules for the performance of sacrifices, nor do they comment on the ceremonial in the Brāhmaṇa style. They are mainly devoted to an exposition of the mysticism and symbolism of the sacrifice and priestly philosophy. Meditation, rather than performance, is the spirit of their teaching, and they naturally substitute a simpler ceremonial for the complicated one of the Brāhmaṇas. We cannot definitely say whether the theory of the *Āśramas* was deliberately formulated by Brahmanism with a view to accommodate the new doctrines that were raising their heads against the older canon of the Brāhmaṇas and the philosophy of the sacrifice.[8] But it must be admitted that the Āraṇyakas or "Forest-texts" came in exceedingly handy, as ideally suitable Vedic texts for the daily study of the forest-hermits, as distinguished, on the one hand, from the student and householder who could do justice to the cult of the Vedic sacrifice set forth in the Brāhmaṇas, and on the other, from the ascetic who could dedicate the rest of his life to the contemplation of Brahman—the Absolute expounded in the Upanishads.

Important service was rendered by the Āraṇyakas when they stressed the efficacy of the inner or mental sacrifice as distinguished from the outer or formal sacrifice, consisting of oblations of rice, barley or milk. They thus helped to bridge the gulf between the "way of works" (*karmamārga*), which was the sole concern of the Brāhmaṇas, and the "way of knowledge" (*jñāna-mārga*) which the Upanishads advocated. The Āraṇyakas further lay down *Upāsanās* (or courses of meditation) upon certain symbols and austerities for the realization of the Absolute, which by now had superseded the "heaven" of the Brāhmaṇa works, as the highest goal of the devout. These symbols form the link between the Brāhmaṇas and the Upanishads as they are borrowed from the sacrifices. Finally the compromise between the two "ways" of *karman* and *jñāna* was consummated when *karman* was made subsidiary to, and a preparatory stage for, *jñāna* in the Āraṇyakas and Upanishads.

---

1. For specimens of these hymns cf. Ch. XX. pp. 411-15.
2. Cf. *Śāṁkhāyana Gṛ. S.*, I. 2-18.
3. *HIL*, I, p. 128.
4. For the English translation of the hymn cf. Ch. XX. pp. 413-14.
5. *HIL*, I, p. 150.
6. Cf. *IP*, I, pp. 118 ff.
7. *SBE*, XLIII, pp. xiv-xxiv.
8. Belvalkar and Ranade, *HIP*, II. p. 84. For further elucidation of this topic see Ch. XXVI.

CHAPTER XXIII

SOCIAL AND ECONOMIC CONDITIONS

1. SOCIAL CONDITIONS

1. *Family Life*

The very use of the term *kula,* which does not occur as an uncompounded word before the period of the Brāhmaṇas, suggests a system of individual families, each consisting of several members, under the headship of the father or eldest brother to whom belongs the *kula* (originally "home or house of the family," then by metonymy "the family" itself). As distinguished from *gotra* it seems to mean the undivided family living under one roof.

The case of the sale of Śunaḥśepa in the *Aitareya Brāhmaṇa* (VII. 12-18) suggests that the son was under the absolute control of the father, but the story may only reflect the horror evoked by the father's heartless treatment of his son. The father as a rule did not arrange the marriage of his son or daughter (*Jaiminīya Upanishad-Brāhmaṇa,* III. 12. 2). The relationship between father and son was one of great affection. The kissing of a grown-up son on the head on important occasions as a token of love is a custom found in *Śāṅkhāyana Āraṇyaka.* Adoption was resorted to, not only in the absence of natural children, but also to secure the addition of a specially qualified member to the family, as in Viśvāmitra's adoption of Śunaḥśepa.

Certain special terms show that it was considered improper for younger brothers and sisters to marry before their elders. The brother and his wife played the part of guardians of the sister in the absence of the father. Quarrels between brothers are mentioned. The family was sometimes large enough to include the great-grandfather as well as the great-grandsons. Among relations are mentioned the wife's brother, the sister's son, the cousin (*bhrātṛivya*), the maternal uncle, etc.

An entire hymn in the *Atharvaveda* is devoted to the praise of hospitality (IX. 6), and the *Aitareya Āraṇyaka* also lays stress on it. The guest-offering is an integral part of the daily ritual of the household.

2. *The Caste-System*

The term *varṇa* is used definitely in the sense of "caste," without reference to colour, in this age. The system of Caste, whose beginnings may be traced in the broad fourfold classification of society in the Rigvedic age (*ante,* pp. 387 ff.), developed during this period in various directions. Many causes contributed to the rise of sub-castes and other caste-divisions. Guilds of workers tended to crystallize into castes, as occupations became more or less hereditary; as examples we may cite the chariot-makers, the smiths, the leather-workers, and the carpenters. The peculiar family constitution or the *gotra* tradition, whereby exogamy as well as endogamy regulated marriage connections, and whereby a man should normally marry a woman of equal birth, i.e. within his caste, but not of the same *gens* or within the *gotra*, was another factor in the development of complications and distinctions in the Caste-System. The original race-feeling or the contrast which the *Ārya varṇa* (Vedic Aryans) felt between themselves and the *Dasyu-varṇa* (aborigines), and which was sought to be mitigated by the incorporation of the conquered population into the framework of Aryan society by admitting them into the fourth class or caste, left its mark in the shape of the rule of hypergamy, whereby an Aryan could marry a Śūdra wife but the Śūdra never an Aryan wife. The same rule was also gradually applied in marriages between the three Aryan classes, and while a Brāhmaṇa would normally marry a Kshatriya or a Vaiśya girl, and the Kshatriya, a Vaiśya girl, the male of a lower class could not ordinarily marry a girl of a higher class. This peculiar feeling as to mixed marriages is fundamental to all caste-divisions, and may be looked upon as the third factor in caste-elaboration during this age.

As has been noted in Chapter XIX (p. 400), it was the third caste-group, that of the Vaiśyas (called also *viś* or *viśya*), which by virtue of its occupations came into the closest touch with the fourth caste-group, that of the Śūdras. The latter was continually receiving accretions from the conquered aboriginal population and could not therefore keep up its cultural purity to the Aryan level. There arose, therefore, the necessity of clearly distinguishing the Aryan Vaiśya from the Śūdra who was a doubtful Aryan. An evidence of this precaution is seen in the variants of caste-names for the last two groups, namely as *Ārya* and *Śūdra*, found in some passages in the *Taittirīya, Kāṭhaka, Vājasaneyi*, and *Atharvaveda Saṁhitās*.

Along with their functions and duties, the privileges and status of the four castes were being differentiated minutely in the religious and social spheres. The *Śatapatha Brāhmaṇa* prescribes varying sizes of funeral mounds for the four castes. The deities to whom victims of the different castes are offered in the Purushamedha are different. Different degrees of politeness are noticed in the modes of address prescribed for the four castes.

The Śūdra class was naturally the hardest hit in these invidious distinctions, but the texts are not consistent in the position they assign to it. If, for example, the *Śatapatha* (III. 1. 1. 10) says that a Śūdra is not worthy of being addressed by a consecrated person, the stories of Satyakāma Jābāla and Jānaśruti in the Upanishads show that the teaching of philosophy was not withheld from him. The Śūdra cannot milk the cow for the Agnihotra-milk according to the *Kāṭhaka Saṁhitā* (XXXI. 2), but the *Śatapatha Brāhmaṇa* (V. 5. 4. 9) gives the Śūdra a place in the Soma sacrifice, and the *Taittirīya Brāhmaṇa* prescribes formulae for establishing the sacrificial fire for the *rathakāra* also who was counted a Śūdra. The *Aitareya Brāhmaṇa,* however, lays down the most reactionary doctrine. It describes the Śūdra as *yathā-kāma-vadhya* (fit to be beaten with impunity), who could be expelled at will and who is always the servant of another. It is also declared that the Śūdra has no rights of property as against the *rājanya*, especially the king. How far these extreme views were actually followed in practice it is difficult to say.

The Vaiśya class (*Viś*) was engaged in agriculture, pastoral pursuits, industry, and trade, and paid tribute to the king and the nobles, in return for the protection given to them. A late passage (VII. 29. 3) in the *Aitareya Brāhmaṇa* gives rather a low estimate of him with reference to the Kshatriya, when it says that "he is to be lived on by another and to be oppressed at will." Although things might not have been really so bad as this, there is no doubt that the position of the Vaiśya was steadily deteriorating in this age.

The Kshatriya class was composed of the king's relations, his nobility, his retainers and other chiefs of petty states. They fought for the protection of the country and maintained peace. They received revenue in kind from the people or masses (the Vaiśyas mainly) during war. For their normal or peace-time subsistence some of them were probably granted villages, because the Grāmaṇī seems to have been more often a nominee of the king rather than a popularly elected officer, and probably the post was hereditary in such cases. Others had their lands cultivated by tenants. In war, they were helped by the people, who fought alongside them.

While it is generally recognized that the Brāhmaṇa and the Kshatriya have undoubted precedence over the Vaiśya and Śūdra, there is not the same unanimity in respect of the relative position of the first two.[1] The more common view is that the Brāhmaṇa is superior to the king, as recorded in the *Vājasaneyi Saṁhitā* (XXI. 21) and the *Śatapatha, Aitareya* and *Pañchaviṁśa Brāhmaṇas.* The Brāhmaṇa is dependent on the king (*Śatapatha Br.* I. 2. 3. 3) and takes a lower seat by his side, but is superior to the king. A Kshatriya can never get along without a Brāhmaṇa while a Brāhmaṇa can; nay, the power of the Kshatriya is derived from the Brāhmaṇa (*Śatapatha Br.* IV. 1. 4. 6; XII. 7. 3. 12). On the other hand, the *Kāṭhaka Saṁhitā* (XXVIII. 5) says that the Kshatriya is superior to the Brāhmaṇa, while the *Aitareya Br.* (VII. 29) rates the Brāhmaṇa rather low, describing him as a receiver (of gifts), a drinker (of Soma) and as liable to be removed at will (by the king). Though this is not the common view of this age it explains some facts very satisfactorily; the fact, for example, that many kings were seers of hymns and sacrificers, and some of them were even instructors of Brāhmaṇas in the Brahmanical lore.

Brāhmaṇas are contrasted with the members of the three other castes as the privileged eaters of the oblation. According to some scholars the Brāhmaṇas were divided into two classes—the Purohitas of the kings, who guided their employers by their counsel, and the ordinary village priests, who led quiet lives.[2] In the view of the present writer these were not separate classes as such. Any one of the ordinary priests could come into contact with the king when they were engaged in some great festival and could be selected for the post of Purohita, if found pre-eminent and distinguished for his learning. The post remained hereditary, only if the son was as well qualified as the father. Imprecations against royal oppressors of Brāhmaṇas in the *Atharvaveda* and the statement therein that kings that persecute the Brāhmaṇas do not prosper, suggest on the one hand that the persecution of Brāhmaṇas was not unknown, and on the other, the gradual consolidation of the prestige of the priesthood. Even though a passage in the *Aitareya Br.* (VII. 29. 4) exalts the Rājanya above the Brāhmaṇa whom (it says) the former can control, the references to the *viśaḥ* only, as the subjects of the king (*Tāṇḍya Brāhmaṇa*), suggest that the Brāhmaṇa class received preferential treatment and enjoyed certain privileges and exemptions denied to the other caste-groups. The greed and cunning of the Brāhmaṇas and many prerogatives claimed by them are reflected in the *Atharvaveda* and other texts (ante, pp. 412, 422), but they may not be a true picture of the class as a whole. There can be hardly any doubt that many of them deserved the highest position in society by their character and intellect.

The most glaring evil of the caste-system, namely the doctrine of the impurity communicated by the touch or contact of lower castes (known as "untouchability" today), had not yet reared its ugly head. Restrictions on inter-dining are known, but not on the basis of caste. Great importance is attached to purity of descent in the Saṁhitās and Brāhmaṇas, but there are instances of Brāhmaṇas of impure descent such as Kavasha, Vatsa, and Satyakāma Jābāla. On the whole it is quite clear that caste had not yet become a rigid system, and none of the three factors which definitely characterize it today, viz., prohibition of inter-dining and inter-marriage, and determination by hereditary descent, was yet established on a secure basis.

3. *Marriage and the Position of Women*

There are evidences that marriage did not normally take place before puberty. As regards restrictions on marriage, it was banned within the circle of agnates and cognates, but the *Śatapatha Brāhmaṇa* (I. 8. 3. 6) allows marriages within the third or fourth degree on either side. Though marriage within the *gotra* was not explicitly prohibited, marriage outside the *gotra* must have been more frequent. Brothers and sisters were not to marry before their elders; so the order of birth was generally respected. The re-marriage of a widow was allowed, as seen from the *Atharvaveda* IX. 5, 27, 28. Polygamy undoubtedly prevailed. The *Maitrāyaṇī Saṁhitā* mentions the ten wives of Manu. The king has four wives, the *mahishī* (the official or chief wife), the favourite one (*vāvātā*), the *parivṛktī* or the neglected one (owing to the absence of a son?), and the *pālāgalī* (daughter of a court official?). The instances of Kavasha and Vatsa, as well as that of Jānaśruti in the *Chhāndogya Upanishad*, who offers his daughter in marriage to a Brāhmaṇa, indicate that hypergamy was permitted during this period. The wife wedded first must necessarily have claimed all the privileges of a wife in the religious and social life of the couple, but the two wives of Yājñavalkya were apparently on a footing of equality. The verses from the *Atharvaveda* quoted above (p. 412) indicate the prevalence of polyandry. Conjugal morality generally stood on a high level, but the infidelity of the wife was certainly not unknown. The ritual of the Varuṇapraghāsa (in the *Maitrāyaṇī Saṁhitā* and the *Śatapatha* and the *Taittirīya Brāhmaṇas)*, in which the wife of the sacrificer is questioned as regards her lovers, is evidently a rite to expiate unchastity (even platonic or purely mental) on the part of the wife. The son of a *Kumārīputra* (son of a maiden) is mentioned in the *Vājasaneyi Saṁhitā* which refers also to illicit unions of Śūdras and Āryas, both male and female. But all these may be looked upon rather as exceptions that prove the rule of a high standard of ordinary sexual morality. The metronymics in the lists of teachers in the *Bṛihadāraṇyaka Upanishad* may be explained as the relic of an ancient sociological feature rather than as evidence of recognized immorality. After all the society is human, and while we should not entertain highly exaggerated notions of unfailing chastity during the age, disproportionate importance need not be attached to isolated cases, or peculiar and exceptional customs and institutions.

The sale of a daughter was known, but viewed with disfavour. Dowries were generally given. The various types of marriage detailed in the later law books had not been formulated as yet. The story of Chyavana in the *Jaiminīya Brāhmaṇa* is an instance of the gift of a maiden for services rendered. The elements of the marriage ceremony described in the marriage-hymn of the *Ṛigveda* are reproduced without much change in the corresponding *Atharvaveda*-hymn, which adds only one important feature, which later became essential, namely the bridegroom causing the bride to mount a stone before grasping her hand. The poetic picture of an ideal family life in which the newly-wedded wife becomes the mistress of her husband's home, as depicted in the *Ṛigveda*, holds true for the texts of this period also, and this ideal was possibly often realized. The term *patnī* regularly applied to the wife in the Brāhmaṇas is indicative of her equal share in the social and religious side of the husband's life, while the term *jāyā* refers only to her conjugal position. Gradually, however, she lost this important position, as a priest was more and more employed to offer the oblations in certain ceremonies instead of the wife. This deterioration of her status and dignity went so far as to result in woman being classed with dice and wine, as one of the three chief evils (*Maitrāyaṇī Saṁhitā*, III. 6. 3). On the whole, judging from references in the *Taittirīya* (VI. 5. 8. 2) and the *Kāṭhaka Saṁhitās*, it appears clearly that woman, who held a high position in the age of the *Ṛigveda Saṁhitā*, had fallen on evil days in this age (*ante*, Ch. XX, p. 424).

It is true that sometimes high praise is showered on her in the texts of this period. Thus it is said that she is half her husband and completes him (*Śatapatha Br.* V. 2. 1. 10). But in spite of this praise she is not allowed to take part in political life, by attending the assembly like men. According to the *Aitareya Brāhmaṇa* (III. 24. 7), a good woman is one who does not talk back. In the *Śatapatha*, there is actually the rule that the wife should dine after her husband. The relative position of the two sexes is reflected in the keen desire for male progeny. This may be regarded as natural in a patriarchal society where relationship was recognized through the father. But this natural predilection exceeds all bounds of propriety or morality when we read in the *Aitareya Brāhmaṇa* (VII. 15) that a daughter is a source of misery and a son alone can be the saviour of the family. The *Atharvaveda* (VI. 11. 3) also deplores the birth of daughters.

The *Atharvaveda* (XVIII. 3. 1) merely refers to the ancient practice of *satī* (window-burning) and the *Ṛigveda* does not countenance it. So it appears that this custom was not very prevalent during the Vedic age. The Vedic texts also tacitly admit the non-existence of the custom, by discussing the question of widow re-marriage, which is permitted by some texts and prohibited by others.

4. *Education*

With the development and elaboration of the institution of the sacrifice and the growth of a vast literature connected with it, the problem of the preservation of this literature became very acute, particularly because during the age under discussion the whole of it (the *Saṁhitās* and *Brāhmaṇas*, including the *Āraṇyakas* and *Upanishads* appended to them) was looked upon as *Śruti* or revealed literature. The Vedic literature must therefore have formed the chief subject of instruction and the vital part of education. Naturally, then, the process of imparting the knowledge of the sacred hymnology and sacrificial ritual must have become more and more systematized during this age. Literary education was transmitted only orally, i.e. by word of mouth from teacher to pupil. We find an echo of this system in the famous frog-hymn of the *Ṛigveda*, quoted above (*ante*, p. 349). The art of writing was very probably known to the Vedic Indians,[3] but that it played no part in the educational system of ancient India is accepted by all.

The *Atharvaveda* (XI. 5) refers to a *brahmachārin* (Vedic student) gathering sacred fuel for fire-worship and bringing alms (begged from door to door) to the teacher. There are also prayers in the *AV* for liturgical employment at the ceremony of Initiation (*Upanayana*). *Svādhyāya* or the daily portion or lesson of Vedic study is referred to in the *Saṁhitās* of the *Yajurveda*. In the *Kāṭhaka Saṁhitā*, a rite for the benefit of one who, though not a Brāhmaṇa, has recited or studied the *vidyā*, is mentioned, and the well-known fact that Kshatriya kings like Janaka were not only keen students of the Vedas, but also great philosophers renders it almost certain that members of the Kshatriya and Vaiśya castes received the sacrament of the *Upanayana* and went through part (at least) of the period of studentship, although normally the Kshatriya would study the art of war. Vedic study, service to the teacher, and chastity were the principal duties of a *brahmachārin*. The fairly detailed description of the *Upanayana* as a sacrament (*saṁskāra*) in the *Śatapatha Br.* (XI. 3. 3. 1-7) includes all the essential features of the same sacrament and life of studentship which are treated at length in the Gṛihya-sūtras, such as: (1) The formal acceptance of the pupil by the teacher at the request of the former; (2) the entrusting of the pupil to the care of certain deities; (3) the vows and duties to be discharged by the pupil while residing at the house of the *guru*, such as: putting fuel on the fire, sipping water, and begging alms; (4) the dress of the pupil consisting of the *ajina*, the girdle, etc. The description of young Āṅgirasa teaching his elders, in the *Tāṇḍya Br.* (XIII. 3. 23-4), and the stories of Nābhānedishṭha and Bhāradvāja in the *Aitareya* and *Taittirīya Brāhmaṇas*, give us a vivid picture of the educational system of those days, with its insistence on truthfulness, observance of duty (*dharma*), devotion to the *āchārya* or *guru* (preceptor) and to one's parents, hospitality, faith, and generosity. The *Taittirīya Āraṇyaka* even anticipates some minute directions of the type given in the Gṛihya-sūtras, such as: the pupil should not run while it is raining, nor urinate in water, nor bathe naked, etc.

Women probably took part in the intellectual life of the society, but we have no such definite reference in the later *Saṁhitā* and *Brāhmaṇa* texts as we get in the Upanishads. From the *Taittirīya*

Saṁhitā (VI. 1. 6. 5), the *Maitrāyaṇī Saṁhitā* (III. 7. 3) and the *Śatapatha Br.*, we know that women were taught to dance and to sing, which appear to be recognized feminine accomplishments.

Among subjects of study figured arithmetic, grammar, and prosody (*Tāṇḍya Br.*). Language was obviously an important subject of study, since Northerners are mentioned as experts in language and grammar.

There was then no system of state education. The Brāhmaṇa teachers taught students of the three higher castes at their houses, giving them free board and lodging. In return, the pupils served the teacher and gave him fees (*guru-dakshiṇā*). That the education in this Home University was not merely literary, but also included physical and moral training, is seen from the hard daily routine of the pupil and the code of moral conduct prescribed for him, while residing with the teacher.

The existence of Vedic schools in this age, that is, even before the establishment of Sūtra-*charaṇas,* is clear evidence that even in these early times, centres of Vedic learning presided over by a celebrated Vedic teacher were scattered all over the country. The Sāmaveda Sūtras refer to Brāhmaṇa-*charaṇas* (schools) and as many as fifteen *charaṇas* of the Vājasaneyins are known, including the Kāṇva and Mādhyaṁdina ones that have survived. The only Saṁhitā-*charaṇas* known are those of the Bāshkalas and Śākalas for the *Ṛigveda Saṁhitā.* The separate Saṁhitā-and Brāhmaṇa-*charaṇas* originated owing to a difference in the texts of the Saṁhitās and Brāhmaṇas respectively. Whatever we might think of Max Müller's theory of the origin of Saṁhitā- and Brāhmaṇa-*charaṇas,* it is important to note that numerous Vedic schools existed all over the country. The example of the assembly of the learned in the court of Janaka shows that debates (philosophical and literary) were often held under royal auspices.

5. *Amusements and Entertainments*

Music, both vocal and instrumental, and dancing continue to be among the amusements of this age.[4] The *Sāmaveda* is a standing monument to the wonderful skill and originality of the ancients in the science of vocal music. Several professional musicians are known, and the variety of instrumental music in vogue can be inferred from the types of musicians enumerated, such as lute-players. flute-players, conch-blowers, drummers, etc. Among the musical instruments known are the *āghāṭi* (cymbal) to accompany dancing (*RV* and *AV*), drums. flutes, and lutes of various types. and the harp or lyre with a hundred strings (*vāṇa*). Many other instruments, of which we cannot form an exact idea, are also named.

The Śailūsha, included in the list of victims at the Purushamedha in the *Vājasaneyi Saṁhitā*, probably means an "actor" or "dancer." There is a theory that a precursor of the later classical drama existed in this period, support being lent to this view by the supposed reference to the Naṭa-sūtras in Pāṇini.

How deeply racing (especially chariot-racing) had entered into the popular scheme of entertainment is seen from its ritual transformation into a ceremony which, by sympathetic magic, secures the success of the sacrificer. The essential part of the Vājapeya ceremony is a chariot-race, in which the sacrificer is made victorious. Horse-racing was a favourite amusement. A semi-circular course and prizes for such a race are mentioned in the *Atharvaveda*. A formal race is also a feature of the Rājasūya ritual. Dicing was another popular amusement. The number of dice, the method of dice-playing, and the names of the throws are all described in detail in the various texts of this period. A ritual game of dice is played at the Agnyādheya and the Rājasūya ceremonies. So gambling is probably sought to be restricted by elevating racing and dicing to the rank of religious ceremonies. It is interesting to note that a *vaṁśa-nartin*, "pole-dancer" or "acrobat," is mentioned in the *Yajurveda*.

6. *Food and Drink*

Various eatables are mentioned in the texts of this period. The *apūpa* is a cake mixed with *ghī* (clarified butter) or made of rice or barley; *odana* is a mess, generally of grain cooked with milk. Special varieties are those made with water, milk, curds or *ghī*, and beans, sesame or meat, and named appropriately, such as "*tilaudana*," etc. A porridge made of grain, barley or sesame unhusked, slightly parched and kneaded, is called *Karambha*. Rice cooked with milk and with beans is mentioned in the *Śatapatha Brāhmaṇa* and the *Vājasaneyi Saṁhitā*. Fried grains of rice were known. Barley-gruel (*yavāgū*) and decoctions of other grains are also referred to.

Meat-eating seems to be fairly common, as in the Rigvedic age. The *Śatapatha Brāhmaṇa* prescribes the killing of a great ox or goat in honour of a guest. Generally meat was eaten on the occasion of some ceremony or other, but such ceremonies were performed almost every day. Its use is forbidden during the observance of a vow. It appears that the killing of cows gradually came into disfavour. "The normal meat-diet consisted of the flesh of the sheep, the goat and the ox, the usual sacrificial victims. What man ate, he offered to the gods.

Among the chief products of milk may be mentioned clotted curds (*āmikshā*), sour milk (*dadhi*), fresh butter (*nava-nīta*), *payasyā* or curds consisting of a mixture of sour milk and hot or cold fresh milk, butter, mixed with sour milk (*prishad-ājya*), *phāṇṭa*, creamy butter or the first clotted lumps produced by churning, and finally *vājina*, a mixture of hot fresh milk with sour milk. This formidable list of milk-products and their mixtures shows the great popularity of milk as a drink.

Surā, an intoxicating spirituous liquor already known in the Rigvedic age, is often mentioned. Though tolerated as an ordinary drink (the drink of the people in the *sabhā*), it is often condemned as leading to quarrels and as seducing men from the path of virtue like dicing and meat-eating (*AV*, VI. 70. 1). The Sautrāmaṇī sacrifice is of the nature of an expiation or penance for an indulgence in *surā*. The method of its preparation cannot be ascertained. Probably it was prepared from fermented grains and plants. It was kept in skins. The *Yajurveda Saṁhitās* mention a beverage called *māsara*, which appears to have been a mixture of rice and *śyāmāka* with grass and parched barley, etc. *Madhu* primarily means "sweet" as an adjective, and so denotes any sweet food or drink such as the Soma or milk. The sense "honey," though known in the *Ṛigveda*, is only now its most definite sense, and there are taboos against its use by students and women under certain circumstances.

Already in the Brāhmaṇa period, the real Soma plant was difficult to obtain, and so substitutes were being allowed. For example, the *Pañchaviṁśa Brāhmaṇa* (IX. 5. 3) suggests that if *pūtikā*, a substitute for the Soma, cannot be procured, *arjunāni* may be used as a substitute for the Soma. In the *Yajurveda*, the plant is ceremoniously purchased before it is pressed. The plant was sometimes subjected to the technical process of *āpyāyana* (causing to swell) by being steeped in water, thus increasing its yield of juice. These few details, culled from the texts of our period, supplement the almost exhaustive description of the preparation of the Soma which can be gathered from the *Ṛigveda* (*ante*, p. 378).

7. *Dress and Decoration*

Ūrṇā-sūtra (woollen thread) is repeatedly mentioned in the later Saṁhitās and Brāhmaṇas, but *ūrṇā* denoted not merely sheep's wool but probably goat's hair also. Clothes were generally woven of sheep's wool. The fondness of the Vedic people for ornamental or embroidered garments was as keen as in later periods. The dress in this period seems to have consisted of three garments—an under-garment (*nīvi*), a garment proper (*vāsas*), and an over-garment (*adhi-vāsas*), like a mantle or cloak. The *Śatapatha Brāhmaṇa* describes the set of sacrificial garments as consisting of a silk under-garment (*tārpya*), a garment of undyed wool, an over-garment and a turban (*ushṇīsha*). The turban was worn by men as well as by women. A royal head-gear or turban is worn at the Rājasūya and Vājapeya ceremonies by the king. The turban of the Vrātya is referred to. The "sandal" or "shoe" was made of boar-skin (*Śatapatha Br.*). The combination of *dāṇḍopānaha* ("staff and sandals") is mentioned in the *Kaushītaki Brāhmaṇa*. Skins were used as clothing. The frequent use of the variant terms for "warp" and "woof" shows the great development of the art of weaving garments.

The *pra-ghāta* or closely woven ends of a cloth to which is attached the trimming, fringe, or border of a garment (*daśā*) is mentioned. The *Śāṅkhāyana Āraṇyaka* (XI. 4) refers to a garment of (dyed with?) saffron. But uncoloured woollen garments are also mentioned (*Śatapatha Br.*). From the manner of wearing the sacred thread outside, can be inferred the manner of wearing the over-garment which probably passed over the left shoulder and under the right arm. The *Śatapatha Brāhmaṇa* (XI. 5. 1. 1) has an interesting legend to explain why man alone wears clothes. So none but the ascetics could go naked.

The *Taittirīya Brāhmaṇa* mentions an article called *Sthāgara*, probably an ornament made of a fragrant substance. *Śalalī*, the quill of the porcupine, is used now for parting the hair and anointing the eyes. The *Śaṅkha* or conch-shell is used as an amulet (*AV.*). The late *Shaḍviṁśa Brāhmaṇa* (V. 6) mentions the pearl (*Vi-muktā*). A jewel (*maṇi*) strung on a thread was worn round the neck as an amulet. The *prā-kāśa*, an ornament of metal or a metal mirror, is often mentioned in the Brāhmaṇas. The *pra-varta* in the *Atharvaveda* (XV. 2. 5, 9, etc.) probably means an ear-ring. A *nishka* of silver (an ornament worn round the neck) as worn by the Vrātyas is mentioned in the *Pañchaviṁśa Brāhmaṇa*.

8. *Knowledge of Medicine*

The inclusion of a physician in the list of victims at the Purushamedha in the *Vājasaneyi Saṁhitā* (XXX. 10) and *Taittirīya Brāhmaṇa* (III. 4. 4. 1) shows that the profession of the physician had already become well established. But whereas the profession was held in high esteem in the *Ṛigveda*—the Aśvins being called "physicians"—a dislike for it seems to have developed in this age, because in some Saṁhitā and Brāhmaṇa texts of the *Yajurveda*, the Aśvins are looked down upon because as physicians they have to mix too freely with men. From the *Atharvaveda* one can say that although their treatment of diseases is somewhat primitive, consisting as it does of the use of herbs in combination with spells and of water—remedies Indo-European in character—their knowledge of pathology is anything but elementary. The *Atharvaveda* enumerates quite a large variety of diseases and the demons supposed to cause them. *Takman* (a kind of fever) is the subject of five hymns of the *Atharvaveda* and is also often mentioned elsewhere. But it is in the *Atharvaveda* that its symptoms are described in detail (*ante*, p. 418). Consumption, scrofula, dysentery, boils, swellings, convulsions, ulcers, rheumatism, headache, jaundice, cramps, eye-diseases, senility, fractures and wounds, bites of snakes and other harmful insects, poison in general, lunacy, and leprosy are the diseases mentioned in the *Atharvaveda.* The use of sandbags to stop bleeding is interesting. The practice of dissecting animals at the sacrifice was a great help to the knowledge of anatomy which was developed to an appreciable extent. Finally may be noted an interesting remark in the *Śāṅkhāyana Brāhmaṇa* (V. I) that "sickness is particularly prevalent at the junction of the seasons"—a very accurate observation indeed.

2. ECONOMIC CONDITION

1. *Agriculture and Cattle*

According to various texts, such as the *Atharvaveda, Vājasaneyi, Maitrāyaṇī, Taittirīya,* and *Kāṭhaka Saṁhitās,* and the *Taittirīya* and the *Śatapatha Brāhmaṇas,* six, eight, twelve, and even twenty-four oxen were used to drag the plough which must have been large and heavy. The oxen were yoked and harnessed with traces and guided by the goad of the ploughman. The furrow (*sītā*) is often mentioned. The value of the natural manure of animals in the field was very much appreciated (*AV*). Dung (*śakṛit*) and dry cow-dung (*karīsha*) are often mentioned. The plough is described as having a smooth handle, well-lying and lance-pointed (*pavīravat*). There is a special name *kīnāśa* for the ploughman or cultivator of the soil. The *Atharvaveda* gives the credit of introducing the art of ploughing to Pṛithī Vainya, but ploughing is constantly referred to in the texts of this period as practised by the Vedic Aryans, the Vrātyas who were outside the pale of the Vedic religion being described as not cultivating the soil. The *Śatapatha Br.* enumerates the various operations of agriculture, as "ploughing,. sowing, reaping, and threshing." The ripe grain was cut with a sickle. From the *Taittirīya Saṁhitā* and other texts we gather that *yava* (meaning "barley" now) sown in winter was harvested in summer, that rice sown in the rains ripened in autumn, and that beans and sesamum planted at the time of the summer rains ripened in winter. Wheat was known and is distinguished from rice (*vrīhi*) and barley. Groats (*saktavaḥ*) made of wheat-grain are mentioned. Cultivation suffered from the usual pests—the moles that destroyed the seed and the other creatures that harmed the tender shoots. Evidently to prevent these and similar evils the cultivators used charms at the time of both sowing seed and gathering corn (*ante*, p. 416). Similar other spells in the *Atharvaveda* to avert drought and excess of rains show that these inevitable mishaps threatened agriculture then (as now) in spite of some sort of a system of irrigation that sought to minimize its evil effects.

Draft-oxen were generally castrated. Female draft-cattle also were used. A four-year-old ox or cow (*turyavāh*) is mentioned in the *Taittirīya, Maitrāyaṇī,* and *Vājasaneyī Saṁhitās.* The milch-cow (*dhenu*) is contrasted with the bull, and there are special terms for cows, oxen, and calves of different ages, for cows barren or otherwise and in various stages of growth and motherhood, as well as for a cow with a calf substituted for one of her own which had died.

A fairly long hymn in the *Atharvaveda* shows the reverence inspired by the cow, and the death penalty prescribed for cow-killing outside the sacrificial enclosure tells the same tale. Pasture-lands were carefully looked after, and large sheds or stalls were erected for accommodating cattle. On the whole, the cows were taken extremely good care of. The origin of the sanctity of the cow lay in the inestimable value of the cow for purposes other than eating, and the occasional mythological identification of the cow with the earth or Aditi helped the process which culminated in the full-fledged deification of the cow in later times.

2. *Trade and Commerce*

Rich Vaiśyas (*śreshṭhins*), who had acquired wealth in trade or agriculture, and who were probably the headmen of guilds, are often referred to. That money-lending was a flourishing business is indicated in various ways. *Kusīdin* is a designation of the usurer in the *Śatapatha Br.*, and *Kusīda* has the sense of a "loan" in the *Taittirīya Saṁhitā.* The rate of interest is not specified. No regular system of currency or coinage appears to have been introduced yet, as no coins definitely belonging to this period have been unearthed and no specific and undoubted reference to coins occurs in the literature of the period. The *māna* is a measure of weight equivalent to the *Kṛishṇala* (i.e. the berry of the *guñjā*) which was a unit of weight. The *śatamāna,* a piece of gold equivalent in weight to a hundred *Kṛishṇalas,* must have been in use as currency among the merchants. The *nishka* also had become by now a unit of value in addition to the old-time unit, the cow. The profession of the merchant was often hereditary, as the term *vāṇija* ("son of a *vaṇij*") in the sense of a merchant shows. The haggling of the market, already known in the Rigvedic age, had now become such a pronounced feature of commerce that a whole hymn of the *Atharvaveda* (III. 15) aims at procuring success in trade through clever bargaining. Garments, coverlets, and goat-skins are among the articles of commerce and market commodities (*AV*).

The sea was undoubtedly known and there was probably some amount of sea-borne trade. In the texts of this period, *samudra* is frequently used in the definite sense of the "sea." The *Aitareya Brāhmaṇa* speaks of the "inexhaustible sea" (V. 16. 7) and "the sea as encircling the earth." The eastern and western oceans (mentioned in the *Śatapatha Brāhmaṇa)* are probably references to the Indian Ocean and the Arabian Sea.

3. *Occupations and Industries*

The principal occupations and professions and the various arts and crafts were distributed among, and assigned to, the various groups of people in accordance with the scheme of the caste-system, which had by now taken root in Vedic society and was being elaborated and complicated by the rise of mixed castes. For example, agricultural and pastoral pursuits were mainly in the hands of the Vaiśyas. The professions of teaching and officiating as priests at the sacrifices (Śrauta or Gṛihya) were confined to the Brāhmaṇas. The fighting profession was mainly the monopoly of the Rājanya or Kshatriya class. Service of all kinds—menial or otherwise—fell to the lot of the fourth class—that of the Śūdras. This is but a rough distribution, and the division was not rigidly adhered to, a member of one caste not rarely following the occupation of another.

Although hunting did not form the chief source of livelihood of any particular class, it was practised for procuring sustenance and for the protection of herds and flocks from wild beasts; and it was also occasionally indulged in as a pastime and sport, chiefly by members of the Rājanya class, as in the Rigvedic age (*ante*, p. 401). Among the victims at the Purusha-medha are found many curious technical names of persons maintaining themselves on hunting and fishing. Birds were caught in nets (*jāla*) and the net was fastened on pegs (*AV*, X. 1. 30; VIII. 8. 5).

Fortunately a very comprehensive list of the professions, occupations, arts, crafts, and industries of this period is to be found in the list of victims at the Purusha-medha as given in the *Vājasaneyi Saṁhitā* (XXX) and the *Taittirīya Brāhmaṇa* (III. 4). The *anu-Kshattṛi*, a special type of attendant on the doorkeeper or on the charioteer, the *anu-chara*, an attendant in general, a drummer, a worker in thorns cut up and used to plait mats, a smith, a ploughman, an astrologer, a cow-killer (or butcher?), a herdsman, a maker of bow-strings, a carpenter, a gatherer of wood, a fire-watcher (*dāva-pa*), a hand-clapper, who presumably scared away birds from the fields by making a noise, a female embroiderer or a basket-maker, a jeweller, the yoker and unyoker of horses, the maker of *surā*, an elephant-keeper and a worker in gold—all these figure in the list of victims in the Purushamedha. In the other texts of this age are mentioned a few additional callings, viz., a ferryman or poleman, a washerman (*mala-ga*), a menial (*purusha*), a potter, a usurer or money-lender, a blower, a barber, a boat-propeller, a cook, a messenger, and a footman running by the side of a chariot. To this multiplicity of occupations must be added the arts and crafts mentioned in Chapter XIX, as there was no appreciable break in the economic life of the Vedic Aryans from the age of the *Ṛigveda Saṁhitā* down to the age of the *Brāhmaṇas*, save that there was a more extensive knowledge and use of different kinds of metals.

4. *House-Building and Means of Transport*

The "House" (*harmya*) was large enough to contain not only a large family, but also pens for cattle and sheep, and evidently had many rooms with a special place for the Gārhapatya fire which was kept continuously burning. The door with a fastener is often mentioned. Houses apparently were generally built of wood as in the Rigvedic period. The method of constructing them is not definitely known. Probably four pillars were erected, propped up by beams leaning against them at an angle. Ribs of bamboo-cane (*vāṁśa*), a ridge, and a net or thatched covering over the bamboo ribs probably made up the roof. Grass in bundles was used to fill in the walls which were finished with reed work. The *dhana-dhānī* ("treasure-house") mentioned in the *Taittirīya Āraṇyaka* (X. 67) probably indicates a special type of room or house. The *Atharvaveda* mentions *patnīnāṁ sadana* or a part of the house called women's quarters. A seat with a pillow or cushion or coverlet, a bed, and a couch are among the articles of furniture mentioned.

As regards means of transport, the draft wagon (*anas*) is distinguished from the chariot (*ratha*) used for war and sport. The axle-box of a conveyance is mentioned. Since the *Atharvaveda* (XV. 2. 1) mentions *vi-patha*, a rough vehicle used for bad tracks, it can be inferred that there were some well-made roads. The wagon was drawn by oxen generally, but riding of horses and elephants was in use. Ships and boats plying on rivers and seas were a popular mode of transport.

---

1. For a detailed discussion on the relation between the Brāhmaṇas and Kshatriyas in this age, cf. Ghoshal, *History of Hindu Political Theories*, pp. 44-52.
2. *Ved. Ind.*, II, p. 255; *CHI*, I, pp. 127-8.
3. Cf. the author's paper "The spoken words in Sanskrit Literature" (*BDCRI*, IV). Cf. also Dr. S. K. Chatterji's view (*ante*, p. 157). There is, however, a sharp difference of opinion on the antiquity of the art of writing in ancient India (*ante*, p. 395).
4. These three are referred to as the threefold *Śilpa* in the *Kaushītaki Brāhmaṇa*.

BOOK SEVEN

THE AGE OF THE UPANISHADS AND SŪTRAS

CHAPTER XXIV

LANGUAGE AND LITERATURE

I. THE UPANISHADS

THE word *upanishad* is derived from the root "*upa-ni-sad*" which means "to sit down near some one." This no doubt refers to the pupil's sitting down near his teacher at the time of instruction. The prefix "*upa*" may also be taken to connote the pupil's "approaching" the teacher to request him to impart his doctrine. The word in course of time gathered round it the sense of secret communication or doctrine which was imparted at such sittings. Later on the word also came to be applied to the texts which incorporated such doctrines.

The number of treatises called Upanishads is quite large, but some of them are not quite as old as the others. The oldest Upanishads are partly included in the Āraṇyakas or the "forest texts" and partly appended to them. As a branch of Vedic literature even these texts are regarded as "breathed out" by Brahman and only "visioned" by the Vedic seers. The Upanishads are usually called Vedānta, or "the end of the Veda," not only because they came at the end of the Vedic period, or that they were taught at the end of Vedic instruction, but also because the later philosophers found in them the final aim of the Veda.[1]

As noted above (Ch. XX, p. 424), some of the Upanishadic texts in fact form the component parts of the Brāhmaṇas. These are the *Aitareya Upanishad*, the *Kaushītaki Upanishad*, the *Taittirīya Upanishad*, the *Mahānārāyaṇa Upanishad*, the *Bṛihadāraṇyaka Upanishad*, the *Chhāndogya Upanishad*, and the *Kena Upanishad*. All these Upanishads, with the exception of only the *Mahānārāyaṇa Upanishad*, belong to the earliest stage in the development of these texts. They are very much akin to the prose of the Brāhmaṇas and are certainly older than Buddha and Pāṇini.

The second category of the Upanishads represents a slightly later stage, but even these are pre-Buddhistic. They distinguish themselves from the first category in their form which is mostly or entirely metrical. Then, again, these texts have very often come down to us as independent texts. To this category belong the *Kaṭha*, the *Śvetāśvatara*, the *Mahānārāyaṇa*, the *Īśa*, the *Muṇḍaka* and the *Praśna Upanishads*. Though these texts also expound the Vedānta doctrine, they are not altogether free from Sāṁkhya and Yoga view-points.

The *Maitrāyaṇīya Upanishad* which is attributed to a school of the *Black Yajurveda* and the *Māṇḍukya Upanishad* of the *Atharva-*

veda belong to the post-Buddhistic period. Their language, style, and contents show a later origin, and the great philosopher Sankara does not mention them. But due to their connection with certain Vedic schools they may be styled, together with the twelve mentioned above, as Vedic Upanishads.

The remaining Upanishads which have come down to us either independently or in larger collections have very little connection with the Veda. Some of them contain very little that may be called philosophical, and some are more akin to the Purāṇas and the Tantras than to the Veda. According to their purpose and contents the non-Vedic Upanishads may be divided into six categories: (1) such as present Vedānta doctrines, (2) those which teach Yoga, (3) those extolling the ascetic life, (4) those which glorify Vishṇu as the highest deity, (5) those which give the same position to Śiva, and (6) the Upanishads of the Śāktas and other minor sects. Some of these, like the *Jābāla Upanishad* quoted by Śaṅkara, the *Paramahaṁsa Upanishad*, the *Subāla Upanishad* quoted by Rāmānuja, the *Garbha Upanishad*, the *Atharvaśiras Upanishad* already mentioned in the Dharma-sūtras as a sacred text, and the *Vajrasūchikā Upanishad* may perhaps belong to a greater antiquity than the rest. All these Upanishads are generally called the Upanishads of the *Atharvaveda*, perhaps because it was easier to refer them to that Veda, their connection with the other Vedas not being easily demonstrable, and because the *Atharvaveda* itself was shrouded in comparative obscurity and mystery. The total number of the Upanishads is very large, and one of the latest, the *Muktikā Upanishad*, enumerates 108 Upanishads classified according to the four Vedas.

The position of the Upanishads at the end of Vedic literature should by no means be taken to indicate that the intelligentsia of the period began to interest itself in philosophical speculations only when they got wearied of their earlier ritualistic activities. The Upanishads are in fact the legitimate development of that scepticism, the earliest traces of which are found even in the Rigvedic hymns. Though these treatises mark the culmination of the earlier line of investigation into the nature of the ultimate reality, yet, due to the nature of their subject matter and the genuine spirit in which the enquiry is carried on, they also constitute a beginning in this direction. The spirit of their contents being anti-ritualistic,[2] it may be quite legitimate to suppose that the earlier philosophical activity originated with those outside the pale of the priestly class.

It is also evident that the Kshatriyas took a leading part in this new line of enquiry. They had now secured a firm footing in the land by defeating the non-Aryans and, as noted above (Ch. XXI, p. 434), obtained a high status and pre-eminent position in society as ruling chiefs and high administrative officials. We can easily guess how the intelligent Kshatriyas with their restless mentality had grown jealous of the Brāhmaṇas and attempted to gain a tactical superiority over them by assigning a deeper significance and meaning to the very sacrificial rites which were elaborately developed by them as the principal element in their religion. That the early philosophical thoughts in the Vedic literature had their origin in the intelligent interpretation which was sought to be put on what might otherwise appear as meaningless Vedic ritual, is abundantly clear. The various discussions between the Kshatriyas and the Brāhmaṇas recorded in the Upanishads leave no reasonable doubt about it.

This supposition is completely borne out by the evidence we gather from the Vedic literature. The references in the Brāhmaṇa texts already inform us that the members of the warrior class had betaken themselves to enquire into the true significance of sacrifice. The story of king Janaka of Videha and the sage Yājñavalkya, which appears in the eleventh book of the *Śatapatha Brāhmaṇa,* is the most instructive in this respect. It shows no doubt the superiority of the warrior-intellect over the priestly one, at least in some isolated instances, but it also proves that even then the warriors as a class were regarded as intellectually inferior to the priestly class (who had as it were appropriated the monopoly of thinking), and as such were not always expected to interfere in intellectual matters. But when we come to the Upanishads we find that the members of the non-priestly class grew more and more inquisitive into the true nature of the world. Thus in the *Chhāndogya Upanishad* (IV. 1-3), Raikva, a "Brāhmaṇa" not by caste but by his knowledge, instructs king Janaśruti. The same Upanishad (IV. 4) shows Satyakāma Jābāla, of dubious descent, to be a worthy recipient of knowledge as he does not swerve from the truth. The king Pravāhaṇa instructs the Brāhmaṇa Gautama in the new doctrine of transmigration (*Chhāndogya,* V. 3, etc.). This story, together with the one in which king Aśvapati Kaikeya instructs five Brāhmaṇas in the doctrine of Ātman (*Chhāndogya,* V. 11. ff.), shows that these two doctrines which did not go well with Brahmanical theology were first conceived among the warrior class.

The principal contents of the Upanishads, at any rate of the more important among them, are philosophical speculations. The philosophers of the Upanishads are actively interested in an earnest enquiry into the ultimate truth that lies behind the world of creation.[3] They have variously expressed their findings in the identity of Brahman—that highest principle which manifests itself in the motley of creation and which receives all things back at the time of dissolution—and Ātman which is the individual self. This has been pointedly recorded in the famous dictum of identity *"Tat tvam asi,"* where *"tat,"* meaning "that," stands for Brahman, and through it the universe, and *"tvam,"* meaning "thou," for Ātman or the individual self.

To quote the words of an Upanishadic sage on the point:

"This my Ātman in my inmost heart is smaller than a grain of rice, or a barley corn, or a mustard seed, or a millet grain. ... This my Ātman in my inmost heart is greater than the earth, greater than the sky, greater than the heavens, greater than all spheres. In him are all actions, all wishes, all smells, all tastes; he holds this All enclosed within himself; he speaks not, he troubles about nothing;—this my Ātman in my inmost heart, is this Brahman. With him, when I depart out of this life, shall I be united. For him to whom this knowledge has come, for him, indeed, there exists no doubt. Thus spake Śāṇḍilya, yea, Śāṇḍilya."[4]

The famous story of Uddālaka Āruṇi and his son Śvetaketu shows us how in that period the learning of the Vedas, without learning that doctrine "by which that which is unheard becomes heard, unthought becomes thought, and unknown becomes known," was regarded as futile. This doctrine was expounded by the father to his son. We are told that originally only the Existent was here without a Second. It then developed into the material world by itself. With Ātman it penetrated into all beings, and therefore when a man dies he is united again with the Existent. As the juices collected by the bees lose consciousness of their diversity, similarly all the creatures when combined in the Existent lose consciousness of the multiplicity of their forms in the universe; just as from the invisible quintessence of the seed springs up the huge fig-tree, so also from the minute ultimate reality proceeds the diverse world; just as the salt dissolved in water cannot be seen and yet its presence can be felt by taste, similarly the Existent, though invisible, is present in the world and can be realized by the consciousness of *"tat tvam asi."*[5] The true nature of Ātman is explained in the *Chhāndogya Upanishad* not as the Purusha in the eye or in the reflected image, not as the spirit that roams in the dreams, not even as the soul in the dreamless and profound sleep, but as the immortal and intelligent spirit in man.[6]

The ethical doctrine of *Karman,* connected with the doctrine of transmigration, is beautifully developed in the *Bṛihadāraṇyaka Upanishad.* With pointed examples the doctrine is thus set forth:—

". . . Just as an embroidress undoes a small portion of a piece of embroidery, and out of it creates a different, quite new and more beautiful design, so man, when he has stripped off his body and has rid himself of non-knowledge, creates for himself a different, quite new and more beautiful form, that of the spirit of an ancestor or of a Gandharva, of a Brahman or of a Prajāpati, of a god or of a man, or that of that some other being.... As he has acted, as he has lived, so he becomes; he who has done good, is born again as a good one, he who has done evil, is born again as an evil one. He becomes good through good action, bad through bad action. Therefore it is said: 'Man here is formed entirely out of his desire, and according to his desire is his resolve, and according to his resolve he performs the action, and according to the performance of the action is his destiny.'"[7] The ethical basis of the Upanishadic doctrine as expressed in the simile "As water does not stick to the leaf of a lotus-flower, so evil action does not stick to him who knows this (that the Self is Brahman)" (*Chhāndogya*, IV. 14. 3) is not to be construed to mean that knower was given all laxity. The simile rather shows that the knower was regarded as inherently incapable of evil actions.

The spirit of sincerity permeates throughout these philosophical chapters in Indian literature. The knowers are as earnest in their search after truth as the ignorant are anxious to know what is beyond. Their eager quest is expressed in the *Bṛihadāraṇyaka*, I. 3. 28: "From the unreal lead me to the real. From darkness lead me to light. From death lead me to immortality." All distinctions of caste, social status and earthly power are set aside when the highest knowledge is to be sought. The story of Nachiketas who prefers the knowledge of the ultimate reality to the pleasures of long life, long progeny and immense wealth and power is the best illustration to the point.[8] Says he:—

> "Ephemeral things! That which is a mortal's, O End-maker,
> Even the vigour (*tejas*) of all the powers, they wear away.
> Even a whole life is slight indeed.
> ....
> ....
> —This, in truth, is the boon to be chosen by me ...
> This thing whereon they doubt, O Death:
> What there is in the great passing on—tell us that!"

This earnest desire to know the truth above all is quite in keeping with what was regarded as the highest object of life in those days, viz., seeking union with the Brahman. No work, however good, could help in effecting this union. The only means to achieve it was to realize the identity of the soul with the Brahman.[9] This growing indifference to the pleasures of the world and belittling them when compared to the supreme joy to be experienced in the unity with the Brahman, however, laid the foundation of the profound pessimism which pervades later Indian thought and literature.

The enormous power which these philosophical poems have exercised over the minds of Indians for centuries together is not so much due to the fact that they were regarded as divine revelation, but because "... these old thinkers wrestle so earnestly for the truth, because in their philosophical poems the eternally unsatisfied human yearning for knowledge has been expressed so fervently." The Upanishads do not contain "superhuman conceptions," but human, absolutely human attempts to come nearer to the truth—and it is this which makes them so valuable to us. As to the influence of the Upanishads on humanity at large we may do no better than quote the view of a distinguished European scholar:—

"For the historian, however, who pursues the history of human thought, the Upanishads have a yet far greater significance. From the mystical doctrines of the Upanishads one current of thought may be traced to the mysticism of the Persian Sufism, to the mystic-theosophical logos-doctrine of the Neo-Platonics and the Alexandrian Christians down to the teachings of the Christian mystics Eckhart and Tauler, and finally to the philosophy of the great German mystic of the nineteenth century, Schopenhauer."[10]

2. THE SŪTRAS

The word *sūtra,* by which a special class of literature is designated, originally means "a thread." Secondarily it denotes that type of literature which is made up of short sentences running through a topic like a thread. A *sūtra* has thus come to mean a short rule, in as few words as possible, giving a clue to the learning stored in a particular topic forming a part of a particular book. Both by their form and object the Sūtras form a class by themselves. The system of oral instruction which formed the basis of education in those days very probably necessitated this peculiar fashion of summarizing the entire exposition to help its easy memorizing. It is also not improbable that the intricacies of Vedic ritual, which were to be scrupulously observed in every small detail, contributed to a certain extent to the development of this form of literature. If, therefore, a non-initiate finds here clarity sacrificed at the altar of brevity, it is only natural. But the definition of a Sūtra clearly says that a Sūtra should be brief in form but at the same time unambiguous in its meaning (*svalpākshararn = asandigdham* . . .).

The class of literature which comes under this head does not form part of the Vedic literature, but is in close association with it. It is not the Veda, a divine revelation, but the Vedāṅga, "the limbs of the Veda," constituting works of human authorship. Though these Vedāṅgas include a number of exegetical sciences like Śikshā (phonetics), Kalpa (ritual), Vyākaraṇa (grammar), Nirukta (etymology), Chhandas (metrics), and Jyotisha (astronomy), all of them have not come down to us in the *sūtra* style. These six Vedāṅgas refer to the six subjects that help the proper understanding, recitation, and the sacrificial use of the Vedas. Taken as a whole, therefore, the Sūtra form of literature is post-Vedic, as is also shown by its language. In contents, however, they may be traced back to the period of the Brāhmaṇas which occasionally deal with etymology, grammar, and astronomy alongside the ritual. Though some of the exemplars of this literary activity are later in date, the period which typifies this aphoristic literature may be taken to be pre-Buddhistic.

1. *Śikshā*

The traditional list enumerating the six Vedāṅgas assigns the first place to Śikshā or the science of phonetics. The word originally means only "instruction," and then specially such instruction as is imparted for the correct pronunciation, accentuation, etc., of the Vedic texts. These works are therefore closely related to the Saṁhitā texts, but in a way they are related to the ritual also; for in the performance of a sacrifice the correct recitation of the *mantras* has as much importance as the correct order of the sacrificial acts themselves. The *Taittirīya Upanishad* (I. 2) mentions this Vedāṅga for the first time, and the Sūtra texts belonging to it are at least as old as the Kalpa-sūtras.

The oldest text-books dealing with this science are the Prātiśākhyas[11] which, as their name suggests, belonged to every *Śākhā* or recension of a Vedic Saṁhitā. Thus we have at present a *Ṛigveda Prātiśākhya* ascribed to Śaunaka, perhaps a later revision in verse form of an earlier Sūtra text, a *Taittirīya Prātiśākhya Sūtra*, a *Vājasaneyi Prātiśākhya Sūtra* ascribed to Kātyāyana, and an *Atharvaveda Prātiśākhya Sūtra*, supposed to belong to the school of the Śaunakas. The *Pañchavidha Sūtra* shows the manner in which the Sāmans are to be sung at the sacrifice, and the *Pushpa-sūtra*, a kind of Prātiśākhya, is meant for the Uttaragāna of the *Sāmaveda*. All these works instruct the students in the correct pronunciation, accent, euphonic changes which the sounds undergo in the composition of words, and such other topics as come under Vedic phonetics.

These texts are the earliest specimens, if we exclude the occasional excursions of the Brāhmaṇa texts in this field, of the activities of Indians in the science of linguistics. Moreover the rules with which they have fixed the manner of the Saṁhitā recitation have helped in the accurate preservation of these texts even to the detail of a syllable. We need not doubt that the *Ṛigveda-Saṁhitā*, as we find it in our printed editions of today, is in any way different from the one which Śaunaka learnt centuries ago from his teacher.

Of later origin and of much less importance are some short treatises on phonetics ascribed to such important persons as Bharadvāja, Vyāsa, Vasishṭha, and Yājñavalkya. The *Vyāsa-śikshā*, which is directly connected with the *Taittirīya Prātiśākhya*, is comparatively older than the other works of similar nature. The *Pāṇinīya śikshā* may be old in its contents though its present form is rather late.

Closely related to the Vedāṅga literature, though not actually forming part of it, are the Anukramaṇīs or "lists" or "catalogues." To Śaunaka are ascribed the catalogues of the *Ṛigveda* hymns as well as of their *Ṛishis*, their metre, and their deities. The *Sarvānukramaṇī* of Kātyāyana is a work in the Sūtra form giving for the *Ṛigveda* the first words of every hymn, the number of verses, the name and the family of the hymn's *Ṛishi*, the deities, and the metre. The *Bṛihaddevatā*, ascribed to Śaunaka, gives in a metrical form not only a catalogue of the gods worshipped in the different hymns of the *Ṛigveda*, but also myths and legends connected with these deities. The work on account of its antiquity, is therefore important from the point of view of the development of narrative literature in India. The *Ṛigvidhāna*, again ascribed to Śaunaka, gives in a form similar to that of the *Bṛihaddevatā* the magic power that one can obtain by reciting the hymns or the verses of the *Ṛigveda*.

2. *Kalpa*

The oldest Sūtra works are the Kalpa-sūtras which deal with the ritual and are thus directly connected with the Brāhmaṇas and the Āraṇyakas. According to the subject-matter dealt with they are divided into two branches, the Śrauta-sūtras and the Gṛihya-sūtras. The former deal with the great rites taught in the Brāhmaṇas and involving the services of a number of priests, whereas the latter teach the domestic sacrifices and other duties in the daily life of a householder. The former are so called as they are based on Śruti, but both the Gṛihya- and the Dharma-sūtras are called Smārta, as they are based on Smṛiti (tradition).

The Śrauta-sūtras teach the laying of the three sacred sacrificial fires, the new and full moon sacrifices, the animal sacrifices and the Soma-sacrifice with its manifold varieties. These texts are highly valuable, not only for the understanding of the cult of the sacrifice, but also for the study of the history of religion.

The Gṛihya-sūtras on the other hand cover a comparatively wider field, since they give instructions regarding the various ceremonies that are to be performed at the different stages in the life of a person. The order of arrangement in a Gṛihya-sūtra is determined by its subject-matter which refers to the ideal life of a householder. Most of them begin with the marriage ceremony and then go on to describe those that are connected with the birth of a child, beginning with the ceremonies performed at the time of conception. The various other ceremonies such as *Annaprāśana* (first taking of rice), *Chūḍākaraṇa* (tonsure), *Upanayana* (initiation), etc., are then described in the order of their natural sequence, the funeral rites naturally coming at the end. There are thus described a large number of domestic customs and usages, and in this respect the value of the Gṛihya-sūtras to the student of ancient folk-lore can never be over-estimated. These customs have their parallels in the manners and customs of the other Indo-European peoples, a fact which goes to prove that "the relationship of the Indo-European peoples is not limited to language, but that these peoples, related in language, have also preserved common features from prehistoric times in their manners and customs."[12]

The Gṛihya-sūtras also describe the five "great sacrifices," i.e. the daily sacrifices to the gods, demons, fathers, man and the Brahman. The first three of these comprise the simple offerings of food and a libation of water, whereas the "sacrifice to man" is nothing but hospitality shown to a guest, and the "sacrifice to the Brahman" constitutes the daily study of the Veda. Further, these texts also deal with the customs and ceremonies connected with such occasional and seasonal functions as house-building, farming, gardening, and digging of tanks and wells, as also the magical rites that are designed to ward off evil omens (e.g., if a dove or owl sits on the house or the bees make honey therein) or to cure the ailing of disease, and love magic. Connected with the funeral rites are also the ancestral sacrifices (*śrāddhas*) which by their importance soon developed into special texts known as the *Śrāddhakalpas*. In spite of the minor differences in detail the Gṛihya texts show a remarkable uniformity in the household ritual of the orthodox Aryans in those days. With regard to the Gṛihya and Śrauta ceremonies Max Müller observes that "... though the latter (i.e. Śrauta) may seem of greater importance to the Brāhmaṇas, to us the former will be more deeply interesting, as disclosing that deep-rooted tendency in the heart of man to bring the chief events of human life in connection with a higher power, and to give to our joys and sufferings a deeper significance and a religious sanctification."[13]

The third class of text-books which are perhaps a continuation of the Gṛihya-sūtras are the Dharma-sūtras dealing with the customary law and practice. The difference (between the Dharma- and Gṛihya-sūtras) is that "the weight in the Dharmas is laid on the wider relation of man to the state, so that those sections which deal with the family become condensed and subordinate."[14] They enumerate the duties of the castes and the stages in life (*āśrama*) in great detail. We also find here the beginnings of the civil and criminal law. The important subjects covering the civil law are taxes, inheritance and the position of women. Under the latter come assaults, adultery, and thefts as the principal topics. It must be noted that the rules of punishment are largely based upon caste-considerations, so that for having committed the same offence, a Brāhmaṇa may pass unscathed, but a Śūdra may even receive capital punishment. The differences of opinion that are noticeable in the different texts are due, partly to differences in their age and locality of origin, and partly also to the various schools in which these texts were studied.

The fourth allied group of the Sūtras is that of the Śulva-sūtras which are directly attached to the Śrauta-sūtras. The word Śulva means "a measuring string," and these texts give minute rules regarding the measurement and construction of the fire-altars and the place of sacrifice. They may thus be regarded as the oldest books on Indian geometry.

The Śrauta- and the Gṛihya-sūtras are also of great value from the point of view of the correct understanding of the Vedic passages. These Sūtras, besides giving instructions for the mechanics of the ritual, also enjoin the use of certain Vedic *mantras* for recitation. It is true that very often the *mantras* show little connection, except perhaps the verbal, with the sacrificial acts which they are to accompany; but sometimes they do supply a clue to the correct explanation of a prescribed text. Such *mantras* are included either in full or in part in the body of the Sūtra texts and thus exhibit their connection with certain Vedic schools; for the Sūtras belonging to a particular Saṁhitā would quote passages from that particular Saṁhitā only with some initial words, but with the full text of the *mantras* taken from other Saṁhitās. The *Gobhila Gṛihya-sūtra,* however, eschews all such *mantras* and puts them in a special prayer-book called the Mantrabrāhmaṇa, and the *Āpastambīya Gṛihya-sūtra* does the same in the Mantrapāṭha.

Of all the different Vedic schools only the Baudhāyana and the Āpastamba schools, belonging to the Black *Yajurveda*, give under the general title of Kalpa-sūtra all the four types of Sūtra texts mentioned above. The uniformity which runs through them makes it quite probable that Baudhāyana[15] and Āpastamba were themselves actual authors of these two Kalpa-sūtras. The schools of Bhāradvāja which give us the Śrauta and the Gṛihya-sūtras and those of Satyāshāḍha Hiraṇyakeśin which give us the Śrauta-, Gṛihya- and the Dharma-sūtras are both in close relation with the school of Āpastamba. To the *Maitrāyaṇī-Saṁhitā* belong the Śrauta-, Gṛihya- and the Śulva-sūtras of the Mānava school and also the *Kāṭhaka Gṛihya-sūtra*.

Of the other Vedic schools we do not get, at any rate at present, a Kalpa-sūtra comprising all the four types of Sūtras referred to above.[16] Whether they existed at one time or not is a moot point. Thus to the White *Yajurveda* belong a *Kātyāyana Śrauta-sūtra,* a *Pāraskara Gṛihya-sūtra* and a *Kātyāyana Śulva-sūtra.* The *Āśvalāyana* and *Śāṅkhāyana Śrauta-* and *Gṛihya-sūtras* belong to the *Ṛigveda.* With the *Sāmaveda* are connected the *Lāṭyāyana* and *Drāhyāyaṇa* Śrauta-sūtras and a Śrauta- and Gṛihya-sūtra of the *Jaiminīya* school. The Gṛihya-sūtras of Gobhila and Khādira also belong to the same Veda. The *Atharvaveda* gives a *Vaitāna Śrauta-*

sūtra and Kauśika-sūtra. The former is of a very late date and is tacked on to the *Atharvaveda* in order to bring it in line with the other Vedas.[17] The latter, however, is much older in date and in character is only partly a Gṛihya-sūtra, for it deals with magical rites also.

The Śrāddhakalpas and Pitṛimedhas dealing with the ancestral sacrifices have been already referred to above. Some of these texts, however, are quite late productions. The important texts belonging to this category are the *Mānava-śrāddhakalpa* and those belonging to Śaunaka, Paippalāda, Kātyāyana, and Gautama. Of the Pitṛimedha-sūtras we have those of Baudhāyana, Hiraṇyakeśin, and Gautama.

To the post-Vedic ritual literature belong the Pariśishṭas or "addenda" which elaborate in greater detail some of the rites that are briefly mentioned in the texts to which they are appended. Of these, the *Gṛihyasaṁgraha-Pariśishṭa* and the *Karmapradīpa* attached to the *Gobhila Gṛihya-sūtra* are more important. The Pariśishṭas belonging to the *Atharvaveda* are equally important since they throw valuable light on such subjects as the magical practices, omens, and portents. The *Prāyaśchittasūtra* which deals with the expiatory rites is one of the oldest Pariśishṭas.

Still later are the Prayogas, Paddhatis, and the Kārikās dealing very elaborately with some special rites such as the marriage customs, burial of the dead, and sacrifices to the manes, but they do not belong to this period.

It is difficult to assign any precise date to the Kalpa-sūtra texts. The dates of the principal Śrauta-sūtras (viz., those of Āpastamba, Āśvalāyana, Baudhāyana, Kātyāyana, Śāṅkhāyana, Lāṭyāyana, Drāhyāyaṇa and Satyāshāḍha) and some of the Gṛihya-sūtras (Āśvalāyana, Āpastamba, etc.), have been fixed between 800 and 400 B.C. The Dharma-sūtras of Gautama, Baudhāyana, Vasishṭha and Āpastamba have been placed by eminent scholars like Bühler and Jolly between the sixth and fourth (or third) centuries B.C., though others assign a somewhat later date. But although none of the extant Dharma-sūtras is older than 600 B.C., there is no doubt that there were works of this class belonging to an earlier period. For not only the oldest text, viz., *Gautama Dharma-sūtra,* probably belonging to sixth century B.C., refers, both directly and indirectly, to other works of this class, but even Yāska's *Nirukta* seems to allude to them. On the whole the Kalpa-sūtras may be roughly placed between the eighth and third centuries B.C.[18]

3. *Vyākaraṇa*

The only representative that has come down to us of this Vedāṅga is the *Ashṭādhyāyī* of Pāṇini, which belongs to a later period.

The Vedic grammar in this work receives only a sectional treatment at the hands of Pāṇini, his principal object being the description of the "*bhāshā*," the ordinary language of the people, and not the sacred language of the "seers." The earlier exegetical works in this field are lost to us. The *Uṇādisūtras* teaching the formation of nouns from roots, and the *Phiṭsūtras* dealing with accent, are the representatives of the earlier treatises in the field of grammar before Pāṇini. The greater number of words explained by the *Uṇādisūtras* are Vedic, and Professor Max Müller observes that ". . . originally the *Uṇādisūtras* were intended for the Veda only, and that they were afterwards enlarged by adding rules on the formation of non-Vedic words."[19]

4. *Nirukta*

Of this Vedāṅga connected with etymology we have the sole representative in Yāska's *Nirukta*. It appears that some centuries after the composition of the Saṁhitās, these texts began to be unintelligible, and to facilitate their understanding it was deemed necessary to have lists of rare and obscure words. These lists were styled the *Nighaṇṭus*, and Yāska's treatise is a commentary on such lists, prepared not by himself but by his predecessors. Yāska certainly had forerunners in this field who commented on such lists, but none of their works has come down to us.

5. *Chhandas*

The literature comprising this Vedāṅga on metrics is equally meagre. The *Nidānasūtra* in ten Prapāṭhakas belongs to the *Sāmaveda* and deals with metre as also with the component parts of the *Sāmaveda*. It has been ascribed to Patañjali by some ancient teachers. Piṅgala's work on metrics is regarded by the indigenous tradition as a Vedāṅga of the *Ṛigveda* and *Yajurveda*. But it is a late work belonging to the early post-Vedic period since it deals with the Vedic as well as non-Vedic metres.

6. *Jyotisha*

There is no work available at present dealing with ancient astronomy in the sūtra style. The *Jyotisha-Vedāṅga* is a later work of a practical utility. It gives some rules for calculating and fixing the days and hours for the different sacrifices. It is really unfortunate that the earlier works of this Vedāṅga as also of others should have been lost to us. Some of the astronomical theories and mathematical calculations worked out by the Vedic Aryans are really startling, considering the age and surroundings in which they originated. But at present the only source is the Vedic Saṁhitās and the Brāhmaṇas, particularly of the *Yajurveda*, from which we may derive our knowledge of these.

3. THE LANGUAGE

1. *The Upanishads*

The language of the Upanishads is more akin to the Classical than to the Vedic Sanskrit. The following traces of the older usage are, however, noticed now and then: (*a*) Nom. Plural in "*asas*" of nouns ending in "*a*"; "*Janāsaḥ*" (*Kaṭha,* 1.1.19); (b) Nom. Plural in "*ā*" of neuter nouns ending in "*a*": "*trī cha śatā trī cha sahasrā*" (*Bṛih.* III. 9. 1); (*c*) Instru. Sing. in "*ā*" of Fem. nouns ending in "*ā*": "*deshā*" (*Chhānd.* VI. 13. 1); "*manīshā*" (*Kaṭha,* II. 6. 9; *Śve.* III. 13); (d) Nom. Plural in "*īs*" of Fem. nouns ending in "*ī*"; "*mānushīḥ*" (*Taitt.* III. 10. 2); (*e*) Loc. Sing. without termination of nouns ending in "*an*": "*akshan*" (*Bṛih.* II. 2. 2); "*Ātman*" (*Bṛih.* II. 3. 6; *Kaṭha,* II. 4. 1); "*vyoman*" (*Taitt.* II. 1); (*f*) the older form of the pronoun "*tat*" namely "*tyat*" (*Bṛih.* II. 3. 1).

A peculiar practice of employing the Dative in place of Gen.-Abla. of some Fem. nouns ending in "*ā*" or "*ī,*" as also of the pronouns "*tat,*" "*etat*" and "*yat*" is noticed in the Upanishads: Thus we get "*teshām saṁkḷiptyai*" (= Abla.) "*varsham saṁkalpate*" (*Chhānd.* VII. 4. 2); "*bhūtyai na pramaditavyaṁ*" (*Taitt.* I. 11. 1); "*etasyai devatāyai sāyujyaṁ jayati*" (*Bṛih,* I. 5. 23); "*jāyāyai kāmāya jāyā priyā bhavati*" (*Bṛih.* II. 4. 5); "*vīṇāyai tu grahaṇena śabdo gṛihīto bhavati*" (*Bṛih.* IV. 5. 10); "*tasyai vāchaḥ pṛithivī śarīraṁ*" (*Bṛih.* I. 5. 11); "*Asyai vidyutaḥ sarvāṇi bhūtāni madhu*" (*Bṛih.* II. 5. 8); "*yasya priyo bubhūshed yasyai vā*" (*Kaushī,* II. 4).

In the case of the Verb, older Moods like the Subjunctive and the Injunctive have almost fallen into disuse. They are met with only as exceptions in the older Upanishads, i.e. the *Bṛih.* and the *Chhānd.* Thus we get "*asat*" (*Bṛih.* V. 5. 1); "*ichchhāsai*" (*Bṛih.* VI. 1.10); "*prāpam*" (*Bṛih.* V. 14.7) and "*upa sīdathāḥ*" (*Chhānd.* VI.13. 1). Imperative forms in "*tāt*" standing for the third person sing. are found twice in *Bṛih.*: "*ayaṁ tyasya rājā mūrdhānaṁ vipātayatāt*" (*Bṛih.* I. 3. 24) and "*abhayaṁ tvā gachchhatād Yājñavalkya*" (*Bṛih.* IV. 2. 4). The Ātmane and the Parasmai Padas are not yet definitely restricted to certain roots as in the Classical language and so we get forms like "*adhyeti,*" "*adhyeshi*" (*Chhānd.* V. 11 2: 6); "*adhīhi*" (*Chhānd.* VII. 1. 1); "*manvāni*" (*Chhānd.* VIII. 12. 5); "*aikshat*" (*Kaṭha.* II. 4. 1). Irregular present forms like "*bhuñjāmaḥ*" (*Chhānd.* IV. 12.2); "*kṛiṇvate*" (*Śve.* II. 7); perfect forms like "*pasparśuḥ*" (*Kena.* 27); passive forms like "*vyaśīryat*" (*Chhānd.* V. 15. 2) and "*parimuchyanti*" (*Muṇḍ.* III. 2. 6) are also occasionally met with. As in earlier Vedic Saṁhitās, prepositions are sometimes separated from their verbs: "*parā asya bhrātṛivyo bhavati*" (*Bṛih.* I. 3. 7); "*ud asmāt prāṇāḥ krāmanti*" (*Bṛih.* II. 1. 11); "*anu mā śādhi*"

(*Bṛih.* IV. 2. 1); "*ā cha gachchheyuḥ upa cha nameyuḥ*" (*Chhānd.* II. 1. 4).

Sandhi has become pretty regular so far as prose passages are concerned. A few irregularities of the Sandhi are found in the metrical portions.

The Upanishadic language is characterized by a few features whose presence is due to the need of conveying dry philosophical ideas with ease and clarity. Some of these are: (1) Abundant use of simple homely similes and metaphors; (2) repetition of an idea almost in the same words and expressions to ensure firm grasp and recollection; (3) use of riddle-like expressions which a man loves to master and reproduce with a feeling of superiority; (4) description of minute details to create and sustain interest; (5) short stories to attract attention before introducing a dry philosophical discussion; and (6) corroboration of a philosophical concept by means of popular beliefs and facts to excite curiosity and create faith.

2. *The Sūtras*

As has been already noticed, the Sūtra works are written in a peculiar terse style which may be traced to the prose of the Brāhmaṇas; for these latter texts are usually written in short sentences, almost entirely without the use of relative and conditional clauses. The Sūtras, however, employ long compounds and gerunds to economize the use of syllables. It may be said on the whole that the language of the Sūtras approaches very near to the norm set up by Pāṇini. Herein too are to be found occasionally words and forms belonging to the Vedic period and also some Prākritisms and solecisms. Yet the language of the Sūtras does not show the same latitude as is evinced in the epic language.

In phonology a possible change of "*ṛi*" > "*a*" is exemplified in "*aṇika*" (< "*ṛiṇika*" ?) (*Āp. Dh. S.* I. 6. 19. 1). The change of "*n*" > "*ṇ*" so peculiar to the MIA stage may be witnessed in "*ṇāma*" (*Āp. S. S.* X. 14. 1), "*eṇam*" (*Āp. S. S.* XIV. 27. 7), "*anulepaṇa*" (*Āp. Dh. S.* I. 3. 11. 13), etc. Some confusion between the sibilants is met with in "*vaśīyān*" for "*vasīyān*" (*Kau.* S. 4. 15); "*pāṁśu*" for "*pāṁsu*" (*Kau. S.* 27. 18, 29. 21). The MSS of the *Kauśika-sūtra* frequently write "*ts*" for "*chh*": Thus we get "*avatsādya*" for "*avachhādya*" (*Kau. S.* 24. 10). Occasionally "*y*" is written for "*j*" as in "*yunaymi*" (*Kau. S.* 3. 1). Then again Tamil-Malayalam "*ḷ*" for "*ḍ*" is found in "*Kāraḷi*" (*Jai. G. S.* I. 14).

The dat. sg. of fem. nouns in "*ā*," "*ī*" and "*ū*" has an ending "*-ai*" as in "*dakshiṇāyai*" (*Āp. S.S.* II. 8. 3). The instr. sg. "*vidyā*" occurs in *Āp. Dh. S.* I. 11. 30. 3. In the same Sūtra II. 1. 1. 17-18 "*dāra*" is used in singular. The shortening of a long vowel before terminations is found in "*patnibhis*" (*Āp. S.S.* 14. 15. 2), "*grāmaṇibhis*" (*Āp. S.S.* 20. 4. 3). The *Bṛihaddevatā* (II. 8, 12, III. 92) gives "*patnayaḥ*" as nom. pl. The nom. pl. "*gāḥ*" is found in *Āp. S.S.* 10. 26. 7. The loc. sg. in "*-an*" of the bases ending in "*-an*" is available in "*ahan*" (*Āp. S.S.* 9. 2. 1), "*ātman*" (*Āp. S.S.* 6. 28. 20; *Kau. S.* 72. 42), "*dhāman*" (*Bau. S.S.* 10. 59, etc.), "*charman*" (*Bau. S.S.* 6. 28, 15. 17).

The forms "*ādadāti*" (and "*dadāti*") for "*ādatte*" occur in the *Vaikhānasa Smārta Sūtra* 9. 2. 4, etc. The unaugmented forms occur very often in the *Bṛihaddevatā*; cf. "*bodhayat*" (IV. 115), "*sīdat*" (IV. 113), etc. The optative in "*-īta*" is also met with, cf. "*dayīta*" (*Āp. S.S.* 5. 25. 18), "*prakshālayīta*" *Āp. Dh. S.* I. 1. 2. 28), "*dhārayīta*" (*Mānava G. S.* I. 1. 10), "*kāmayīta*" (*Bau. S.S.* II. 1), "*upanayīta*" (*Kau. S.* 17. 31. 31, etc.). The opt. pl. "*-īran*" is found in "*upakalpayīran* (*Bau. S. S.* 25. 12).

Absolutives in "*-am,*" a peculiarity often observed in the Brāhmaṇas, are found in such instances as "*anavakrāmam*" (*Āp. S.S.* II. 13. 7), "*abhishekam*" (*Bau. S. S.* II. 9), "*ayujakāram*" (*Hiraṇyakeśi Pitṛimedha Sūtra* 2. 1). Other irregular forms of absolutives are "*śchotya*" (*Kau. S.* 53. 18), "*kshipya*" (*Kau. S.* 30. 18). "*tyājya*" (*Āgniveśya G. S.* 3 11. 2), "*sāntvya*" (*Bṛihaddevatā*, IV. 3), "*saṁgṛihītvā*" (*Bṛihaddevatā*, II. 48).

In sandhi also occasional departure from the grammarian's norm is found in the removal of hiatus by crasis in "*patnyāñjalau*" from "*patnyā(ḥ) añjalau*" (*Kau. S.* 6. 17), "*daivateti*" from "*daivata iti*" < "*daivate iti*" (*Kau. S.* 6. 34, etc.).

---

1. Winternitz, *HIL*, I, p. 234.
2. *Muṇḍaka Upanishad* (I. 2. 7.) declares sacrifices as "unsafe boats" and the fools who cling to it go again to old age and death.
3. "What is the cause? Brahma? whence are we born? Whereby do we live? And on what are we established? Overruled by whom, in pains and pleasures, do we live our various conditions, O ye theologians?" *Śvetāśvatara Upanishad*, I. I. Tr. by Hume, *Thirteen Principal Upanishads*, p. 394.
4. *Chhāndogya*, III. 14. Tr. by Winternitz, *HIL*, I, p. 250.
5. *Chhāndogya*, VI. 1 ff.; also cf. the *Bṛihadāraṇyaka*, II. 4.
6. *Chhāndogya*, VIII, 7-12.
7. *Bṛhadāraṇyaka*, IV. 4. Tr. by Winternitz, *HIL*, I, p. 259.
8. *Kāṭhaka Upanishad*, I. 20 ff. Tr. by Hume, *Thirteen Principal Upanishads*, pp. 344 f.
9. *Ahaṁ Brahmā asmi* (*Bṛihadāraṇyaka*, I. 4. 10).
10. Winternitz, *HIL*, I, p. 266.
11. The origin of the Prātiśākhyas is thus accounted for by Max Müller. "During the Brāhmaṇa period the songs of the Veda were preserved by oral tradition only, and as the spoken language of India had advanced and left the idiom of the Veda behind as a kind of antique and sacred utterance, it was difficult to preserve the proper pronunciation of the sacred hymns without laying down a certain number of rules on metre, accent, and pronunciation in general. The necessity, however, of such a provision could hardly have been felt until certain

differences had actually arisen in different seats of Brahmanic learning." *HASL*, second edition, p. 117.

12. Winternitz, *HIL*, I. p. 274 and fn. 2.
13. *HASL*, second edition, p. 205.
14. Hopkins, *CHI*, I, p. 229.
15. Dr. Winternitz points out that Baudhāyana is sometimes called a *pravachana-kāra*, and that *pravachana* is perhaps the term for a literary type which comes midway between the Brāhmaṇas and the Sūtras. See *HIL*, I, p. 278, fn. 3.
16. For a detailed account of the Śrauta-sūtras, cf. Ch. XII, pp. 235. ff.
17. This point has been discussed above, in Ch. XII. p. 243.
18. *KHDS*, I, pp. 8-9; *SBE*, II, XIV, Introduction.
19. *Op. cit.*, p. 151.

CHAPTER XXV

POLITICAL AND LEGAL INSTITUTIONS

I. POLITICAL THEORY

The political and legal ideas of the period are presented to us, in a collected form, in the Dharma-sūtras. This is a distinct advantage, as hitherto we had to depend for them merely on isolated passages scattered in the different Saṁhitās and Brāhmaṇas. Although none of the existing Dharmasūtras is probably older than 600 B.C., they are no doubt based on earlier works of this class and have preserved strata of earlier thought. It is remarkable that the older Dharma-sūtras are singularly free from the revolutionary ideas in religion associated with Buddhism and other heterodox or sectarian religious sects, and do not contain any trace of the great territorial kingdoms which arose in India in the fifth and fourth centuries B.C. We are, therefore, justified in treating the Dharma-sūtras as reflecting the ideas of the closing period of the Vedic Age.

The Dharma-sūtras do not contain any systematic exposition of legal principles and political doctrines such as we find in the Dharmaśāstras and Arthaśāstras of the later age. Nor does their conception of law and politics conform to our present ideas on the subject. As we shall see later, they "cover far more than law and do not cover the whole of law." As regards politics they view the state or society as an organic whole, in which the different elements, such as the king and the people, play their part according to Dharma or Law, imposed or at least sanctioned by the Divine Will. Life is also regarded as a whole without any sharp distinction between public and private, or individual and collective. As a matter of fact the collective organization of society dominates over the idea of individual persons. Each individual has his duty and responsibility, rather than rights and privileges, fixed by law and custom, and this applies as much to the king as to his meanest subject. Each man has a recognized function, which he inherits as a member of a group rather than selects of his own accord. To perform this function successfully is his highest object in life, a duty not merely political, social and moral, but also religious in character. For on this depends not only his well-being in this life, but also his salvation in the next world. Like the modern collectivist theories (such as Fascism) this view raises society above individuals, and strikes at the very root of personality or individuality; but there is an important difference. For the allegiance here is not to any party or political principle, but to Dharma conceived as an eternal and immutable Law or Order, which is divine in character and does not emanate from human will.

Such is the background against which the State is conceived in the Dharma-sūtra. It lays down the duty of the king and the people, and does not worry about the rights of the latter and checks against the tyranny of the former. For failure to do his duty the king is sure to be visited with adequate penalties both in this world (by way of expulsion) and the next. This was considered to be a sufficient deterrent, and we do not hear of the popular assemblies called *sabhā* and *samiti* which in days of old regulated the affairs of state and controlled the power of the king.

A comprehensive view is, however, taken of the life and duty of a king. A high intellectual and moral discipline and military training are prescribed for him. "He must be fully instructed in the threefold (sacred sciences) and in logic, and learn the management of chariots and the use of the bow; he shall be holy in acts and speech, pure, and of subdued senses." He shall not live better than his *gurus* and ministers. His essential functions and duties are "to protect the castes and orders in accordance with justice," and "to take measures for ensuring victory," specially when danger from foes threatens the kingdom. His duty of affording "protection to all created beings" is very liberally interpreted. He must support the learned Brāhmaṇas and the poor and needy of all classes, and none in his realm must suffer hunger, sickness, cold, or heat, be it through want or intentionally. He must be impartial towards his subjects and do what is good for them. It is further laid down that "that king only takes care of the welfare of his subjects in whose dominions, be it in villages or forests, there is no danger from thieves." That this was no mere pious wish but conceived as a fundamental duty of the state, would appear from the injunction that if the stolen property is not recovered he shall pay its value out of the treasury.[1] Save and except the legal taxes the king was not authorized "to take property for his own use from the inhabitants of his realm" (*Vas. Dh. S.* XIX. 14). The taxes were regarded as "pay" received by the king for protecting his subjects. It amounted to one-sixth (of their incomes or spiritual merit) (*Bau. Dh. S.* 1. 10. 18. 19).

The high position of the Brāhmaṇa in the State is indicated by several injunctions. According to Gautama (VIII. 1) "a king and a Brāhmaṇa deeply versed in the Vedas, these two uphold the moral order in the world." It is also declared (XI. 1) that the king is master of all, with the exception of the Brāhmaṇas. The Brāhmaṇas were also exempt from taxes. The Purohita or domestic priest exercised high power and privileges and the king was also to "take heed of that which astrologers and interpreters of omens" told him, for "the acquisition of wealth and security depended also upon that."

The king had to act in religious and many other matters according to the advice of the Purohita. An interesting aspect of the dependence of the king on the Purohita even in military matters is seen in ritual literature. The Purohita guarantees success to the king's arms by his prayers. The view of Geldner[2] that these prayers were offered in the *sabhā* or assembly-house, while the king fought on the battle-field, is not countenanced by the Gṛihya-sūtras. It is true that the *Śāṅkhāyana Gṛihya-sūtra* lays down that Vedic recitations were not to be carried on in any army-camp, but ritual actually steps forth on the field of battle, and the result is rather amusing. In the *Āśvalāyana Gṛihya-sūtra* (III. 12) we find that "when a battle is beginning," the Purohita stands to the west of the king's chariot and mutters appropriate *mantras* from the *Ṛigveda* while he makes the king put on his armour and hands over to him bow and quiver. The Purohita also recites *mantras* over the horses, when the king actually starts for battle, and also when he ties to the king's arm the guard (by which the arm is protected against the bow-string). He then mounts on the royal chariot and the king repeats the *mantras,* while driving, touching the drum, and, finally, shooting off his arrows. It is also laid down that the king "should commence the battle in the formation invented by Āditya or by Uśanas." It would almost appear that the ritual even dictated military tactics to the king.

The influence of the Purohita in moderating the autocratic zeal of the king cannot be lost sight of in any appraisal of the political theory of those days. The number of priests at the court of a king may be many, but there is only one Purohita. Nay, one Purohita may even do service for more than one king, for example Jala Jātūkarṇya was the Purohita of the kings of Kāśi, Videha, and Kosala, according to the *Śāṅkhāyana Śrauta-sūtra* (XVI. 29. 5).

We also hear of an influential body of Brāhmaṇas forming a *Parishad.* Although its chief function was to advise the king on intricate and disputed points of law, it was probably a general body of advisers on all matters, religious, political, and judicial. For in a Sūtra of Pāṇini (V. 2. 112) the king is called *Parishad-bala* (one whose strength lies in Parishad), and we definitely hear of administrative functions exercised by *Parishad* in later times. This *Parishad* was composed of at least ten (Brāhmaṇas), viz., "four men who have completely studied the four Vedas, three men belonging to the three orders (a student, a householder, and an ascetic), one who knows the Mīmāṁsā, one who knows the Aṅgas, and a teacher of the sacred law." These men must be "well instructed, skilled in reasoning, and free from covetousness."[3]

The term *Parishad* has an interesting history. In the Upanishads it means "a gathering of specialists discussing problems of philosophy"; in the *Gobhila Gṛihya-sūtra* (III. 2. 40) it means a council sitting round a teacher. The use of this name in the Dharma-sūtras for an advisory body of the king in judicial and probably also administrative affairs, is perhaps significant of the changed conception of state and society, to which attention has been drawn above.

The Dharma-sūtras usually view the king as the primitive ruler of a petty state. There is a rule, for example, in *Gautama* (V. 30-31) that a Madhuparka (a mixture of curds and honey) should be offered to certain relations, if they come after a year, but to a king, who is a Śrotriya (proficient in the Vedas), as often as he comes. But if the king is not a Śrotriya, only a seat and water should be offered. Again a king was to make way for a Śrotriya (*Gau. Dh. S.* VI. 25), a Brāhmaṇa (*Āp. Dh. S.* II. 5, 11, 5-6) and a Snātaka (*Vas. Dh. S.* XIII. 59). Further, Gautama (XII. 43) implies and Āpastamba (I. 9. 25. 4) expressly says that a king shall personally strike a thief with the cudgel carried by the latter.

These passages convey the idea of a petty chief. But there are others which indicate the greatness and majesty of the king. According to Āpastamba (II. 10. 25. 2-15) he "shall cause to be built a town, a palace, with a hall in front of it, in the heart of the town, and an assembly-house at a little distance from it." The palace hall served as a guest-house, and provided rooms, a couch, food, and drink. The assembly-house was used for the purpose of playing dice, and men of the three higher castes were allowed to play there. Even this picture shows that the king was a homely ruler and did not occupy an isolated position of grandeur and majesty, such as is indicated by the pompous details of the Rājasūya and Aśvamedha sacrifices described at great length in the Śrauta-sūtras. The king was, of course, entitled to the homage of all except the Brāhmaṇas and wielded great power and authority. There is one rule which throws considerable light on the status and position of the king. According to Vasishṭha (II. 49. 50) all interest on moneys lent ceases to accrue on the death of the king and until the coronation of the new king. This is probably a recognition of the principle that the king represents the state, and all state-regulations derive their power and authority from him alone. This is an abstract principle of great importance, but we do not find its logical application in any other instance.

That kingship had come to be normally hereditary in the period of the Sūtras is seen from the tendency to associate the king's son in the monarchy—a tendency which has already received ritual sanction. The *Āśvalāyana Śrauta-sūtra*, for example, in its description of the Rājasūya (IX. 3) tells us that the Hotṛi narrates the *ākhyāna* of Śunaḥśepa to the anointed king seated with his son and ministers on a golden seat. That the monarchy was occasionally elective is at the same time shown by the legend in the *Nirukta* (II. 10) of the Kuru Brothers, Devāpi and Śantanu, which, though of doubtful character as a legend, retains its value as evidence of the contemporary practice of selecting, as king, one member of the royal family to the exclusion of another less suitable in an emergency. The field of selection could also extend to the entire nobility.

The Sūtra VI. 2. 59 in Pāṇini shows that a Brāhmaṇa could sometimes become a king. Again the sacrifices prescribed in the Śrauta-sūtras for an oppressed and disgruntled Rājanya or Vaiśya to acquire supreme power suggest that kingly power was not very stable and kingship was not confined to the royal family.

The insecurity of royal power during this period is also illustrated by the many references to kings expelled (*apa-ruddha*) from their kingdoms and striving to regain their sovereignty by means of spells (*Kauśika-sūtra*, XVI. 30).

2. ADMINISTRATIVE ORGANIZATION

The duties of the king, briefly sketched in the Dharma-sūtras, give us for the first time some definite idea of the scope of administration. His supreme duty, as noted above, was the protection of the people, and maintenance of the rules of Caste and Order. As a corollary to this, he must punish the thieves and other criminals as well as those who stray from the path of duty laid down in the Śāstras. His authority and jurisdiction thus extended practically over the entire activities of his subjects. One of his most important duties was to decide legal disputes. He was to protect the interests of a minor until he attained majority. He was also to support learned priests, the widows of his soldiers, those who are exempt from taxes (to be specified later) and Brahmachārins. He must preserve fruit-bearing trees. He must make an equal division of the booty secured in battle and distribute it equitably among those who shared the risks of war with him. He must prevent the use of false weights and measures.

For carrying on the administration the king appointed a regular heirarchy of officers. According to Āpastamba (II. 10. 26. 4) the king "shall appoint men of the first three castes, who are pure and truthful, over villages and towns for the protection of the people." These officials were to appoint subordinates possessing the same qualities. They were to protect the towns and villages from thieves and must be made to repay what is stolen within their jurisdiction. These passages, though brief, hold out the picture of a regular administrative machinery which was set up for the security of life and property.

One of the most important branches of administration was that for the collection of taxes. The texts do not make it quite clear whether the same officials who protected the towns and villages also collected taxes, or if there were others specifically employed for the purpose. But in any case the long list of taxable commodities shows a developed state of administrative organization. We come across a general statement that the king was entitled to a sixth part of the income or spiritual merit of his subjects (*Bau. Dh. S.* 1. 10. 18. 1; *Vas. Dh. S.* 1. 42). But Gautama (X. 24-35) gives a long list of taxes, viz., one-sixth, one-eighth, or one-tenth of the agricultural produce, the variation probably being due to difference in the quality of land, one-fifth of cattle and gold, one-twentieth of merchandise, and one-sixtieth of roots, fruits, flowers, medicinal herbs, honey, meat, grass, and firewood. The artisans and other manual workers had to do one day's work every month for the king, and there were similar rules in respect of owners of ships and carts. One-tenth was levied on goods imported by sea (*Bau. Dh. S.* 1. 10. 18. 14). Certain categories of persons were exempted from taxation. The list is a fairly large one and is differently given in the different Dharma-sūtras, this lack of uniformity being a general feature with respect to most of the topics treated. Exempt from taxation, according to Āpastamba (II. 10. 10. 26. 10-17), are a learned priest, women (according to Vasishṭha, only special categories of them like unmarried girls, wives of servants, widows who have rejoined their families, etc.), ascetics, students, infants, old men, the blind, dumb, deaf, and diseased persons, and Śūdras who live by washing the feet. To this list Vasishṭha (XIX. 23) adds one who has no protector, and a servant of the king.

As regards military matters, the king must be always prepared for war. He should lead his fighting hosts personally to battle, and be brave and fearless in the field. Very noteworthy is the high ethical standard of the rules of battle. The use of poisoned weapons is strictly prohibited. One must not kill those who are helpless, ask for mercy, or offer submission by eating grass like "cows" (which was the ancient equivalent of the "white flag").

The village was the basic administrative unit. The inhabitants of the village may be roughly classified into four groups. First may be mentioned the Brāhmaṇas and the Kshatriyas who did not cultivate the land themselves, but some of whom had a proprietary interest in it by virtue of royal grants. Secondly there were the cultivating owners, mostly Vaiśyas. To the third group belonged various artisans such as the chariot-makers (*ratha-kāra*), carpenters (*takshan*), smiths (*karmāra*) and others who formed the bulk of the village population. Lastly there were the Śūdras and other labourers who tilled the soil or did other menial work as day-labourers. All equally were under the authority of the king, and had to render tribute in various forms, such as food or service, either to the king or to such members of the royal family or household who paid a visit to the village. The head of the village was the *Grāmaṇī* (leader of the Grāma) who discharged military duties in times of war and civil duties in times of peace. Whether the post of the *Grāmaṇī* was hereditary, and whether the officer was nominated by the king or elected by the village council, cannot be definitely stated. The varying local customs make it likely that all these modes of appointment in the case of a *Grāmaṇī* were current in different parts of the country. The royal officials, mentioned above, who are said to have protected villages or towns, probably acted as police-officers and were different from *Grāmaṇīs*.

Another official named in the Sūtra texts of this age (as also in the Saṁhitās and Brāhmaṇas), is the *Sthapati*. From the fact that the Śrauta-sūtras of Kātyāyana (I. 1. 12) and Āpastamba (IX. 14. 12) mention a Nishāda-sthapati, the word may be understood in the sense of "Governor." Other passages in the same Śrauta-sūtras, however, point to the "Chief Judge." It is very likely that the *Sthapati* combined in his office both the executive and judicial functions.

3. LAW AND LEGAL INSTITUTIONS

As we have seen above, there is no clear evidence in the earlier age of organized criminal justice administered by the king or by a judicial tribunal, and the prevalence of the system of wergeld (*vaira-deya*) rather suggests that the injured party took the law into its own hands. It is in this period that we for the first time meet with the theory that a crime is a disturbance of the public peace and that, therefore, the penalty for the crime in the shape of fine must be paid to the king or to a Brāhmaṇa authorized by him. Similarly it is in the Dharma-sūtras that we find the real beginnings of civil and criminal law. But as already noted above, the conception of law was very different from that of the present day. There was no code of positive law emanating from the authority of the king. The Veda, the tradition (Smṛiti), and practice of those who know (the Veda) are said to be the threefold sources of law each evidently being superior to the one mentioned later), and "if authorities of equal force are conflicting, either may be followed at pleasure" (*Gau. Dh. S.* I. 1-4). This obviously left a great deal to be settled by usages, conventions, precedents and customs. No wonder, therefore, that the rules and customs of different castes, communities, families, and localities are expressly recognized as having the force of law. It is also laid down that the communities (*vargas*) of "cultivators, traders, herdsmen, money-lenders and artisans have authority to lay down rules for their respective classes" and a right to expound them in the royal court of justice (*Gau. Dh. S.* XI. 20-22; *Vas. Dh. S.* I. 17).

Further, many activities of social and religious nature, which lie beyond the jurisdiction of a modern law-court, are brought within the scope of law, and penance and loss of caste are prescribed as penalties both for offences of this nature (e.g. eating the flesh of forbidden animals, neglect of the Vedas, drinking spirituous liquor, incest) as well as for heinous crimes such as theft, homicide, causing abortion, adultery, etc. (*Āp. Dh. S.* I. 7. 21. 8 ff; *Gau. Dh. S.* XXII). In some cases, penance and loss of caste are imposed in addition to other punishment, but in others they alone are prescribed, and penance is supposed to wash off the guilt of even the most heinous crimes like adultery with a teacher's wife or drinking spirituous liquor, for which death by a painful process is also laid down as an alternative punishment (*Āp. Dh. S.* I. 9. 25. 1-10).

That the king himself personally administered civil and criminal justice appears from certain indications in the Sūtras (*Gau. Dh. S.* XII. 43). The administration of justice was to be regulated by the Vedas, the Dharmaśāstras, the Aṅgas, and Purāṇas (*Gau Dh. S.* XI. 19), due regard being paid to local and family usage or (in other words) to the laws of districts, castes, and families which the king must learn from those who in each case have authority to speak (*Gau. Dh. S.* XI. 20-22). It seems to have been permissible for the king to delegate his judicial authority or at least the supervision of punishments to a royal officer or a Rājanya who could act as an *adhyaksha* (overseer). Difficult cases were referred to the *Parishad* whose composition has been mentioned above. When it failed to arrive at any satisfactory solution in doubtful cases, the king referred the matter to a Śrotriya or Brāhmaṇa of high learning (*Gau. Dh. S.* XXVIII. 50). The theory of *daṇḍa* ("the rod of punishment") as the symbol of penal powers vested in the king had now fully developed.

Under criminal law, assault, theft, and adultery are the main general topics discussed in the Dharma-sūtras. The *Nirukta* (VI. 27) gives a list of seven sins ("crimes") among which the slaying of a *bhrūṇa* is mentioned. *Bhrūṇa* is generally interpreted as "embryo," but later tradition takes it to mean "Brāhmaṇa" also. The killing of a Brāhmaṇa alone is murder—the most heinous crime. The *Vasishṭha Dharma-sūtra* mentions cases of manslaughter where "the slayer commits no crime by killing an assassin" (III. 15-18). The *Āpastamba Dharma-sūtra* (I. 10. 28. 1-3) discusses and defines "theft" as follows: "He who under any conditions whatsoever, covets (and takes) what belongs to another commits a theft (according to Kautsa, Hārīta, Pushkarasādi and Kaṇva), but some exceptions are noted by Vārshāyaṇi. For example, food for a draught-ox or seeds ripening in the pod, if taken only in moderate quantities, do not constitute theft."

The punishment for theft is rather severe, sometimes even death. The thief with loosened hair and carrying a cudgel presents himself before the king. The king with his own hand hits him with that very cudgel. If the thief dies, he atones for his sin. The thief may expiate his sin also by throwing himself into a fire or starving himself to death; but if he is forgiven by the king or if the king fails to strike him, the guilt falls on the king. It appears that this punishment of death became operative only when the thief was caught red-handed.

Generally speaking, physical chastisement or expulsion from the country was the penalty for crimes. The fines of the later age are known, but had not yet become systematized. Caste-interest is a factor in the regulation of the severity of the punishment. Whereas, for example, a Śūdra would receive capital punishment with confiscation of his property for homicide or theft, a Brāhmaṇa would only be blinded. For abuse (or defamation) the amount of the fine varies with the caste of the offender and the offended party. With the gradual reduction of fines, according to the descending scale of caste of the offended, a Brāhmaṇa goes scot-free if he abuses a Śūdra; but "a Śūdra who intentionally reviles twice-born men by criminal abuse, or criminally assaults them with blows, shall be deprived of the limb with which he offends" (*Gau. Dh. S.* XII. 1). In general the discriminatory penalties and punishments laid down for the Śūdras make painful reading (*Āp. Dh. S.* II. 10 27. 9, 14-15, etc.), and even if we assume that they were not usually resorted to in practice, they throw a lurid light on the arrogance of the upper classes and the helpless condition of the down-trodden lower grades of society. Some relics of barbarous punishments are preserved in the Dharma-sūtras such, for example, as those prescribed by Āpastamba for adultery (I. 9. 25. 1-2; I. 10. 28. 15). The penalties prescribed for deserting a wife are also rude and primitive. The husband has to put on an ass's skin, with the hair turned outside, and beg in seven houses, saying, "Give alms to him who forsook his wife." That shall be his livelihood for six months (*Āp. Dh. S.* I. 10. 28. 19; see below, Ch. XXVI, p. 506). A drinker of spirituous liquor is to drink boiling liquid until he dies (*Āp.* I. 9. 25. 3). One redeeming feature, however, should be mentioned. Gautama (XII. 17) prescribes that if a learned man offends, the punishment shall be very much increased. How one wishes that this very salutary principle were extended to considerations of caste, so that the discriminatory penalties would be just reversed!

The law of manslaughter shows that in spite of the public organization of criminal justice during the Sūtra period, the system of private vengeance, moderated by the wergeld (*vairadeya*), was still in force Thus although the crime of murdering a Brāhmaṇa is too heinous to be expiated by a wergeld, one thousand cows constitute the wergeld for killing a Kshatriya, one hundred cows in the case of a Vaiśya, and ten cows for killing a Śūdra (*Āp. Dh. S.*

I. 9. 24. 1-4). The cows are apparently to be a compensation to the relations of the murdered man so that they may not press for the punishment of death to the offender. Over and above this payment to the relations, Baudhāyana (I. 10. 19. 1. 2) prescribes the payment of a bull to the king, probably partly as appeasement for the infringement of his peace, and partly as reward for his intercession with the relations. Among other Aryan nations, too, this method of compensation for murder is found. The *Āpastamba Dharma-sūtra* (II. 5. 11. 3) alone mentions ordeals, but in a very general way.

Though *dharma* or law (civil and criminal) is properly the sphere of the *Dharma-sūtras,* we find occasional notices of certain legal topics in Sūtra texts earlier than the *Dharma-sūtras.* The *Nirukta* (III. 4) says that women were not entitled to partition or inheritance, and uses the technical term *dāyāda* "heir," the term *dāya* being established soon after the *Ṛigveda* in the sense of "inheritance" or "a share of the father's property which is divided among his sons either during his life or after his death." Similarly the *Śāṅkhāyana Śrauta-sūtra* (XV. 27. 3) refers to "inheritance" in the technical sense. The Gṛihya-sūtras again refer to courts of justice in connection with the *vaśīkaraṇa* rite which aims at secretly winning over the court and the assessors or jurors to one's side. Failing this, the rite would seek to deprive the judge of the power of speech (so that no judgment could be delivered). The Gṛihya-sūtras also touch upon legal matters incidentally, as when they state the rule that one of the occasions for kindling anew the domestic fire is the time of the division of the inheritance, or the rule that the site of a house should be undisputed property.

Detailed rules of inheritance of landed property occur for the first time in the Dharma-sūtras. A few typical and illustrative rules alone may be cited. *Sapiṇḍa* males (those related within six degrees) are heirs in default of near relations like sons, and *Sakulyas* (remote relations) inherit in default of *Sapiṇḍas.* The widow is not entitled to inheritance, though, according to some authorities, the wife's share consists of her ornaments and gifts from relations. According to Āpastamba, a daughter inherits only in default of sons, teacher, or pupil. The king inherits in default of these, who are all expected to keep the spiritual good of the deceased in view while spending the inheritance. Very possibly, and more often than not (though not necessarily), the division of property took place during the lifetime of the owner, rather than after his death.

Some authorities hold that among sons only the eldest one inherits. *Apastamba Dharma-sūtra* (II. 6. 14. 7) refers to a local law whereby the eldest son receives (in some countries) gold or black cattle or the black produce of the soil(?), in other words the best chattel. But the rules in the Dharma-sūtras are not consistent in this matter, and it is laid down also that the father may divide equally among all his sons.

Whereas earlier authorities are content with the mention of the vague term "sons" in the matter of inheritance, it is the latest Dharma-sūtras like that of Vasishṭha which give a classification of the "twelve" sons into two groups, (1) the heirs and kinsmen, and (2) kinsmen but not heirs, in the manner of the later formal law-books.

The whole matter of inheritance is rather vague, there being no universal law regulating it. Different rules are given by the various texts and legal authorities, and they were evidently authoritative in different localities or families.

Lost property is to be proclaimed by a crier, and if the owner does not turn up within one year, the king takes it giving a certain percentage (25 per cent) to the finder, unless the latter is a Brāhmaṇa, who keeps the whole of it. All treasure-troves belong to the king, but the rules are not unanimous on the point, and whereas, according to one authority, any finder gets one-sixth, according to another authority, if the finder be a learned Brāhmaṇa, the king shall not take it (*Vas. Dh. S.* III. 13-14).

Title to property can be established by documents, witness, and possession. If the documents are at variance, the evidence of old men and of guilds and corporations may be called in (*Vas. Dh. S.* XVI. 10-15). The categories of property which are not lost, even though enjoyed by others, are interesting; viz., a pledge, a boundary, the property of minors, an (open) deposit, a sealed deposit, women, the property of a king (and) the wealth of a Śrotriya. So women are property. Eight other kinds of property which have been enjoyed by another person for ten years are lost to the owner (*Vas. Dh. S.* XVI. 17-18). The king himself is the trustee of the property of a minor.

The legal rate of interest is roughly the equivalent of fifteen per cent per annum; but the influence of caste is noticeable even in this matter, and different rates of interest are payable by different castes. Neither a Brāhmaṇa nor a Kshatriya may become a usurer. The lending business, therefore, was a sort of monopoly of the Vaiśyas.

---

1. For the duties of the king enumerated above, cf. *Gautama* Dh. S. X, XI, and *Āpastamba Dh.* S. II, 10, 25, 10-15.
2. *Ved. Stud.*, II. 135.
3. The constitution of the *Parishad* is laid down, with slight variations, in *Gau. Dh.* S. XXVIII, 48-49; *Vas. Dh.* S. III. 20; *Bau Dh.* S. I. 1. 1. 7-8.

CHAPTER XXVI

RELIGION AND PHILOSOPHY

1. THE UPANISHADS[1]

Long before the period of the Brāhmaṇas, the thought-ferment which culminated in the rich philosophical speculations of the Upanishads had come to the surface in certain *RV*-hymns (X. 129, etc.) which express doubts concerning the efficacy of the priestly cult and the current belief in gods. The philosophical hymns of the *AV* and some portions of the *YV Saṁhitās* carry on (though only in a symbolic form) the tradition of these sceptics and doubters, who were certainly not the priests. Not only in the Upanishads but also in the Brāhmaṇas, there is clear evidence of the fact that kings and warriors share the honours, if not the monopoly, of the intellectual and literary harvest of these days with the Brāhmaṇas who had to go to them very often for instruction. Nay, even women and people of doubtful parentage took part in this intellectual life and very often possessed the highest knowledge. It was probably these non-priestly circles opposed to the Brahmanic way of works (*Karma-mārga*) that formed the chief recruiting ground for forest hermits and wandering ascetics, who kept aloof from the sacrificial ceremonial of the Brāhmaṇas by renouncing the world and followed the "way of knowledge" (*Jñāna-mārga*). Buddhism represents, very probably, one fruit of such protestant activity. It was in the nature of things impossible that the Brāhmaṇas should be confined to the opposite camp and, as noted above (Ch. XXII, p. 451), their supreme genius for compromise and adjustments of differences probably led later to the formulation of the wonderful theory of *Āśramas* or different stages of Aryan life. (1) In the first one lives with a teacher and learns the Veda as a *Brahmachārin;* (2) as a householder (*Gṛihastha*) he next founds a household, begets children and himself offers sacrifices (*gṛihya* and *śrauta*) or has them offered; (3) when grown old, he leaves his house and village for the forest, where as a *Vānaprastha* (forest-hermit) he offers only a minimum sacrificial service and devotes himself mainly to meditation upon the mystical and symbolical significance of the sacrifice. The Āraṇyakas, as noted above, are eminently suitable to the hermits as text-books. The oldest Upanishads speak of these *Āśramas* only as three types or branches of life, but not as successive stages. It is only in the late Upanishads, the Great Epic, and the Dharmaśāstras, that the theory of successive stages of life is formulated and is developed further by the addition of a fourth stage, that of the *Saṁnyāsin* who gives up even sacrifice, in fact, all good works, and as an ascetic, renounces the world to meditate on the Absolute (*Brahman*), with a view to realize it or achieve union with it. In the early period, the last two stages probably formed a single stage. Anyway, the unbelievers in ritualism who preferred the *Jñāna-mārga* to the *Karma-mārga* of the priests were completely placated by this scheme, which allowed them scope in the last two stages or *Āśramas*.

If one single doctrine were to be selected from the old Upanishads as representing the quintessence of Upanishadic philosophy, and if we were asked to sum it up in one sentence, that sentence would be: "The universe is *Brahman*, but the *Brahman* is the *Ātman*." The conception of the world-soul, *Ātman* has developed from that of the world-man (in the *RV*), and the earlier conception of the personal creator, Prajāpati, has grown into the Upanishadic one of the impersonal source of all being, namely *Brahman*. The two streams meet in the following manner: *Ātman* in the *RV* is "breath"; in the Brāhmaṇas it comes to mean "self" or "soul," and through the identification of the *Prāṇas* (vital airs), which are supposed to be based on the *Ātman*, with the gods, an *Ātman* comes to be attributed to (and pervades) the universe (as in the *Śatapatha Br*. XI. 2. 3), the conception having already attained to a high degree of abstraction. On the other hand, *Brahman* (neuter), which in the *RV* means only "prayer," or devotion, in the oldest Brāhmaṇas, signifies already "Universal holiness" as manifested in prayer, priest, and sacrifice; from this to the holy principle animating all nature in the Upanishads is but a short step. This word "*Brahman*" epitomizes, as it were, the whole evolution of religious and philosophical thought in India. This unity of *Brahman* (the cosmic principle) and *Ātman* (the psychical principle) or (in other words) the identity of the individual *Ātman* with the world-*Ātman* expressed by the Upanishadic dictum "*tat tvam asi*" ("Thou art That"), is very tersely explained by Deussen:[2] "The Brahman, the power which presents itself to us materialized in all existing things, which creates, sustains, preserves and receives back into itself again all worlds, this eternal, infinite, divine power is identical with the *Ātman*, with that which, after stripping off everything external, we discover in ourselves as our real most essential being, our individual self, the soul." The Upanishads, piling, as they do, metaphor on metaphor on this conception, are unceasingly struggling to help an understanding of the true nature of the pantheistic Self. Ajātaśatru explains to Gārgya Bālāki[3] that the true *Brahman* is to be sought only in the knowing and intelligent Spirit (*Purusha*) in man, i.e. in the *Ātman (the self)* out of which emanate all worlds, all gods, all beings. The *Ātman* thus takes the place of the more personal Prajāpati as a creative power. The beautiful dialogue between Yājñavalkya and Maitreyī (*Bṛihadāraṇyaka Up*. II. 4) expresses the doctrine that the *Ātman* is one with the Universe and that everything exists only in so far as it is the cognitive self. No wonder, one of the later Upanishads (*Śvetāśvatara* IV. 10) should contain the notion (which in later Vedānta became so prominent) that the material world is an illusion (*māyā*), produced by *Brahman* as by a conjurer (*māyin*).

Prāṇa plays an important part in the psychology and metaphysics of the Upanishads. *Prāṇa* is breath of life, life, or life-principle. In the singular *Prāṇa* is a frequent appellation of the *Ātman*. A favourite theme with the Upanishads is a description of this *Prāṇa,* which is identical with the intelligent Self, and of its relations to the *Prāṇas* (plural), i.e. the organs of the soul (breath, speech, sight, hearing, and the organ of thinking). The reciprocal action between these organs of the soul and the corresponding five forces of Nature—wind, fire, the sun, the quarters of heaven and the moon—is also often touched upon. This explains the frequently recurring psychological fable of the quarrel among the *Prāṇas* regarding seniority. This *Prāṇa* doctrine is also responsible for much poetic speculation on the vicissitudes of the individual *Ātman* in the conditions of waking, sleeping, dreaming, and death, and its wanderings in the Beyond, up to the point of its emancipation, i.e. complete absorption in the *Brahman.* Thus, in a passage of poetic beauty, unsurpassed perhaps in the literature of the world, the *Bṛihadāraṇyaka Up.* (IV. 3-4)[4] tells us of the fortunes of the soul and incidentally develops the doctrine of the transmigration of souls, and in close connection with it, the ethical doctrine of *Karman* (action) which, with the infallibility of a law of nature, must produce its consequences (its reactions on the ethical plane must be equal and opposite?) and regulate the new birth, which thus depends on a man's own deeds and makes man truly "an architect of his own fate." This is the germ of the Buddhist doctrine which, while denying the existence of soul altogether, allows *Karman* to continue after death and determine the next birth. The *Chhāndogya Up.* gives us the most detailed account of this theory of transmigration. The forest-ascetic, equipped with knowledge and faith, enters after death the *devayāna* (the path of the gods) which leads to absorption in (i.e. oneness with) *Brahman* or deliverance. The householder who performs sacrifices and works goes by the *pitṛiyāṇa* (the path of the Fathers) to the moon, where he abides till the consequences of his actions are exhausted, and then returns to earth, where he is first born as a plant and then as a member of one of the "*dvija*" (or three higher) classes. This is a kind of double retribution, first in the next world (which is traceable to a survival of the old Vedic belief about future life), and then by transmigration in this. The wicked are born again as outcastes, dogs, or swine. The *Bṛihadāraṇyaka* (VI. 2. 15-16) gives a similar account.

The *Kaushītaki Up.* (I. 2-3) gives a somewhat different itinerary, according to which, after death all go first to the moon. From here, some go by the path of the Fathers to *Brahman,* while others return to various forms of earthly existence from man to worm. The earliest form of this theory is found in the *Śatapatha Brāhmaṇa* which speaks of repeated births and deaths *in the next world,* both for the man who has correct knowledge and performs a certain sacrifice, resulting in his attaining immortality, and for the ignorant defaulter, who ultimately becomes the prey of death. In the Upanishadic version, the rebirth takes place in this world. So it is not necessary to suppose (though it may not be impossible) that the theory was picked up by the Vedic Aryans from the animistic views of the aborigines. Some hymns of *RV* (X. 16. 3; 58. 1-12) contain hints of animism.

A very sound ethical idea underlies the Upanishadic doctrine of the *Ātman*[5] the logical and beautiful conclusion of which must be that it is the Universal Soul which we love in each individual, and that the recognition of this *Ātman* must lead to love for all creatures. But it is the doctrine of *Karman* that represents the preponderance of the moral element in the Upanishads as compared to the Brāhmaṇas. Nevertheless, moral precepts are met with in a few passages only as, e.g., in the famous *Taittirīya Upanishad* (I. 11) inculcating truthfulness, duty, etc., and in the *Bṛihadāraṇyaka Up.* (V. 2) preaching self-restraint, generosity, and compassion. The reason is not far to seek. The highest object—union with Brahman—is attainable only by cognition, by giving up non-knowledge, i.e. all works good and bad. Sacrifices and pious works can only lead to newer births, but knowledge alone lifts one above the maze of *Saṁsāra* to the One and Eternally True. This conception of "knowledge" or "cognition" has evolved out of "the knowledge of some secret doctrine or other sacrificial science" on which insistence is laid in the Brāhmaṇas and Āraṇyakas. The longing for this true knowledge, leading to the disregard of all pleasures, finds poetical expression in the legend of Nachiketas (*ante*, p. 475) in one of the most remarkable and beautiful Upanishads, the *Kāṭhaka,* but in the *Maitrāyāṇīya Up.* (I. 2-4), one of the latest, it leads to an utter contempt of the world and that pessimistic trait of thought which recurs so often in the Buddhist as well as later Indian literature. The fact is that although at bottom the old Upanishads are not pessimistic, describing as they do *Brahman* and *Ātman* as *ānandamaya* ("consisting of joy"), belief in the unreality of the world must ultimately lead to contempt for it.

Thus we find in the Upanishads vigorous and creative philosophical thought clothed in the language of poetry. No wonder they make a powerful appeal to the heart and the head. The thinkers seek earnestly for the truth and so their thoughts become a fervent expression of the ever unsatisfied human yearning for knowledge. All the philosophical systems and religions of India, heretical or orthodox, have sprung up from the Upanishads. The theological-philosophical systems of Śaṁkara, Rāmānuja and others are founded on the *Vedānta-Sūtras* of Bādarāyaṇa which in their turn are reared on the doctrines of the Upanishads. Reference has already been made above (pp. 475 ff.) to the profound influence exercised by the Upanishads on human thought outside India.

We may now represent a few fundamental tenets of the Upanishads in the form of propositions[6] in the manner of Deussen. (1) The *Ātman* is the knowing subject and as such can never become an object for us and is therefore itself unknowable. It can only be defined negatively. When later Vedānta defined it as *being, thought,* and *bliss* (*sach-chid-ānanda*) on the basis of the frequent references to these separate elements scattered in the older Upanishads, it is nothing but a negative characterization, because *being* is rather a *not-being* in an empirical sense, *thought* is the negation of all objective being, and *bliss* is the negation of all suffering. (2) As the *Ātman* is the metaphysical unity expressing itself in all empirical plurality—a unity found only in our consciousness— it is the sole reality. To know the *Ātman* is, therefore, to know everything. There is really no plurality; there can be no *becoming;* "change" is a mere name. (3) The pantheism of the Upanishads is but a compromise between the two opposite points of view—the metaphysical one which does not recognize any reality outside of the *Ātman,* i.e. consciousness, and the empirical one according to which a manifold universe exists external to us. The *Ātman* being the Universe, it remains the sole reality although the universe is real. But what distinguishes Upanishadic pantheism from that of Europe is the subtle distinction made by the Upanishads when they state that the universe is in God, but never that the universe is God. God (or *Ātman*) is transcendent as well as immanent. (4) Thus when it is stated that the universe is the *Ātman,* the identity remains very obscure. This obscurity was sought to be removed by borrowing the well-known empirical category of causality and representing that the *Ātman* is the chronologically antecedent cause and the universe is its effect, its creation.

2. THE SŪTRAS

Side by side with the high philosophy of the Upanishads, laying stress on knowledge and meditation as the means to emancipation, we find a continuance of the old sacrificial rituals of the Brāhmaṇas throughout the period under review. The Śrauta- and Gṛihya-Sūtras (ante, p. 478) are our chief sources of information regarding the ritualistic religion of the age, and some important features of the rituals described in them are noted below.

As a rule, the Śrauta sacrifices required the use of three fires. The number of priests was sixteen or seventeen, not counting the actual performers of minor ritual acts such as the slaying of the animal victims and other menial functions in a fairly complicated ritual. Prayers to more than one god—nay, a very large number of gods—accompanying the ritual acts, were another characteristic. Sometimes, as in the Āprī litanies, the order of the deities invoked was the same whatever the families that addressed them. Among the sacrifices, some are the norm (*prakṛitis*) which others (the *vikṛitis*) follow as a model. For example, the new and full moon sacrifices serve as the norm for a sacrifice of the Ishṭi type and for the animal sacrifice in its form as offering to Agni and Soma. The latter becomes the norm for other and more elaborate animal sacrifices. Agnishṭoma is the *prakṛiti* or norm of the Soma sacrifice in all its variations including the Dvādaśāha, while the Sattras are based on the latter. Among the details of performances in every sacrifice some are subsidiary (*aṅga*) and common to many sacrifices, while others (*pradhāna*) are special or peculiar to it only. A peculiarity of the Soma sacrifice is the singing of the Sāmans or melodies based on verses of the *Ṛigveda*, each of which could be sung to different melodies. When, however, more than one verse is sung to one melody, we have a Stotra usually made up of triplets or Pragāthas. The Stomas further are forms or ways of chanting Stotras, of which there are numerous varieties. The Stotra is followed by a Śastra which is a recitation of the Hotṛi or his assistants. Broadly speaking, there are two types of Śrauta sacrifices, the Soma sacrifices characterized by the singing of the Sāmans, and the Haviryajñas marked by the absence of Sāman-singers. The animal sacrifice is midway between the two. It does not employ the Sāman-singers and so should be deemed a Haviryajña, but, on the other hand, is a vital part of the Soma sacrifice.

The Gṛihya or domestic ritual[Ca] is so called because it centres round the domestic fire or the fire which is established in the home and is maintained by the householder. It was the duty of the householder and his family, including wife, son, daughter, and pupil, to see that it was kept constantly burning and alive. If it ever went out, it had to be rekindled ceremoniously by friction, or borrowed from the house of a wealthy person or of the performer of many sacrifices. The normal occasions for the establishment (with proper ceremony) of the domestic fire were marriage, the division of property of the family, the *samāvartana* ("the return of the student after the completion of his period of studentship"), the death of the head of the family (when the eldest son kindled a new fire), and a continuous break of twelve days in the maintenance of the fire. As a rule, the householder himself performed the domestic sacrifices, the wife being allowed to act for him, if necessary, at the morning and evening libations and at the evening Bali. The employment of a Brahman is optional, though he must be requisitioned at the Śūlagava (spit-ox) and Dhanvantari sacrifices. When the householder did not call in the Brahman, a straw puppet or a sunshade and garment were placed on the vacant seat in the south which would have been occupied by the Brahman if he were employed. The marriage formulas were muttered by the bridegroom himself if he were a Brāhmaṇa, otherwise by the Brāhmaṇas on his behalf. In the offerings to the gods the position of the sacrificer's sacred thread was over the left shoulder and under the right arm-pit, but exactly the reverse in the offerings to the Pitṛis. The domestic offerings receive the name *"pāka"* in distinction from the Śrauta. *Pāka* means "cooked food," or as an adjective, "simple." Whatever the original sense (and neither is unsuitable), the term is comprehensive enough to include offerings of milk, curds, melted butter, rice, barley, sesame, barely-gruel, porridge, and even the flesh of animals, though these were offered on very rare and special occasions. Varieties of butter (butter at various degrees of temperature) are used, the butter-offering being of a simple type. The fore-offerings and after-offerings, the kindling-verses or instruction-formulae (*nigadas*) and the invocation of the Iḍā which are well-known features of the Śrauta offerings are conspicuous by their absence in the *Pāka* ("simple" or "baked") offerings. The few occasions for an animal sacrifice are marriage, offerings to the manes and the guest-reception. The only special animal sacrifice is the Śūlagava (spit-ox), which inclines more to the Śrauta type.

It is necessary to make a few general observations on certain important aspects of the Vedic sacrifice and the element of magic in the ritual. It is impossible to accept the view that all worship of the gods is to be traced to the cult of the dead, being but an imitation of the mode of providing for the dead. The human worshipper, realizing his weakness and utter helplessness, leans, as it were, for support on the all-powerful gods—a support which he seeks to canvass by the offering of gifts. This is the essential nature of the Vedic sacrifice. This divine help and the power of magic were both invoked through the sacrifice, in the inevitable struggle with the forces of evil or the demons. Magic and religion are never confused in the Vedic religion. The fear of the living for the dead plays an important part in the cult of the dead, but it must be remembered that there is no direct fear of the spirit of the dead, to whom no hostile nature is attributed. It is rather the fear of death—the fear of the great change—that has affected them. This explains why the whole cult of the dead in Vedic ritual is marked by love and deep regard for the dead ancestors, and why providing nourishment for them is a matter that claims the respectful attention of the living all his life.

Keith thinks that "in the *Ṛigveda* and in the later period alike, the cult of the gods is marked by the absence of any temple or house of the god, even of the simplest kind."[7] This view may, however, be justly questioned. If by "temple" we understand "a sacred place set apart for purposes of worship and devotion to a deity," then the *agnyagāra* (*Gobhila Gṛihya-sūtra*, I. 4. 5) or fire-temple, inside or outside which *bali* oblations could be offered, is such a temple. A god's house is mentioned in the Gṛihya-sūtras along with a forest as the place where a student observing the *Mahānāmnīvrata* is to fast. When a Snātaka is advised to go round "god's houses" (keeping his right side to them), if they are met with on the way, temples seem to be meant. The truth is that though temples probably existed, they played no important part in the ritual of the sacrifice, the essence of which lay in an invocation of the god to come to the place of the sacrifice and to partake of the food and drink there kept ready for him.

If the hymns of praise, the music, and the dance in the ritual can be understood as fitting reception for the god invited, other features such as chariot-racing, dicing, archery, ribaldry, mimic fights, etc., can be explained better as examples of the employment of sympathetic magic than as part of the entertainment provided for the gods. Such magic elements abound in the Vedic sacrifice.

Offerings are made in the hope of favours expected from the deity. The god accepts the offerings and becomes strengthened, and the prosperity of the sacrificer is in proportion to the prospering of the god. This theory of the sacrifice results in an exchange of gifts, but the initiative in this exchange generally comes from the worshipper rather than from the god. That is to say, there are only a few thank-offerings (comparatively speaking) in the ritual of this age or the earlier ones. The *Āśvalāyana Gṛihya-sūtra*, (IV. 1. 1 ff.) prescribes the offering of a Soma or animal sacrifice, when a person, who has established the three sacred fires, falls ill and then leaves his residence and goes out of the village to bring pressure on the three fires: he naturally takes these fires with himself and they cure their worshipper, being eager themselves to go back to the village. The view of Keith[8] that vows of the kind, "Do this and I will offer to thee," are not common in the Vedic religion is not quite correct, and is probably based on the absence of explicit statements. But the offering of first-fruits, the sacrifice offered on the birth of a son or on the acquisition of a thousand cattle, and the feast to the dead at the marriage ceremony should perhaps be accounted as thank-offerings. The subtle distinction that the keeping of a promise (to offer a sacrifice), explicit or implicit, is not a thank-offering is not legitimate in Vedic religion.

Gradually, however, the belief in the magic power of the sacrifice grows to such an extent as to overshadow and ultimately eclipse the belief in the efficacy of the good-will of a deity. In the organization and elaboration of sacrificial ritual, during this and the Brāhmaṇa age, a particular mental outlook is noticeable, which construes the sacrifice as a potent weapon of magic.

The magic power of the sacrifice could be employed to wash away sin. To take but one example out of many, the *Kātyāyana Śrauta-sūtra* (XIX. 5. 13) tells us that in the Sautrāmaṇī offering, a vessel containing a special preparation is made to drift away on water with the sins of the performers. The sin is treated like a disease, and the concept of this sin or evil is comprehensive enough to include errors in the sacrifice, un-common occurrences in the home or outside, and all unaccountable phenomena of Nature. The Prāyaśchitta (or expiation) offerings, overlaid with magic practices of a simple kind, and culminating in gifts to the priests, occupy a very large space in the Sūtras, both Śrauta and Gṛihya.

The purifying power of a public confession and the usefulness of a warning to others of the identity of the sinner may be elements of belief in some strange and peculiar practices connected with the removal of sin, such as the proclamation by the husband of his sin against his wife, while begging for alms clothed in an ass's skin (*see ante*. p. 495). The murderer drinks out of the skull of the murdered man, puts on the skin of a dog or an ass, and lives on alms, confessing his guilt before all. These practices are mentioned in the Dharma-sūtras of Āpastamba, Gautama, and Baudhāyana, as also in the *Pāraskara Gṛihya-sūtra*.

We need not discuss here at length the problem of the original theory of the sacrifice—whether the magic art of perpetuating the life of the herds and of vegetation, and even of man, was the essence of the sacrifice, and whether the gift-theory was original or secondary. We may only note that when the *Kauśika-sūtra* (XIII. 1-6) prescribes a magic rite in which portions of the bodies of some animals and human beings, such as a lion, a tiger, a Kshatriya and a Brahmachārin, are to be eaten to acquire certain qualities, not totemism but the conception of sacramental communion is hinted at. Similarly the idea of a common meal as a means of producing harmony is clearly seen in the same Sūtra (XIII. 6). The rule in the Gṛihya-sūtras that nothing is to be eaten without making an offering of a portion of it, is but an illustration of the conception of communion. When the newly-married couple share food together from an offering made by the husband, we see an instance of the belief in the community produced by the sacrifice. But the theory that the sacrifice is a communion of men, both among themselves and with the god, whether through the direct rite of eating with him or as a sacrament through eating a victim which has become impregnated in some measure with the deity, is not enunciated in the formulae of the ritual.

The important rôle played by the fire in a sacrifice is too obvious to be emphasized. The fire is the intermediary who conveys the sacrifice to the gods and at the same time an effective means of chasing away evil spirits. The all-important position of the fire in the domestic ritual is evidenced by the fact that the fire is a witness to, and sanctifier of, every domestic sacrament or rite, and receives an oblation or prayer at every important stage of the ritual. The cathartic function of the fire is to be seen in the burning of the grass covering the altar at the end of the offering, lest, imbued with a superhuman character, it should harm anyone by contact. The *omentum* is burnt before being offered to other deities, evidently with a view to purifying it and imparting to it an agreeable savour.

The fire-offering, however, was not the only type of offering. Food for the dead was placed in pits according to an ancient and universal custom. Gifts to water-deities were naturally thrown into the waters and the offerings to Rudra and other demoniac figures may be deposited in anthills or hung on trees or merely thrown in the air.

A comparison of the Śrauta ritual with its three fires with the Gṛihya ritual with its one fire suggests some interesting hypotheses regarding the origin of this triad of fires. Certain ceremonies are common to both the cults, such as the morning and evening Agnihotra and the new and full moon sacrifices, the difference being one of elaboration only. Certain cereal and animal offerings are also common to both the cults. Every householder had to keep one fire in the house to carry on (mostly by himself) the domestic cult. The kings, the nobles, and the rich people who could afford it, maintained the three fires, employing a number of priests for the performance of the Śrauta cult. The family rites as such must be performed only in the domestic fire, while the Soma sacrifice cannot be performed without the triad of fires. The name Gārhapatya ("of the householder") of one of the three Śrauta fires suggests that the latter three have developed out of the one domestic fire, because like the domestic fire the Gārhapatya alone was continually kept, the other two —the Āhavanīya and Dakshiṇa—being derived from it when necessary. A man going on a journey takes formal leave of the Gārhapatya first, which is another point of contact with the ceremonial of the domestic fire. The Āhavanīya is the fire for the actual offering and the Gārhapatya for cooking the food to be offered to the gods; the Dakshiṇāgni, by its place in the south, was, in the beginning, probably intended to drive away the evil spirits, and later, to receive the offerings intended for such spirits and for the fathers.

As a rule the sacrifice is for an individual, the Yajamāna ("sacrificer"), who provided the "sinews" of the sacrifice and the gifts for the priests. There is only one exception to this rule, namely the Sattras or "sacrificial sessions," lasting for a year or longer, where the entire host of officiating priests are themselves the sacrificers, it being taken for granted that all are Brāhmaṇas. The merit of the offering in these Sattras belongs to all the sacrificers, while any error or evil done belongs to the perpetrator only.

As Agni is the Purohita as well as Hotṛi priest in the *Ṛigveda*, the Hotṛi was the most important priest in those days. Later on, with the elaboration of the ritual, the Purohita, who was the superintendent or overseer of the sacrifice, became a different priest from the Hotṛi and called the Brahman, to whom the duty of superintending the whole sacrifice was naturally assigned. In the Śrauta-sūtras of Śāṅkhāyana, Āśvalāyana, and Kātyāyana, the list of priests is as follows: the Hotṛi, Potṛi, Neshṭṛi, Agnīdh, the Adhvaryu, the Brahman and the Upavaktṛi (who appears in place of the Praśāstṛi in the otherwise identical list in the *Ṛigveda*) and the Achchhāvāka (who is later admitted to a share in the Soma). Another passage of the *Kātyāyana Śrauta-sūtra* (IX. 8. 8 ff.) gives another list in connection with the morning pressing of the Soma: the Hotṛi, two Adhvaryus, two Praśāstṛis, Brahman, Potṛi, Neshṭṛi, and Āgnīdhra. The second Adhvaryu becomes the Prati prasthātṛi and the second Praśāstṛi becomes the Achchhāvāka later. The Hotṛi originally combined the two functions—the performance of the offering and the recitation of the accompanying *mantra*—but the functions were later separated. In the ritual text-books of our age, two kinds of offerings are to be distinguished—the *yajatayaḥ* in which there is one reciter and performer, i.e. the Adhvaryu, so called because his manual duties are the more important, and the *juhotayaḥ* in which there is the Hotṛi to recite and the Adhvaryu to perform the manual acts. The Hotṛi recites a variety of verses but, in a large number of offerings, only two types of verses, the Puronuvākyā which invites the god to be present at the offering intended for him, and the Yājyā which is recited just when the Adhvaryu is about to throw the offering into the fire. He also recites the Nivids, which are inserted in the hymns and are invitations to the god, with a bare enumeration of his titles, to come and intoxicate himself with the Soma. Although, in their present form, the Nivids are later than the *Ṛigveda*, they are, in essence, the oldest form of the invitation to the gods, from the point of view of the evolution of the liturgical employment of rubrics in the ritual. The Adhvaryu is in charge of the practical performance of the various manual acts of the ritual and has to mutter a certain number of formulas, normally in prose, to the accompaniment of the performance. He was assisted by the Agnīdh, whose main duties were concerned with the kindling of the fire. The Hotṛi, the Adhvaryu with his assistant, the Agnīdh, and the Brahman, the general overseer, sufficed for the minor sacrifices and the new and full moon offerings. For the animal sacrifice, the

Hotṛi required an assistant named variously Upavaktṛi or Praśāstṛi or Maitrāvaruṇa, and for the Soma sacrifice, the services of the Potṛi and the Neshṭṛi were requisitioned. The Brāhmaṇāchchhaṁsin, in the ritual of our period, is but a Hotraka or an assistant of the Hotṛi. The position of the Brahman enumerated in the list given above becomes all-important in this age. He recites practically nothing. He takes his seat by the chief fire-altar and is engaged in general supervision. He makes good every flaw in the sacrifice by his silent meditation. The Udgātṛi, Prastotṛi and the Pratihartṛi were Sāman-singers, whose chants fall into two classes. One is composed of those addressed to Soma Pavamāna and based on verses mainly drawn from the ninth Maṇḍala of the *Ṛigveda.* The other class consists of chants addressed to the ordinary gods to whom libations are offered at the three pressings of the Soma. The chant based on certain Ṛik-verses is followed up immediately by the Hotṛi's recitation of those very Ṛik-verses. This correspondence or parallelism is insisted upon in the ritual. For the Soma sacrifice, as many as sixteen priests are prescribed, the Kaushītakins even prescribing a seventeenth.

In the ritual of this age, the choosing of the priests (*ṛitvigvaraṇa*) has become a well-developed formal ceremony. The sacrificer and the invitees both satisfy themselves as to the worthiness and qualifications of the other party, before extending and accepting the invitation. An interesting feature of the formal questions and answers used in the ceremony is the care taken by the priests to see that they are not invited because other priests who had been employed had struck work for some reason, leaving the sacrifice unfinished. The sacrificer has to be a member of one of the three higher castes. His duties in this age are very light. He repeats certain formulae, throws the offerings into the fire, and observes certain restrictions along with his wife. Above all, it is he who pays the Dakshiṇā (fee), appropriate to each sacrifice.

We may now briefly refer to the relation of magic to this ritualistic religion. Magic is not earlier than religion, though they are inextricably blended in India. As has been noted already (*ante;* Ch. XXII, p. 442) the *Atharvaveda* is the first book that makes use of magic mixed up with theosophy, though it is priestly and not purely popular magic. In the Brāhmaṇas magic practically pervades the whole ritual. The transition is best exemplified in the changed conception of the sacrifice, which was originally an appeal or prayers to the gods, but became the supreme power in the universe controlling even the gods and granting all wishes. The potencies to be treated by magic are both personal or actually alive, and impersonal, i.e. spirits. The means of magic are the words and figures or representations of things which are used, either as substitutes for, or in addition to the articles connected with, the objects of magical treatment. Special times, such as evening or night, and places such as grave-yards or cross-roads are prescribed. The chief source-books for our information regarding magic are the *Atharvaveda* and the *Kauśika-sūtra* belonging to that Veda, the *Sāmavidhāna Brāhmaṇa*, the *Ṛigvidhāna*, the *Pariśishṭas* of the *Atharvaveda* and other minor texts.

The averting of evil influences is accomplished by propitiation, or banishment by any means fair or foul, such as the use of water for washing them off, the use of noise, the holding of a staff, and the gesture of shaking off and transfer of the evil to someone else. The use of amulets is recognized as an excellent means of protection. Mimetic magic, the magic spell, and even the magic sacrifice are all known and prescribed in the Sūtra texts. The theory of divination is known, and a variety of means is employed. Omens are drawn from the movements of animals. The interpretation of dreams is also an interesting feature of Vedic magic, and experts in the interpretation of omens are known. The ordeal is nothing more than an application of the theory of divination. Although not many characteristic and essential practices of the later Yoga philosophy are traced in ritual literature, the fivefold divisions of breaths or vital airs is known. Perspiration is induced in the *Dīkshā* ceremony, as a means of awakening the ecstatic state, but the various sitting postures familiar to the later Yoga are not known.

It would appear from the above discussion that religious thought during the period under review does not, on the whole, present a very consistent picture because of the contradictory legacies it was heir to. The polytheism of the Saṁhitās had narrowed down to Upanishadic monism. At one end was sacrifice and ritual, at the other was the abstruse and profound philosophy of the Upanishads. The conception of rebirth was inextricably mixed up with ideas of a happy heaven and a horrid hell. Spiritual barrenness of the people at large was the natural result. No wonder formulae, observances, and sacraments became the order of the day!

But even though only sacrificial rites and duties are found systematized in the *Kalpa-sūtras*, ethical purity was not neglected and indeed was regarded as the *sine qua non* in the path of *Karman*. Inner ethical virtues such as purity, perseverance, forbearance, and kindness to all were prescribed along with religious rites by the *Gautama Dharma-sūtra* (VIII. 20-23) for example, and are even ranked higher than mere ritualistic ceremonial. Self-restraint is the mother of all virtues and is to be ceaselessly cultivated in this life, since the present life is but a preparation for the real, happy life after death. Here we find the doctrine "Man is the architect of his own fate," in the truest sense of the phrase. This *Karman* discipline does not rule out desire as the motive power of action. Only it is focussed on the acquisition of happiness in a future life. *Dharma* (religious merit), *Artha* (the acquisition of wealth), and *Kāma* (the enjoyment of the present life) are the *Purushārthas* ("human values" or the "aims of man"). Worldly aims and efforts to secure them are not scorned but harnessed to the fulfilment of higher aims in the next life. *Dharma* bears fruit in a future life and is extra-empirical in its technical aspect, in the sense that it can be ascertained only from a divine or traditional code.

---

1. For a general account of the Upanishads, and particularly their chronological classification cf. Ch. XXIV.
2. *The Philosophy of the Upanishads*, p. 39.
3. *Kaushitaki Upanishad*, IV, and *Bṛihadāraṇyaka Up.*, II. 1.
4. Cf. Ch. XXIV, pp. 470. ff.
5. Some quotations from the Upanishads on this subject are given in Ch. XXIV, p. 470.
6. Cf. Deussen, *Op. cit.*, pp. 396 ff.

6a. For an account of these rituals, cf. Ch. XXIV, pp. 474 ff.

7. *RPVU*, p. 258.
8. *Op. cit.*, p. 260. fn. 5.

CHAPTER XXVII

SOCIAL AND ECONOMIC CONDITIONS

I. SOCIAL CONDITIONS

1. *Family Life*

THE family life was the framework on which society rested, and the Gṛihya-sūtras that deal with the domestic sacrifices and other duties performed by the householders supply valuable information regarding it.

As in the age of the Later Saṁhitās and Brāhmaṇas, the family was normally a joint one with the most senior married member or householder as the head. But partitions often took place as the rules in the Gṛihya-sūtras regarding the kindling of the domestic fire show. Among the occasions mentioned there for fresh formal kindling are the division of the inheritance or the death of the head of the family, in which case the eldest son kindled it. Seniority in age constituted an important claim for respect in the family. The directions about the *Vaiśvadeva-bali*—one of the daily domestic sacrifices—that it need not be repeated every time the food was cooked, and that it may be offered from the kitchen of the chief householder or from that of the member whose food was ready first, show that the joint family was big enough to necessitate cooking at different kitchens. The fact that a rite is prescribed for one desirous of a large family shows that the people liked to have many children. Male additions to the family were preferred to female ones. An interesting formality in the family life of these days is the manner in which the father greeted the children in the house after his return from a journey, the mode of greeting being different for male and female children. The high sense of responsibility and duty expected to be shown by the head of the family towards the other members is seen in the Gṛihya-sūtra rule that he was to take his food only after feeding all the children and old persons, as well as any female residing under his protection, and any pregnant lady in the house. The respect and authority that the father commanded is shown by the fact that the Dharma-sūtras, describing in detail the acts of courtesy which a son owed to his father, mention that he is allowed to eat the remnants of his father's food. The father on his part is expected to be kind. The heartless conduct of the father in the story of Śunaḥśepa is condemned in the *Śāṅkhāyana Śrauta-sūtra*. The spiritual succession from father to son is almost taken for granted by the Upanishads. The gradation of the relations in a family is given, as it were, in the *Chhāndogya*

Upanishad (VII. 15. 2), where father, mother, brother, and sister are mentioned in succession.

2. *The Caste-System*

The period of the Sūtras witnessed the gradual hardening of the caste-system in general and the deterioration of the position of the Vaiśyas and Śūdras in particular. We can trace this process step by step if we follow the evidence of the three broadly distinguishable chronological strata in the Sūtras, namely (1) the Śrauta-sūtras with which may be conveniently considered the evidence of the Sūtras of Pāṇini also; (2) the Gṛihya-sūtras; and (3) the Dharma-sūtras.

From the evidence of the *Śāṅkhāyana Śrauta-sūtra* which records that the Vājapeya sacrifice—a sacrifice of which the chariot race forms an integral part—was at one time a sacrifice for a Vaiśya as well as a priest or king, it is clear that the position of the Vaiśya is deteriorating now and Caste distinctions are hardening. The power of the Brāhmaṇas is growing. They are exempt from taxes and could, on occasions, be kings, but Kshatriyas could hardly become priests. The prestige and influence of the Purohita in the state are considerable. Pāṇini's division of the Śūdras into *niravasita* and *aniravasita* shows that certain degraded Śūdras with unclean habits like the Nishādas were forced to reside outside the limits of the village or town. The Śūdra was denied the privilege of *saṁnyāsa* ("renunciation"). The *rāshṭra* or nation consisted only of the three higher Castes, the Śūdras being excluded from it. Although some Caste-sections were degraded, it is not quite certain if the Mixed Castes had arisen in this period.

The Gṛihya-sūtras clearly differentiate the status, occupations, obligations, duties, and privileges of the four principal Castes in matters both spiritual and secular. A different age is prescribed for each of the three higher castes for the various sacraments, such as the *Chūḍākaraṇa* (the tonsure ceremony of the child) and the *Upanayana* ("initiation") ceremonies. One is not sure whether these different prescriptions were adjustments necessitated originally by the differences of mental calibre and moral fibre in the various caste-groups (for the *Upanayana* ceremony, for example). Different seasons are also prescribed for the different castes. The differentiation extends even to such minor things as the girdle, the staff, the skin, and the garment to be used by the student, and the *Upanayana mantra* to be recited by him. The story is the same with regard to most of the sacraments such as the naming of the child, the building of a house, marriage, and even such unessential matters as *anulepana* or salving which is part of the *snāna* ceremony signifying the completion of the period of studentship. Even in the giving of gifts, the Caste determined the nature of the gift as much as the financial condition of the giver.

The Brāhmaṇas in particular have now become a well-organized priesthood. Among their special duties and privileges are the study and the teaching of the Veda, sacrificing for themselves and others, and the receiving of gifts. The feasting of learned Brāhmaṇas to invoke their blessings is, without exception, laid down as the concluding feature of every sacrament. That this feasting was originally more a disinterested homage to the noble qualities of the spiritually-minded Brāhmaṇas, than a sop to a worldly-minded priesthood, is clear from the rules that the invitee must not be a relative and that the invitations must not be arranged in a bargaining spirit. The general trend of the Gṛihya-sūtra prescriptions is that if the privileges of a Brāhmaṇa were many, he deserved them, and inspired respect and confidence as much by his high ethical standard as by the responsibilities and duties he owed to the other classes.

The Rājanya or Kshatriya class, among the rest, came closest to the Brāhmaṇa class in power and prestige, the two together being as it were the moral and material props of society. It was but natural that the cultural and social status of the Vaiśyas should gradually deteriorate, because by virtue of their occupations, namely agriculture, cattle-breeding and commerce, they came into close contact with the Śūdras. But the popular notion that the Vaiśya class had very little in common with the two higher classes in religious and sacramental matters is erroneous, though it has crystallized in the *Bhāgavadgītā* verse (IX. 32) which puts women, Vaiśyas, and Śūdras in one and the same category of people to whom eligibility to absolution through *Bhakti* (devotion) is conceded by the Lord. According to the Gṛihya-sūtras, when the domestic fire is to be kindled for the first time, it may be borrowed from the house of a Vaiśya rich in cattle, or from the house of one who performs many sacrifices, be he a Brāhmaṇa, a Kshatriya or a Vaiśya.

When we come to the Śūdras, however, we find that a wide gulf separates them from the three higher classes. The mixture of non-Aryan elements was probably responsible for this, as the word Ārya has a racial as well as moral connotation in this period and meant practically "reborn," that is, a member of the three higher castes. The privilege of performing the sanctifying sacraments (excepting that of marriage which took place in his case without the recitation of *mantras*) is denied to a Śūdra, and this was at once the cause and effect of his low position. But the Śūdra was certainly not a *pariah.* He enjoyed the status of a regular member of the household, and as a servant he was employed in all departments of the household not excluding the kitchen.

If the *Upanayana* ceremony was neglected for three generations in a family—whether Brahmaṇa, Kshatriya or Vaisya—the members became outcastes whose very sight was inauspicious and who probably lived outside the village or town. But the *Vrātya-stoma* ceremony of expiation and penance could secure for the outcastes readmission into the Aryan fold. Thus the horrors of an age-long and irremediable outcasting were unknown in the days of the Gṛihya-sūtras.

The Dharma-sūtras show that caste distinction has outstripped its proper limits and has even invaded the field of civil and criminal law (*ante*, pp. 495 ff.). The legal rate of interest and fines were graded according to the castes and a Śūdra received capital punishment for a crime like homicide for which lighter punishments were awarded to members of the higher castes. The contact of the three Aryan castes with the Śūdras through intermarriage was bound to lead to the rise of mixed castes, and the difference of occupations must have resulted sooner or later in an increase in the number of such mixed castes. Whether the mixed castes had arisen as early as the period of the later Saṁhitās is not certain. The enumeration of different classes or categories of victims in the Purushamedha chapters of the *White Yajurveda*, for example, may refer to different professions rather than castes. Similarly, for the period of the Śrauta-sūtras and Pāṇini, all that can be said is that certain caste-sections were degraded, but for the period of the Gṛihya- and Dharma-sūtras the existence of Mixed Castes cannot be doubted. The *anuloma* type of marriage, sanctioned by the Sūtras, whereby a member of higher caste could take unto himself a wife or wives of the lower castes, in addition to one of his own caste, must necessarily lead to new caste-divisions, although in the beginning, for some time, the rule that the progeny of such *anuloma* unions belonged to the *varṇa* or caste of the father arrested such a tendency. The Dharma-sūtras give the names of the mixed castes that arose not only as a result of the permitted *anuloma* marriages, but also as a result of the prohibited *pratiloma* marriages (where the husband's caste was lower than that of the wife) which apparently took place not rarely. The *Vasishṭha Dharma-sūtra* (XVIII. 1), for example, tells us that the offspring of a Śūdra male and a Brāhmaṇa female becomes a *Chāṅḍāla* who was to be treated as an outcaste. The sacramental direction of the Gṛihya-sūtras raise an interesting problem in this connection by mentioning rarely, if ever, the mixed castes. The rules seem to be framed only for the Brāhmaṇa, the Kshatriya, and the Vaiśya. One can understand that the progeny of *pratiloma* marriages should be excluded from the sacraments, but if *anuloma* progeny was also excluded, then a very large number of people would be denied the spiritual benefit of the sacraments. Apparently the *Āpastamba Gṛihya-sūtra* is of this view when it omits all reference to the *rathakāra* (the offspring of an *anuloma* marriage)in its Upanayana rules. The *Baudhāyana Gṛihya-sūtra,* which includes the *rathakāra* in the initiation rules, seems to reflect the earlier view. The following stages may, therefore, be distinguished in the treatment of the mixed castes in the Sūtra period from the sacramental point of view. In the earliest, perhaps the progeny of *anuloma* marriages was absorbed in the father's *varṇa* and thus became eligible for the sacraments as a Brāhmaṇa, Kshatriya, or Vaiśya. The next stage was probably reached when some important intermediate castes, like that of the *rathakāra,* received a separate treatment in the sacramental rules. The third stage is reflected in the exclusion of the *rathakāra* and other mixed castes from the sacraments.

It has to be recognized, however, that the caste-system even in this period had not become as wooden and exclusive as it is now. Inter-dining and inter-marriage (in the *anuloma* form) were not prohibited, though it is difficult to decide whether and how far change of caste was permissible. Even outcastes who had performed the prescribed penances could be readmitted to the Aryan fold. Nor were the castes so strictly separated or ramified into so many caste-divisions as obtain today. We see in the Dharma-sūtras the beginning of the formal theory of defilement resulting in the taboo of all contact on the part of a pure man of the upper castes with an impure man, namely, a member of the lowest caste. For example, we see in the Dharma-sūtras of Vasishṭha, Gautama, and Āpastamba the idea of impurity communicated by the touch or contact of inferior castes, which is reflected in the purification rendered necessary in the case of contact with a Śūdra and implied in the prohibition of eating in company with men of lower castes.

3. *Marriage and the Position of Women*

As already mentioned above, the *anuloma* system of marriage (i.e. between a male of a higher and a female of a lower caste) prevailed in this period. The low status of the Śūdra wife is reflected in the directions given in the Śrauta-sūtras that a sacrificer is allowed to cohabit with a *savarṇā* wife (of the same caste as his own) but not with the Śūdra one. The rules of Pāṇini regarding *Abhivādana* (salutation as a mark of respect to elderly persons in the house) show that the presence of wives of the lower castes (especially the Śūdra one) in a family and the consequent inevitable association of the higher caste ladies with them in the house has brought down the general level of womanly culture and led to a deterioration in their social status.

Among the Gṛihya-sūtras, only the *Āśvalāyana Gṛihya-sūtra,* and most of the Dharma-sūtras, mention eight forms of marriage. Of these, two call for an explanation, viz., the *paiśācha,* in which a girl is carried off while her relatives are sleeping or are indifferent, and the *rākshasa* in which the girl is abducted after a fight with her relatives. Probably the names of these marriage forms are derived from the names of the tribes among whom those peculiar marriage customs prevailed. That such immoral practices should be dignified as "forms" of marriage may be due to the desire not to deny some kind of a social status to the unfortunate girl-victim and her progeny, once the regrettable occurrence had taken place and was beyond recall. The Gṛihya-sūtras give detailed rules regarding the proper seasons for marriage, the qualifications of the bride and the bridegroom, and the various stages of the marriage ceremony. The bride should not be a *sapiṇḍa* relation of the bridegroom's mother nor belong to the same *gotra* as his own. The bridegroom should be a young man with intelligence, character and good health, and should, above all, come from a good family.

The various stages of the marriage ceremony are as follows: (1) the wooers formally go to the girl's house; (2) when the bride's father has given his formal consent, the bridegroom performs a sacrifice; (3) early in the morning of the first day of the marriage celebrations the bride is bathed; (4) a sacrifice is offered then by the high priest of the bride's family and a dance of four or eight women (not widows) takes place as part of the *Indrāṇī karman;* (5) the bridegroom then goes to the girl's house and makes the gift of a garment, unguent, and mirror to the bride who has been bathed as mentioned already; (6) the *Kanyā-pradāna* or the formal giving away of the bride now takes place, followed (7) by the *Pāṇi-grahaṇa*, the clasping of the bride's right hand by the bridegroom with his own right hand; (8) the treading on stone; (9) the leading of the bride round the fire by the bridegroom; (10) the sacrifice of fried grains; and, the most important ceremony of all, (11) the *saptapadī* (the couple walking seven steps together as symbolic of their lifelong concord) follow in due order. Finally the bride is taken in all ceremony to her new house. It must be taken for granted that the offering of oblations to the fire and the feasting of Brāhmaṇas take place at every important stage in this as in other ceremonies.

As regards the age of the bride, the prescriptions of the Gṛihya-sūtras differ. The older texts which describe the consummation of marriage as the *Chaturthī-karman*, or the ceremony of the fourth (night immediately after the marriage), evidently imply that the bride is of mature age. The more modern Gṛihya-sūtras and the Dharma-sūtras, however, lay down the rule that the bride should be *nagnikā* (*lit.*, naked), i.e. one who has not yet had her monthly period or one whose breasts are not yet developed. Evidently the only reasonable explanation of the incongruity is that the earlier practice is reflected in the older texts.

The prevalence of polygamy is implied in the *anuloma* system of marriage. The elements of bride-price (*śulka*) are discernible in the Āsura form of marriage, where the father of the bride is gladdened with money, and there are hints of a dowry in the Brāhma and Daiva forms of marriage where the father gives away the daughter after decking her with ornaments.

The prayers and rites of the ceremony clearly indicate that matrimony was a holy bond, and not a contract, and that progeny (especially male progeny) was the goal of marriage. As in the preceding age, the birth of a daughter was not welcome, and this fact in a way reflects the comparatively inferior position of women in society. All the sacraments, except that of marriage, are performed in the case of women without the recitation of Vedic *mantras*, and the *Upanayana* is not performed for them.

The woman, however, held an honoured position in the household. That a life of merriment, song, and dance was not denied to her is seen from certain sacraments in which women are asked to dance and sing. The presence of women who are not widows is particularly desired in marriage and other sacraments. The *Gobhila Gṛihya-sūtra* allows the option that the wife may offer the morning and evening oblations in place of the husband, because "the wife is as it were the house." That there were wives who desired to keep their husbands under control is clear from a rite prescribed for the purpose.

Since the Dharma-sūtras treat of the widow's right in the property of her husband, the possibility of the general prevalence of *satī* is ruled out. The *Vasishṭha Dharma-sūtra* speaks of the marriage of widows under certain circumstances, and the son of a remarried woman is one of the twelve sons enumerated in the Dharma-sūtras. So the remarriage of widows was not as strictly prohibited as it appears to have been in later days. In the marriage rules of the Dharma-sūtras local customs were recognized. The *Baudhāyana Dharma-sūtra*, for example, states that marrying the daughter of a maternal uncle is a southern custom. The custom of *niyoga* (levirate) or appointment of widows is recognized by the Dharma-sūtras which give detailed rules laying down the circumstances under which it is permissible. Some of the later Dharma-sūtras, however, condemn it.

On the whole the Dharma-sūtras take a more lenient attitude towards women than the Smṛitis of a later age or the customs and practices of the present day. Baudhāyana (II. 2. 4. 6.) quotes the injunction, which also occurs in the *Manu-smṛiti* (IX. 81), that "a barren wife should be abandoned in the tenth year, one who bears daughters (only) in the twelfth, one whose children (all) die in the fifteenth, but she who is quarrelsome without delay." But Āpastamba (II. 5. 11. 12-14) forbids the husband to take a second wife unless the first wife has no male child or neglected her religious duties. According to Vasishṭha (XXVIII. 2-3) a wife shall not be abandoned "even though she be quarrelsome or tainted by sin, or have left the house, or have suffered criminal force, or have fallen into the hands of thieves." Even a wife, who has committed adultery, becomes pure and is taken back by her husband after she has done proper penances (*Vas. Dh. S.* XXI. 8-10). As noted above (Ch. XXV, p. 495), Āpastamba (I. 10. 28. 19) imposes severe penalties on a husband "who unjustly forsakes his wife." On the other hand "a wife who forsakes her husband has only to perform a penance" (*Āp. Dh. S.* I. 10. 28. 20). This is a singular instance where the law or custom accords more favourable treatment to the wife than to the husband. Again, "a father who has committed a crime causing loss of caste must be cast off, but a mother does not become an outcast for her son." Similarly, the male offspring of outcasts are (also) outcasts, but not the females, who may be married, even without a dowry, by a twice-born (*Vas. Dh. S.* XIII. 47. 51-53). It is interesting to note that according to Baudhāyana (IV. 1. 15-16) "if a damsel has been abducted by force and has not been wedded with sacred texts, she is to be treated like a maiden and may be lawfully married to another man." Lastly, there is a general agreement among the Dharma-sūtras that a grown-up maiden, if not given in marriage in proper time by her father, may choose her own husband after waiting for three years (or months). At the same time the general principle is already enumerated in the later texts that "the males are the masters of women." "Their father protects them in childhood, their husbands protect them in youth, and their sons protect them in age; a woman is never fit for independence" (*Vas. Dh. S.* V. 1-2. *Bau. Dh. S.* II. 2.3.44-45).

4. *Education*

The Upanishads are a living testimony to the high intellectual attainments of the age. The stories of Śvetaketu Āruṇeya and Satyakāma Jābāla in the *Chhāndogya Upanishad* and the well-known passage in the *Taittirīya Upanishad* (I. 11) containing instruction (*anuśāsana*) given to the student at the end of his studies, show that the educational system maintained the high standard and lofty ideals of the preceding age (*ante*, p. 474). Some special features of the educational system are prominently brought out in the Upanishads. We find, for instance, that the highest position in society is willingly yielded to the intellectual aristocracy. Kshatriya kings like Janaka were famous for their learning, and respect was paid to them by all including the Brāhmaṇas. There are many instances on record where even the Brāhmaṇas learned the sacred knowledge, particularly philosophy, from the Kshatriyas. The story of Āruṇi, in the *Bṛihadāraṇyaka Upanishad*, shows that even old men became pupils. But the most pleasing feature is the frequent reference to women teachers, many of whom possessed the highest spiritual knowledge. The famous dialogues between Yājñavalkya and his wife Maitreyī (*Bṛih.* IV. 5) and Gārgī Vāchaknavī (*Bṛih.* III. 6. 8) show the height of intellectual and spiritual attainments to which a woman could rise. The stories of these noble and gifted ladies stand in sad contrast to the later age when even the study of Vedic literature was forbidden to women under the most severe penalty.

The Upanishads contain several lists of subjects of study, and these give us a good idea of the wide range of knowledge in those days. One such list[1] mentions not only Veda, Itihāsa, Purāṇa, and spiritual knowledge (*Brahma-vidyā*), but also grammar, mathematics (*Rāśi*), chronology (*Nidhi*), dialectics (*Vākovākya*), ethics (*Ekāyana*), astronomy, military science, science of snakes, and knowledge of portents (*Daiva*). There are a few more branches of knowledge mentioned in this list whose exact scope or nature cannot be defined, such as *Pitrya* (science relating to the manes), *Deva-vidyā* (etymological interpretation of divine names or knowledge of gods), *Bhūta-vidyā* (demonology or science of elements), and *Devajana-vidyā* (dancing and music or mythology). It is extremely unfortunate that we have no texts preserved regarding many of these subjects. But the list shows how a very comprehensive view of education was developed at the close of the Vedic Age. It also demonstrates that the six subjects comprised in the Vedāṅgas, to which a detailed reference has been made above (Ch. XXIV, p. 477), formed only a small portion of the curriculum of study, and not the whole of it, as is popularly believed.

The Sūtras give us a detailed account of student-life, which commenced with the *upanayana* (initiation). This ceremony, the essential features of which have been described above (Ch. XXIII. p. 459), in all probability originally signified the formal reception of an adult youth as a regular member of the (Aryan) tribe, a custom that prevailed among all primitive people. But, as described in the Gṛihya-sūtras, it is dominated by priestly interest, and this is not unnatural, as in this age, education was entirely under the control of the priestly class, and *upanayana* meant also the formal initiation into an educational career of boys of the three higher castes, at the ages respectively of eight, eleven, and twelve. The youth to be initiated wears a new upper garment or skin (which is to be that of a deer, goat or cow, according to his caste), a lower garment of a suitable colour, a staff of the prescribed length, and a threefold twisted girdle. According to some Gṛihya-sūtras he wears a sacrificial cord also. This equipment constitutes the educational uniform, as it were, of the youth.

Moral training formed the very pivot and the backbone of the educational system, and development of character was the one ideal that dominated it. The numerous vows and observances obligatory on the pupil (*Brahmachārin*) after the *upanayana*, which was a kind of initiation by the *Guru* (teacher) into a new spiritual life, entailed on him the most rigorous discipline for a prescribed period, during which he was to live religiously as a student in the house of his teacher. His daily routine is begging alms, collecting fuel, looking after the sacrificial fires, tending the house (of the teacher), learning, and practising austerities. The maintenance of chastity was obligatory on the *Brahmachārin*. Thus the ancient universities were residential, and a more perfect tutorial system was followed than is possible in any modern university, the pupil being under the observation of the *Guru* all the twenty-four hours. The daily begging of alms, on which the student lived, was for the inculcation of "plain living and high thinking," and had probably little or nothing to do with the financial status of the pupil or of the teacher with whom he resided. Attention may be drawn in this connection to some interesting practical and thoroughly human aspects of the educational system of this age as reflected in the *Taittirīya Upanishad* (I. 11.). After the admonition "let the *āchārya*, the parents, etc., be your gods" comes the frank admission that the preceptors, as human beings, may have their weaknesses, but it is not these but their good points that have to be copied by the pupils. A very practical streak is revealed in the advice to the pupil to continue the family-line by marrying and begetting children, to attend to *kuśala* or well-being (in a wordly sense), to make gifts and practise charity, for fear (*bhaya*) of public opinion or out of shame *(hriyā)*, if not out of the generosity of the heart.

The intellectual side of education was developed through the numerous subjects of study referred to above. Naturally more particulars are given of the study of the Vedic literature. It centred round the preservation by means of recitation, of the Veda of the particular *Śākhā* to which the pupil and the teacher belonged, or of as many Vedas as could be mastered by the student. Memory was a specially valued faculty and was most assiduously cultivated. The period of studentship is normally fixed at twelve years or until the pupil has mastered the Veda, though it may extend to much longer periods such as twenty-four or twenty-eight years, nay even for life in exceptional cases. The extent of the daily lesson is described, among others, in the Gṛihya-sūtras of the *Ṛigveda*. The pupil is to recite either the hymns belonging to each *Ṛishi* or each Anuvāka of the short hymns (*Kshudra-Sūktas*) or an Anuvāka or one verse in the beginning of each hymn. This option was a very useful and practical concession which enabled students, who did not aspire to become Vedic scholars, and (probably and chiefly) students of the Kshatriya and Vaiśya castes, to fulfil nominally their duty of learning the Veda. The Gṛihya-sūtras proceed on the assumption that all the three higher castes are to go through a period of studentship, but more often than not, the Kshatriya studied the art of war and the elementary knowledge of administrative functions. There are, however, traditions regarding the Kshatriyas studying philosophy and having taken a prominent part in the evolution of the doctrine of Brahman. As for the Vaiśyas it is unlikely that they were engaged in the intellectual life of the day, and at least in their case, this very practical device of a nominal fulfilment of the duty of Vedic study was very useful. A student who knew the first and last hymns of a *Ṛishi* or of an Anuvāka was, by a sort of fiction, considered to have known the whole portion belonging to the *Ṛishi* or the whole Anuvāka.

The rite prescribed for victory in debates shows that literary debates were very common and were held in special assembly-halls which used to be crowded.

The Vedic term commenced with the *upākarman* (inauguration) ceremony which was performed some time during the bright fortnight of the month of *Śrāvaṇa* (July-August) when the herbs appear, or during the rainy season. The Vedic study then went on for four months and a half or five months and a half or six months, at the end of which came the *utsarga* (discharge) ceremony which formally closed the first term in the month of Pausha or Māgha. After this there is a break of study for five or six months (this appears to be the long vacation of the ancient University), or according to the Dharma-sūtras, the Vedas may be studied during the bright fortnight and the Vedāṅgas during the dark one. This almost year-long recitation was subject to numerous interruptions (*anadhyāyas*) or "no-lesson" intervals, the special occasions for which were births and deaths, portents, miracles, lightning, thunder, rains or eclipses, and the normal occasions for which were the 14th and 15th days of the two fortnights, the last days of the seasons, etc. The large number of these interruptions is not surprising, as the ancients held that it was better that there was no recitation at all, rather than that a slight error should creep into it, get repeated in the transmission by word of mouth, and later become an integral part of the Veda itself. The preservation of the Vedic literature by a meticulously correct and scientific method of recitation, down to the minutest part of it, viz., the syllable, was their chief concern, because in the beginning, Vedic texts were not available in a written form and even later were not usually reduced to writing. Impure places were to be avoided for the recitation. Personal purity and good health were also essential conditions for study. After the completion of the whole course came the ceremony of *samāvartana* after which the student, now called a *snātaka* (i.e. one who has taken a ceremonial *bath* marking the termination of his studentship), can either enter upon the married state and found a household or (in exceptional cases) remain celibate, his principal duty being now the management and support of his family from which he was so long absent.

The *samāvartana,* however, does not spell the end either of Vedic study or of moral training. The *snātaka* can carry on both either in the rôle of a teacher or student. The *svādhyāya* or daily recitation of Vedic texts is part of the fivefold daily routine, consisting of the performance of the five *mahāyajñas* (Great Sacrifices), of the married *snātaka* in the capacity of a householder, and comprises portions not only of the Saṁhitās, Brāhmaṇas, and Kalpa-sūtras, but also of the Gāthās, Nārāśaṁsīs, Itihāsas, and Purāṇas. In the Dharma-sūtras of Vasishṭha and Āpastamba there is an inhibition against learning a language spoken by barbarians, and the study of *śabda-śāstra* (philology) is condemned in the *Vasishṭha Dharma-sūtra* (X. 20).

The teacher is the central figure, the very pivot of the educational system with which the State had very little to do. He introduces (*upa-nī*) the boy to studentship, and is in sole charge of his moral, mental, and physical upbringing. The teacher, who was a *snātaka,* provided in his own house for the boarding and lodging of a certain number of pupils, and received from them, in return, daily service during the period of studentship and, at the end of it, gifts voluntarily given by the pupils. Though, thus in a measure, the teacher was compensated for his labours, the relationship between the teacher and pupil was in no sense mercenary, but sacred and almost spiritual. Very often the father himself was the teacher, and the student received education at home. The teacher was the friend, philosopher, and guide to the pupil. The initiation of the boy into studentship by the teacher marked, as it were, his second birth (in a spiritual sense), whence the term *dvija* ("twice-born") was applied to the three higher castes, who only had the privilege of *upanayana.* The pupil was to show the very greatest respect to the teacher. It was not, however, merely a one-sided discipline. The teacher also observed certain vows and rules while he taught.

That physical training was an integral part of the educational scheme is clear from the unmistakable trend of the numerous prayers for the grant of vigour and strength that form part of the *upanayana* ceremonial. The begging of alms, morning and evening, the gathering of fuel-sticks, and the manual labour involved in the worship and tending of the fire made for sufficient hard work or exercise for the student. The recitation of the vedic texts was a strenuous vocal exercise. But the *prāṇāyāma* or control of breath, which formed part of the daily *sandhyā* (morning, noon, and evening prayers) adoration, was not only an ideal exercise for the lungs, but also one that penetrated to all parts of the body as any careful student of Yogic exercises can testify. Lastly must be noted the fact that the *daṇḍa-pradāna* (handing the staff to the initiated boy) was a regular ceremony, and the staff was certainly an excellent weapon for self-defence.

5. *Manners and Morals, Habits and Customs*

Hospitality not only continues to be recognized as a binding social obligation, but is raised to the status of a religious duty, for an offering of food to the guest attains to the rank of a sacrifice as one of the five daily *mahāyajñas*—the *atithi-yajña* or "guest sacrifice"—which the householder must perform. There is a formal definition of an *atithi* or guest, and an authorized list of important guests, which includes a teacher, a *Ṛitvik* (an officiating priest), a king, a snātaka, a father-in-law, and a son-in-law. Though a guest could arrive at any time it was understood that a wedding and a sacrifice were the recognized (or official) occasions for their reception in the grand style. A seat (or a special enclosure, if the guest is *persona grata*), water for washing the feet, *argha* water, water for sipping, and the *madhuparka* (a mixture of curds, honey, and *ghī*) are first offered to him. After this, food containing meat is to be offered to him, and if the occasion is a special one (such as a sacrifice or a wedding), a cow is offered and it is for the guest to have it killed for him or to set it free.

The Gṛihya-sūtras, while prescribing the code of conduct for a *snātaka*, give us a fairly detailed account of the manners and etiquette of those days. Only a few rules can be cited here. A scentless wreath is not to be worn. Girls must not be subjected to banter or ridicule. Walking or bathing naked or running without sufficient justification are prohibited. There is a taboo on certain words in the language of a *snātaka* ensuring linguistic purity.

Great insistence is laid on moral purity. Self-restraint is the keynote of the ethical code prescribed for the householder. Human nature, of course, is the same in all times and climes, and warnings against the faithlessness of companions, pupils, servants, and wives are conveyed indirectly through rites prescribed for their prevention. Purity of mind is as much inculcated as purity of body. Abstinence of all kinds and respect for elders and for self are valued qualities.

The ancient Indians did not cultivate cleanliness as a mere habit. They had developed a passion for it. The sipping of water (*āchamana*) and washing of feet are insisted on everywhere as a preliminary to any, even the most trivial, ritual act. The *pavitrakas* (strainers or purifiers made of grass), the use of which is so marked in the ritual, are symbols of purity and cleanliness. If a bird befouled the person of a *snātaka*, or an unknown drop of water fell on him, *mantras* were to be recited by way of expiation. The habit of early rising is also well cultivated.

Life in this age was so thoroughly ritualized that it is difficult to distinguish habits from sacraments. Thus the many rites prescribed for the safety and good health of the mother and child, before and after delivery, may be looked upon as records of remarkable usages also. The rite of *Sīmantonnayana* or parting of the hair in the middle in the fourth or seventh month of pregnancy is an interesting custom. The child is given two names of which one is to be kept secret. The occasional counting of years, not from birth but from conception, is a practice that has a parallel in the Buddhist ordinances. The Gṛihya- and the Dharma-sūtras recognize the force of local custom, and allow it to modify or sometimes even override some of their rules. The father's greeting to the son, when either of the two has returned from a journey, which takes the form of smelling or kissing him on the head, is also a noteworthy custom.

6. *Amusements and Entertainments*

As in the preceding age, dancing, and both vocal and instrumental music, were well cultivated. In the *Sīmantonnayana* ceremony mentioned above, the wife is asked to sing a song merrily, and in the marriage ceremony the bridegroom sings a *gāthā* after the treading on the stone by the bride. The vogue of the musical recitations of the *Sāmaveda* is responsible for the rule in the *Gobhila Gṛihya-sūtra* that the *Vāmadevya gāna* may be sung, by way of a general expiation, at the end of every ceremony. The lute players are asked to play the lute in the ceremony of "parting the hair," and four or eight women (not widows) perform a dance in the marriage ceremony. The restrictive rule that a *snātaka* is not to practise or enjoy a programme of instrumental or vocal music or dance, shows their popularity. It seems that the game of dice was looked upon as a popular entertainment, since a common gaming hall is one of the official public buildings of a town.

The reference in the *Maitrāyaṇīya Upanishad* to a *naṭa* (actor) changing his dress and painting himself proves the popularity of dramatic shows in this age.

7. *Food and Drink*

Rice and barley were evidently the staple articles of diet as they were to be offered into the Gṛihya fire every morning and evening. Wheat was probably not eaten daily, as it is mentioned but rarely. Beans (*māsha*), kidney beans (*mudga*), mustard seed (*sarshapa*), and sesamum were known.

Milk and its products were very liberally used (*ante*, p. 461). The various forms of butter (due to its varying temperature) were distinguished for purposes of the ritual as: clarified (*sarpis*), melted (*ājya*), and solid (*ghṛita*) butter. Among other esculent things may be mentioned honey and *kshāra-lavaṇa* (saline food), which is supposed to be an irritant and an excitant, and therefore to be eschewed in the interests of celibacy.

The culinary art was fairly well developed. The different processes or operations through which the grains passed before being cooked or eaten are indicated in words like *akshata-dhāna* (unbroken grain), *lāja* (fried grain), and *saktu* (ground grain). Washing the rice-grains, husking them, baking them, and sprinkling *ājya* over them, and then taking them out of the oven are the different stages mentioned in the preparation of a *sthālīpāka*. The preparation of a *Puroḍāśa* (sacrificial cake) implied great skill in baking as it was baked on a pan with varying number of hollows (resembling saucers) which gave a variety of forms to it. An *Apūpa* was a cake baked on a flat vessel. Boiled rice (*odana*) eaten with *ghi*, milk-rice (*pāyasa*) which seems to be a preparation very much akin to *dudha-pāka* so popular in Gujarāt now, *kṛisara* (boiled rice mixed with sesamum seeds), *dadhimantha* and *madhu-mantha* (cooked ground grains mixed with curds and honey respectively), and rice and barley gruel are other preparations known. The scum of boiled rice made a very light liquid food. Vegetable food (*śāka*) is mentioned as a substitute for flesh-food (*māṁsa*).

But people in this age were by no means vegetarians. They ate flesh freely, not excluding even beef which was prohibited later owing to the growing reverence for the cow. Flesh-food must be served to the Brāhmaṇas invited to a *Śrāddha* dinner, vegetable food being allowed only in its absence. Similarly in the ceremony of the first feeding of the child with solid food, among the various foods enumerated in order of merit, the flesh of a goat, partridge, or another (specified) bird, and fish come first, boiled rice mixed with *ghi* coming last. Similarly food offered to a guest of consequence *must not be without flesh*. The merit of vegetarian diet is, however, recognized in the rule that a student should abstain from flesh.

In spite of condemnation in the earlier texts (*ante*, p. 462) and severe penalties laid down in the Dharma-sūtras, *surā* continued to be a favourite intoxicating drink. The four or eight women who give a dance at the marriage ceremony are to be regaled with food and *surā*. In the *Anvashṭakya* ceremony, *surā* is to be offered along with the *piṇḍa* offerings to female ancestors. The *Śrauta* ritual is naturally full of references to the Soma drink in the numerous Soma sacrifices, and the *Gṛihya* ritual in the fitness of things ignores it.

8. *Dress and Decoration*

Two pieces of clothing—one the *uttarīya* or upper, and the other the *Antarīya* or lower—constituted the dress proper (the simple two-piece suit) of males and females; the lower garment being put on first and then the upper one. If one could afford only one garment, then a part of the lower garment may be turned into and worn as an upper garment. In the case of a student, the skin of a deer or goat made a very holy upper garment. The *āprapadīna paṭa*, mentioned by Pāṇini, is a garment that reached down to the ankles. A longish piece of cloth wrapped round the head in the fashion prescribed by local custom constituted the ceremonial head-wear or turban. The same piece could be used informally to veil the head. Red turbans and clothes were used for magic rites and silk ones (*kshauma*) for sacrificial purposes.

Woollen blankets were in use. In the list of garments prescribed for the *upanīta* (the initiated boy) figure cotton, woollen, linen, and hempen cloth. Silk was also used (as there is a reference to the silk-worm giving silk). Upper garments were dyed with the juice of *lodhra* flowers or with madder or indigo. Black clothes were also worn (as they are forbidden for one practising the *Śākvara* vow). The colour scheme of dyed garments prescribed for the *upanīta* is interesting; reddish yellow, light red, and yellow for the Brāhmaṇa, the Kshatriya, and the Vaiśya respectively. The art of washing was, of course, known, though a particular sanctity attaches to a brand new (*ahata*) garment.

A pair of garments, a turban, ear-rings, shoes, a bamboo staff, and an umbrella complete the full dress (of a *snātaka*, for example). The *daṇḍa* (staff) is not only a weapon of defence in the ordinary sense, but also a magic wand for warding off evil. The staff of the *upanīta* boy was to be of palāśa, bilva, or nyagrodha (or udumbara) wood. according to his caste. It had to be of a standard height. In one Gṛihya-sūtra (the *Āśvalāyana*) there is an invocation to the shoe not to pinch. So shoes have had a tendency to pinch in all times and climes!

Two important sacraments—the *Chūḍā-karman* or tonsure ceremony for the child, and the *Godāna* or the ceremony of hair-cutting at the age of sixteen or eighteen—give us a clear idea of development of the tonsorial art as known and practised in those days. Among the details of the *Chūḍā-karman* are the use of a mixture of hot and cold water to moisten the hair, the tangled locks of which are disentangled with a porcupine's quill—the hair-comb of the ancients—the anointing of the hair with fresh butter, the holding of a mirror before the boy, the use of the razor (with a copper or wooden handle) which makes a sound while it is being plied by the barber on the head, and the leaving of a lock or locks (*Chūḍā*) according to local custom or family usage. A layer of *Kuśa* grass is kept ready to receive the hair that is cut off. In the *Godāna* ceremony, the beard and the hair, both on the head and under the armpits, are shaved and the nails clipped. Generally a top-lock was kept, as a clean-shaven head was not fashionable. The *Āśvalāyana* and *Śāṅkhāyana Gṛihya-sūtras,* strangely enough, prescribe both these rites for girls. Probably local custom determined what quantity of hair was to be kept and in what fashion in the case of both boys and girls. The *Sīmantonnayana* ceremony (of parting the hair of a pregnant woman mentioned above) clearly shows that the two (shaving) ceremonies did not much affect the growth of hair on a girl's head. Does this ceremonial parting of the hair in pregnancy suggest that unmarried girls and married women who were not mothers did not part their hair but merely brushed it back?

It is noteworthy that the toilet and make-up of the ancient Indians were not as simple as we fondly imagine. Collyrium (*añjana*), an eye-salve, and other salves for anointing the body before the bath and the nose and mouth after the bath, *sthāgara* (a fragrant application) (see *ante*, p. 463), a bath-powder, and ground sandalwood are among the toilet requisites mentioned in connection with the "bath" ceremony which entitles a student who has completed his studies to become a *snātaka* (graduate) and settle down as a householder by marrying if he so chooses. Garlands and *kuṇḍalas* (an ear ornament) are put on after the *snāna* (bath). Three gems strung on a wollen or linen cord make at once an ornament and a charm for a bride when tied round her body. A perforated pellet of sandal or *Bādara* wood, overlaid with gold and worn round the neck, and a *Bādara-maṇi* or pellet of *Bādara*-wood tied to the left hand, are among the other known ornaments worn by both males and females with distinction.

9. *Health and Hygiene*

A keen desire to live a long and healthy life of a hundred years was the natural outcome of the optimistic and robust outlook which the ancient Indians had on life. Their healthy slogan was "prevention is better than cure." Consumption seems to have been a notorious affliction. Epilepsy (*Kumāra* or *Apasmāra*), to which children were particularly liable, was very much dreaded and its popular name *Śvagraha* indicates that it was supposed to be a seizure or attack by a dog-demon. Among the symptoms are stiffness of the body and much crying aloud. Another peculiar illness, to which again boys were particularly susceptible, was named *Śaṁkha* in which the patient utters tones resembling the sound of a *Śaṁkha* (conch) when blown. These diseases were sought to be cured by propitiating the demons by means of rites and ceremonies which afford a glimpse into the curious superstitions and magical belief of the period. From the number of rites prescribed during the period of pregnancy, it seems that a safe delivery was a matter of great concern. Headache and poisonous bites are among the minor ailments receiving ritual treatment.

That there were centenarians is seen from the rules in the ceremony of *Udakadāna* or the offering of water libations to the deceased. Fasts are so often recommended in the ritual that the inference becomes irresistible that the ancient Indians were fully aware of their beneficial effects on health.

A knowledge of hygienic principles may be inferred from many a rule in the Gṛihya-sūtras. Cleanliness is most stringently enforced and the free use of water is recommended at every step in the ritual for cleansing purposes. A regular daily bath is insisted on. Floors are to be swept, sprinkled over with water, and smeared with cow-dung. There is a peculiar mixture prescribed for smearing the floor and walls of the lying-in chamber, which must have been an effective disinfectant. A *snātaka* is not to spit or eject phlegm in the neighbourhood of water. That special places were set apart to receive dirt, accumulated waste, and sweepings is seen from the direction to offer a *bali* on such "heaps of sweeping." Easing was to be done on ground covered with grass and not on the bare ground. That cow stables and cemeteries were located outside the village or town is seen from the rule which enumerates them among landmarks in a journey along with a forest, a boundary-tree, etc.

2. ECONOMIC CONDITION

1. *Agriculture and Cattle*

The fact that there is a domestic rite synchronizing with each stage in the agricultural life of the people, and practically none associated with urban life, shows that the Indians of those days lived mostly in villages, and that the village agriculturist was the true representative of ancient India. There are rites for putting the bulls and oxen to the plough, for sowing, and for honouring *Sītā* (*lit.*, the "Furrow") or the Goddess of Agriculture. There is a sacrifice offered to Kshetrapati or the Lord of the Field. The Āgrayaṇa sacrifice is the religious ceremony of partaking of the first fruits of the harvest. There are further sacrifices signalizing the other agricultural operations such as threshing, the reaping of the crop, and putting it into the barn.

Rice and barley seem to be the staple crops from the reference to the two harvests—that of barley in the hot season and of rice in autumn. From the direction to the *snātaka* to live on the gleanings of uncultivated corn it may be easily inferred that there were extensive stretches of uncultivated land and forest, and wild rice and grains used to grow on untilled tracts. That a cultivated field was measured by the quantity of seeds that could be sown in it is seen from the term *prāsthika* in Pāṇini, applied to a field that accommodated a *prastha*-full of seeds.

The cattle were an invaluable possession. "Make us rich in cows" is almost the burden of the *mantras* that accompany the various Gṛihya rites. All the three higher classes were engaged in cattle-keeping in their own way. There are ceremonies like the *Śūlagava* and the *Bauḍhyavihāra* for propitiating Rudra and his hosts, so that they may avert evil from cattle and the fields. Cattle served, in a way, as the standard of value or as a medium of exchange, because kings kept their own herds and gave away thousands of cows as *dakshiṇā* (sacrificial fees). The *Dārshadvata* sacrifice, described in the Śrauta-sūtras, is virtually a description of the tending of the cows of a Brāhmaṇa in Kurukshetra for one year. The Gṛihya-sūtras prescribe a number of minor rites on the following occasions:—

(1) When the cows are led to the pasture lands;
(2) When they run about;
(3) When they return; and
(4-5) before, and after, their entry into the cow-pen.

The Śrauta-sūtras prescribe sacrifices for the acquisition and recovery of lost cows. Prayers and rites for prosperity in cattle and their good health abound in the Gṛihya-sūtras. There is a ceremony for cattle-breeding called *Vṛishotsarga* on the release of a (stud-) bull among the cows. *Yakshmā,* a wasting disease affecting cattle, was very much dreaded. It was a custom to brand the cows.

But the cows were not prized merely as property. A feeling of reverence for them is rapidly growing. A suspension of study (*anadhyāya*) is ordered in the presence of cows that have eaten nothing. Persons riding in a chariot are to do homage to a cow, if met with on the way. Paradoxically enough, in the eyes of the ancient Indians, this veneration of the cow is not only not inconsistent with the cow-sacrifice prescribed in funeral ceremonies, on the occasion of a guest-reception, or the *Śūlagava* (spitox) sacrifice, but is, in a sense, responsible for it. Nevertheless, the feeling of reverence for the cow went on steadily gathering volume, and the rule for sacrificing a cow was often relaxed by the admissibility of an alternative or substitute ritual whereby the cow was saved.

2. *Trade and Commerce, Arts and Industries*

There is a rite called *paṇyasiddhi* (ensuring success in trade) in which a portion of the particular article of trade is cut off and sacrificed in the fire with the prayer: "If we carry on trade to acquire (new) wealth by means of our (old) wealth, may Soma... prosper that." (*Hiraṇyakeśi G. S.* I. 15. 1). The Vaiśya class was engaged in trade and commerce. The Sūtras of Pāṇini refer to imports from the north and his *vaṁśādi gaṇa* mentions several forest-products such as *Vaṁśa, Kuṭaja, Ikshu* (sugar-cane) and *Madya* (liquor). The Gṛihya-sūtra rule that the relations of a deceased person are not to cook in the house, but to buy food during the period of the death-impurity, shows that food could be bought either from public eating houses (?) or private individuals. A system of coinage or currency was probably in vogue, though quite a large volume of trade was managed by way of exchanges in kind. Pāṇini mentions coins like *Pāṇa, Kārshāpaṇa, Pāda,* and *Vāha* and measures and weights like *Āḍhaka, Āchita, Pātra, Droṇa,* and *Prastha.* But, as noted above, Pāṇini's date is uncertain, and he probably belonged to a period later than 600 B.C.

Implements and vessels of copper, iron, stone, and earthenware are mentioned and must have been locally manufactured. Golden spoons and brass gongs were in use. Silver was also known. Upper and lower millstones, mortar and pestle, cups, ladles, dishes, spoons, and swords were required for domestic as well as ritual use. Baskets made of leaves are referred to. *Kaṭas* or rush mats made of *Vīriṇa* grass were offered as seats for the married couple. The varieties of cloth worn were cotton, linen, woollen, silken, and hempen. That spinning and weaving were daily occupations of the people is clear from the rule that the initiated boy is to put on a garment spun and woven on the same day, and from the prayers offered to "Goddesses who spun and wove" (*Āpastamba G. S.* IV. 10.10). A *Chātrā* or spindle is mentioned. A flourishing dyeing industry may be inferred from the prescription of garments of different colours for the initiated boy.

Many of the occupations, professions, arts, crafts, and industries have been already incidentally referred to in the previous sections (also cf. *ante,* Ch. XXIII, pp. 466-7). We may notice here the profession of the butcher, who was so indispensable in the animal sacrifice that there was actually a priest called *Śamitṛi* who did the necessary slaughtering to the accompaniment of sacred verses. Manual labour was so highly prized that it was compulsory for a student as a householder (*snātaka*).

3. *House-building and Means of Transport*

The fact that the Gṛihya-sūtras include the ceremony of house-building among sacraments to be performed by the rich and the poor alike, leads to the obvious inference that in those days of vast open spaces and long stretches of jungle, a site for a house and building materials were available to a poor man of three higher classes at a nominal cost. The site should be undisputed property. It should be non-saline and with trees, herbs, or at least grass, growing thereon. It should not be hollow or undermined and be of the colour prescribed for the particular caste. From the directions given, we gather that a spacious house contained an assembly or drawing room a provision-room, and a resting or retiring room, with a nursery and privy standing detached from the main building. Measuring the site, digging the pits for the posts, two of which were erected in each of the four directions, setting up the door-jambs and the gable, putting up the beams and the grass or thatch on the roof, are some of the operations detailed. The position of the main door is carefully specified. The setting up of the water-barrel—evidently an arrangement for water supply—is part of the house construction. The repairs and renovation of the house are to be effected every year with ceremony about the same time as the *Divālī* holidays of the Hindus. From the directions to erect huts and enclosures in the course of a day, it seems these could be improvised with ease. The consecration ritual for ponds, tanks, wells, covered reservoirs of water, and gardens, shows that these were public works for general use though they seem to have been constructed by individuals rather than by the state; for the ritual is of the domestic type.

Bridges, roads, cross-ways, and squares where four roads meet are referred to. Among the means of transport may be mentioned the very popular, light two-wheeled wooden carriage (*ratha*). Horses and oxen (even cows occasionally) were the common draught animals, the elephant being employed for a state journey or a procession. Horses, asses, camels, and elephants were ridden for purposes of travel. Rivers were crossed by rafts and boats, and if necessary by ships.

---

1. The list is given in *Chhāndogya*, 7. 1, 2 and is repeated several times in the following sections. The interpretation of the technical terms denoting different branches of knowledge is not always easy. Max Müller takes *Brahma-vidyā* as three of the Vedāṅgas (viz., *Śikshā*, *Kalpa*, and *Chhandas*); *Devajana-vidyā* as "the sciences of the genii, such as the making of perfumes, dancing, singing, playing, and other fine arts"; *Pitrya* as "the rules for the sacrifices for the ancestors"; and the Veda of the Vedas as grammar (*SBE*, I, pp. 109-10).

GENERAL BIBLIOGRAPHY

I. ORIGINAL SOURCES

(A detailed account of the literature of the age has been given in Chapters XII, XVI, XX, and XXIV. A select list of important texts, with translations, is given below. Further accounts of the individual texts will be found in Winternitz *History of Indian Literature,* vol. I and the other Histories of Literature mentioned in section II, B of this bibliography.)

Aitareya Āraṇyaka: Text ĀSS. No. 37, Poona, 1898. Ed. with a trans. by A. B. Keith. Oxford, 1909.

Aitareya Brāhmaṇa: Ed. Th. Aufrecht. Bonn, 1879.
Ed. K. S. Agashe. Poona, 1896.
Trans. by Keith. HOS, Vol. XXV. Cambridge, Mass. 1920.

Āpastambīya Dharmasūtra: Ed. by G. Bühler (Bombay Sanskrit Series), 1892, 1894.

Āpastambīya Śrautasūtra: Ed. by R. Garbe. Calcutta, 1882-1902.

Ārsheya Brāhmaṇa: Ed. by A. C. Burnell. Mangalore, 1876.

Āśvalāyana Gṛihyasūtra: Ed. by A. G. Stenzler, Leipzig, 1864.

Atharvaveda: Ed. R. Roth and W. D. Whitney. Berlin, 1856.
Ed. with Sāyaṇa's Comm. by S. P. Pandit. Bombay, 1895-8.
Trans. by W. D. Whitney. Cambridge, Mass., U.S.A., 1905.
Trans. in part. M. Bloomfield. SBE, Vol. XLII. Oxford, 1897.

Baudhāyana Dharmaśāstra: Ed. by E. Hultsch. Leipzig, 1884.

Baudhāyana Gṛihyasūtra: Ed. by R. Shama Sastri. Mysore, 1920.

Baudhāyana Śrautasūtra: Ed. by W. Caland. Calcutta, 1904-23.

Bṛihadāraṇyaka Upanishad: Ed. with trans. by O. Böhtlingk. Leipzig, 1889.

Chhāndogya Upanishad: Ed. with trans. by O. Böhtlingk. Leipzig, 1889.

Daivata Brāhmaṇa: Ed. by Jivananda Vidyasagara. Calcutta, 1881.

Gautama Dharmasūtra: Text ĀSS, Tr. SBE, II.

Gopatha Brāhmaṇa: Ed. by Rajendralal Mitra and H. Vidyabhushan. Calcutta, 1872.

Kapishṭhala Kaṭha Saṁhitā: Ed. by Raghu Vira. Lahore, 1932.

Kāṭhaka Saṁhitā: Ed. by Von Schroeder. Leipzig, 1900-11.

Kātyāyana Śrautasūtra: Ed. by Vidyadhara Sarma. Benares, 1933-7.

Kaushītaki Brāhmaṇa: Ed. by E. B. Cowell. Calcutta, 1861. Trans. by Keith. HOS, XXV. Cambridge, Mass., 1920.

Khādira-Gṛihya-sūtra: Ed. by A. Mahadeva Sastri and L. Srinivasacharya. Mysore, 1913.

Maitrāyaṇī Saṁhitā: Ed. by Von Schroeder. Leipzig, 1881-6.

Nirukta: Ed. with Durgāchārya's Comm. by V. K. Rajavade. Poona, 1921-26. Ed. and trans. by L. Sarup. Two vols. Lahore.

Pañchaviṁśa Brāhmaṇa: Ed. by A. Vedantavagisa. Calcutta, 1869-74.

Pāraskara Gṛihya-sūtra: Ed. by Gopal Shastri Nene. Benares, 1926.

Ṛigveda: Saṁhitā and Pada text with Sāyaṇa's Comm. Ed. by F. Max Müller (second edn.). 1890-2. Saṁhitā and Pada text with Sāyaṇa's Comm. critically edited by Vaidika Saṁśodhana Maṇḍala, Poona. Four vols. 1933, etc. Trans. by H. Grassmann. Leipzig, 1876-7; R. T. H. Griffith. Benares, 1896-7; in part, by Max Müller. SBE. vol. XXXII, Oxford, 1891, and H. Oldenberg, SBE, Vol. XLVI. Oxford, 1897.

Sāmaveda: Ed. with trans. by Th. Benfey. Leipzig, 1848. Ed. by Satyavrata Samasrami. Calcutta, 1873.

Sāmavidhāna Brāhmaṇa: Ed. by A. C. Burnell. London, 1873.

Saṁhitopanishad Brāhmaṇa: Ed. by A. C. Burnell. Mangalore, 1877.

Śāṅkhāyana Āraṇyaka: Ed. by Friedlander. Berlin, 1900 (I-II); E. B. Cowell. Calcutta, 1861 (III-VI); A. B., Keith. Oxford, 1909 (VII-XV). Trans. by A. B. Keith. London, 1908.

Śāṅkhāyana Śrautasūtra: Ed. with Comm. of Varadatta-suta Ānartiya and Govinda, by A. Hillebrandt. Calcutta, 1886-9.

Śatapatha Brāhmaṇa: Ed. by A. Weber. London, 1885. Trans. by J. Eggeling. SBE, XII, XXVI, XLI, XLIIII, XLIV. Oxford, 1882-1900.

Shaḍviṁśa Brāhmaṇa: Ed. by Jivananda Vidyasagara. Calcutta, 1881. Ed. by H. F. Eelsingh. Leyden, 1908.

Taittirīya Brāhmaṇa: Ed. by R. Mitra. Calcutta, 1855-70.

Taittirīya Saṁhitā: Ed. by A. Weber. Berlin, 1871-2: with the Comm. of Mādhava, Calcutta. 1854-99.

Taittirīya Upanishad: Ed. with Comm. of Śaṅkara. ĀSS, fifth edn. Poona, 1929.

Vājasaneyi Saṁhitā: Ed. with Mahīdhara's Comm. by A. Weber. London, 1852.

Vaṁśa Brāhmaṇa: Ed. by A. C. Burnell. Mangalore, 1873. Ed. by A. Weber. *Ind. Stud,* IV. pp. 371 ff.

Vasishṭha Dharmasūtra: Ed. by A. A. Führer. Bombay, 1916.

Yajurveda: *See* Taittirīya Saṁhitā, Kapishṭhala-Kaṭha-Saṁhitā, Kāṭhaka Saṁhitā, Maitrāyaṇī Saṁhitā and Vājasaneyi Saṁhitā.

Translations of Collected Works

1. The principal Upanishads have been translated by F. Max Müller in SBE, I, XV, and by R. A. Hume in *Thirteen Principal Upanishads*, Oxford, 1921.
2. The Gṛihya-sūtras of Śāṅkhāyana, Āśvalāyana, Pāraskara, Khādira, Gobhila, Hiraṇyakeśin and Āpastamba have been translated by H. Oldenberg in SBE, XXIX and XXX.
3. The Dharma-sūtras of Āpastamba, Gautama, Vasishṭha and Baudhāyana have been translated by G. Bühler in SBE, II and XIV.

II. MODERN WORKS

A. Histories of Ancient India (which prominently deal with the Vedic Age).

1. *Cambridge History of India*. Vol. I. Cambridge, 1922.
2. DUTT, R. C. *History of Civilisation in Ancient India*. London, 1893.
3. MOOKERJI RADHAKUMUD *Hindu Civilisation*. London, 1936.
4. OLDENBERG H. *Ancient India* (second edn.). Chicago, 1898.
5. RAPSON, E. J. *Ancient India*. Cambridge, 1914.
6. RAYCHAUDHURI, H. C. *Political History of Ancient India* (fourth edn.). Calcutta, 1938.

B. *Histories of Literature*

1. FARQUHAR, J. N. *An Outline of the Religious Literature of India*. Oxford, 1920.
2. FRAZER, R. W. *Literary History of India*. London, 1898.
3. HENRY, V. *Les Litteratures de l'Inde*. Paris, 1904.
4. KANE, P. V. *History of Dharmaśāstra*. Three vols. Poona, 1930, 1941, 1946.
5. MACDONELL, A. A. *History of Sanskrit Literature*. London, 1900.
6. MAX MÜLLER, F. *History of Ancient Sanskrit Literature* (second edn.). London, 1860.
7. OLDENBERG, H. *Die Literatur des alten Indien*. Berlin, 1903.
8. PISCHEL, R. *Die indische Literatur, "Die Orientalischen Literaturen," Die Kultur Gegenwar*, I, vii. Berlin und Leipzig, 1906.
9. VAIDYA, C. V. *History of Sanskrit Literature*, vol. I: Śruti (Vedic) Period. Poona, 1930.
10. WEBER, A. *History of Indian Literature* (Eng. Trans. by J. Mann and Th. Zachariae) (second edn.). London, 1882.
11. WINTERNITZ, M. *History of Indian Literature* (Eng. Trans. by Mrs. S. Ketkar), vol. I. Calcutta, 1927.

C. *General Works*

1. IYENGAR, P. T. S. *Life in Ancient India*. Madras, 1912.
2. KAEGI, A. *The Rigveda*, Trans. by R. Arrowsmith. Boston, 1886.

8. MACDONELL, A. A and KEITH, A. B. *Vedic Index*. London.

4. MUIR, J. *Original Sanskrit Texts*. London.

5. OLDENBERG, H. *Rigveda forschung*. Berlin, 1905.

6. PISCHEL, R. and GELDNER, K. F. *Vedische Studien*. Stuttgart, 1889-1901.

7. ROTH, R. *Zur Litteratur und Geschichte des Veda*. Stuttgart, 1846.

8. VON SCHROEDER, L. *Indiens Literatur und Kultur*. Leipzig, 1887.

9. ZIMMER, H. *Altindisches Leben*. Berlin, 1879.

BIBLIOGRAPHY

CHAPTER III

Archaeological Explorations and Excavations

1. The publications of the Archaeological Survey of India, viz.:
Reports by Cunningham (23 vols.).
Annual Reports and Reports of Circles (since 1902-3).
Memoirs (67 vols.).
New Imperial Series.

2. *Archaeological Survey Reports of Indian States* (Baroda, Gwalior, Hyderabad, Mysore, Jaipur, etc.).

3. CUMMING, SIR JOHN. *Revealing India's Past* (London, 1939). (It gives a complete bibliography of Archaeological publications up to 1939.).

4. DIKSHIT, K. N. *The Progress of Archaeology in India in the past 25 years.*

5. DIKSHIT, K. N. *An Outline of Archaeology in India* (included in "An Outline of the Field Sciences of India" published by the Indian Science Congress, Calcutta, 1937).

CHAPTER IV

The Geological Background of Indian History

1. BROWN, J. C. *Catalogue of Pre-historic Antiquities in the Indian Museum at Calcutta,* Simla, 1917.

2. BURRARD, SIR S. G. and HERON, A. M. *The Geography and Geology of the Himalaya Mountains.* Delhi, 1932.

3. CUNNINGHAM, A. *Ancient Geography of India.* Trubner, London, 1871.

4. DE TERRA, H. and PATERSON, T. T. *Studies on the Ice Age in India and Associated Human Cultures.* Carnegie Inst., Washington, 1939.

5. FOOTE, R. B. "Discovery of Pre-historic Remains in India." *Geol. Mag.* London, I. X, 1873.

6 HAYDEN SIR H. N. "Relation of the Himalayas to the Indo-Gangetic Plain and the Peninsula." *Rec. Geol. Surv. Ind.*, vol. XLIII, Pt. 2, 1913.

7. MITRA, P. *Prehistoric India.* Calcutta University, 1927.

8. OLDHAM, C. F. "The Lost River of the Indian Desert," *CR*, vol. LIX, 1874.

9. OLDHAM, R. D. "The Structure of the Indo-Gangetic Plains." *Mem. Geol. Surv. Ind.*, vol. XLII, 1917.

10. PILGRIM, G. E. "The Siwalik Primates and Their Bearing on the Question of Evolution of Man." *Rec. Geol. Surv. Ind.*, vol. XLV, 1915.

11. WADIA, D. N. *Geology of India.* Macmillan, London (third edn.), 1939.

12. WADIA, D. N. "Post-Tertiary Hydrography of Northern India." *Nat. Inst. Sc. Ind.*, vol. IV, 4, 1938.

CHAPTER V

The Geographical Background of Indian History

Imperial Gazetteer of India. Oxford, 1907-9.
HOLDICH, T. H. *India (Regions of the World Series)*. Oxford, 1905.
HOLDICH, T. H. *The Gates of India*. London, 1910.
MACKINDER, H. J. *Eight Lectures on India*. London, 1910.
MORRISON, C. A. *A New Geography of the Indian Empire*. London, 1909.

CHAPTER VI

I. *Flora*

1. BISWAS, K. *Presidential Address*. Sec. of Botany, Ind. Sc. Congress, 1943.
2. BART, B. C. *Agriculture and Animal Husbandry in India*. Silver Jub. Session, Ind. Sc. Cong., 1937.
3. CALDER, C. C. *An Outline Vegetation of India*. Silver Jub. Session. Ind. Sc. Cong., 1937.
4. CHATTERJEE, D. "Studies in the endemic flora of India," *JRASB(S)*, V, 19 ff.
5. DAS GUPTA, A. *Economic and Commercial Geography*, 1941.
6. HOOKER, J. D. *A sketch of the flora of British India*, 1904.
7. HOOKER, J. D. *Imperial Gazetteer of India*, vol. I (Botany), 1909.
8. HOOKER, J. D. and THOMSON, J. *Introductory Essay to the Flora Indica*, 1855.

2. *Fauna*

1. *Fauna of British India*.
2. GHARPUREY, K. G., LT.-COL. *The Snakes of India*. Bombay, 1937.
3. *Imperial Gazetteer of India*. I, 1909.
4. RAO, H. S. *An Outline of the Fauna of India*. Calcutta, 1937.
5. SALIM ALI. *The Book of Indian Birds*. Bombay, 1941.
6. WHISTLER, HUGH. *Popular Handbook of Indian Birds*. London, 1935.

CHAPTER VII

Palaeolithic, Neolithic and Copper Age

(Cf. also Bibliography to Ch. IV.)

1. BROWN, J. C. *Catalogue of Pre-historic Antiquities in the Indian Museum at Calcutta*, 1917.
2. CAMMIADE, L. A. and BURKITT, M. C. "Fresh Light on the Stone Age in South-east India." *Antiquity*, IV (1930, pp. 327-39).
3. CHAKRAVARTI, S.N. The Pre-historic periods in India. *JUB*, X. Part I (1941).
4. CHAKRAVARTI, S. N. "An Outline of the Stone Age in India." *JRASB(L)*, X, pp, 81-98.
5. DAS GUPTA, H.C. "Bibliography of Prehistoric Indian Antiquities." *JASB*, XXVII, 1931, No. 1.
6. DE TERRA, H. "The Siwaliks of India and Early Man." *Early Man*. 1939.

7. De Terra, Hellmut' Movius and Hallam L. "Research on Early Man in Burma." *Transactions of the American Philosophical Society*, vol. 32, Part iii (1943), pp. 343-5.

8. Foote. *Indian Prehistoric and Protohistoric Antiquities, Notes on their Ages and Distribution*, 1916.

9. Ghurye, G. S. "Megalithic Monuments," *NIA*, VI, pp. 26-57, 100-39.

10. Karve and Sankalia. *Preliminary Report of the Third Gujarat Expedition*, Poona, 1945.

11. Rea, A. R. *Catalogue of Prehistoric Antiquities from Adichanallur and Perumbair*, 1915.

12. Sankalia, H. D. *Investigations into Prehistoric Archaeology of Gujarat*, Srī-Pratāpsimha Mahārājā Rājyābhisheka Granthamālā, Memoir No. IV, Baroda, 1946.

See also Proceedings of the Science Congress, Archaeological Reports (see under Ch. III).

CHAPTER VIII

Race Movements and Prehistoric Culture

1. Anderson, J. D. *Peoples of India*. Cambridge, 1913.

2. Bagchi, P. C. *Pre-Aryan and Pre-Dravidian in India*. Calcutta University, 1929.

3. Baines, A. *Ethnography*. Strassburg, 1912.

4. Caldwell. *Comparative Grammar of the Dravidian Language*.

5. Caldwell. *The Census of India* (Reports for 1901, 1911, 1921, 1931, 1941).

6. Chanda, R. P. *The Indo-Aryan Races*. Rajshahi, 1916.

7. Chatterji, S. K. "Non-Aryan Elements in Indo-Aryan." *JGIS*, II, 42.

8. Chatterji, S. K. "Dravidian Origins and the Beginnings of Indian Civilization." *MR*, Dec. 1924.

9. Crooke, W. *The Tribes and Castes of the North-West Provinces and Oudh*. Calcutta, 1896.

10. Guha, B. S. *An Outline of the Racial Ethnology of India*. Calcutta, 1937.

11. Guha, B. S. *Racial Elements in the Population* (Oxford Pamphlets on Indian Affairs, No. 22; Oxford University Press, Bombay, 1944).

12. Iyengar, P. T. S. *Pre-Aryan Tamil Culture*. Madras, 1930.

13. Risley, H. H. *Tribes and Castes of Bengal*. Calcutta, 1891-2.

14. Risley, H. H. *The People of India* (second edn.). London, 1915.

15. Thurston, E and Rangachari, K. *The Castes and Tribes of Southern India*. Madras, 1909-10.

For a full descriptive bibliography on the question of non-Aryan elements in the civilization of India, cf. Constantin Régamey, "Bibliographie Analytique des Travaux relatifs aux Éléments anaryens dans la civilization et les langues de l'Inde" in *BEFEO*, vol. 34, 1935, pp. 429-566.

CHAPTER IX

The Indus Valley Civilization

1. APTE, D. N. *Hindī-Sumerī Saṅskṛiti* (in Marathi). Poona, 1928.
2. ARAVAMUTHAN, T. G. *Some Survivals of the Harappa Culture*. Bombay, 1942.
3. AYYAR, R. S. V. *The Indo-Sumcro-Semitic-Hittite Problems*. Madras, 1932.
4. BANERJI, R. D. "Dravidian Civilization." *MR*, Sept. 1927, pp. 304-14; Nov. 1927, pp. 552-9.
5. BANERJI, R. D. "The Indian Affinities of the Ainu Pottery." *JASB*, XXIII, pp. 269-72.
6. BANERJI-SASTRI, A. *Asura India.* Patna, 1926.
7. BANERJI-ṢASTRI, A. "Remains of a pre-historic civilization in the Gangetic Valley." *JBHS*, III, pp. 187-91.
8. BEASLEY, H. G. "The Script of Mohenjo-daro, Harappa and Easter Island." *Man*, XXXVI, No. 199.
9. BHANDARKAR, D. R. "Śiva of prehistoric India." *JISOA*, V, pp. 74-7.
10. BHANDARKAR, D. R, *Some Aspects of Ancient Indian Culture*. Madras, 1940.
11. BILLIMORA, N. M. "Excavations of prehistoric places in Sind." *JSHS*, II, pp. 9-17.
12. BILLIMORIA, N. M. "The Script of Mohenjo-daro and Easter Island." *ABORI*, XX, pp. 262-75.
13. BROWN, W. NORMAN. "The Beginnings of Civilization in India." *JAOS*, LIX, Supp., pp. 32-44.
14. CADELL, SIR P. "Who are the Descendants of the People of Mohenjo-daro?" *Anthrop. Soc. Bom, Jub.* Vol., pp. 20-30.
15. CARLETON, P. *Buried Empires*. London, 1939.
16. CHANDA, R. P. "The Indus Valley in the Vedic Period." *MASI*, No. 31. Calcutta, 1926.
17. CHANDA, R. P. "Sind Five Thousand Years Ago." *MR*, LII, pp. 151-60.
18. CHANDA, R. P. "Survival of the prehistoric Civilization of the Indus Valley." *MASI*, No. 41. Calcutta, 1929.
19. CHAUDHURI, N. M. "The Pamirian Alpines in the Indus Valley in Chalcolithic Times." *CR*, June, 1945.
20. CHAUDHURY, N.C. *Mohenjo-daro and the Civilization of Ancient India with reference to Agriculture*. Calcutta, 1937.
21. CHILDE, V. G. *New Light on the Most Ancient East*. London, N. Y. 1934.
22. DIKSHIT, K. N. *Prehistoric Civilization of the Indus Valley*. Madras, 1939.
23. EHRENFELS, BARON OMAR. ROLF "The Indus Civilization and Ethnographic Research in the Mediterranean Basin." *JSHS*, IV, pp. 90-8.

24. Fabri, C. L. "The Age of the 'Indus Valley Civilization'." *CS*, VI, pp. 433-6.

25. Fabri, C. L. "Un element mesopotamian dans l'art de l'Inde." *JA*, CCXVII, pp. 298-302.

26. Fábri, C. L. "Exploration of prehistoric mounds in Baluchistan." *ABIA*, 1929, pp. 14-8.

27. Fábri, C. L. "Latest Attempts to read the Indus Script." *IC*, I, pp. 50-6.

28. Fábri, C. L. "Mesopotamian and Early Indian Art." *Études d'orientalisme*, Paris, 1932, pp. 203-53.

29. Fábri, C. L. "The Punch-marked Coins: a survival of the Indus Civilization." *JRAS*, 1935, pp. 307-18.

30. Fábri, C. L. "A Sumero-Babylonian Inscription discovered at Mohenjodaro. *IC*, III, pp. 663-73.

31. Frankfort, H. *Archaeology and the Sumerian Problem*. Chicago, 1932.

32. Frankfort, H. *Cylinder Seals*. London, 1939.

33. Frankfort, H. "The Indus Civilization and the Near East. *ABIA*, 1932, pp. 1-12.

34. Friederichs, H.F. *Der Alte Orient*. 1933.

35. Friederichs, H. F., and Müller H. W. "Die Rassenelemente im Indus-Tal während des 4. und 3. vorchristlichen Jahrtausend und ihre Verbereitung." *Anthropos*, XXVIII, pp. 383-406.

36. Gadd, C. J. "Seals of Ancient Indian Style found at Ur." *PBA*, XVIII, pp. 1-22.

37. Ganguly, K. K. "A Note on the Nose-ornament in Mohenjodaro." *IC*, V, pp. 342-3.

38. Goetz, H. *Epochen der indischen Kultur*. Leipzig, 1929.

39. Gordon, D. H. and Gordon M. E. "Survivals of the Indus Culture." *JRASB(L)*, 1940, pp. 61-71.

40. Guha, B. S. "New Light on the Indus Valley Civilization." *SC*, II, pp. 49 f.

41. Hargreaves, H. "Excavations in Baluchistan, 1925." *MASI*, No. 35, Calcutta, 1929.

42. Heras, H. "Chanhu-daro and its Inscriptions," *St. Xavier's College Mag.*, Feb. 1937.

43. Heras, H. "Further Excavations at Mohenjo-daro." *NR*, Jan. 1939, pp. 64-75.

44. Heras, H. "Karnatak and Mohenjo-daro." *KHR*, IV, pp. 1-5.

45. Heras, H. "The longest Mohenjo-daro Epigraph." *JIH*, XVI, pp. 231-8.

46. Heras, H. "Mohenjo-daro—The most important archaeological site in India." *JIH*, XVI, pp. 1-12.

47. Heras, H. "Mohenjo-daro, the People and the Land." *IC*, III, pp. 207-20.

48. HERAS, H. "The Numerals in the Mohenjo-daro Script." *NIA*, II, pp. 449-59.

49. HERAS, H. "The Religion of the Mohenjo-daro People according to the Inscriptions." *JUB*, V, pp. 1-29.

50. HERAS, H. "A supposed Sumero-Babylonian Inscription discovered at Mohenjo-daro." *IHQ*, XIII, pp. 697-703.

51. HERAS, H. "Two Proto-Indian Inscriptions from Chanhu-daro." *JBORS*, XXII, pp. 308-20.

52. HERAS, H. "Tree Worship in Mohenjo-daro." *Anthrop. Soc Bom., Jub. Vol.*, pp. 31-9.

53. HERAS, H. "Were Mohenjo-Darians Aryans or Dravidians?" *JIH*, XXI, pp. 23-33.

54. HERTZ, A. "The Origin of the Proto-Indian and the Brāhmī Scripts." *IHQ*, XIII, pp. 389-99.

55. HEVESY, G. DE. "Sur une Ecriture Océanienne paraissant d'origine néolithique." *Bulletin de la Société Prehistorique. Française*, 1933, pp. 433-49.

56. HEVESY, G. DE. "On a Writing Oceanique of Neolithic Origin." (Eng. Version.) *JIH*, XIII, pp. 1-17.

57. HEVESY, G. DE. "Osterinselschrift und Indus-schrift." *OLZ* XXXVII, pp. 665-73.

58. HROZNY, B. *O Nejstarsím Stěhování Národů A O Problému Civilisace Proto-Indické*. Praha, 1939.

59. HUNTER, G. R. "Mohenjo-daro—Indus Epigraphy." *JRAS*, 1932, pp. 466-503.

60. HUNTER, G. R. *The Script of Harappa and Mohenjo-daro and its Connection with other Scripts*. London, 1934.

61. JAYASWAL, K. P. "The Punch-marked Coins: a survival of the Indus Civilization." *JRAS*, 1935, pp. 720 f.

62. JAYASWAL, K. P. "The Wikramkhol Inscription." *IA*, LXII, pp. 58-60.

63. JOSEPH, P. "The Extent and Influence of the Indus Civilization." *JOR*, XI, pp. 246-50.

64. KEITH, A. BERRIEDALE. "The Aryans and the Indus Valley Civilization." *Ojha Vol.*, Sect. I, pp. 58-66.

65. KEITH, SIR ARTHUR. "The Ancient Mesopotamia of India," *ILN*, Dec. 19, 1931, pp. 1000-4.

66. LAW, N. N. "Mohenjo-daro and the Indus Civilization." *IHQ*, VIII, pp. 121-64.

67. LÜDERS, H. "Philologie, Geschichte and Archaeologie in Indien." *ZDMG*, N.F., VIII., pp. 1-20.

68. LÜDERS, H. "Die Ausgrabungen von Mohenjo-Daro." *ZDMG*, NS, XIII, p. 22 f.

69. MACKAY, E. J. H. "Arts and Crafts in the time of Mohenjo-Daro." *IAL*, XIII, pp. 73-89.

70. MACKAY, E. J. H. "Bead Making in Ancient Sind." *JAOS,* LVII, pp. 1-15.

71. MACKAY, E. J. H. *Chanhu-daro Excavations* (1935-36). New Haven, 1943.

72. MACKAY, E. J. H. "Early Culture at Chanhu-Daro." *Discovery,* Sept. 1937 pp. 286-9.

73. MACKAY, E.J.H. "Excavations at Chanhu-Daro in 1935-36." *ABIA,* X, pp. 20-4.

74. MACKAY, E. J.H. "Excavations at Chanhu-Daro." *JRSA,* 1937, pp. 527-45.

75. MACKAY, E. J. H. *Further Excavations at Mohenjo-Daro.* 2 vols. Delhi, 1938.

76. MACKAY, E. J. H. "Further Links between Ancient Sind, Sumer and Elsewhere." *Antiquity,* V, pp. 459-73.

77. MACKAY, E.J.H. *The Indus Civilization.* London, 1935.

78. MAHIRCHAND, BHERUMAL. *Mahan-jo-Daro.* Karachi, 1933.

79. MAJUMDAR, N. G. "Explorations in Sind." *MASI,* No. 48. Delhi, 1934.

80. MARSHALL, SIR JOHN. *Mohenjo-Daro and the Indus Civilization.* 3 vols. London, 1931.

81. MERIGGI, VON. P. "Zur Indus-Schrift." *ZDMG,* 1934, XII, pp. 198-241.

82. MITRA, PANCHANAN. "Racial and Cultural Interrelations between India and the West at the Dawn of the Age of Copper." *IHQ,* XI, pp. 699-709.

83. MORGAN, J. DE. *Prehistoric Orientale.* 3 vols. 1925-7.

84. MÜLLER, H. W. and HEINZ, E. F. "Die Rassenelemente in Indus. *Anthropos,* Band XXVIII. Wien, 1933.

85. OTTO, E. "Die Indus-Schrift. Ihre Entzifferungs-und Einordnungsversuche." *Zentralblatt für Bibliotek,* Wesen. LIII, Heft 3, pp. 109-14.

86. PETRIE, SIR FLINDERS "Mohenjo-daro." *AE,* June 1932.

87. PICCOLI, G. "A Comparison between signs of the 'Indus Script' and Signs in the Corpus Inscriptionum Etruscraum." *IA,* LXII. pp. 213-5.

88. PRAN NATH. "The Scripts on the Indus Valley Seals, I and II." *IHQ,* VII, Suppl., pp. 1-52: VIII, Suppl., pp. 1-32.

89. PRAN NATH. "The Script of the Indus Valley Seals." *JRAS,* 1931, pp. 671-4.

90. PRAN NATH. "Sumero-Egyptian Origin of the Aryans and the Rigveda." *JBHU,* I, pp. 303-58.

91. PRASHAD, B. "Animal Remains from Harappa." *MASI,* No. 51. Delhi, 1936.

92. PRASHAD, B. "Cattle of the Indus Valley Civilization." *CR,* Jan. 1935.

93. PUSALKER, A. D. "Authors of the Indus Culture." *ABORI,* XVIII, pp. 385-95.

94. RAWLINSON, H. G. and VENKATESWARA, S.V. "The Indus Valley Civilization: Two Views." *AP,* 1934. pp. 84-90.

95. ROSS, A. S. C. "The direction of the Mohenjo-Daro Script." *NIA*, II, pp. 554-8.

96. ROSS, A. S. C. "The Numeral Signs of the Mohenjo-Daro Script." *MASI*, No. 57. Delhi 1938.

97. ROY, BINODE BIHARI. "Harappa and the Vedic Hariyupia." *JBORS*, XIV, pp. 129 f.

98. SANKARANANDA, SWAMI. *Rigvedic Culture of the Pre-Historic Indus.* Vols. I-II. Calcutta, 1943, 1944.

99. SARKAR, S. S. "Disposal of the Dead at Harappa." *SC*, III, pp. 632-4.

100. SARUP, L. "The Ṛigveda and Mohenjo-Daro." *POC*, VIII, 1-22, also, *IC*, IV, pp. 149-68.

101. SASTRI, S. SRIKANTHA. "Proto-Indian Ceramics." *IHQ*, XVI, pp. 511-23.

102. SASTRI, S. SRIKANTHA. *Proto-Indic Religion.* Bangalore, 1942.

103. SASTRI, S. SRIKANTHA. "Studies in the Indus Scripts." *QJMS*, XXIV, pp. 224-30; 335-42.

104. SASTRI, S. SRIKANTHA. "Hieroglyphic Hattili and Proto-Indic Scripts." *BV*, IV, pp. 1-17.

105. SHEMBAVNEKAR, K. M. "The Identity of the Indus Valley Race with the Vāhīkas." *IHQ*, XII, pp. 477-84.

106. SPEISER, E. A. "On some important Synchronisms in Prehistoric Mesopotamia." *AJA*, XXXVI, pp. 465-71.

107. SPEISER, E. A. *Mesopotamian Origins.* Philadelphia, 1930.

108. STEIN, SIR AUREL "An Archaeological Tour in Waziristan and Northern Baluchistan." *MASI*, No. 37, Calcutta, 1929.

109. STEIN, SIR AUREL. *Archaeological Reconnaissances in North-Western India and South Eastern Iran.* London, 1937.

110. STEIN, SIR AUREL. "An Archaeological Tour in Gedrosia." *MASI*, No. 43. Calcutta, 1930.

111. STEIN, SIR AUREL. "An Archaeological Tour in Upper Swat and Adjacent Hill Tracts." *MASI*, No. 42. Calcutta. 1930.

112. STEIN, SIR AUREL. "The Indo-Iranian Borderlands: Their Prehistory in the Light of Geography and of Recent Excavations." *JRAI*, LXIV, pp. 179-202.

113. SUR, A. K. "Indian Script Paleontology." *CR*, 1933. pp. 261-5.

114. SUR, A. K. "Origin of the Indus Valley Script." *IHQ*, IX, p. 582.

115. THOMAS, E. J. "Interpretation of the Indus Seals." *IHQ*. XVI, pp. 683-8.

116, THOMAS, F. W. "Mohenjo-Daro and the Indus Civilization." *JRAS*, 1932, pp. 453-66. (Review.)

117. VATS, M. S. *Excavations at Harappa.* 2 vols. 1940.

118. VENKATESWARA, S. V. "The Antiquities of Harappa and Mohenjo-Daro." *AP*, 1930, pp. 11-15.

119. WADDELL, L. A. *The Aryan Origin of the Alphabet: Disclosing the Sumero-Phoenician parentage of our Letters ancient and modern.* London, 1927.

120. WADDELL, L. A. *The Makers of Civilization in Race and History.* London, 1929.
121. WOOLLEY, C. L. *The Sumerians,* 1928.
122. WOOLLEY, C. L. *Ur of the Chaldees.* London, 1929.

CHAPTER X, XI

The Aryan Problem and Indo-Irānian Relations

1. BRANDENSTEIN. *Die erste indogermanischen Wanderung,* Wein. 1936.
2. CHILDE, V. G. *The Aryans.* New York, London, 1926.
3. CHRISTENSEN, A. *Kulturgeschichte des alten Orients.*
4. GILES, G. P. Articles in *Encyclopaedia Britannica* (Aryans, Indo-European Languages).
5. HERZFELD, E. *Iran in the Ancient East.* 1941.
6. *Hirt-Festschrift.* *Heidelberg.* 1936.
7. HIRT, H. *Die Indogermanen, ihre Verbreitung, ihre Urheimat, und ihre Kultur.* Strassburg. 1905 and 1907.
8. JACKSON, A. V. W. *Notes and Allusions to Ancient India in Pahlavi Literature,* etc. Festschrift Ernst Windisch (pp. 209-12).
9. MEYER, E. *Geschichte des Altertums.*
10. MUCH H. *Die Heimat der Indogermanen in Lichte der Urgeschichtlichen Forschung.* Jena, 1904.
11. NEHRING. *Studien Zur indegermanischen Kultur und Urheimat.*
12. REINACH, S. *L'Origine des Aryens.* Paris, 1892.
13. SPIEGEL, F. *Die arische Periode und ihre Zustande.* Leipzig, 1887.
14. SCHRADER, O. *Reallexikon der indogermanischen Altertumskunde.* Strassburg, 1901.
15. SCHRADER, O. *Sprachvergleichung und Urgeschichte.* Jena, 1906-7. (Eng. trans. by F. B. Jevons under the title *Prehistoric Antiquities of the Aryan Peoples.* London, 1890).
16. SCHRADER, O. *Die Indogermanen.* Leipzig, 1911.
17. TAYLOR, I. *The Origin of the Aryans,* London, 1889.
18. TILAK, B. G. *Orion.*
19. TILAK, B. G. *The Arctic Home in the Vedas.*

CHAPTERS XIII-XV

Aryan Settlements in India and Traditional History

(For Original Sources see under General Bibliography.)

MODERN WORKS

1. BANERJI SASTRI, A. *Asura India,* Patna, 1926.
2. BHANDARKAR, D. R. "Aryan Immigration into Eastern India." *ABORI,* XII, pp. 103-16.

3. Bhandarkar, D. R. "Lectures on the Ancient History of India." *Carmichael Lectures,* 1918. Calcutta, 1919.
4. Bhandarkar, D. R. *Some Aspects of Ancient Indian Culture.* Madras, 1940.
5. Chakladar, H. C. "Aryans in Eastern India in Rigvedic Age." *MR,* Jan. 1930, pp. 40-44.
6. Chakladar, H. C. "Eastern India and Aryavarta." *IHQ,* IV, pp. 84-101.
7. Cunningham, A. *The Ancient Geography of India.* Ed. by S. N. Majumdar. Calcutta, 1924.
8. Das, A. C. *Rigvedic India.* Vol. I. Calcutta, 1921.
9. Dey, N. L. *The Geographical Dictionary of Ancient and Mediaeval India* (second edn.). London, 1927.
10. Dikshitar, V. R. R. "Anthropo-Geography of Vedic India." *JMU,* 16, pp. 23-37.
11. Dikshitar, V. R. R. "Aryanization of East India (Assam)." *IHQ,* XXI, pp. 29-33.
12. Dutt, N. K. *Aryanization of India.* Calcutta, 1925.
13. Kirfel, W. *Das Purāṇa Pañchalakshaṇa.* Bonn, 1927.
14. Law, B. C. *Rivers of India.* Calcutta, 1944.
15. Law, B. C. *Tribes in Ancient India.* Poona, 1943.
16. Pargiter, F. E. *Ancient Indian Historical Tradition.* London, 1922.
17. Pargiter, F. E. *Dynasties of the Kali Age.* London, 1913.
18. Pradhan, S. N. *Chronology of Ancient India.* Calcutta, 1927.
19. Rangacharya, V. "Pre-Musalman India," vol. II, Part I. *Vedic India.* Madras, 1937.
20. Stein, M. A. "Indo-Iranian Borderlands." *JRAI,* LXIV, 179-202.
21. Stein, M. A. "On Some River Names in the Ṛigveda." *JRAS,* 1917. pp. 91-9.
22. Woolner, A. C. "The Ṛigveda and the Punjab." *BSOS,* 6, 549-54.

CHAPTERS XII, XVI, XX and XXIV

Language and Literature

(See Histories of Literature under General Bibliography.)

1. Arnold, E. V. *Vedic Metre.* Cambridge, 1905.
2. Bloomfield, M. *The Atharvaveda.* Strassburg, 1899.
3. Fürst, A. *Der Sprachgebrauch der älteren Upanishads.* Göttingen, 1915.
4. Hillebrandt, A. *Ritual—Litteratur.* Strassburg, 1897.
5. Macdonell, A. A. *Vedic Grammar.* Strassburg, 1910.
6. Wüst, Walter. *Stilgeschichte und Chronologie des Ṛigveda.* Leipzig, 1928.

CHAPTERS XVII, XXI, and XXV

Political and Legal Institutions

(For Original Sources see under General Bibliography.)

1. BASU, P. *Indo-Aryan Polity*. London, 1925.
2. BENI PRASAD. *Theory of Government in Ancient India*. Allahabad, 1927 (Chs. I, II).
3. DIKSHITAR, V. R. R. *Hindu Administrative Institutions*. Madras, 1929.
4. GHOSHAL, U. N. *A History of Hindu Political Theories*. London, 1923 (Chs. I, II).
5. GHOSHAL, U. N. *History of Hindu Public Life*. Part I. Calcutta, 1945.
6. JAYASWAL, K. P. *Hindu Polity*, Calcutta, 1924.
7. JOLLY, J. *Recht und Sitte*. Strassburg, 1896. (Eng. trans. by Dr. B. K. Ghosh under the title: *Hindu Law and Custom*. Calcutta, 1928,)

CHAPTERS XVIII, XXII, and XXVI

Religion and Philosophy

(For Original Sources see under General Bibliography.)

1. BARTH, A. *The Religions of India*. London, 1882.
2. BARUA, B. M. *A History of Pre-Buddhistic Indian Philosophy*. Calcutta, 1921.
3. BERGAIGNE, A. *La Religion Védique*, Paris 1878-83.
4. BLOOMFIELD, M. *The Religion of the Veda*. New York, 1908.
5. DAS GUPTA, DR. S. N. *History of Indian Philosophy*.
6. DEUSSEN, P. *The System of the Vedanta* (Eng. trans.). Chicago, 1912.
7. DEUSSEN, P. *Philosophie des Veda*, Leipzig, 1894.
8. DEUSSEN, P. *Die Philosophie der Upanishads*. Leipzig, 1899. (Eng. trans. Edinburgh, 1919.)
9. HILLEBRANDT, A. *Vedische Mythologie*. Breslau, 1891-1902.
10. HOPKINS, E. W. *The Religions of India*. Boston, 1895.
11. KEITH, A. B. *Religion and Philosophy of the Veda and Upanishads*. Cambridge, Mass, 1925.
12. MACDONELL, A. A. *Vedic Mythology*. Strassburg, 1897.
13. MONIER-WILLIAMS, M. *Religious Thought and Life in India*. London, 1891.
14. OLDENBERG, H. *Die Religion des Veda*. Berlin, 1894.
15. RADHAKRISHNAN, SIR S. *History of Indian Philosophy*. 2 vols. London, 1923, 1927.
16. RANADE, R. D. *Constructive Survey of the Upanishadic Philosophy*. Poona, 1926.

CHAPTERS XIX, XXIII, and XXVII

Social and Economic Conditions

(For Original Sources see under General Bibliography.)

1. AIYANGAR, K. V. RANGASWAMI. *Ancient Indian Economic Thought.* Benares, 1934.
2. ALTEKAR, A. S. *Education in Ancient India* (second edn.), Benares, 1944.
3. APTE, V. M. *Social and Religious Life in the Gṛihya Sūtras.* Ahmedabad, 1939.
4. BANERJEE, S. *Hindu Law of Marriage and Strīdhana.* Tagore Law Lectures. Calcutta, 1896.
5. BASU, P. *Indo-Aryan Polity.* London, 1925.
6. DAS, S. K. *Economic History of Ancient India.* Calcutta, 1925.
7. JOLLY, J. *Rechte und Sitte.* Strassburg, 1896. (English trans. by Dr. B. K. Ghosh under the title *Hindu Law and Custom.* Calcutta, 1928.)
8. SAMADDAR, J. N. *Economic Condition of Ancient India.* Calcutta, 1922.
9. SARKAR, S. C. *Some Aspects of the Earliest Social History of India.* London, 1928.

The Caste-System

1. BAINES, A. *Ethnography.* Strassburg, 1912.
2. DUTT, N. K. *Origin and Development of Caste in India.* Vol. I. London, 1931.
3. GAIT, E. A. "Caste" in *ERE,* III (1910).
4. KETKAR, S. V. *The History of Caste in India.* Ithaca, N. Y. 1909; London, 1911.
5. MUIR, J. *Original Sanskrit Texts,* vol. I.
6. OLDENBERG, H. In *ZDMG,* LI, pp. 267-90.
7. SENART, E. *Les Castes dans l'Inde.* Paris, 1896.
8. WEBER, A. *Indische Studien,* X.

APPENDIX

CHAPTER IX

In the absence of any definite vestiges of a system of fortification in the Indus Valley excavations so far, it was naturally assumed that the Indus Valley civilization was politically and socially far ahead of the contemporary civilizations in the West, and had developed "a democratic bourgeois economy" (*ante*, p. 170) devoid of citadel rule. Recent excavations in Harappā, however, besides supplying other valuable data, have shown that the Indus Valley civilization had its fortifications and was as militant and centralized as any of its day (*Ancient India*, No. 3, pp. 61 ff.).

In the mound towards the West at Harappā, rising 50 feet above the level of the plain, high projecting masses of decayed mud-brick indicate the presence of former defences. Recent digging has shown that a defensive wall with a basal width of 40 feet and a height of upwards of 35 feet, built of mud-bricks, stood on a great rampart 10 to 20 feet high consisting of mud and debris with a mud-brick core. The wall, externally revetted with a facing of baked brick, was reinforced at intervals by rectangular towers or salients representing an elaborate system of enfilade. There were probably two gateways, one on the western side and the other at the northern end, the latter representing the main entrance. The defences fall into three main periods of construction: the original baked brick revetment was rebuilt after a long period of weathering and other damage, and the north-west corner was considerably thickened. This new work was built with complete bricks, unlike the older work which was constructed largely of brickbats. During the next period, the north-west corner was reinforced by an additional salient, and two entrances of the western gate system were wholly or partially blocked. Finally, roughly-built dwellings, constructed above a layer of debris and associated with the intrusive ceramic of a later period, came to occupy the western terraces.

The cuttings across the defences enable us to trace the origin, development and decline of the Harappā culture. It appears that after a preliminary occupation of the apparently unwalled town, associated with a variant or alien culture, the Harappan people built a citadel with imposing defences. These were reconditioned after a considerable time during the heyday of the Harappā culture, when craftsmanship was at its height. The period of decline is seen in the further reinforcement of the reconstructed fortifications and the blocking of a gateway, indicating that the city was on the defensive. Finally, a part of the site, above layers of the debris, was occupied by inhabitants of an alien culture.

The situation of Harappā and Mohenjo-daro, pre-eminent among numerous prehistoric sites between the Arabian Sea and the foot of the Simla Hills, already indicated that the Harappā civilization was of a centralized type similar to those in Sumer and Egypt. In both, the detached mound on the west is the highest and most imposing in the site, roughly a parallelogram in shape, approximately 400 yards long and 200 yards wide. The mound at Mohenjo-daro is known as the *stūpa* mound and includes such remarkable structures as the Great Bath, Collegiate Building, and the Pillared Hall, which find no parallel elsewhere in these cities. It may reasonably be assumed that the mound was a centre of religious or administrative life on a large scale. The counterpart of this mound at Harappā, almost identical in size and orientation, is not a mere coincidence, and the assemblage, in its close vicinity, of a serried line of barracks or cooly quarters, working platforms and granaries, suggests a centralized and disciplined citadel rule. Whether the government was in the hands of a priestly order, as was often the case in Sumer, or of a ruler of royal standing, it is not yet possible to say.

Dr. Acharya considers Mohenjo-daro, with its irregular shape, to correspond with the *Droṇaka* fortress of the *Mānasāra's* plans (*B. C. Law Volume*, Part II, p. 281). It is not yet definite whether the fortifications surrounded the entire area of the town or were confined only to the west. In the latter case, the probable reasons may be that the important buildings were grouped on that side and that the villagers feared attacks from the west.

Recent excavations of a cemetery of the Harappā culture present yet another analogy between the cities of the Indus and the Euphrates. The dead were buried in an extended position with their heads towards the north and surrounded by large quantities of pottery of normal Harappan type. Grave-pits were 10 to 15 feet in length, 2½ to 10 feet in width, and were dug to a depth of from 2 to 3 feet from the contemporary surface. The grave furniture occasionally included toilet objects, besides pottery and personal ornaments. In some graves were found a few decayed animal bones besides a human skeleton. There was one coffin-burial, at present unique in India, but common at Ur, Kish and other places in Mesopotamia in the third millennium B.C. The skeleton, enclosed in a reed shroud, was placed within a wooden coffin, 7 feet long and 2 to 2½ feet wide. The presence of a lid is suggested by streaks of sticky black substance running over the toes, and the use of preservatives is inferred from the light green substance found over and around the body. This burial, no doubt, represents the customary mode in Sumer during contemporary and previous epochs; but it is not yet known whether this isolated burial was of an Indian or of a Sumerian merchant in India.

It may be mentioned that Dr. Wheeler does not include "post-cremation burials" (*ante*, p. 193) as a method of the disposal of the dead in the Indus Valley, "since," according to him, "there is no evidence whatsoever that these have anything to do with human burial" (*Ancient India*, No. 3, p. 83).

SELECT BIBLIOGRAPHY (1946-1948)

1. BARUA, B. M. "Indus Script and Tantric Code." *B.C. Law Volume*, Part II, pp. 461-7.
2. BARUA, B. M. "Trends in Ancient history." *CR.*, Feb. 1946, pp. 79-93.
3. HERAS, H. *Mīn-Kaṇ*. Bombay, 1947.
4. MACKAY, E. *Early Indus Civilizations*. London, 1948.
5. PIGGOTT, S. "The Chronology of Prehistoric North-West India." *Ancient India*, No. 1, pp. 8-26.
6. PIGGOTT, S. "A New Prehistoric Ceramic from Baluchistan." *Ancient India*, No. 3, pp. 131-142.
7. PUSALKER, A. D. "Mohenjo-daro and Ṛigveda." *Bhārata-Kaumudī*, Part II, pp. 551-63.
8. WHEELER, R. E. M. "India's Earliest Civilization; Recent Excavations in the Indus Basin." *ILN*, Aug. 10, 1946.
9. WHEELER, R. E. M. "Harappa, 1946: the Defences and Cemetery R. 37". *Ancient India*, No. 3, pp. 58-130.
10. WIJESEKERA, O. H. DE A. "Rigvedic River-Goddesses and an Indus Valley Seal." *Kunhan Raja Presentation Volume*, pp. 428-41.

Map 1

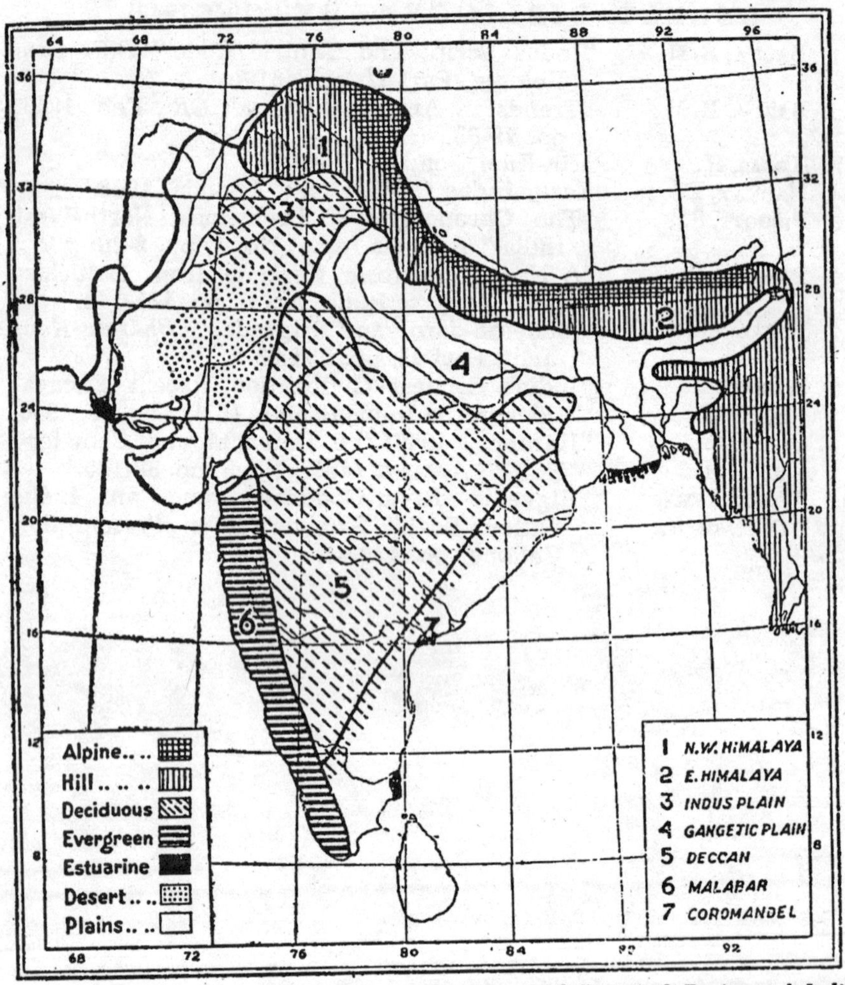

Map of India showing types of Forest Vegetation and Botanical Regions of India

Map 2

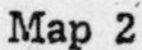

ANCIENT INDIA
Showing local & tribal names in Vedic literature and the Chalcolithic sites in Sind
Chalcolithic Sites .... ▲
KAMBOJA
GANDHARI
PAKTHA
KEKAYA
YADU
SIBI
MARU
KHANDAVA
SRINJAYA
SALVAS
MATSYA
SATVANT
NISHADA
DAKSHINAPATHA
VIDARBHA
ANDHRA
KIKATA
MAGADHA
VIDEHA
PUNDRA
KOSALA
PANCHALA
CHEDI
VATSA
USINARA
TURGHNA
BALHIKA
DRUHYU
ANU
TURVASA
Mohen-jo-Daro
Harappa
Kausambi
Yamuna
Ganga
Miles

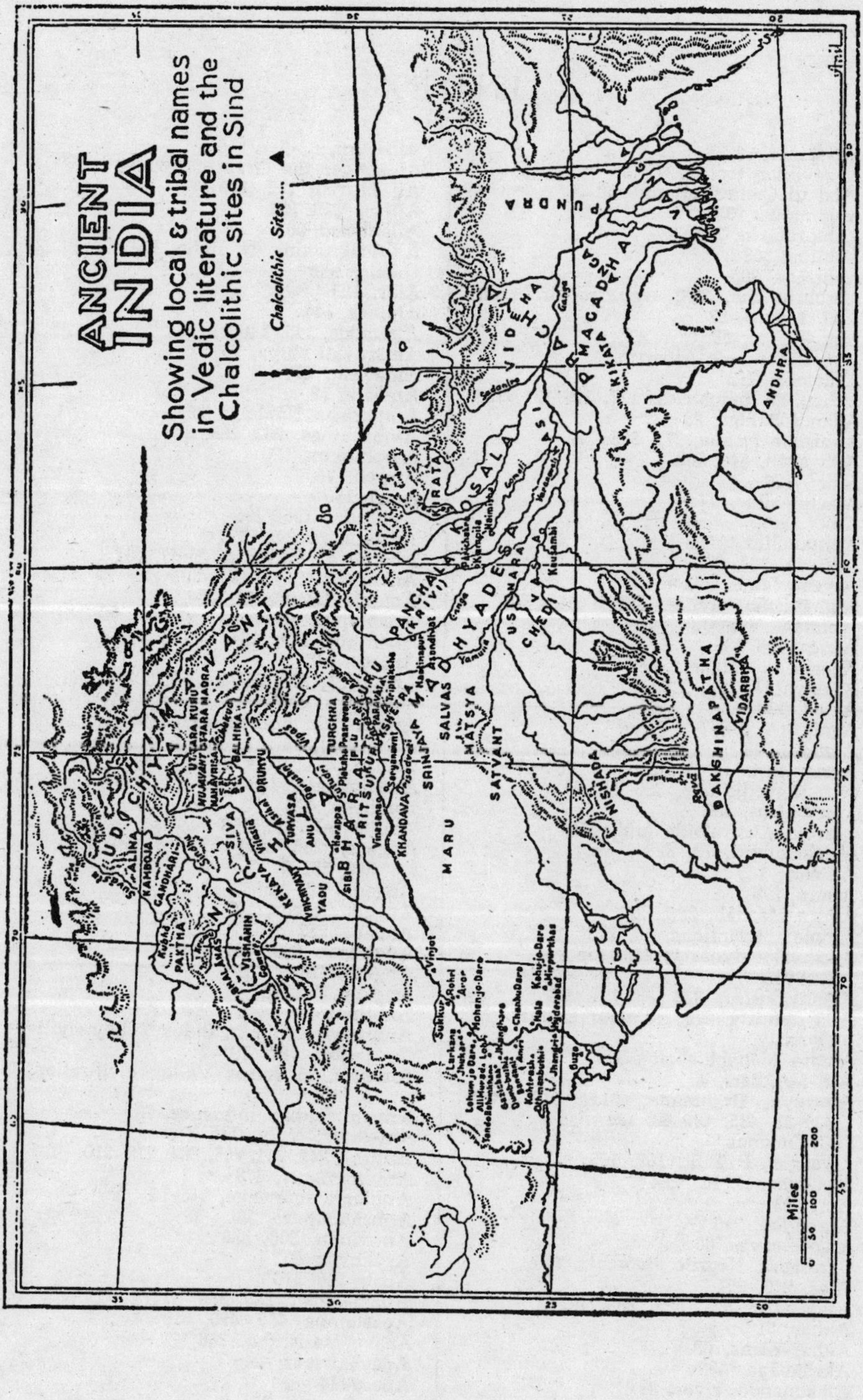

INDEX

INDEX